Na pamiątkę

Ewa, Roman, Krystyna,
Marta i Mateusz

Kostrzyn, 4.07.2004

POLAND

MANORS · CASTLES · PALACES

Roman Marcinek

Kraków 2002

30-110 Kraków, ul. Kraszewskiego 36
tel./fax: (0-12) 421-22-28, e-mail: biuro@kluszczyński.com.pl

Internet sales:
www.kluszczyński.com.pl

Consultant: **Dr Stanisław Kołodziejski**

Editorial supervision: **Jadwiga Marcinek**

Translated by: **Władysław Chłopicki** (pp. 3-5 and 50-112) and **Marta Kapera** (pp. 6-49)

Cover design: **Anna Gałuszka**

Map of Poland: **Mariusz Kędzierski**

Photographs:
R. Cieślik: 63 bottom; **M. Ciunowicz**: 6 top, 15t, 20t, b, 25b, 47b, 51b, 66b, 83b, 85t, 98t, b, 99t, b; **R. Czerwiński**: 10b, 12t, 13t, 14t, 31t, 36t, b, 41t, 44t, b, 46b, 48t,b, 52t, 58t, b, 61b, 65t, 72b, 77t, 79t, 84t, 102t, b, 112t, b; **M. Grychowski**: 10t, 12b, 19t, b, 31b, 34t, b, 37b, 40t, b, 42t, b, 45t, 49b, 56t, b, 60b, 61t, 63t, 68t, b, 70b, 73t, 79b, 81t, 82t, 84b, 85b, 86t, 89t, b, 90t, b, 100b, 103t, b, 108b; **S. Klimek**: 14b, 16t, 18b, 25t, 27t, 39b, 50t, 52b, 55b, 107t, b, 109t; **M. Kowalewski**: 23b, 51t, 53t, b, 88t, 93b, 96t, 97t, 106b; **J. Kozina**: 6b, 17b, 23t; **S. Markowski**: 7t, 8b, 11t, b, 18t, 22t, b, 24b, 27b, 29t, b, 35t, b, 47t, 50b, 55t, 62t, 70t, 71t, 76t, b, 77b, 80t, 82b, 83t, 87t, 88b, 91b, 92b, 106t, 108t, 109b, 110t; **S. Michta**: 33t, b; **Z. Moliński**: 69b, 73b, 78t, b, 86b, 92t; **J. Moniatowicz**: 24t, 38t, b, 39t, 59t, b, 64t, b, 94b, 96b, 97b, 101t, 104t, b; **P. Pierściński**: 7b, 13b, 16b, 17t, 28t, b, 30b, 41b, 43b, 54t, b, 57b, 62b, 71b, 72t, 111t, b; **K. Pollesch**: 32b, 80b; **W. Stępień**: 8t, 9b, 37t, 60t, 87b, 91t, 93t; **S. Tarasow**: 15b, 21b, 26b, 30t, 32t, 43t, 46t, 49t, 66t, 67t, b, 69t, 74t, b, 75t, b, 94t, 95t, b, 100t, 101b, 110b; **Agencja B&W**: 9t, 26t, 45b, 57t, 65b, 81b, 105t, b.

DTP
Fabryka Grafiki s.c.
30-147 Kraków, ul. Trawiasta 3
tel./fax: (0-12) 637-13-12
e-mail: fabryka@fabrykagrafiki.com

ISBN: **83-88080-94-6**

Foreword

In the early Middle Ages, it was only the rulers who had the right to erect castles since they were the guarantee of their military advantage and the symbol of their sovereignty over the land. At the turn of the 13th c. also bishops started to build their strongholds within the confines of their estates, while private owners were allowed to raise castles only in the latter half of the 13th c. By the end of the century and in the following decades, fortified residences started to crop up as the centres of landed estates. At the outset they were small buildings, but gradually they began to match royal castles in size, spatial layout and fortification systems. The military efficacy of medieval castles was constantly improved as the owners took excellent advantage of their physical location. Nowadays when you look at some of them, it makes you wonder how it was technically possible to erect them at the time when no construction machines were yet even in sight. Castles in Poland give you a thorough overview of the consecutive phases of development of fortification systems, a good picture of the neighbourly impact of Bohemia and the state of Teutonic Knights, or the decorative art from Rhineland and Ruthenia.

In the modern period, the lordly residences gradually tended to lose their defensive functions and were turned into palaces, to meet the contemporary taste. The Royal Castle of Wawel was an unattainable model in Poland then, but there were continual attempts to overshadow its splendour. In the 17th c., Renaissance villas and Mannerist castles were replaced with massive, richly decorated Baroque residences. The edifices such as Krzyżtopór Castle or palaces of the "overlords" from eastern Poland were symbols of power and glory. The most eminent noble families spent fortunes in order to emphasise their standing and rank. The outcome was genuine gems of architecture created by best artists, usually imported from abroad. In such countryside residences and their immediate surroundings cultural life flourished, with the remote capital of Warsaw remaining only the symbol of the state. Collections of paintings, sculptures, arts and crafts, prints and books were amassed, meticulously preserved and enlarged by consecutive generations in order to give testimony to the significance and good taste of the family ancestors. The nicely alliterative saying "Wart Pac pałaca a pałac Paca", which circulated in those times, concerned the famous 17th-c. royal chancellor Krzysztof Pac, who had the Belvedere palace built for himself in Warsaw, but it could be applied to other prominent magnate families, the Radziwiłłs, Lubomirskis, Potockis and others as well. Their courtly etiquette, theatricality of customs and an inflated sense of pride did require a suitable setting.

The residences went through a path of evolution from the Italian *palazzo in fortezza* to the vast and open layout influenced by the French *entre cour at jardin* model. In the Baroque palaces the official functions prevailed, and the most resplendent interiors were located usually on the upper floor, where the owners' apartments were separated by the great hall. Sometimes, from habit only, these residences were referred to as castles but their defensive role was in fact the lowest priority. New preferences of the owners were visible in the palaces as well since at the turn of the 16th c. the culture of landed gentry underwent a surprising change. The Polish-Lithuanian Union moved the borders of the Republic far to the east, and a large population of Orthodox Christians and Muslims found themselves within the Polish state. Fascinated with the opulence of the Orient, the Polish landed gentry tended to adopt the Eastern fashion, particularly in the clothing and daily habits, as well as the Oriental love of tapestries and tents. This could not have remained without impact on the decoration of palace interiors. Reading Roman authors, Polish nobles found the descriptions of a mysterious nation of the Sarmatians, which used to raid the lands between the Vistula and the Dnieper. It is in these horseback warriors that the landed gentry saw their ancestors, creating a rather bizarre Sarmatian myth. To live up to it, the Polish "Sarmatians" wore long, buttoned-up undergowns and open overcoats, gold-encrusted sashes, curved sabres, scaled cuirasses and hussar wings; their heads were half-shaven and their moustaches sweeping.

By the end of the 18th c. the neo-classical palaces ousted the Baroque residences with their glitzy splendour. The most fashionable English designs were followed in their construction. The shift in the lifestyle, from public to private, when more time was spent at home with the family and friends, was of particular significance. The residences became places of quiet repose, thus in the planning of the layout of the rooms more attention was paid to its practicality. The official spacious rooms were located solely on the ground floor and were adjoined by smaller private apartments. Palaces were surrounded with landscape parks which constituted a romantic backdrop to the residences. The Baroque axial layout and perspective were supplanted by scenic landscapes and the slightly artificial "naturalness" of the surroundings, but they came back in the 19th c., along with the historicist fashion. Neo-Baroque urban mansions or small, romantic, neo-Gothic castles set among lakes and fields became symbols of good taste and love for tradition.

The simplified model of the neo-classical palace, reduced to the single-storey manor house of an elongated shape with the columned portico as a decorative element, turned into a stereotypical solution which from then on became unequivocally associated with the Polish landed gentry residence. Initially, the manor had been the administrative centre of a landed estate, consisting of residential and farm buildings, surrounded by yards and simple earthwork bulwarks. It had to withstand raids of angry neighbours and offer effective resistance to hostile bands of robbers passing across the country. In time, the term *manor* was transferred to a residence of the landed estate owner. *Manor houses* in turn became the suburban residences which did not have any administrative functions. The oldest Polish manors which have been preserved date back to the 16th c. and derive from the medieval type of residential towers. In the 16th-18th c. the manor was primarily the abode of more or less affluent landed gentry, as well as magnates and even royals. Manor houses, urban mansions, castles or storage towers gradually evolved, assuming newer architectural forms and more open character. Annexes, two-layer roofs, attics, porticos and columns were the typical features. Manor houses were usually built from round larch, fir or pine logs which formed massive walls; they had a stone underpinning with a single storey and a large-size roof on top. The roofs were shingled, or sometimes thatched. The author of the anonymous brochure, entitled *A Brief Lesson in Building Manors, Palaces, Castles in Agreement with Heavens and the Polish Custom,* published in Cracow in 1659, persuaded the Polish landed gentry to construct their houses from "masonry" due to its "durability and anti-fire safety." Close architectural links can be observed between the manor house (particularly belonging to poorer landed gentry) and the dwellings of peasants. The typical manor house consisted of a kitchen, a bedroom and a common room (also called a knights hall).

Until the Second World War, the families of landed gentry lived in the manors. Under the Agrarian Reform Decree enforced by the Communist authorities after the war, manors were confiscated, abandoned by owners or used haphazardly without appropriate management and maintenance, and thus gradually falling into disrepair. Nowadays they require conservation, together with their surroundings, since they are pride of the countryside and monuments of national culture. The image of the ancient manor house have become an inseparable part of Polish history and tradition; Poles turned back to it in the late 20th c. as architectural inspiration for modern residences raised in the newly independent country. It is doubtful, however, if they will earn the regard and status enjoyed by their predecessors, high enough to find their way to top literary works.

On top of all that, it must be remembered that all those palaces, manors and castles were people's homes with which the most delightful memories were linked. It was those memories that inspired the owners to inscribe mottoes in the friezes of their palaces, such as the one from Horace: "That corner of the world smiles for me beyond all others."

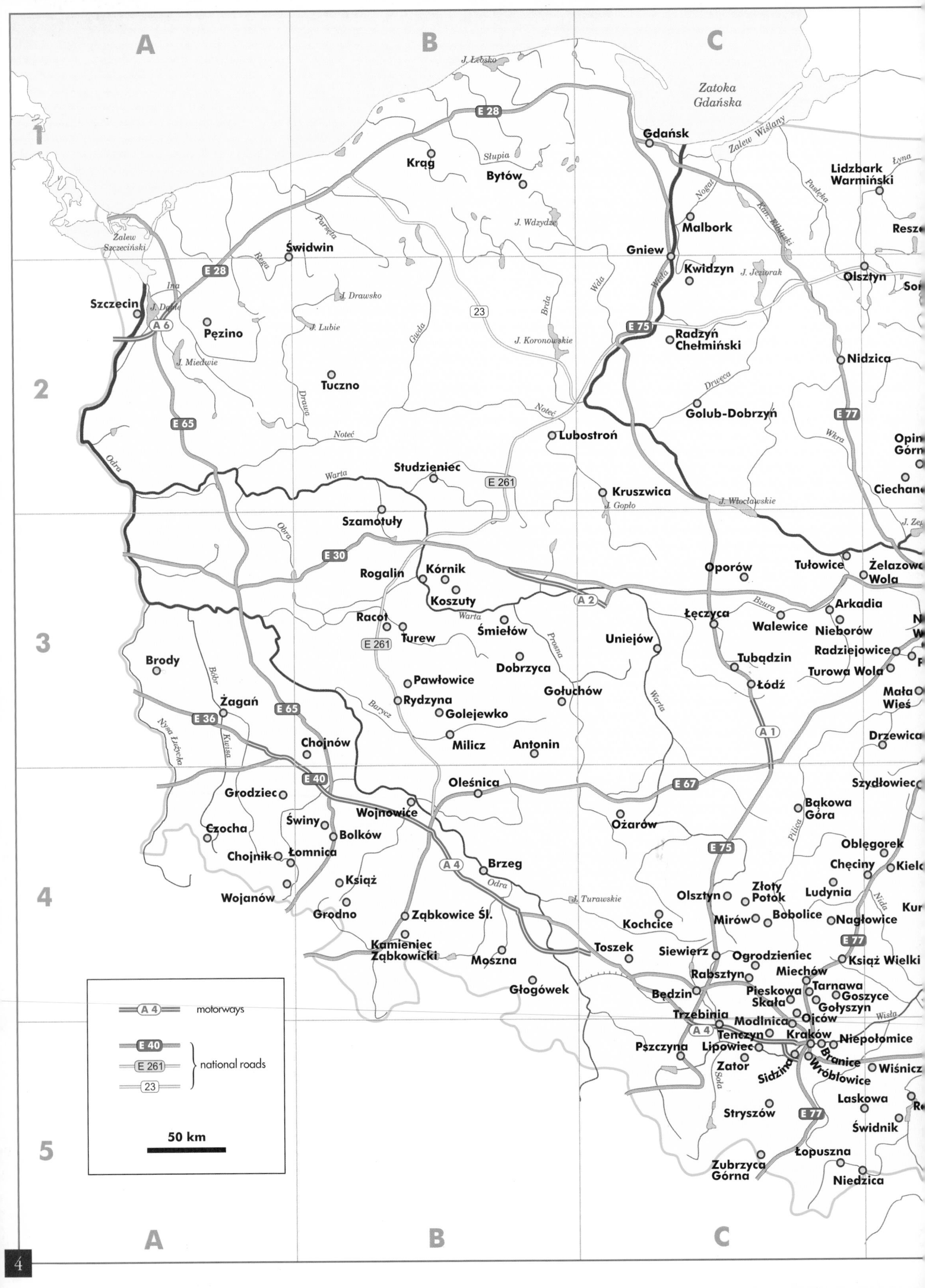

A
B
C
1
2
3
4
5
J. Łebsko
Zatoka Gdańska
E 28
Gdańsk
Zalew Wiślany
Słupia
Krąg
Bytów
Lidzbark Warmiński
Łyna
Pasłęka
Nogat
Malbork
Kan. Elbląski
Parsęta
J. Wdzydze
Zalew Szczeciński
Świdwin
Gniew
Kwidzyn
J. Jeziorak
Olsztyn
Rega
E 28
Ina
J. Drawsko
Wda
Wisła
Szczecin
J. Dąbie
23
Brda
A 6
Pęzino
J. Lubie
Gwda
E 75
Radzyń Chełmiński
J. Koronowskie
J. Miedwie
Nidzica
Tuczno
Drwęca
Drawa
Noteć
Golub-Dobrzyń
E 65
E 77
Lubostroń
Noteć
Wkra
Odra
Warta
Studzieniec
E 261
Kruszwica
J. Gopło
Ciechanów
J. Włocławskie
Szamotuły
Obra
E 30
Rogalin
Kórnik
Oporów
Tułowice
Żelazowa Wola
Koszuty
A 2
Racot
Warta
Bzura
Arkadia
Turew
Śmiełów
Prosna
Łęczyca
Walewice
Nieborów
Uniejów
E 261
Radziejowice
Brody
Dobrzyca
Tubądzin
Turowa Wola
Bóbr
Pawłowice
Łódź
Żagań
Rydzyna
Gołuchów
Mała Wieś
E 36
E 65
Golejewko
Barycz
Nysa Łużycka
Kwisa
Warta
A 1
Milicz
Antonin
Drzewica
Chojnów
E 40
Oleśnica
E 67
Szydłowiec
Grodziec
Bąkowa Góra
Wojnowice
Ożarów
Świny
Pilica
Czocha
Bolków
Oblęgorek
Chojnik
Łomnica
E 75
A 4
Brzeg
Chęciny
Kielce
Książ
Złoty Potok
Odra
Wojanów
Olsztyn
Ludynia
Nida
J. Turawskie
Grodno
Ząbkowice Śl.
Mirów
Bobolice
Nagłowice
Kochcice
Kamieniec Ząbkowicki
E 77
Toszek
Siewierz
Ogrodzieniec
Moszna
Książ Wielki
Rabsztyn
Miechów
Głogówek
Tarnawa
Będzin
Pieskowa Skała
Goszyce
Gołyszyn
Trzebinia
Ojców
Wisła
A 4
Modlnica
Tenczyn
Kraków
Niepołomice
Pszczyna
Lipowiec
Branice
Zator
Sidzina
Wróblowice
Wiśnicz
Soła
Laskowa
Stryszów
E 77
Świdnik
Łopuszna
Zubrzyca Górna
Niedzica
A 4 motorways
E 40
E 261
23
national roads
50 km
A
B
C

List of Contents

Hunting lodge in Antonin

ANTONIN

In the region of Wielkopolska, many interesting quasi-historic residences were built according to the designs of leading German architects, e.g. the arcaded palace in Rokosowo or the neo-classical hunting lodge in Antonin. Antonin, a romantic residence of Duke A. Radziwiłł, was the first (1821-24) Polish project based on the design of K.F. Schinkel. He favoured romantic trends in architecture, with elements of neo-classical and neo-Gothic styles. In his opinion, the antiquity and the early Middle Ages represented two comparable styles, while Gothic architecture, in opposition to the antiquity, was a symbol of the victory of spirit over matter. When planning the summer residence in Antonin, the architect had to consider the fact that it was to serve as an official seat of Duke Radziwiłł, who composed music to Goethe's *Faust* and was a supporter of arts (although at the same time he brought the family estate of Nieśwież to ruin), and in 1815-31 was the Governor of the Grand Duchy of Poznań. The Duchy was one of several territories into which Poland had just been divided by the diplomats having a good time at the Congress of Vienna. Though the position of the Governor was given to Radziwiłł, who was affined with Prussian aristocrats, he could only perform minor administrative functions. However, the appearance of the Duke and Governor's court in Wielkopolska invigorated those who liked to show off in high society, which in turn fostered the construction of appropriately splendid residences.
Schinkel designed a palace whose framework was set on a foundation of brick and stone. The construction work was supervised by H. Haberlin. The timber building was raised on the ground plan of the Greek cross. Its main part holds an immense, octagonal reception hall covered with a broach roof and supported by a pillar-cum-chimney. The hall is a few storeys high and surrounded by galleries. Adjacent to the main part of the building stand four smaller, square ones. Three of them hold apartments and the fourth one a staircase. The solutions adopted in the design of the palace resemble those of hunting lodges or ecclesiastical architecture. The structure of the building was to correspond to its function, which made Antonin palace a good example of *architecture parlante*. The surrounding landscape park gradually turns into a large forest with many huge oaks. The nearby utility buildings represent the "Tirolean" style. In the vicinity, on the island in the pond, stand the remnants of the marble tomb of Duke Radziwiłł's daughters, and on the way to Mikstat, an old family chapel of the Radziwiłłs, built in 1836-38 in neo-Romanesque style, and probably designed by Schinkel as well. In 1827 and 1829 Antonin was visited by Frédéric Chopin. For the Duke's daughter, whom he taught to play the piano, he composed *Polonaise in C Major Opus 3*, and dedicated *Trio in G Minor Opus 8* to the Duke himself. The composer personally chose the piano for his pupil, and her father ordered it in Paris.

BARANÓW SANDOMIERSKI

Baranów Sandomierski lies on the Vistula, in the plain of Tarnobrzeg. Its tourist attraction is the castle of the Leszczyński family, one of the most beautiful Mannerist buildings in Poland. It replaced a 15th-c. structure probably built by Jakub Grzymała, a Crown official in Sandomierz. In 1569 Palatine Rafał Leszczyński began the construction of the eastern wing. The crucial stage of the project was carried out under the supervision of Santi Gucci in 1591-1606.
The owner of Baranów was then Andrzej Leszczyński, the Palatine of Kujawy. The complex consists of the castle and bulwark fortifications. The castle itself is rectangular, has four cylindrical towers in the corners, an inner courtyard, cloisters and a two-sided staircase. The centre of the façade is occupied by a protruding entrance adorned with an attic. Baranów castle proves the incredibly strong

Hunting lodge in Antonin: Interior

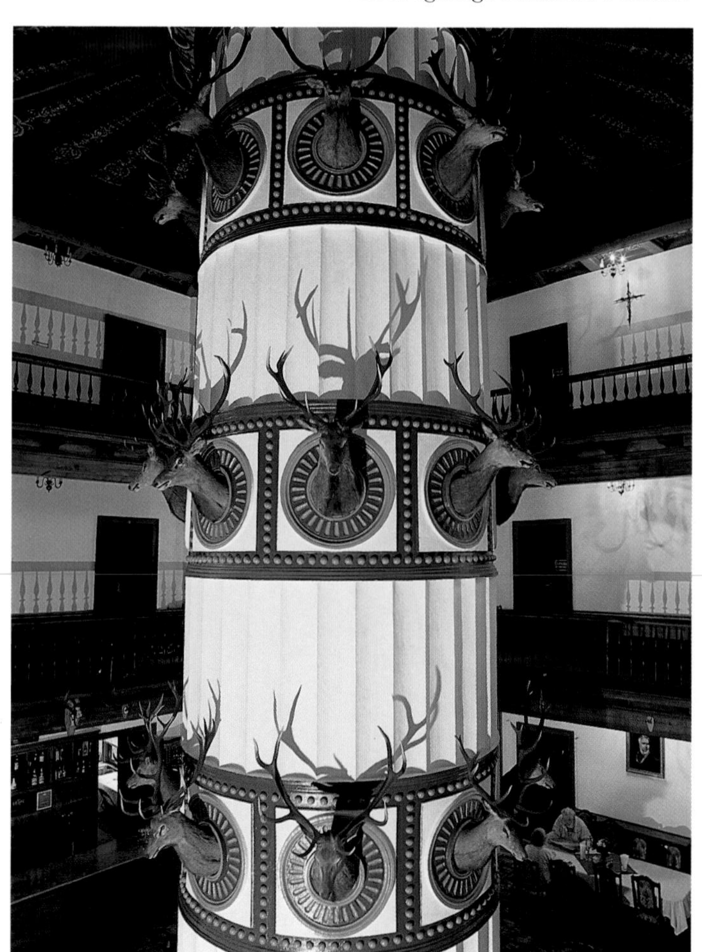

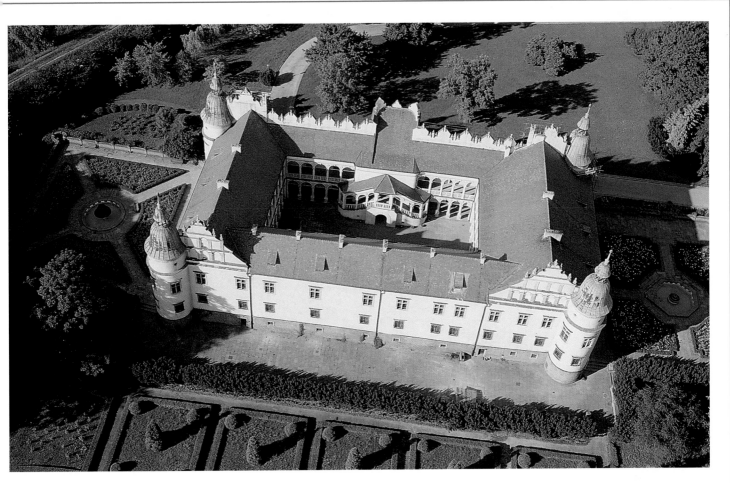

Castle in Baranów Sandomierski

influence of the royal castle on Wawel Hill, especially its arcaded courtyard. The cloisters of Baranów castle are elegant in design and meticulous in detail. Especially noteworthy is the masterful masonry of the portals, where delicate floral motifs merge with dragons' mouths. The ornaments are ascribed to the school of Santi Gucci. Both storeys are decorated with Ionic columns, Gucci's favourite ones. (In Pińczów, taking advantage of the qualities of local stone, Gucci established two workshops for stonecutters and sculptors, where decorative elements were prepared and then transported even to distant construction sites.) The castle is adorned with fancy gables and attics. The impressive stucco on the ceiling of the north-eastern tower is the work of G. Falconi.

The castle was enlarged in 1695, as commissioned by Józef Karol Lubomirski, to the design of Tylman van Gameren. It should be stated that this architect, whose name was Polonised as Gamerski, shaped the Polish taste for architecture in the second half of the 17th c. He came from Utrecht and began his artistic education in the Netherlands, but in the late 1650s left for Venice, where he studied chiefly painting. Before 1663 he was employed as the court architect of Jan Sebastian Lubomirski and since then concentrated almost solely on architecture. Van Gameren reconciled the elements of classicising Dutch Baroque with the inspirations of Italian and French art. In Baranów, under his supervision, the western part of the castle was rebuilt, the interiors were modernised and the equipment was changed. In the upper storey of the western wing an additional arcaded passageway appeared, and the chambers were decorated with stuccoes and paintings. Also, the fortification system was taken care of.

Unfortunately, the castle was seriously destroyed in the fire of 1850: numerous objects of art were burned as well as the priceless manuscripts of the poet Ignacy Krasicki. At the beginning of the 20th c. the residence was renovated, based on the design by Tadeusz Stryjeński. In the restoration work, among others, two painters, Jacek Malczewski and Józef Mehoffer, were involved. After the war the castle was devastated, but many years of restoration brought back its previous splendour. The park, blending with the flat landscape along the Vistula, was arranged in the 20th c., replacing old bulwarks.

Castle in Baranów Sandomierski: Courtyard

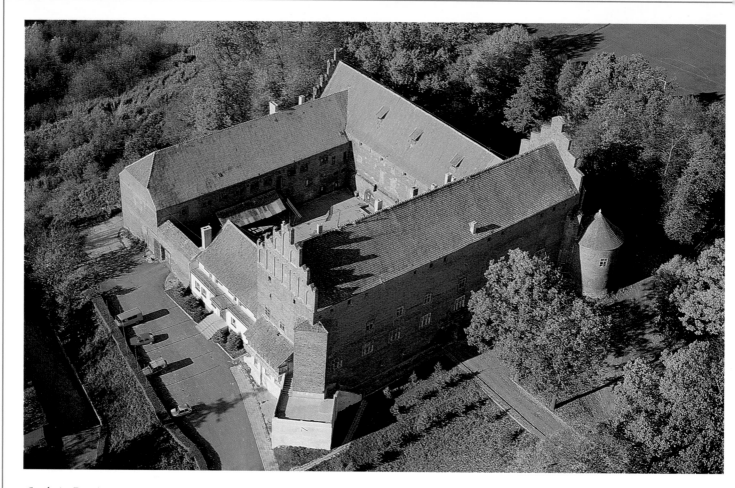

Castle in Barciany

Barciany

In Barciany stands a reconstructed castle of the Teutonic Knights, built ca 1380 in the middle of treacherous marshes by order of the Grand Master Winrich von Kniprode, who decided to establish here a commandery. Only for a short time was the castle the residence of the Bishop of Pomezania. Therefore it represents an interestingly archaic way of castle construction and its austere, towerless design shows one of the stages in the development of medieval fortresses. A previously existent structure was razed to the ground probably by an outburst of violence of local Prussian peasants, infamous for that in 1310 they baked over the coals the local representative of the Teutonic Order, Herman von Harttangen. The new, rectangular castle was built of brick on a small hill.

Bąkowa Góra

Bąkowa Góra lies near Przedborze, on a slope of a hill over the picturesque Pilica River. The manor house was built in the second half of the 18th c. for the Małachowski family. It is a one-storey building, covered with a shingled mansard roof. The interiors hold interesting examples of masonry. It is supposed that the late Baroque design was authored by Rev. J. Karśnicki, known as a prolific designer.

Będzin

The attraction of Będzin is an ancient castle, erected on the site of a previous earth-and-timber structure from the 11th-12th c. In the second half of the 13th c. a cylindrical tower and in the 14th c. a rectangular one were added. Probably under King Kazimierz the Great the lower castle was built. It is not surprising that Będzin castle was repeatedly fortified: it was the borderline castle between Poland and Silesia. Still, the 1564 inspection report describes the castle as desolate. Extensive reconstruction work was undertaken in 1616, following a fire that ruined part of the building, and later after the Swedish invasion of 1655. Just before the disintegration of the Polish state in the 18th c., the inspectors wrote: "In this castle, the wall cracks, some demolished and some damaged parts threaten with imminent collapse." In 1834 the castle was renovated in the Romantic, neo-Gothic vein to the design of F.M. Lanci, to house a school for coal-miners.

Manor house in Bąkowa Góra

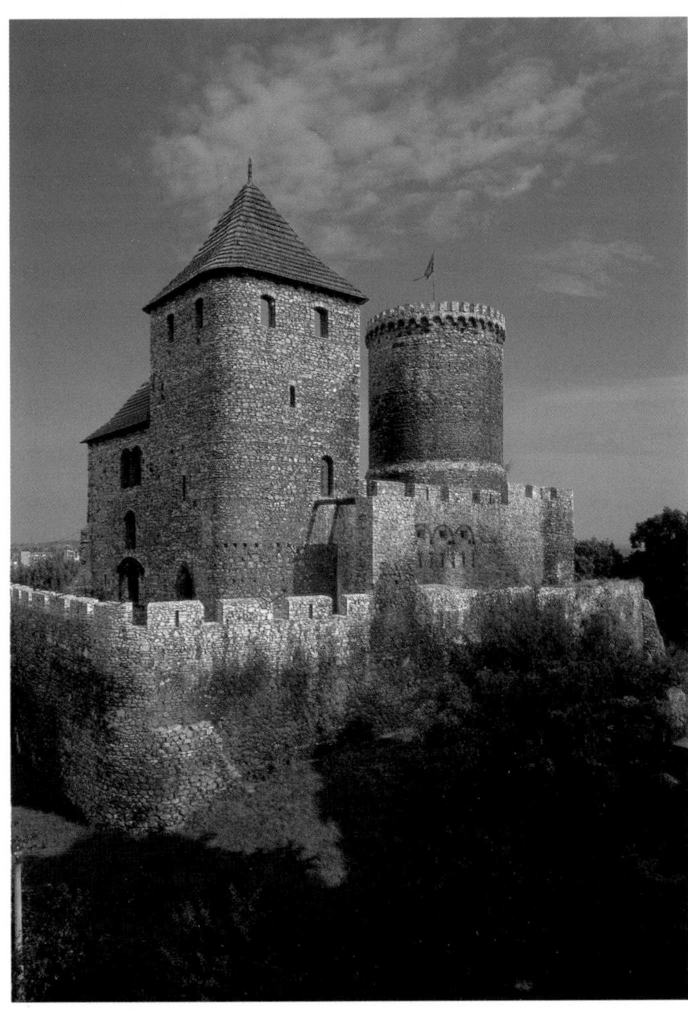

Brody

As the anecdote has it, the interest of King August III in the matters of the state was limited to the question: "Brühl, do I have money?" The Prime Minister answered, "Yes, Your Majesty," and modestly added that so did he. Henryk Brühl, the king's confidante, held several dozen positions and offices. He was, for example, the chairman of the Privy Council, manager of the royal library, commander of a few regiments of cavalry and infantry, supervisor of the king's privy treasury. Besides, he administered many regions of Poland and from 1731 supervised the finance and internal and foreign policy of Saxony. In 1740 Count Brühl purchased Brody for 160 thousand talers. The last of the Brühls who resided in Brody was Fryderyk August Franciszek Hubert Benedykt Johann Brühl. In Brody one can admire the late Baroque construction and landscape designs commissioned by the Minister, as well as the army barracks, pharmacy, inn, and other houses of the same style. They were built in 1741-53 by J. C. Knöffel, chief builder of the Saxon king.

The palace itself was erected earlier, in 1680, under U. Promnitz, by the architect G. Franck. Knöffel modified it as a horseshoe-shaped structure covered with a mansard roof, and varied the design by adding flank buildings. The Baroque Polish Gate was built in 1753 to celebrate the arrival of King August III, who came here to hunt. Unfortunately, the halcyon days of Brody under the Brühls were soon over. In September 1758, during the Seven Years' War, Frederick II, hostile towards the Saxon-Polish Prime Minister, had the residence burned down to the ground. The town never regained its previous prosperity despite the efforts of Brühl's son, the royal administrator of Warsaw. However, the palace as such and the surroundings were thoroughly renovated. In the autumn of 1945 the palace burned again, set on fire by the Red Army soldiers. The area of the park around the palace is almost 100 hectares. It was established in 1670-1726 by the Promnitz family in the French manner, and then changed by the Brühls into a landscape park. The dimensions, according to Knöffel's design, are 3 kilometres in length and 1 kilometre in width, and the park's attractions are a lake and a pheasant farm.

Castle in Będzin

Brody: Palace and town

Białystok

Białystok is situated at the edge of the primeval Knyszyn Forest, which once was the favourite hunting grounds of the Jagiellons. The town began to prosper when it was chosen as a place of residence by Hetman Jan Klemens Branicki, the last to bear the Gryf coat of arms. He was a mediocre commander and a poor politician, but a connoisseur of art. Flatterers exaggerated, calling his Białystok palace "the Versailles of Podlasie", and the contented magnate presented them with rings and snuffboxes. The late Baroque complex (palace surrounded by gardens) was erected as early as in 1691-97 by Tylman van Gameren, on the site of a 16th-c. castle. Branicki, aided by J.Z. Deybel and J.H. Klemm, the Polish Crown army colonel, extended it in 1728-58 into a residence with several courtyards, surrounded by a geometrical garden with canals and statues. The designer of the splendid staircase (from 1753-55) was G. Fontana, and the sculptures in the rooms are by Jan Chryzostom Redler (1755-58). The complex included also a gatehouse (1758), arsenal (18th c.), and the Guests' Palace (1771). An additional attraction was the French garden. Not much is left of the glamorous interiors, although almost all the rooms used to be richly decorated with drawings and sketches. Branicki even bought a printing press so as to copy various views of his beloved garden by a dozen. After the fire of 1944, the palace was reconstructed.

Palace in Białystok

Bobolice: Castle ruins

Bobolice

The castle in Bobolice was mentioned in the chronicles by Jan of Czarnków and Jan Długosz, who numbered it among the keeps founded by Kazimierz the Great. Nowadays it is a picturesque ruin, where only a trained eye can detect traits of medieval fortifications. The castle was of a distorted shape, as required by that of the limestone hill. Its uppermost part was a cylindrical tower. Among the remains of the walls, made of local limestone, one can find the outer wall, which followed the irregular outlines of the hill. The castle may have been destroyed during the invasion of Archduke Maximilian Habsburg (1587) or during the Swedish wars. In the 17th c. King Jan Sobieski stayed in Bobolice on his way to relieve Vienna, and the army had to spend the night in tents. Eventually, the castle was completely abandoned at the beginning of the 18th c. The remains of the walls and tower were looked after from 1958 on. The best-preserved part is the two-storey tower.

Castle in Bolków

Bolków

The majestic castle of the dukes of Jawor and Świdnica overlooks the town and the valley of the Nysa Szalona. It is one of the most beautiful mountain castles in Poland. The construction started in the late 13th c. by order of Duke Bolesław II the Bald. The only extant structure from that period is a unique, massive tower with a 25-metre spike, the only such tower in Poland. The castle held the treasury of the duchy. In 1245 the Czech forces, led by the knights from Czerna, stormed the walls four times, but all in vain. Neither was the castle captured during the Hussite wars. It was only conquered by the Bohemian king George of Podebrad. In 1540 it was rebuilt in Renaissance style to the design of J. Parr: the interiors were refurbished and the walls decorated with sgraffiti and the typically Silesian attics. A new building, called the women's house, was added as well as outer walls and bulwarks. In its extended shape, the castle occupied the area of 7,600 square metres, so it was one of the largest in Silesia. In 1703 it became the property of the Cistercians from Krzeszowice, and when the order was suppressed, it fell into disrepair.

Branice

Branice, situated in the neighbourhood of Cracow, was the seat of the influential Branicki family. A small but interesting building is connected with them. Its foundations were laid in the early 16th century, wVhen a defensive residential tower appeared on the site, and it acquired its present shape probably around 1603.

The initiative to enlarge the residence is ascribed by researchers to the royal administrator of Niepołomice, Jan Branicki. He commissioned the modernisation work to the Cracow workshop of Santi Gucci. The mastery of these craftsmen is manifest in the late Renaissance interior decorations of the upper room, especially in the relieved mantelpiece from 1603. Near the mantelpiece one can also see an excellent portal decorated with acanthus leaves and a cartouche with the coat of arms of the Branicki family.

In the vicinity of the 17th-century residence stands a one-storey neo-classical manor, rebuilt in the late 19th century by Tadeusz Stryjeński. Both are surrounded by a former landscape park, which has retained some features of the original layout.

Residential tower in Branice

Brzeg: Castle courtyard

BRZEG

To stress the grandeur of Brzeg castle, some call it a "miniature of Wawel castle." But this place needs no lofty phrases. After the division of the Wrocław Duchy in 1311, Brzeg was the capital of the Duchy of Legnica and Brzeg, which in 1329 became a Bohemian dominion. The last of the Piasts ruling here, Duke Jerzy Wilhelm, died in 1675, and with him died the greatness of this once prosperous town when it came under the rule of the Habsburgs. The ducal seat in Brzeg was mentioned as early as in 1235, and the castle was probably built ca 1300. Perhaps even before 1342 it was extended by Duke Bolesław III. The chapel, i.e. the old collegiate church of St Jadwiga, was erected in 1368-71. The chapel stands now in the southern corner of the rectangular complex; it holds sepulchres of the Piasts from the local dynastic line.

In 1541, Duke Fryderyk II began to reshape the castle in Renaissance style. The work was commissioned to Franciszek and Jakub Parr (Bahr), who employed a team of masons, stonecutters and sculptors, some from Italy and some from Silesia. The modernisation supervisor, Jakub Parr, came from Milan, and in Brzeg he was the superior of the guild of Italian masons. When Fryderyk II died in 1547, his project continued under Jerzy II. The old Gothic castle was completely remodelled. The result was a compact, four-winged complex with an inner courtyard and cloisters; the northern wing was built in 1556-58. The arcaded yard and the decorations of the gate belong to the greatest achievements of Renaissance architecture in Silesia. After the death Wilhelm, the last Silesian Piast, in 1675, the Duchy of Brzeg came under the Austrian rule.

The castle suffered seriously under the gunfire of the Prussian army in 1741. For decades afterwards, the victors used it for storage. It was only a dozen or so years ago that, after a long restoration, the residence regained its previous beauty. Especially impressive is the entrance building, whose façade with figural decoration from 1556-60 is one of the masterpieces of Silesian Renaissance, and the work of Silesian sculptors: A. Walther, K. Kuhne and J. Werter, supervised by Franciszek Parr. Over the entrance stand two life-size statues of the founder and his wife Barbara, and stone statues of squires holding huge armorial shields.

Brzeg: Decoration of castle gate

Bytów

In 1329 the area of Bytów was bought by the Teutonic Knights and at the end of the century they began to build here the westernmost fortress on their territory. The construction, completed in 1405, was supervised by M. Fellenstein. The fortress was intended as a base for large troops of mercenaries. The corners were reinforced with four towers: the Mill Tower, the Gunpowder Tower, the Rose Tower and the Lower Tower. Following the battle of Grunwald, King Władysław Jagiełło gave the castle to Duke Bogusław VIII, but in 1657 it was taken over by Elector Frederick William I. The fortifications were modernised after 1500 under the supervision of F. van dem Werder. Temporarily, Bytów functioned as a residence of dukes' sons. Between 1560 and 1570 the Duke's House, and in 1570 the Duke's Chancellery were erected. In the 17th c. the castle was reshaped again, but it served now only as a residence of dukes' wives or widows. In the 19th c. it was turned into a prison and court.

Bytów: Castle of Teutonic Knights

Chęciny: Castle tower

Chęciny

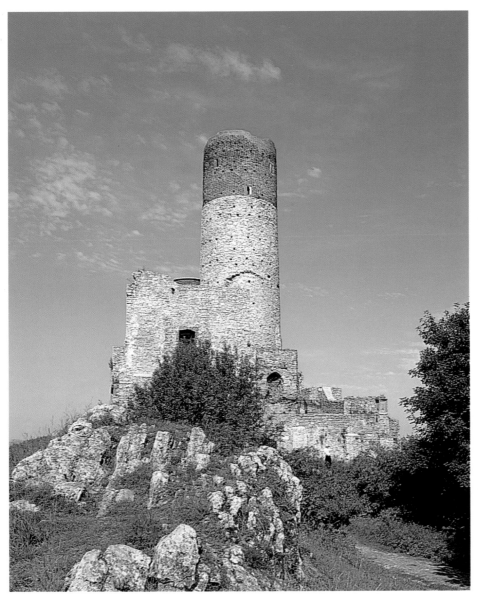

Chęciny lies near Kielce. The landmark of the area is the ruins of the castle situated high upon a rocky hill. From up there, one could easily control the crossing of merchants' routes. The fortified castle was probably built by Bishop Jan Muskata in the late 13th c. From 1308 the fortress belonged to King Władysław the Elbow-High, who captured it from the rebellious Bishop. The castle was several times enlarged. In 1318 Archbishop Janik transferred here the treasury of Gniezno Cathedral. The years 1310, 1318 and 1331 saw the assemblies of Polish dukes and noblemen; the last date is considered to mark the first Polish parliamentary assembly. In the next centuries Chęciny served as an important military and administrative centre. Traditionally, it was also the residence of royal widows. In 1425 King Władysław Jagiełło sent his son Władysław to Chęciny so that, in this secluded place, he could await the end of the plague which spread over the kingdom. Queen Bona deposited here her jewels. Chęciny is a typical upland castle which took advantage of the natural defences of the area. The upper castle has an irregular polygonal shape, two cylindrical towers, a gatehouse with a drawbridge and treasure vaults. On the western side, the lower castle and the rectangular tower were put up. When the Jagiellonian dynasty died out, the interest in Chęciny expired. In 1607 the castle was seriously damaged by a fire. It returned to its previous form, but in 1657 it was ravaged by the Hungarian troops of Duke George Rakocsy. Although rebuilt then again, after the devastations of the Northern War it fell into ruin.

Chojnik: Castle ruins

Chojnik

The area of Jelenia Góra is watched over by Chojnik castle, perched on high rocks above a 150-metre precipice of the "Hell Valley." In medieval times the castle was the seat of the Piasts ruling the Duchy of Jawor and Świdnica. They also founded here the oldest building, perhaps even from the late 13th c., whose remnants are the upper castle with a cylindrical tower and a small adjacent hall. Additionally, Duke Bolko the Short fortified Chojnik as it guarded his territories against the Bohemian state, ruled by John of Luxembourg. Between 1393 and 1634 the castle was owned by the Schaffgotsch family. Gotfryd Schaff founded the chapel of SS George and Catherine (finished in 1405), which was situated over the entrance to the upper castle. The chapel's bay window was decorated with coats of arms and openwork of red sandstone. The extant Renaissance elements are attics shaped as semicircular crests. About 1560, an enormous outwork was built north of the castle. More fortifications were added in the 17th c. In 1675 the castle was set on fire by a lightning and burned down, which marked the beginning of its collapse. Probably this medieval structure could not have been reconstructed because it had no supply of drinking water apart from rain water, which was collected in three stone cisterns.

Chojnów: Gate of ducal residence

Chojnów

Chojnów is a medieval town on the Chojnów Plain. The Gothic keep of the dukes of Legnica and Brzeg burned down in 1508, therefore in 1546-47 Duke Fryderyk III replaced the damaged structure with a tripartite Renaissance residence. The façade boasts a portal with a relief representation of the ducal couple: Fryderyk III of Legnica and Katharina of Mecklenburg, their coats of arms, and a foundation plaque. The modernisation was commissioned to the Italian workshop of F. Parr (Bahr) operating in Silesia. During the Thirty Years' War (when the town was captured by the Swedish in 1642) and then in 1661, the residence was destroyed by fire. But at the beginning of the 18th c. it was still inhabited. Its remains were several times reshaped and thus the original design was obliterated. The process was aggravated by the fire started in 1813 by the French soldiers. In the 19th c. the premises served as offices of the Prussian administration.

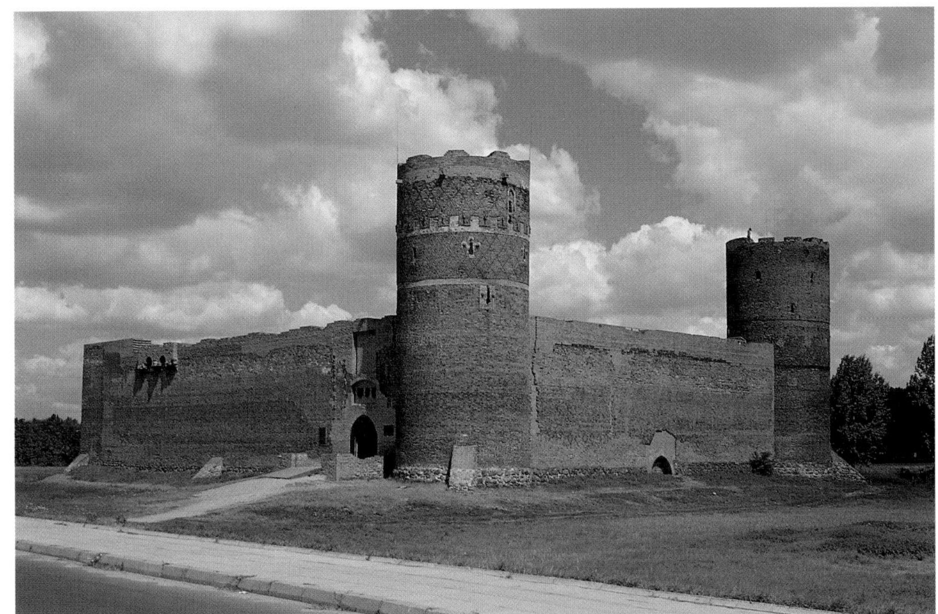

Castle in Ciechanów

Ciechanów

Ciechanów is famous for its castle, built in the 1420s on riverside marshy meadows by the Mazovian dukes. It was their residence and also it protected the border with the territories of the Teutonic Knights. When Mazovia was incorporated into Poland in 1526, the castle became the property of Queen Bona, who made it one of her favourite abodes. Afterwards, it could not enjoy an equally considerate manager. When in 1648 Queen Ludwika Maria Gonzaga, wife to Władysław IV, spent here the night, one of her retinue, the Lithuanian Chancellor A. Radziwiłł, wrote: "We stayed for the night in Ciechanów, which can be rightly called the capital of rats." Destroyed by the Swedish troops in 1657, the castle remained in ruins for a long time and it never regained its former functions. It was used as offices for the local administration. After the collapse of the Polish state, the Prussians demolished the palace. The extant parts are the perimeter wall and the two towers.

Czersk

In the 1st half of the 13th c. Konrad of Mazovia appointed his castellan to reside in Czersk. His decision stressed the rank of the castle, which had existed from the end of the 11th c. From 1247, Czersk was the seat of Mazovian dukes, the second (besides Płock) administrative centre of the region, and the capital of the duchy: Warsaw became the capital of Mazovia only in 1413 by order of Duke Janusz of Mazovia. In Czersk one can find remnants of a Gothic residence from the turn of the 15th c. Masonry work started under Janusz the Elder. The ramparts were lowered; an outer wall was raised instead and towers were added. When Mazovia was incorporated in Poland, in 1526 the castle was taken over by Queen Bona. It became a residence and was deprived of its defensive character: it was not so important any more as the raids of the Lithuanians had been long forgotten. For Queen Bona, a palace was erected and vineyards were arranged on the slopes of the hill. But when the ducal seat was removed to Warsaw, and the river Vistula changed its course, Czersk lost its significance. The castle with several towers fell into ruin after the attack of the Swedish (1656), the army of the Duke of Transylvania, George II Rakocsy, and the Prussians. In the 19th c. the castle was abandoned and subsequently vandalised as it was treated as a useful store of building materials.

Ducal castle in Czersk

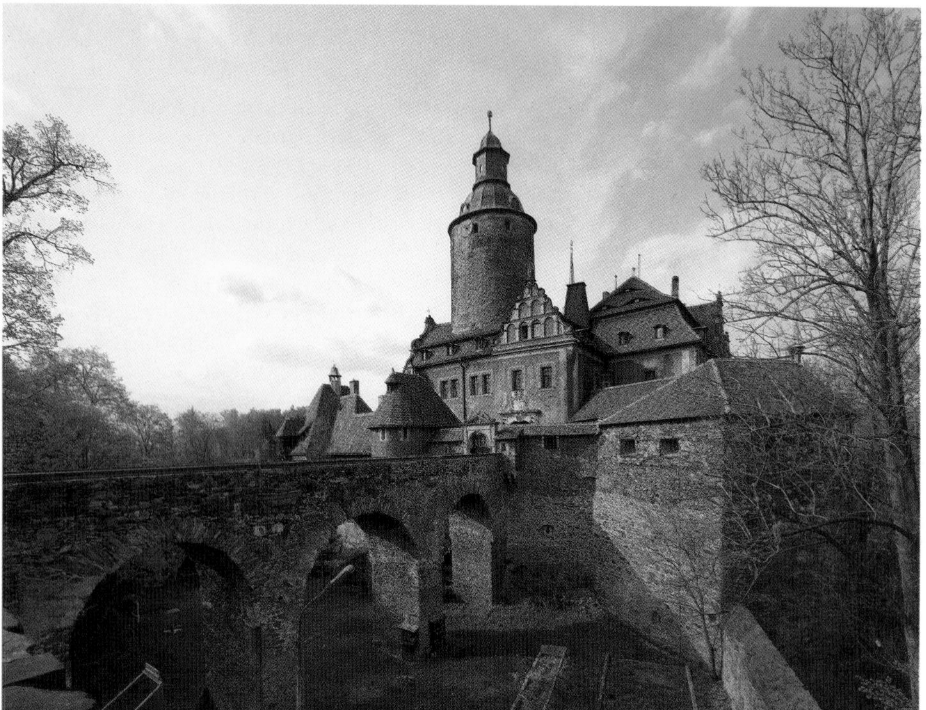

Castle in Czocha

Czyżów Szlachecki

In a small village at the border of the Sandomierz Upland stands a late Baroque palace of the castellan of Połaniec, A. Czyżowski. It was built in 1740-51 and reshaped in 1781--1820. Specialists in the history of architecture consider it an exemplary replica of Habsburg residences, in the 18th-c. fashion of the Polish countryside. In its design, the palace resembles the residence of the Lubomirski and Czartoryski families in Puławy. The remodelling from the turn of the 19th c. was probably the achievement of the Jesuit architect Józef Karśnicki. Although his design preserved the then outdated corner annexes, it also introduced rococo gables and mansard roofs. The outstanding feature of the façade is the sculpted decoration by T. Hutter (ca 1731--46). The entrance portal is extant as well, with a representation of figures of bound slaves. In front of the palace, a statue of Hercules is to be found. The building underwent renovation in the 1920s and then 1980s.

Czocha

This mysterious castle, with its maze of corridors, secret dungeons and passages, is positioned on a high rock over the Kwisa. In the 1st half of the 14th c. it belonged to the dukes of Jawor and then it became a fief of the Bohemian crown. The Gothic fortress was remodelled in the 16th c. In the mid-17th c. only the tower was left intact. Even the moat was adapted for a menagerie, and a huge bridge spanned over it (this timber structure collapsed in 1719 under the weight of the cortege which followed the coffin of the castle's owner). The great fire of 1793 put an end to Czocha's prosperity, destroying also the rich archives. At the beginning of the 20th c. a splendid Tudor-style library was established here. The castle acquired its present, neo-Romantic shape during the extension works of 1904-14, conducted by B. Ebhardt. Czocha was later bought by the family von Gütschoff. The interiors were reconstructed and refurnished in their original style. This was not the first renovation; no wonder that the castle changed into a kind of labyrinth. Not without good cause, it is mentioned in many stories about the jewels of the Romanov dynasty, about the experiments of the missile constructor Werner von Braun and secret documents hidden here towards the end of the Second World War. One gets inside through a semi-circular gate, flanked by two bulwarks. The entrance is adorned with an impressive portal which shows the genealogy of the previous owners, and the façade is topped with a statue of Athena carrying a shield with an image of Medusa.

Palace in Czyżów Szlachecki

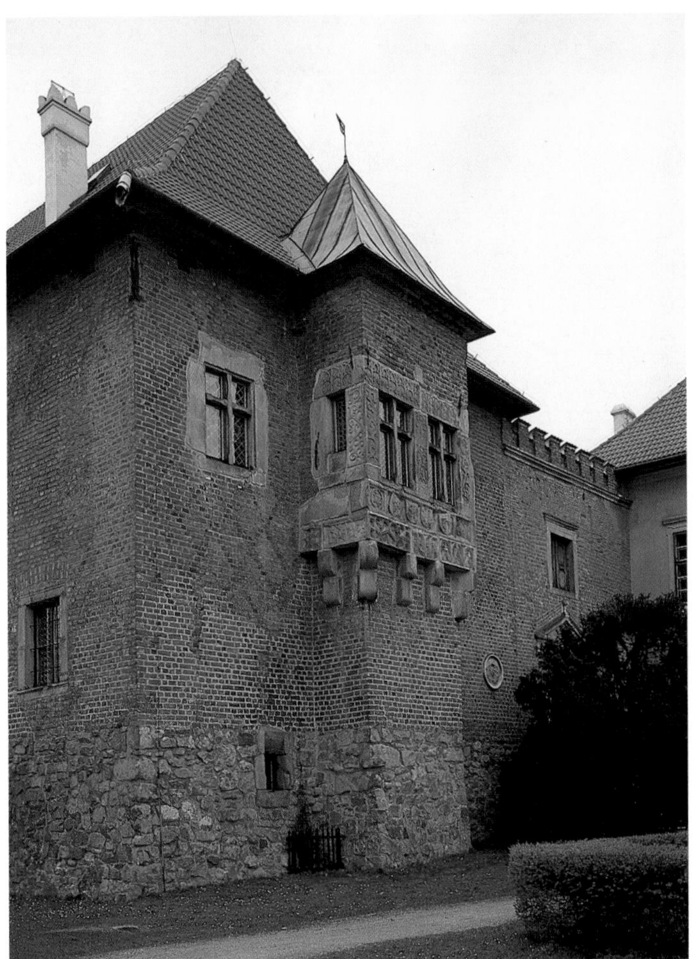

Dębno

The appearance and the surroundings of Dębno castle almost ideally mirror our notions of old, legendary feudal halls, filled with ancient weapons. The defensive residence, as it exists now, was built around 1470-80 and it was founded by Crown Chancellor Jakub Dębiński. The castle is one of the best examples of small, Gothic buildings with a rectangular yard and probably the first one that was not protected by any additional defence walls. The interiors owe a great deal to the secretary of King Stephen Báthory, Ferenc Wesseleny, who, having received the castle in 1583, refurbished it in Renaissance style. The evidence of his excellent taste is, for instance, 16th-c. portals. The picturesque castle, whose late Gothic construction is extremely attractive and whose abundant architectural details fascinated the painter Jan Matejko, was thoroughly renovated in the 1970s.

Dobrzyca

Dobrzyca boasts a unique neo-classical palace, built for Augustyn Gorzeński in 1795-99 to the design of Stanisław Zawadzki. The two-winged building is shaped like a builder's square: Freemasons' symbol of rights and responsibilities, which was probably imposed on the designer by the founder. The interiors were decorated after 1800 by Antoni Smuglewicz and are noteworthy for their murals imitating architectural details. The stuccoes were made under the supervision of Italian artists. In the palace, Gorzeński gathered a collection of contemporary sculpture, e.g. by A. Canova. Many objects were donated by King Stanisław August (e.g. the mantelpiece of black stone, the coronation portrait by M. Bacciarelli, sculptures, furniture). The collonaded portico of the palace looks upon the garden. The highlight of the landscape park, which is situated at the confluence of two arms of the Patoka stream, is the Masonic lodge modelled on the Roman Pantheon.

Dębno: Castle projection

Palace in Dobrzyca

Manor house in Dołęga

Dołęga

Near Dębno, in the area of Tarnów, lies the small village of Dołęga. The larch-wood house was raised in 1845 for Teodor Pikuziński. It is shaped like a horseshoe, plastered and covered with a shingled gable roof: a typical modest country residence of a noble family. The front has a porch supported by two pillars. During the 1863 Uprising the house functioned as a meeting base for the insurgents and a makeshift hospital for the wounded who managed to steal across the border. Two Polish generals were hosted then in the manor. At the turn of the 20th c. the house was visited by the artists Stanisław Wyspiański, Adam Asnyk and Włodzimierz Tetmajer. In 1973, the last owner Jadwiga Tumidajska handed the property over to the state so that it should hold a museum (in 1945 the privately-owned estate was not divided among peasant families as its area was too small). Inside, one can see a drawing room with old furniture, photographs, paintings (e.g. by S. Wyspiański) and the residents' memorabilia. In the study-cum-bedroom the majority of exhibits come from the time of the 1863 Uprising, e.g. weapons and an insurgents' standard. Among the traditionally furnished rooms, one should note that of Professor Michał Siedlecki, a famous biologist, oceanographer and traveller. The manor complex in Dołęga, besides the timber house, includes also a chapel in the park. It is said that the insurgents, before combat, took their soldiers' vows here. Behind the orchard stands a big granary, removed from the old estate of the Sanguszko family in Chyszów.

Drzewica

Drzewica lies near Opoczno, among the gloomy, sandy plains of the area of Radom. The first records from the 13th c. mention it as a village and then a town owned by the Ciołek-Drzewicki family. Drzewica was famous for its smithies. F. Carosi, who travelled around Poland in the 18th c., saw in Drzewica (which then belonged to Filip Szaniawski, a local official) a huge furnace and two hammer forges, "equipped as adequately as possible so that one could not find better equipment in any country." It must have really been so, because the smithies in Drzewica survived the disintegration of the Polish state and produced weapons even at the time of the 1830 Uprising. The continuator of this tradition has been the well-known company Gerlach. The prosperous owners of Drzewica had an impressive Gothic-Renaissance castle, built in 1527-35, originally

Drzewica: Castle ruins

as a residence for the Archbishop of Gniezno, Maciej Drzewicki. The fortifications did not match the size of the residence and the towers, situated in the angles of this very high structure, were not suitable for flank fire. The designer apparently had not heard about bulwarks. His building replaced a medieval defensive structure, whose remnants were found by specialists in historic architecture in the walls of what is extant now. Drzewica castle was built of sandstone on a rectangular ground plan. Square towers were placed obliquely in the corners. One of the towers had a large and a small pedestrian gate. A two-storeyed palace stood in the western part of the courtyard. The opposite side was occupied by a three-storey utility building, which in the early 19th c. was converted into a chapel. The residence is memorable for the richness of late Gothic and Renaissance brick gables. In the 18th c. the town and the castle were the property of the Sołtyks and then of the Szaniawskis. The palace was taken over by a Bernardine convent, and in 1787 it was visited by King Stanisław August. The residence fell into ruin after the fire of 1814 and the nuns moved to the village of Święta Katarzyna. The walls have been preserved till now in good shape; one can even see the outlines of two moats and an earthen rampart.

Gdańsk Dwór Artusa

The Guild Hall was a special meeting house for a relatively large group of merchants and patricians. The tradition of establishing such a hall (literally "Arthur's court", in Polish "Dwór Artusa") derives from Arthurian legends, which upheld the Round Table as an ideal of equality and concord. The Guild Hall in Gdańsk was put up in 1476-81. It was managed by seven guilds consisting of various groups of opulent and influential residents of the town, renowned craftsmen and scholars. The walls were covered with carved panelling and the murals above it depicted Biblical and mythological scenes. Each guild lavishly decorated their part of the building with benches, wall panelling, paintings and sculptures (the richest furnishings were bought by the guilds of St Reinold, St Christopher and the Three Magi). From the stellar ceiling, supported by four columns, there were suspended elaborate ship models. In 1616-17 the Gothic building was given a Mannerist Dutch style southern façade, facing the street of Długi Targ, designed by Abraham van den Blocke and adorned with statues. They represent ancient military leaders (Scipio Africanus, Themistocles, Camillus and Judas Maccabaeus) or allegories of Might, Justice and Plenty. In the same period the Neptune Fountain was placed before the Guild Hall (the extant statue is a late Baroque one, by K. Stender). The modest late Gothic façade facing the north, restored to its original shape in 1842, is crowned with a triangular openwork gable. In 1742 the Guild Hall began to serve as a commodity and stock exchange and it maintained this function till the Second World War; the building was completely renovated in 1997. The interiors are filled with objects of art donated by the guilds between the 15th and 19th c.. One of the most precious is Europe's highest, five-tiered stove (10.6 metres high) built by G. Stelzener of decorated tiles as well as the inlaid and carved benches for guild members. A memorable exhibit is the relief of St George fighting the dragon (by Hans Brandt, ca 1485).

Gdańsk Guild Hall: Detail of the stove

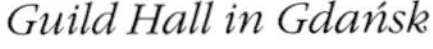

Guild Hall in Gdańsk

Gniew

Gniew lies on a high bank of the Vistula. In 1276-1464 it was ruled by the Teutonic Knights, who received it from the Pomeranian Duke Sambor. In 1283 the Knights arranged here a makeshift fort, using building materials from the demolished Pottenberg castle in the area of Chełmno. The structure surmounted the steep slopes facing the Vistula and its tributary Wierzyca. Later on the castle was extended. The Gothic residence of Teutonic commanders, later on of Polish royal officials, was rectangular, had four angle towers and was surrounded by a wall. When it became the residence of the Grand Master M. Küchmeister, it was enlarged. The assembly house and the neighbouring area were ringed by fortifications, towers and two gates. The castle was twice destroyed by the Swedish. In 1626, in the battle of Gniew, the charges of the Polish hussars broke under the fire of Swedish muskets and artillery: the troops of King Gustavus Adolphus could take their revenge for the lost battle of Kircholm. In 1667-96 the administrator of Gniew was Jan Sobieski. For his beloved wife Marysieńka he commissioned a Baroque palace, while the old castle underwent renovation. Another restoration came in 1772 and it resulted, among others, in the demolition of medieval vaulting. In 1875-79 the castle was turned into a prison. The conversion project was aimed at a partial remodelling in Gothic style. Also, new angle turrets were added. After 1918 the building housed local administration offices, but in 1921 it was destroyed by a fire. Preservation work commenced only in 1969.

Gniew: Castle of Teutonic Knights

Głogówek

The castle in Głogówek, sited on a high slope, overlooks the town and the river valley. Till 1532 it was under the rule of the Piasts from Opole. During the Hussite wars the castle became a base of the utraquists, religious radicals. In the 16th-17th centuries, on the foundation of the Piasts' castle, a new residence of the Oppersdorf family was raised. A symbol of their rank and self-importance is the portal, richly decorated with coats of arms and statues. In the first stage of the project, a three-winged building appeared (the western wing being the main one), and an outer ward and park were arranged. In the second stage, after 1584, under Duke Jerzy II, the three-winged building was enlarged: four cylindrical towers were added. During the Swedish wars, Głogówek gave shelter to King Jan Kazimierz. In the 1730s, when the estate was in the possession of the Moravian line of the Oppersdorfs, the residence began to acquire its late Baroque shape and so its Renaissance features were gradually erased. In 1806 the castle in Głogówek became the residence of Ludwig van Beethoven, who also gave concerts here and composed his *Fourth Symphony*, dedicated to Count Franz von Oppersdorf. In the mid-19th c., in the times of E. Oppersdorf, the aristocratic residence was reshaped in neo-Gothic style with neoclassical elements, modelled on the designs by K. F. Schinkel. It was destroyed in 1945.

Głogówek: Courtyard of the upper castle

Golejewko

The oldest record concerning Golejewko comes from the famous bull of Pope Innocent III, issued in 1136 in Pisa. At the turn of the 13th c., Golejewko was a castellan's residence: its traces can still be found in the vicinity of the park. In the 17th c. the castle was extended in Renaissance style by the Chojeński family and afterwards it became the property of the Rogaliński family. The extant appearance of the building reflects the tastes of Count Marceli Czarnecki, who in the mid-19th c. laid out the design of the whole complex. In 1848 Antoni Czarnecki added a neo-Renaissance palace, but preserved the 17th-c. gatehouse.

Golub-Dobrzyń

On 4th July 1228, Konrad of Mazovia ceded the area of Dobrzyń to the Prussian Knights of Christ, a faction of the Knights of the Sword. The Prussian Knights had a papal permit to fight the heathen Prussians. Soon it became obvious that so small an order could hardly defend Dobrzyń against the attacks of the pagans. Hence their mission was taken over by a more powerful order, the Teutonic Knights, who grew in might in close vicinity, on the other side of the Drwęca River. They initiated contacts with Konrad, who, having obtained a promise that Mazovia should be safeguarded against the raids of the Prussians, gave the Teutonic Order the area of Chełmno. It became the centre of the Teutonic state and, for Poland, a source of problems arising later in Prussia, Pomerania and Warmia. At the beginning of the 14th c. Commander Konrad Sack built in Golub a Gothic castle. The fortress watched over a ford in the river and was frequently under siege. Between 1329 and 1333 it was stormed by Polish and Lithuanian troops invading the area of Chełmno. It was also besieged in 1410 and 1422 during the "war of Golub". Having captured the castle, King Władysław Jagiełło had some of the fortifications pulled down. In 1460, during the Thirteen Years' War, Golub was both beleaguered and defended by the Czechs, that is mercenaries on the side of the Teutonic Knights and of the Polish king. In 1611-25 the castle was rebuilt and adorned with a harmonious Mannerist attic; it served as a residence of Princess Anna Vasa. After the First Partition, the buildings housed local administration offices and later on a field hospital. In 1867 the castle was destroyed by a hurricane and fell into ruin. Only in 1955-69 was it renovated and partly reconstructed. Nowadays we can admire its beautiful original shape: it is a square structure with and inner courtyard and cloisters of wood, four angle turrets and two towers at the front (the southern tower comes from before 1422). The wing holds a chapel from 1310, notable for its stellar ceiling, and a chapter. At present Golub-Dobrzyń hosts knights' tournaments that are famous all over Poland.

Palace in Golejewko

Golub-Dobrzyń: Castle of Teutonic Knights

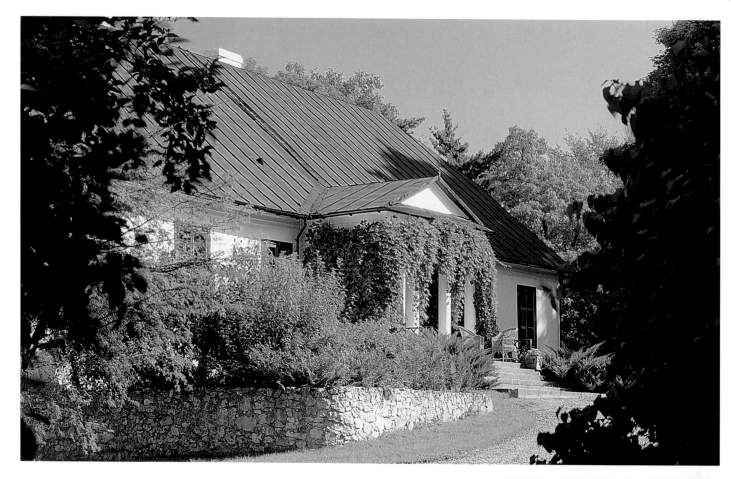

Manor house in Gołyszyn

Gołyszyn

In the picturesque landscape of the uplands stretching from Cracow to Częstochowa stands a small, stone-and-timber manor house from the first half of the 19th c. With a porch at the front and a jerkin head roof, it provides an example of a provincial treatment of the typical neo-classical design. The embellishments are stone and marble portals. The place gained a unique character thanks to its decorated stoves from the mid-19th c. The house is situated on a slope over a tributary of the Dłubnia. It may be accessed by a country road which ends with a driveway around the front lawn. The house is surrounded by a landscape park.

Goszyce

The manor house in Goszyce, in the Plain of Miechów, belongs to the oldest timber structures of the kind. It looks so old that the tradition and many publications obstinately date it back to the times of King Jan III Sobieski (others prefer a later date, the early 18th c.). The main part of the building is square and has two annexes. The house is covered with a mansard roof and has a small attic supported by two columns. Thus it represents a classic Polish manor house: a mute witness of the past in a charming neighbourhood. The walls were made of vertically arranged logs. In the 19th c. the manor was owned by the Zawisza family. The fame of the old house was then slightly overshadowed by that of the new one, built in 1890, which achieved historical recognition as a base of the mounted patrol of the First Cadre Company led by Władysław Belina-Prażmowski. In August 1914 the soldiers of the Polish Legions, who fought for the independence of the Polish Republic, spent here their first night before they took the field. The event is commemorated by a plaque which was unveiled personally by Marshal Józef Piłsudski.

Gołuchów

Gołuchów is famous for its splendid residence which developed from a castle into a palace and then into a museum. The original structure was a defensive castle with four angle towers, surrounded by a moat. It was built ca 1560 by Rafał Leszczyński and extended at the beginning of the 17th c. From 1846 it was owned by Wincenty Kalkstein and in 1853 sold to Jan Działyński, who

Manor house in Goszyce

Gołuchów Castle: Bedroom

in 1871 passed the residence over to his wife Izabela nee Czartoryska (d. 1899). After Działyński's death, the renowned family expired. And no wonder since he never stepped over the threshold of her bedroom, although Izabela was an acclaimed beauty. The entailed estate of Gołuchów was taken over by Witold Czartoryski, and his family owned the palace till the Second World War.

The present style of the palace (French neo-Renaissance) is the result of the 1872-85 remodelling ordered by Izabela Działyńska to the design of Eugene Viollet-le-Duc, inspired by the castles on the Loire. The project was carried out by Zygmunt Gorgolewski and Maurice Ouradou (Violet-le-Duc's son-in-law). The palace had two storeys, an open yard, four angle towers, arcades in the upper storey and a terrace. The atmosphere of the past was evoked by original sculptures and architectural details from the 15th-16th c., brought from France and Italy. The palace held the art collection of the Czartoryski family (some exhibits came from Hôtel Lambert in Paris), including a famous collection of antique vases. The objects of art were dispersed during the Second World War and only some of them were later regained. In the museum one can see, among others, unique Gothic furniture. Since 1962 the renovated residence in Gołuchów has been a branch of the National Museum. The building stands amid a large arboretum and a 162-hectare park laid out in 1876-99 by A. Kubaszewski and crossed by the Trzemna Stream. The historical complex includes, besides the residence, numerous adjacent buildings: the exquisitely designed Czartoryski Palace (1890-96) with splendid interiors, a distillery (1872-74), a counting house (1885-87), a mausoleum, that is the old chapel of St John the Baptist, and other buildings.

Castle in Gołuchów

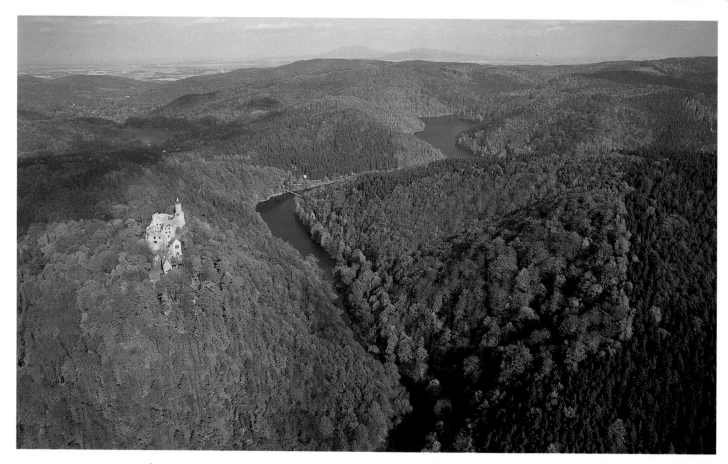

Grodno Castle in Zagórze Śląskie

Grodno

On the verge of the Sowie Mountains stand the ruins of the Gothic ducal castle Grodno. It was built in the 13th-14th c. by Bolko I and Bolko II, rulers of the Duchy of Świdnica and Jawor. However, the tradition says that the castle was erected under Bolesław the Tall in 1198. The castle guarded the border between the Duchy and Bohemia. This stone building with a small rectangular tower occupied an elongated platform atop a steep hill. The rulers of Świdnica and Jawor kept the castle till the death of Duchess Agnieszka in 1392, when it was taken over by Bohemian kings and later by feudal lords. In the 15th c. it was a den of merciless robber-barons. In 1545 the castle was purchased by the administrator of the Duchy, Mathias von Logau, who began to enlarge it. He had the upper castle girdled with a perimeter wall fortified with bulwarks. At the same time, the tower's octagonal upper storey was built and attics were added onto the façades of lodging quarters. The Gothic upper castle was supplemented with a Renaissance lower castle. In the northern part, a second yard appeared, and opposite the main entrance, a third one with a gatehouse. The lower yard was surrounded by a wall with five bulwarks. The extant Renaissance relief portals of grey sandstone date back to that period. In 1570, the north-western curtain wall gained a late Renaissance gatehouse decorated with beautiful sgraffiti and a sundial (from 1716). Eventually, the 170-metre long complex spread over the entire hilltop. During the Thirty Years' War, the castle was defeated by the Swedish and partly destroyed. The year 1679 saw the rebellion (later on violently suppressed) of local peasants against the castle's owner, Baron Jerzy Eben from Strachowice near Legnica. The next owners did not care about the condition of the castle. They abandoned it in 1774 and since then it gradually deteriorated. In 1869, hit by a lightning, the tower burned down. The castle was saved from utter destruction by a historian from Wrocław, Johann Büsching, who in 1824 began the renovation. In 1868-69 some parts of the castle regained their Gothic shape.

Grodno Castle: Sgraffito decoration

Castle in Grodziec

Grodziec

Grodziec hill is a relic volcanic hill. In the 15th-16th c. the Piasts from Legnica put up here their second residence. In 1473, under Duke Fryderyk I, an elongated hexagonal structure was built. The extension work, in Renaissance style, continued under Fryderyk II (1522-24). During the Thirty Years' War, the castle was a base of the famous commander of the Empire, Albrecht Wallenstein. Stormed by Protestant forces, Grodziec was destroyed. In 1675 the reconstruction was started by the Duke of Brzeg, Jerzy IV Wilhelm. In the 18th c. the castle fell into ruin. At the beginning of the 20th c. it was reconstructed again.

Jabłonna

Jabłonna boasts a Baroque and neo-classical palace of the Poniatowski family, built in 1774-79 to the design of Merlini. The village was purchased by the future Primate M. J. Poniatowski, who established here his residence. Also Duke Józef Poniatowski had a liking for it. The façade is crowned by a tower covered with a cupola with a ball. The back, facing the garden, is dominated by the round projection of the Ball Room. The structure of the building is clearly Baroque, but the decorations were made in neo-classical style. The complex includes also two neo-classical pavilions (1780-82), an orangery (1781-84) and a Chinese arbour, all designed by S. B. Zug. The "royal house" on the left provided accommodation to King Stanisław August when he visited the Primate, his brother. The palace was rebuilt for the Potocki family by H. Marconi in 1837-38. He did not modify the design of the buildings, but only the arrangement of the rooms. To commemorate his achievement, he erected a triumphal arch in the garden (ca 1842). The palace is surrounded by a large park from the 18th c., reshaped in 1827-37. It was in Jabłonna that the historic Round Table negotiations were originally to take place in 1989, and the piece of furniture itself was designed to fit in the Ball Room.

Palace in Jabłonna

Palace in Kochcice

KOCHCICE

Kochcice was owned by the Kochcickis from the Middles Ages till the Thirty Years' War. Following the War, Protestant Silesian nobility, who felt connected with Poland, were deprived of their estates and influence and their role was taken over by Catholic German families who supported the Habsburg rule. Kochcice prides itself on a three-storey rectangular palace which was once renowned for the elegance of the façade and exquisite interior decorations. The façade of this neo-Baroque building is noted for the richness of its architectural design and for the ornaments. The terrace offers a view of the nearby ponds. The most beautiful hall of the residence, profusely stuccoed, is the Mirror Room, or the Ball Room. Let us remember, however, that Kochcice palace is an almost contemporary building. F. von Ballestrem bought the property in the early 20th c. and gave it over to his youngest son. In 1900-03 the new owner began to supplement it with utility buildings, stables and a distillery. Only in 1906-09 did he put up his new residence in the vicinity of the old one. He surrounded the palace with a park and landscape and geometrical gardens. He commissioned mosaics in the rooms, arranged the Ball Room and the chapel. Ballestrem considered himself a Silesian and a loyal citizen of the Republic of Poland; during the Second World War he refused to accept German citizenship. After 1945, the residence was ravaged by looters and soldiers of the Red Army.

JANOWIEC

Janowiec, a late Gothic-Renaissance castle of the Palatine of Lublin and Ruthenia, Piotr Firlej, is positioned on a high slope over the Vistula. It was put up in the 1st half of the 16th c. From an austere bulwarked fortress, in the 2nd half of the 16th c. and in the early 17th c., it was transformed by the Tarło and Lubomirski families into a great aristocratic residence. The project was carried out by Santi Gucci. The castle had a pentagonal courtyard, arcades to the south, a huge bulwark in the corner and smaller towers. The palace occupied the southern part of the complex; it was a two-storey building with five resplendent halls in the upper storey. Burned down by the Swedes in 1656, the castle was rebuilt in the 17th c. by T. van Gameren. The additions were, for instance, a projection on the northern side (with two storeys of enormous reception halls), a chapel (1676) and arcades; the interiors were decorated in Baroque style. In 1783 Janowiec was bought by M. Piaskowski. After his death the residence gradually dilapidated, and the new owners did not live in it. In 1928 it was purchased by L. Kozłowski, who began to renovate it. He remained the castle's owner even under the Communist regime, but gave up the renovation project. In 1975 he sold the ruins to the museum in Kazimierz Dolny, and in the next year restoration work commenced.

Castle in Janowiec

Kamieniec Ząbkowicki

When you look at the marble floors in the Congress Hall of the Palace of Culture and Science in Warsaw, remember that they were torn out from the palace of the Hohenzollerns in Kamieniec Ząbkowicki. The medieval village developed at first thanks to the neighbourhood of the monastery of the Austin monks, then Cistercians. And it could have lived on, unperturbed by historical events, if it had not been for the beautiful surroundings which attracted several monarchs. Nowadays the landscape is dominated by the neo-Gothic palace of Duke Albert Hohenzollern, or rather by what has remained of it. The residence was erected to the design of a famous architect from Berlin, K. F. Schinkel (and his partner F. Martius), on a high hill bought in 1812 by a Dutch princess. Her successor was Marianne of Orange, wife to Frederick Henry of Prussia. In the first design commissioned by Marianne (1838), the architect used Renaissance and Gothic motifs; in the second design he limited himself to neo-Gothic ones. The palace, whose construction began in 1839, was to virtually grow out of greenery. Red brick was used as in medieval architecture, which stressed the importance of colour in the design of the building. Stone elements excellently contrasted with the brick background. The scale of the project was rather impressive: the complex embraced the palace and outbuildings, vast gardens with many terraces, fountains and pergolas, baths on a hill and a mausoleum in the gardens. In this way Europe's largest neo-Gothic residence was put up on the rectangular ground plan which measured 75 by 50 metres. The angles were fortified with 34-metre high towers. The palace building has two storeys. Its wings flank a rectangular, arcaded inner courtyard. An arcaded passageway was built to join the wings of the palace with the staircase and the gardens. The interiors, as designed by Schinkel, have palm ceilings, modelled on those in Malbork castle. The garden with terraces (1858) was designed by J. P. Lenne, the director of the Royal Gardens in Berlin. The project was implemented till the autumn of 1865 and the cost of the investment amounted to five tons of gold. The palace held numerous objects of art, including a collection of paintings by Flemish masters, brought here by the Hohenzollerns. The valuable art objects were stolen in 1945 by the Red Army. The looted castle, in an act of sheer stupidity, was burned down.

Castle in Kamieniec Ząbkowicki

Kamieniec Ząbkowicki: Castle ruins

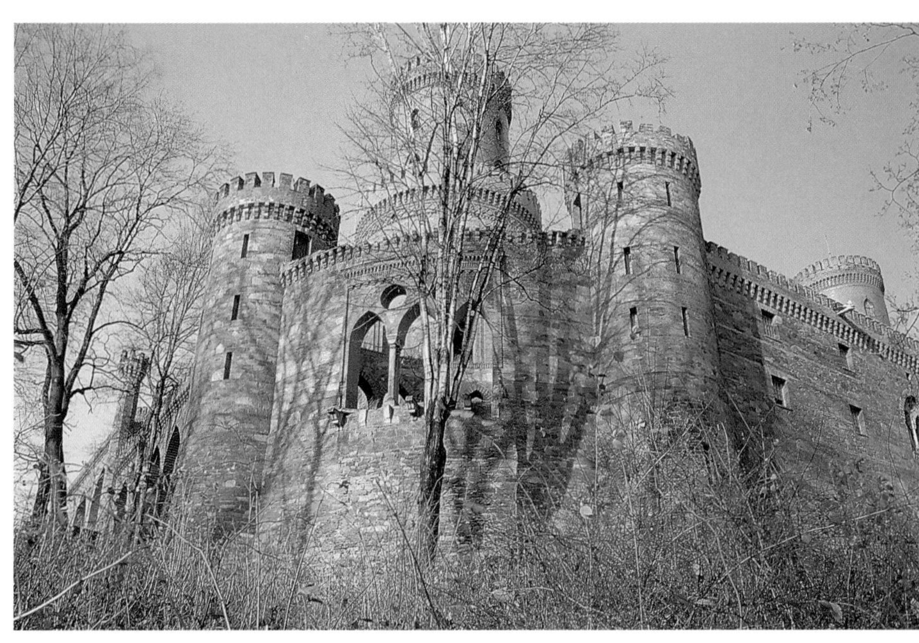

Kielce

The most imposing historical building in Kielce is the Baroque bishops' palace, erected for J. Zadzik in 1637-41. By building the palace, he fulfilled his ambitions: King Władysław IV apparently promoted but actually marginalised Zadzik by depriving him of the Chancellor's position and nominating him the bishop of Cracow. The authorship of the design is not certain; the documents mention T. Poncino, but he was more of a skilful mason than an architect or designer. So it is supposed that the palace was designed by G. Trevano. Poncino, an Italian, settled in Poland ca 1620. First he worked for the Vasa dynasty. With time, he became the chief mason of Warsaw. Kielce palace apart, he extended the collegiate church in Łowicz and erected there the Bernardine church. He also supervised the construction of the Cistercian church in Ląd and the Jesuit church in Poznań. He was one of the most important builders of early Baroque buildings. His work contributed to the propagation of the architectural forms typical of early 18th-c. Baroque buildings in Warsaw. The bishops' palace is arranged along three main axes, has two storeys and four hexagonal angle towers. It was put up in a conspicuous place: on a rocky hill, next to the then collegiate church. The central axis of the structure is accentuated by the arcaded entrance loggia and the windows of the great hall in the ground floor. The front towers are distanced from the main body of the building, which broadens the façade. The back towers are incorporated into the main body of the building and they hold apartments. Adjacent buildings appeared in 1720-46. A characteristic decorative element is obelisks: symbols of glory of contemporary rulers. The founder of the palace commissioned T. Dolabella to commemorate the crucial events in which Zadzik participated as the Chancellor: the treaty with Sweden, the imprisonment of the Shuysky Tsars and the banishment of the Arians. The palace houses a museum where one can find old portraits, furniture and handicraft. Especially memorable is the upper dining room, decorated with several dozen portraits of bishops and metropolitans of Cracow. The upper floor rooms boast polychrome ceilings. The residence in Kielce is practically the only one that has survived without any modifications since the 1st half of the 17th c. When the

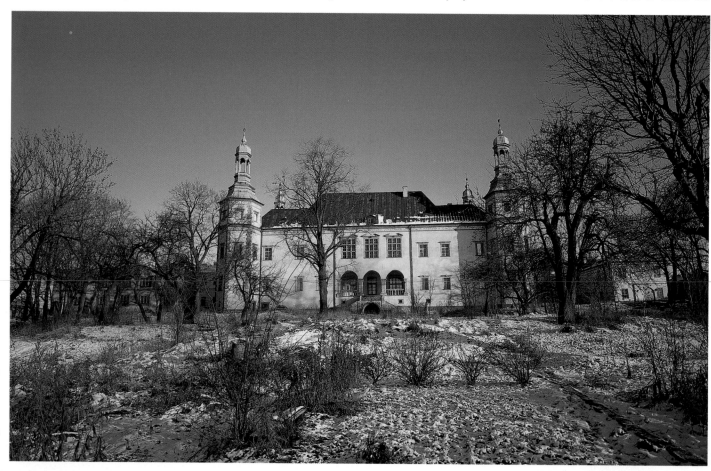

Kielce Palace: First Prelates' Room

Palace of Cracow bishops in Kielce

estates of bishops were nationalised in 1789, the palace became a seat of various institutions, e.g. in 1816-27 of the Coal Mining Board and the first technical university in Poland; and in 1867-1914 of the authorities of the Kielce province. The deterioration of the building came to an end only when Poland regained independence after the First World War. The cupolas on the towers, which had been dismantled by the occupants, returned to their previous places and the interiors were refurbished (beam-framed ceilings and friezes were revealed then). In 1919-39 and 1945-70 the residence provided offices to the local administration, and from 1971 on belonged to the National Museum.

Manor house in Koszuty

KOSZUTY

Koszuty lies a few kilometres from Kórnik. It was the seat of the Koszucki family, who owned the village from the 14th c. till the end of the 17th c., when it was acquired by the Rekowski family. In the 17th c. the Koszuckis had a wooden manor house built, which was demolished in the second half of the 18th c. On the old foundations, a new manor was put up with a carcass of timber and clay. It had Baroque features and a centrally positioned, masoned oval parlour. A characteristic element of the design is brick and stone annexes and a shingled roof. In this shape, the manor house served one of the heroes of the 1794 Uprising, General A. Kosiński. From 1850, the house and the land belonged to a Polish nobleman, Napoleon Rekowski. The next owner was his daughter Maria Rekowska, who in 1875 married Witold Kosiński. When Maria and Witold died without an heir, the estate went back to the Rekowski family and in 1945 it was taken over by the State Treasury. At present, in the larch house coming from the 18th c. and rebuilt in the 19th and 20th c., one can see interesting interiors. The present shape of the building is the result of the 1902 renovation. One can visit several fully furnished rooms: service and dining room, guests' room, parlour, the lord's, the lady's and the children's room. The exhibited furniture, paintings and bric-a-brac make it possible to recreate the appearance and the atmosphere of a manor house from the turn of the 20th c. Highly valuable are the memorabilia collected by the Kosiński family: the bust by A. Canova (ca 1790) and a well-known painting *Arrival of General Dąbrowski in Rome* by J. Suchodolski.

Koszuty: Interior of manor house

Kozłówka Palace: Façade

KOZŁÓWKA

Kozłówka palace is the most important one in the region of Lublin. The large complex of palace-cum-gardens was built in 1735-42 in late Baroque style by G. Fontana for the Bieliński family. In 1879-1907 the palace was reshaped, as commissioned by K. Zamoyski, in neo-Baroque style. Additional buildings appeared such as the chapel (modelled on the Versailles chapel; its organ was made in 1907 by the company of E. F. Walcher from Ludwigsburg), the theatre, an outbuilding and an entrance gate. The interiors have retained their design, decorations and original furnishings from the turn of the 20th c.. During the reconstruction of 1898-1911, the rooms were redecorated with neo-rococo and neo-Regency plafonds, marble mantelpieces, Meissen porcelain stoves and ornamental oak-wood floors. They were filled with furniture of various styles, from neo-Baroque to Empire, and adorned with many paintings, sculptures, sketches and drawings. On the walls there hung paintings and mirrors in lush gilt frames, the windows were embellished with curtains and lambrequins of silk damask and embroidered velvet. Nowadays the handicraft collection includes: china from Meissen and Sevres, porcelain services, jewellery and trinkets, e.g. an agate figurine of a boar made by C. Faberge. Among the palace interiors, one should note a resplendent staircase with a neo-rococo railing and richly decorated with stucco and marble. Zamoyski's study boasts the oldest painting in the palace: a landscape dated 1672 by O. Hams. The largest room in the palace is the Red Parlour, from which three exits used to lead onto the terrace (nonexistent now). In the Parlour, Zamoyski gathered portraits of Polish kings and hetmans, giving prominent places to the representations of his predecessors. According to the 19th-c. fashion, the dining room was arranged in somewhat hefty Baroque style. Opposite the windows stand Gdańsk wardrobes from the 17th and 18th c., filled with tableware. Kozłówka is the only residence turned into a museum in the whole region of Lublin. The collection of painting, sculpture, sketches and drawings contains family portraits, historical scenes (by F. Smuglewicz and J. Oleszkiewicz), landscapes and many copies of European masterpieces. The section of decorative arts embraces rare glass services (one of them decorated with the coat of arms of the Zamoyskis). The old coach house was converted into Poland's only gallery of art of social realism, with monuments standing outdoors. The complex is surrounded by a large park from the 18th–19th c., where one can find a romantic grave and a monument commemorating Napoleon's soldiers. The majority of the furniture and furnishings remain in the places they occupied under the Zamoyski family: no other aristocratic residence has been preserved in such a good condition.

Kozłowka Palace: Staircase

Kórnik

Kórnik Castle: Moresque Hall

Kórnik is one of those places where a visitor is not sure whether to see the residence or the gardens first. It was always the property of the great families of the Wielkopolska region. First mentioned by records in 1362, it belonged subsequently to the Górka, Działyński and Zamoyski families. Now, on an island surrounded by a broad moat stands a palace, the former castle of the Górkas, which was completely rebuilt by commission of T. Działyński in 1845-60 to the design of late K. F. Schinkel. The German architect was inspired by the fashionable romantic Gothic style from England. The fashion also gave rise to the legend about the White Lady who in the night stepped down from the portrait of Teofila nee Działyńska. Following the orders of the owner, the castle was adapted to function as a museum and a library; at the same time it acquired some features of a defensive structure: the walls were crenellated and fortified with towers, and a bridge was suspended over the moat. The palace rooms, including the magnificent Black Room or the Moresque Hall, boast furniture, paintings (e.g. by A. Grottger, J. P. Norblin, M. Bacciarelli), artistic handicraft, ethnographic exhibits and hunting trophies. The showcases hold objects of historical importance, old silverware, porcelain and faience, and textiles. Among the exhibited furniture, valuable objects are 17th- and 18th-c. Gdańsk and Brittany wardrobes, inlaid and encrusted cabinets, closets and chests of drawers. The collection includes also a great deal of jewellery and goldware (goblets, cups, tankards, tableware, cutlery, snuffboxes, ecclesiastical art objects, buttons, belts, rings, seals and watches). In the precious collection of arms and armour one should note a complete hussar's armour (17th c.), a Gothic suit of armour (16th c.), hussars' spears (17th c.), maces and pistols (18th c.), rifles (17th c.), curved swords and hunting crossbows (16th c.).

Kórnik is the only fully preserved aristocratic residence in the region of Wielkopolska. Part of it is Kórnik Library, which is of much importance for Polish culture as a valuable collection of manuscripts (e.g. a MS of *The Forefathers,* part III by A. Mickiewicz), incunabula and old prints. The Library was established by the Działyński family and now counts ca 350 thousand volumes. The most precious section consists of 30 thousand old prints (from the 15th-16th c.) and 15 thousand MSS (from the 12th c. on). The palace may also be considered a monument to W. Zamoyski, patriotically and socially minded aristocrat. He inherited Kórnik from the Działyński family, extended and modernised it. In 1889, with his own financial resources, he bought from the Hungarian government a part of the Tatra Mountains with the lake of Morskie Oko. In 1925 he donated the whole area as well as Kórnik and its collections to the Polish nation, instituting a foundation whose aim was to continue the previous owners' activities, i.e. to enlarge the Library and the museum collections and open them to the public. At present Kórnik palace formally belongs to Kórnik Library owned by the Polish Academy of Sciences, and so does the museum. The complex is surrounded by a geometrical park from the 18th c. and a landscape park, including an arboretum laid out after 1830 by T. Działyński and in 1953 taken over by the Polish Academy of Sciences. Now it is Poland's largest dendrological park (49 hectares; 4 thousand species of trees and bushes). A memorable sight is the blooming magnolias and Poland's oldest taxodium, a symbol of the Kórnik arboretum, with its roots growing above the ground. One can also observe here an apparently impossible phenomenon: pears growing on a willow, strictly speaking, on a Caucasian willow-leaf pear. An 18th-c. pavilion houses a dendrological museum with an unusual collection of cones. The complex additionally embraces late Baroque outbuildings from the mid-18th c. and from 1791, and farm buildings from the second half of the 18th c. and the first half of the 19th c.

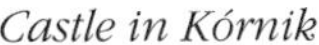

Castle in Kórnik

Wawel Castle: Arcaded courtyard

KRAKÓW WAWEL

The name "Wawel" remains an enigma to linguists; it has such an ancient origin that any knowledge of its etymology is impossible. Some scholars derive the name from an old Polish word *wąwel*, which meant a dry place surrounded by marshes, others think it must be connected with the tribes that inhabited the territories of present-day Poland before the arrival of Slavs. A defensive settlement on top of Wawel Hill must have existed under the Vistulanian state (9th c.). The remnants of non-ecclesiastical buildings (*palatium*) and of the pre-Romanesque rotunda of St Mary (or of SS Felix and Adauctus) come from the 10th c. In the year 1000 a bishopric was established in Cracow and it had its seat on Wawel Hill as well. The first monarch to choose Wawel as his permanent residence was Kazimierz the Restorer. The oldest section of the Gothic castle was a defence tower built of unhewn stone. In the 19th c. it was called the Tower of Władysław the Elbow-High, but its founder was more probably Wenceslas II of the Bohemian Premyslid dynasty. Next, a stone perimeter wall was raised, which protected all the buildings scattered around a yard. In the mid-14th c. King Kazimierz the Great put up a massive castle (still enlarged under Queen Jadwiga and King Władysław Jagiełło) and, allegedly, two towers: Jordanka and the Thieves' Tower. The remains of the Gothic structure are the Danish Tower and the Hen's Foot (15th c.). The latter tower is characteristic of Wawel Castle. Originally, it was a *Dansker*, that is a medieval toilet which stood far outside the walls. Under Kazimierz the Great, Wawel was the seat of various state offices and institutions, and perhaps also of the Cracow Academy (after 1364). Under Kazimierz the Jagiellon new towers were built: the Senators' Tower and the Sandomierz Tower.

The royal residence flourished during the reign of Zygmunt the Old, who decided to transform the Gothic castle into a Renaissance residence fit for a ruler of a great European power. The project was commenced by the builder and sculptor F. Fiorentino, who in 1502-07 rebuilt the castle's western wing as the Queen's House. When Zygmunt succeeded to the throne, in the years 1507-36 he carried out his projects with the help of Fiorentino (till 1516), Master Benedict (1521?-29) and, most importantly, B. Berrecci (1530-36).

Wawel Hill in Cracow

Wawel Castle: Birds Room

The result of their work was a residence with a spacious arcaded courtyard. The majority of Gothic buildings were demolished and new wings were raised; the southern wing had only arcades and the back wall, without any residential quarters. The arcaded courtyard – with slender columns in the first floor, reception rooms in the *piano nobile*, murals based on classical themes and roof covered with coloured tiles – was unparalleled in beauty, not only in Poland, but also abroad, even in Italy. The imposing interiors of Wawel complement the grandeur of the architecture. The most resplendent room is the Audience Hall, also called the Envoys' Hall. It boasts a coffer ceiling decorated with wood polychrome heads from 1531-35, a collective portrait of the contemporary inhabitants of Cracow. The Tournament Room and the Troops Parade Room are decorated with friezes by H. Dürer and Antoni of Wrocław. In the Senators' Room one can see arrases depicting the biblical Deluge. It was King Zygmunt August who, in order to adorn the interiors, ordered in Brussels a set of magnificent Flemish tapestries, which are mistakenly referred to as arrases, i.e. tapestries from Arras. Some of them form series, e.g. Adam and Eve in Paradise, Noah's Ark, or the Babel Tower; others represent imaginary landscapes and mythological animals, heraldic symbols, royal monograms and grotesque motifs. Worth noting is the collection of trophies gained during the Relief of Vienna, e.g. Turkish standards and tents. Other collections present old painting (with exhibits donated by Prof. K. Lanckorońska), valuable furniture, ceramics and china (especially precious is china from Saxony donated by T. Wierzejski, and the porcelain objects from China and Japan that were owned by Tsarina Catherine II are priceless). From the arcaded courtyard one can enter the Treasury. Since the 14th c. these rooms, untouched by Renaissance-style reconstruction, were used as a storage place for jewels, money and documents. After the suppression of the Kościuszko Insurrection (1794), the Prussian troops that occupied Cracow broke in and stole Polish coronation insignia, which they destroyed in 1810-11: the gold was melted in the mint and the jewels were sold. Only a small portion of the priceless Treasury collection has been preserved. Nowadays the most important exhibit is the coronation sword of Polish kings called Szczerbiec ("the notched sword"), which allegedly belonged to King Bolesław the Brave. The fire that destroyed the castle in 1595 was one of the reasons why the royal court moved to Warsaw. King Zygmunt III Vasa rebuilt some sections of the castle and introduced early Baroque decorations in the interiors. Wawel Castle still held the Treasury and the state archives, and the Cathedral maintained its function of the coronation church and the place of royal burials. From that time on, the castle did not undergo any serious reconstruction. A decisive blow to the glorious residence was the Swedish invasion, as it was barbarously pillaged and burned (1655 and 1702). During the Partitions, Wawel fell into ruin and in 1846 the Austrians converted it into army barracks. They pulled down medieval walls and towers and replaced them with heavy brick bastions, which made Wawel look like a citadel threatening the town. Only the Cathedral fulfilled its function of the shrine of the nation. The reconstruction of Wawel Castle when it was repurchased from the Austrian army in 1905 was a nationwide undertaking. The renovation started in 1911 and continued between the wars. In 1920 the castle was proclaimed the property of the Polish State. During the Second World War the Nazis tore down former kitchen buildings that closed the outer yard on the side of the Cathedral and instead they erected a hefty edifice which now holds offices and the Wawel museum workshops.

Wawel Castle: Tournament Room

Cracow: Decius' Villa

Kraków Willa Decjusza

A villa is a detached house in a garden, built in a pleasant neighbourhood, usually in a suburb. The tradition of raising villas goes back to ancient Rome, where a villa denoted a country residence surrounded by a large farm. The fashion revived in the Renaissance, when the great Italian architect Andrea Palladio produced several exquisite designs.

Since Polish-Italian ties were then extremely strong, similar edifices were soon to appear in Poland. Some of them are still extant, for instance Decius' Villa from the late Renaissance, situated in the Cracow suburb of Wola Justowska, so named after by the secretary of King Zygmunt the Old, Iustus Decius from Alsatia, who bought it in 1528. He remodelled the existent late Gothic building as a Renaissance villa and surrounded it with a large park which was lauded in Latin verse by the poet Klemens Janicki.

Decius could afford a great deal. As the King's trusted diplomat, lessor of a mint and owner of mines, he did not have to limit his expenses. No wonder that he commissioned the construction project to the most eminent Italian architects that worked in Cracow, e.g. to B. Berrecci's collaborator, G. Cini from Siena.

Decius' family owned the villa till 1576. Around 1620 it was reconstructed for Stanisław Lubomirski, one of the most powerful magnates in Poland. According to the design, the rooms were regularly arranged and the building had a through hall, corner projections and a three-tier arcaded loggia. The elegant façade is the most unique and beautiful element of the building. Nowadays the edifice is the seat of the European Academy which carries out research and organises conferences on European cultural heritage.

Kraków Rydlówka

"In his tightly buttoned frock coat, he stood the whole night leaning against the door frame and looking with his steel-blue, weird eyes. Close by, the wedding bustled." This is how the writer Tadeusz Boy-Żeleński remembered the playwright Stanisław Wyspiański on the night of 20 November 1900, when the poet Lucjan Rydel married Jadwiga nee Mikołajczyk, a peasant's daughter from the suburb of Bronowice.

The mésalliance would probably have been soon forgotten if it had not been for the genius of Wyspiański, who managed to transform the social event into one of the greatest visionary dramas in Polish literature, *The Wedding*. The Mikołajczyk family had even earlier connections with artists. In the summer of 1890 the painter and poet Włodzimierz Tetmajer married their second daughter Anna. The house where the wedding party took place is still to be found in the district of Bronowice and is called Rydlówka (Rydel's house). It was built by the poet Włodzimierz Tetmajer in 1894; the house was constructed of timber logs by local carpenters and thatched. But soon, in 1902, Tetmajer bought from a peasant called Dzieża a neo-classical manor house from 1862, previously owned by the Franciscans. He renovated it and put up another brick building, his studio. After the war, the house was devastated by careless lodgers. Only in 1992 could the rightful owners reclaim the house and raise funds to comprehensively renovate it.

The house described in *The Wedding* was abandoned at the moment of the Tetmajers' removal. The artist hosted there his friends, e.g. for over a year his residing guests were the painter Henryk Uziembło and his family and another painter, Jan Skotnicki. The subsequent remodelling to the design of Filip Pokutyński was finished in 1912. During the First World War the Rydels had to leave their house, where Austrian officers were billeted. Now it is turned into a museum where visitors can admire the wedding room reconstructed according to the stage directions in Wyspiański's play.

Cracow: Manor house in Bronowice

Cracow: Manor house in Biały Prądnik

Kraków Biały Prądnik

The manor house in the district of Biały Prądnik replaced a previous Renaissance suburban villa. Many of them appeared in the neighbourhood of Cracow under the Jagiellons, in the historical Golden Age of Poland. The house of Samuel Maciejowski, bishop and humanist, was erected before 1547. It was a place of recreation and intellectual dispute for scholars and writers. This group of intellectuals was described in *The Courtier* by the bishop's secretary, Łukasz Górnicki. The book was modelled on Castiglione's work and devoted to the question of moral reform. The evening sessions in the bishop's house proved to be as stimulating as the meetings at the ducal court in Urbino. Similar trends were promoted also by Bishop Andrzej Zebrzydowski, who in 1551 established an Italian garden. The successive bishops renovated and enlarged the building till, under the Partitions, it was appropriated by the Austrian authorities (who later on auctioned it to a private owner). At that time the building had two storeys and was flanked by two towers. Unfortunately at the beginning of the 19th c. this design disappeared: the building was devastated by the Russians in 1769 and rebuilt in a new form. Remodelled several times between 1812 and 1846, it finally acquired its present shape of a manor house with a portico supported by columns and a two-layer roof. In the 20th c. the neo-classical façades of the side buildings were reconstructed. What remained of the 16th-c. building is the Golden Room and the Fireplace Room. In 1809 the manor house was inhabited by General Henryk Dąbrowski.

Kraków Krzesławice

Krzesławice used to be a village in the parish of Pleszów, now it is a surprising place, considering the location: it lies halfway between the centre of the industrial district of Nowa Huta and steelworks. The manor house of the painter Jan Matejko is a building with a shingled roof. It stands in a devastated park where the painter himself planted lindens, larches, poplars and beeches. In 1788 Krzesławice was purchased by H. Kołłątaj, one of the supporters of the Enlightenment in Poland. Soon, because of new developments in politics, he was deprived of the estate, which was given over to K. Głębocki, counsellor to the Targowica Confederates, notorious for their treason to the Polish state. In the early 19th c. the estate was managed by the Kirchmayers. From them, in 1876, the house was bought by Matejko with the money he had earned from the sale of one of his paintings. The painter renovated the house as a summer residence and grew flowers around, he also built a studio. In 1893 Matejko's son sold Krzesławice. In 1957 the last owner ceded the house to the Society for Fine Arts. Now it holds a small museum with some interesting memorabilia such as Matejko's easel, a closet for his sketches and a piano.

Cracow: Manor house in Krzesławice

Krasiczyn

Gazeta Warszawska, a Warsaw daily, lamented in 1842: "If this castle was in England or in Germany, multitudes of visitors would come to see it, and a detailed description accompanied by sketches would make this most secluded place known to all the world." However, Poland is not England. Palatine M. Krasicki, who inherited the Gothic castle in Krasiczyn, began a thorough renovation. As a result, at the end of the 16th c. the castle turned into a fortress of an irregular rectangular shape. It had four bulwarks in the corners and before the entrance in the west stood a gate and a tower. The building, anyway, was to be perceived rather as a palace as it had an arcaded yard. The entire construction project, divided into several phases, lasted from 1589 to 1633. The castle may owe its final shape to G. Appiani. In the name of piety and respect for feudal hierarchy, the towers were called the Divine, the Papal, the Royal and the Noble Tower. The largest is the Divine Tower with a cupola on top and huge sgraffito decoration on the walls. The other towers are adorned with attics, while the Royal Tower, thanks to its little ornamental turrets, resembles a king's crown. Unfortunately, nothing has been saved of the old equipment such as carved ornaments and furniture, tapestries, fine portals and mantelpieces, a gallery of painting, or meticulously decorated ceilings. Numerous memorabilia showed that Krasiczyn castle had been visited by the Vasa rulers. But in 1852, during the preparations for an aristocratic wedding, the castle burned. The fire destroyed the treasures accumulated by many generations. In the ashes, peasants could find pieces of gold and silver from the tapestries and jewellery that melted in the fire. And the excellent chapel was devastated in 1939 by the Red Army.

Kruszwica: Tower of Mice

Kruszwica

In Polish tradition, the borderline between legendary and historical times lies in the area of Lake Gopło. There, on a narrow promontory stands Kruszwica, which is associated with the beginnings of the first royal dynasty in Poland, the Piasts. Unluckily, the octagonal, 32-metre Tower of Mice is not, contrary to children's beliefs, the place where the bad king Popiel wanted to find shelter and where voracious mice finally put an end to his reign and his dynasty. The Tower is the remnant of a structure that was raised in the 14th c. by King Kazimierz the Great. The complex consisted of a bailey, the main tower and living quarters. After subsequent fires in 1519 and 1591, the building was reconstructed and reshaped by royal administrators of the area, who resided here. After Kruszwica was captured by the Swedes in 1655 and then burned in 1657, the castle was finally abandoned and fell into ruin. In the 18th and 19th c. the walls were almost completely demolished.

Castle in Krasiczyn

Castle in Krąg

Krąg

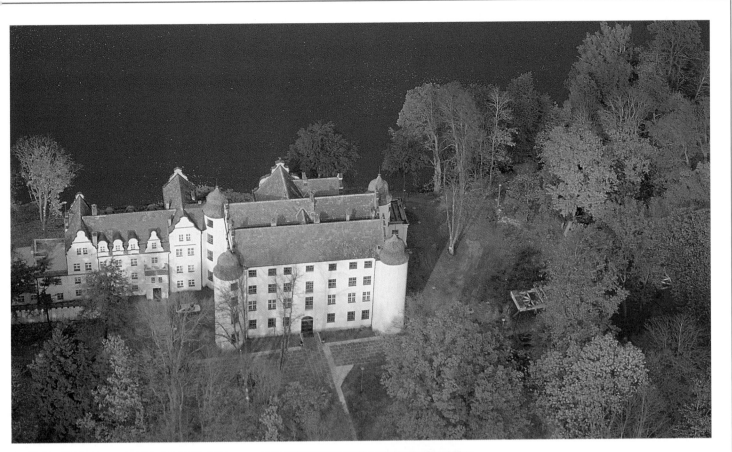

In the present day, the 16th-c. castle in Krąg, situated on the bank of a lake, houses a tastefully furnished, luxurious hotel. Krąg was the seat of the Podewilses (a Pomeranian noble family connected with the court of the dukes of Szczecin) from the 15th c. until 1860, when the estate was sold to Hugo von Löwen. From 1884 till the 1940s the castle belonged to the family von Rippenhausen. The beginnings of the residence in Krąg date back to the times of Peter von Podewils, who established here the management centre of his landed estates. The castle's form developed in several phases. In the 15th c. a castle of unknown design was constructed here. About 1580 a reconstruction started and afterwards the castle became a Renaissance defensive structure. Following the Thirty Years' War, in the middle of the 17th c. the design of the castle was firmly established and at the end of the 19th c. the rectangular, compact castle gained upper floors and a side wing. Its northern façade was remodelled and the interiors were refurbished. The residence is surrounded by a landscape park arranged in the 19th c. Within the park, on the south-eastern bank, one can find preserved remains of the early medieval castle. In the Renaissance-Baroque chapel, which stands in the park too, you can see rococo sepulchres: a marble one of A. von Podewils (1697) and a tin one of H. von Podewils (1696). Another attraction of the park is a drawbridge that was transferred here from Łeba.

Książ Wielki

Mirów castle in Książ Wielki is an exceptional building. Specialists in old architecture consider it the first wooden residence on the Polish territory. It was erected in 1585-95 for the Bishop of Cracow, Piotr Myszkowski, by a recognised Italian architect Santi Gucci. The form of the symmetrical structure, which reflects purely Italian influences and is deprived of any defences, is varied by projections holding halls and staircases. Marble was used everywhere in profusion. Before the palace one can find a yard with symmetrically positioned Mannerist buildings and behind it, a geometrical park. The light form of the side buildings is contrasted, as Mannerism loved contrasts, with the massive body of the palace. For over two centuries, Mirów was the centre of the entailed estate of the Myszkowski family. Its extant design is the result of the 19th-c. renovation supervised by an architect from Berlin, Friedrich Stüler, as commissioned by Marchgrave Aleksander Gonzaga Myszkowski. The project, however, was never completed and eventually Marchgrave removed to the nearby Chroberz. Mirów became desolate.

Mirów Castle in Książ Wielki

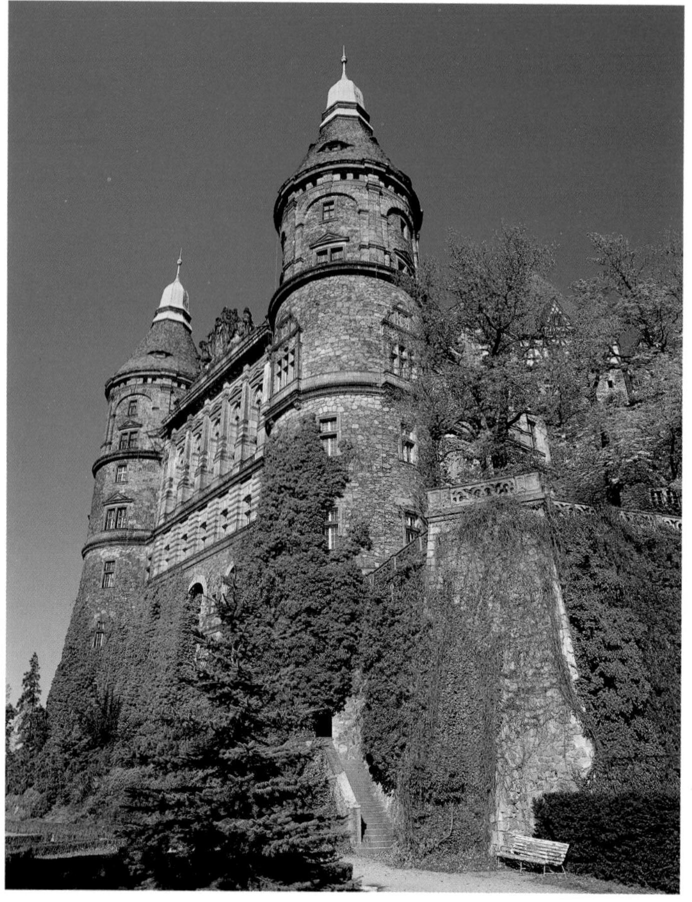

Książ Castle: Eclectic façade

Książ

Książ, which lies within the limits of the town of Wałbrzych, is one of the largest historical buildings in Poland. It has over 400 rooms but few of them are open to the public. The castle is situated on a high mound over the meandering Pełcznica and the deep ravine of the Ogorzelec Stream, in the area that is protected for the beauty of its landscape. It was built in the late 13th c. by Bolko I, the Duke of Świdnica and Jawor (who signed himself as "the Duke of Silesia and the owner of Książ"), and served as a ducal residence for decades onwards. The fortified structure (called Fürstenberg, and from the end of the 14th c. Fürstenstein) was of an irregular shape and had a square tower at the entrance. Till 1392 the castle belonged to Bolko II's widow, Agnieszka. After her death the Duchy was ruled by the Bohemian king Wenceslas IV. From 1387 it was a feudal domain. Throughout history, it had to oppose the attacks of the Hussites, of the Hungarians of Matthias Corvinus and, during the Thirty Years' War, of mercenaries of various origins. The Gothic-Renaissance palace, built in 1548-55, was commissioned by a powerful Saxon family, the Hochbergs, who resided here from 1509, that is from the moment when Książ was reclaimed from the hands of robber barons, till the Second World War. Along with the castle, the Hochbergs acquired a large landed estate which towards the end of the 16th c. embraced thirty-one villages, the towns of Boguszów and Mieroszów as well as Świebodzice with its coal-mining areas. In 1560 Konrad II Hochberg was appointed the administrator of the region and later the Emperor's counsellor. In 1603 Konrad III managed to ensure that Książ should become his hereditary property. With time, the residence evolved. Between 1718 and 1734 a large late Baroque edifice was raised in front of it, to the design of the architect F. A. Hammerschmidt, whose collaborators were the painter F. A. Scheffler and the sculptor J. G. Schenck. In consequence, the castle was

Książ Castle: Aerial view

Książ Castle: Maximilian Hall

transformed into a luxurious residence with many resplendent halls, e.g. the Maximilian Hall. The old fortifications were razed and replaced with elegant gardens, new entrance gates and utility buildings. In 1772 Jan Henryk IV obtained the Prussian king's permission to establish in Książ a *fideicommissum*. The income from the estate financed, among others, further decoration work in the castle. In the 1790s, Jan Henryk VI employed for that purpose the architect C. W. Tischbein. In the 19th c. the role of the castle's owners grew more important. In 1848 the Hochbergs became affined with the family von Pless from Pszczyna in Upper Silesia, and in 1855 they received the ducal title. They were also constantly present at the court in Berlin. From 1855 the gardens and adjacent areas were rearranged and the castle's library was transferred to the lower gatehouse. The famous stables and larch-timber manege were built. The western part of the castle gained a new wing with cylindrical towers and an impressive façade of red sandstone. In 1908-23, on the initiative of Jan Henryk XV, a monumental neo-Renaissance section with two towers was raised, and the 49-metre main tower received a neo-Renaissance finial. There appeared new lifts, chapels, fountains, two cinemas, a Japanese garden, etc. Książ at that time was the largest private residence in Europe, and the British Duchess Daisy, courted and wooed by monarchs, was received here with proper pomp. Hochberg's marriage, scandalous divorce and the next marriage attracted the attention of the rag press of all Europe. Daisy gave him three sons: Jan Henryk, Aleksander and Bolko. Bolko died in unexplained circumstances in 1936. His brothers left for Great Britain when the Second World War broke out. Jan Henryk served in the RAF and Aleksander joined the Polish Army in the West. The castle was confiscated by the Nazi authorities. The idea to adapt it as one of Hitler's residences proved disastrous. The project was never completed, but when tunnels were dug under the castle, the interiors were also devastated: the Nazis stole part of the precious art collection, excellent furniture and library collection. The original interior decorations were demolished, wainscotting removed, plafonds, stuccoes and other ornaments destroyed. Till the end of the war the length of the underground corridors totalled 900 metres. They were bored even 55 metres below the courtyard. The purpose of this underground complex has not been sufficiently explained yet, but the project went on till 8th May 1945. Later on the castle and its neighbourhood were devastated and pillaged by the Red Army. When the soldiers abandoned the residence, it remained unrestored till 1956. It was only after many years of renovation that it partly regained its previous beauty.

One enters the castle through a portal over which an armorial shield of the Hochbergs is placed. On the same side of the yard, in the lower castle, there are two adjacent utility buildings from the 18th c. and several residential buildings. Over a bridge decorated with stone sculptures, one approaches the reception yard, laid out in the 18th c. From here you can have a good look at the Baroque façade of the palace which is covered with a mansard roof. In the Maximilian Hall jutting out from the façade, one should note high, pilaster-flanked windows. Worth seeing are also the Knights' Room, Konrad's Room, the Crooked Room, the Hunters' Hall and the Parlours (Green, White, Chinese and Baroque). One of the memorable places in the castle is the Black Yard. Its walls are decorated in neo-Renaissance style and the most interesting wall shows the coats of arms of the former owners. Also the terraces are uniquely arranged, especially the water terrace with twenty-seven fountains and beautiful lawns. The French style Baroque gardens (to be found in the suburb of Lubiechów) attract visitors with antique-like sculptures scattered throughout and the palm house from 1911-14, whose interiors are laid out with tablets of lava brought here from the slopes of Etna. In the 18th c. the forest that partly encompassed the castle was turned into a romantic landscape park, where the Old Castle stands: an equally romantic ruin from 1797, designed by Tischbein. In the vicinity of the castle one can also find a state-owned farm of studhorses.

Książ Castle: Neo-Renaissance Black Yard with heraldic decoration

Krzyżtopór

Before Louis XIV started to build his residence in Versailles, Krzyżtopór castle was said to be the largest and the most luxurious one in Europe. It was K. Ossoliński, the Palatine of Sandomierz, who had this fortified residence erected in the village of Ujazd. It was to testify to the power and prosperity of his family. Here even horses had mangers of marble. The castle was called Krzyżtopór ("cross and axe") as on either side of the entrance gate there were relief representations of the cross as a symbol of Christianity and the axe as the heraldic emblem of the Ossolińskis. How proud must have been the man who put these two symbols on a par! The construction of the residence reportedly cost the exorbitant sum of 30 million zloties and was completed in 1644. The supervisor of the project was L. Senes, the court architect of the Ossoliński family. The design could have originated among the architects of Rome, but the author remains unknown. The complex was built as a regular, pentagonal defensive structure of the latest Italian type. Besides residential quarters, it also comprised gardens. The intricate spatial arrangement and the decorations alluded to the measurement of time. It is not entirely true that the design was symbolic of various periods of time (4 towers for the 4 seasons of the year, 12 halls for 12 months, 52 rooms for 52 weeks, 365 windows for 365 days), but this does not diminish the grandeur of the residence. The furnishings were supplemented with painted decorations. The local tradition says that the castle had a special reception room whose ceiling was an aquarium: fish of different colours swam above the guests' heads. The Ossolińskis could take pride in their imposing residence only for ten years or so. In 1655 it was captured by the Swedes and in 1657 burned by them. Later on nobody was able to restore it (it was partly inhabited only till 1770) and it stayed a ruin: a monstrous reminder of the power and pride of the past.

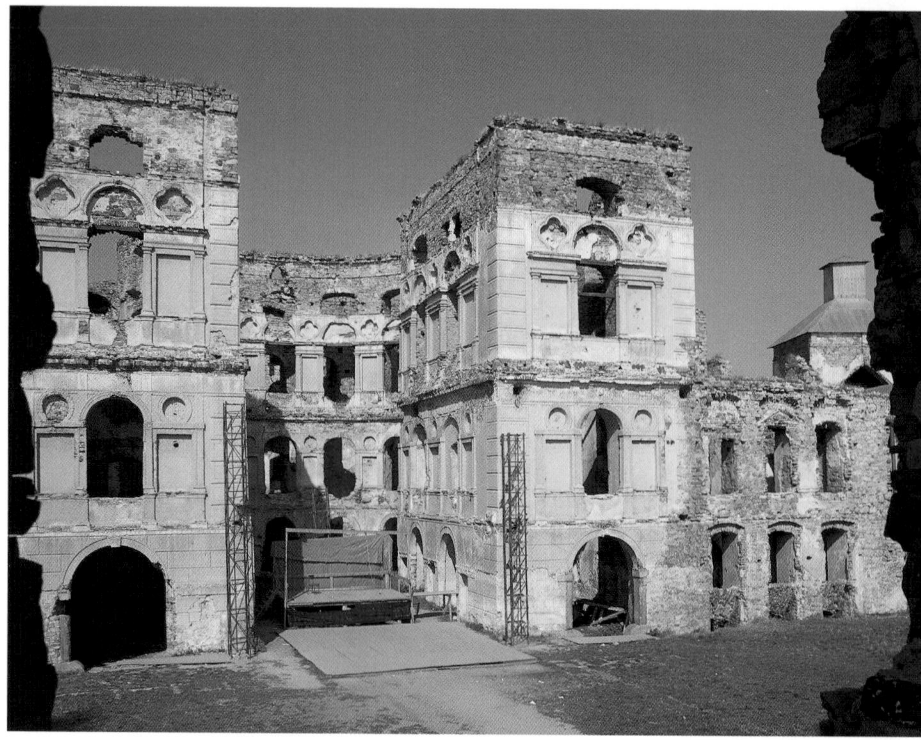

Krzyżtopór: Palace ruins

Kwidzyn

Between 1285 and 1587 Kwidzyn was the seat of the chapter of the bishopric of Pomezania. In 1440 the Prussian Union was instituted here to oppose the Teutonic Order. When Prussia was secularised and the bishops converted to Lutheranism (1526), the seat of the chapter was administered by Protestant

Krzyżtopór Palace

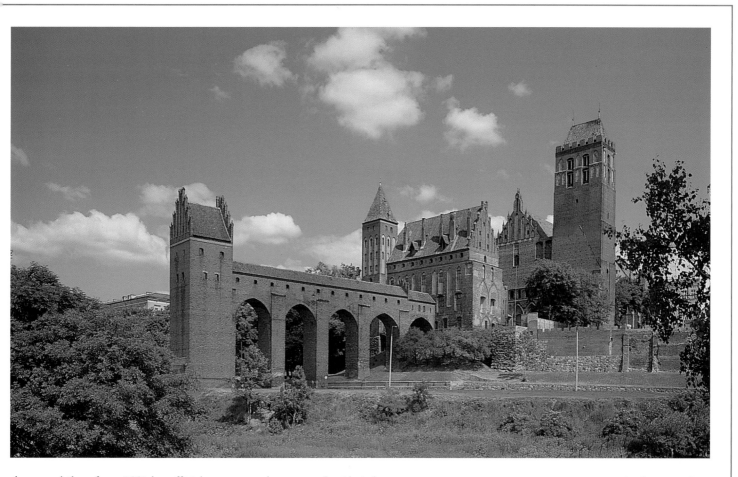

clergy and then from 1551 by officials appointed by the duke. The Gothic complex of the castle and cathedral, which tower over the valley of the Vistula, is the most precious historical monument of the town. The castle, built on a square ground plan, comes from 1322-47 and was partly demolished in the second half of the 19th c. Its unique feature is a huge tower (German *Dansker*) which is distanced from the main section and connected with it by a passage supported by five arches. It is hard to believe that such an enormous tower served primarily as a toilet. Originally, the castle was rectangular and had angle towers but the Prussian troops destroyed it in 1789, and only the northern and western wings and the *Dansker* were preserved. Another remnant of the medieval structure is the Well Tower on the northern side. In the cellars and in the second storey one can see Gothic (stellar and cross-ribbed) ceilings.

Castle in Kwidzyn

Palace in Kurozwęki

KUROZWĘKI

Kurozwęki palace belongs to those residences where one can observe an evolution from a feudal castle through a defensive residence to a neo-classical residence. The first castle of the Kurozwęcki family was remodelled in the early 17th c. by the Lanckoroński family. The courtyard was equipped with two storeys of arcades and the rooms were finally of an equal height, which accounted for the fact that for two centuries Kurozwęki was one of the buildings which ostensibly resembled Wawel Castle. In 1747 S. Lanckoroński died without an heir, and in 1752 his widow married M. Sołtyk. About 1770 Sołtyk commissioned renovation works (probably based on the design by F. Nax), which endowed the residence with neo-classical features as well as perceptibly Baroque motifs. According to the architect's design, the front section held the Ball Room, where a ball was given to King Stanisław August Poniatowski on his return from the meeting with Tsarina Catherine II in Kaniów. Especially for the King, modifications were introduced in the Dining Room, the Red and Green Parlours, the Library and the adjacent Study. The last construction project was carried out in Kurozwęki after 1918. After 1945 the complex dilapidated. It was restored as late as in the 1990s, when it was returned to the Popiel family. The complex stands in a park rearranged in 1811-25 by Zulauf and more thoroughly in 1859-73 by Dionizot.

Laskowa

The village of Laskowa, founded in the 16th c., lies in the northern part of the Beskid Wyspowy, in the valley of the Łososina. The large wooden manor house was built in 1677 for the Laskowski family. A typical Polish design was adopted. In 1689 Laskowa was bought by the Bishop of Cracow, Jan Małachowski, who gave the house to the supervisors of the estates of the Congregation of the Mission, or the Lazarists. They arrived in Poland in 1651, invited by Queen Maria Ludwika, and till the end of the 18th c. took over the task of managing the majority of diocesan seminaries. Appropriately enough, in the 18th c. they converted the drawing room into a chapel of the Immaculate Conception of the BVM. This elongated room has therefore a ceiling lavishly embellished with carved and polychrome ornaments (in the central oval, Christ is represented amid garlands and angels). In the same period, some farm houses such as a granary and stables, still extant, appeared around the manor house. All of them are surrounded by the former landscape park. In the late 18th c. the estate was bought at an auction by a private owner and after the Second World War the land was divided among peasant families. The house served as the local administration office and then was turned into a youth hostel. Now it is privately owned again. This old country manor of Polish nobility, with is well-proportioned shape and a two-layer roof, is an epitome of a modest house which was not intended to be a dazzling residence, but a place from which all the farm jobs were supervised. In the past there used to be many such places in Poland. Those that have survived till today are unique.

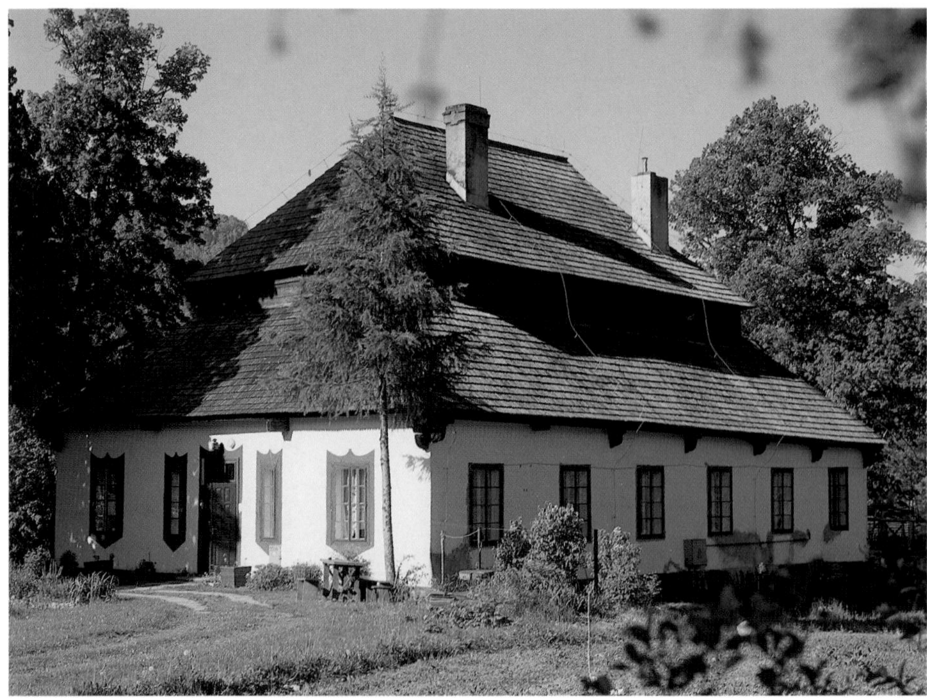

Manor house in Laskowa

Lipowiec

Centuries ago, travellers going from Cracow to Oświęcim almost automatically averted their eyes from the walls of Lipowiec castle, ominously towering over the road. Here, on a high rock surrounded by woods, stood a fearsome *domus correctionis*. The detainees were blasphemers, undisciplined clergymen and incorrigible heretics who were carefully watched over by the owners of Lipowiec, the bishops of Cracow. The most famous of the prisoners was a professor of the Cracow Academy, Franciszek Stankar. This Italian from Mantua not only distributed anti-Catholic publications listed on the Church index, but also managed to escape from Lipowiec. The legend says that the jailor's daughter fell in love with him, that he escaped using ropes and that, romantically, they eloped and were chased. Actually, the "escape" of Stankar was unofficially negotiated between Protestant nobility and the representatives of the bishop. They agreed upon the professor's release from prison on condition that neither of the parties should be compromised. Reshaped and fortified throughout centuries, the castle served as a defensive residence as well as an administrative centre of the area. Its earliest days have not been so far satisfactorily researched. According to the chronicler Jan Długosz, the village Lipowa (identified as Lipowiec) at first belonged to the Gryfita family and then to the Benedictines from Staniątki. At that time highway robbers erected a castle nearby, which served as a base for their forays to the surrounding villages. When captured, the fortress was passed on to the Cracow bishopric. A new structure to replace the robbers' den was allegedly erected in the second half of the 13th c. by Bishop Prędota, one of the initiators of the canonisation proceedings of St Stanislaus, the Bishop of Cracow martyred in the 11th c. At first the fortress was just a single cylindrical stone tower girdled by fortifications of earth and timber. After subsequent modernisations, two-storey residential quarters appeared around a pentagonal yard. The entrance was situated in a spacious gatehouse. At the end of the 15th c., the outer ward with wooden utility buildings was also surrounded by fortifications. The complex was affected by serious catastrophes in the 17th c. In 1629 a fire broke out, destroying practically all the timber buildings, the houses that stood before the gate and some sections of the upper castle. The keep, rebuilt and fortified

Lipowiec: Ruins of bishops' castle

anew after the disaster, was taken in 1655 by the Swedish troops of General Wirtz, who, when forced to evacuate the castle, burned it. The Swedish had to leave Lipowiec because of the attacks of the irregular troops of Kasper Karliński operating in the Beskidy. As a property of the Cracow bishopric, the castle survived till 1789, when, during the Partitions, it was confiscated by the Austrian authorities. Under the new owners, the castle fell into ruin. The final blow was the fire of ca 1800 which destroyed the roof and seriously damaged the walls. Conservation work to preserve the remains commenced in 1961 and ended in 1975. Thanks to the effort of restoration experts, the site is now open to the public.

Liw

On the way from Sulejówek to Węgrów one can visit the castle in Liw, lying among marshy meadows. Before Mazovia was incorporated in Poland, it was the residence of the Duke, his administrator or the castellan. The extant form of the castle, with its gatehouse and living quarters, is the result of reconstruction work. The castle was put up towards the end of the 14th c. by Janusz the Elder to supersede an earlier, earth-and-timber structure which guarded the ford on the Liwiec, which formed the border between Mazovia and Lithuania. The castle was constructed before 1429, when Master Niclos, the builder, presented the Duke with the bills for his commission. In the early years of its existence, the castle complex was almost square and consisted of the crenellated perimeter wall, the main building and another smaller building. The castle was accessed via a low, rectangular gate tower. In 1549-70, by order of Duchess Anna and Queen Bona, the residence was expanded. The gate tower had four storeys and loopholes – apparently all in vain, since in 1656 and 1703 the castle was captured and burned by the Swedish. Anyway, it continued to function as an administrative and judiciary centre. In 1782, in order to replace one of the buildings, a Baroque residence was raised for the royal administrator of the area. In 1831 the Polish and Russian forces fought at Liw, near the ford. Captain Wysocki, one of the leaders of the Uprising, gained here his fame as a commander. During the Second World War the Germans preserved the ruins thanks to the ruse of a local amateur archaeologist who persuaded the Nazi authorities that the castle had been owned by the Teutonic Knights. Now the castle holds a museum: an arsenal with a splendid collection of arms and armour (15th-20th c.).

Castle in Liw

Ludynia

It is not easy to find your way to Ludynia. The village is situated at the Chęciny-Włoszczowa road, not a busy one. The village boasts an 18th-c. manor house which is the incarnation of all our notions about the past. When we look at it, we can imagine ourselves listening to the yarns of an old "resident", that is an elderly person who was supported by the owners, or reading stories of the long-forgotten writer I. Chodźko. The house mirrors the way of living of Polish nobility at its best. It was lucky enough to survive the post-war turmoil, it was even renovated, but it did not have a careful manager. Only in the 1990s was it bought by people who, besides saving its walls, succeeded in saving the atmosphere of peace and stability that is associated with old houses. Next to the manor house stands a 16th-c. storage house made of stone, covered with a shingled roof, and equipped with a chime. It is called the "Arian prayer house" as the Arians operated in the neighbourhood. One can find here some more traces of Polish history. After the lost battle of Szczekociny in 1794, General Tadeusz Kościuszko is said to have stayed in Ludynia. During the tragic 1863 Uprising the insurgents fought here a Cossack troop; a simple cross commemorates those who died in action. The complex is surrounded by a park with some fine old trees. The patriotic aura of the manor house in Ludynia was discovered by the crew shooting the film *Springtime* based on a novel by S. Żeromski: Ludynia plays Nawłoć, the family home of the protagonist Cezary Baryka, an idealistic character who lived his turbulent life dreaming of independent, welfare Poland.

Manor complex in Ludynia

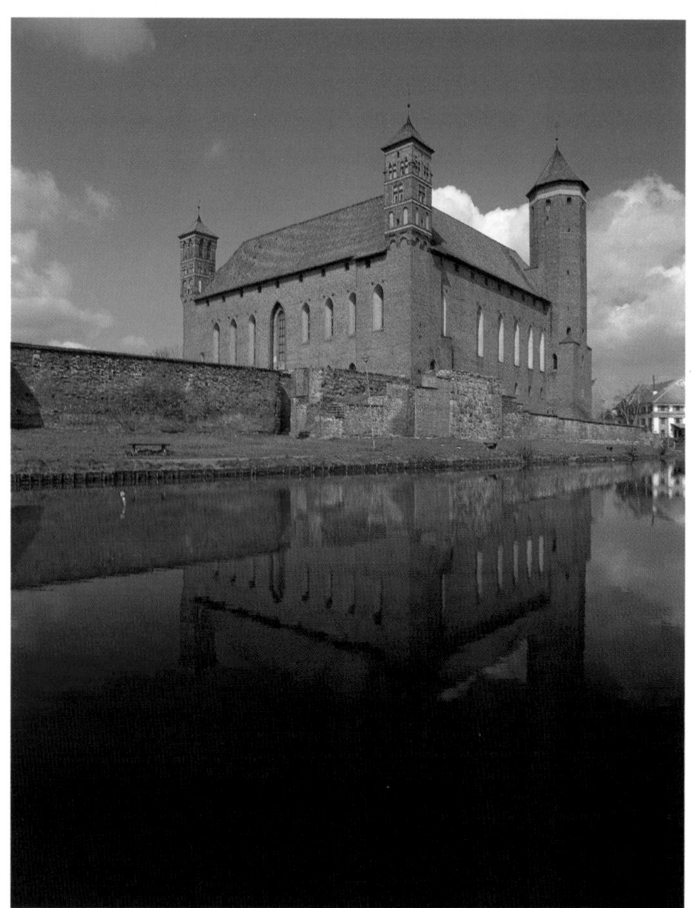

Lidzbark Warmiński

Lidzbark Warmiński, the main town of the region of Warmia, used to be called Lecbarg and later Heilsberk. It was originally an important settlement of the pagan Prussians. In 1348-1400 the Teutonic Knights built here a fortress which in 1454 was taken over by the burghers. Between 1350 and 1795 the castle was the residence of the bishops of Warmia, who differed from the rest of Church hierarchy in that they joined pastoral functions with administrative ones. After Warmia was incorporated with Poland (1466), the castle was inhabited by Bishop Jan Dantyszek and Bishop Marcin Kromer. In 1749, in the castle library, Adam Grabowski discovered the medieval chronicle by Gallus Anonymus. Lidzbark castle belongs to the most beautiful medieval residences in Poland. It is positioned between the rivers Łyna and Symsarna on a platform whose end is occupied by the castle and the rest by the outer ward, separated from the castle by a moat. The construction started under Bishop Jan of Meissen (1350-55). After 1497 new additions were angle turrets. The fortress looks rather austere on the outside, but inside it offers a surprising variety of forms. Particularly charming is the courtyard with two storeys of arcades with arches supported by granite pillars. As to the chambers, one should note the Great Refectory and the chapel with rococo ornaments carved in wood. In the majority of chambers and in the cloisters, Gothic murals are preserved. Between 1666 and 1673 Jan Stefan Wydżga raised a Baroque palace. One of its wings was in 1741-66 rebuilt by Bishop Grabowski. New murals in the Great Refectory and in the private dining room were commissioned by Bishop Ignacy Krasicki, the last Polish governor of Warmia before the Partitions. An attractive proof of the Bishop's architectural initiatives is the orangery from 1711-24, extended ca 1770. It was especially admired by the visitors, not only because it was larger than the art gallery but

Bishops' castle in Lidzbark Warmiński

Lidzbark Wamiński: Castle courtyard

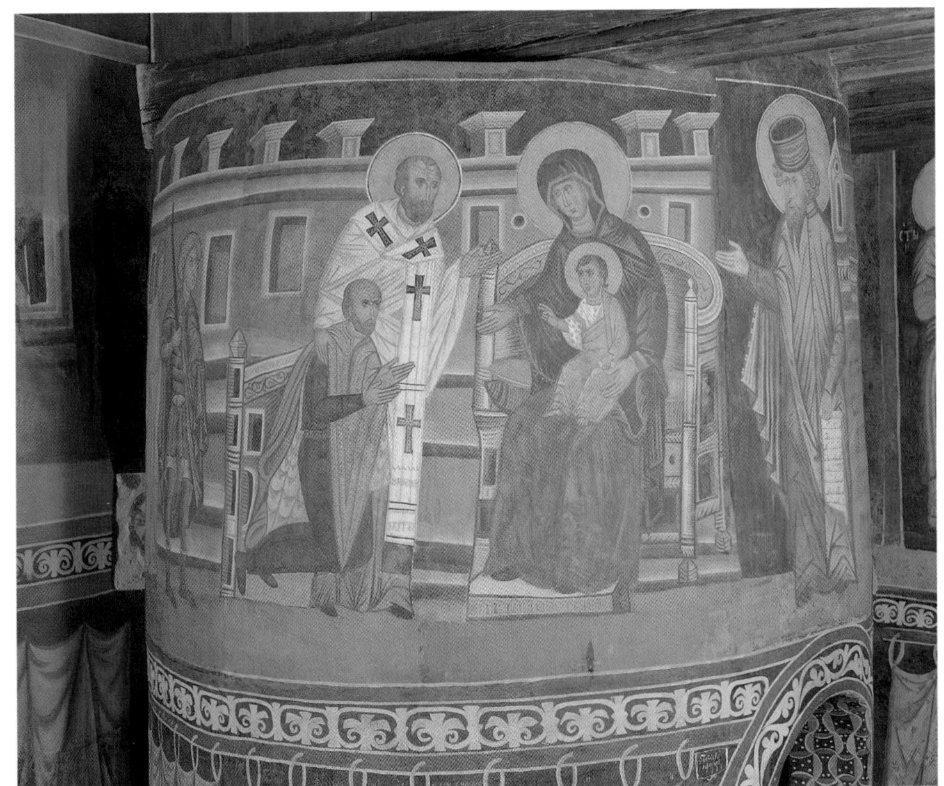

Lublin: Murals in the Chapel of Holy Trinity

also because "cauliflowers and pineapples grew there abundantly, even in winter." Once in February Krasicki wrote: "I swear to you that my garden is in full bloom; I'm just coming from there, bathed in the fragrance of jasmines and roses." The garden took pride in Italian grapevine, "Astrakhan apples" and forty species of roses. Thousands of tulip bulbs were transported here from London, Amsterdam, Haarlem and Hamburg. Constant work went on in the promenades, bridges and dykes. The Bishop's court in Heilsberk was indeed modelled on the ducal courts of Italian Renaissance.

Lublin

The origin of the castle is connected with the nomination of the castellan in Lublin in the 12th c. In the first half of the 13th c., in the upper section of the castle, a brick tower was erected, which was the first part of the future complex built here ca 1370 by King Kazimierz the Great so as to protect the strategically important town. Around 1520 Zygmunt I started to convert the castle into a magnificent royal residence. The town could be accessed from the castle via the Tower Gate, reshaped in 1785 by D. Merlini. In consequence of 17th-c. wars, the castle was destroyed: only the tower and the chapel were preserved. In 1823-26 Ignacy Stompf rebuilt the castle as a neo-Gothic prison. Since 1954 a museum has functioned there.

The most precious part of the complex is the Gothic, brick Chapel of the Holy Trinity (called the Castle Chapel) with Byzantine-Ruthenian frescoes, the best-preserved of the kind in Poland. In the Chapel, a mass of thanks giving was offered after the Polish-Lithuanian Union of Lublin in 1569. The Chapel was founded by Kazimierz the Great and put up in 1370-85. It has two levels supported by a single pillar. Under the presbytery, a vault is situated. That the chapel was a defensive structure is testified by the gallery with weapon emplacements that surrounds the apse. Commissioned by King Władysław Jagiełło, Master Andrzej and other Ruthenian painters covered the walls at the upper level with Orthodox-style paintings. The foundation inscription on the chancel arch informs that the project was completed on 10th August 1418. The representations include those of Christ Pantocrator, cherubs, seraphs, archangels and angels (on the ceiling) and a series of portraits of prophets (high on the walls of the nave). The most important scenes from the Gospels are depicted below and Passion scenes are painted in the presbytery. Other murals are portraits of saints and scenes presenting the founder, King Władysław Jagiełło, on horseback or kneeling before St Mary, who is seated on a throne (the latter representation is to be found in the staircase leading to the gallery). In the 18th c. the paintings were plastered over and then re-discovered in 1899. In 1903 a long-standing project of uncovering and renovating the frescoes began, and was completed as late as in 1997.

Castle in Lublin

Lubostroń Palace: Interior of the rotunda

LUBOSTROŃ

Lubostroń was the property of General Skórzewski. Among morain hills, his son began to build a palace complex. Till 1800 the village was called Piłatowo, and the later name denotes "a lovely retreat" (in Polish *lube ustronie*). The owner did not hide who he wanted to please. The frieze of the portico bears a Latin inscription: "To myself, friendship and posterity." The residence was erected in 1795-1800 to the design of S. Zawadzki. The interior stuccoes are by M. Ceptowicz and the murals by A. Smuglewicz. The building was to resemble the famous Villa Rotonda, built near Vincenza at the end of the 16th c. by Palladio. Lubostroń palace is almost perfectly symmetrical: the centre is occupied by parlours encompassed by a three-storey rotunda and ornamented with figural stuccoes, and the rotunda opens up onto four façades with porticoes of Ionic columns. Skórzewski used the columns that were originally made for the Church of the Divine Providence in Warsaw which was never raised because of the disintegration of the Polish Republic. The reception apartments of Lubostroń palace are to be found in the ground floor and they ring the central rotunda. The stucco decorations depict episodes from the history of Poland, especially those that exemplify the Polish dominance over the Germans in the past. In the study, Smuglewicz painted ancient and Italian landscapes; in the library, Pompeian motifs; and in the upper floor hall, a panorama of fancy Egyptian ruins. The cupola is topped with the statue of Atlas by W. Marcinkowski. An interesting addition to the palace is other neo-Gothic buildings. The main one, called the Old Palace, was built at the end of the 18th c. and its design is ascribed to Zawadzki. The stables and coach houses date back to the early 19th c. In the park, which was designed ca 1800 by O. Teichert, one can see the remnants of the orangery and the library. The last private owner of Lubostroń was Count Zygmunt Skórzewski. Afterwards, the palace was taken over by a state-owned travel agent and defaced by the presence of shoddy holiday lodges.

LUSŁAWICE

In the 16th c. Lusławice, situated in a secluded spot in the valley of the Dunajec, was an important settlement of the Arians, who in 1570 established here their college and printing house. In Lusławice their leader Socinus (Fausto Paolo Sozzini; 1539-1604) worked and died, and A. Taszycki built here a fortified

Palace in Lubostroń

Manor house in Lusławice

prayer house which later served as the manor's store. It is a small building, part of the interesting manor complex. Since 1976 it has been owned by the composer K. Penderecki. Behind the wall stand a neoclassical 19th-c. manor house, a 19th-c. neo-Renaissance pavilion and an octagonal mausoleum of Socinus. The beautiful house is a one-storey building whose façade has a porch and a portico supported by four columns. The interiors offer stucco-decorated plafonds by M. Stachowicz, a painter from Cracow who was popular at the beginning of the 19th c. All the buildings of the complex are located within a carefully designed landscape park. The store functions as an exhibition hall for painters and other artists. It should be remembered that the *fin de siecle* painter J. Malczewski was once a resident at Lusławice.

ŁĘCZYCA

Łęczyca was one of the most important towns in the development of the Piast realm, but it is more readily associated with legends about the devil called Boruta than with any vital legislative achievements. In 1180 King Kazimierz the Just convened in Łęczyca a meeting of the highest officials whom he commissioned to reform the state and the 1285 synod, presided over by Archbishop J. Świnka, voted through the precedence of Poles in nominations for the Church positions. At first Łęczyca was the capital of the Duchy, then of the Palatinate, and flourished in the 14th c. So as to safeguard the town, it was surrounded with massive defence walls and a new, Gothic castle was erected. It occupied the south-eastern corner of the fortifications and was separated from the town by a moat. The defence walls were at least ten metres high. In the mid-15th c. the castle burned down and was rebuilt between 1563 and 1565. After the Swedish invasions in the 17th c. the castle fell into disrepair and its halcyon days never returned. In the 19th c. it was treated only as a site providing free building materials. After the Second World War it was turned into a museum.

Łęczyca Castle: Main tower

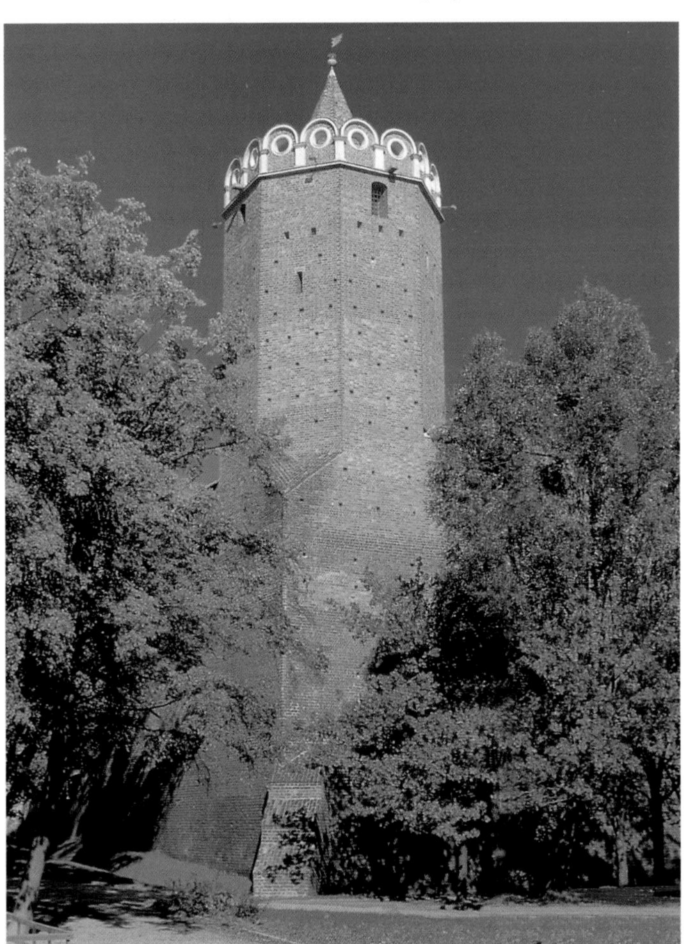

Palace in Łańcut

ŁAŃCUT

The liberties of the nobility, so beloved of Poles in the old days, had an odd tendency to degenerate into wilfulness or even lawlessness. Many brawlers walked in the aura of dubious glory, but none of them surpassed the notorious owner of Łańcut, Stanisław Stadnicki (1551?-1610), a living symbol of power, barratry and rebelliousness. Because of his cruelty, Stadnicki was nicknamed the Devil. In 1608 the private army of Łukasz Opaliński and Anna Ostrogska captured Łańcut castle, putting an end to the owner's misrule. In 1628 it became the property of Stanisław Lubomirski, who between 1629 and 1641 had it remodelled as a beautiful, early Baroque *palazzo in fortezza*. The project was probably supervised by M. Trapola. The building was ringed by bulwarks and deep moats. The defensive angle towers were transformed into ornamental ones. G. Falconi's stuccoes in the Zodiac Room come from the same period. In the late 17th c., employed by Sebastian Lubomirski, Tylman van Gameren worked in Łańcut, but his task was just to modernise the fortification system. In 1745 the property was inherited by Stanisław Lubomirski (1719-83). Together with his wife Izabela, he established one of the first aristocratic courts, hosting many VIP refugees from the revolutionary France, e.g. the future King Louis XVIII. Three times a week, chamber concerts were given, conducted by the student of Joseph Haydn, P. Haensel. Also the palace theatre frequently staged plays, for instance the comedies by Jan Potocki. The owners did not neglect the castle. Reconstruction projects went on for years and the meritorious designers were S. B. Zug, C. Kamsetzer and later C. P. Aigner. The present shape of the building is the result of Aigner's work and the 1889-1912 restoration. The last private owners of Łańcut (from 1816 to 1945) were the Potocki family, who endowed the residence (with the help of A. Banque and A. Pio from Vienna) with its present, eclectic design. Alfred I Potocki (1786-1862) earned his place in the history of Łańcut by that he turned it into an entailed estate, which prevented the division of land among inheritors. Alfred II (1822-89) paid little attention to the

Łańcut Palace: Gardens

Łańcut Palace: Column Hall

condition of the residence; he spent most of the time in Vienna and in Lvov (as he was the governor of the province of Galicia). He was especially favoured by Austrian Emperor Francis Joseph, who visited Łańcut several times. Alfred II's lack of care was made up for by Roman Potocki (1851-1915), the initiator of the last modernisation project. Alfred III (1886-1958) was one of the richest people in Europe. During the Nazi occupation, he saved many inhabitants of Łańcut from being transported as slave labourers to Germany. He also financed everyday dinners for 400 people. When the outcome of the Second World War became obvious, he sent to Vienna several hundred chests containing the most valuable objects of art, and left the castle a week before the arrival of the Soviets. The residence was defended against looting by the servants. The interiors (with an immense collection of art, handicraft, arms and armours and the splendid library) remained intact after the war and now attract multitudes of visitors. One can find here resplendent reception halls and a suite of rooms of different functions and in different styles: the Chinese Apartment, the Small Pompeian Parlour, the Mirror Study, the Winter Dining Room, the Yellow Bathroom, etc. Extremely impressive are the first floor halls: the Billiards Room, the Dining Room over the Gate, the Ball Room and the Great Dining Room, designed by Aigner. One should have a look at the Library and the neoclassical Column Hall with the statue of Eros by A. Canova (1787), which is a sculpted representation of the juvenile Henryk Lubomirski. Around the castle spread vast gardens. At the beginning of the 19th c. some sections of them were rearranged, especially the geometrical garden from about 1770, which lay within the fortifications. In 1890-1904, outside the fortifications, an extensive landscape park, an Italian garden and a rose garden were laid out, and an orchid house and palm house were built. Among the park buildings, the most important one, put up in 1902, held stables and a coach house. Here a unique collection is gathered of horse-drawn carriages: ceremonial carriages, coaches, equipages, travelling carriages, chaises, phaetons and carts for afternoon rides, racing or hunting.

Łańcut Palace: Parlour

Łomnica: Widows House

ŁOMNICA

The village is situated in the picturesque Jelenia Góra Basin at the confluence of two rivers. It was first mentioned in 1305; in 1645 the estate passed into the hands of the Habsburg officer Tomagnini, whose descendants ruled here for 80 years. It was at their time, in the early 18th c., that the Baroque residence was erected here. The construction was the work of the architect M. Frantz. The original shape of the residence was largely obliterated, however, by the late 19th c. remodelling. In 1737 Łomnica was purchased by the merchant C. Mentzel from Jelenia Góra and in 1798 inherited by his son. It was their idea to build the second manor house, called Widows House. In 1841 the Łomnica estate was entailed on the diplomat G. von Kuester, whose descendants owned it until 1945. The scenic location of the complex and the magnificent view of the Karkonosze mountain range is a definite advantage of the place. The sizeable park used to reach as far as the gardens of Wojanów Palace which spread on the opposite bank of the Bóbr.

ŁOPUSZNA

The 14th-c. village situated at the banks of the Dunajec at the foothills of the Gorce is remarkable thanks to its historical complex of wooden buildings comprising a beautiful late 15th-c. church and the manor house of the Tetmajer family with outbuildings, although the contemporary plastering and whitewashing makes the wooden construction of the manor house hardly visible. The manor was built at the turn of the 19th c. and acquired by the Tetmajers, together with the village, in 1824. It soon became an active centre of national revival; it hosted e.g. the writer S. Goszczyński, who authored the earliest description of the place. The grange might have existed already at the time when W. Poradowski received the village from King Stefan Báthory in 1575 as a reward for the courage he had shown on the battlefield. The manor house, which was the property of the castellan of Sącz, H. Przyłęcki, in the 17th c., was a defensive construction, indispensable in the area at the time. Today the building and a reconstructed small Baroque attic are covered with an attractive mansard roof, while the house next door (moved from the other end of the village) has retained the traditional two-layer roof. Well-preserved 19th-c. farm buildings are another highlight of the complex. Today, the manor house has been restored, with the effects of the 1892 remodelling removed, and houses the Museum of Polish Landed Gentry, a branch of the Museum of the Tatras.

Manor house in Łopuszna

Palace of the Poznańskis by night

ŁÓDŹ
PAŁAC POZNAŃSKICH

Residences of factory owners are the most impressive, or rather the most richly decorated, houses in Łódź; they were originally located at some distance from the city centre, next to the factories with which they formed separate urban complexes. The cotton company of I. K. Poznański was one of the largest textile factories not only in Łódź, but also in the whole of Europe; a jocular saying circulated at the time that Poznański together with his chief rival, K. Scheibler are able to buy out the Kingdom of Poland, except that they see no business in it. The construction of the factory complex in 1876-80 was overseen ex officio by H. Majewski, the head engineer of the city of Łódź. The design was highly original at the time: the front building was erected from unadorned brick with neo-Renaissance elements, the hall covered with glass roof which was propped against cast iron supports. Among the factory buildings was also one of the four palaces of the Poznańskis. Their residences have always drawn attention because of the ab undance of eclectic decoration. When they had been erected, they overshadowed the residences of all other factory owners.

The edifice at Ogrodowa Street is the most impressive and directly linked with the gigantic factory, which was raised in 1888-98; enlarged in the early 20th c. it received a monumental neo-Baroque architectural form, which clearly referred to the pompous fashion of the 2nd Empire. Many prominent architects were hired at the construction site, e.g. J. Jung and D. Rosenthal. Splendid and rich interior design combines the historicist styles of late 19th c. and that of Art Nouveau. This seems to confirm the anecdote in which Poznański, when asked what style he wished his residence to be, replied: "Poznański can afford all styles."

Originally the palace had the official and commercial roles: at the ground floor there were storage rooms with sturdy vaults supported by cast iron supports. Later remodellings were always linked to the changes in ownership: in the 1920s and 30s it was the seat of the Voivodeship Office, while in 1975 the main part of the building was taken over by the newly established Historical Museum.

Łódź: Palace of the Poznańskis

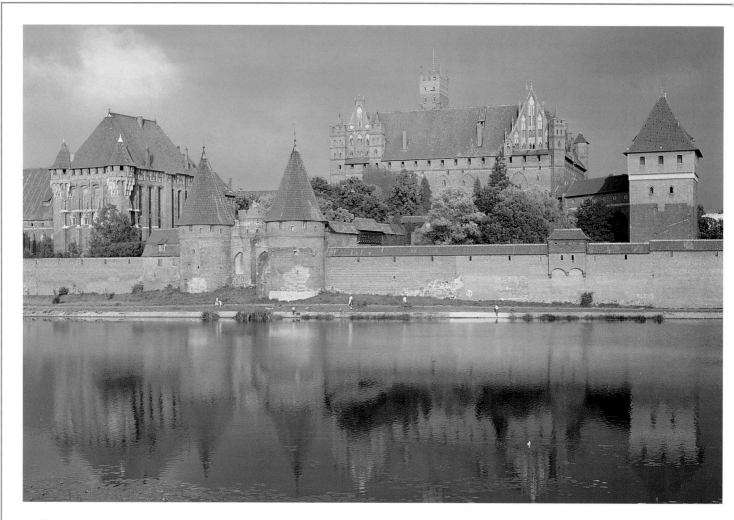

Malbork: Castle of the Teutonic Knights

Palace of the Grand Masters

MALBORK

Malbork Castle, once the seat of the Grand Master of the Order of the Knights of the Hospital of St Mary of the Teutons in Jerusalem (more widely known under the name of the "Teutonic Knights") is the largest castle in European lowlands. But only such a castle could be suitable for the most powerful chivalric order, the formidable war machine admired by the medieval world. The Teutonic Knights evolved out of a German hospital fraternity established near Acre in 1190, during the Third Crusade. Among its principal tasks was the protection of German pilgrims to the Holy Land and warring with unbelievers. The lands of the order were divided into districts and commanderies. In 1211 the Teutonic Knights received property in Transylvania from the Hungarian King Andrew II and were entrusted with the defence of the borders against the nomadic tribe of the Cumans. When they showed too much independence, however, they were driven out. In 1226, the Teutonic Knights contacted Prince Konrad of Mazovia, who invested them with the province of Chełmno (Kulm) in exchange for protection against pagan Baltic tribes. Teutonic Knights have always had bad press in Poland – and not without a reason. Polish-Teutonic relations consisted of a string of wars, broken treaties, treacherous acts and mutual accusations. But leaving emotions aside, Teutonic rule did bring about progress in those territories through the introduction of new forms of state organisation, colonization of rough country by founding new villages and towns, and – most importantly – through building impregnable fortresses. The stone and brick structures were derived from Sicilian and Norman models: quadrangular castles with an inner courtyard, surrounded by walls and a moat, and a bridge which led into the foreyard.

The construction of Malbork Castle began in 1274 on the initiative of H. von Schönenberg on the river island which had been purchased

Refectory

from the Pomeranian Duke Sambor. In thirty years the Order Assembly House was erected (in time transformed into the High Castle) with the Chapel, Chapter House, Dormitory, Refectory, inner courtyard and the foreyard. A long and high parapet walk linked the angle tower with the *Dansker* (fortified tower, which was at the same time a toilet). In 1309 Malbork, called Marienburg (St Mary's town) by the Teutonic Knights, became the capital of the Teutonic State, but the Grand Master himself settled there only in 1324. The complex was gradually enlarged, reaching the size of nearly 700 metres along the Nogat. Malbork was considered to be impregnable. Indeed, King Władysław Jagiełło, after the victory at Grunwald in 1410, failed to capture Malbork. In order to accomplish this feat half a century later, his son Kazimierz resorted to bribing mercenaries in the service of the Teutonic Knights. Following the Treaty of Toruń (Thorn) (1466), Malbork was incorporated into Poland and for several centuries remained the seat of a Crown administrative district and one of the largest national arsenals. The castle gradually fell into disuse and decline and after the First Partition of Poland in 1772, it was transformed into a Prussian barracks and vandalised. In 1817 restoration works began, supervised initially by K.F. Schinkel and F. von Quast. Painstakingly restored in 1882-1921, it was subsequently damaged during the Soviet offensive of 1945, particularly the eastern parts. Conservation has lasted ever since; in 1997, the castle was entered onto UNESCO's World Heritage List.

This formidable Gothic stronghold consists of three parts: the High Castle (1276-80, remodelled in 1331-44), the Middle Castle with the Great Refectory (1318-24) and the Grand Masters Palace (1383-99), and the Outer Castle (14th c.). The High Castle is a typical monastic castle on a quadrangular plan with the inner courtyard and cloisters. Surrounded by deep moats and several rings of walls, the castle had many impressive interiors, including the Chapter House and the castle church with the underlying Chapel of St Anne (serving as Grand Masters' burial chapel). The entrances to both are marked by beautiful figurative Gothic portals made of artificial stone. The church, 38 metres long and 14.4 metres high, was built in 1331-44. The chancel, protruding from the outer face of the walls, obtained a triangular crowning with a huge, 8-metre high, outward-facing figure of the Blessed Virgin Mary.

The former foreyard of the High Castle was also enlarged and turned into a sizeable Middle Castle, the actual administrative centre of the Teutonic State. The most interesting part of the Middle Castle is the Great Refectory with room for at least 500 people (the hall is 15 m long, 30 m wide and nearly 10 m high, with the vaults supported on three pillars; when Malbork was seized by the Prussians, the hall served as a horse-drill area). Another architectural gem is the Grand Masters Palace, which occupies the outer end of the castle's western wing. This is a most elegant residence, in which concern for prestige seems to take precedence over defence considerations. At the beginning of the 17th c. some of the rooms were even converted into royal suites. The rooms were heated by hot air which was supplied through a network of passages from stoves in the cellars, where large stones were kept in high temperature. The Middle Castle also houses two refectories designed for summer and winter use. The former is elaborate in design with palm vaults supported on a slender granite pillar. The Outer Castle was enlarged in the 14th c. and the first half of the 15th c. in order to house the Armoury. Very little of the original interior decoration has been preserved.

Wise and Foolish Virgins: Details of the portal

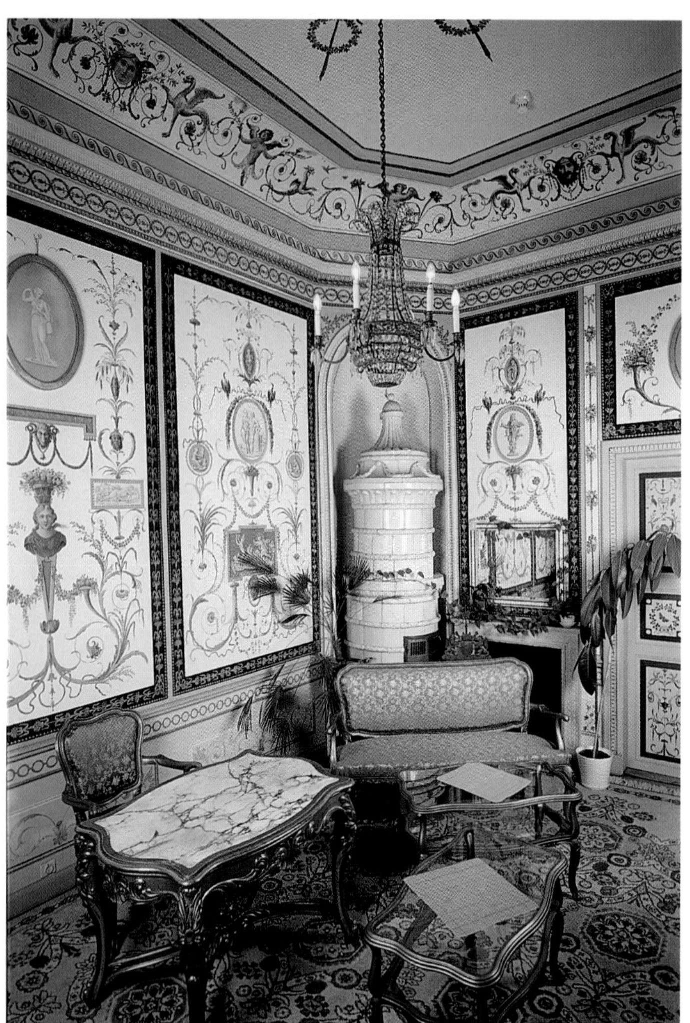

Mała Wieś: Palace interior

Mała Wieś

The Palatine of Rawa and Mazovia, Bazyli Walicki, spent his youth at the court of Louis XVI. Upon his return, he married Róża Nieborska, who in her dowry brought him the estate of Mała Wieś. They decided to replace the small wooden manor house with a genuinely French style neo-classical palace and park. The palace complex was raised in 1783-86 to the design of H. Szpilawski, including the main section of the palace (a two-storey building on a rectangular plan with a columned portico in the middle and an elegant ground floor) and the connected neo-classical pavilions. This type of design soon became the dominating model of Polish countryside residence until the mid-19th c. The complex was remodelled in the first half of the 19th c. by F. Lessel. Later it belonged to the Polish noble family of the Lubomirskis; among the owners were a 19th c. Polish government minister as well as the Mayor of Warsaw in the 1920's and a senator of the reborn Republic of Poland who died in 1943 murdered by the Nazis.

The interior of the house is decorated with murals, while in the Golden Room there is also stucco decoration crafted in the late 18th c. and around 1808. In the Pompeian Room grotesque motives coincide with ancient scenes and allegories, while in the Warsaw Room there are views of Warsaw and Naples (in illusionist frames). The view of the Polish capital, clearly inspired with works of Canaletto, can be admired as if from an open gallery: the artist framed the panorama in columns and railings.

Landscape gardens were laid out first around the palace and later expanded and cultivated in the 19th c. In the latter half of the 19th c. the prominent Polish naturalist A. Waga was a frequent visitor to the palace and contributed many rare species of trees and bushes. The palace, demolished in 1945-50, was restored in 1980. Today it is one of the official residences owned by the Polish government and is not accessible to visitors. The interiors have been furnished with stylish furniture and valuable textiles, some of which have been deposits of the National Museum in Warsaw.

Façade of the palace in Mała Wieś

Miechów

In 1162 Jaksa from Miechów, a pious pilgrim to the Holy Land, founded here the Romanesque monastery and church of the Equestrian Order of the Holy Sepulchre of Jerusalem. Compared with that, the manor house "Zacisze," seems a modern structure. In fact, however, it dates back to 1784, the testimony to which is the date carved on a ceiling beam. The one-storey manor house was built from larch timber and covered with two-layer shingled mansard roof. Two dormers make the whole construction slightly archaic. Front and back entrances are marked with pillar-supported porches. Zacisze is a now rare example of an urban manor house, which was given traditional and elegantly proportional form by the 18th-c. architect. The interiors feature two brick fireplaces from the late 18th c.

Manor house in Miechów

Milicz

Located at the ford on the route from Wrocław to Wielkopolska, Milicz grew in importance when in 1492 a free estate was carved out from the Duchy of Oleśnica. The entail was ruled by the Kurzbach family and after 1590 by the Maltanz family. The ruins of the 14th-c. castle of Oleśnica Dukes have been preserved in Milicz; the castle belonged to Konrad I and his son Konrad II, who in 1358 bought and enlarged the former bishops' castle. Following the attack of Hussite troops in 1432, the castle was destroyed and then abandoned. In the 17th c. the Maltanz family gave the building a more elegant shape so that it no longer had its defensive function. The largest of the castle towers was three-storey high and was supported by one great pillar. In 1772 Milicz was visited by King Frederic II. He donated to his minister, a Maltanz, a collection of valuable musical instruments which remained with the family until 1945. The castle was destroyed in a fire in 1797. The palace and park of the Maltanzes erected in 1797-98 to the design of K.G. Geissler is a valuable historical monument. Landscape gardens, the first in Silesia, were laid out around the building. They were 50 hectares in area, and the watermill stream supplied the ponds with water. In 1813 Tsar Alexander I stayed in the Milicz Palace, while the members of the anti-Polish coalition: Kings of Sweden and Prussia, the Russian Tsar, and Austrian and English diplomats, used to meet in nearby Żmigród. In the winter and spring of 1945, furniture, candelabra, lamps, carpets, clocks and paintings were looted from the castle.

Palace in Milicz

Mirów

Mirów Castle, situated in Jurassic Uplands, retained its defensive capability until the mid-18th c. This is probably the most gloomy of the "Eagle's Nests": its walls seem to grow out of limestone rocks typical of the area. The castle was probably one of a chain of strongholds raised by King Kazimierz the Great to reinforce the Polish-Silesian border. The first written source which mentioned the edifice dates back only to the 15th c., however. Made of stone, the castle was divided into the upper castle, the high tower, and the lower castle surrounded by perimeter walls. The entrance consisted of the gate and drawbridge. There was a watchtower and the residential keep as well.

Modlnica

Modlnica is one of the oldest settlements in the Cracow area: there is a folk tradition which links its origin with St Adalbert (Wojciech), who was to stop and pray (Pol. *modlić*, hence the name) here. The beautiful late 18th-c. house of the Konopkas is an outstanding example of the traditional Polish manor house: the columned portico with the date (1813) and a triangular pediment in front, and receded columns at the back, the façade decoration, and the high mansard roof. The interior design includes decorative ceilings, stuccos, parquets and fireplaces. The construction of the manor house in its present form dates back probably to 1784 as the date on the cellar vault testifies. It was founded by J. Konopka and built by K. Kriszkier, master of the Cracovian guild of masons and bricklayers. What remains from the Renaissance manor of the Salomons is the eastern wall and a small keep. The surrounding park, with a terraced layout and magnificent old trees, dates back to the Renaissance period in its oldest parts. The Modlnica manor house was a favourite meeting place of Cracow's cultural and intellectual elites.

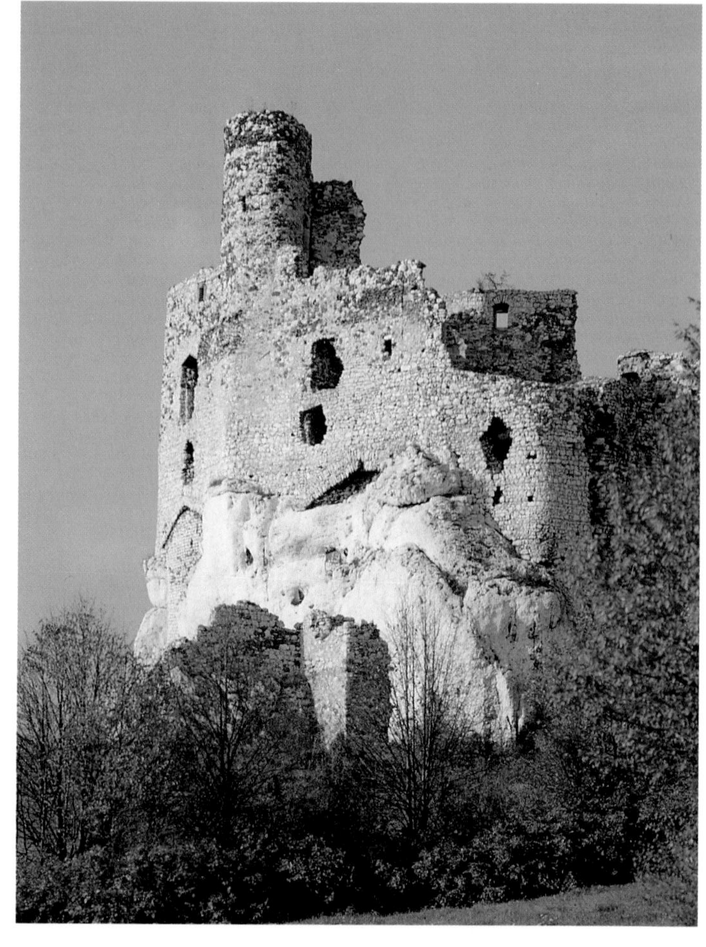

Mirów: Castle ruins

Manor house in Modlnica

Moszna

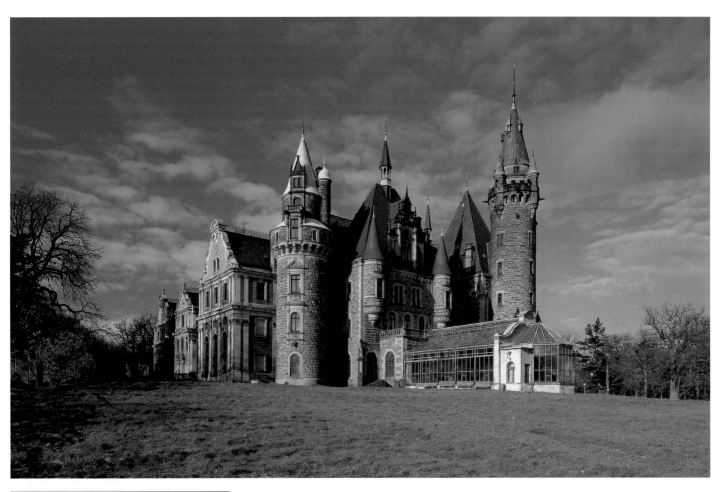

Moszna is one of those eclectic castles-cum-palaces whose owners, designers and restoration initiators lost all moderation. The whole structure bristles with turrets, chimneys and dormers to such an extent that it seems another embodiment of the Disneyland castle of the Sleeping Beauty.

The village of Moszna is located in the region of Opole; its name derives from that of the Mosce or Moshin family, who arrived here in 1309 or 1310. Two medieval castle sites are testimony to those ancient times. The eclectic castle, located in the nature park, replaces the earlier, Baroque palace which was destroyed by fire in 1896 and rebuilt and enlarged by the wealthy industrialist F.H. von Thiele-Winckler right afterwards.

The U-shaped edifice consists of three parts: the small neo-Baroque palace on a rectangular plan with a projection façade and two pseudo-medieval wings. The sizeable eastern wing was erected prior to 1900, while the western wing was constructed in 1912-14. Under the roof with 99 turrets there are as many as 365 rooms, among which are the library, built especially to mark the arrival of Emperor William II, although he was not considered to be very fond of reading, and the Chapel with excellent acoustics, which occasionally serves as a concert hall. At the beginning of the 20th c., a part of old cellars was discovered in the gardens: local romantic legends associate it with a mythical castle of Knights Templar and the underground passages allegedly leading to the stronghold in Chrzelice. Today the palace houses a sanatorium.

Palace in Moszna

Nagłowice

After 1545 the village of Nagłowice was the property of the writer Mikołaj Rej, the great promoter of the Polish language, whose work is documented by the museum organised in the manor house. In 1784 it was purchased by K. Walewski, who in 1800 erected the neoclassical building. It was rather unfortunately remodelled around 1878: spacious quasi-wings were added, which formed a kind of internal yard in front of the columned portico.

Manor house in Nagłowice

Palace in Nieborów

Nieborów

Arcadia was the mythical country extolled by Virgil's bucolics as an ideal of simple and happy life; Greek myths located it in remote wooded mountains of Peloponnesus. The memory of it remained with European culture for very long. In time it took the shape of fashionable Romantic parks in which the elegant ladies and chivalric gentlemen spent time flirting and reading poetry. The best tailors sewed quasi shepherds' costumes from the most expensive fabrics, sheep were brushed clean and their hooves and horns were painted gold, village girls were transformed into forest nymphs (naturally with limited success). The actors of these open-air games walked among the ruins which had been built as such, lay by the rustling artificial streams, and tried to nurture a spark of melancholy sitting among randomly collected stones and sculptures.

Poland was not immune to this fashion. The Arcadia Park near Łowicz is proof that vision combined with money can transform the Mazovian plain into an ancient paradise. The park – planned in the then fashionable Anglo-Chinese style – was established by Duchess H. Radziwiłł in 1778-1821. She hired the most prominent architects, S. B. Zug and W. Jaszczołd, to work on her estate. Riverside pastures and woods were incorporated into the park's layout, featuring large meadows, a pond and a mount. The structures erected in the park draw on both ancient tradition (Elysian fields and Temple of Diana from 1783; hippodrome and aqueduct from 1784) and Romantic inspiration (a mount with the Gothic House and Gallery from before 1800, Archpriest's House from 1783), and feature sculptures and stone fragments of both classical and domestic provenance. The park pavilions were decorated by such masters as J.P. Norblin, A. Orłowski and M. Płoński. The Duchess could afford to pay any price, so she was

Arcadia: Temple of Diana

Library at the Palace

able to accumulate one of the largest collections of ancient art in Poland, which turned into a magnet for connoisseurs, experts and snobs from the entire country.
The nearby Nieborów boasts a Baroque palace complex which was built by T. van Gameren in 1690-99 as a residence for Primate M. Radziejowski. Van Gameren designed a palace with two towers, which in time was surrounded by a garden of 40 hectares, partly geometrical and partly landscaped. Ca 1800, S.B. Zug designed the adjacent buildings of the complex (including the orangeries). In the park a collection of sculptures, statues and stone fragments was created, which, apart from ancient Roman exhibits, includes four stone female statues from the 12th c. (nicknamed "Nieborów gammers") that were brought here from the Ukrainian steppes. In the 18h c. the residence had a number of owners. In 1774 the Palatine of Vilna, M.H. Radziwiłł, purchased the palace from the Great Hetman of Lithuania M.K. Ogiński. It is then that Nieborów had its halcyon days; the family employed S.B. Zug, the author of the final shape of the palace complex. The residence was visited several times by King Stanisław August, and the local gallery features his coronation portrait by M. Bacciarelli.
In the interiors, the family gathered a magnificent collection of paintings, including over six hundred exhibits, a collection of drawings and sketches, interesting coins and medals and a large library. Not less valuable are the furnishings: furniture, tapestries, glassware and pottery of European best manufacturers. In 1831 M.G. Radziwił inherited the place after his father's death. But as general of Napoleon's army and one of the leaders of the 1831 Polish insurrection, he could not take over the estate. The insurrection was crushed by the Russian army, he was sent to Siberia, and the estate was requisitioned by force of the Tsar's decree. Only in 1840 could he get the Warsaw court to annul the confiscation, whereupon he claimed the estate back to stop looting and damage.
In 1881, the Radziwiłł family began manufacturing faience and majolica in a former brewery. Their factory remained in operation (with some interruptions) until 1906. Its products constitute the core of the display organised in the palace. In the 1920s, the last of the Radziwiłł family who owned Nieborów, Duke Janusz, ordered to top the palace with another storey (to the design of R. Gutto) and to remodel the interiors. The palace, however, continued to thrive in its dignified atmosphere until it was swept by "the new." In January 1945, the Duke was arrested by the Soviets and deported with his family to a place near Moscow. After a few years he returned from the labour camp, but the Communist authorities did not allow him to get anywhere near Nieborów. His wife died in the gulag.
Just as Łańcut or Wilanów, Nieborów was lucky to survive the horrors of the Nazi occupation and the post-war destruction triggered by the agrarian reform. Now it forms a branch of the National Museum in Warsaw and its historical interiors are open to the public. The halls and cabinets of the palace, the Venetian Room and the Yellow Cabinet, the Library and the Palatine's Bedroom have retained the charm of old Poland. The surviving part of the original Radziwiłł collection includes paintings from their gallery, a valuable library and a collection of antique sculptures.
In Polish literature Nieborów is known primarily thanks to the poem called "Niobe," which is a lyrical confession of the belief in the permanence of art. K.I. Gałczyński wrote it in the palace in 1950, inspired with the Roman copy of the touching Greek sculpture which stood in the hallway – the bust of the grief-stricken mother who was forced by the gods to watch the death of her children (a gift of Tsarina Catherine II for Duchess U. Radziwiłł).

The Red Room

Nidzica: Castle of the Teutonic Knights

Nidzica

The castle in Nidzica was built overlooking the old trade route from Mazovia. This border stronghold was the seat of the local administration head who was subordinate to the Teutonic commander from Ostróda. The construction was started after 1370. The rectangular Gothic brick castle is one of the most spectacular works in the Teutonic military architecture. In the western wing most official rooms were located, decorated with star vaulting. In the middle part of the suite there was a refectory, while the northern part comprised the castle administrator room; 15th-c. frescos were discovered on the walls. In the 15th c. the stronghold received two low semicircular outworks. The castle had been preserved in excellent condition until the First World War and 1945 when it was damaged in the fighting.

Niepołomice: Castle arcades

Niepołomice

The town of Niepołomice grew around the castle built by King Kazimierz the Great by the old bed of the Vistula and the Niepołomice Forest, the latter now thinned although still vast in area. The castle bustled with life especially in the Jagiellonian times as a holiday spot for the monarchs, a venue of political and diplomatic encounters, and a royal hunting lodge. Thoroughly remodelled in 1550-71 as well as in 1585 and 1637, it is a splendid example of a Renaissance residence. The castle was modernised by King Zygmunt August and became another regularly planned residence with arcaded courtyard, second only to Wawel Castle, which contributed to popularising the Italian-style architecture among Polish nobility. The walls of the King Kazimierz castle were mostly demolished and a sizeable hunting lodge resulted, which was a good functional match to a suburban villa, a concept fashionable at the time. It is from this time that the present layout derives, with the gateway and the arcaded three-level courtyard. The arcades used to be wooden; the brick and stone structures were founded by S. Lubomirski in 1637. Despite the transfer of the royal seat to Warsaw and the devastation by the Swedish army, the palace remained the favourite royal hunting venue. After the Partitions it fell into disrepair (the second floor was dismantled after 1800), and it has been renovated only recently. At present the former royal gardens are being rearranged.

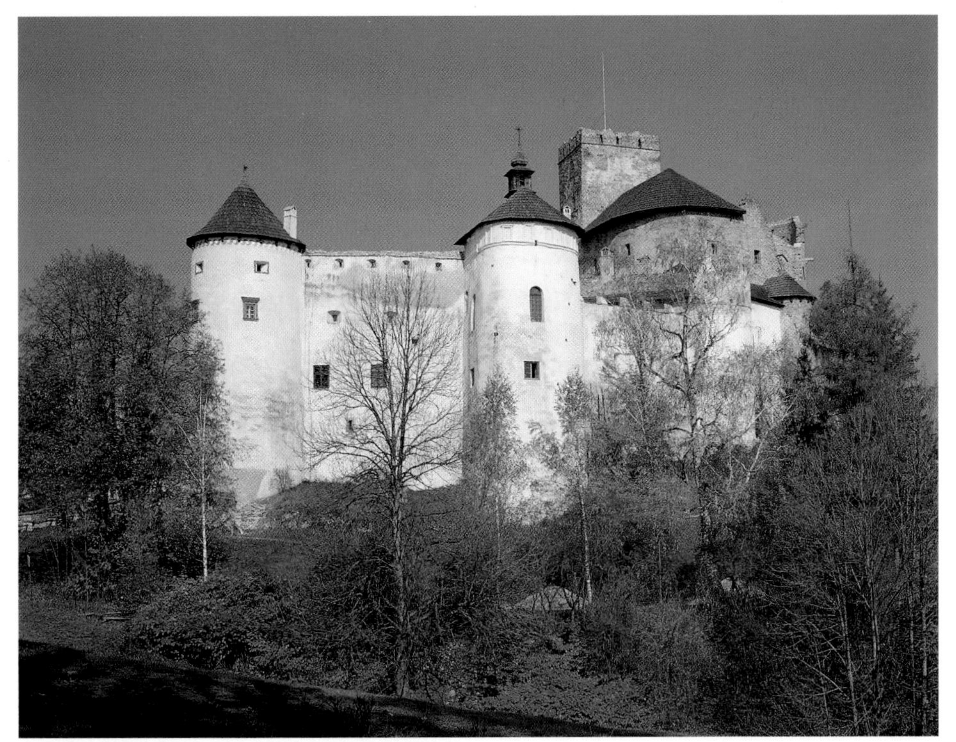

Castle in Niedzica

Niedzica

In the Pieniny mountain range scenic views and vigorous folklore blend together in harmony with the historical monuments dating back to the times of Polish, Czech and Hungarian kings, St Kinga and the hermits. The royal castle of Czorsztyn used to be the southernmost point in the Crown lands, separated by the river from the Hungarian Dunajec castle (the present Niedzica). The latter ruled over the Spisz, one of the most fascinating geographical and historical lands in the Carpathians, where the Polish, Slovak, Hungarian, Spisz German, Jewish and Ruthenian influences intermingled for centuries.

The oldest part of the castle, dated rather broadly to the late 13th c. or early 14th c., consisted probably of wooden houses and the well cut in the rock. The construction of brick and stone castle is attributed to W. Drugeth before 1330, when the "upper castle" was built comprising the irregular stone perimeter wall and the residential quarters. In 1412, it was the scene of an important political event: P. Schwarz of Łomnica, the treasurer to Emperor Sigismund of the House of Luxemburg, collected from King Władysław Jagiełło's envoys a loan of over 2 million Prague grossi, against the security of 13 towns of the Spisz region, ceded to Poland. In the 15th c., Niedzica Castle with the associated villages passed into the hands of the Hungarian Zapolya family and then the Polish Łaski family. In 1533-35, the Zapolyas fought a private war against the Habsburgs and the castle became a hideout for robber-knights. In 1589, O. Łaski sold Niedzica to the Horvath family; they modernised and enlarged the castle, which assumed a form close to its present appearance. Over the centuries the castle was transformed from a medieval mountain stronghold (the high castle with the keep) into a Renaissance residence (middle and lower castles) with an attractive courtyard and picturesque exterior decorated with parapets. The work on the fortress was completed in 1601. The next owners were the Italian Joanelli family (ca 1670) and, towards the end of the 18th c., the decaying residence returned to the Horvaths. The last Niedzica lords (1858-1944) were the Salamon family.

Gruesome legends are associated with the castle's dungeons, torture chambers and executions of highland robbers that used to take place there. There is also the exciting story of a quipu supposedly found at the castle, identifying the place where an Inca treasure is said to be hidden! The Niedzica castle was also the stronghold of feudalism: the relics of serfdom in the Spisz villages were abolished only in the 1920s. After the Second World War, the castle was thoroughly restored and opened for tourists. Unfortunately, the dam built in its immediate vicinity has somewhat marred the landscape.

Nowa Wieś: Manor house complex

Nowa Wieś

Nowa Wieś is situated at the edge of the Warsaw Plain. The neo-classical brick manor house was built in the early 19th c. for the Borowski family. After 1821, the next owner, Tomasz Gąsowski, most probably introduced considerable architectural changes. The one-storey building was erected on a rectangular plan and covered with a shingled hipped roof. A four-columned, rather low portico was added around 1844 to the design of the subsequent owner, Adolf Sucha, himself a prominent architect. The back façade with a rectangular niche and the windows divided by half-columns looks more attractive than the front. A group of historical 19th-c. manor buildings have been preserved as well, e.g. the wooden granary, in a small mid-19th-c. park. Fragments of the decorative stonework from the former romantic pavilion raised by the Gąsowskis and the 1823 park chapel were incorporated into the manor gate. This was the way to preserve small Ionian pillars and decorative sandstone cones.

The neo-classical burial chapel from 1830 (reconstructed after 1945), located outside the village, complements the manor. The local legend links the manor and its patriotic tradition with the chapel erected on the tomb of 1863 insurrection soldiers for whom, as was often the case with 19th c. manors at the time of the Partitions of Poland, the manor was to offer shelter and support. Currently the building houses the Horticultural Institute.

Oblęgorek

This village in the Świętokrzyskie Mountains is home to the biographical museum of the 19th-c. patriotic novelist and Nobel Prize winner H. Sienkiewicz. It was established in 1958, in accordance with the will of the writer's descendants, who donated the house to the nation. The study of Sienkiewicz has been meticulously reconstructed, with the original furniture and the writer's favourite trinkets. The museum also houses family memorabilia, manuscripts and prints. The collection had been put on show in the manor house of the Tarłos, purchased for the writer from the contributions of grateful Poles and offered to him in 1900 to mark an anniversary of his writing career. In 1902, following the renovation, Sienkiewicz moved in, but he stayed here only in the summer. The eclectic hunting lodge had been raised in 1895, designed by H. Kunder in Romantic historicist style with a round tower and a corner annexe. The cartouche with the Sienkiewicz family coat of arms crowns the entrance and the stone knight figure tops the gable.

Oblęgorek: Manor house of H. Sienkiewicz

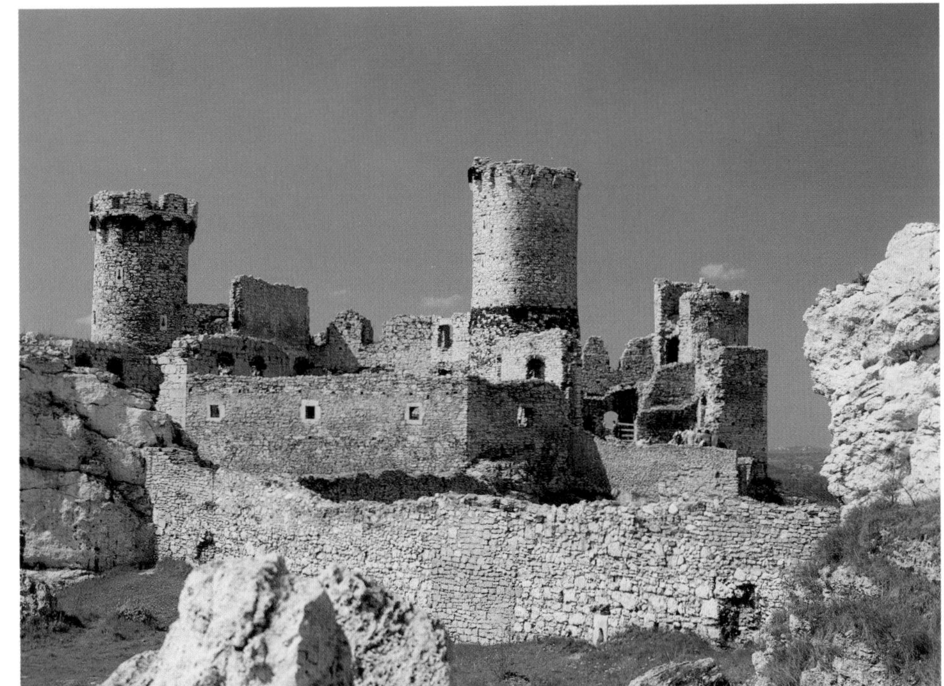

Ogrodzieniec: Castle ruins

Ojców

The Prądnik Valley is one of the most spectacular sites in Europe with regard to its natural beauty and cultural legacy. Small in area, it contains some 200 caves and a number of peculiar rock formations, and is extraordinarily rich in plant species. The castles in Ojców and Pieskowa Skała are characteristic features of the landscape. They originally constituted a property of the Crown, and Ojców was the administrative centre of the royal estate. The castle had been built by King Kazimierz the Great, but its later enlargements were the domain of the royal administrators. The place fell into complete ruin only at the turn of the 19th c. and in 1829 its walls started to be dismantled. The preserved octagonal tower, raised at the crest of a rocky outcrop, was the core of the original stronghold; the wall running along the hilltop with the entrance gate dates back to the 14th c. too.

Ogrodzieniec

Perhaps the most majestic of the "Eagles' Nests", the series of strongholds which once guarded Polish borders, is at Ogrodzieniec. The castle was built in 1530-45 for S. Boner, the Burgrave of Cracow and a trusted advisor to King Zygmunt the Old. Boner was a banker of Alsatian descent who made a swift career in Poland. He had a residence built which, with its numerous towers, deliberately mimicked medieval castles, and it was only the irregular shape of the inner courtyard and the form of the fortifications that betrayed the castle's more modern provenance. Ogrodzieniec came under attack several times. It was first captured in 1587 by the troops of Archduke Maximilian, the Habsburg pretender to the Polish throne. During the Swedish invasion in the 1650s, the residence was captured again. Somewhat unusually, however, the Swedes did not cause any significant destruction to the castle. After the war, it was restored by the new owner, S. Warszycki, who had it surrounded by an outer wall with a gate and a drawbridge. It was only in 1702 that the castle suffered severe damage, when it was set on fire by the Swedish troops of King Charles XII. Afterwards, it gradually fell into ruin, and in the early 19th c. local people began to dismantle its walls for building materials. The sombre ruins gave rise to local legends about a monstrous dog guarding hidden treasure. These inspired A. Janowski to establish the Polish Tourist Society in 1906.

Castle in Ojców

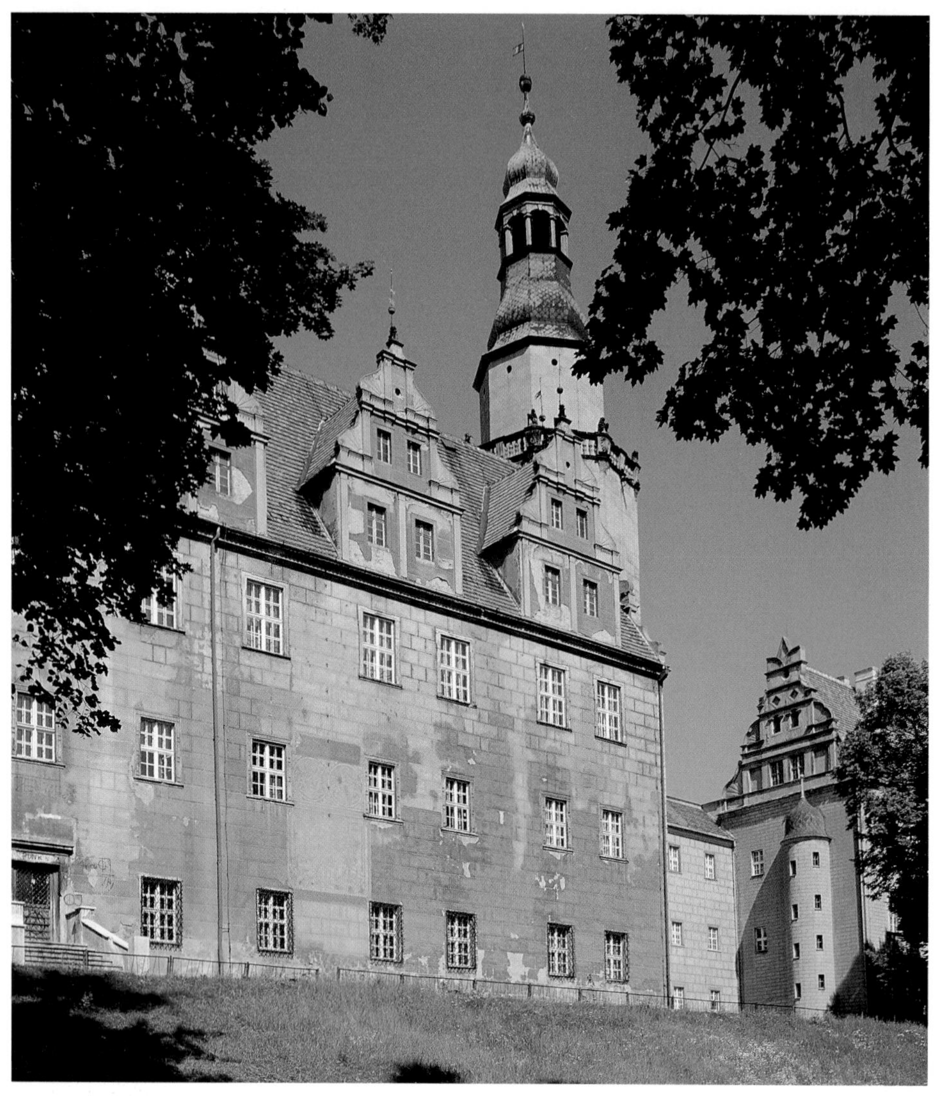

Castle in Oleśnica

The castle dominating the town replaced an older structure from the second half of the 14th c. Two enlargements and remodellings were effected during the time of Jan of Podebrad: around 1542-56 the north-western wing was remodelled, while in 1559-63 the gatehouse palace was built and the tower was raised by the builder K. Cuneo. Finally, in 1585-1610, during the reign of Rudolph II, the castle was remodelled again by B. Niuron; the remarkable overhanging galleries in the courtyard were designed by him. Placed in a niche above the gateway is the statue of Duke Jan of Podebrad by J. Oslew from 1554. The artist also built the tomb of the Duke and his wife at the parish church (14th-15th c.), which was linked to the castle with a covered cloister (1613-16). At the time of its heyday, the ducal court was an important cultural centre in Silesia, and its library was considered one of the best. It took pride in a copy of the Bible sent here by Martin Luther, who had himself added many side notes for Duke Jan. Unfortunately, the Golden Age was followed by the age of disasters: the sieges in 1627, 1640, 1642 and 1648 (it was then that the Swedish general A. Wittemberg issued an order to destroy the city "as completely as possible") intermingled with fires (1630) and attacks of the plague (1631 and 1634). In the second half of the 17th and 18th c., the residence was modernised again and a new, Baroque interior decoration was added. The major conservation works were completed in 1891-1906 restoring the original Renaissance shape to the castle. Oleśnica has thus survived the historical turmoil – picturesque and well-preserved.

Oleśnica

During the period of Fragmentation (12th-14th c.), Oleśnica was the property of the Wrocław branch of the Piast line. In 1255, Duke Henryk III offered it the municipal charter, based on the law of Środa Śląska. The early medieval settlement had existed here as far back as the 11th c., however; in a 1247 document Oleśnica was mentioned as the castellany seat, although most probably only a burgrave resided here. In the 12th c. the monastery of the order of Irish Benedictines, the only one in Poland, was established here. In 1312, the town became incorporated into the newly established Duchy of Oleśnica. In 1492, after the death of Duke Konrad the White, the town passed into the hands of the Podebrad family, and in the second quarter of the 17th c. it became part of the realm of the Württemberg-Weitlingen Dukes. After they had expired in 1752, the place was inherited by Frederick August from Brunswick, and in 1805 it was taken over by his nephew, the Prussian king, Frederick II. From 1876 on, the vast estate was entailed on the consecutive heirs to the Prussian throne.

Castle courtyard: Detail

Castle in Olsztyn

Olsztyn

The town of Olsztyn is situated in the centre of the Warmia and Mazury region. In 1346-53, a Gothic Allenstein castle belonging to the Warmia Chapter was erected in the river bend. It was built on a rectangular plan and enlarged in several phases: the northern and southern wings are Gothic, while the eastern wing is Baroque. Nicolaus Copernicus was the administrator of the chapter estate in 1516-19 and 1520-21; during the war of Poland with the Teutonic Knights in 1521, he was responsible for defence preparations of the Olsztyn Castle (preserved on the wall is a diagram of the equinox, possibly left by the famous astronomer). In the late 16th and the 17th c. the castle was repaired: new vaults were constructed in the castle residence, the interiors were remodelled, St Anne's Chapel was built. In 1772, after Warmia had been incorporated into Prussia, the estate of the chapter and diocese was secularised. In 1821 and 1827, part of the castle interior was damaged in fires. In 1909-11 the building housed offices. In some of the rooms the Gothic style was restored, and new elements were added to the Baroque wing. Today the castle houses the museum which boasts the sundial constructed by Copernicus. A stone gammer stands in the middle of the courtyard, dating back to the time of old Prussians and their pagan rites.

Olsztyn koło Częstochowy

The village of Olsztyn, not far away from Częstochowa, is linked with one of the most genuinely "Roman" episodes of Polish history. In 1587, the Archduke Maximilian, the Habsburg pretender to the Polish throne, sieged the castle defended by Burgrave K. Karliński. Not able to overpower the castle defence, the German landsknechts used Karliński's 6-year-old son as a human shield. When the soldiers approached the castle gate, Karliński grasped the canon's fuse, shouted out "I was not born a father, but I was born Polish," and fired the cannon. Seeing that, Maximilian gave up and the Archduke's army withdrew. The determination of Karliński is testimony to the significance of the Olsztyn castle for Poland at the time. The castle was erected most probably in the second half of the 13th c. and enlarged during the reign of King Kazimierz the Great. It was gradually transformed into a large defence complex consisting of three basic parts: the upper (on the rocky hill, with the cylindrical defence tower), middle and lower castles. In 1399, the Olsztyn estate gained the status of the landed property reserved for the most deserving noble families. The consecutive owners developed the military capability of the stronghold until the Swedish invasion of 1655-56 brought about the ultimate fall of the castle. The restoration was not undertaken since in the meantime, due to the development of artillery, the fortresses of this type had lost most of their military value, and the costs would have been enormous. The abandoned castle, once the pride of the Crown, was now turned by local peasants into pigsties. Conservation work was initiated in 1995.

Jurassic Uplands: Ruins of Olsztyn Castle

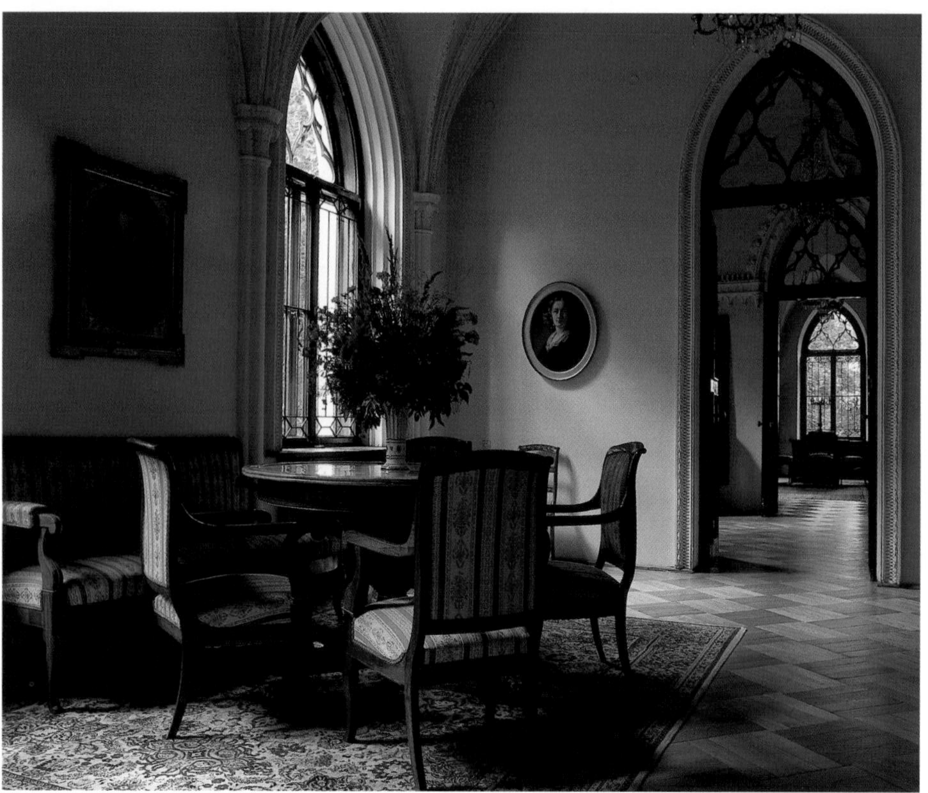

Suite of castle rooms

is covered with delicate stucco decoration. The interiors available to visitors include the hallway, the Anteroom, the Dining Room, the Red Room, the Ancestors Room, Napoleon's Room, and the Poet's Bedroom. On display are furniture and arts and crafts in the Duchy of Warsaw style, portraits of the poet and his family, his memorabilia and photographs. The former chapel, now Napoleon's Room, contains the most beautiful vaults and stuccoes, as well as portraits of Napoleon, General Kościuszko, Duke J. Poniatowski, and other Polish generals. The palace is surrounded with a landscape park with the statue of Zygmunt Krasiński, the only one in Poland (the work of M. Welter from 1989).

A wooden manor house used to stand next to the palace; it was dismantled by the Krasińskis, who in 1908 announced a competition for the design of a new one. The designs which were awarded all represent the manor-house construction style: one-storey buildings with high-pitched roofs and columned porticos. The manor house was never built, however, as the First World War broke out. The late 19th c. neo-classical parish church houses the crypt of the Krasińskis.

Opinogóra

In Opinogóra, the neo-Gothic Krasiński palace (erected following the design of H. Marconi) houses the Museum of Romanticism, the only one of the kind in Poland, which was opened to the public in 1961. In the Middle Ages, there was a hunting lodge of Mazovian Dukes here. From the 17th c. on, the village was practically in the hands of the Krasiński family; formally, however, W. Krasiński obtained the position of the administrator of the area from Napoleon only in 1811 (together with the title of the Earl of the Empire). The owner was certainly an extraordinary man, although his personality was far from uniform. He was Chairman of the Society of Friends of Poland, and co-founded the Polish Light-Cavalry Regiment of Imperial Guards. He became its leader, and the soldiers, proud and highly valued, enthusiastic and eager to fight, started the long campaign which was to bring them from the Atlantic coast and the famous Somosierra battle in Spain to the walls of the Kremlin. At the time of the Russian-dominated Kingdom of Poland, Krasiński, already as a Russian army general, obeyed the policy of St Petersburg and opposed the Polish 1831 insurrection; in 1855-56 he was the Governor of the Polish Kingdom.

His decisions determined the fate of his son, the poet Zygmunt Krasiński. He was forced to make a dramatic choice "between the father and the fatherland"; he was torn between the defence of tradition and the unbiased assessment of the contemporary dilemmas, and was ostracised by his friends because he had failed to take part in the national insurrection. The poet developed the idea of the mission of the Polish nation in the moral revival of the world. He opposed the revolutionary movements which he considered to be embodiments of the destructive presence of evil in history; he favoured tradition-based "organic" development as a unified "action" of the entire nation, supervised by aristocracy. He held disputes with his father against the background of the beautiful palace in Opinogóra, which Zygmunt had received from him as a wedding gift in 1843.

Krasiński residence had been built in 1828-43, remodelled in 1894 by J. Huss and restored in 1958-61 and 1973-74. This is a neo-Gothic building with a terrace on the south side, a portico, a stepped gable and an octagonal tower in the south-western corner. Part of the exterior

Castle in Opinogóra

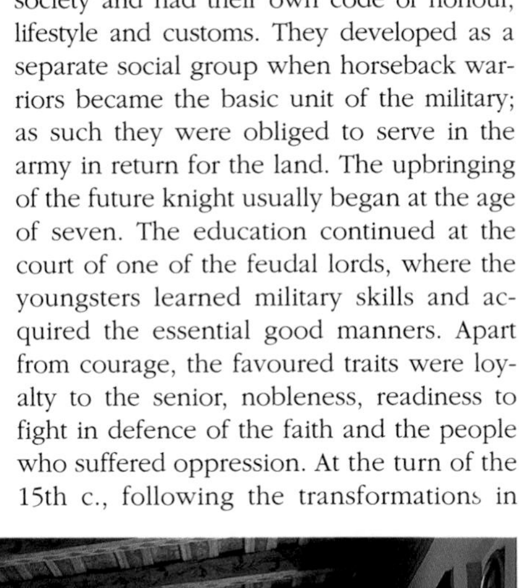

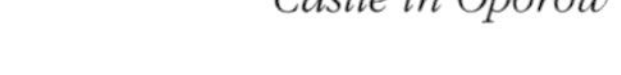

Castle in Oporów

Oporów

The late Gothic castle at Oporów near Kutno is one of the smallest but the most picturesque Polish strongholds. Its shape and wide water-filled moats around it almost ideally fit the commonly held image of knights' residences which used to be scattered around the old Polish Republic – that of village manors teaming with family legends and valuable furnishings rather than that of gloomy castles surrounded with historic battlegrounds. It must be remembered that in the Middle Ages the knights were the elite of the feudal society and had their own code of honour, lifestyle and customs. They developed as a separate social group when horseback warriors became the basic unit of the military; as such they were obliged to serve in the army in return for the land. The upbringing of the future knight usually began at the age of seven. The education continued at the court of one of the feudal lords, where the youngsters learned military skills and acquired the essential good manners. Apart from courage, the favoured traits were loyalty to the senior, nobleness, readiness to fight in defence of the faith and the people who suffered oppression. At the turn of the 15th c., following the transformations in military art, the knights lost in significance and they started to turn into landed gentry. The knights' residences evolved in a similar way.

In the late Middle Ages, Oporów, first a village then a town, was the centre of the Oporowski estate. One of the most prominent owners of the place was M. Oporowski, first the Chamberlain (1411-19), then the Palatine of Łęczyca (1419-25). The oldest document mentioning the fortified residence here dates back to 1418. The castle was given its final shape in 1434-39 by Primate W. Oporowski and consisted of several buildings as well as the Eastern Tower and the Chapel Tower, all set in a quadrangle around a small yard. From the 17th to the 20th c. the castle was remodelled several times, although its original form has been largely preserved (one of the architects hired for the task in 1877-78 was Z. Gorgolewski). The castle, encircled by a wide moat filled with water, served as a spacious, comfortable residence rather than a defensive castle. From the early 17th c. on, a number of noble families resided here following the Oporowskis, including the Tarnowskis, the Korzeniewskis and the Orsettis, most of whom only confined themselves to small construction works and repairs. Today the museum displays the castle's interiors. In the 1960s, the Renaissance polychrome ceilings were restored as well as the Gothic portals and window frames. The castle is surrounded by a large landscape park laid out in the mid-18th c. and cut up with scenic streams and canals.

Knights Hall

Ożarów: Wooden manor house

Ożarów

Located in the vicinity of Wieluń, Ożarów boasts a wooden manor house from the mid-18th c. The Baroque building was raised from best larch timber by the owner of the village, the castellan of Wieluń W. Bartochowski, at the top of a small hill. The one-storey structure with the attic was built on a rectangular plan with an axial hallway. It is covered with a high two-layer shingled roof . The main section of the building adjoins small square annexes, also covered by high roofs. Inside, the beamed ceiling has been preserved, with the date on the dining room beam (1757); the interior is furnished in 18th-c. style with the original furniture. The present manor house replaced the earlier one, which had been in a poor state as far back as 1669. The Ożarów estate was owned by the Bartochowski family and their relatives until 1883, when it was purchased by H. Meske. After 1945, the building together with the park and the woods was taken over by the state.

The manor house is a good example of an unpretentious residence of local landed gentry. It is not deprived of artistic ambitions, though; it clearly resembles the north-Italian Palladio-style villas as their simplified replica. The bell-shaped tops of the annexes also resemble those of the manor at Czarnożyły, which has not been preserved. In 1970-80, the Ożarów manor was restored. On display in the museum, opened in 1981, are various artefacts of the landed gentry culture, with the furnishings of the drawing room, alcove, hunters' room, study and dining room. The furniture includes not only the Baroque wardrobes, trunks, and chests of drawers, but also hunting trophies, china and silver. The original Polish overcoat belts, weapons and, most importantly, 18th- and 19th-c. portraits of Wieluń landed gentry contribute to the unique atmosphere of the place. A fireplace has been preserved too, with late Baroque ornaments, as well as a 19th-c. neo-Renaissance tiled stove.

Drawing room

Palace in Otwock Wielki

Otwock Wielki

The Baroque palace in Otwock Wielki was designed by Tylman van Gameren in 1682-89 for K. Bielański. He erected a spacious two-storey building at the river island, with two projection façades: one at the front with a triangular pediment depicting a Bacchanalia scene and a polygonal one facing the garden. It was here that King August II conducted negotiations with Swedish deputies, while in 1705 Bielański entertained Tsar Peter the Great in the manor. The palace was enlarged by G. Fontana in the mid-18th c. In 1824, however, it was damaged by floods. Renovated only in 1850 to the design of J. Skarbori, it passed into the hands of F. Jezierski in 1871. The restoration work from 1947 and 1975 saved the 18th-c. stuccoes and murals which adorn elegant first floor rooms, including the former drawing room and ballroom. Of particular interest is the series of ten murals which illustrate quotations from Horace's work, as well as classic panoramas in the Landscapes Room and the fireplace with stucco decoration depicting a phoenix raising from the ashes. The façade features the coats of arms of the first owners of the palace. The park with the 17th-c. formal garden was enlarged and rearranged in the 18th and 19th c. The palace is closed to the public as the building is owned by the Chancellery of the President of Poland.

Pawłowice

In Pawłowice, an imposing palace in neo-classical style was built in the second half of the 18th c. for A. Mielżyński, the royal administrator of the area. In 1779-83 it was remodelled to the design of K.G. Langhans, the subsequent designer of the Brandenburg Gate in Berlin, who added slightly rounded galleries and annexes. The portico was adorned with a parapet and statues in the classical spirit. In the garden-side projection façade there is a rounded drawing room which is decorated by panels with plant and musical motives. The most impressive part of the palace is the ballroom, with 24 columns, mirrors and floor inlays. The study with costly silk wall decorations has luckily survived too. The interior decoration was designed by J.B. Kamsetzer. Surrounding the palace is a large 18th-c. park.

Palace in Pawłowice

Manor house in Petrykozy

PETRYKOZY

Petrykozy is a small village in the Rawa Upland. The pride of the place is a single-storey brick manor house which is situated in the vicinity of cascade-linked ponds. Typically for Polish manor buildings, it is covered with a two-layer shingled roof. It was erected in the first half of the 19th c. for the Janasch family. Before 1850, it was plastered and decorated with porches, which are supported on Tuscan-style columns. In the 1920s and 30s it belonged to Count Edward Broel-Plater. The manor buildings are surrounded with a small, well-kept park from the second half of the 19th c.

PĘZINO

In the opinion of experts, the castle of Pęzino, near Stargard Szczeciński, is one of the most valuable monuments of military architecture in Western Pomerania. In the 14th c. it was the property of the Boreck family, and in 1382 it was purchased by B. von Schulenburg, a district commander of the Knights Hospitallers. At the turn of the 15th c., they erected there a castle on water, surrounded by two rivers, which was the seat of their commandery in 1483-92. In 1493 it returned to the Borecks and in 1703 it passed into the hands of the Puttkamer family. In 1657, the commander of the Polish troops in the Polish-Swedish war, Hetman Stefan Czarniecki, had his headquarters here. The oldest, Gothic part of the castle was built of brick and stone, on an irregular rectangular plan with a huge tower protruding from the south-western corner of the walls. The tower is quadrangular to the level of the top of the walls and then cylindrical, the highest part having toppled before 1674. The residential quarters in the eastern wing were remodelled in the late Gothic spirit in the early 16th c., retaining framed mullioned windows and decorative gables. In 1600, the northern wing was added, which was late Renaissance in style, with narrow bays, gables and decorative chimneys. In 1853-55, the eastern wing obtained a neo-Gothic part. From the south, a forecastle is attached, 30 x 40 m in size, with a chapel erected at the time of M. Boreck. The remaining buildings have the timber-framed construction. The water-mill, dams and ponds on the Krąpiela river add a scenic element to the historical complex.

Pęzino Castle

Castle courtyard

Castle in Pieskowa Skała

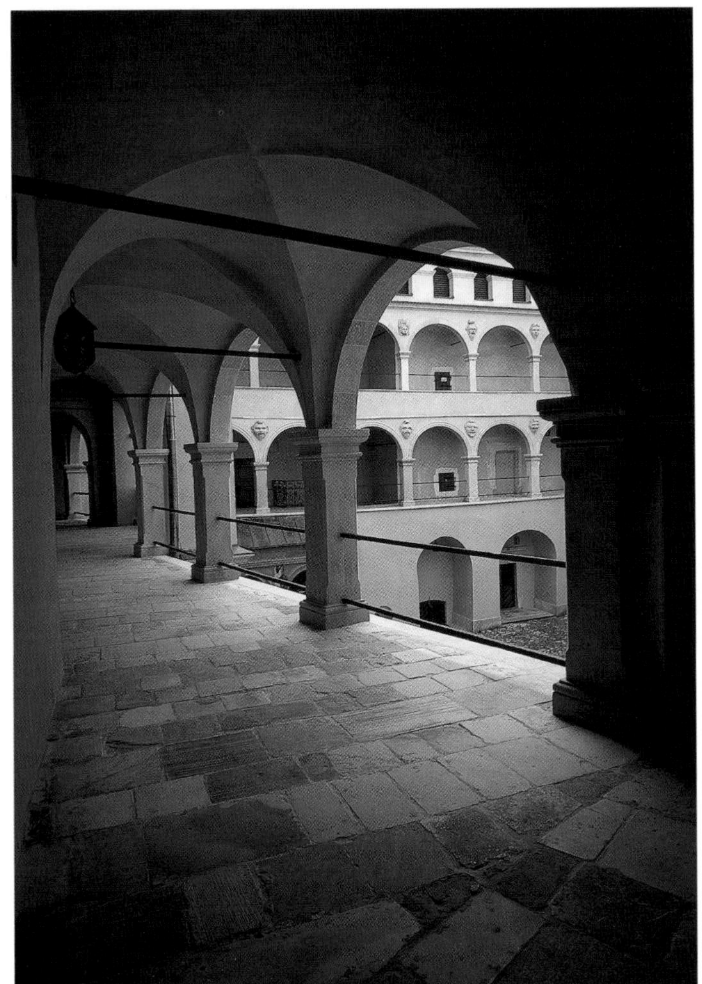

Pieskowa Skała

The castle at Pieskowa Skała was founded by King Kazimierz the Great and in 1377 King Louis the Great donated it to P. Szafraniec. The Szafraniec family kept it until the early 17th c. Remodelled in Renaissance style, the castle became one of the most beautiful residences in Małopolska. In 1557-78 S. Szafraniec erected a quadrangular castle with a trapezium courtyard inside. The three-level arcaded and pillared cloisters turned the residence into a palace. A panoramic loggia and a clock-tower were added in front of the building. After the death of J. Szafraniec in 1608, the palace frequently changed hands. The Zebrzydowski family introduced considerable changes in the spatial layout of the castle. It was surrounded with a modern fortification system. In 1640-55, M. Zebrzydowski erected two powerful bastions on the eastern flank, linked by a curtain wall with the entrance gate. In this way the castle gained the second, as if external courtyard. He also built a chapel and added two upper floors to the castle. Unfortunately, it suffered considerable destruction at the hands of the Swedish invaders in 1655 and 1702. Even so, it has always attracted attention of visitors on account of its scenic location. Thanks to the restoration work conducted around 1760 by H. Wielopolski, the castle regained the residential character, with the new theatre hall inside. In 1902, the castle, partly destroyed by fire, was purchased by a joint-stock company (set up on the initiative of writer A. Dygasiński), which opened a guest house here. On 8 August 1914, J. Piłsudski, commander of Polish troops, stopped here on his way to the Russian-occupied Kingdom of Poland. During the Second World War, the building served as a temporary shelter for war orphans, while following the Warsaw Uprising it hosted refugees from the destroyed city.

Thoroughly restored after the war, it now functions as a museum – a branch of the Wawel collections. In its present shape, it is a good example of a Renaissance fortified residence with some Mannerist details, at the same time preserving medieval elements, as well as Baroque and 19th-c. historicist buildings.

Radzyń Chełmiński

Radzyń Chełmiński is situated to the southeast of Grudziądz, in the Chełmno Lake District. In the 13th c. it was one of the administrative centres of the Duchy of Mazovia. In 1231 it was donated to the Teutonic Knights, who in 1234 began to build a castle; it was most likely then that Radzyń obtained municipal rights. The stronghold was erected on the thin strip of land between two lakes (they have dried out since) on the trade route from Grudziądz to Wąbrzeżno, Golub and Toruń. The castle, which has been preserved, is regarded as one of the prominent examples of a fortified structure, with quadrangular angle towers, surrounded by an external wall and a moat. It was built from brick in the 14th c. in the early stage of the expansion of the Order of Teutonic Knights, when they erected primarily the wooden-and-earth fortifications and settlements with churches. In time stone and then brick buildings started to appear. The first castle, on an irregular plan was raised in Toruń, while in the early 14th c. the monastic type of castle took shape. It was in Gniew and Radzyń castles that the model of regular quadrangle with the inner, sometimes arcaded, courtyard came into being. The front wing contained the entrance gate in the middle, and the second floor of the side wings housed two main halls: the Chapel in the eastern and the Chapter in the western wing. The other wings contained the refectory, dormitory, kitchen and other rooms, while the ground floor and the top floor had storage and other subsidiary functions. The watchtower was built in one of the corners of the quadrangle. The perimeter wall constituted the first defensive line. In the Teutonic workshops new construction technologies were forged: the lower parts of the walls were made from stone while the upper parts were brick walls; the artificial stone came into use as early as at the end of the 13th c. In 1440, Radzyń Chełmiński joined the anti-Teutonic Prussian Union, and after the 13-year-long war with the Teutonic Order had broken out, it passed into the Polish hands. In 1456, it was looted by the Knights, but in 1466 it was finally incorporated into Poland. During the wars with Sweden, the castle and the town were repeatedly destroyed, and the castle fell into ruin. This is what it looks like today too.

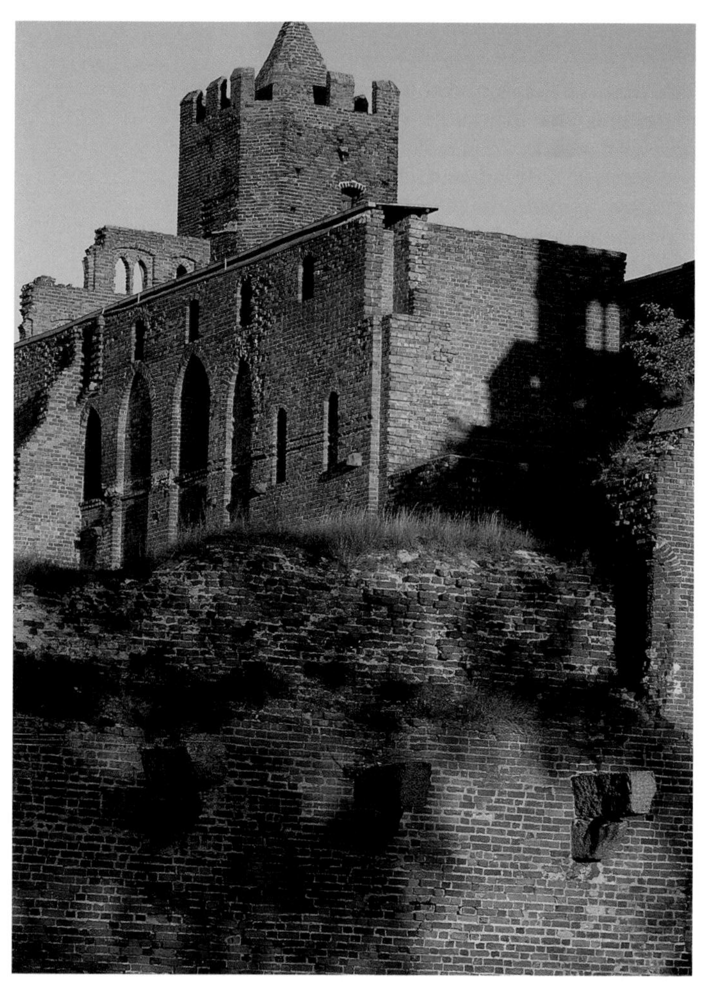

Radzyń Chełmiński: Castle of the Teutonic Knights

Palace in Radzyń Podlaski

Radzyń Podlaski

Radzyń had been royal property until 1534, when King Zygmunt I the Old presented it to his administrator M. Mniszech (later, his granddaughter, Maryna, became the main protagonist of the false Dmitri story and the Russian Tsarina). An impressive palace of Radzyń can now be admired surrounded by a spacious park. It was the result of the rococo remodelling, carried out in 1750-95 to the design of G. Fontana by order of E. Potocki (general of Lithuanian artillery), of the former Baroque-style residence of S. Szczuka (1685-1709; the work of A. Locci), which in turn had replaced a 15th-c. Kaznowski castle. Fontana was the best man for the job: he was fond of subtl e and delicate forms. The residence in Radzyń is a good example of a skilful combination of French spatial planning and rococo architecture.

The complex consists of the palace built on a horseshoe plan with the perpendicular wings embracing a large courtyard. Both the central axes meet in the middle of the Yard of Honour, the cross line linking the palace with the town. The façade is divided into parts by flat pilasters. A decorative tower gate was built into the western wing of the palace, which faces the town. The side wings may seem to have been given priority as they are marked with effective helm-topped gates. The coats of arms of the Potockis and M. Kątska, wife of E. Potocki, only add to their splendour. Features typical of French architecture are noticeable in projection crowns and sculpture-adorned parapets. The sculptural decoration in stone is the work of J.C. Redler (e.g. *The Four Tasks of Hercules*). The eastern wing used to house the stables and the coach-house. The formal garden was designed by J.D. Knackfus, who planned it around the 300-year-old larch trees. The Orangery, designed by G. Fontana, features at the top of the central projection the sculpture titled *Apollo's Chariot Drawn by Three Stallions.*

The canal and the pond was designed by P.R. de Tirregaille. For the aristocracy of the late Baroque period, this French architect and army officer was of the same significance as Tylman van Gameren a century earlier. He worked for Hetman Branicki in Białystok, as well as for the Palatine of Kiev, F.S. Potocki, in Lvov. He also designed the palace and garden complex in Krystynopol, the manor in Perespa, as well as the urban mansions of the Czackis and Bielskis. He advised the Uniate Archbishop of Lvov on the construction of St George's Cathedral. In 1763 he left for Berlin where he worked for King Frederick II. In 1831-1920, the palace was the property of the Szablewski family, who sold it to the state. In July 1944 the German army set fire to the castle, but it was reconstructed in 1950-69. The restoration work is still in progress.

Front façade of the palace

Manor house in Radziejowice

Radziejowice

After the 14th c., the village was owned by the Radziejowskis, then Prażmowskis, Ossolińskis (after 1705) and Krasińskis (1782-1945). The surrounding woods were the natural habitat of aurochs (the last female of the species died in 1627) and the royal hunting ground. The Baroque palace of Cardinal M. Radziejowski (raised in 1678-84) was remodelled in neo-classical style by order of the Krasiński family. The palace is surrounded by the romantic, sentimental park laid out in 1817, with diverse elements such as clearings, tree groups, a pond with irregular shoreline and an island, a wharf, bridges, benches, sculptures. Facing the palace is a neo-classical wooden manor house with a columned portico and a shingled roof from the turn of the 19th c., designed by J. Kubicki. It is in this house that several scenes were shot to the film entitled *Pan Tadeusz*, based on the epic poem by the best Polish Romantic poet, A. Mickiewicz.

Reszel: Bishops' Palace

Reszel

In 1241, the Teutonic Knights erected a wooden watchtower here, although the name of Reszel is of old-Prussian origin. Later the town passed into the hands of bishops of Warmia (1254), who combined the spiritual and secular power over the region. The construction of the castle, situated on a steep slope of a gorge, was commenced in 1350 by order of Bishop Jan of Meissen. It was built on a square plan. Following 1360, the southern wing, the angle tower and the gate tower were raised, while after 1505 the corner gate and two northern towers were added. In the 15th c. residential quarters and the chapel with the star vault were located on the second floor of the eastern wing. The southern wing contained the bishops' quarters, a small and large refectory, a room for the debt collector. After the castle passed into the Polish hands in the mid-15th c., it lost its defensive role and became the administrative centre. In 1503-10, Copernicus stayed in Reszel as an advisor to the bishop, while later the castle hosted the historian M. Kromer and Cardinal A. Báthory, the nephew of King Stefan Báthory. The building fell into disrepair in the 18th c. In 1772, after the Prussians occupied Warmia, the castle was turned into a prison. It was remodelled in 1806, and in 1807 the prisoners set fire to the castle on hearing the news that Napoleon's troops were approaching Reszel. It was in ruins until 1820s when it was rebuilt and has remained unchanged until today.

Palace in Rogalin

ROGALIN

The countryside around Poznań abounds with oak-lined alleys and lush-green parks. In the beautiful scenery of extensive meadows and romantic oxbow lakes stands the Raczyński Palace. The family acquired Rogalin in the mid-18th c. and the construction of the present palace, to the design of I. Graff, was initiated in 1770 by K. Raczyński. In 1782-83, the slightly rounded Palladian galleries were added. The work was continued by Raczyński's son, Edward, who had the interiors of this magnificent, if somewhat heavy building decorated by D. Merlini and J.B. Kamsetzer. In 1788-89 Kamsetzer remodelled the staircase, while Merlini designed the first floor drawing room. In the first-floor ballroom – now called the Armoury – there is a collection of rare military exhibits, along with historical memorabilia and family heirlooms of the Raczyńskis. The southern annexe of the palace houses a museum of interiors, with a collection of old furniture and bric-a-brac. In the gallery building, put up in 1910, part of E. Raczyński's collection of Polish and European painting is on display. The palace is approached from a forecourt, with stables and a paddock at its sides. In the coach-house, there is an interesting collection of carriages and harnesses.

The old chestnut-lined alley, the triple-arch bridge and the formal garden blending with the landscape park and then with riverside meadows – it is a wonderful place. Everything has been carefully planned here. The most decorative element of the gardens is the Garden Lounge, which is framed with a panoramic mound (Parnassus). Lanes spread radially from the centrally-situated flowerbed, running among rococo stone sculptures. Together with the adjacent greens, the park forms a unique arboretum comprising 960 oak trees, the largest of its kind in Europe. In 1820, a mausoleum chapel, closely modelled on the Roman temple at Nîmes, was built at the edge of the park to house the burial crypt of the Raczyńskis. Neo-classical annexes and other manor buildings from 1776-1820 make the picture of the place complete.

ROŻNÓW

The neo-classical 19th-c. manor house of the Stadnicki family stands next to the remains of the fortress of J.A. Tarnowski. The front faces the driveway, while the back façade is more effective with the receded portico supported on ten columns. The interior features murals attributed to M. Stachowicz. Of interest are the preserved woodwork and three fireplaces made from marble-like stone.

Manor house in Rożnów

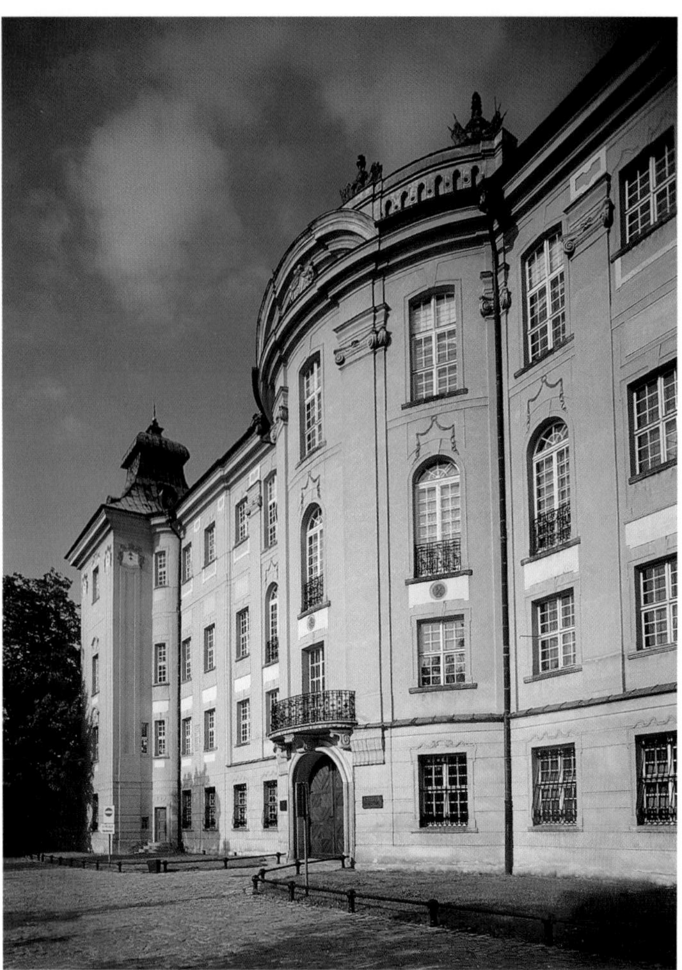

Palace in Rydzyna

Rydzyna

The monumental residence at Rydzyna is surrounded by a large landscape park. The town received its municipal charter in 1422, and in the 15th c. it was owned by Jan of Czernina. In the 17th and 18th c., it was the seat of the Leszczyński family. The town has retained its Baroque layout, in which the castle on an artificial island surrounded by a moat figures prominently. There is an interesting church of St Stanislaus, designed by K.M. Frantz and decorated by I. Graff.

The first defensive castle in Rydzyna was built in the 15th c. In time it was replaced by a Baroque palace, known as the "castle", which was erected in 1685-95 for Palatine Rafał Leszczyński to a design by J.S. Bellotti. Together with the surrounding park and the neighbouring area it was the largest aristocratic residence in the region of Wielkopolska. In its quadrangular ground plan with projecting corner towers and the central courtyard, the architect incorporated the foundations of an earlier edifice from the first quarter of the 15th c. In the early 18th c. the palace was restored after the raid by the followers of Elector of Saxony August II, who without scruples set on fire the fine residence of his rival to the Polish throne, Stanisław Leszczyński. The works were supervised by P. Ferrari, who lived in Rydzyna. The interiors were richly decorated with murals by M. Palloni and sculptures by A. Schlütter. The election winner, King August II, liked to spend time in the renovated castle. Here he had all he wanted: lovers, wine barrels, and hunting grounds. And not only that: he also summoned his Council of State here, received messengers of Tsar Peter the Great, the Khan of the Tartars and the Sultan of Turkey.

In 1738, Rydzyna was sold by the former king Stanisław Leszczyński to A.J. Sułkowski. The work of Ferrari was continued in 1742-45 (under the guidance of K.M. Frantz) and in 1766-96 (I. Graff). The castle then received the new roof, the rococo decoration of the façade, and the impressive main entrance structure. The son of Sułkowski continued the work on the decoration of the palace and its surroundings. The annexes received neo-classical façades, the ballroom was decorated, the orangery buildings and stylish pavilions in the formal gardens were erected. In 1775, Rydzyna became the centre of the Sułkowski estate, a cultural and educational centre with the court theatre and a Piarist secondary school. The construction work ceased after the Second Partition of Poland. The courageous J. Sułkowski, the adjutant of Napoleon, brought war splendour to the Rydzyna branch of the family as he died a heroic death in Cairo. The last of the Sułkowskis from Rydzyna died heirless in 1909. The estate with the castle was taken over by the Prussian authorities. On the basis of the former Sułkowski entail, a foundation was established in 1924, which had educational purposes. In 1927-28, part of the building was adapted for a school. Unfortunately, the residence burnt down during the Second World War. The conservation work was completed only in 1989. Today the palace houses a luxury hotel.

Rzeszów

Rzeszów, once a private town founded in the 13th c., was owned by the Rzeszowski family (until 1583), and then successively by the Ligęzas (17th c.) and the Lubomirskis (mid-17th-18th c.). A number of interesting buildings have been preserved from their time, one of which is the Rzeszów castle from the late 17th c. The initially simple residence was remodelled by the castellan of Sandomierz, probably after 1620, using the existing curtain walls in the process; what resulted was the quadrangular castle with the arcaded courtyard inside.

After 1637, a further enlargement was supervised by the new owner of the castle and the town, Jerzy Sebastian Lubomirski. He was the magnate who embodied all the vices and virtues of the nobility. He fought with the Cossacks, but he soon fell out with King Jan Kazi-

Rydzyna Palace: Ballroom

mierz. This was of great significance during the Swedish "Deluge" of Poland; he refused to surrender to the Swedes, and, after many hesitations, he supported the Polish king and distinguished himself in the fighting of 1656. In 1660 he defeated the Russians in the battle of Cudnowo. His later conflict with the royal couple resulted in his mutiny. He was a prominent military leader and politician, but he used his talents to harm the interests of the state. His excessive ambition and low esteem at the royal court led him to plot with foreign powers against Poland. He died soon after the mutiny, deprived of the offices he had held.

The castle of Rzeszów along with its fortifications was remodelled again after 1667 by order of Hieronim August Lubomirski. The Baroque design with neo-classical touch was authored by Tylman van Gameren with the quadrangular plan of 65 m x 71 m. In the 18th c., a six-storey helm-topped tower was erected over the gate located on the axis of the western wing. The domed chapel was built in the south-east corner of the building. The castle has two courtyards: the external courtyard, which was situated between the perimeter wall and the castle walls, and the internal one. The exterior defensive walls contain four corner bastions and moats which spread over the area of 2.5 hectares. The castle has retained the defensive character (according to the Italian *palazzo in fortezza* tradition), which was highly suitable in the turmoil of the Carpathian border area. In 1820 it was purchased by the Austrian government and turned into a court building and a prison. The latter moved out only in 1981. The castle has recently been thoroughly renovated. It is now the seat of the Regional Court and the Justice Museum. Another Rzeszów residence of the Lubomirskis, the Summer House, is worth mentioning as well. It was raised prior to 1744 to the design of K.H. Wiedemann. It is a typical residence *entre cour et jardin* in French late Baroque style.

Castle in Rzeszów

SANDOMIERZ

The 14th-c. castle built by King Kazimierz the Great replaced the earlier 11th-c. settlement. The castle is separated from the town by a deep gorge. The town was first mentioned in the Chronicle by Gallus Anonymous from the early 12th c. as one of the main ducal residences (*sedes regni principales*). From the 12th c. it served as the seat of the castellany, in the 12th-13th c. a principality capital during the Fragmentation, while from the 14th c. it was the seat of the Palatine. The rich town attracted looters, e.g. Tartars raided it twice, in 1241 and 1259.

Castle in Sandomierz

Not much has remained from the early Gothic building, and a few relics were uncovered only as a result of the archaeological excavations. The effective Renaissance remodelling was carried out by the architects Benedict from Sandomierz and Santi Gucci. The works were started under the reign of King Zygmunt I and carried on for almost a century. The quadrangular castle began to take shape in 1564-65, while the residential wings were still under construction in the late 16th c. and early 17th c. The final effect must have been magnificent, but it was totally ruined by the Swedes, who blew up the castle in 1656 – one of them took the decision when the Poles storming the town seemed to be getting the upper hand in the battle. The western wing suffered the least damage and that is why King Jan III Sobieski ordered its reconstruction in 1680-88. The free-standing palace which resulted has been preserved with little modifications until today despite the war damage inflicted in the late 18th c. at the time of the Confederation of Bar. It contained the rooms of the regional administrator, court rooms, chancellery, archives and treasury, as well as other essential services. After the Third Partition of Poland, the Austrians turned the castle into a criminal court building and a prison, which lasted there until 1959, when the building became a museum with an interesting collection of 17th-19th-c. silver and European tin exhibits.

SIDZINA

The neo-classical manor house became part of Greater Cracow already some years ago, but the place still has no trace of urban atmosphere. It has a long and inspiring history. The date 1803 on the beam by no means refers to its beginning. The first building in the village was noted as early as 1198. Among the owners were Benedictines from nearby Tyniec Abbey, Piotr Szafraniec, the owner of the castle at Pieskowa Skała, and the Cracow Academy. The present building was raised by the Benedictines and confiscated by the Austrians in 1816. It was then auctioned off to reinforce the so called "religious fund." The original wooden manor house was repeatedly remodelled but it never lost its characteristic shape, with the four-columned Doric style portico and the stone veranda.

Manor house in Sidzina

SIENIAWA

Sieniawa is situated in the lower San valley. In the 17th c. it was an important river port and acquired its municipal rights in 1676. Among many historical monuments, the town boasts the Baroque palace of the Sieniawski and then Czartoryski family from the 18th c. with 18th-19th-c. formal gardens. Another highlight is the ruins of the defensive castle with powerful bastions, which was erected in the 17th c. by Marshal Mikołaj Hieronim Sieniawski. The palace replaced the orangery with rare tropical trees, which was built in 1718-26. The Baroque palace was erected in 1720 to the design of J. Spazzio, the court architect of the Sieniawskis, and then extended in 1743-45 by the Czartoryskis: the former main building, which roughly equalled the size of the present ballroom, received side pavilions. In 1760, the residence had 13 rooms: the spacious hall, the hallway and 11 rooms: 6 in the Duchess's suite and 5 in the Duke's suite. In the early 19th c., the Czartoryskis took nearly permanent residence in Sieniawa. In 1818 they hosted Tsar Alexander I, who was on his way back from the meeting of monarchs in Aachen.

The palace was thoroughly remodelled in 1881-83 to the design of B. Podczaszyński. It largely affected the side wings: new storeys, staircases and bathrooms were built and new rooms were added in the northern wing. The roof was reshaped and covered with sheet metal. In the 19th c., the family turned the palace into one of the centres of political, cultural and intellectual life of the province of Galicia. There were plans to transform the building into a resplendent Versailles-type of residence, the evidence of which are designs of A. Bitner from 1901 which have never been carried out. The First World War brought large-scale destruction to Sieniawa, including the palace. Duke Adam Ludwik Czartoryski transformed part of the palace into an Austrian field hospital for soldiers afflicted with infectious diseases.

In the 1920s and 30s, the damaged building was not used for residential purposes. The last owner of Sieniawa lived in the nearby wooden manor house, called the Summer House. In the 1930s, restoration works began in the interiors, but they were interrupted by the outbreak of the Second World War. Demolished by the Nazis and vandalised in the post-war period, the palace quickly fell into ruins and was restored only in 1984-86. The exposition in one of the rooms features extraordinary funeral wreaths made of thousands of little beads and small ceramic plates imitating flowers. The most elaborate composition consists of 1.5 million elements (!).

Palace in Sieniawa

SIEWIERZ

Situated on the right bank of the Czarna Przemsza, Siewierz, the former capital of the Siewierz Duchy, probably dates back to the 11th c. It was ruled by Silesian Dukes until 1443 when the Duke of Cieszyn, Wenceslas I, sold the Duchy of Siewierz to the Bishop of Cracow, Zbigniew Oleśnicki. In 1443-1790 it was ruled by bishops of Cracow. All the towns and over a dozen villages in the Siewierz and Koziegłowy areas were private property of the bishops. The rest was held by the landed gentry of Siewierz, which became proverbial in the old Polish Republic for their poverty and me-

Siewierz: Ruins of Bishops' Castle

diocrity. The bishops castle of Siewierz housed the town and country courts. What has remained until today are ruins of the 14th-c. Gothic residence of the bishops (remodelled ca 1530-74), huge walls and the barbican (late 16th c.). In the 17th c. the edifice gradually fell into disrepair which is documented by the inventory from 1645. The Swedish invasion only contributed to the devastation. After the 1655 war damage, the last attempt was made to rebuild and extend the castle; from then on, the subsequent inventories register only its decline. The last owner to reside here was Bishop Feliks Paweł Turski, who abandoned the totally ruined castle in 1800.

SORKWITY

The palace and park is situated on a small strip of land between two lakes. An old Prussian watchtower reputedly had been in existence here before. The defensive location enticed the Teutonic Knights to put their castle here as well in the 14th c. In 1451, the estate was taken over by J. Przebędowski, who in turn sold it over in 1469 to J. von Schleiben. In 1788 the Major of the hussars, J.Z. Bronikowski von Oppeln built a manor house in Sork wity. In 1850-56, the Mirbach family (the owners of the estate after 1804) raised a neo-Gothic palace here, falling to a fashion for historicist architecture which had come from England and swept through Germany. Built on a horseshoe plan, the palace consisted of a number of buildings of different height and size which were integrated and overshadowed by an octagonal corner tower. The façades were topped with sentimental pseudo-crenellation and decorated with turrets. The surrounding landscape park was laid out at approximately the same time. There was a coach-house here as well shaped so as to resemble the castle tower. In 1914 the Russian troops set fire to the palace, which destroyed all furnishings and the collections. The palace was reconstructed in 1922-23 under the supervision of the Berlin architect O. Rüger. The last heir to the Sorkwity estate was Baron B. von Paleske, adjutant to Emperor William II, related to the Mirbach family. The war saved the exterior of the palace, only the furnishings of the interior were looted. After the war, the palace housed a state farm, which "inherited" the former huge farm of 5770 hectares (in 1904), and in 1957 it was taken over by the tractor factory "Ursus."

Palace in Sorkwity

Stryszawa: Drawing room in the manor house

Stryszów

The village of Stryszów is situated at the foot of Mount Chełm in the range of Beskid Makowski. Its manor house is one of the most interesting examples of old residential buildings in the region. It was erected in the late 16th c. or early 17th c. The founder was a member of Suski, Jagniątkowski or Pisarzewski family, who were successive owners of Stryszów. The northern part of the manor house dates back to that time. In 1739, the building was partly destroyed. The new owner, Kazimierz Wilkoński, soon began restoring it. The former Renaissance defensive manor was turned into a nobleman's country house, Baroque in style. The rooms and the chapel were decorated with Baroque polychrome. In the mid-19th c., Julian Gorczyński carried out another modernisation and enlargement of the house. To the north of the building, a spacious landscape park was laid out. In 1969, the manor house was turned into a branch of Wawel Castle collections. Thanks to the furniture and other exhibits brought from Wawel, the visitors can admire typical 19th-c. residence interiors: drawing room, dining room, study and bedroom, which were the rooms considered most elegant in old Polish residences.

Studzieniec

Studzieniec lies at the edge of Gniezno Lake District. It was the estate of the Studzieński family already in the Middle Ages (first mentioned in 1365). The Baroque manor house is the most valuable historical building, an interesting example of the combination of the architecture native to Wielkopolska region and the Pomeranian tradition. It was probably erected in the third quarter of the 18th c., when it was owned by Count K. Raczyński. It was built on a rectangular plan with projecting annexes. The external and internal walls are timber-framed, filled in with brick and plastered. The house is covered with the two-layer shingled roof and surrounded with a rather neglected landscape park.

Studzieniec: Timber-framed manor house

Manor house in Sucha

Sucha koło Siedlec

Sub veteri tectu, sed parentali (Under an old, but familial roof), says the inscription over the portico of this delightful Mazovian larch manor house. It was built in 1743 and for two hundred years remained the property of the Cieszkowski family. The corner annexes and the columned portico, added in early 19th c., have been preserved from the original building. The rest has been reconstructed. Inside, the original beamed roofs and the Dutch-tile stove have remained. The current owner, Prof. M. Kwiatkowski, has restored the building, furnished it with period furniture and founded the Museum of the Polish Manor House. In the vicinity, he gathered many historical country buildings, such as wooden huts, a bell tower, an inn and a Dutch-style windmill. On the other side of the yard there is an octagonal manege, sheds and another inn, while beyond the gate there is another manor house and an 18th-c. presbytery.

Szamotuły

Only a brick tower from 1518, which probably used to adjoin the castle gate, remains from the medieval Szamotuły stronghold. It is linked with a romantic legend of the unfortunate Black Princess, that is Halszka of Ostróg, born in 1539 as the daughter of Duchess B. Ostrogska nee Kościelecka and King Zygmunt the Old. The unhappy fruit of the mother's egoism and the dowry-related intrigues of Lithuanian, Polish and Ruthenian nobles was kept in this tower by her husband in 1559-73. In 1549, the tower was remodelled by J. Czeterwan, the bricklayer from Poznań, and in 1869 it was partly reconstructed. Today the castle of the Górkas has two perpendicular wings and houses a museum, established in 1958, where you can admire reconstructed interiors of this aristocratic residence. The rooms of the lord and the lady of the castle have been furnished with high-quality furniture.

Szamotuły: Halszka Tower

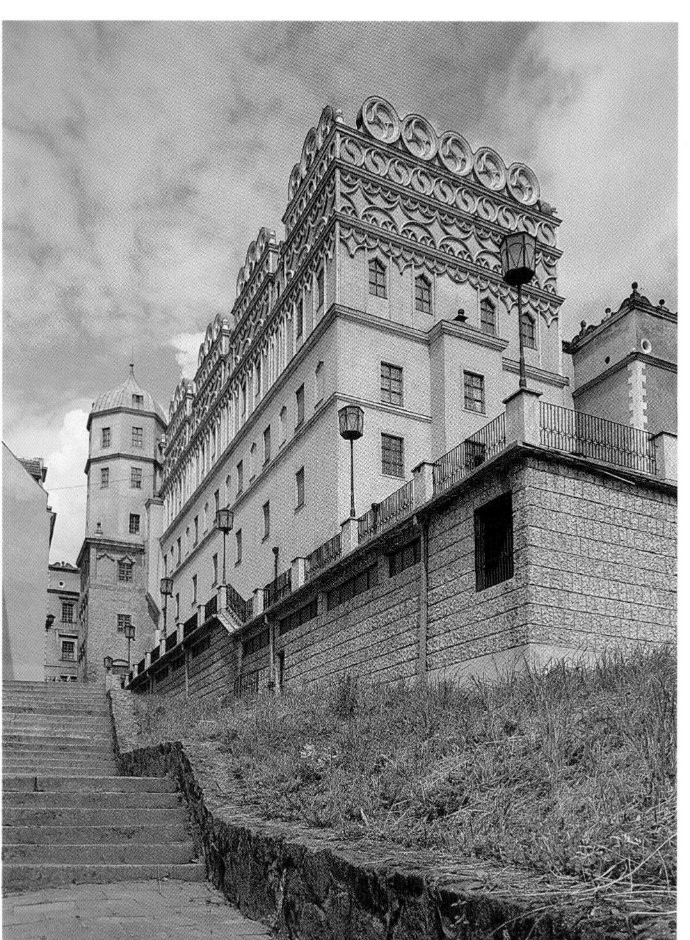

Szczecin: Castle of Pomeranian Dukes

Szczecin

The castle of the Pomeranian Dukes from the Piast dynasty, raised on the high left bank of the Odra, towers over the Old Town. Initially, the seat of the Dukes could have been situated elsewhere, in the area of Mariacki Square or at the Trzygław Hill. Duke Barnim III started erecting the brick castle in the first half of the 14th c. Only parts of its cellars and the foundations of St Otto's Chapel have lasted until today. After 1365 an angle tower was raised and the southern wing, called the Big House, extended; the latter was then remodelled in 1428-34 and then around 1490 when it became a four-storey structure topped with tracery-decorated gables. Later it was remodelled a number of times, particularly in 1530-38, at the time of Duke Barnim IX, when it became late Gothic in style (design of F. Nussdörfer), and the Prison Tower and the Clock Tower (now with K. Nietard's chronometer from 1693) were topped with additional storeys. Motives from that building can still be observed in the bottom part of the Prison Tower. In 1551 the castle burnt down, and in 1575-81 it was enlarged into a Renaissance residence of Duke Johann Frederic (the works were supervised by A. Guglielmo). The western and northern wings together with the Chapel, the Bell Tower, and the arcades of the main courtyard date back to that time. The quadrangular plan was complemented in 1616-19 by Duke Philip II with the western wing designed as a museum (Armoury, Library, Curiosity Collection). Since 1637, when the last duke of the Gryfita family had died, the castle went into decline; after 1720, it lost most of the Renaissance decorative elements: the arcades and parapets were dismantled, the vaults were removed, staircases remodelled and the rooms divided up to suit the needs of the offices which the castle housed at the time. The southern wing was totally pulled down and raised from scratch. The whole building was thoroughly modernised again in the late 19th c. and early 20th c. In August 1944, the castle was destroyed during the bombing raid of the Allies. The reconstruction works started in 1958.

Castle in Szydłowiec

SZYDŁOWIEC

Szydłowiec, situated in the Iłża Foothills, was the centre of the estate owned by the Odrowąż family, who took the surname of Szydłowiecki. It received the municipal rights probably in the 14th c. In 1427 the sources mention the manor house of Jakub and Sławek, the presumed ancestors of the Szydłowiecki family. The Szydłowiecki castle is one of the most magnificent aristocratic residences in Poland. In 1515-26, M. Szydłowiecki, who was the royal treasurer at the time (1515-32), turned the former defensive castle into a Renaissance residence: the three-wing palace was created, closed from the south with the curtain wall. The eastern wing, designed for official purposes, consisted of a three-storey house, while the northern one was residential, and adjoined the western wing with another suite of rooms. The older tower was combined with the western wing into one structure. The castle, situated on the artificial island, surrounded with the moat and waters of the Korzeniówka, could equal any contemporary residence with its splendour. The interiors were furnished with rich stone portals, polychromed coffer ceilings, painted friezes, multicoloured tile stoves and decorative mosaic floors. In 1548, the castle was inherited by the Radziwiłł family, thanks to the marriage of the daughter of K. Szydłowiecki and M. Radziwiłł Czarny, and remained with the family until 1802 when it was bought by A. Sapieżyna, who then sold it to the government of the Kingdom of Poland. Both at the time of the Radziwiłł family and that of the last owner the residence was enlarged and decorated further. The remodelling carried out in 1619-29 by the Radziwiłłs consisted in adding a staircase with the loggia to the eastern wing. Two multi-sided terrace-topped annexes were adjoined to the outer corners of the same wing probably at the same time. In the 20th c. the palace was partly reconstructed, and today it houses the Museum of Folk Musical Instruments and the Szydłowiec Cultural Centre with a good library. The large permanent exposition focuses on the present state of the Polish holdings of folk musical instruments.

SZYDŁÓW

Szydłów boasts the 14th-16th-c. stone perimeter walls best preserved in Małopolska, together with two castle entrance gates. The town received its municipal rights probably in the early 14th c. The earliest elements of the castle most likely date back to that time. The town walls were raised by King Kazimierz the Great. The local church is of his foundation as well – it was part of the penance imposed on him for ordering to drown the curate from Cracow Cathedral, M. Baryczka, who had vocally condemned his immoral demeanour.

On top of the hill, sloping towards the river, there are ruins of the repeatedly remodelled, irregularly shaped castle, surrounded with town walls (from the west) and castle walls (from the east and south), with the gatehouse on the eastern side erected by King Zygmunt III. Consecutives fires dealt considerable blows to its splendour. In 1565, King Zygmunt August ordered the town income from wine and alcohol production to be assigned to the repair of the castle and the walls (this money must have been considerable, as the walls have stood ever since). In 1630, the town and the castle was set on fire by a group of marauding soldiers. The damage was so extensive that the necessary reconstruction funds had to be allocated by the Sejm. The castle suffered damage at the hands of the Swedes too and fell into disrepair in the 18th c. The remains of the walls were to be dismantled and in 1822 the materials were put up for auction. Later however, the castle and the remaining walls were secured and maintained. In 1945-47, in the act of romantic imagination the walls were topped with crenellated parapet, which had never existed before.

Szydłów: Knights Hall

Castle in Szymbark

SZYMBARK

At the time of the Golden Age of Poland, contemporary with the reign of the Jagiellonian dynasty, new architectural trends and new construction technologies were advanced. In the residences of landed gentry, the medieval idea of the donjon coexisted with Renaissance decorative trends. In the region of Małopolska, the castle keep was frequently surrounded with angle towers. Such a castle was able to fight back the attacks of both a band of robbers and a hostile neighbour. This is what the masoned residence of the Gładysz family was like in Szymbark. From the 14th-17th c., the village was the property of the Gryf family, who gradually and courageously colonised the hilly area. The Renaissance manor house with the overhanging towers in the corners was raised in the mid-16th c. In 1589-90, it was remodelled and decorated. The purity of style was disturbed by 19th-c. modifications and was restored only in the 1980s when e.g. the Renaissance parapet was reconstructed.

ŚMIEŁÓW

One of the most effective neo-classical palaces of the Wielkopolska region was built in 1797 by S. Zawadzki by order of the Gorzeński family. The building with the columned portico and drawing room on the central axis was flanked by slightly rounded wings with rectangular annexes. The interiors have retained their original appearance, including the murals from 1800, probably the work of A. and F. Smuglewicz. In 1886, the residence was purchased by F. Chełkowski. Today the building houses a branch of the National Museum, featuring manuscripts of the Romantic poet A. Mickiewicz and his portraits. The interiors are furnished in Biedermaier style and decorated with paintings and 19th-c. crafts. The collection was founded by J. Chełkowski, who gathered all the memorabilia related to the stay of the poet in Śmiełów in 1831. He had intended to cross the Partition frontier and take part in the Polish November Insurrection. Ultimately, however, he limited himself to flirting and hunting. Searching for the traces of Śmiełów in Mickiewicz's poems, particularly in the epic poem *Pan Tadeusz*, Chełkowski did not refrain from blending fiction and reality: the manor garden, the local inn, and the palace in Żerków were supposed to be models for the places significant in the poem. The most convincing of the comparisons is said to be the coffee-making ritual in Śmiełów which closely resembled that described by the poet.

Palace in Śmiełów

Manor house in Świdnik

Świdwin

The Gothic castle stands on the sandy patch, on the right bank of the Rega. In the 13th c., the Brandenburg Margraves gave the settlement the municipal rights, and by the end of the century they founded their easternmost stronghold there which was to keep the Pomeranians in check. In 1319, the knights N. Olafson and W. von Wedel received the estate. In 1384, the area of Świdwin was purchased by the Teutonic Knights, who installed head of the local administration in the castle. The transaction was highly beneficial for the Order: they thus received an ex-territorial enclave situated by the route to Brandenburg. The new owners remodelled the castle beginning from the late 14th c.. The new seat of the administration was now three-storey high, and the official rooms were accessed from the staircase from inside of the wooden arcades adjoining the façade. The chapel was built on the eastern side of the same storey. The gate tower was raised and remodelled. Following 1445, the region of New March, with Świdwin, passed into the hands of Elector Frederic II. About 1520 the gate was remodelled again and the foreyard was added. In 1540--1808, the building was owned by Knights Hospitallers, who refashioned the Gothic wing (1704-58) and erected other buildings with the façades in Baroque style with the neo-classical touch. After the order was secularised, the castle housed public offices. It burnt down in 1945 and was reconstructed in 1962-68.

Świdnik

The manor house in Świdnik was raised in 1752 by the Sędzimir family, who then owned the village. It is a timber construction with some stone and brick parts, plastered and shingled. It consist of the rectangular main section with the hipped roof with an attic and corner square annexes. The two-storey fireplaces are an interesting feature: one with an ornamental frame and a sculpted mask, and the other more plain, built into the overall design. There is a small masoned chapel nearby, dating back most likely to the mid-18th c. The manor house is surrounded by an old park with an old cellar, which seems to have been part of the church of Polish Antitrinitarians (also called Arians) from 1560-80. The Świdnik manor has its equivalents in Slovakia: the manors in Kromolov and Vyzni Kubin.

Castle in Świdwin

Świny

The castle in Świny is one of the few in Silesia which has been conquered neither by the Hussites nor by the Swedes. The defensive town was erected in the mid-13th c. on a rocky, wooded peninsula. In 1245-72, the noble family of the Świnkas, from which the influential Archbishop of Gniezno J. Świnka originated, settled in the former castellany. The preserved 13th-14th-c. tower was doubtless their oldest residence. The entrance was through the Gothic portal, the knights hall was on the ground floor, while wooden steps led to higher storeys. Subsequent owners enlarged the castle and the most significant remodelling was carried out in 1720s. As a result, the castle was turned into a late Renaissance fortified residence. A new palace was erected, defended with semicircular outworks, as well as two flanking towers on the fortified walls of the lower castle, a bastion and the new forecastle buildings. The entrance consisted of a drawbridge, while the castle gate was crowned with a portal with the Świnka coat of arms on top. After the death of J.Z. Świnka in 1664, the building was inherited by the lateral line of descent, whose last representative was Count G. E. von Schweinichen (he died in 1702). In 1713, the estate passed into the hands of his son-in-law, S.H. von Schweinitz. In 1769 the castle was abandoned, and the storm of 1868 and the fire of 1876 contributed to its final demise. The last pre-Second World War owners of the place were the von Hoyos-Sprinzensteins. Since 1991, it has been private property.

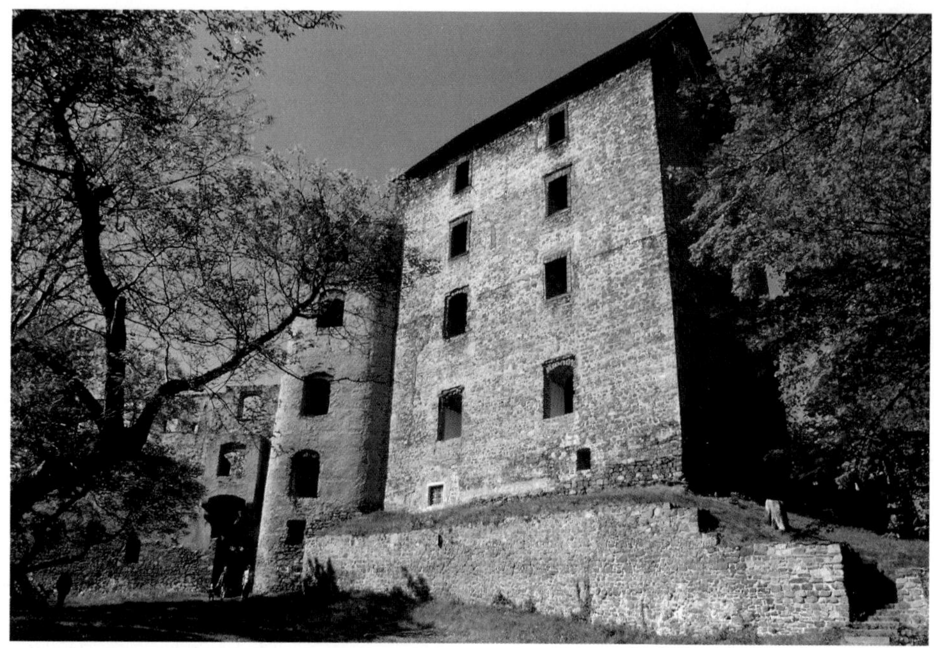

Castle in Świny

Tarnawa

The partly larch timber, partly stone manor house in Tarnawa, nearly completely hidden in the lavish greenery, dates back to 1784. It was built for the administrator of the Mieroszewski family estate. After the insurrection of 1831, the Russian government turned the estate into the property entailed on the officials of special merit. They in turn leased it to the Poles, one of whom was M. Novák (after 1888). In 1897, Z. Novák, the future initiator of the Jurassic Landscape Park on Małopolska Uplands (established in 1947), was born here. He bought the manor house in 1925 along with the small estate which had been left after the land reform. The house was remodelled, nearly without interfering with the original appearance. Restored in 1982-83, it is now family property. The park was laid out as landscape park in the 19th c. and then, around 1930, turned into a mixed layout with alleys and clearings. The lime-lined driveway is an additional picturesque asset of the place.

Manor house in Tarnawa

Rudna: Ruins of Tenczyn Castle

Tenczyn

The scenic Rudno village is famous for the ruins of Tenczyn Castle which dominate over the area from a high hill. The defensive residence was erected by the Toporczyk noble family from Morawica in the early 14th c. The heart of the Gothic castle was probably the sturdy keep and the residential buildings together with the chapel. The owners must have been quite proud of it as in the course of time they changed their name to Tęczyński (after the castle). Around 1570 the austere castle was turned into a Renaissance residence, which consisted of residential wings surrounding the arcaded courtyard and of fortifications with round flanking towers and bastions. Gradually enlarged and decorated, it passed into the hands of the Opaliński family in 1639. In 1655 it was occupied by the Swedes, who on their way out in 1656 looted the castle and set fire to it, as was their custom then. The reconstruction carried on by subsequent owners never brought back its former splendour. It was considered fit for residential purposes only until the mid-18th c.; in 1768 it was already referred to as the ruins. In 1784, King Stanisław August visited and admired the castle, and the poet A. Naruszewicz wrote about it as "testimony to the passing of things human." The Gothic gate tower, the chapel and the walls with three flanking towers have been preserved. The outlying defensive gate tower and the shooting gallery date back to the 16th c., while the pentagonal casemate bastions were erected in the early 17th c.

Toszek

The 15th-c. castle of Racibórz and Opole Dukes is situated at the edge of Racibórz Basin. The place is sometimes linked to the ancient town of the Opolanie tribe, although no remains of early medieval fortifications were found during excavations on the castle hill. In the 12th c. the town of Toszek obtained the status of separate castellany within the Opole province.

The stone and brick castle was erected probably at the turn of the 15th c. The damage caused by the Hussite raid in 1429 was repaired by the Oświęcim Duke Przemysław in the second half of the 15th c. The medieval castle stood on top of the hill surrounded by a moat. The only entrance was through a drawbridge. In 1532, the stronghold was the property of the Habsburgs, who sold it to the von Reder family for 36 thousand talers. After the fire of 1570 the Reders turned the castle into a Renaissance residence. A house with two angle towers was erected and the entrance was modernised with a new gatehouse. The later owners of Toszek, the Colonna family, carried out another thorough remodelling in 1650-66, with the help of an Italian architect, G. Seregno The castle stables he had designed serve as a cinema hall today.

Then Toszek had several other owners, including the Kotuliński and Posadowski families, who also changed and modernised it. The remodelling was an ongoing process, as the castle fell victim to frequent fires and looting raids. In 1677 there was a fire; that was followed by the Seven Years' War and then the 1807 campaign. The devastating fire of 1811 contributed to its final undoing, and the owners moved to the "lower manor house." The preserved parts were reconstructed in the 1920s and in 1956-63, and since then the castle has housed a local cultural centre.

Legend has it that the vitality of the castle, which was reconstructed so many times, is due to the presence of the Golden Duck in deep dungeons, who lays her eggs there and takes care of the castle. The legend was taken seriously as late as in 1841, when in the castle sale contract it was stipulated that in the case the Duck was found, it would become the property of the former owner.

Castle in Toszek

Trzebinia

The town of Trzebinia gives you the foretaste of industrial and mining areas of Upper Silesia. It grew as a mining settlement and was linked to exploitation of lead ores containing silver in the 15th-18th c. The Zieleniewski family manor house dates back to the 15th c. when it was the property of K. Kesinger. The defensive structure presumably existed even earlier and was home to Karwacjan family. In 1415, M. Kesinger obtained a privilege for mining metal ores from King Władysław Jagiełło and founded a mining settlement which was then leased by various other noble families. Today the manor house is neo-classical in style after the late 18th-c. remodelling. As a result of repeated modernising works (the last of which was carried out in 1925), the two-storey building has the hallway axis moved slightly to the left. Most of the ground floor rooms have rounded-off ceilings, while the upper-level rooms were topped with beamed ceilings. After the Second World War, the building was nationalised; never maintained for decades, it fell into such a dreadful state that it was only fit for dismantling. The beautiful park was vandalised too, with only some ancient trees having been preserved. The reconstruction work started in 1990. The edifice is not a typical Polish manor house, in spite of the presence of such characteristic features as the two-layer roof and four-columned portico facing the driveway (reconstruction), as it unusually has the upper floor. Another unique feature of Trzebinia manor is surprisingly spacious cellars.

Manor house in Trzebinia

Tubądzin

The 18th-c. neo-classical manor house of the Walewski family in Tubądzin houses an interesting and well-arranged Museum of Manorial Interiors. The manor house – once the abode of landed gentry – is perhaps the most characteristically Polish type of residence, noted for its specific structural features and unpretentious appearance. An early manor house was typically a one-storey timber building with a shingled roof. Its interior would be divided into a kitchen, bedrooms and a common room (knights hall). The size, layout, decoration and furnishings depended on the wealth of the owner. In the 16th c., some manor houses were already built of stone and brick. At the same time, annexes began to appear at the corners and the roof assumed the characteristic "Polish mansard" form. Many old manors, thanks to their suitable location and surrounding ramparts or solid fences with gates, served a defensive function.
The Tubądzin Museum presents the manorial interiors of the turn of the 20th c. with the living room, the drawing room-parlour, the library and the study-bedroom, furnished in the 18th-19th-c. style and adorned with 17th-20th-c. portraits of the Walewskis, and arts and crafts collection including artefacts from glass, china, and precious metals as well as old prints. The last owner and founder of the museum was K.S. Walewski. The Nobel Prize winner, writer W.S. Reymont, was a frequent visitor in Tubądzin.

Manor house in Tubądzin: Interior

Tuczno

A fishermen village existed here already in the 10th c., while in the 13th c. it was a border town of the Duchy of Wielkopolska. The beginnings of the stone and brick castle date back to the first half of the 14th c. It was erected by the influential Pomeranian family of von Wedels (or Wedel-Tuczyńskis, after the castle), who owned the estate until 1739. The stronghold was situated on a hill between two lakes. The original plan was a trapezium which consisted of the perimeter wall with

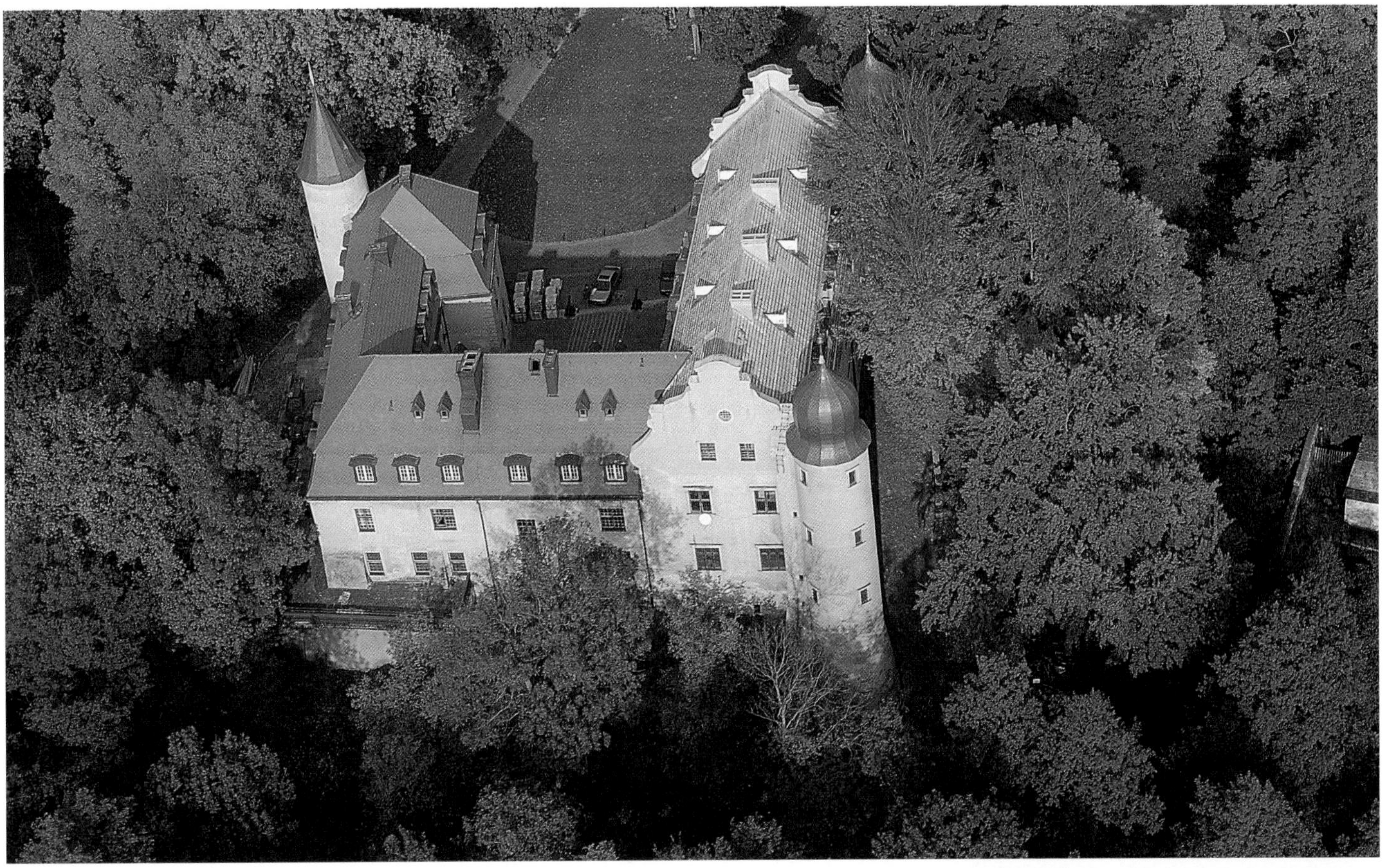

Castle in Tuczno

the gate from the north and the residence inside. Buttressed on the corners, the building was finally pulled down in 1581 and replaced by a residential edifice with two round flanking towers and the parapet. The remodelling undertaken in 1680s by S. Wedel resulted in the retaining of the defensive character of the building, which was encircled with 7-metre-high walls. But still, this was now more of a residence than a castle. The Baroque wings added in 1608-31 formed a horseshoe shape around the courtyard which opened up to the north when the northern wall had been demolished. After the death of the last heir, the castle passed from hand to hand and became more and more neglected. The buildings were partly destroyed in 1945 and then burnt in 1947. Reconstruction works were carried out in 1966-76 when the Renaissance form of the eastern wing and part of the interior was restored and the Gothic-and-Renaissance cellars were opened to visitors.

Manor house in Tułowice: Garden façade

TUŁOWICE

The large neo-classical manor house in Tułowice, on the edge of Kampinoski National Park, is visible from a large distance. A chestnut and maple-lined alley leads from the main entrance gate to the driveway in front of the house. The estate was formed when part of the landed property belonging to A. Lasocki, the castellan of Sochaczew, was carved out for his daughter. The manor house was erected at the turn of the 19th c., probably to the design of H. Szpilowski. Although there is no direct evidence to support this hypothesis, the stylistic similarity with other works by the same architect is undisputed. The one-storey house with the second storey in the middle section only is made from brick and plastered. A characteristic feature is the placement of a row of high columns at the back entrance, not at the front, where an unpretentious projection façade was built with two pairs of Tuscan-style pilasters topped with a triangular pediment. F. Lasocka lived in the manor until 1822 when the estate was sold off to K. Linowski, son of a Polish senator. After his death, Tułowice passed into the hands of the Orsetti family and in 1857 it was bought at the auction by the Górskis. Later the owners changed very frequently, but the manor and the surrounding park stayed intact until the post-Second-World War land reform. The current owner has restored the building in its original, historical shape.

Turew: Palace façade

Turowa Wola

A manor house built in the early 20th c. by order of the Ostromęcki family dominates its flat surroundings from a small hill. It was an unpretentious but decent house for a landowning noble family, set in peaceful surroundings, with the columned portico as the only architectural decoration. The building, renovated in 1980s, is accompanied by farm buildings, such as a turn-of-the-20th-c. brick stable. The formal gardens laid out in the late 19th c. by S. Celichowski are a highly welcome touch.

Turew

Turew is known as the place where General Dezydery Chłapowski established a unique large landed estate in 1820-30. Back at home after the Napoleonic Wars, he began to introduce modern farming techniques: deep ploughing (he bribed and coerced his farm hands to use the ploughs he had imported from Scotland), cultivation of fodder crops, large-scale animal farming, lining the fields with wind-protecting trees and shrubs. Other landowners respected him, but when they saw him sow clover for the first time, they considered him a madman. But it was he who was right, and the young agriculturists he had taught went across the country with their progressive ideas, reaching its even most remote corners, where the "elites" still believed in throwing spells, not in crop rotation.

Turew, with its neo-Gothic palace, provides a model of landscaping based solely on natural elements. Chłapowski wrote: "A loving owner does not think so much about living off the land, as about its improvement, advancement and adornment." The two-storey mid-18th-c. Baroque palace was refashioned in 1820-30 and decorated with a neo-Gothic annexe in the form of a tower. The neighbours were astonished when Chłapowski removed the coat of arms and had it replaced with a clock. The interior design dates back to 1770-80 and is attributed to I. Graff. In 1846-47 the neo-Gothic chapel of Virgin Mary (with epitaphs of the Chłapowski family) was erected side by side with the residence.

Manor house in Turowa Wola

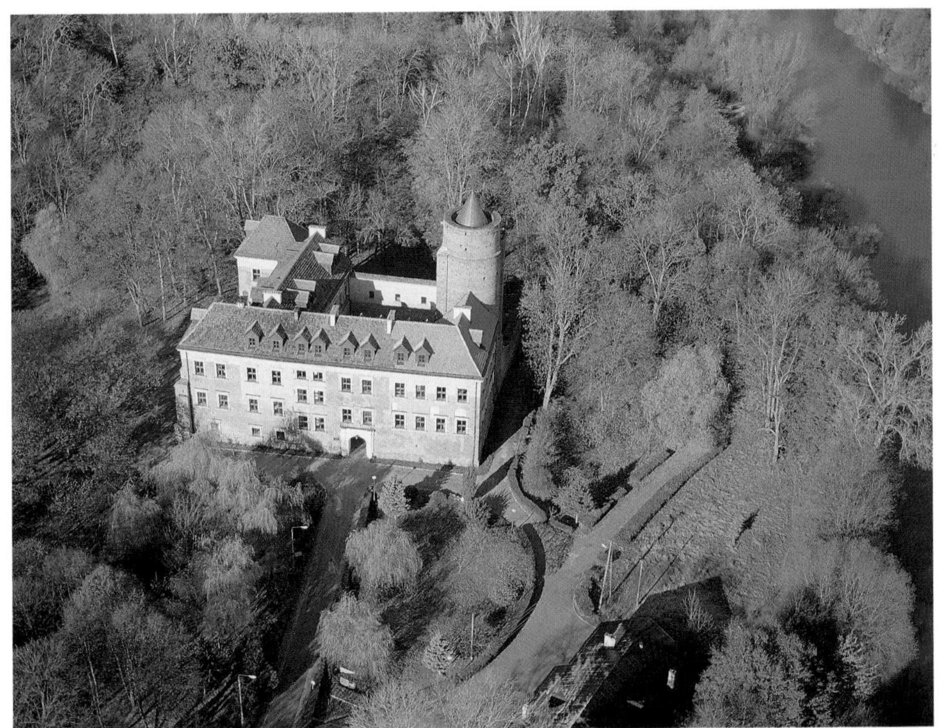

Uniejów: Bishops' Castle

Walewice

The place is known for the Baroque and neoclassical palace of the Walewski family raised in 1783 to the design of H. Szpilowski. He created a solution typical of the residences of landed gentry: a building on a rectangular plan with a columned portico and the elegant suite of rooms on the ground floor. One-storey galleries link the palace with side pavilions. Surrounding the palace, which was remodelled in the 19th and 20th c., is a landscape park laid out in 1886. One of the most famous Polish romance stories is linked with the palace; in their own interest, the entire Polish nation kept their fingers crossed. When Mrs Maria Walewska gave birth to Alexander, the natural son of Napoleon I, some people seemed to have taken it for granted that now Napoleon would consider the affairs of Poland to be of primary importance. The imperial chamberlain A. Walewski, the husband of the unfaithful Maria, was among those who believed otherwise. And no doubt he was to be proven right.

The last modernising works were carried out in 1900-09. The 18th-c. landscape park was rearranged in 1860-70 by A. Denizot: there you can admire an ancient oak, 7,8 metre in diameter, bearing the name of Dezydery. The palace is surrounded by 18th-c. farm buildings.

Uniejów

Uniejów turned into a private town of Gniezno archbishops in 1331 due to the decision taken by J.B. Skotnicki, and this legal situation remained in force until the late 18th c. A castle was erected on the left bank of the Warta, which until the 16th c. was one of the principal residences of the archbishops. Archbishop Skotnicki built it in the mid-14th c. as a Gothic-style stronghold. This son of the Palatine of Cracow was educated in Bologna and soon climbed higher and higher in Church hierarchy, enjoying the trust of the monarchs as well. In 1381, the castle was occupied by Bernard from Grabów and the archbishops' treasury looted. The robber was so impudent that he persisted until Archbishop J. Suchywilk granted him impunity and promised not to search for the stolen valuables. Around the middle of the 15th c. the castle was considerably enlarged, but it was captured again in 1492 by W. K. Gruszczyński during his feud with Bishop Z. Oleśnicki over the town of Koźmin. In 1638-45, Archbishops Wężyk and Łubieński finally transformed the castle into a Renaissance-Baroque residence, erasing traces of its defensive nature. After Church estates were secularised in the late 18th c., most of the buildings were abandoned; only in 1836 was the place donated by the Russian government to General A. Toll, who had distinguished himself in suppressing the Polish November Uprising. The Toll family effected another remodelling, laid out the park and remained in Uniejów until the First World War. The western perimeter wall, linking both the 15th-c. residential towers, was dismantled and replaced with a terrace which opened with a wide stairway towards the garden. In the 1920s and 30s there was a guest house in the castle, but the Second World War and the ensuing period caused considerable damage to the building. In 1956-67, it was reconstructed and adapted for archives and then a hotel and a restaurant. Today only a 25-meter-high tower and the northern part of the perimeter wall remain from the old Gothic castle of the archbishops. Nonetheless, the whole complex still looks impressive.

Palace in Walewice: Portico

Warszawa Zamek Królewski

Unlike Poznań, Gniezno or Cracow, Warsaw has no ancient roots. It was first mentioned in documents only in the early 14th c. However, its central location was an asset that Polish monarchs came to appreciate in time. Upon the incorporation of Mazovia into the Crown in 1526, the unpretentious residence of Dukes of Mazovia became a royal castle and in 1569 a venue for the meetings of the Sejm. This is why a thorough Renaissance remodelling of the castle was undertaken (supervised by G.B. Quadro, J. Parr and others), which led to the merging of former ducal courts into a regularly shaped building decorated with a tower on a circular plan (later called Władysław Tower) housing Deputies Room, Senators Room and other rooms.

The crucial turning point in its history was the 1609 final decision of King Zygmunt III to transfer the royal court from Wawel to Warsaw. Poland's rulers took great care in improving their new seat, and to this end they enlisted the services of the best architects, including G. Trevano, M. Castelli, C. Tencalla, A. V. Locci. Northern, southern and western wings were erected with the magnificent city tower, which turned the castle into a grand edifice centred on a large courtyard. The elegant interiors were decorated e.g. with T. Dolabella's historical paintings. The rooms were thoroughly remodelled under the reign of King Władysław IV (after 1637) to the design of G.B. Gisleni and C. Tencalla. The partly preserved interior of the Marble Room (1640-43), i.e. the waiting room located in front of the royal audience room, gives a good idea of early Baroque architecture. The castle was looted and vandalised in the times of the "Swedish Deluge" and restored during the reign of Jan III Sobieski. But not for long. In 1704, the Swedes stormed Warsaw again: this time the destroyed parts of the castle included the theatre hall and the chambers of the Sejm. Renovation and remodelling lasted throughout the 18th c. The building gained many splendid rooms: the Throne Room, the Ballroom, the Knights Hall (with A. Le Brun's sculpture *Chronos*), the Audience Room, and many studies.

The castle owed its new shape above all to King Stanisław August Poniatowski – a mediocre ruler, but a great connoisseur and patron of art. To be sure, critics blamed the King for extravagance, claiming

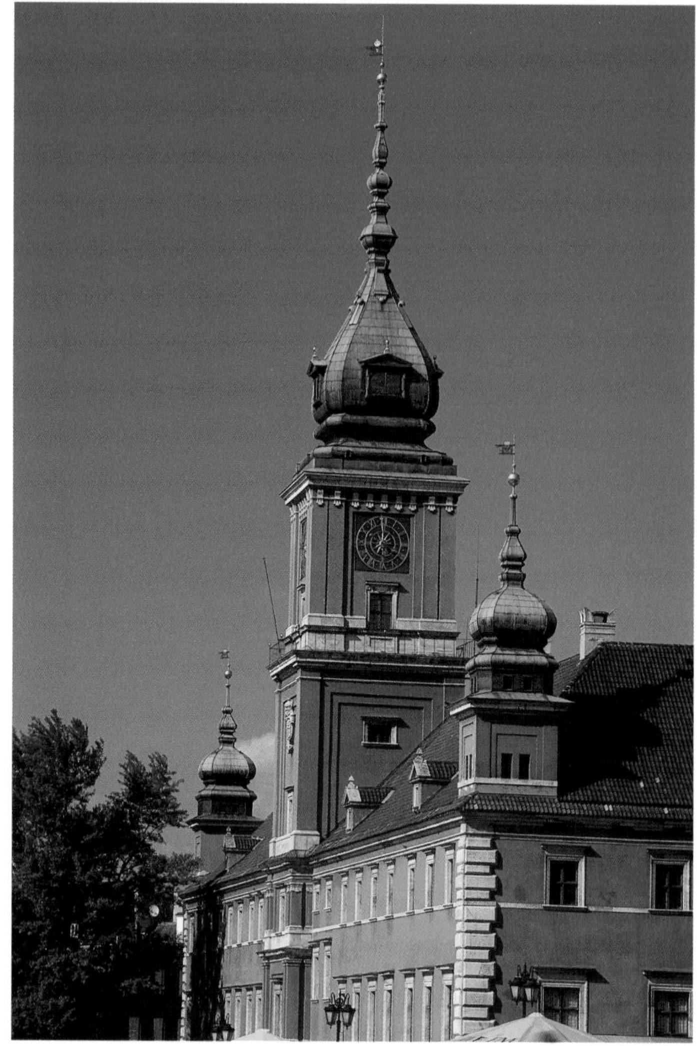

Warsaw Castle: Clock tower

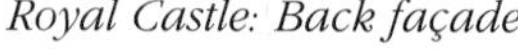

Royal Castle: Back façade

Ballroom

that the amounts spent without adequate planning of the reconstruction effort would have been sufficient to build four other castles from scratch, but the work of G. Fontana, D. Merlini and G. B. Kamsetzer was breathtaking in its effect. This was complemented by the exquisite art collection accumulated by the King, including gold artefacts, statues and paintings (among others, by M. Bacciarelli, Canaletto and J. B. Plersch). But first and foremost, in those years the castle was the arena of a battle for the future of Poland and the scene of a belated attempt to avert its impending fall – it was here that the Constitution of 3 May 1791 was adopted. The castle fell into disrepair during the period of Partitions (which supposedly had been foretold by a spectre haunting the Audience Room, where Hetman S. Żółkiewski once threw the captive Russian Tsar Vasili Shuysky at the feet of Zygmunt III). The art objects were dispersed among private collections and many were taken away to St Petersburg. During the November Uprising of 1830 Tsar Nicholas I was dethroned in the Senators Room and after the Uprising had been crushed, he had it demolished. The rooms in the "former royal castle," as the official name had it, were gradually converted into offices and military quarters. Only on 11 November 1918 was the white-and-red flag flown from the castle tower – a symbol of an independent Poland reclaiming the castle, the capital city and the state. After renovation, part of the building was used as apartments for luminaries of culture and science. In 1926, the castle became the official residence of the President of the Republic. When the restoration works were almost completed, the Second World War broke out. In December 1944, the German sappers wiped out the castle, already damaged in 1939, from the face of the earth. Some furnishings were rescued by employees of the National Museum. The decision to rebuild the castle was taken immediately after the war, but it was not put into practice until the early 1970s. Meticulously restored, the castle gradually builds up its Polish art collection. Today the Royal Castle is successful in reconciling its diverse functions and serves the Polish state, science and culture. The exhibited objects are furniture, coins and medals, sculptures, bronze- and silverware. Some of them were restored to the castle after many years. The most precious paintings, apart from those by J. Matejko and Canaletto, most cherished by Poles, are Rembrandt's *The Scholar at his Desk* and *The Girl in a Hat*. They come from the former collection of King Stanisław August and were graciously donated to the castle in 1998 by K. Lanckorońska.

Throne Room

Ujazdów Castle

WARSZAWA ZAMEK UJAZDOWSKI

The castle was once a summer palace which had been raised for King Zygmunt III Vasa on a steep river bank in suburban Ujazdów. Initially, there was a 16th-c. royal hunting castle here. The early Baroque royal palace was erected in 1624-32 most probably by M. Castelli. The two-storey building, built on a nearly square plan with hexagonal corner towers and a courtyard surrounded on two sides by cloisters, is an example of "Vasa style." In 1635-40, King Władysław IV ordered the remodelling of the garden wing. In 1683, the Sejm handed the palace over to Stanisław H. Lubomirski, who used the design of Tylman van Gameren to turn it into a magnificent residence. In the castle gardens he set up an Arcadia park, a zoological garden and a bathhouse.

During the reign of King Stanisław August, who purchased the palace, it was refashioned by D. Merlini and E. Schroeger. The interiors were remodelled e.g. by J.B. Plersch, who painted grotesque decorations (1768). Abandoned by the ruler for the sake of nearby Łazienki and donated to the city of Warsaw in 1784, it was turned by S. Zawadzki into the barracks of Lithuanian Infantry Guards (prior to 1789). Later it housed a hospital. During the Second World War it burnt down and was dismantled in 1954. Reconstructed after 1973, today it houses the Modern Art Centre.

WARSZAWA PAŁAC KRASIŃSKICH

Miodowa Street is an excellent proof of the old splendour of Warsaw. On the edge of the Krasiński Gardens stands a magnificent three-storey Baroque Palace of the Krasiński family (also known as the Palace of the Polish Republic). It was commissioned by J.D. Krasiński, Palatine of Płock and royal administrator of Warsaw, as his Warsaw residence. The magnate bought several adjoining plots of land, which allowed him to lay out a spacious courtyard and the formal gardens, which still carry the name of his family. The palace, which has never been completed because of the death of both the founder and the architect, was erected in 1677-93 to the design of van Gameren as a typical palace *entre cour et jardin*, with three projection façades; the central one was marked with a pediment and decorated with sculptures glorifying the Krasiński family (the work of the Gdańsk artist A.Schlüter). The façade is crowned with stone statues personifying the Roman public virtues. The same themes dominated in the interiors superbly decorated e.g. with a collection of tapestries. The murals were authored by M. Palloni. In 1765 the state bought the residence from the Krasińskis and several central offices were located here, e.g. the National Education Commission. The remodelling was supervised by G. Fontana (1766-76) and D. Merlini (1783-84). In the 19th c. the palace housed the courts. The building burnt down in 1939. During Insurrection of 1944 it was the headquarters of the Polish "Parasol" Battalion. Reconstructed in 1948-61, it now houses Special Collections Department of the National Library.

Krasiński Palace

WARSZAWA PAŁAC POD BLACHĄ

When in 1789 Duke Józef Poniatowski arrived in Warsaw to enjoy himself, he soon became the talk of the town as did his carriage drawn by eight horses in one row and his spirited ride around the town in imitation of Lady Godiva (after he had lost a bet). The Prince Charming is usually associated with the Tin-Roofed Palace, although he moved here only a few years after his arrival. The building adjacent to the Royal Castle (whose name derives from the roofing rare in the 18th c.) was created as a result of the remodelling of a large townhouse into a residence of the Lubomirski family. First the main section was erected and in 1716 the wings were added which embraced the unique courtyard. In 1777 the palace was purchased by King Stanisław August Poniatowski and incorporated into the castle complex. In 1779-84, D. Merlini built the royal library wing thus linking both buildings. In 1794 the King handed the building over to Duke Józef. Then it became the venue of revelries and frolicking, which was observed by Warsaw burghers with dread, although not without some degree of admiration. In 1820 a descendant of the Duke sold the residence to Tsar Alexander I and from then on the palace shared the fate of the castle. In 1926-39, it housed the offices of the Chancellery of the President of the Republic. Conservation works were carried out by A. Szyszko-Bohusz in 1935-37, but their effects were destroyed by the Nazis, who set the building on fire in December 1944. Reconstructed in 1948-49, it now houses a museum with a collection of oriental tapestries which were donated to the Royal Castle by T. Sahakian.

WARSZAWA PAŁAC PREZYDENCKI

The President's Palace stands out among many large buildings at the Royal Route. The work on the edifice, designed by C. Tencalli, was commenced in 1643 by Hetman S. Koniecpolski. In the 17th and 18th c. the palace was owned by the Lubomirski and Radziwiłł families, and in the 19th c. it became the seat of the Tsar's governors. In 1694-1705 and 1720-22 the residence was remodelled by the most prominent architects active in Warsaw at the time. It acquired new wings and its main section was reconstructed in late Baroque style. In the 19th c. the front façade was remodelled in the neoclassical fashion, while the back façade was turned Renaissance. The original structure have been preserved intact, although the interiors perished in the fire of 1852. After 1918 the palace was the seat of the Chancellery of the Council of Ministers and since 1994 it has served as the residence of the President of the Republic of Poland. The second floor is taken by the President's apartments.

Tin-Roofed Palace

President's Palace

Warszawa Królikarnia

Outside the close town centre is Królikarnia (literally "Rabbitry"). In the 18th c., it used to be a royal manor situated on a steep river bank surrounded by hunting grounds. The open spaces were used for military exercises. In 1732 a large parade of Polish and Saxon troops was held on the Królikarnia and Czerniaków fields, which was watched by the King, deputies and senators. In 1782-89, for the comfort of shooters fatigued by hare chases, D. Merlini erected here an elegant, neo-classical palace (commissioned by K. Thomaitis). Merlini's arrangement followed Palladian principles, so the building is constructed on the plan of a circle within a square and capped with a cupola. The kitchen annexe was modelled on the Roman tomb of Cecilia Metella. Lavish feasts were organised here, King Stanisław August frequently visiting the place. In 1816 the palace was bought by M. Radziwiłł, who exhibited here his collection of paintings including those by J. Ruisdale and P. Potter. In 1849, the collection of the Pusłowski family was placed in the palace. Unluckily, the palace was damaged in the 1879 fire. It was rebuilt in 1880-83 to the design of J. Huss, with a hospice housed in the annexe. Besides, in the vicinity of the Królikarnia palace there is an interesting historicist chapel based on Lombardian motives, designed by W. Bobiński around 1860. In September 1939, during the battle between the Polish Army and the Wehrmaht, the park surrounding Królikarnia and the palace itself became the scene of fierce fighting. The building was rebuilt from the war damage in 1964. At present it houses a museum of the sculptures of X. Dunikowski.

Królikarnia

Warszawa Pałac Sapiehów

It is from the barracks of Sapieha Palace that the 4th Line Infantry Regiment of the Kingdom of Poland marched to join the 1830 Uprising. This favourite regiment of the Russian governor Duke Constantine showed courage in the battles of Olszynka and Ostrołęka, and in the battle of Warsaw. From 1500 soldiers only 200 lived to the end of the uprising. It was also the personal tragedy of the Duke: his beloved army with which all his aspirations had been connected came out against him.

After Tsar Alexander I, wishing to win support of the Poles, had agreed that separate Polish army should continue to exist, he appointed none of the Russian generals but his younger brother Constantine to be its commander. The organisation of the troops was managed by the Military Committee, which consisted of distinguished Polish officers and soon fell into conflict with Duke Constantine. For the latter the army was a favourite toy, but also a guarantee of a relatively independent position in Warsaw. Military parades on the Saski Square in the presence of the Grand Duke were later a characteristic feature of the military life of the time. The conflicts between him and the generals were due both to the Duke's domineering character and the clash between the liberal model of the Napoleonic troops and the brutal tradition of the Russian army. The barracks were housed in the Sapieha Palace purchased by the army in 1817 and remodelled in 1818-20 by H. Minter.

The attractive late Baroque edifice had been raised in 1731-34 and 1739-46 by J.S. Deybel from Salzburg. It was a typical *entre cour et jardin* layout with the central palace of subtle architectural divisions and harmonious proportions, which left it monumental nonetheless. The three-storey building was topped with openwork parapet and decorated with sculptures. At the time of King Stanisław August the palace was the venue of constant feasts, balls and theatre performances. The abandoned building was rented in 1810 by the army. As a result of the remodelling by Minter the rococo decorations were removed and the fine residence was turned austere and neo-classical. Later the stables and a rather chaotic yard were added. In 1931 the building was turned into a military hospital which burnt down during the 1944 Insurrection. The reconstruction carried out under the supervision of J. Zachwatowicz restored the original form of the palace.

Palace of Sapieha family

Staszic Palace

WARSZAWA PAŁAC STASZICA

The large edifice of Staszic Palace, designed in 1830 by B. Thorvaldsen, dominates over the statue of Copernicus at the end of Krakowskie Przedmieście. From the very beginning it was intended as the headquarters for the Society of the Friends of Science, modelled after similar western societies. The latter, however, were usually established and founded by rulers, whereas the Polish society was created as a group initiative of the Warsaw elite to bring together rich noblemen interested in science and, usually impoverished, scholars. The society organised lectures and competitions, supported industry and agriculture with up-to-date information, ran a public library and published scientific studies. Thanks to its efforts the grammar of the Polish language was codified. The founder of the Palace, the scholar and civic leader S. Staszic, lived in its annexe until 1826.

The building was erected in 1820-23 on the site of the dismantled church of the Dominicans. The design was authored by A. Corazzi, who also created other large public buildings in Warsaw, such as the palaces for the Government Commission for Internal Affairs (1823), the Government Commission for the Mazovian Voivodeship (1824), and the Bank of Poland (1832). The most impressive edifice raised by Corazzo from public funding was the National Theatre (1824-33), then considered one of the most aptly constructed theatre buildings in Europe. The palace of the Society of the Friends of Science was erected in a mature neo-classical style. The Society was dissolved by Tsar Nicholas I in 1832 and the confiscated building was adapted for the seat of Lottery Management and in 1862 a secondary school for boys moved in here. In 1892-93 the building was thoroughly remodelled by the Russian architect Pokrovsky in over-ornamental Byzantine-Ruthenian style. An Orthodox church was placed in the middle of the building to commemorate the Shuyskis, the Russian Tsars buried here in the "Moscow chapel" – it used to be part of the church which stood earlier on the site. During the remodelling carried out in 1924-26 by M. Lalewicz, the neo-classical style of the palace was restored. The architect was not faithful to Corazzo's design, however: he failed to reconstruct the side projections and shaped the dome slightly differently. In the 1920s and 30s, the building was the seat of the Warsaw Scientific Society again. After the Second World War, in 1946-50, it was reconstructed under the supervision of P. Biegański. The architect also designed the new wings surrounding the internal courtyard.

WARSZAWA PAŁAC OSTROGSKICH

The visitors to Warsaw should associate this house at Tamka with the legend of a Golden Duck every guide will tell you. More importantly, in the former Ostrogski palace one can find a museum managed by Frédéric Chopin Society. The exhibits include the piano on which Chopin composed his works in the years 1848-49 and a collection of his musical autographs. Chopin's oeuvre embraces chiefly solo piano pieces: 3 sonatas. 4 ballads, 3 scherzos, 27 etudes, 25 preludes, 19 nocturnes, 16 polonaises, 57 mazurkas, 19 waltzes, 4 rondos, 4 variations, 1 fantasia and several other single pieces. Since 1927, on the initiative of J. Żurawlew, the Chopin Piano Competition has been organised, the world largest review of Chopin's music.

The palace itself was raised – in its lower part – as early as in the 16th c. by order of the affluent Ostrogski Dukes from eastern Poland. The works were continued in the late 17th c., and were completed already by the new owners, the Gnińskis. Tylman van Gameren was hired to fashion a Baroque residence on a high terrace over the cellars. In 1720 the palace passed into the hands of the Zamoyski family, who modernised the interiors following the concept of G. Fontana. Remodelled in the 19th c. the building later housed military storerooms, war hospital and Health House. In 1859, the town authorities opened the Music Institute here (later renamed Conservatory). The house was burnt down by the Germans in 1944. Today it has been reconstructed in the late 18th-c. style.

Ostrogski House

Warszawa Belweder

Behind the Łazienki palace is the building of the Military School, from which young conspirators on the November night starting the Uprising of 1830 marched to Belvedere – the small palace was then the residence of the Grand Duke Constantine. The attack ended in failure and the action evoked controversy among Polish generals and the troops. The conspirators initiative was saved by craftsmen who joined in and by the hesitant attitude of the Duke himself, who rejected the offer of the frontal attack of the loyal part of the Polish army and the Russian troops on the mutinied soldiers and withdrew from Warsaw.

Built in 1659 on the steep river bank for Chancellor K. Pac, with panoramic view of the city, Belvedere was refashioned around 1740, and in 1767 was the property of King Stanisław August. In the annexes there was a ceramics manufacture, established in 1770 as the Royal Faience Factory. The "Turkish set," made in 1777 as a gift to Sultan Abdul Hamid I, was particularly renowned for its artistry. In the 19th c. it was a favourite residence of those in power. On the Duke's orders, J. Kubicki remodelled the palace in 1818-22 into a neo-classical country residence with the portico and perpendicular wings. He erected decorative pavilions in the park: the Egyptian Temple, the Temple of Diana and the neo-Gothic Orangery. When Poland regained independence in 1918, the castle was taken over by the head of the Polish state, Marshal J. Piłsudski, who lived here and died in 1935. The world press reported then: "On Sunday May 12 at 11 am, the Marshal remained mostly unconscious, regaining consciousness only for short moments. In the evening he received the Extreme Unction. He died at 8:45 pm in his bedroom on the first floor of the Belvedere Palace."

In May 1920, at the time when the country was threatened by the Bolshevik offensive, Piłsudski received in Belvedere his staunchest political opponent, R. Dmowski, who had just returned to Poland after five years absence to serve his country. After the meeting, the latter commented: "Piłsudski is doubtless a great man, although we totally differed in our opinions." The Marshal said this of Dmowski: "He is the only politician with whom I would like to discuss things, although we differ fundamentally in our views on the future of Poland". This is what you can call top class politicians! During the Second World War the building served as a residence of Governor H. Frank and thus survived. In 1945-52 B. Bierut, the puppet President favoured by the Russians, lived here and so did afterwards several Chairmen of the State Council. Between 1989-94, The Polish President resided in Belvedere. At present it hosts the most distinguished officials visiting Poland.

Warsaw: Façade of the Belvedere Palace

Belvedere: Pompeian Room

Myślewicki Palace: Dining Hall

WARSZAWA
PAŁAC MYŚLEWICKI

The expression "the style of King Stanisław August" was introduced only in 1916 by the philosopher W. Tatarkiewicz. In this way the masterpieces which were created with the personal contribution of this controversial monarch as well as the works influenced by the Warsaw court received a deserving name. The style was rather conservative, far removed from the avant-garde achievements of the time, and was formed by the personal taste of the ruler. In architecture and interior design, the King tended towards neo-classicism, while in painting and sculpture he was more faithful to Baroque and rococo styles.

An early example of this style is Myślewicki Palace in Łazienki, which, until the Palace on Water was completed, had been the most impressive building of the complex. It was designed and built in 1775-76 by D. Merlini. This Italian architect was one of the most prominent representatives of Polish neo-classical style. In 1761 he was appointed Royal Architect, and upon the death of G. Fontana in 1773, Architect of the Republic of Poland. He greatly contributed to the creation of a new type of elegant interior design, the best examples of which may be found in the palaces of Łazienki. Myślewicki Palace is a small residential pavilion in which guests of the King would stay. Although in designing it, Merlini applied neo-classical solutions, the building still had rococo-style decorations. They are particularly visible in the interiors which were designed by the Italian sculptor G. Monaldi (*The Statue of Flora*) and the painter J.B. Plersch. Particularly noteworthy is the dining room, where in 1778 the artists placed three large murals: *The View of the Bridge and Castle of San Angelo in Rome, The Casino of Pius VI in the Vatican* and *The View of Venice*. Panoramas, side by side with arabesque-grotesque decorations, were the most popular type of elegant interior decoration at the time. When composing them the painters freely used the existing drawings and illustrated books. Since King Stanisław August was nearly obsessed with constant remodelling, Myślewicki Palace was not immune to the trend. Initially a square villa with a large niche in front, it was refashioned into a palace with slightly rounded two-storey wings. It is an excellent example of the favourite style of the King, suspended between the neo-classical and the late Baroque. Today, the meticulously reconstructed building is used for official occasions.

Łazienki Park: Myślewicki Palace

Palace on Water

WARSZAWA ŁAZIENKI

The famous Łazienki is a charming palace in park surroundings, situated in the district of Ujazdów spreading from Ujazdowskie Avenue to the banks of the Vistula. In the second half of the 17th c., Tylman van Gameren built a Baroque pavilion on a rectangular island for the Grand Marshal of the Crown, H. Lubomirski. In 1764, the entire property was bought by King Stanisław August for part of the enormous sum of over one million Polish zloties he had received from the Sejm to remodel the royal residences. His summer residence in Łazienki (Pol. baths), named after the pavilion located in the large forest which used to house the royal baths at the time of the Vasa dynasty, became then his favourite venue. It is here that he found shelter from the everyday tumult of the city and the political squabbles. In 1772, a major remodelling began, aiming to transform Łazienki into a summer residence fit for the King, a task which took 20 years to complete. The external appearance of the building, thereafter called Palace on Water, was radically altered – in neo-classical style. In 1784, the southern façade was remodelled, while the northern one was completed in 1788. Among the architects and artists commissioned to do the task were D. Merlini, J. B. Kamsetzer and J. B. Plersch. The palace was a pearl of architectural art, an expression of the King's exquisite taste, combining traits of late Baroque and neo-classical styles. It is in this constantly adorned residence that the best paintings from the royal vast collection were exposed.

Łazienki has nothing of the pomp of the Versailles: it was conceived as a place of quiet and joy. The Pompeian murals were painted by V. Brenna, while the stucco decoration were the work of F. Baumann to the design of C. P. Aigner (1800-05). Over the entrance the following motto was inscribed: "This house abhors grief, loves peace, recommends country life and wishes to host honest people." Łazienki Gardens were modelled on English landscape gardens by J. Schuch. They embraced a number of buildings, such as Myślewicki Palace (1775-78),

Island Theatre and Palace on Water

the Old Orangery (now Poland's largest museum of sculpture) and the charming Island Theatre (1790-91), a work by Kamsetzer reminiscent of the Hadrian Villa at Tivoli. The bridge over one of the ponds was designed by Merlini and adorned with the monument of King Jan III Sobieski (1788). The White Cottage used to be the residence of the future king of France, Louis XVIII, when he remained in exile, the Hermitage was the lodging of Lady Lhullier, the fortune teller at the court.

After his abdication, the King bestowed Łazienki to his nephew Duke Józef Poniatowski, after whom it was inherited by J.M. Tyszkiewiczowa. In 1817, she in turn sold it to Tsar Alexander I, and in 1818 part of the park was donated to the Botanical Gardens. In the 19th c. Łazienki retained much of its splendour (after 1831 it was a Tsar's residence) and survived almost intact until 1939. A monument to Chopin (designed by W. Szymanowski) was put up in 1926 next to the pond, the genius of music sitting under a willow, the tree typical of the Mazovian plain. In 1944, the Germans set fire to the residence, gutting its interiors, but, thanks to a happy coincidence, it was not blown up. After the war it was faithfully and meticulously restored, together with all the pavilions in the park, and the 18th c. atmosphere can be felt again. Thanks to the King, Warsaw acquired modern look and became a truly European capital;

Dining Hall with Aphrodite Statue

Palace on Water: Rotunda dome

The Royal Castle and Łazienki could compete with any royal residences across Europe. The king was doubtless an art connoisseur, but was he a really generous patron? In fact, only three percent of his spending was allocated to supporting art. Bacciarelli received a yearly allowance which was roughly one third of the money offered to an average royal concubine. He could not get more as the King, always a spendthrift, was notoriously short of money. No wonder, if you take into account the fact that he had to maintain a court of nearly 300 people. The concubines took their fair share indeed. Well-known was the performance of the play *The Arrival of Cleopatra*, organised by the King for one of his lovers in Łazienki Gardens. Most resources, however, went to bribe the king's political supporters; they were about two thirds of the royal budget. The list of beneficiaries included some artists and writers as well, but compared with the "political" spending it was more like alms money. The funds allocated for the establishment of the Academy of Fine Arts seem comparatively small too. On the other hand, the King cannot be accused of not seeking savings: the masses said for the souls of his parents were paid for from public funds. Strolling around Łazienki Gardens, we must admit that three percent though it was, the King has spent it very wisely.

Wilanów Palace

Pałac w Wilanowie

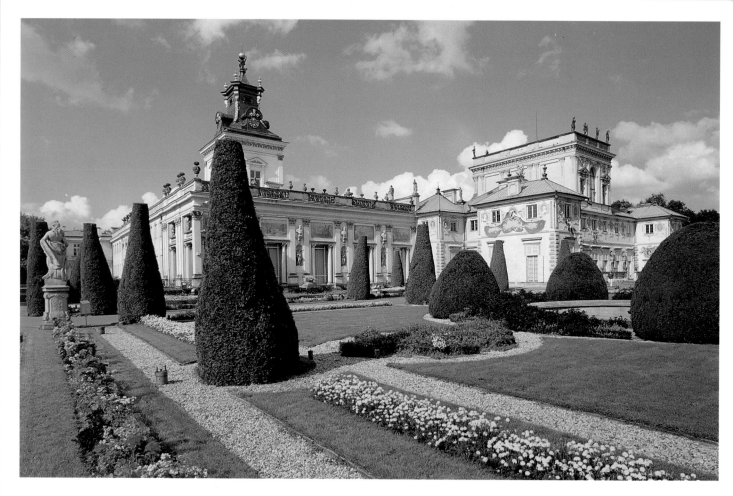

Belwederska and Sobieskiego streets lead to one of the most beautiful Polish residences, situated in Wilanów. Its greatest attraction is the sumptuous palace built for King Jan III Sobieski on the foundations of the former Leszczyński Palace from the first half of the 17th c. For him, the last warrior-king on the Polish throne, Wilanów was a place of rest after battles with the enemies of Poland. The Wilanów Palace was designed not only as one of the monarch's residences, but also as a monument to his martial glory and a seat of beauty, virtue and knowledge.

In the Polish tradition, Sobieski embodies all the best features of the flamboyant "Sarmatian" tradition, which was cherished by the greater part of the nobility. The interiors of the palace were furnished with precious objects, and many of them are still extant: paintings, fabrics, furniture, silverware, pottery, precious weapons. The King valued Italian and French products, and – as the Sarmatian king should – adored those from the Near and Middle East: Persian carpets and tapestries, cloth of gold, Turkish velvet-covered saddles ornamented with gold tin, turquoise and nephrite, broad oriental swords and guns laid with ivory. Many of Wilanów's rooms and memorabilia are intimately connected with the king and his beloved French wife Marie-Casimire, affectionately called Marysieńka. The most spectacular interiors are the Royal Apartments, the Mirror Gallery, the Library, the Etruscan Cabinet, the Grand Crimson Room and the Garden Gallery. Some of these are decorated with murals by the King's protégé, J. E. Siemiginowski. The beautiful bedchamber plafond *Eos* was painted by J. Reisner, who endowed the nude goddess with the features of the beautiful queen Marysieńka. Incidentally, the bedroom is not the only place permeated with erotic and hedonistic atmosphere, so much valued in the Baroque era.

The palace, whose two wings encompass a spacious courtyard, was built around 1680 to the design of A.V. Locci and enlarged in

Wilanów: Baroque formal gardens

Palace Dining Hall

1692. The oeuvre of Locci, inspired with classical art and Baroque buildings of Rome, is a good example of full-blown Baroque in Polish architecture. The architect was one of the wealthiest artists of his time. Apart from numerous prestigious positions, he also held the estate in the vicinity of Warsaw – the King knew how to return favours. In Wilanów he first designed the manor house with side annexes; then a storey was added to the main section and garden galleries with octagonal towers were adjoined; finally the central building was topped with a superstructure, and a large courtyard and the garden with a retaining wall, canals, ponds and bowers were laid out. Locci endowed the royal summer residence with a twofold nature: sacred (the portal of an ancient temple in the front façade) and rural (the back façade). The palace was also remodelled in 1722-25 (G. Spazzio), 1730-33 (J. S. Deybel) and 1848 (F. M. Lanci).

King Jan III dreamed of establishing a dynasty, but his sons' personalities were incomparable to his. The quarrelsome Prince Jacob, instead of gaining favour of the nobility, became infamous for his scandalous bearing. In 1695, he hired murderers to kill a state official, who fortunately managed to save his life. Jakub, however, had to seek refuge as far as Silesia to avoid his father's anger. He returned immediately after the King's death and occupied the Wilanów palace. When the Queen's retinue arrived, Prince Jakub ostentatiously slammed the door in his mother's face and announced he had no intention to share the estate. No wonder then that the winner in the next royal election was not called Sobieski.

The palace was inherited by consecutive noble families. S. Kostka Potocki, officially the royal master of the pantry, housed his collections here (Greek art, 17th- and 18th-c. painting, copies of ancient sculptures), founded the archives and the library. In 1805 he opened part of the interiors to the public: this was one of the first museums in Poland. He was by no means an ordinary person. He collected Etruscan vases, he designed the façade of St Anne's church in Warsaw (together with C. P. Aigner), he conducted archaeological works in Laurentum near Rome, which was documented by the drawings of V. Brenna, he was also one of the founders of the Society of the Friends of Science. Each successive family of owners remodelled the interiors in their own fashion, so very little is left of the objects previously owned by King Jan III.

During the Second World War, the art collection was plundered by the Nazis, who also ruined the park. Fortunately, most of the missing works of art were later recovered. After restoration, the palace became a branch of the National Museum. The interiors were restored in the style of the period of King Jan and Queen Marysieńka. From the reign of King August II, the Grand Dining Hall designed by J.S. Deybel around 1730 has been preserved. A good part of the collection dates back to the time when the Potockis took charge of the place, e.g. the painting gallery or the collection of ancient vases. Furniture, china, glass and silverware are well-represented in the museum as well. Wilanów has thus become one of the most interesting palace interiors in the country. It also serves as an official residence for the Polish diplomatic service (the visitors included the Ethiopian Emperor, Haile Sellasie, and the Iranian Shah, Reza Pahlavi). The palace is surrounded with a formal garden from 1682, supplemented in 1799-1801 with landscape sections. It reaches as far as the bank of the Vistula, gradually merging with the riverside meadows and alder forest. Nostalgically, many people perceive a similarity between this landscape and that of former Polish eastern territories which were so dear to King Jan III.

Study Room

After 1554 the place was owned by two consecutive families, and in 1593 the castle and the estate were purchased by S. Lubomirski, who talked Emperor Rudolph II into granting him the title of "the Lord of Wiśnicz." The construction works carried out in 1615-21 by order of his son gave the residence its final impressive shape. The Baroque residence designed by M. Trapola consisted of a regular pentagonal complex of buildings with corner towers and a slender arcaded loggia. The work of Trapola were the impressive new-Italian-style fortified ramparts and bastions with an early Baroque gate. A domed chapel was built too, decorated with stuccoes by J.B. Falconi. The family sarcophagi are still housed in an underground crypt. In 1616, King Zygmunt III Vasa allowed S. Lubomirski to set up the town of Nowy Wiśnicz in the vicinity of the castle, on the land which had formerly belonged to Stary Wiśnicz and the village of Rogozie. The Lubomirskis obtained a municipal charter for it based on Magdeburg Law. It thus received the right of storage and release from duties across the country. This attracted a group of active merchants and started the most prosperous period in the town's history. The private troops of the Wiśnicz Castle consisted then of 650 soldiers (including 200 dragoons, and 400 Hungarian infantrymen), who had 80 canons at their disposal. During the Swedish invasion (called "the Deluge" in Polish history), Lubomirski was loyal to the Polish king, but he handed the castle over to the Swedes, thus trying to save it from destruction. From the castle, the oversees invaders could then control the turbulent foothill area. Withdrawing, they broke their word, however, and looted the castle; rumour has it, they needed some 150 wagons to take the spoils away.

The residence never regained the former glory, not for the lack of efforts of the consecutive owners. In October 1707, during the Northern War, it was the stronghold of General Z.J. Rybiński, who sent around his armed reconnaissance troopers to control Cracow and Sandomierz lands. Wiśnicz suffered considerable damage at the time of the Confederation of Bar. It remained the property of the Lubomirskis until the mid-18th c. when it passed into the hands of the Sanguszko, Potocki and Zamoyski families. It lost its role of the landlord's residence in 1780 and was entirely abandoned in 1831, after a devastating fire. The repair works undertaken by the Lubomirski Family Union, which had re-purchased the ancestry residence in 1901 and owned it until the Communist nationalisation and land reform of 1945-46, saving it from total ruin. Renovation works have been carried on until today.

Wiśnicz Castle

WIŚNICZ

The Palatine of Cracow S. Lubomirski was one of the most powerful Polish magnates of the first half of the 17th c. His residence in Wiśnicz, remodelled in a truly magnificent style, is testimony to his power. The fortified castle overlooking the river valley was already mentioned in the invoices from the Bochnia salt mine from 1396-97. Initially, the castle consisted of a quadrangular perimeter wall with a square tower. The structure raised in the 15th c. by the influential Kmita family was a regular four-wing building with the courtyard and three towers. In the 16th c. P. Kmita turned the stronghold into a Renaissance residence. King Zygmunt August stayed here in 1550 with his wife Barbara, and it is here that his short-lived happiness with his beloved wife (the best example of femme fatale Poland has ever had) was cut even shorter, as the Queen's enemies served her with a poison.

Cartouche with Lubomirski's coat of arms

Palace in Wojanów

Wojanów

From the early 19th c., the Jelenia Góra Basin was a highly snobbish place. It was considered – and rightly so – to be a place equally attractive as Potsdam or the Rhine valley. The royal and ducal families: the Hohenzollern and Radziwiłł families, Hessian dukes, Orange princes and others, chose it for their summer residences. They were followed by aristocracy and high officials. In a letter to L. Radziwiłł, her friend, the Hessian Duchess Marianne thus expressed her joyful expectation: "So we will celebrate a wonderful meeting in our beloved Silesia." The estate with a view on Mount Śnieżka, one of the symbols of the relatively young Prussian state, was a boost to prestige. The residences were surrounded with vast gardens, which the Duchess I. Czartoryska, an authority on horticulture, thus described in 1816: "The preference for landscape gardens is noticeable everywhere, particularly in details: wonderful arable fields, excellent selection of trees, a highly sophisticated layout of shrubs and plants lined up along the roads and paths. Following these you can reach various interesting buildings."
Wojanów on the Bóbr, situated at the foot of a mountain range, had every chance to attract fine residences. Indeed, several interesting buildings can be found within a small area. The oldest of them is a knights castle, the picturesque ruins of which top the Koziniec Hill today. Overlooking the river, there is a once Baroque palace (1603-07), destroyed in 1642 by the Swedes, and reconstructed by C. von Zedlitz. In 1667, the palace in Wojanów was listed among the most impressive buildings in Silesia. In 1833, it was thoroughly remodelled by K.F. Schinkel and rather unfortunately "improved" in 1900. The palace adjoined a spacious park (designed by the famous landscape architect, J.P. Lenne), which reached the Bóbr. In 1839, the Wojanów estate was purchased by King of Prussia Frederic William III for his daughter Louise (in the sales contract it was mentioned that "the palace was built in a medieval style with turrets"); by the end of the 19th c. it passed into the hands of Maria zu Wied.
On the opposite bank of the river rises the huge eclectic Boberstein Castle (Wojanów-Bobrów), which looks like the embodiment of the place of action of your typical Gothic novel. The maze of stairs, parapets, balconies and turrets makes you think that it was designed by someone who abhorred even the smallest stretch of smooth surface. Count K. von Rothkirch, who commissioned the castle, surrounded it with a high perimeter wall with towers and the majestic entrance gate. Today the neo-Renaissance edifice houses institutions working to support European integration.

Wojnowice

Wojnowice in the vicinity of Wrocław takes pride in the magnificent Renaissance manor house on an isle surrounded with a wide moat. It is an example, rare in Poland, of a late medieval *Wasserburg*, castle on water, which has been preserved intact.
In Wojnowice, the castle of this type is particularly impressive. Built in 1513-30 for Nikolaus von Scheibitz, it was soon bought by the rich Boner family. The Wrocław burghers were eager to own such a palace as this was considered a sign of affluence. The new owners had the construction completed, with a small inner courtyard, in 1545-62. They held it until 1576, and their coat of arms may still be seen today in the castle gate. The quadrangular castle was built from brick, only door frames and other details were made from sandstone. The large windows were framed in carved stone and the steep roofs were shingled. By the entrance gate a slender tower was erected and topped with crenellation. The wings received stepped gables and Renaissance arcades were added to part of the courtyard. There was a new decorative well too. *Dansker* bays have been preserved on the eastern façade, and Renaissance ceilings can be seen in some rooms. Unfortunately, part of the drawbridge was replaced in the 19th c. with a fixed construction.
The castle is a proof that medieval strongholds – anachronistic from the military point of view – were still in vogue in the 16th c., adding splendour to the owner's name and used as backdrop for party games. Later (until 1945) the castle was the property of several other patrician families. Today it houses guest rooms of the Art Historians' Society.

Wojnowice Manor

Wróblowice

The 19th-c. neo-classical wooden manor house used to be far away from Cracow, now it has been incorporated into the city. The manor stands where the Augustinian estate used to be; only the old ponds are missing. The rectangular one-storey building is probably the simplest example of the manor form: purely utilitarian, deprived of anything that could be considered dispensable decoration. An exception was made for the portico supported on wooden columns – they were considered essential features of a manor house. A few traces of the 19th-c. decorative garden may still be found in the neglected landscape park. Until 1939 it abounded with climbing roses, trimmed hedges, benches, and vine crept onto the porch.

Manor house in Wróblowice

Zator

The ducal castle in Zator was erected in 1445-47. After the Partitions it was purchased by P. Dunin, who restored the building. In 1836, F.M. Lanci, the Italian residing in Poland, redesigned it by order of the Potocki family. He was influenced by medieval English architectural style and gave the castle the romantic neo-Gothic shape. The interiors were adorned with stuccoes, and the southern annexe was turned into a neo-Gothic loggia. Two pairs of rooms on both sides of the ground floor are worth noticing, richly decorated in 1836 with murals and stuccoes in "Pompeian style." On the left of the hallway are the Hunters' Room and the Golden Room with complex vaults from the turn of the 19th c. Traces of 14-karat gold may be seen on the walls of the latter. Several marble fireplaces in neoclassical style have been preserved as well, the vault of the hallway is still decorated with beautiful murals, while several rooms are adorned with inlaid doors. The castle had been the residence of the Potocki family until the Second World War. The rooms housed a remarkable historical collection: memorabilia of the monarchs (Queen Bona, Stefan Báthory, Jan III Sobieski, August II the Strong, Napoleon I), military exhibits, painting gallery (works by Leonardo, Canaletto, Bacciarelli), collection of sculptures and Egyptian and Greek statues. During the Second World War, the building was damaged and the collections were looted by the Nazis.

Palace in Zator: Ground floor room

Ząbkowice Śląskie: Castle ruins

Ząbkowice Śląskie

The gloomy ruins in Ząbkowice Śląskie will stimulate your imagination better if you remember the castle's German name: Frankenstein. Although the link of this place with the monster born in the imagination of Mary W. Shelley is doubtful, horror lovers could not care less and will certainly search among the ruins for traces of the mad Geneva student and the lonely monster creature he has created. Sizable ruins of the ducal residence, which replaced an earlier medieval castle, rise on a steep river bank. Dominated by the parapet of the gate tower and the tall keep, the castle has few Gothic remains, most of which were erased during the works carried out on the initiative of the Duke of Ziębice, Charles I from Podebrad.

Ząbkowice belonged to the Duchy of Wrocław (until 1290), Świdnica (until 1322), and then Ziębice. The castle was first mentioned in the document from 1321: it then guarded the Czech frontier. In the second half of the 14th c. it was the seat of the Luxemburg family, and in 1397 it was handed in to Jan, the Duke of Opawa and Racibórz. After the damage suffered during Hussite wars and the siege of the castle by Wrocław burghers (1443), the castle, which was the property of Czech noble families, passed into the hands of King George Podebrad, then his family and King Mathias Corvinus. After the death of the King in 1491, Henry the Elder of the Podebrad family sold the town and the nearly totally demolished castle to the Czech Chancellor, Jan of Schellenburg. The Renaissance remodelling was designed by B. Ried. In 1524-32, most of the old walls were dismantled and the quadrangular structure was erected with two towers and two cylindrical artillery outworks in the corners. The Renaissance building, made from sandstone and stone on the square plan, had an arcaded courtyard, one of the earliest at this side of the Alps. The residence was said to have no match in Silesia at that time. The earthwork bastions it was surrounded with did not save it from war damage. In 1632 the castle was sieged three times by troops of the Emperor until it surrendered for lack of food. In 1642, it was captured by the Swedes, then recaptured by the Habsburgs and blown up. In 1651 and 1661, the building was partly remodelled for the seat of the royal administrator of the region. In 1728 it was abandoned and in 1784 partially burnt.

Złoty Potok

The village of Potok, situated on a stream (as the name suggests) and surrounded by forests, has been referred to as "Golden" (Pol. *złoty*) since the time of the poet Zygmunt Krasiński. After 1785, Potok was owned by the Duke of Courland J. E. Biron, friend of Tsarina Anna, and his son, and then by three other noble families. In 1851, General W. Krasiński, father of the poet, bought the village and the neighbouring town of Janów. Zygmunt was delighted with the beautiful views he enjoyed there. He decided to name the stream sources after his children, he renamed the Green Pond the Midsummer Night Pond, and called the rocky outcrops the Devil's Bridges and Twardowski Gate. The large pond in the park is called Irydion (after one of the poet's dramas). The one-storey neo-classical manor house of the Krasińskis, erected in 1829 with a columned porch, houses now the biographical museum of the poet. After the fire in 1952, which partly destroyed the house, it was thoroughly restored and partly reconstructed.

Next to the manor house, in the park, stands the Raczyński Palace (it was the dowry of the poet's daughter, Maria), which is now the seat of the Management of Jurassic Landscape Parks. In the palace, built around 1856 and remodelled at the turn of the 20th c., there is a nature museum. Stone lions holding the shields with the coats of arms of the Krasińskis and the Raczyńskis stand guarding the entrance. The park boasts a romantic bridge over the artificial cascades of the Wiercica stream and about one hundred species of trees and shrubs, including a Japanese larch and a Turkoman elm. It was laid out by K. Raczyński, who in 1934 also founded a private nature reserve in the Wiercica valley.

Manor house in Złoty Potok

Zubrzyca Górna

The Polish Upper Orava located on the southern slopes of the Beskid Wysoki mountain range is an interesting and picturesque land. It was once part of the no-man's land on the Polish-Hungarian border, first colonised in the 16th c. by J. Turzon. Religious conflicts dealt a blow to his plans. The peasants of Upper Orava offered the armed resistance against the intended imposition of Protestantism on the area. As a token of appreciation for his role in the victory in the struggle, M. Moniak, the headman of Zubrzyca Górna, received knighthood. The Moniaks then erected a manor house which has been preserved until today. It is the central point of Orava Ethnographic Park in Zubrzyca Górna, which was established in 1937 thanks to the bequest to the State Treasury made by the last heirs of the family. The manor house is not a uniform structure, however: its left wing is older and allegedly dates back to the 17th c., while the right wing was built in 1784. The style of the house is strongly influenced by local architectural tradition, and combines the archaic peasant construction style with that promoted by former ambitious village elites. The common room is filled with Biedermaier furniture, but there are smoke holes in the roof, as the manor house was deprived of the chimney – a unique feature indeed. The charming interior introduces the visitor into the atmosphere of the foregone epoch. The right wing is furnished in the style of 19th-c. landed gentry manors, unpretentious as it is. The former farm buildings of the Moniaks, slightly older, have been preserved as well.

Zubrzyca Górna: Manor of the Moniaks

Zwierzyniec

Zwierzyniec is located in the upper valley of the Wieprz, at the edge of Roztocze Uplands. It grew around the hunters' lodge which was also J. Zamoyski's country residence. It owes its present name to the animal hunting reserve which was the nobleman's property too. In the course of time, subsequent owners of the Zamość entailed estate enlarged and adorned their residence in Zwierzyniec, entrusting this task to their architects, gardeners and foresters. In the early 19th c. the administration of the Zamoyski estate was moved to Zwierzyniec. During the German occupation, the Nazi transition camp was set up here. The palace complex has some interesting sights: the Baroque Church on Water situated on an urban isle, founded by T.A. Zamoyski; the former palace of the plenipotentiaries; the historical, but still functioning brewery from 1806; and the complex of estate administration buildings. Zwierzyniec is an interesting example of a non-residential complex which was the efficient centre of administration of a vast area.

Zwierzyniec Palace complex: Church on water

Castle in Żagań

Żagań

On the northern fringe of the vast Lower Silesian forest lies the town of Żagań. This 12th-c. borderland stronghold was made capital of a duchy ruled by the Legnica and Głogów branch of the Piast dynasty in 1427. Its original layout has been preserved. The most interesting sight in the town is the Baroque palace, which belonged in 1674-1700 to the Lobkowitz family. It had probably replaced an earlier, late 13th-c. castle of the Piasts which had probably stood on the same spot. The initial form of the palace was the design of V. Boccaccio and A. Della Porta. In planning the building they made use of fragments of an earlier Mannerist palace from 1627-34. From 1628, the palace was the property of the famous mercenary A. Wallenstein, who had acquired it from the Austrian Emperor, Ferdinand II. The Mannerist residence was defensive in function, erected on a high base surrounded with a moat. The changes introduced by Della Porta brought the departure from the conception of *palazzo in fortezza.* The Żagań residence had received the structure of a Mannerist-Baroque palace built on a square plan with four wings. In 1785 it was taken over by the Duke of Courland P. Biron. In 1792-96, the interiors were redecorated to a design by C. Schulze.

In 1842, when the duchy became the property of D. Talleyrand-Perigord, Żagań attained the rank of one of the best-known courts in Europe. Among the visitors were F. Liszt and G. Verdi, who performed in the palace (the organ played on by Liszt may still be seen in the Assumption Church), and Stendhal, the Napoleon's proxy in the Żagań Duchy, who sought inspiration here. The enlargement plans were not neglected either and a large orangery was erected. The park surrounding the residence was extended and given a romantic form, designed by O. Teichert. The last of the Talleyrands, Duke Bosan II, left Żagań in 1935 for political reasons. After a period of post-war abandonment, when the remains of the furnishings were either destroyed or taken away, the long-lasting restoration works were carried out in the palace in 1965-83.

Also worth seeing is the former Augustinian monastery complex. The highlights of the monastery are the 18th-c. library and the study used by the famous astronomer J. Kepler. The 56-metre-high church tower had the first lightning rod in Europe installed in 1778.

Żagań Castle: Drawing room

Manor house in Żelazowa Wola

Żelazowa Wola

Many scenic places adjoin the Kampinoski Forest and sit on the Vistula banks. The village of Żelazowa Wola, lost amid the Mazovian plains at the edge of the forest, is the best known among them as it is remembered as the birthplace of a musical genius. At the turn of the 19th c., the settlement was the property of the Skarbek family. In 1802, M. Chopin was brought here as a teacher, and here he met his future wife, T.J. Krzyżanowska. It was here, in an annexe to the Skarbek Palace, that Frédéric Chopin was born. Although the Chopins moved to Warsaw already in October 1810, but the composer returned here many times later. He visited Żelazowa Wola for the last time in the summer of 1830, just before his departure abroad, and he never came back again. The palace itself burnt down during the First World War, but the annexe, built in 1810, survived and was renovated in 1930-31. L. Niemojewski gave it the appearance of a one-storey neo-classical country house, now overgrown with vine. It is surrounded by a scenic garden, which was rearranged in 1933-35 by F. Krzywda-Polkowski, and features a monument commemorating the artist. In 1894, the obelisk with the medallion of Chopin was unveiled, on the initiative of the Russian composer M. Balakirev. From the western side there is a hornbeam alley, the continuation of which is the line of linden trees framing the park. Carefully cultivated, the park on the river is scenic and delightful.

The stylish manor interiors with low beamed rooms house a small Chopin Museum. During the summer season, piano concerts are held there. Opening the museum here was the aim of A. Towiański, who had bought the property already in 1859, but he failed to realize his dream. The manor house was purchased from private hands only in 1926 by the Ministry of Religious Affairs and Public Enlightenment. Then in 1928 the most famous annexe in Poland (together with three hectares of grounds) became the property of the Chopin Committee, and after 1953, of Frédéric Chopin Society (the organiser of international Chopin Competitions).

Chopin's manor house: Drawing room

W9-BFQ-562

Navigation

Other Publications:
THE SEAFARERS
THE ENCYCLOPEDIA OF COLLECTIBLES
WORLD WAR II
THE GREAT CITIES
HOME REPAIR AND IMPROVEMENT
THE WORLD'S WILD PLACES
HUMAN BEHAVIOR
THE ART OF SEWING
THE OLD WEST
THE EMERGENCE OF MAN
THE AMERICAN WILDERNESS
THE TIME-LIFE ENCYCLOPEDIA OF GARDENING
LIFE LIBRARY OF PHOTOGRAPHY
THIS FABULOUS CENTURY
FOODS OF THE WORLD
TIME-LIFE LIBRARY OF AMERICA
TIME-LIFE LIBRARY OF ART
GREAT AGES OF MAN
LIFE SCIENCE LIBRARY
THE LIFE HISTORY OF THE UNITED STATES
TIME READING PROGRAM
LIFE NATURE LIBRARY
LIFE WORLD LIBRARY
FAMILY LIBRARY:
HOW THINGS WORK IN YOUR HOME
THE TIME-LIFE BOOK OF THE FAMILY CAR
THE TIME-LIFE FAMILY LEGAL GUIDE
THE TIME-LIFE BOOK OF FAMILY FINANCE

Navigation

By the Editors of
TIME-LIFE BOOKS

The
TIME-LIFE Library of Boating

TIME-LIFE BOOKS, ALEXANDRIA, VIRGINIA

The TIME-LIFE Library of Boating

Editorial Staff for Navigation:
Editor: Harvey B. Loomis
Text Editor: Bryce S. Walker, Jay Brennan, Philip W. Payne
Designer: Lee Stausland
Assistant Designer: James Eisenman
Staff Writers: Richard Cravens, Lee Hassig, Wendy Buehr Murphy, Don Nelson, Richard Oulahan, John von Hartz
Chief Researcher: Nancy Shuker
Researchers: Starr Badger, Holly Evarts, Stuart Gannes, Helen M. Hinkle, Nancy J. Jacobsen, James B. Murphy, Kate Slate, Scot Terrell
Design Assistants: Rosi Cassano, Kaye Sherry Hirsh, Sanae Yamazaki
Editorial Assistant: Cecily Gemmell

Editorial Production
Production Editor: Douglas B. Graham
Operations Manager: Gennaro C. Esposito
Assistant Production Editor: Feliciano Madrid
Quality Control: Robert L. Young (director), James J. Cox (assistant), Michael G. Wight (associate)
Art Coordinator: Anne B. Landry
Copy Staff: Susan B. Galloway (chief), Edward B. Clarke, Eleanor Van Bellingham, Florence Keith, Celia Beattie
Picture Department: Dolores A. Littles

The navigational skills described in this book are essential in piloting a boat in inland and coastal waters. Celestial navigation—the art of establishing position in open water without the benefit of markers or soundings—is explained in another volume of this series.

The Cover: The 12-meter racing sloop *Columbia* shaves past red sea buoy #32 during a practice run on Long Island Sound. This buoy warns of a rock ledge off Stamford, Connecticut, and often doubles as a mark for racers. The buoy light guides sailors at night, and a bell serves as a locator during fog.

The Consultants: Halsey Herreshoff, the navigator for *Courageous* in her successful defense of the America's Cup in 1974, has piloted sailing craft and powerboats for 25 years.

G. James Lippmann, a naval architect, is the executive director of the American Boat and Yacht Council.

Carleton Mitchell has logged more than 50 years as a racing skipper and cruising man, under sail and power, and is the author of seven books and scores of articles on nautical matters.

William Munro, a powerboatman with over 20 years of experience, is a photographer and author of many articles for *Motorboat* magazine and other boating publications.

Correspondents: Elisabeth Kraemer (Bonn); Margot Hapgood, Dorothy Bacon (London); Susan Jonas, Lucy T. Voulgaris (New York); Maria Vincenza Aloisi, Josephine du Brusle (Paris); Ann Natanson (Rome). Valuable assistance was also provided by: Jean Walker (Miami); Carolyn T. Chubet, Miriam Hsia (New York).

Fourth printing. Revised 1978.
Published simultaneously in Canada.
Library of Congress catalogue card number 75-13778.

Contents

The Wayfinding Skills

The Wayfinding Skills

by Halsey Herreshoff

There are no highways at sea. When a boat sails out from the comforting familiarity of the harbor it moves into a wide-open, ever-changing world. Perspectives shift, distances become hard to gauge, and landmarks along the receding shoreline take on a new and often perplexing aspect. Ahead, all kinds of unseen dangers may lurk—sand bars, rocks, sunken wrecks and powerful tidal currents. To keep track of his exact location in this alien environment and to lay a safe course to his next destination, a boatman applies a basic and venerable skill: he navigates.

None of the techniques a navigator uses—especially when calculating his route along coastlines and through inland waters—are particularly mysterious or difficult to master. The navigator simply performs a kind of careful detective work. He reads the clues provided by his compass, his charts, his depth-finding equipment; he gathers evidence from the bearings of buoys and lighthouses; he pries out information from tide tables and coastal piloting guides; he picks up a hint or two from the look of the water or the feel of the wind on his cheek. Then, like a nautical Sherlock Holmes, he weighs all this information, deduces his position and plots his progress on a chart.

The particular kind of detective work a boatman uses to find his way when he is within a day's sail from shore—a process called coastal navigation, or piloting—will be set forth in the pages that follow. In mid-ocean, where there are no landmarks or buoys, another kind of pathfinding, called celestial navigation, comes into play. Here the navigator finds his own position from calculations on the positions of the sun and certain bright stars. This latter technique is described in another book in this series.

Coastal piloting can provide some of the most adventurous and satisfying moments in boating. I remember the sense of pride and pleasure I felt a few summers ago at making a tricky passage to my home port at Bristol, Rhode Island, through one of the thickest fogs I have ever been in. We had set sail right after breakfast from Block Island, about 10 miles south of the Rhode Island coast, aboard my 38-foot sloop, *Alerion.* The wind was blowing in from the southwest, strong and mist-laden, and as we nosed out past the harbor breakwater, the fog closed in. Visibility dropped to 100 feet, and *Alerion* sped onward in a puffy gray world all her own.

But even while wrapped in the dense fog blanket, we enjoyed a comforting sense of knowing exactly where we were. Before leaving the harbor, I had plotted a series of compass courses to various buoys and lighthouses along our route. Our first mark, a bell buoy some three miles to the northeast, marked a stretch of dangerous shoals and severe tide rips. A strong tidal current swept across our course, and unless I allowed for its effect, we could be set down onto the shoals. Now, as *Alerion* slid along through the fog, I checked her speed: 7.2 knots. Knowing the speed and the distance to the buoy, I could figure out the time of our arrival: just 25 minutes away.

At exactly 23 minutes from the Block Island breakwater, the muffled clank of the bell broke through the fog. A minute later the buoy itself hove into view. We were dead on course. With a flicker of pride at this initial victory, I altered course to our next compass heading, toward a lighthouse on the mainland. Again I checked the speed, worked in my estimate of the current's effect and calculated our passage time. Again we arrived at our mark, right on schedule. And so it went until, early in the afternoon, we picked up our mooring in Bristol Harbor at the end of a perfect passage.

Not all my pathfinding attempts—nor those of fellow navigators—have worked out so satisfactorily. Some years ago, as a fledgling 23-year-old lieutenant junior grade in the U.S. Navy, I served aboard a 750-ton minesweeper in the Pacific. One day I was piloting the vessel through a maze of islands and reefs in the Inland Sea of Japan. The visibility was good; nevertheless, we

Master navigator Halsey Herreshoff stands in the cockpit of the 12-meter sloop Courageous, whose courses he plotted during her successful defense of the America's Cup in 1974. Grandson of the illustrious yacht designer Nathanael Herreshoff, the author has spent some 25 years piloting sailing craft and powerboats of all sizes, and is, in addition, an accomplished naval architect.

moved ahead cautiously as the channel meandered among the natural hazards with only occasional buoys to mark the turns.

We had decided to follow the shoreline of a rocky island until it seemed safe to cut for an opening at the far end of the next big promontory. From time to time, I would glance at the chart, and compare its features with the look of the land on either side of us. Suddenly, an alarm went off in my mind. The chart and the landscape did not seem to agree. The depth finder showed the water shoaling rapidly to 27 feet, only twice the minesweeper's draft. Instead of following the channel, we were steaming headlong into a shallow bay. Through inattentiveness, I had lost my place on the chart and was heading in straight for the beach.

Frantically I signaled full power astern and counted some prickly moments until the ship lumbered to a halt. We managed to turn ourselves around and head back to the channel where we belonged, but I emerged from the episode a singularly red-faced junior lieutenant.

In all my later stints as navigator, however, I have been fortunate enough to stay out of serious trouble by being more attentive and consistent than I was that day. Basically, I try to apply a mixture of reasoned calculation and seat-of-the-pants judgments—a combination that has guided mariners for centuries. While today's boat pilot relies on some extraordinarily accurate and sophisticated tools to help him find his way, most of the fundamental concepts and practices of navigation have changed very little since the days of Columbus and Eric the Red.

The very first navigators simply used their eyes, along with a good bit of common sense. They picked out landmarks along the shore, watched where waves broke against rocks, looked for eddies and ripples that might indicate shallows, even hunted in the water's color for clues to the depth of the channel. Past sight of land, the early mariners steered by the stars or the track of the sun from east to west, or by the slant of the prevailing winds.

Some nautical pioneers used more esoteric natural aids. One of the great Viking explorers was a man named Floki Vilgjerdarsson, who discovered Iceland. On his voyages, Floki carried a cage of ravens. When he figured land was near, he opened the cage and released a bird. If it circled aimlessly, land was still far beyond the horizon. But if the raven flew off with a purpose, Floki followed it, knowing the bird would lead him to a landfall.

Lacking the inborn piloting instinct of ravens and other wild fowl—which no one has yet been able to analyze with certainty—human navigators through the centuries have come up with various man-made devices to help orient themselves. Bonfires on mountaintops lighted the seafarers of ancient Greece to harbors in the Aegean. The Egyptians, with a low silty coastline that offered few landmarks, erected a 400-foot-high lighthouse on the island of Pharos, just outside the harbor of Alexandria, in about 280 B.C. Topped by an open chamber where a log fire was kept burning, the lighthouse cast a light about 25 miles out to sea. The structure stood for more than a millennium as one of the wonders of the ancient world, beckoning sailors into port until it collapsed in the 1400s.

Besides referring to prominent markers ashore, early navigators developed a number of onboard navigating aids. The first and most basic was a tool for measuring water depth. In an Egyptian wall painting executed more than 3,500 years ago, a man stands in the prow of a river barge holding a long rod, called a sounding reed, for probing the bottom. Eventually navigators adopted the lead line—a weighted line equipped with graduated markings, and often with a bit of tallow on the end to bring up bottom samples.

By the late Middle Ages, mariners were relying on their lead lines to cross wide stretches of open water. "Ye shall go north until ye sound in 72 fathoms in fair grey sand," reads a set of 14th Century sailing directions on how to get from Spain to England. "Then go north until ye come into soundings of ooze, and then go your course east-north-east." Fourteenth Century lead lines must have been awesomely long; 72 fathoms is 432 feet.

A medieval sailor's most valuable tool, beside his lead line, was his magnetic compass. At first, mariners rigged compasses only in emergencies, when cloudy skies hid the sun or the North Star. The ship's pilot would rub an iron needle against a lodestone, a chunk of iron ore with the ability to magnetize other bits of the same metal. Then he skewered the magnetized needle through a wisp of straw and floated it in a bowl of water, where the needle would point in the general direction of north. Eventually compasses became permanent fixtures, much as they are today, with the needle swinging freely on a pivot. And by the time of Columbus, a calibrated card had been added to the compass for reading direction.

Columbus certainly used such a compass to find his way to America in 1492. He also carried a rough chart, drawn on sheepskin, on which he marked each day's passage across the ocean. His principal method for determining his position was a basic piloting technique called dead (short for deduced) reckoning. By referring to his compass to get his heading, and by measuring his speed and the time sailed, Columbus could calculate his position—at least theoretically—at any given moment.

But the Admiral badly misjudged his progress. His principal timing device was a sandglass, which the helmsman turned every half hour, and his sole method for judging speed was to watch bubbles or patches of seaweed flowing past his hull. Relying on this system, when Columbus reached the West Indies he figured he had sailed 3,466 miles; he thus overestimated the true distance by about 9 per cent.

Dead reckoning became a lot more precise a century later when English navigators came up with the first oceangoing speedometer. The device, called a chip log, consisted of a light towline with a pie-shaped sliver of wood on one end to act as a drag in the water. The line was knotted at regular intervals. Stationed in the stern, the navigator would toss the chip log overboard and let its line pay out astern. As the log hit the water he would set up a 30-second glass and count the knots that slipped through his fingers while the sands ran out. He could then convert his knot count into the ship's hourly speed. And though the chip log has long since disappeared from the navigator's arsenal, the term "knots" survives as the proper designation of a ship's pace measured in nautical miles per hour.

Even with a fairly workable speed gauge, however, the pilots of the old sailing ships often had trouble telling exactly where they were. Unseen currents could carry a ship hundreds of leagues off course, with no one the wiser. Compass needles, too, showed an uncomfortable habit of wandering. So navigators in the past, like sailors today, would try to confirm their dead-reckoned positions by other means. Near shore, they would take sights and make fixes on landmarks and buoys. On the high seas and in unmarked, uncharted areas, they used the techniques of celestial navigation.

As more and more ships sailed out to the far reaches of the earth, the tools and techniques of navigation were sharpened and refined. By the end of the 18th Century, a reliable ship's chronometer had replaced the sandglass. The deviations and variations in readings of compasses were carefully worked out and tabulated. Map makers drew up charts with ever greater precision, defining water depths, land features and compass directions. Each reef and promontory was given its known position on the earth's surface.

The most celebrated contributor to these advances in the art of navigation was an 18th Century British sea captain named James Cook, who mapped out vast stretches of the South Pacific, and also piloted the first ship to go south of the Antarctic Circle. Unlike most seafarers of his day, Cook was a scientist and an accomplished land surveyor. In 1768, the Royal Society sent him to Tahiti, with orders then to sail west in search of a huge continent that many geographers felt lay undiscovered in the Southern Ocean. Cook paused in Tahiti to take some astronomical observations. Then he sailed on to New Zealand and finally reached Australia—the missing continent.

Wherever he made a landfall, Cook surveyed and mapped the coastline.

His maps were not the imprecise and often wildly imaginative sketches set down by most explorers before him, but were charts of painstaking exactness with each detail clearly marked and meticulously positioned. In fact, his chart data was so reliable that some of it was still being used by the British Admiralty during World War II.

Since Cook's time, the only real change in the navigator's techniques has come from the use of electronic devices. Today, besides his charts and compass, a boatman can outfit his craft with electronic depth finders, radar sets to warn of any hazards unseen in storm and fog, and very elaborate radio equipment that can establish his position within a few yards on almost any well-traveled waterway on earth.

The ultimate in modern piloting gear—and certainly the fanciest equipment I have ever used—was lodged in the navigator's station aboard the 12-meter *Courageous,* winner of the 1974 America's Cup. Precise piloting is essential in a 12-meter race, for a skipper's tactical decisions depend on an absolute knowledge of his boat's position at every moment. As navigator on *Courageous,* it was my job to keep tabs on our position and compare it with that of the competing boat.

At the heart of *Courageous'* navigational setup was a digital computer, which analyzed every movement the boat made and predicted how the craft would behave on any heading in any wind condition. Readings from the various instruments aboard—wind gauge, speedometer, compass, heel-angle meter—were fed into the computer at the rate of four times a second. I would fix our starting position and our destination, and punch this information into the computer; the computer would do some quick calculations to disgorge our position. Also, it would help us decide, as we tacked upwind, the exact moment to change course and head for the mark. This last ability is what put us over the finish line first in the key race of the Cup trials against *Intrepid,* to determine which boat would defend the Cup against the Australian challenger. Each of us had won four races; this was the final one.

On the day of the race, a blustery wind blew in from the northeast, bringing with it a thin fog that cut visibility to about a mile. *Intrepid* nosed by us at the start and strode ahead toward the first mark on the course, 4.5 miles to windward. We were close on her tail, moving smartly, but we seemed unable to close the gap. Our main hope was that a piloting lapse would occur aboard *Intrepid.* And that is precisely what happened.

I was keeping a dead-reckoning plot on the chart, and knew that any moment we should come about if we were to arrive precisely on the mark with no distance or time wasted. Unsure in the poor visibility of exactly when to make our move, I punched the computer button for a readout. The computer's reply, couched in mathematical terms, was unmistakable: "Go now." We did—a critical 15 seconds before *Intrepid* made her move. We shaved past the mark in first place, and the race was ours.

Helping to guide *Courageous* to first place in those trials—and to ultimate victory in the America's Cup—provided the high point of my career so far as a navigator. But the satisfactions of everyday piloting can be just as rich: threading an intricate course along a winding channel, fetching a difficult mark in a pea-soup fog, or confirming a position from a set of quick, deft fixes. And on an ordinary cruise no elaborate computerized gear is needed.

Any competent navigator can plot his course with the use of only a few basic tools: compass, depth finder, speedometer or log, a good set of charts, a sharp pencil, a set of parallel rules, a pair of dividers to tick off distances, and a firm surface on which to work. Most important of all is to develop careful, common-sense procedures when putting the tools to work. A good navigator practices whenever he takes out his boat. He gets into the habit, even on easy trips when the weather is fair and the waters familiar, of plotting his course, timing his run, reading his depth finder and checking his position by taking the appropriate fixes. Then, when night falls or when the fog rolls in, he will have the skills and tools to find his way with purpose and conviction.

Soquel Cr.
Capitola
Aptos
Valencia Cr.
Aptos Cr.
Rio Del Mar
Seacliff Beach
SOQUEL COVE
Twin Lakes
Granary Tr
S.P.R.R.
R TRS (KSCO) 1080 kHz
Occ G 6M
HORN
Harbor
Soquel Pt
10 ft Rep (1971)
BW "SC" WHISTLE Mo (A)
NAVAL OPERATING AREA

1 The nautical chart is an essential tool for any boatman, whether he is setting off for new waters or cruising along a familiar coastline whose piloting pitfalls may be too numerous to keep in mind. With a chart, no helmsman need ever encounter the unexpected. The crew of the yawl at left—superimposed against a chart of California's Monterey Bay—might come to this coastal indentation as complete strangers to the area. But using the chart and referring to its numbers and symbols, they would know as they neared land that water depth here decreases from an average of 11 fathoms to two or less, and that the bottom near shore is alternately covered with rocks and anchor-snagging kelp. To orient themselves

THE INDISPENSABLE CHART

as they steered toward a desired anchorage, they could establish their position by taking compass bearings *(page 98)* on the mouth of Soquel Creek and on the pier at Seacliff Beach. In short, the chart could tell these seamen where they were, where to sail, and where not to sail.

Such vital information is available through charts meticulously prepared by government agencies *(page 172)* for all boating areas in the United States. A skipper plying an eight-mile stretch along the Virginia shore of Chesapeake Bay from Cape Henry to Little Creek, for example, has immediate access to more than 500 bits of highly significant data. He can pinpoint water depths ranging from a comfortable 40 feet to a potentially disastrous two. He can see the exact location of a well-dredged channel, with safe lanes for threading through bridge supports. He will note a half dozen sunken wrecks, plus scores of other submerged obstacles—even the site of an unexploded depth charge. Obviously, this area poses some challenging piloting problems. Yet a boatman who properly uses a chart in conjunction with such other navigation aids as buoys and beacons *(pages 46-73)* can safely negotiate this or any other patch of water, even at night or in a fog.

Learning to read a chart is a simple process. Many of the symbols used are self-explanatory, and the government's charts include extensive descriptive material. With a little study, a boat handler can become familiar with the other symbols that locate and identify every conceivable relevant object, from underwater fish traps to a church spire on shore.

Hundreds of new, or revised, charts are published each year, and well over a million are sold annually to recreational boatmen. But even though a chart may be absolutely accurate at the time that it is published and sold, the sea bottom and shorelines are constantly changing—through wave action, wrecks and the sweep of tidal currents. A boatman should always keep his navigation nook stocked with the most recent charts; thus he avoids such dangers as ramming the hulk of an oil tanker recently sunk or running aground in a channel that shoaled in after his obsolete chart was updated.

However, since the waters move more quickly than government cartographers, the boatman should also consult a weekly government publication called *Notice to Mariners,* which announces recent discoveries affecting navigational safety and can be used to supplement and correct chart information between publications. Two other vital publications for chart users are the *Coast Pilot,* which gives detailed sailing directions for various areas, and a pamphlet called, curiously enough, *Chart No. 1,* which catalogues every chart symbol used by United States mariners.

While maneuvering his craft, of course, a skipper cannot keep his eyes glued to a chart. Experienced boatmen always study a chart of the cruising area before leaving the dock, rechecking as needed during the trip. Avid mariners even find considerable enjoyment in reading their charts at home, constantly discovering new facts about the waters they navigate.

By referring to a nautical chart like that in the background at left, crewmen on the yawl could easily pick out navigation aids and hazards as they sail along the California coast.

A Revealing Perspective

A chart gives a sea-level mariner a revealing overhead perspective of the nautical landscape along a given stretch of navigable water. The dominant element tends to be the coastline of any land mass in the area. These coastlines, along with features such as reefs, are rendered with painstaking accuracy, as can be seen by comparing the chart opposite with the photograph of the same region at right.

The photograph depicts parts of two small islands in the Virgin group, a popular cruising ground for Caribbean boatmen. The chart reproduces their coastlines, detailing each bend, point and notch of the islands' coves and promontories. Offshore, the chart portrays rock formations, the surrounding shallows and navigable deep water, with a record of water depths in feet at significant points.

The chart maker's art, interpreting waterway characteristics by means of overhead perspective, also conveys a wealth of other detailed information (shown on the following pages) on shorelines and sea bottom—information that a helmsman must have to navigate safely.

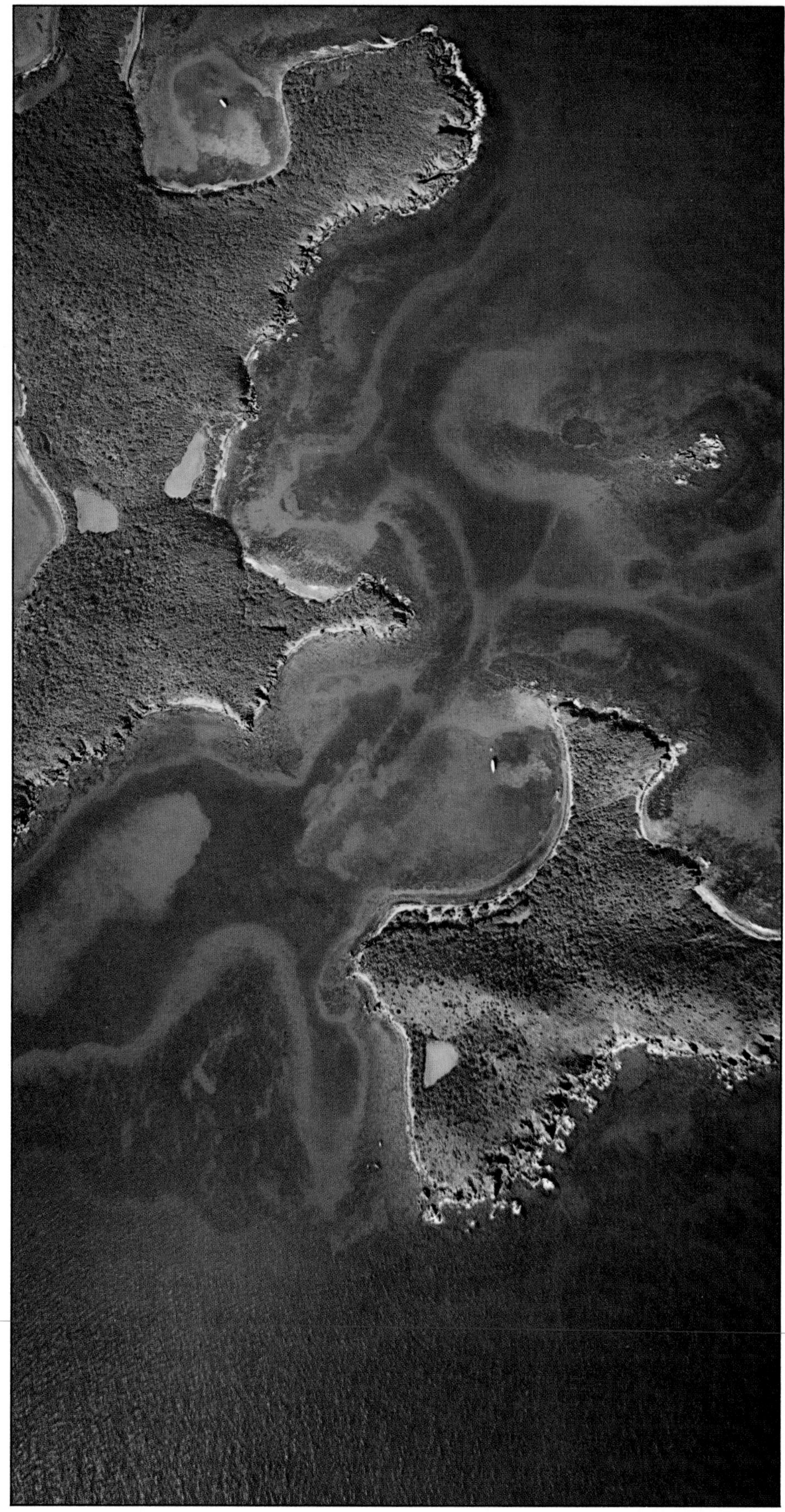

The aerial photograph at right, taken at 6,000 feet, was used by cartographers to chart a section of Great and Little St. James, Virgin Islands. Ragged lines of cliffs, defined by breakers, alternate with smooth beaches along the coastlines. A profusion of rocks, particularly off the southern shore of the smaller island, poses navigational hazards. The two white specks in the coves at the top and center of the picture are anchored boats.

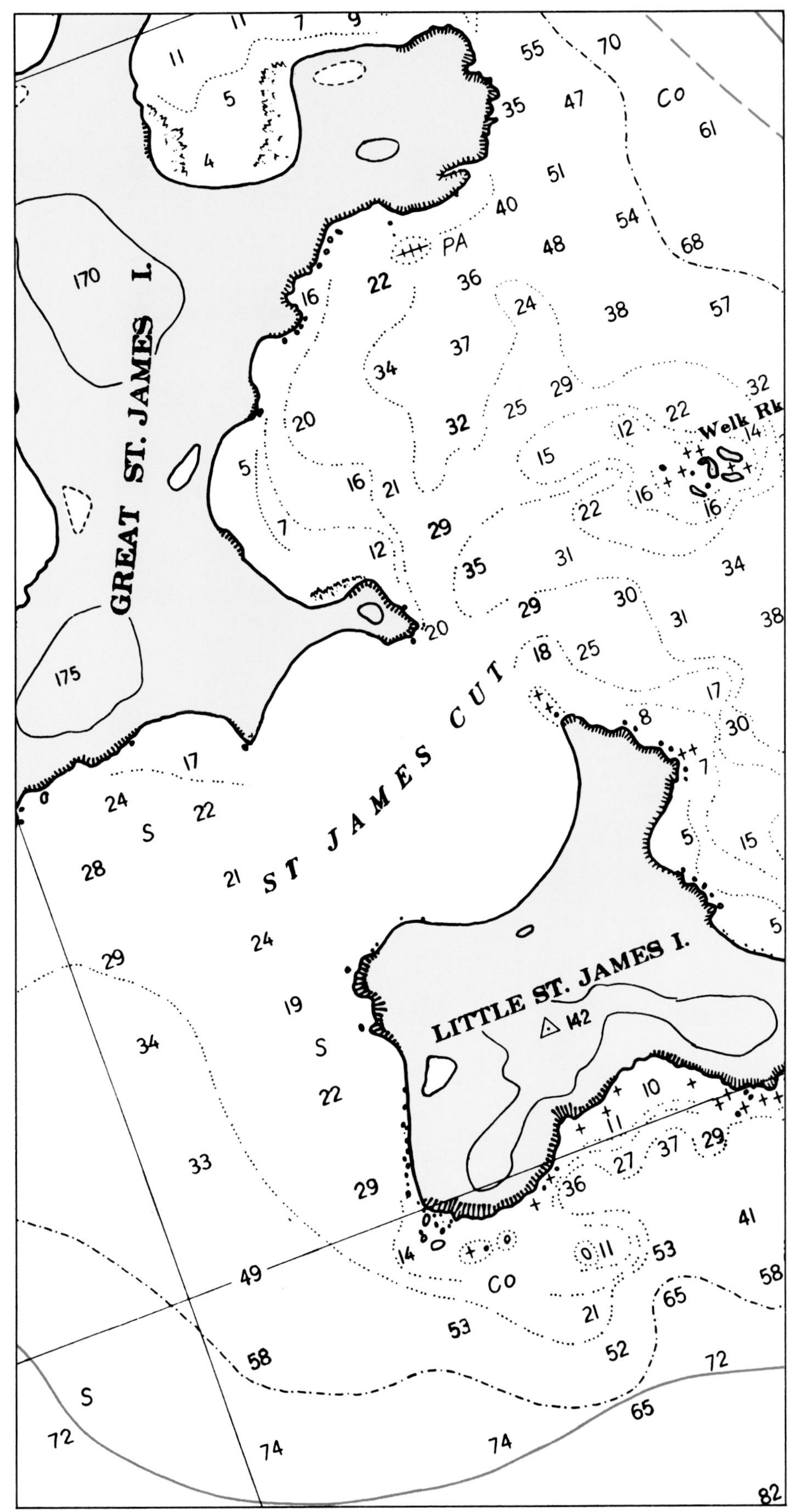

This chart of Great and Little St. James islands duplicates all of the coastal characteristics depicted in the aerial photograph opposite, and includes water depths for the entire area. Hatch marks along the shore indicate bluffs, and the chart points out small but dangerous rocks only a few yards from the beach. Wherever possible—as with Welk Rocks to the east of the islands—the cartographers have even drawn the true shapes of the rocks, though they are 25 yards or less in length.

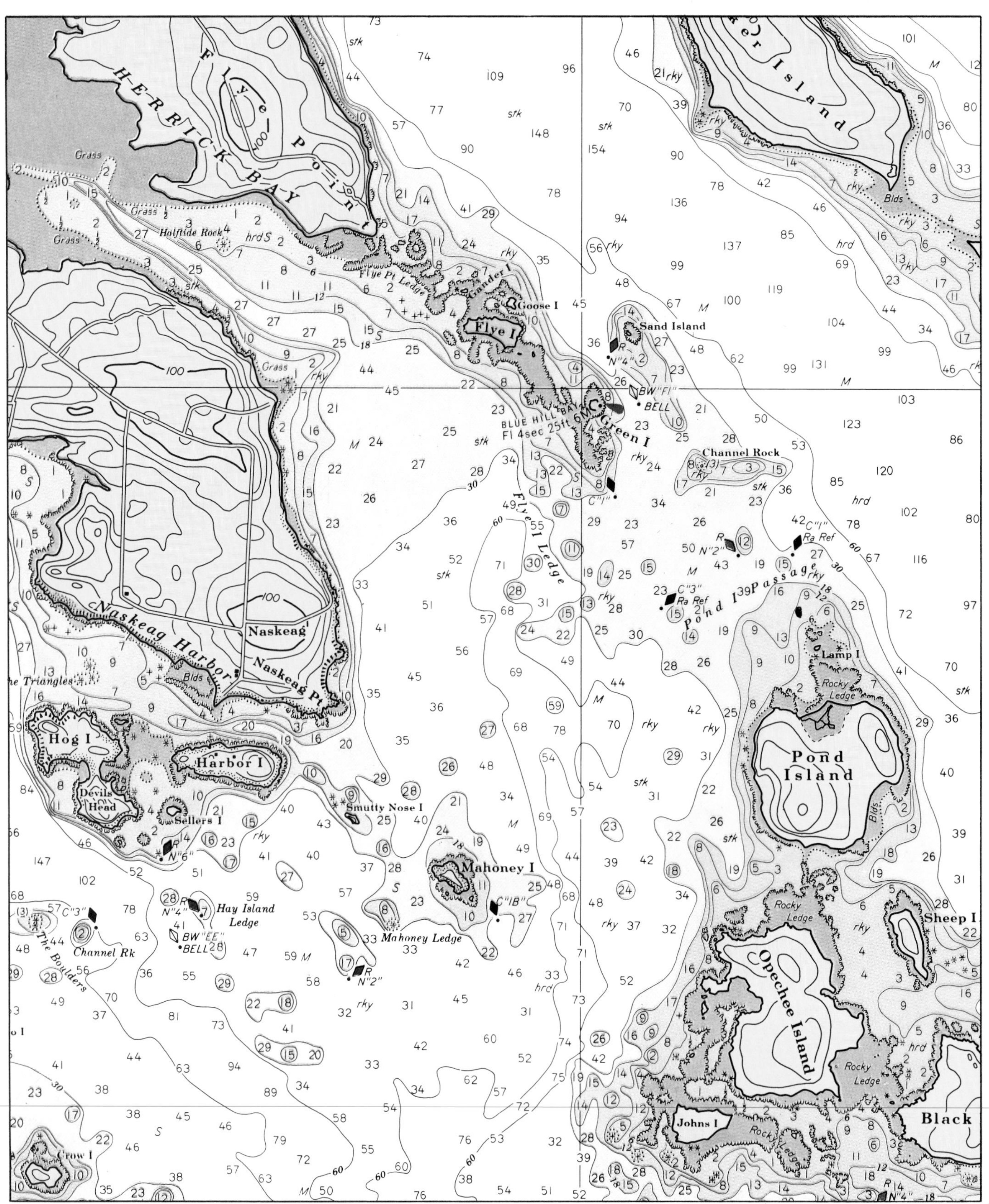

Colors, numbers and contour lines on this chart of a tricky sailing area off the coast of Maine provide an instant key to water depth. All water less than 18 feet deep at low tide is shown here in dark blue, depths from 18 to 30 feet in light blue, and depths over 30 feet in white. Within the tinted areas, contour lines at prescribed intervals help define the depth differences. Each contour line is labeled in italics to show its depth, as can be seen by 12-, 18-, 30- and 60-foot notations on the contour lines just north of Pond Island. Frequent soundings, noted here in feet, give depth readings at mean low water.

The Underwater Terrain

The most vital service a chart performs is to describe the territory beneath the skipper's hull. Using a combination of numbers, color codes, underwater contour lines and a system of abbreviations and symbols, the chart tells a pilot all he needs to know about an area's undersea topography, including where he can safely venture and the sections he should avoid.

Most of the numbers on the chart represent measurements of the water's depth at mean low tide, taken at the spot by a hydrographic vessel. These soundings may be either in feet or in fathoms (a fathom equals six feet); the chart's legend will indicate which unit is used. Contour lines, which connect points of roughly equal depth, profile the bottom's shape; the lines are either numbered *(chart, opposite)* or coded *(chart, below)* according to depth. Color shadings also indicate depth, with the shallowest areas in the darkest tint. Rocks and reefs, and various other characteristics of the bottom, are marked by either standardized symbols or abbreviations, as described at right.

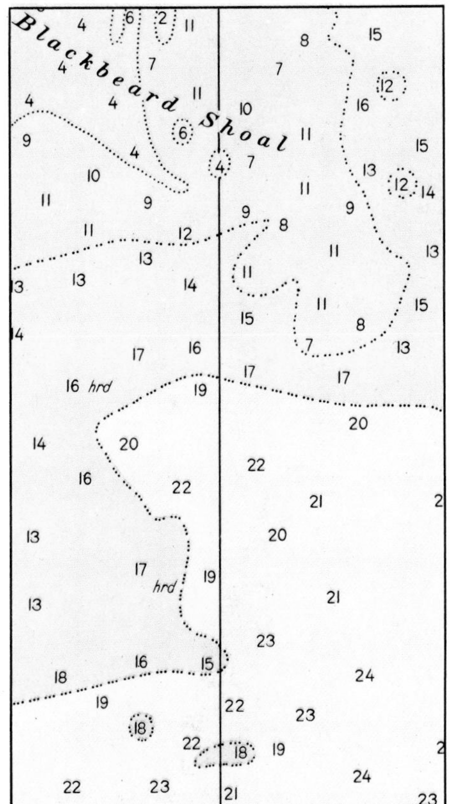

On some charts, as in this excerpt showing Blackbeard Shoal off the Georgia coast, the depth of each contour line is indicated by a system of dots. And even though the individual soundings are in feet, the dots refer to fathoms. Thus lines of single dots enclose areas of one fathom (six feet) or less, while lines of double and triple dots indicate depths of two and three fathoms respectively.

Wrecks, Rocks, Reefs

Cartographers choose from a selection of stylized notations, like the ones shown below, to indicate underwater hazards. A sunken wreck, for example, may be shown either by a symbol or by an abbreviation plus a number that gives the wreck's depth. A dotted line around any symbol calls special attention to its hazardous nature. Since slightly different symbols often indicate the same hazard, the boatman should consult the complete list in the pamphlet entitled *Chart No. 1*, published by the National Ocean Survey and available at both the NOS distribution office *(page 172)* and most marine-supply outlets.

Symbol	Meaning	Symbol	Meaning
5½ Wk; 21 Wk	Sunken wrecks (abbreviation: Wk); a number indicates precise depth in feet at mean low water.	Uncov 2 ft; (2); Uncov 2 ft; (2)	Rocks that are covered at high tide and uncovered at low; height is given in feet above mean low water. Parentheses enclose uncovered height.
	A partly submerged wreck, showing part of its superstructure or hull at mean low water.		Rocks awash at low water.
			Rocks awash at low water.
5 Rk	Sunken rocks (abbreviation: Rk); a number indicates the precise depth at mean low water.	(25)	A rock never covered by water, with height above mean high water.
		Coral; Co; Co; Co	Coral reefs located offshore that are uncovered at mean low water.
Co 3; reef line; rky	Submerged reefs (abbreviations "Co" and "rky" indicate coral and rocky); a number gives the precise depth at mean low water.	Foul	An area fouled by wreckage, rocks or coral.

Bottom Quality

A system of cartographer's abbreviations, used alone or in combination, describes the composition of the bottom, allowing a skipper to pick the best holding ground for his anchor. He should look for hard sand (hrd S), for example, to hold him securely, trying to avoid a rocky (rky) or weed-choked (Wd) bottom that could snag his anchor or allow it to drag.

S	sand	*sft*	soft
M	mud	*hrd*	hard
G	gravel	*stk*	sticky
Sh	shells	*rky*	rocky
Wd	seaweed	*gy*	gray
Grs	grass	*br*	brown

Clear Warnings of Shoal Waters

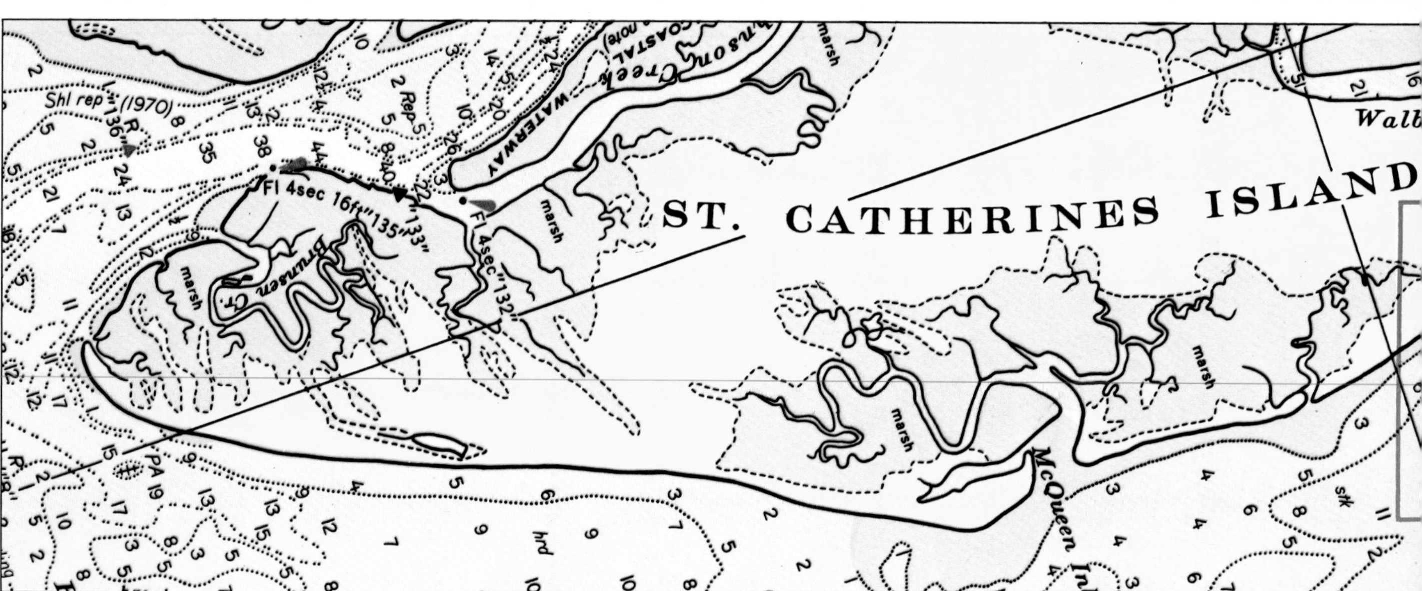

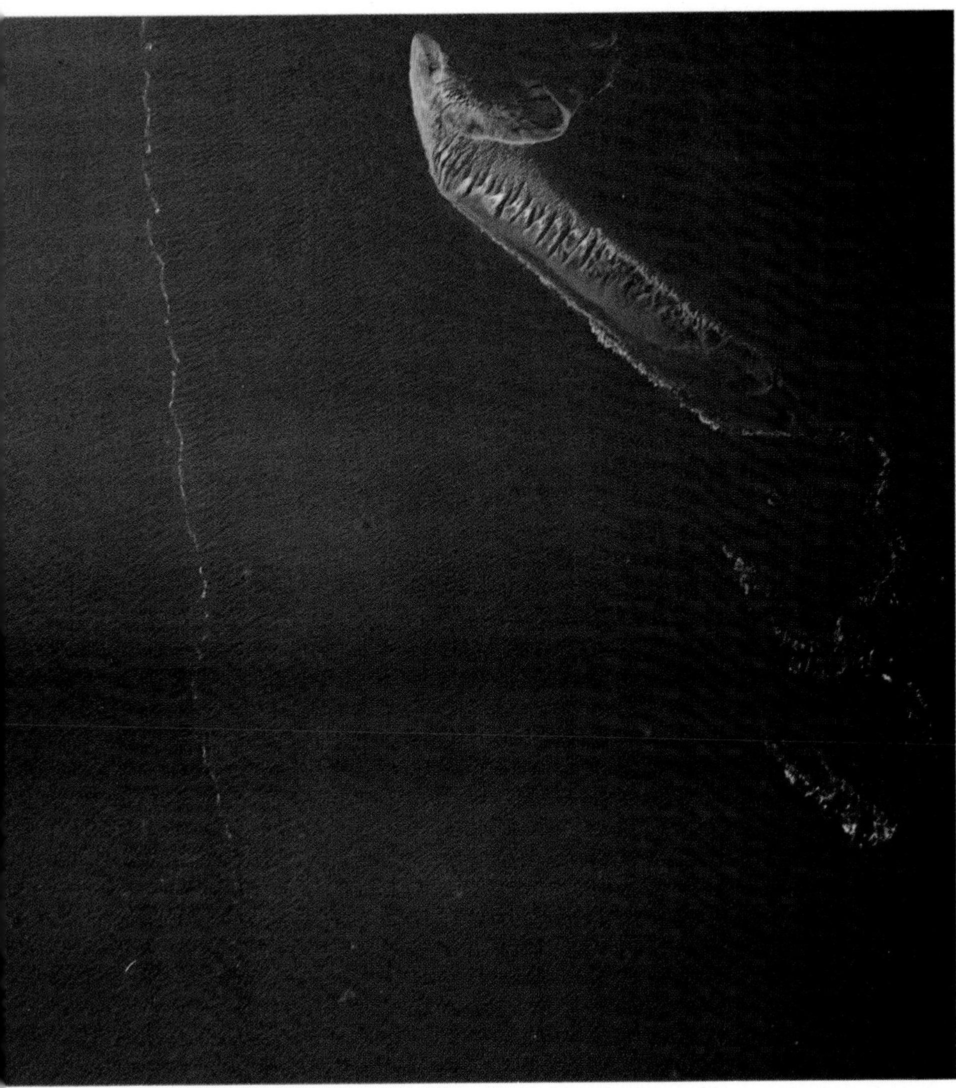

At the inlet to St. Catherines Sound, Georgia, shifting sand bars—which are seen in this aerial photograph as pale slashes—flank the channel and create a constant threat to navigation. But the color codes and symbols on the chart below (marked off with a blue rectangle corresponding to the area covered in the photo) give pilots clear warning of the hazards. The sand bars show up as green areas enclosed by dotted lines, indicating they are uncovered at low tide. Breakers are labeled; hard bottom is indicated by the abbreviation "hrd." "Middle Ground" is the name of a shoal just inside the inlet.

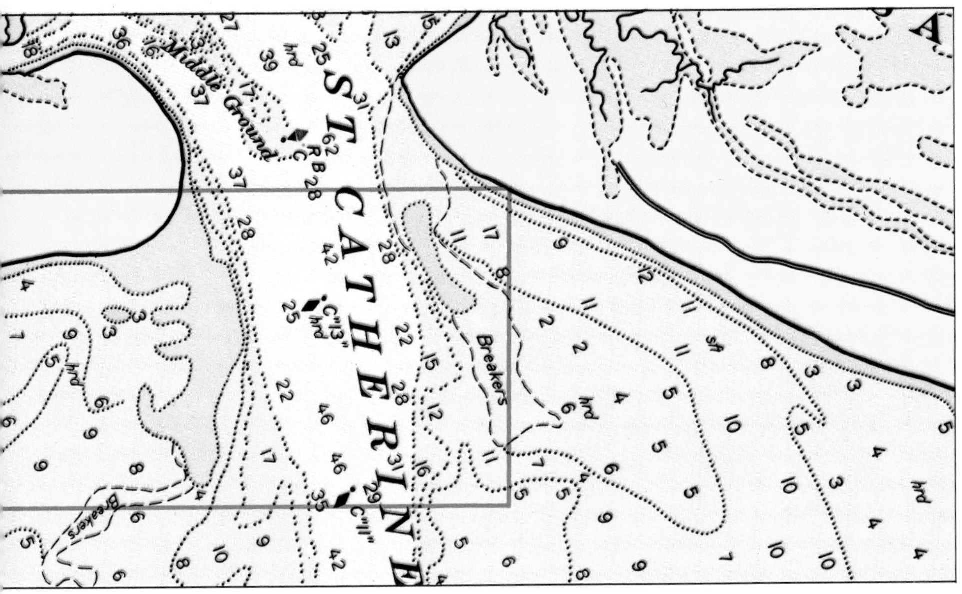

A Key to Prominent Checkpoints

To pinpoint the location of high, man-made landmarks such as water towers, smokestacks, flagpoles and radio beacons, cartographers use the standard symbol of a dot surrounded by a circle. A notation next to the symbol defines the landmark's precise nature—whether, for example, it is a large domed roof or small cupola—as explained in the table of selected landmarks below. If the dot is omitted, the notation will be given in lower-case type—indicating that the landmark's position is approximate.

⊙ CHY	The chimney of a building; the building is not charted, because the more visible chimney gives a navigator a better bearing.	⊙ GAB	A prominent gable on the roof of a building, providing a more precise bearing than would the building as a whole.	⊙ TR	A tower that is part of a larger building.
⊙ STACK	A tall industrial smokestack.	⊙ FP	A free-standing flagpole.	⊙ R TR	A radio tower—either a tall pole or a tall scaffolded structure for elevating radio antennas.
⊙ S'PIPE	A standpipe or a tall cylindrical structure, such as a water tower, whose height is greater than its diameter.	⊙ FS	A flagstaff attached to a building.	⊙ R MAST	A radio mast—a relatively short pole or scaffolded structure for elevating radio antennas.
⊙ TANK	A water tank that is elevated above the ground by means of a tall skeletal framework.	⊙ DOME	The dome of a building. If the building is well known, its name may appear in parentheses; e.g., DOME (STATE HOUSE).	⊙ LORAN TR	A loran tower—a tall, slender structure, braced with guy wires, for elevating loran antennas.
⊙ MON	A monument, such as an obelisk or statue.	⊙ CUP	A cupola—a small dome-shaped turret atop a building.	⊙ TELEM ANT	The large dish-shaped antenna—known as a telemetry antenna—of a missile tracking station.

Structures Drawn to Scale

For low-lying structures such as piers, ramps and bridges—and also for buildings and towns—cartographers have developed shorthand representations such as the ones shown here. Thus, various rectangular or triangular shapes may indicate streets with houses along them; old military forts are shown by an outline of their ramparts. Such symbols are drawn to scale, and depict the landmarks as viewed from overhead. Like all landmark symbols used on nautical charts, these are listed in Chart No. 1.

A grid of streets representing a city or town.	A dam. The tooth-edged line represents the dam structure; the lines below, the runoff.	A water-front ramp; broken lines indicate the portion submerged at mean low tide.
Groups of adjoining buildings; large rectangles are usually shaded, small ones blank.	A military fort.	A pair of jetties; broken lines mark the extent of their underwater foundations.
Individual buildings. Larger symbols are shaded, small ones filled in or left blank.	Short parallel docks projecting out into the water from a curved bulkhead.	A long single pier projecting into the water.

A bascule drawbridge, whose sections swing up like the gates at a railroad crossing.	A swinging drawbridge. The center section turns upon a central pier.

Symbols for Landmarks

Besides a knowledge of the underwater terrain, the mariner needs a clear representation of the coastal landscape; the chart provides it. Coastlines are depicted at both high tide and low, inland topography is defined, and any landmark that might help a navigator fix his position is noted and labeled.

Some of the drafting techniques used to portray the shape and character of coastal areas are shown at right. Contour lines or hatch marks designate slopes and cliffs. Dots or speckles along the shoreline indicate a sandy or boulder-strewn beach. And green tints denote areas that are uncovered when the tide goes out.

A variety of dots, circles and other symbols *(opposite)* give the locations of prominent landmarks. And on some charts —most notably those for foreign waters —churches, temples and mosques merit their own symbols. Samples are shown below, along with stylized drawings of the buildings themselves.

Ecumenical Signposts

Spires make handy landmarks. On United States charts, they are shown merely by a circle. But for foreign waters, chart makers distinguish between religions with the special symbols at left below (the drawings at right are supplied here for convenient identification).

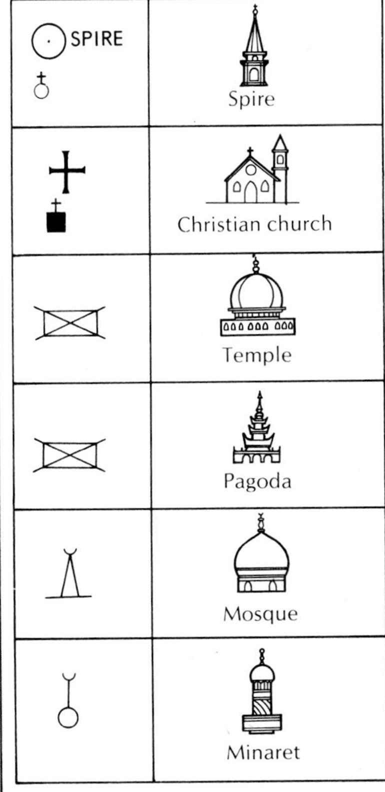

The Look of the Coast

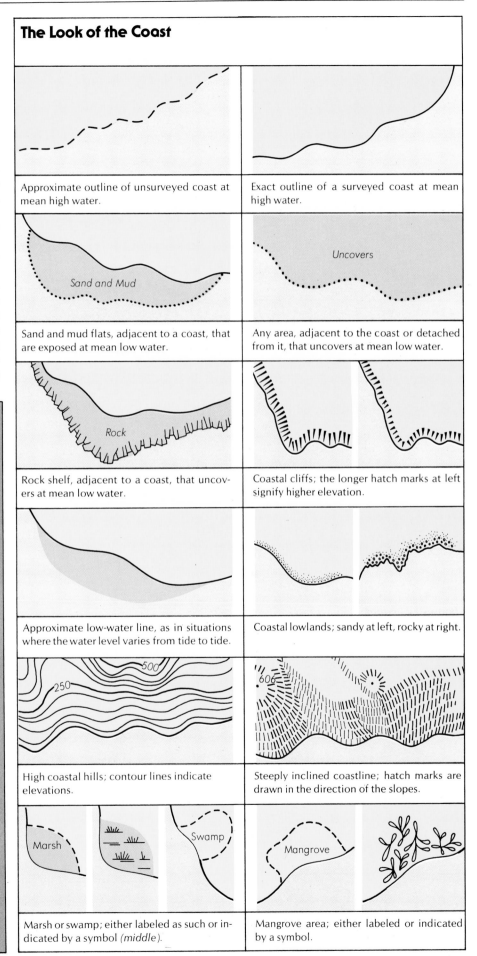

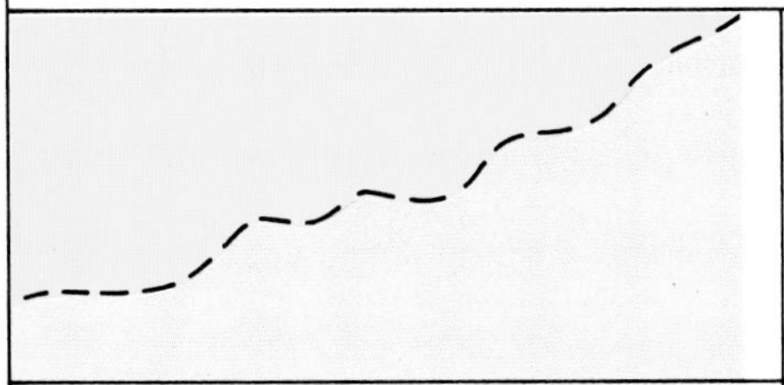

Approximate outline of unsurveyed coast at mean high water.

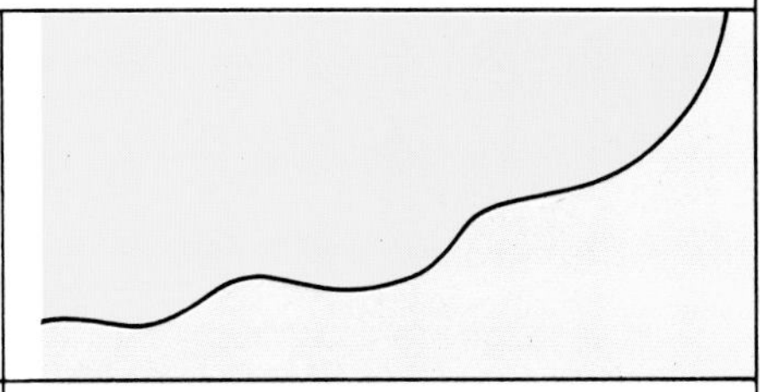

Exact outline of a surveyed coast at mean high water.

Sand and Mud

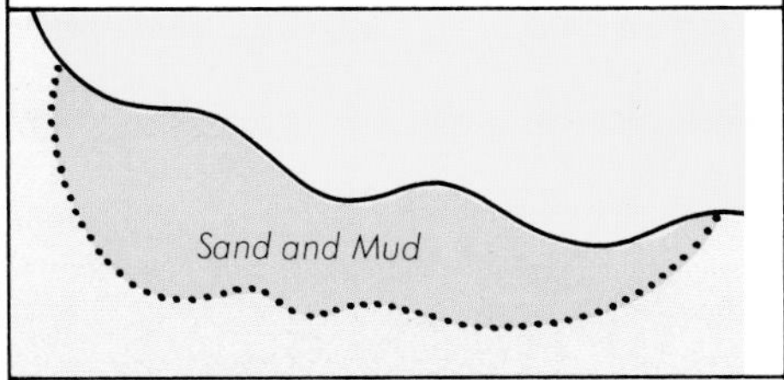

Sand and mud flats, adjacent to a coast, that are exposed at mean low water.

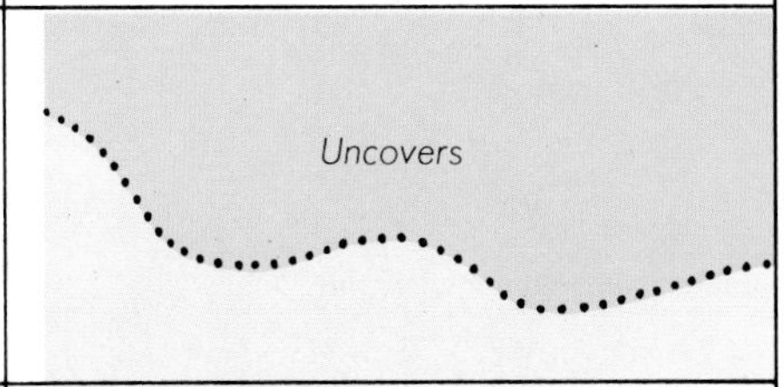

Uncovers

Any area, adjacent to the coast or detached from it, that uncovers at mean low water.

Rock

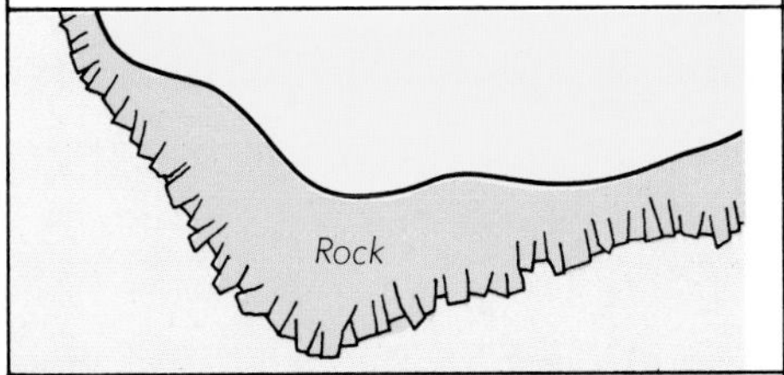

Rock shelf, adjacent to a coast, that uncovers at mean low water.

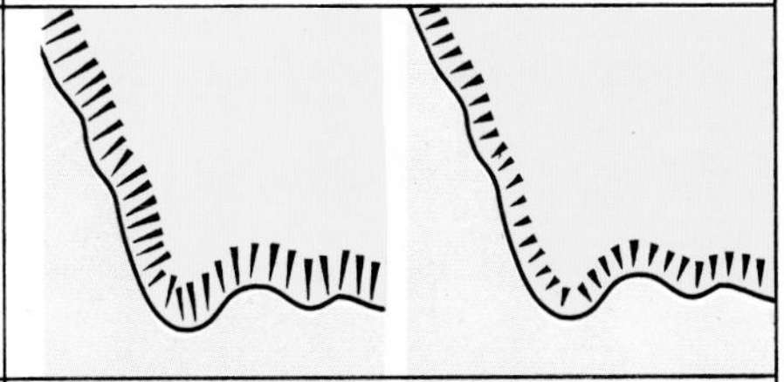

Coastal cliffs; the longer hatch marks at left signify higher elevation.

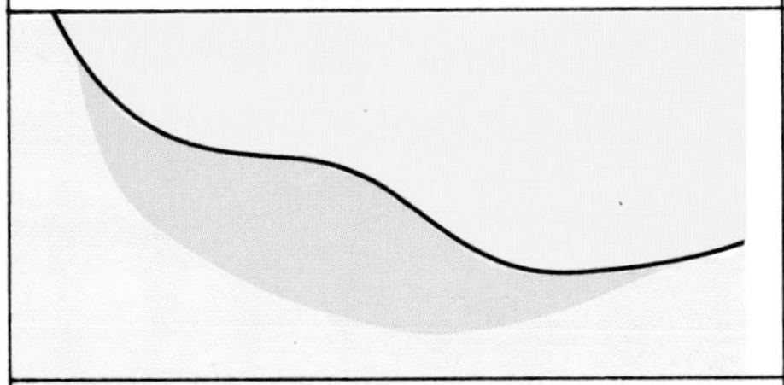

Approximate low-water line, as in situations where the water level varies from tide to tide.

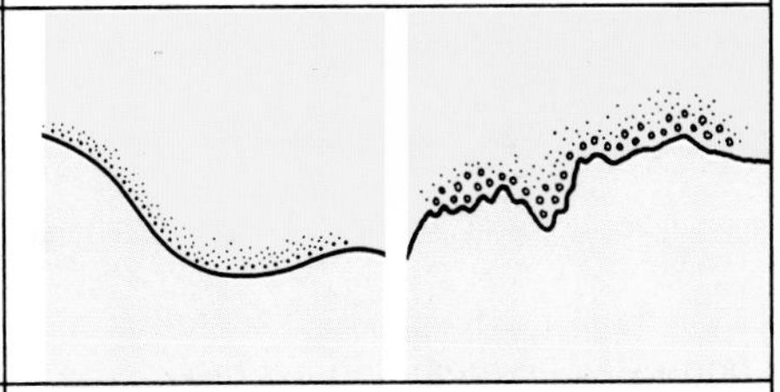

Coastal lowlands; sandy at left, rocky at right.

500 250

High coastal hills; contour lines indicate elevations.

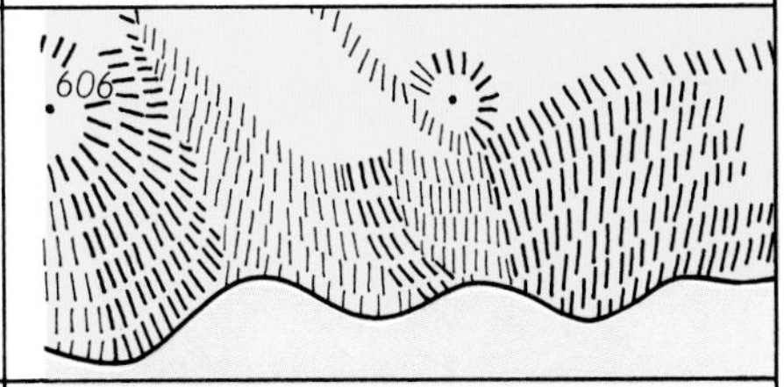

606

Steeply inclined coastline; hatch marks are drawn in the direction of the slopes.

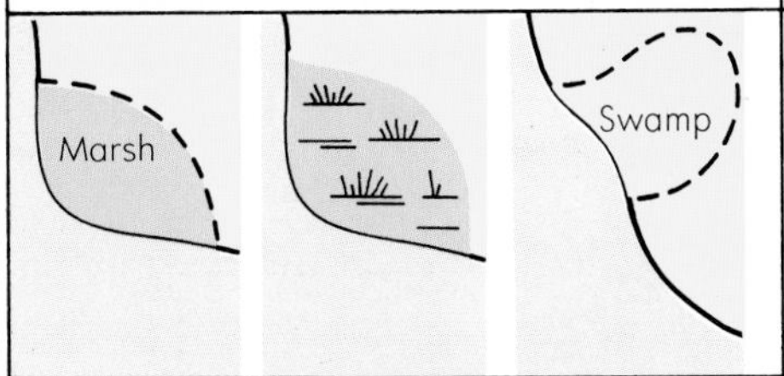

Marsh Swamp

Marsh or swamp; either labeled as such or indicated by a symbol *(middle)*.

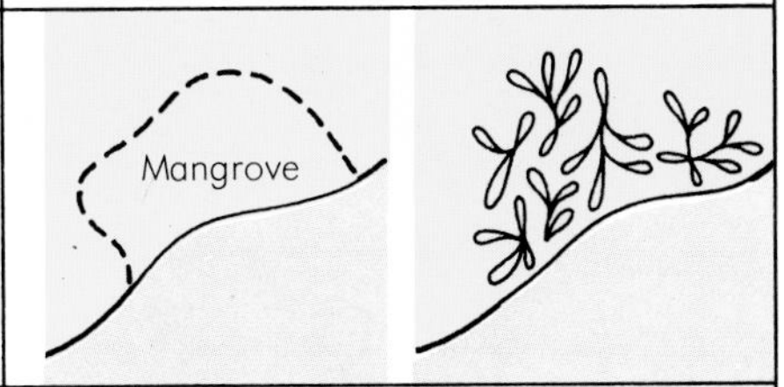

Mangrove

Mangrove area; either labeled or indicated by a symbol.

A Mariner's Match-up

Matching chart symbols to landmarks, a boatman traveling past Santa Cruz Harbor in Monterey Bay, California, can find his position by identifying prominent man-made features on shore. The large letters on the photograph above identify: (A) an 800-yard-long pier, (B) a conspicuous domed structure, (C) a stretch of buildings, and (D) the mouth of a small boat harbor. All four are reproduced (with duplicate letters for easy recognition) on the chart in stylized symbols: a long yellow ramp for the pier, a circle and dot for the dome, a grid for the buildings, and two broken lines for the harbor channel.

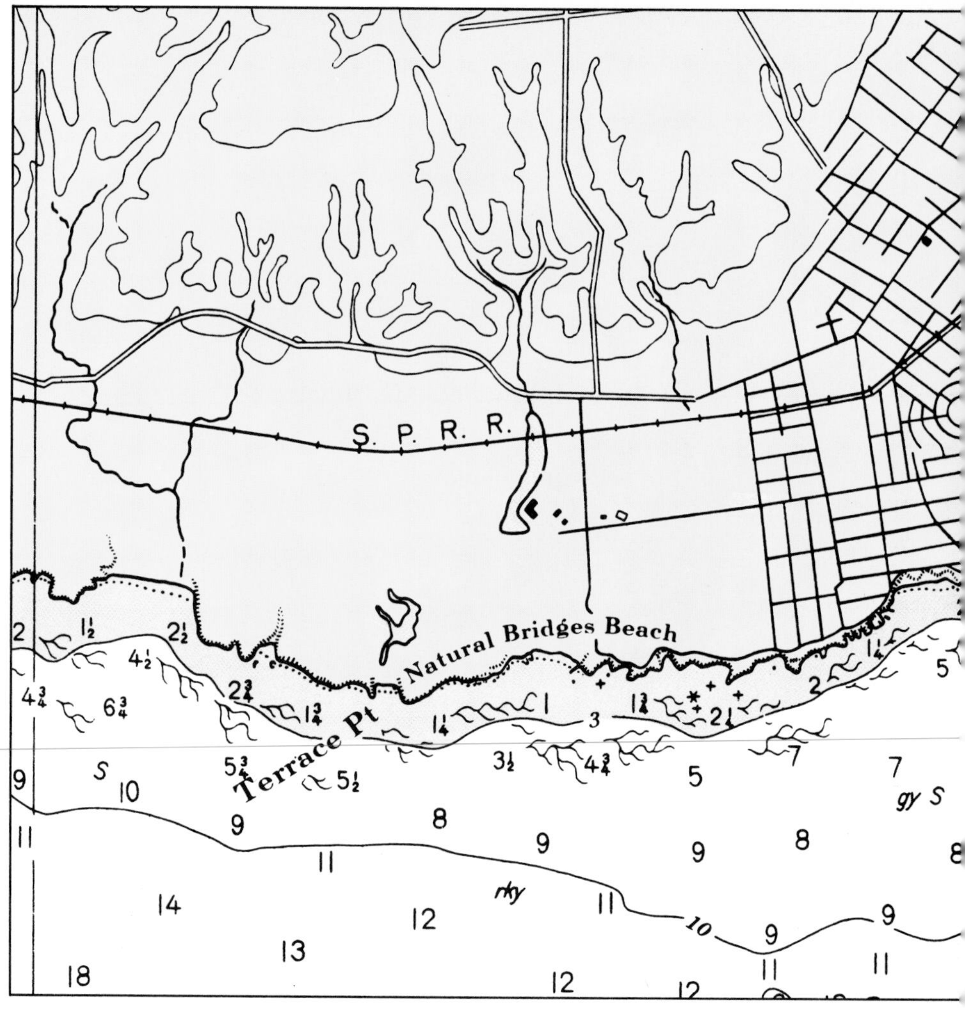

Ca
S. P. R. R.
Granary Tr
Twin Lakes
Seabright
DOME
B
C
Occ G 6M
3¾ HORN
D
(use inset)
Black Pt
R TRS
(KSCO) 1080 kHz
rky
Santa Cruz Harbor
HORN (Apr 15 to Nov 1)
A
Priv 5½ maintd
Fl 5sec
60ft 13M
USE INLAND RULES OF THE ROAD
10 ft Rep (1971)
Soquel Pt
hrd gy S
Pt Santa Cruz
gy S
rky
BW"SC"
WHISTLE
Mo (A)
hrd S

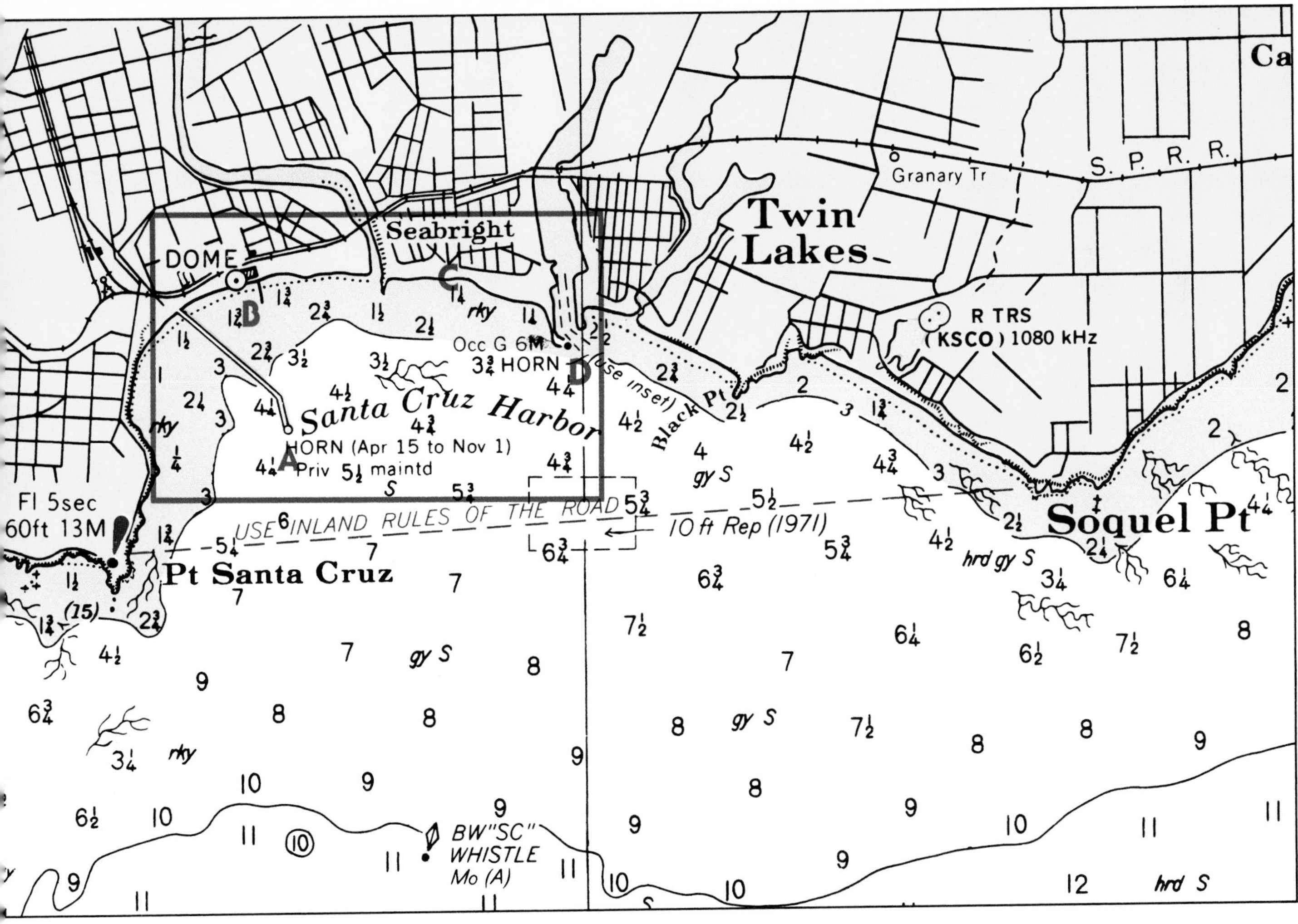

The Prime Locators

A typical nautical chart has built into it a brilliantly simple system for telling a boatman exactly where he is, and the direction and distance from any one place on the chart to any other. The principal element of this master key is a grid *(right)* superimposed over a chart's geographic forms. The grid's horizontal lines run in an east-west direction, and are parallels of latitude; the vertical lines, running north-south, are meridians of longitude. In this system, any location or position can be described or fixed in terms of the point where a parallel and a meridian intersect.

All major parallels and meridians are coded by degrees, counting upward from zero. The zero parallel, or base line of latitude, is the equator. From there, the parallels march north and south in progression until they reach 90° at the poles. The longitude base line, called the prime meridian, passes through Greenwich, England. This site was chosen in 1884 by an international conference of astronomers, largely owing to Britain's status as a maritime power—and because the Greenwich Observatory was the scene of extensive navigational research. From 0° along the prime meridian, longitude is reckoned east and west halfway around the world to a maximum of 180°, where the meridian runs through the Pacific Ocean.

As the chart excerpt on the opposite page shows, each degree is subdivisible into 60 units called minutes, with each minute representing one nautical mile, or about 2,000 yards. And each minute further subdivides into 60 seconds, or multiples thereof.

The basic reference point for calculating nautical directions is north; but a navigator has to contend with two "norths." One is true north, that is, the chart direction to the North Pole—where, on a globe, the meridians converge. The other is magnetic north, the place to which, basically, all compass needles point. These two locations are some distance apart *(globe, right)*; in making calculations, navigators must compensate for the variation.

The grid of latitude and longitude lines that overlays every chart enables a mariner to pinpoint any location on it. Longitude is reckoned by degrees east (E) or west (W) of the prime meridian, which runs through Greenwich, England, and latitude is indicated as north (N) or south (S) of the equator. Thus, the coordinates 20°W 20°N mark a spot just off Africa's west coast (blue dot).

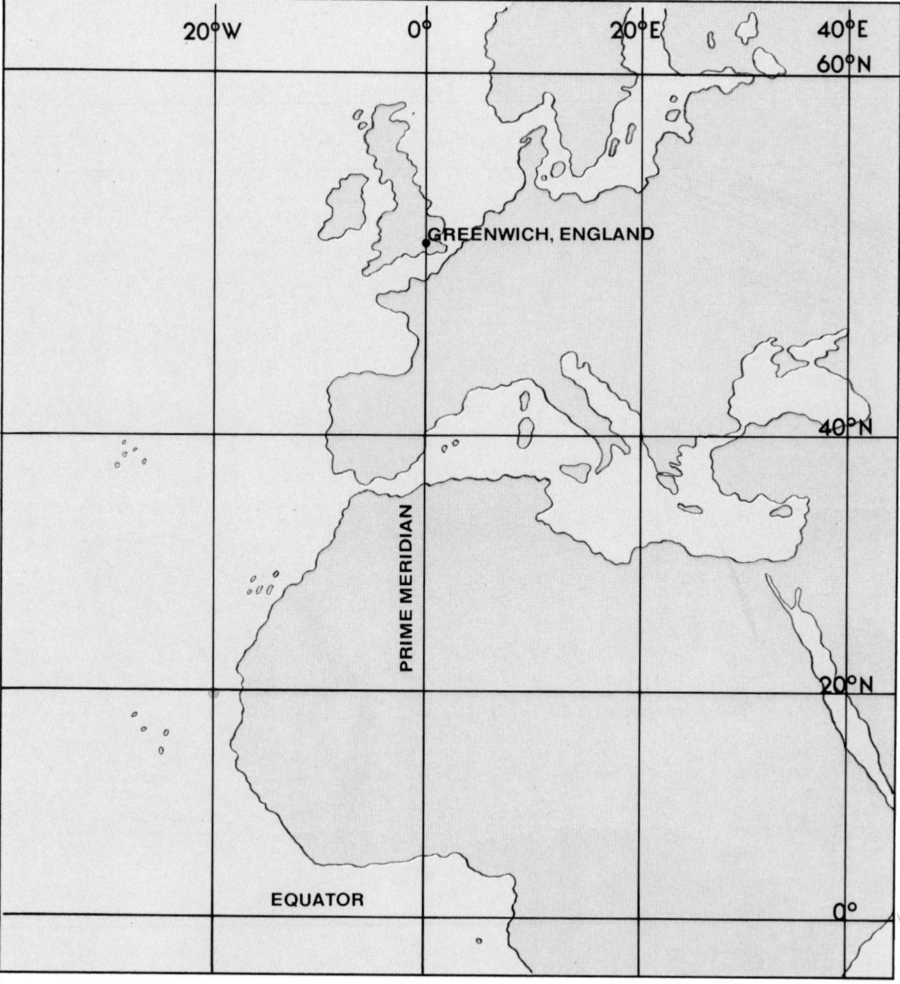

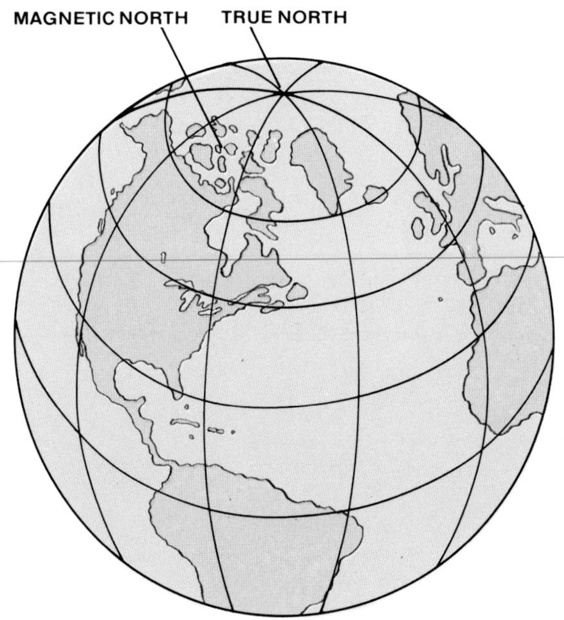

The northern terminus of the lines of longitude represents true north, but the North Magnetic Pole toward which compass needles generally point is 1,000 miles away at Bathurst Island, Canada. Navigators compensate for the variation between the two poles by using a device that is called a dual compass rose (opposite). The amount of variation differs with each locale.

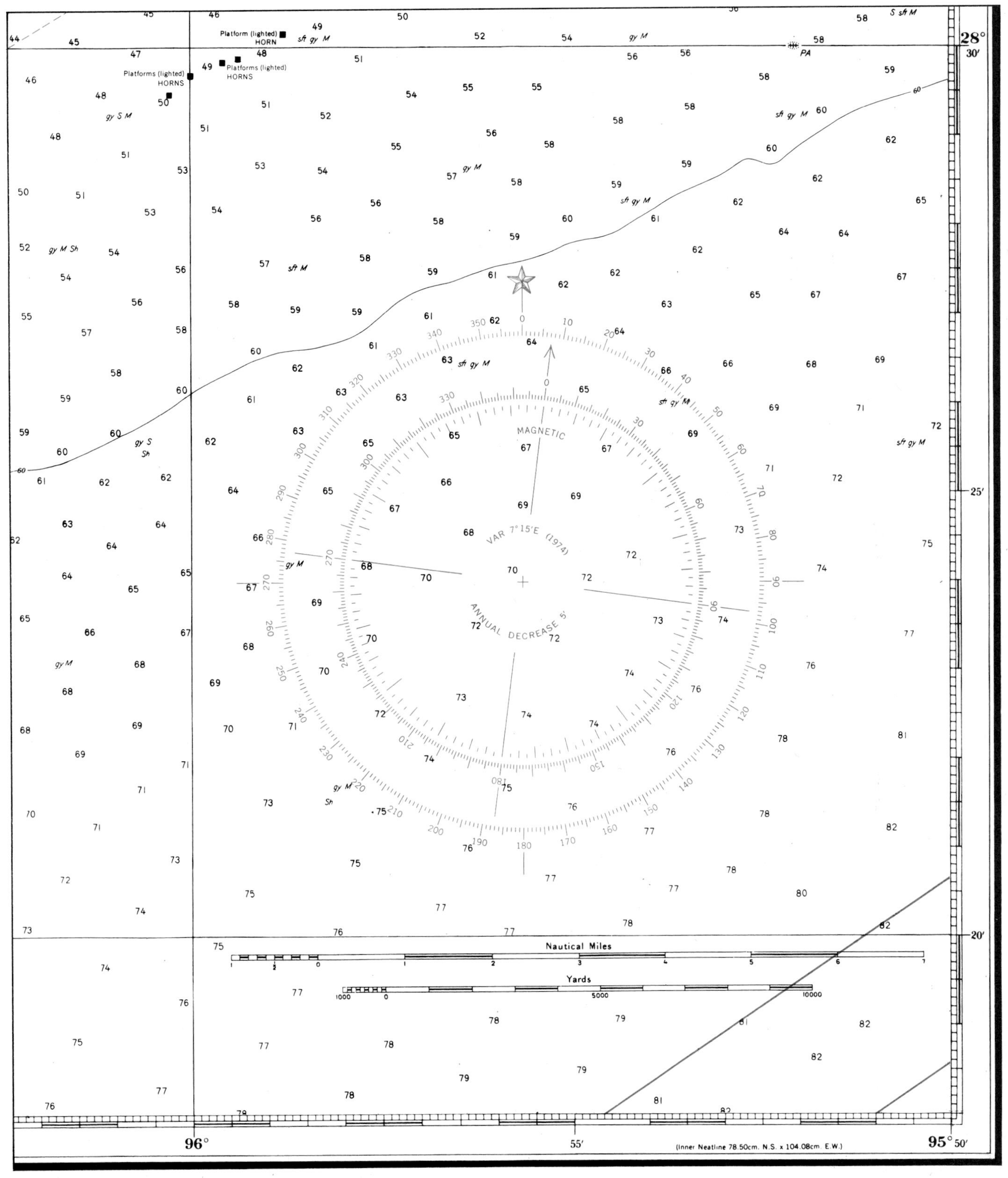

On this chart excerpt, a dual compass rose shows the variation between true north and magnetic north. The zero of the outer rose points to the geographic pole, while the inner circle's zero shows the compass direction to magnetic north. The difference between the two is the local variation, which increases (or decreases, as noted within this rose) each year because the magnetic field that is generated by the earth's moving molten core is in flux. In the margins of the chart are displayed the degrees of latitude (along the right-hand margin) and longitude (along the bottom margin). The margins further divide the area into minutes by means of the alternating lined and blank bands, and into six-second units, or tenths of minutes.

Mercator's Distortion

A chart is a flat representation of a section of the earth's curved surface. There are many ways to depict—or, as cartographers put it, to project—a round surface onto a flat one. The most popular projection for nautical charts is the Mercator, named after the Dutch map maker, Gerhard Mercator, who invented the technique in 1567.

The Mercator flattens out the earth so that lines of latitude and longitude can form a rectangular grid. To achieve this, the projection must stretch those parts of the globe not precisely on the equator. The amount of stretch increases in proportion to the distance from the equator. And wherever the stretch occurs, the distance between points on a chart will appear greater than it is on the earth's surface. The Mercator is devised so that the east-west stretch is balanced with a north-south stretch. Thus the mariner can use the latitude margin *(opposite)* as a scale for measuring all distances correctly.

In making a Mercator projection, a chart maker, in effect, uses one or more triangular earth peelings taken off from a pole to the equator. He then stretches each triangle so that its apex is as wide as its base, and it becomes a rectangle. At the same time, the rectangle is proportionately elongated to balance out the increasing amount of lateral stretch as the latitude approaches the poles.

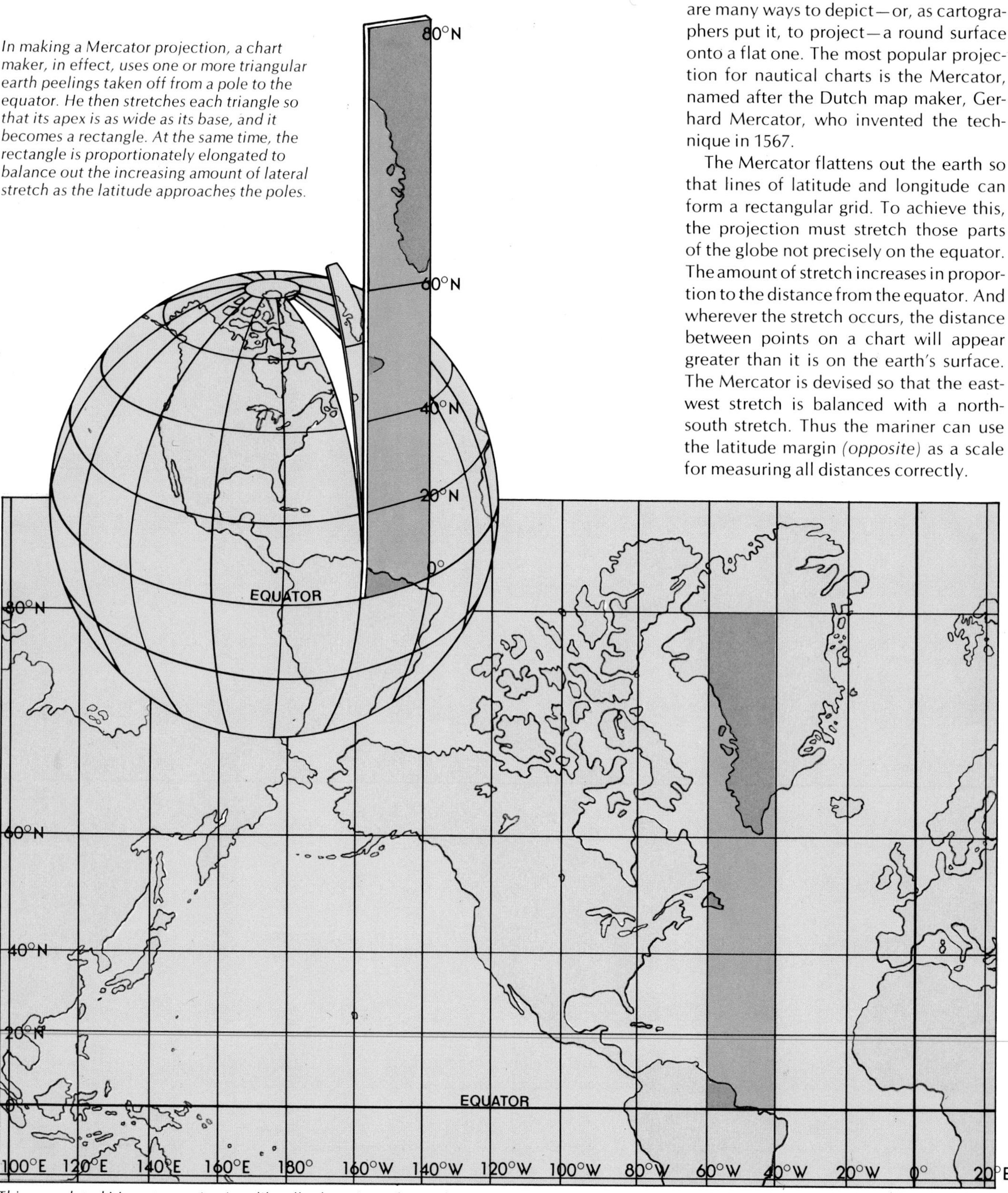

This completed Mercator projection, like all others, is made up of rectangular strips, which represent sections of the earth laid down adjacent to one another. The blue rectangle between 40°W and 60°W duplicates the strip peeled and stretched from the globe at top. In high latitudes the areas become enlarged and distorted. Thus, Greenland appears, proportionately, three times its true size.

Nova Scotian Coast

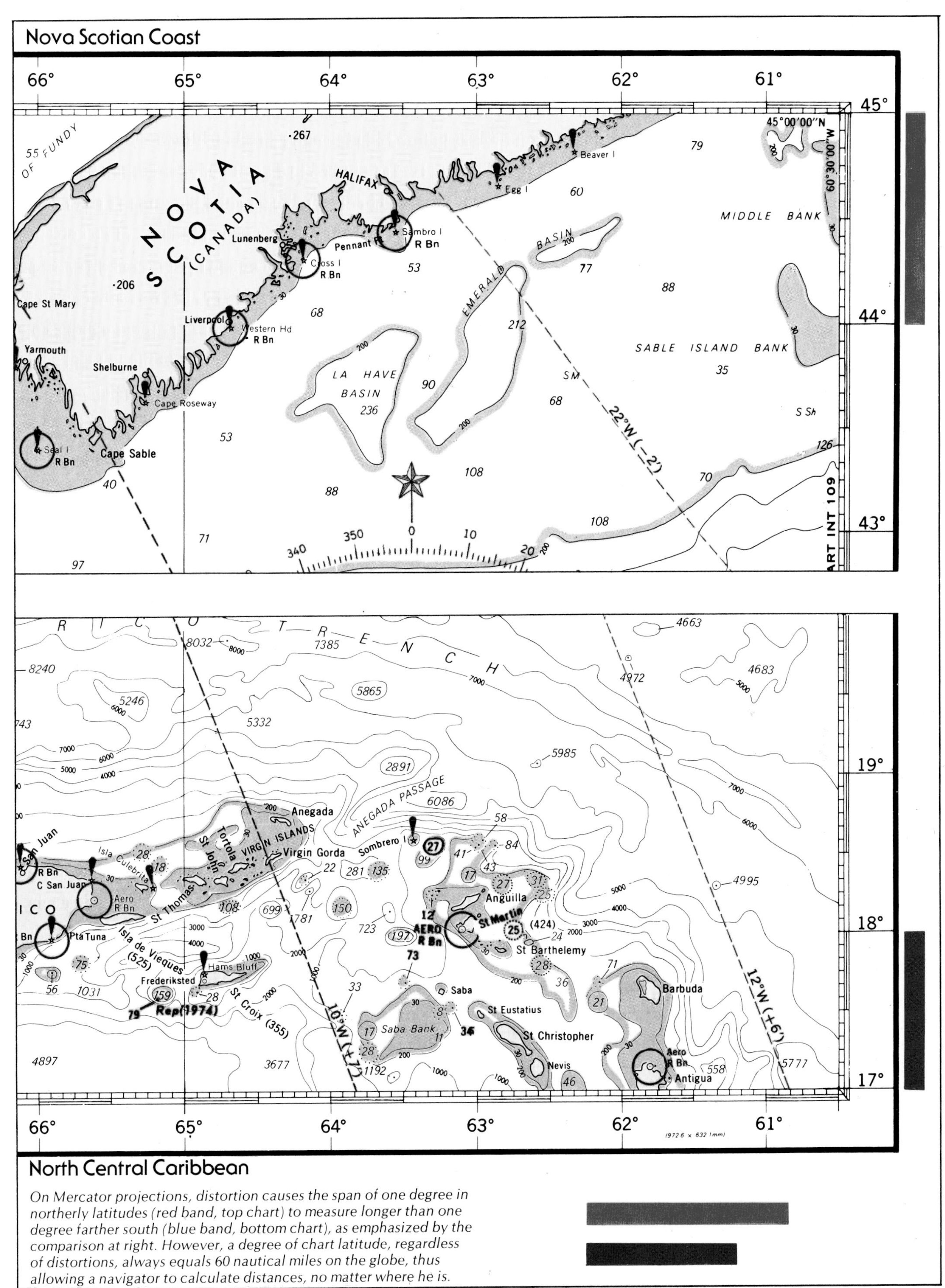

North Central Caribbean

On Mercator projections, distortion causes the span of one degree in northerly latitudes (red band, top chart) to measure longer than one degree farther south (blue band, bottom chart), as emphasized by the comparison at right. However, a degree of chart latitude, regardless of distortions, always equals 60 nautical miles on the globe, thus allowing a navigator to calculate distances, no matter where he is.

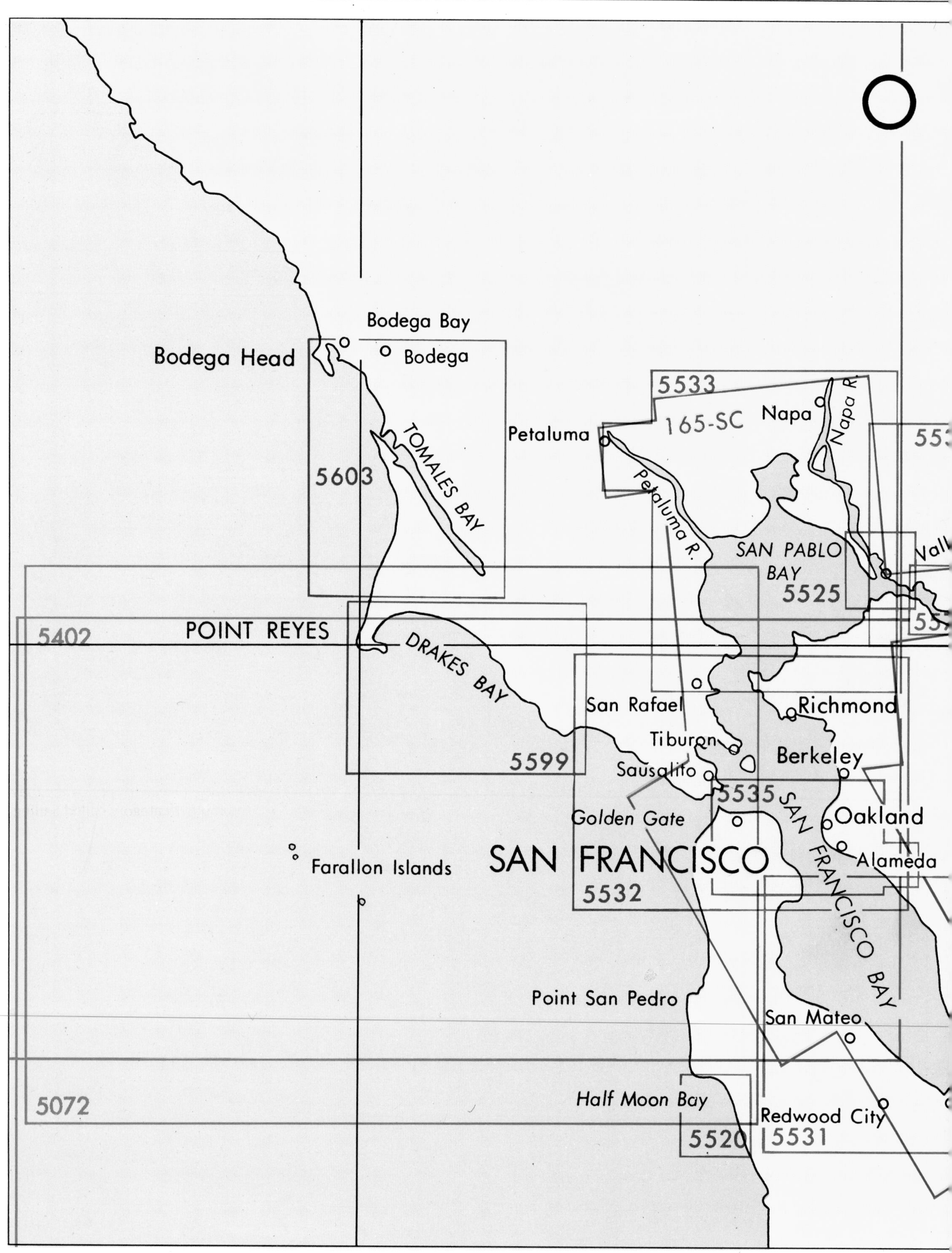
Bodega Bay
Bodega Head
Bodega
5533
165-SC
Napa
Napa R.
Petaluma
TOMALES BAY
5603
Petaluma R.
SAN PABLO
BAY
5525
5402
POINT REYES
DRAKES BAY
San Rafael
Richmond
Tiburon
5599
Sausalito
Berkeley
5535
Golden Gate
Oakland
Farallon Islands
SAN FRANCISCO
SAN FRANCISCO BAY
Alameda
5532
Point San Pedro
San Mateo
Half Moon Bay
5072
Redwood City
5520
5531

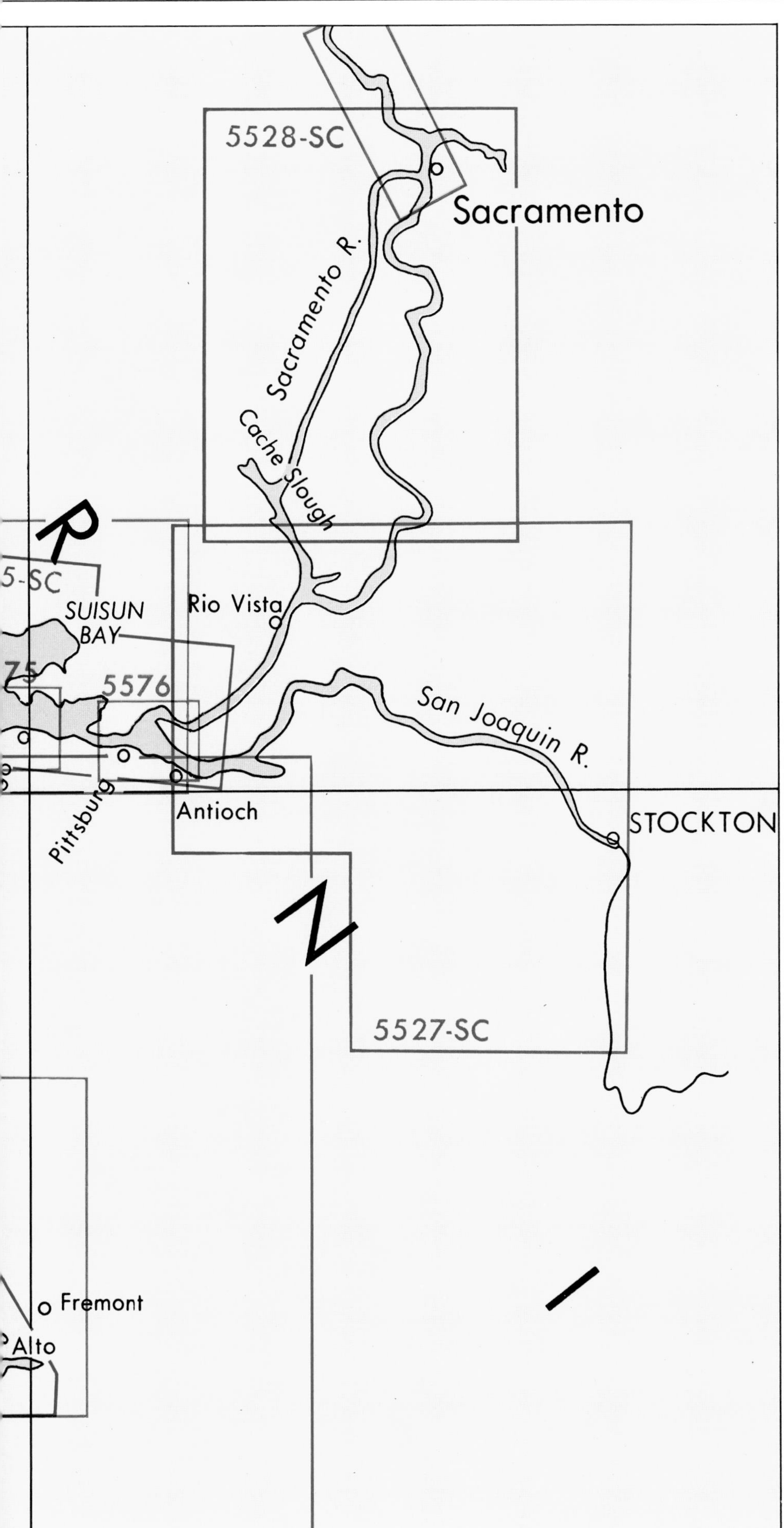

This excerpt from a Pacific Coast chart catalogue shows the charts a boatman may select for navigation in the San Francisco Bay area. For his long-range coastal piloting and overall perspective he would use General Chart 5402 (blue outline). Coastal Chart 5072 gives more detail on the approaches to the Golden Gate. From there, if he were headed for, say, Vallejo, he would get Harbor Charts 5532, 5533 and, finally, 5525 for a look at his anchorage. Alternately he might select Small-Craft Chart 165SC (green outline), which covers all the bays in the area.

A Choice of Charts

Whenever a boatman heads out on a cruise, for a day or a month, he should carry a selection of charts that gives both an overall look at the general area he is traveling, and minute details on every harbor, channel, hazard and aid to navigation he may encounter. In choosing, he can use as a guide the chart catalogues of the National Ocean Survey *(pages 36-37)*, a federal agency that compiles most of the charts covering United States waters.

As the excerpt at left shows, these so-called catalogues are actually large annotated maps on which the areas covered by available charts are outlined in coded colors, each individual chart being designated by a serial number. Normally, the pleasure-boater uses four kinds of charts, which the catalogue outlines in three different colors. Two of these kinds, General Charts and Coast Charts, indicated by blue lines, embrace sizable stretches of water and coastline, and are essential for coastwise piloting. Harbor Charts, outlined in red, provide detailed close-up views of selected inshore areas.

In addition, many skippers carry a stock of Small-Craft Charts, outlined in green, which are designed especially for the recreational boatman. Essentially they are strips of Harbor Charts arranged along the axes of popular waterways, including tidal stretches of major rivers. They show all navigation aids and hazards in precise detail; they also contain tide tables, point out repair facilities and indicate the best cruising routes.

The National Ocean Survey catalogues also offer another category called Sailing Charts. These charts cover broad sweeps of ocean and are most often used for offshore navigation; they are too small in scale to be shown in the excerpt at left. A segment of one is shown overleaf, however, along with samples from other chart categories to illustrate the differences in scale and in detail.

Closing In by Scale

Every chart represents a compromise between showing maximum area and maximum detail. The key to the compromise is scale. The effect of different scales is illustrated here by excerpts from four chart categories, as they zero in on an island *(red arrow on chart at right)* off Maine. As the chart scale increases, the focus narrows, but topographic features become larger and more detailed.

Cartographers describe a chart's scale by a numerical ratio, which defines the unit of chart space showing a corresponding unit of the earth's surface. On the segment at right, the scale is 1:1,200,000; i.e., one inch depicts 1,200,000 inches of actual distance, or about 20 miles.

1:1,200,000 scale. *The Sailing Chart excerpted here encompasses an enormous stretch of water, but gives only scanty information on inshore areas: the island in Blue Hill Bay marked by the arrow appears in rough outline. Like other Sailing Charts, all of which have a scale of 1:600,000 or smaller, this one shows a few major lighthouses, includes offshore soundings in fathoms and is useful solely for making long-range approaches.*

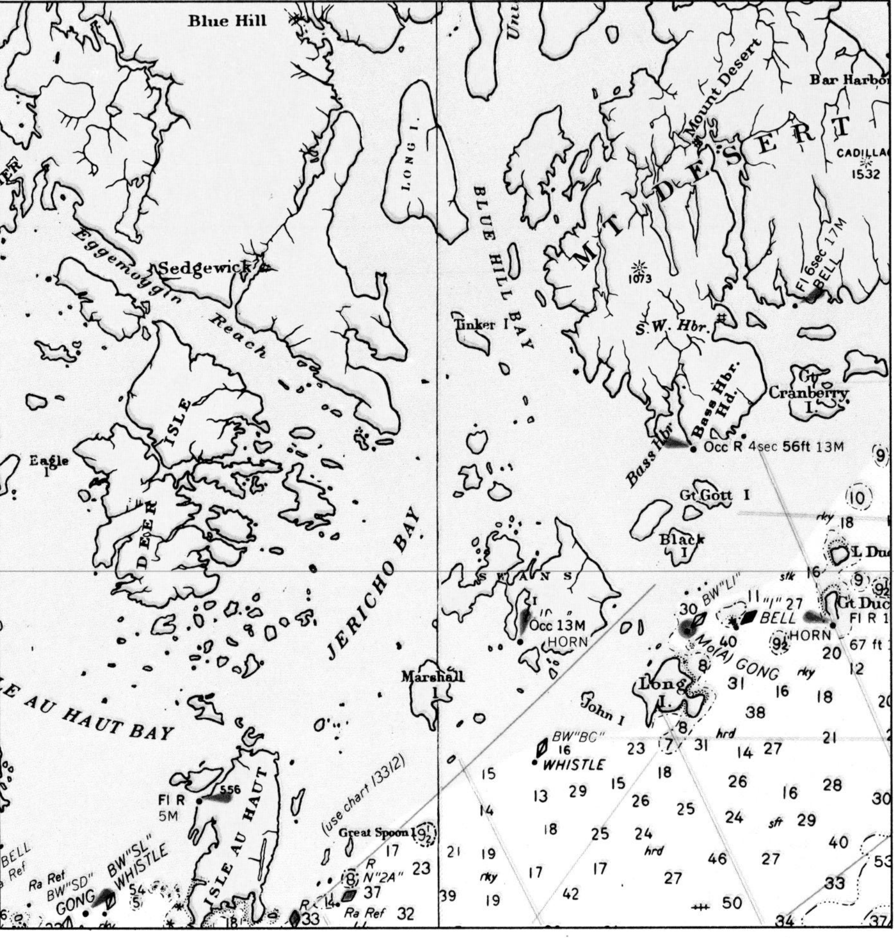

1:378,838 scale. *When scale increases, as with this General Chart, coastal areas are shown in somewhat greater detail. The island in Blue Hill Bay appears larger and has acquired a name: Long Island. But General Charts, ranging in scale from 1:600,000 to 1:150,000, still do not include the precise data that is required for close-in piloting. They are used for plotting courses along a coast—but outside of major rocks and reefs.*

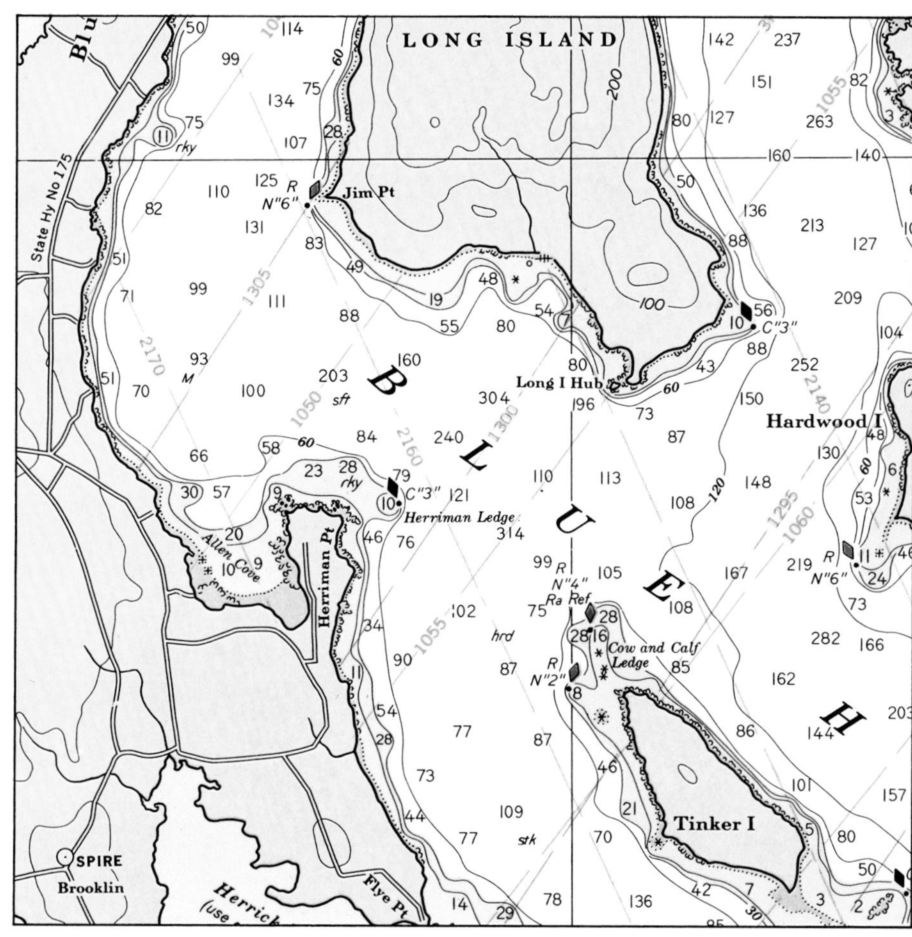

1:80,000 scale. *The amplified scale of a Coast Chart, like the example at left, allows the cartographer to incorporate the major navigational details necessary for inshore piloting. Here, a part of the intricate coastline of Long Island is carefully delineated; depth soundings in feet describe shoal areas and channels, and principal navigation hazards and aids are clearly shown. The perspective is still broad enough, however, to give the navigator an overview of his immediate area.*

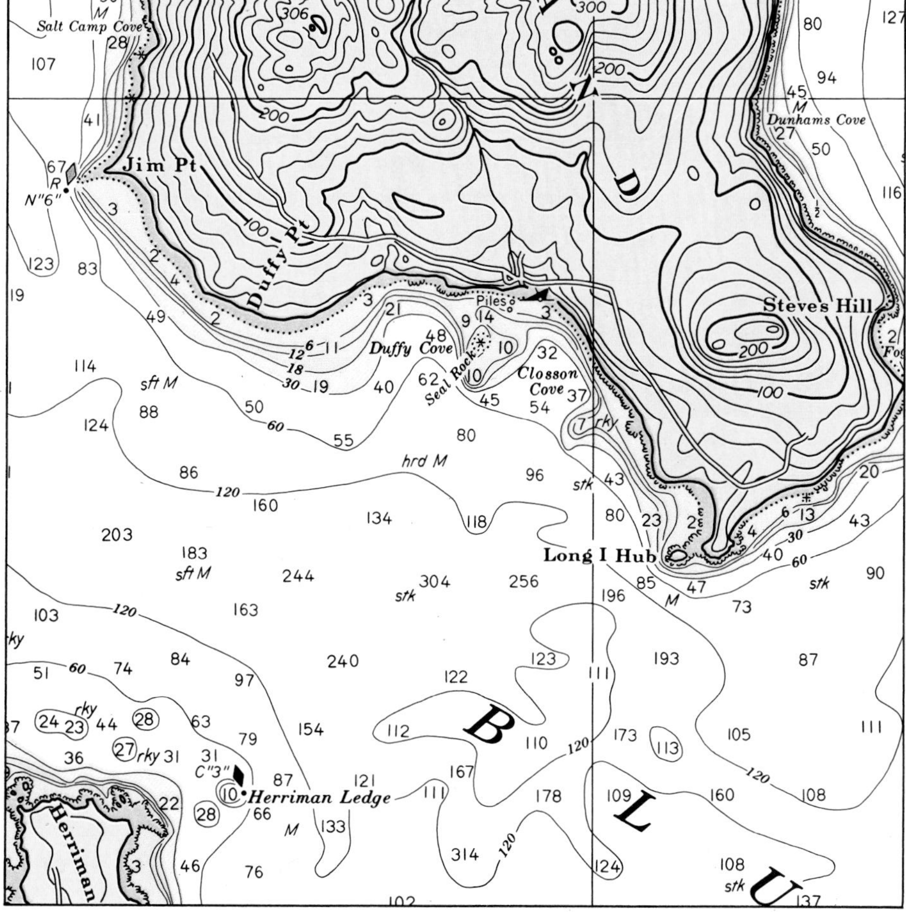

1:40,000 scale. *The closest view of all is provided by a Harbor Chart (Small-Craft Charts are similar in scale), which closely details the coastlines and bottom contours, and includes an elaborate schematic representation of inland topography. Here, Long Island has been scaled up so that even pilings between Duffy and Closson coves are clearly marked. Some Harbor Charts are drawn to an even larger scale than this one; they range from 1:50,000 to 1:5,000.*

Other Looks in Charts

While most cruising grounds in the United States are covered by the standard nautical charts issued by the National Ocean Survey (NOS), some areas require their own charts. Any skipper who travels on lakes, canals or rivers above the tidal zone can turn to specialized charts such as the ones shown here. They are compiled by the Defense Mapping Agency's Hydrographic Center, by the Army Corps of Engineers or by a regional NOS branch called the Lake Survey Center, and they can be purchased by writing to the agency that puts them out *(page 172)*. (For cruising in Canadian waters, you may obtain charts from the Canadian Hydrographic Service.) While these regional charts usually follow the general format of the NOS charts, they show some significant differences.

The Defense Mapping Agency's charts of foreign waters, for example, use data obtained from foreign-government surveys, and thus they sometimes resemble foreign-admiralty charts. Land areas are usually gray, as in the Bahamian chart below; depths may be in meters rather than fathoms or feet. Great Lakes charts *(top right)* and river charts *(opposite, below)* are sometimes marked with preplotted courses along channels or between major navigation marks; but course distances are given in statute rather than in nautical miles *(page 94)*. And while most charts use the standard NOS symbols for rocks, reefs, landmarks, buoys and lighthouses, the river and lake charts compiled by the Corps of Engineers often employ an entirely different set of symbols; they are described on the charts themselves.

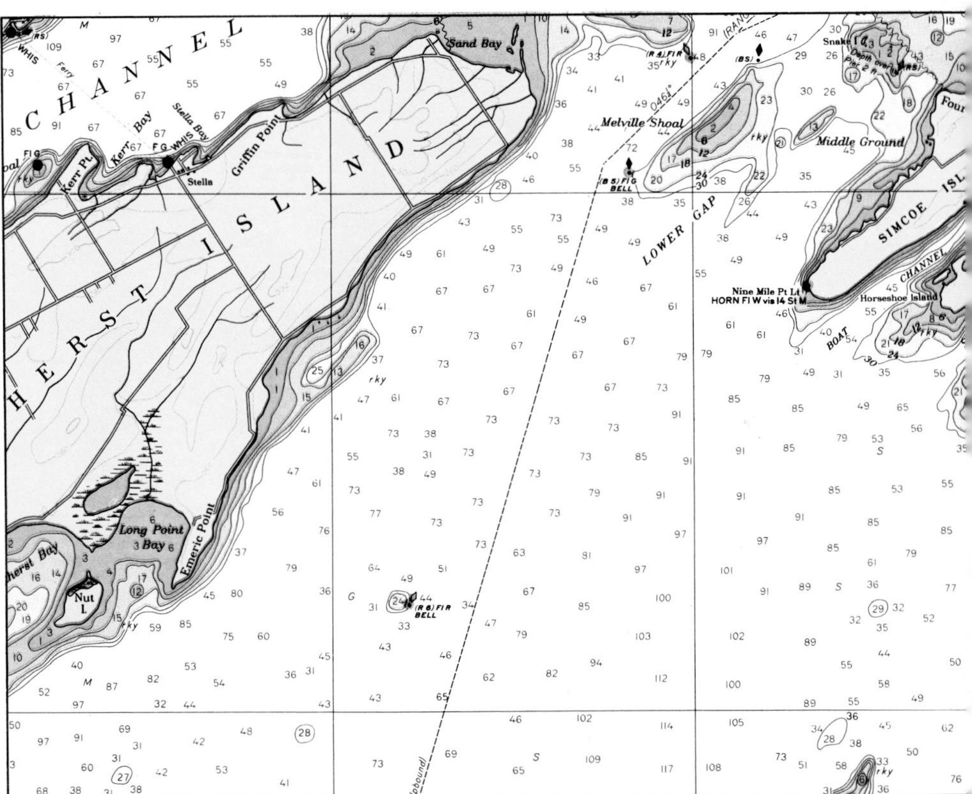

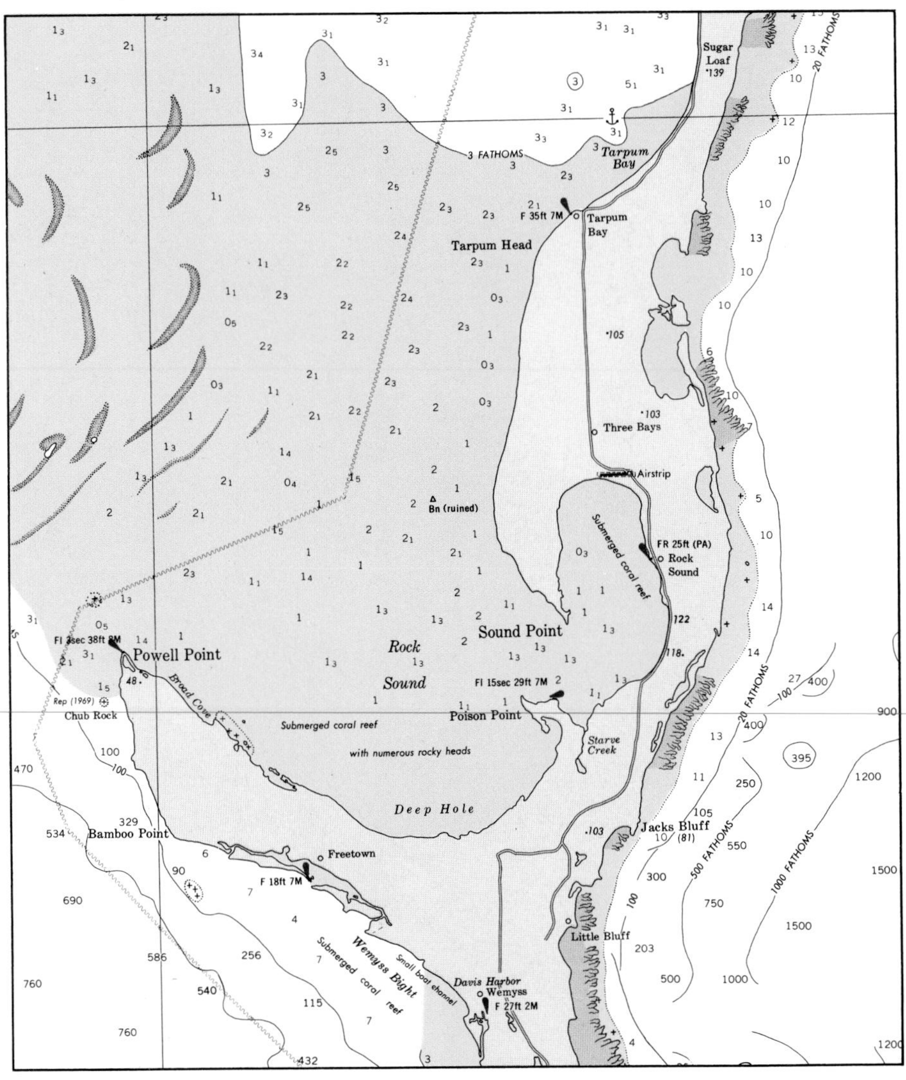

This chart excerpt of a part of Eleuthera Island in the Bahamas is typical of the international charts that are put out by the U.S. Defense Mapping Agency. The land areas are tinted gray, and shallow water is indicated by a distinctive aqua blue. Soundings are marked in fathoms; also, within areas of less than 11 fathoms, a small number next to the fathom mark defines depth to the nearest foot. But the navigator should not rely on such exact measurements, since revisions of these special charts are sporadic, and sand bars may have shifted and channels filled since the last survey.

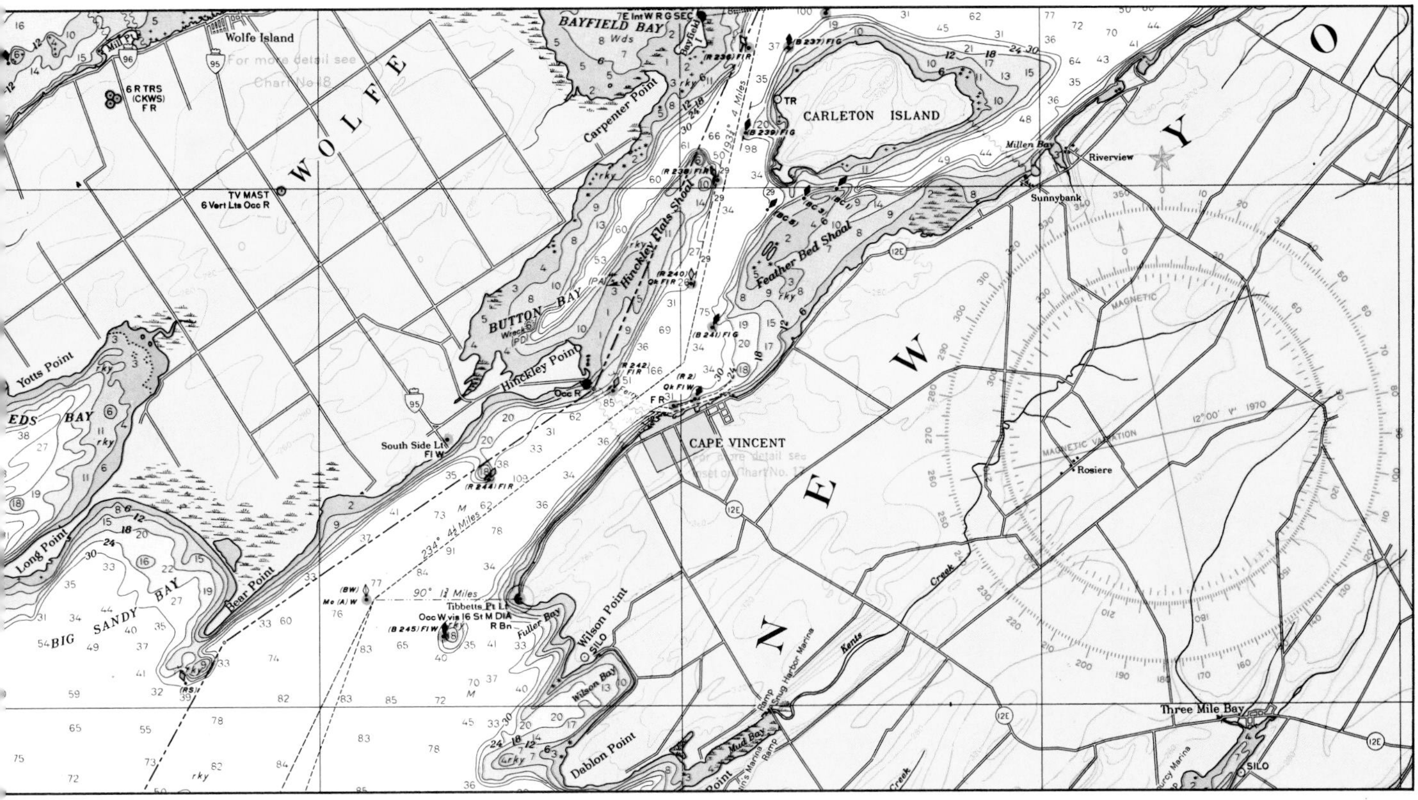

A tricky stretch of northeastern Lake Ontario is shown in this segment of a chart issued by the Lake Survey Center. As in all charts of the Great Lakes, where water level depends on seasonal variations in climate rather than the daily tide, depth soundings are based on an average of historical lows occurring during the winter months. Suggested course headings between major navigation marks and landfalls are shown by light dashed lines, which are accompanied by distances in statute miles and by compass bearings. The heavy broken line running by Wolfe Island is the United States-Canadian border.

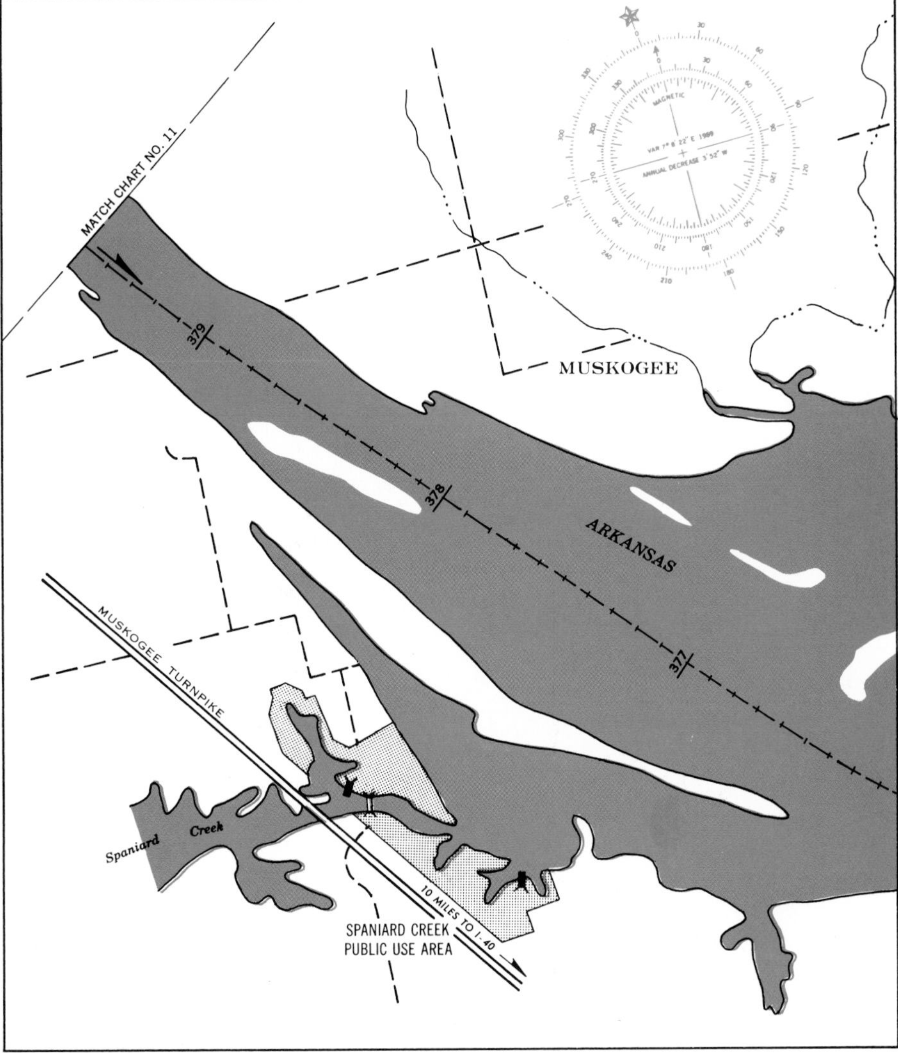

This three-mile strip of the Arkansas River near Muskogee, Oklahoma, is part of an extended river chart put out by the Army Corps of Engineers, which maps most major inland watercourses in the United States. Soundings are omitted because of the continuously shifting bottom contours, but a broken black line gives the safe channel. The line is marked for each statute mile; the numbers indicate the distance to the river's mouth, which is at the Mississippi. As in most river-chart formats, the Arkansas system is traced in separate chart sections, which are bound together sequentially in a booklet.

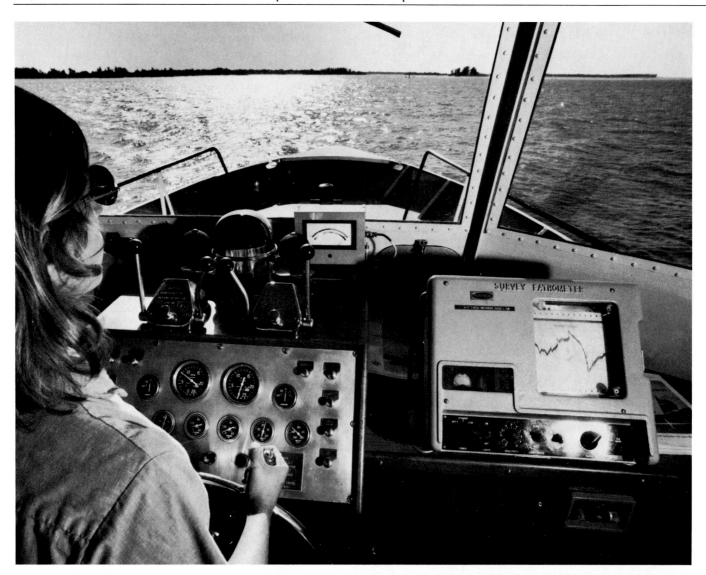

Steering a survey launch along a depth-sounding run, a helmsman stands before a panorama of dials and screens, which appears as complex as the control panel of a small airliner. Each course he runs is precisely predetermined, and the course data are fed into a computer. Underway, he steers by a sensor needle that remains centered in its dial when he is on course. To the helmsman's right, the tracer of a depth finder records a profile of the ocean floor on graph paper, in response to a series of depth soundings.

As the survey launch runs its depth-sounding course, the on-board computer records on magnetic tape the depth-finder readings and their locations, as determined by radio position-fixing equipment linked to the computer. Throughout the run an officer monitors the instruments by periodically checking the computer's tape print-out.

How Charts Are Made

To meet the unending need of mariners for up-to-date charts, specially equipped survey teams like the one on these pages keep a constant eye on the nation's waterways. These professional water watchers are members of the National Oceanic and Atmospheric Administration, which also maintains a staff of 100 map makers *(pages 36-37)* in a group called the National Ocean Survey in NOAA's headquarters in Rockville, Maryland. Together they revise the 971 different charts that are the cruising bibles for 18 million pleasure-boat owners and another 250,000 or so commercial mariners.

Some of the information is collected by planes armed with 400-pound aerial cameras; these aircraft fly more than 50,000 miles annually photographing changing shorelines and river courses. At the same time, a flotilla of powerboats, skillfully manned and lavishly equipped, develops data on water depths and bottom characteristics, as shown here. Cruising at 20 knots, this vessel uses highly sophisticated radio position-fixing equipment, electronic depth finders and computers that pick up information along the lines of meticulously plotted courses.

The results of these surveys—reams of computer print-outs, piles of handwritten notes, fat rolls of sequential nine-inch-square color transparencies—as well as reports from the Coast Guard, the Army Corps of Engineers and alert civilian boatmen, all find their way to the NOS's chart-making center, where cartographers transpose them onto charts.

To double-check the survey boat's position, seamen measure with sextants the angles from three onshore landmarks, and then, by triangulation, determine the launch's exact location at the start and finish of each day. These visual fixes serve to verify the position that the vessel's computer obtains out of its radio position-fixing equipment—which is vulnerable to atmospheric distortion.

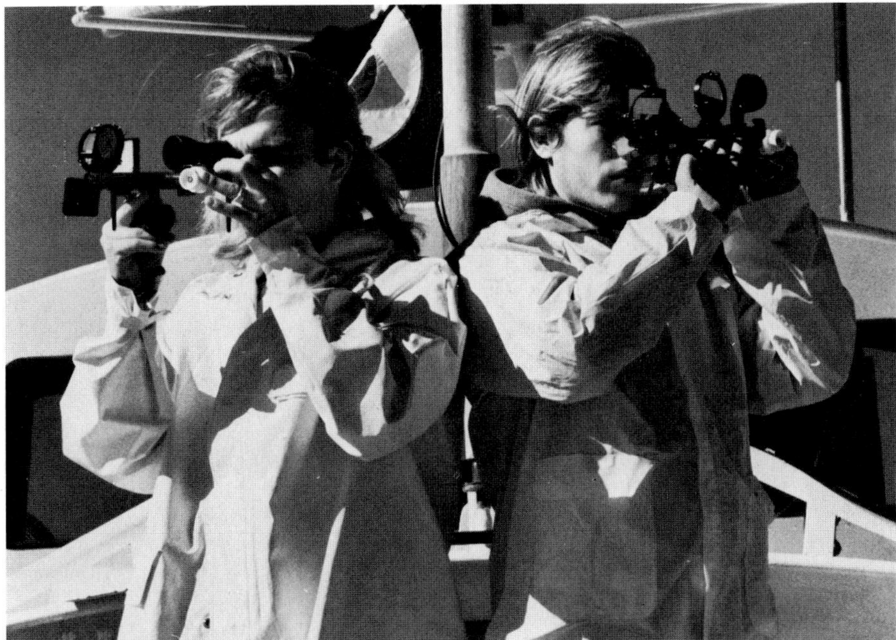

To obtain a specimen of the sea bottom, a crewman lowers a clamshell sampler over the side. When the device touches down, its two halves snap shut, collecting about two cups of material. The crewman then hauls the sampler aboard, examines the contents and marks his findings and their location in a record book. Later, this record of the bottom material (mud, sand or rock), its consistency (soft, sticky or hard) and any significant sea life on its surface (kelp or beds of seashells) will be used to update charts.

Cartographers at the National Ocean Survey office in Rockville, Maryland, work on revising charts—or creating new ones—for every patch of navigable U.S. waters. The map makers revise more than 550 charts annually, including some, like those covering the ever-changing offshore oil-drilling area between the Mississippi River delta and the Texas border, that have to be revised twice every year.

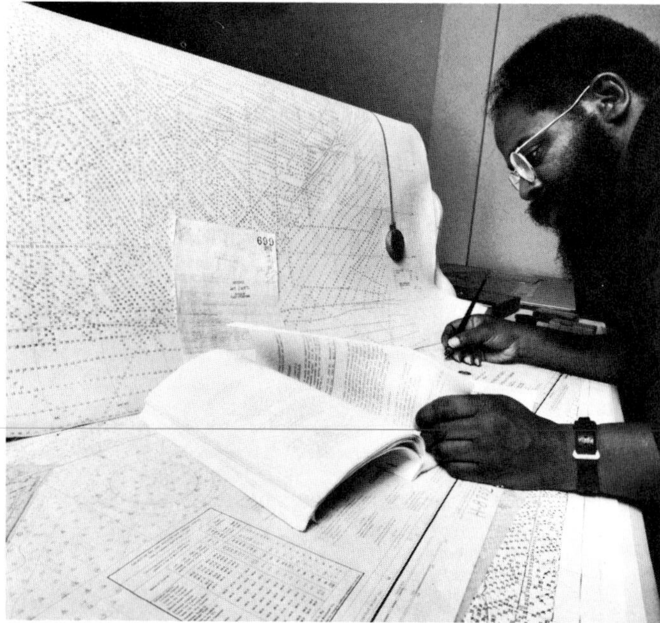

Correlating field data, a cartographer sifts out newly reported depth soundings, bottom information and menaces to navigation, such as submerged rocks and wrecks. Then he transfers them to the master drawing of a nautical chart that is under his right hand.

This cartographer corrects a section of coastline by tracing over the contours of an aerial photograph made to the scale of the chart. Placing the chart and transparent photograph atop a light-table, she records topographic information from the picture.

To transfer information from aerial photographs to a large-scale chart, the cartographer puts two transparencies into an aviograph, a stereo viewer with an attached scribing arm. As the cartographer moves a control handle, a pointer, visible through the viewer, traces the features he wants to transpose, while a pencil on the drawing arm (far right) re-creates the same details on the chart (foreground).

MASTERWORKS OF CHART MAKING

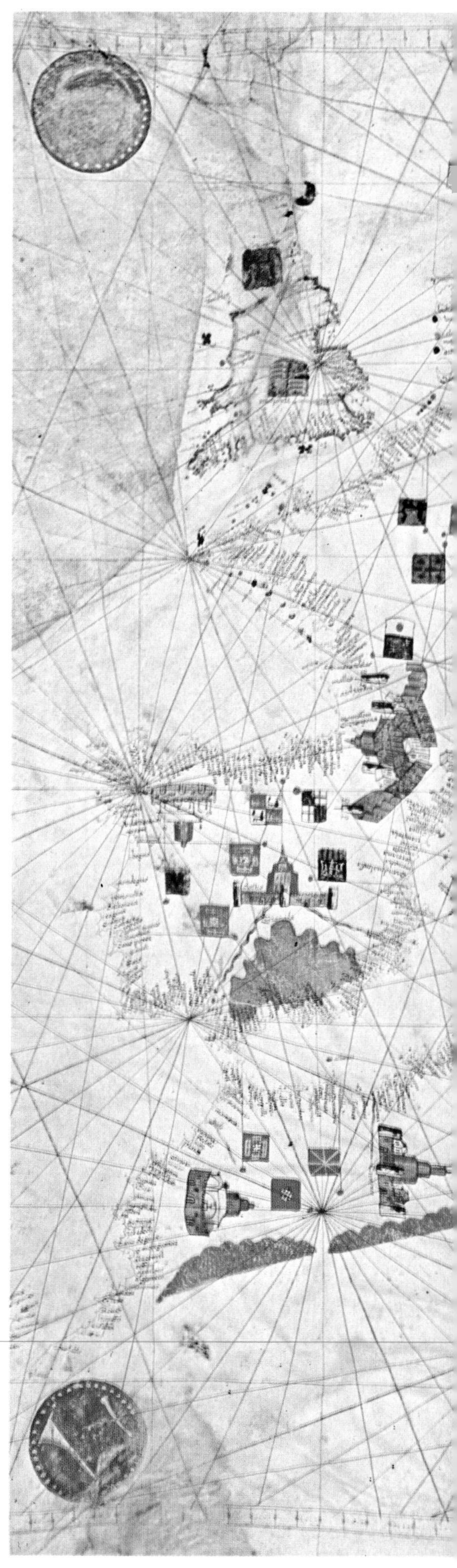

Not long ago, as measured by the main currents of history, most common sailors navigated by either pure guess or luck, or by their own crude sketches of coastlines. During much of the 15th Century the art of the nautical chart maker was not much more than a century old. Columbus had not yet exploded the boundaries of the known world, which still centered around the Mediterranean. But an era of great navigators was aborning. The few existing charts, laboriously created by a handful of talented cartographers, were coveted by kings and queens, and by a few powerful traders and sea captains. These works were treasured instruments of high ambitions; they could help guide fleets to commercial ports or the wealth of new lands.

The chart makers' creations were also remarkable for their artistic beauty. The exquisite example shown at right was drawn by two craftsmen in Barcelona in 1456—only 150 years after the creation of the earliest known nautical chart. The design is overlaid with an interlacing of straight-line navigation routes, called rhumb lines, that radiate from major ports and cities—and from compass roses. The artists added national flags, and miniature illustrations showed the principal buildings—some of them curiously capsized—at centers of trade and worship.

From this elegant base, the science of nautical cartography began to develop in earnest with the great voyages of exploration in the late 15th Century. In Portugal, Prince Henry the Navigator recruited Europe's finest map makers to chart his captains' discoveries along Africa. In Spain, King Ferdinand and Queen Isabella established one of the earliest government cartographic offices. In charge was a hydrographer who kept New World maps under lock and key. One hydrographic appointee was the Italian explorer Sebastian Cabot, who outraged the Spanish court when he tried to sell secret charts to his own country. Thereafter, no foreigner was allowed to hold the post.

The Spanish monarchs had hoped to set up a monopoly on charts, empowering their cartographic office with sole authority to draft and sell charts. But in Spain and Portugal, private map makers bribed seafarers returning from the New World for descriptions of lands, bays and harbors. And a black market in charts flourished in many Iberian seaports.

Though some of the early cartographers were explorers, such as Cabot and Amerigo Vespucci, who actually saw the areas they mapped, most map makers simply interpreted the reports of returning sailors—or plagiarized the work of fellow cartographers. Wherever the information originated, it was closely guarded. The Italian Battista Agnese, whose Pacific chart appears on pages 42-43, was elaborately secretive; neither his contemporaries nor historians ever learned his sources.

As exploratory voyages grew more numerous, cartographers scrambled to keep pace with the sailors—constantly adding new discoveries to their charts. And the science of cartography improved apace. Abetted by improved navigational instruments, Portuguese chart makers were the first to include lines of longitude. By the middle of the 16th Century, most maps had fully developed grids of latitude and longitude superimposed upon the spiderweb networks of rhumb lines.

Although many similarities exist in the products of the early chart makers, distinctive styles emerged in various locales. Catalan charts were noted for their decorative qualities, Portuguese works for their flamboyant colorings, and charts of the Italian school for their Spartan purity of execution. By the late 16th Century, the Dutch craftsmen had become preeminent in Europe; their bold, informative attention to coastal details dominated cartography for more than a century.

This 1456 chart of the Mediterranean was a climactic achievement of the Catalan school of cartography. The coastline and listing of towns and ports (in red) is meticulously accurate. But the artists stylized such features of unconcern to Mediterranean sailors as the Red Sea (lower right) and the Atlas Mountains (scalloped green frond).

This Portuguese chart of Brazil's northern coast was one of the earliest to indicate latitude. Drafted in 1519, the map illustrates explorers' impressions of the new land. The chart maker filled it with colorful birds, a plethora of place names and ferocious cannibals. The most important parallels of latitude—dividing climatic zones—are drawn across the face of the map; others are indicated by the beaded north-south line along the right margin.

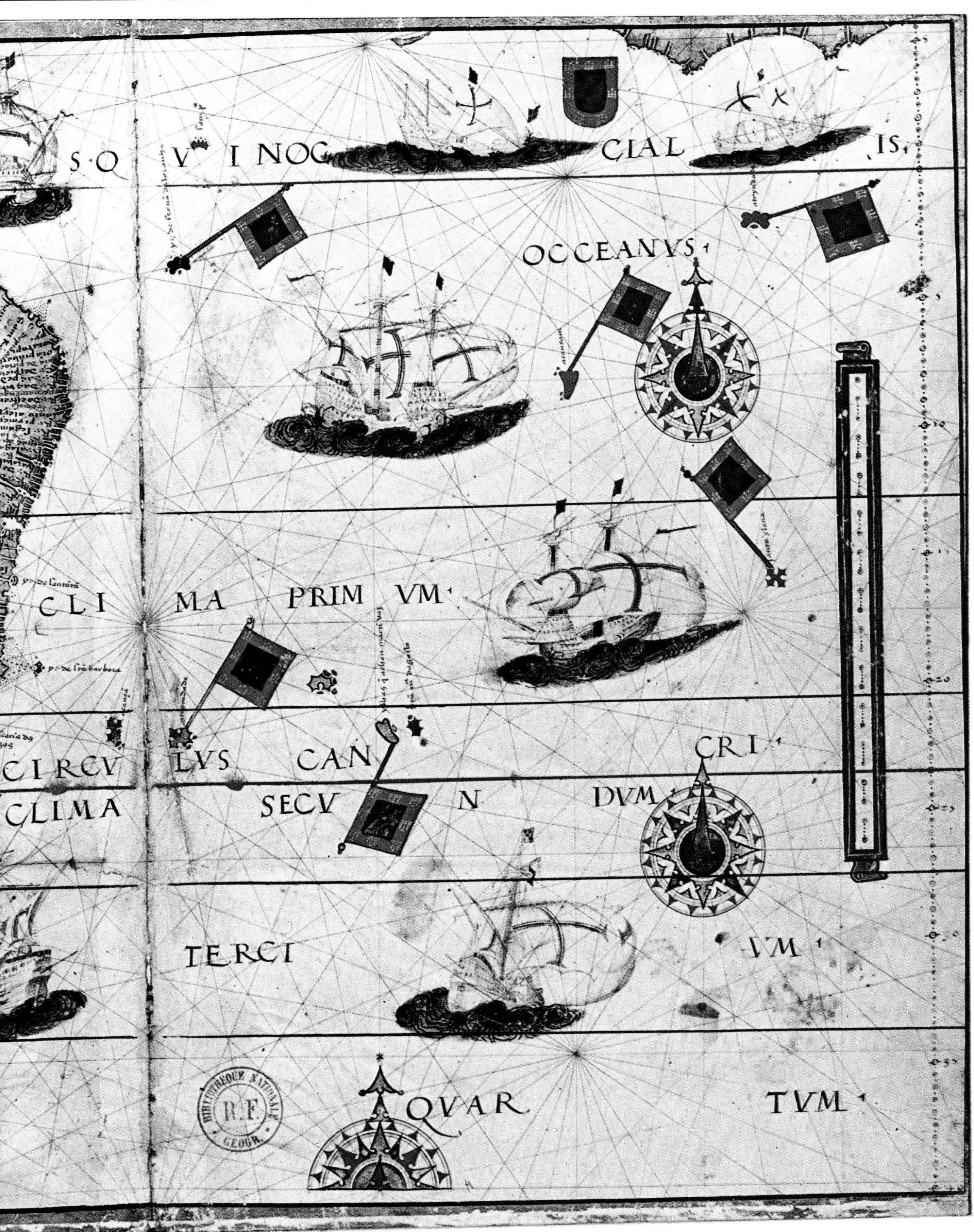

S·Q V I NOC CIAL IS
OCCEANVS
CLI MA PRIM VM
CIRCV LVS CAN CRI
CLIMA SECV N DVM
TERCI VM
QVAR TVM
BIBLIOTHÈQUE NATIONALE R.F. GEOGR.

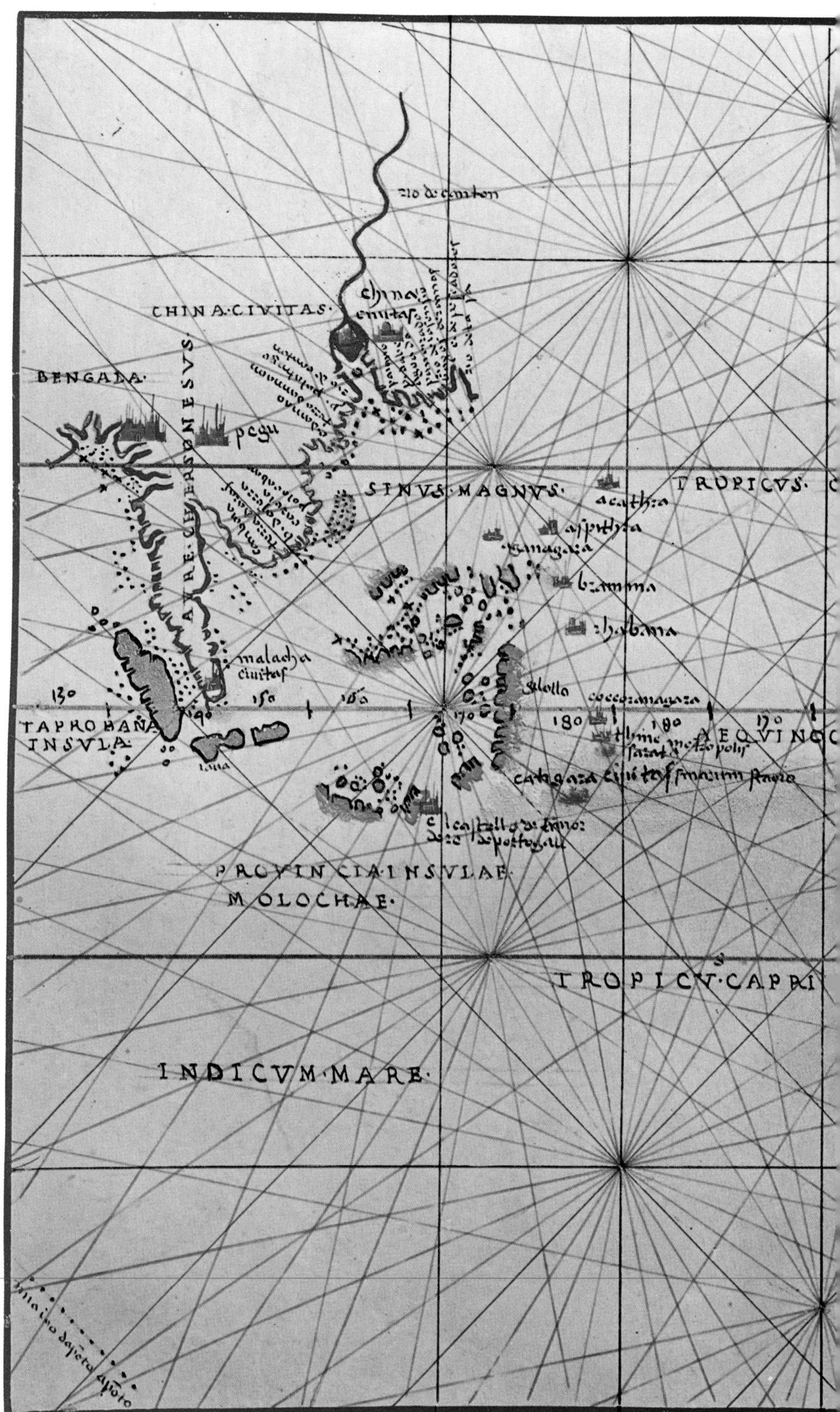

This chart of the Pacific, created in 1555 by a Genoese, Battista Agnese, reveals the state of exploration at the time. China, Ceylon and the Philippines are shown, but Australia and New Zealand had yet to be discovered. The chart includes one of the earliest indications of tides: at the head of the Gulf of California, flecked with a reddish tint, an inscription notes that high-water depth is 11 brazas (a braza is the span of a man's outstretched arms) and low-water depth is eight brazas. Also, Agnese overlaid the map with a grid showing both latitude and longitude —one of the first chart makers to do so.

temititstan nell mexico civitas
cuba
PERV·PROVJCIA
MVNDVS·NOVV
STRICTVM·D EMAGELLANO·

A Aldus verthoont hem tlandt van Bretaignen otrent S: Pouwels, alsmen twe mijlen van lan
Facies littoralis Bri: S. Paulus tanniæ circa fanum D. Pauli, dum 2. miliar. distantia
O. beurac.
Dijnant
Dinant fluuius.
Le taure.
Ysle de Bas
B R I T A N N I
B R E T A
S. Seledor.
S. Brieux.
S. Malo.
Plamconet.
C. de Late
Porterieux.
fluuius
Lantrilis
Banck
Pont rien.
Port blanc
treguer
Ulis
Bribac.
Oreme
Sept. Ysles
Britannische
B R I T A N N I C V S
MERIDIES
ORIENS
OCC
S-W
N-W
S-O
N-O
SEPTETRIO
Iar. sij.
Gromes.
Hispanica miliaria. Spaensche mijlen tot 17½. in ee graedt.
Duijtsche mijlen tot 15. in een graedt
Germanica miliaria 15. vni grad. compet.
Getebrokho.
Cornet.
Garn
C. De gruive

In this 1583 chart of the coast of Brittany, the Dutchman Lucas Janszoon Waghenaer introduced systematic depth indications, pointed out hazardous rocks and shoals, and sketched the coast's profile (top). English sailors admired Waghenaer's work, and for centuries called any collection of piloting charts a waggoner.

2

SIGNPOSTS FOR SAILORS

Dotting the coastal and inland waters of the United States are tens of thousands of objects designed to tell a boatman where he is and where he should or should not go. These aids to navigation, as they are called, communicate their message by almost every imaginable means. Some ring bells or gongs, or sound horns or whistles; others signal their information mainly by shape, color or distinctive markings; some of them are designed to reflect radar or searchlight beams efficiently; and still others reach 10 or more miles across the sea by the use of high-intensity lights or radio waves.

The largest aids to navigation are lighthouses and beacons—descendants of ancient Mediterranean towers that displayed wood or coal fires to warn ships off dangerous shores. Buoys are smaller but much more numerous; they make up about 60 per cent of the total of all nautical signposts. Sturdy tank-mounted structures such as the wasp-waisted model at left are anchored in depths of up to 450 feet. Designed for use in exposed locations, these buoys possess steel skeletons nearly 20 feet tall and are capable of withstanding extreme forces of wind and water that would have hopelessly overmatched their predecessors, the wooden-keg buoys or crude logs used to mark navigable waterways in centuries past. Farther inshore and in channels, simpler cylindrical or conical buoys suffice. In shallow water, the role of buoys is often assumed by signs that are called daymarks; they are displayed on pilings or spars driven into the bottom.

All of these various communicators speak to boatmen by means of a relatively simple language that can be easily deciphered and put to use with the help of charts, light lists *(page 73)* and other publications of the federal and state governments. The various sorts of navigable waters in the United States are subject to four major buoyage systems, which are described in detail on the following pages. The four systems differ from one another in minor respects, but each system operates on the same underlying principle: in concise and compelling language they all try to keep the boatman out of trouble, sometimes by indicating the proximity of specific dangers or, more basically, by offering the navigator a means of determining his location—the fundamental information that spells the difference between simply reacting to danger and anticipating it.

These aids to navigation are carefully maintained—in most cases by the United States Coast Guard—and are steadily replaced with more advanced designs. But they are not infallible. Lights or other electronic equipment can fail. Buoys sometimes drag from their appointed positions, particularly during heavy weather when the navigator is most in need of them. And communication can break down even when the device is functioning properly. Buoys that have been emplaced to warn of a shoal may become a liability if the shoal shifts in a storm. In fog, atmospheric conditions can play all sorts of tricks with sound, altering the apparent direction from which a boatman believes he hears a gong or whistle, for instance, or even changing a whistle's special identifying tones.

A skipper should never rely upon a single navigation mark to give him warning of possible danger. Instead, he should make use of all of the information conveyed to him by all of the aids that he can see or hear, or that he detects with his electronic equipment *(pages 130-133, 136-139)*. When used in this manner and with understanding, the aids to navigation are the seaman's best friends. After the safe negotiation of a long passage in dirty weather, the flashing light on the far horizon that signals "this is the way home" can be the most welcome sign a sailor ever sees.

As fog rolls in toward Santa Barbara, California, a sentinel buoy at the entrance to the harbor employs both light and bell to guide the mariner to a safe return.

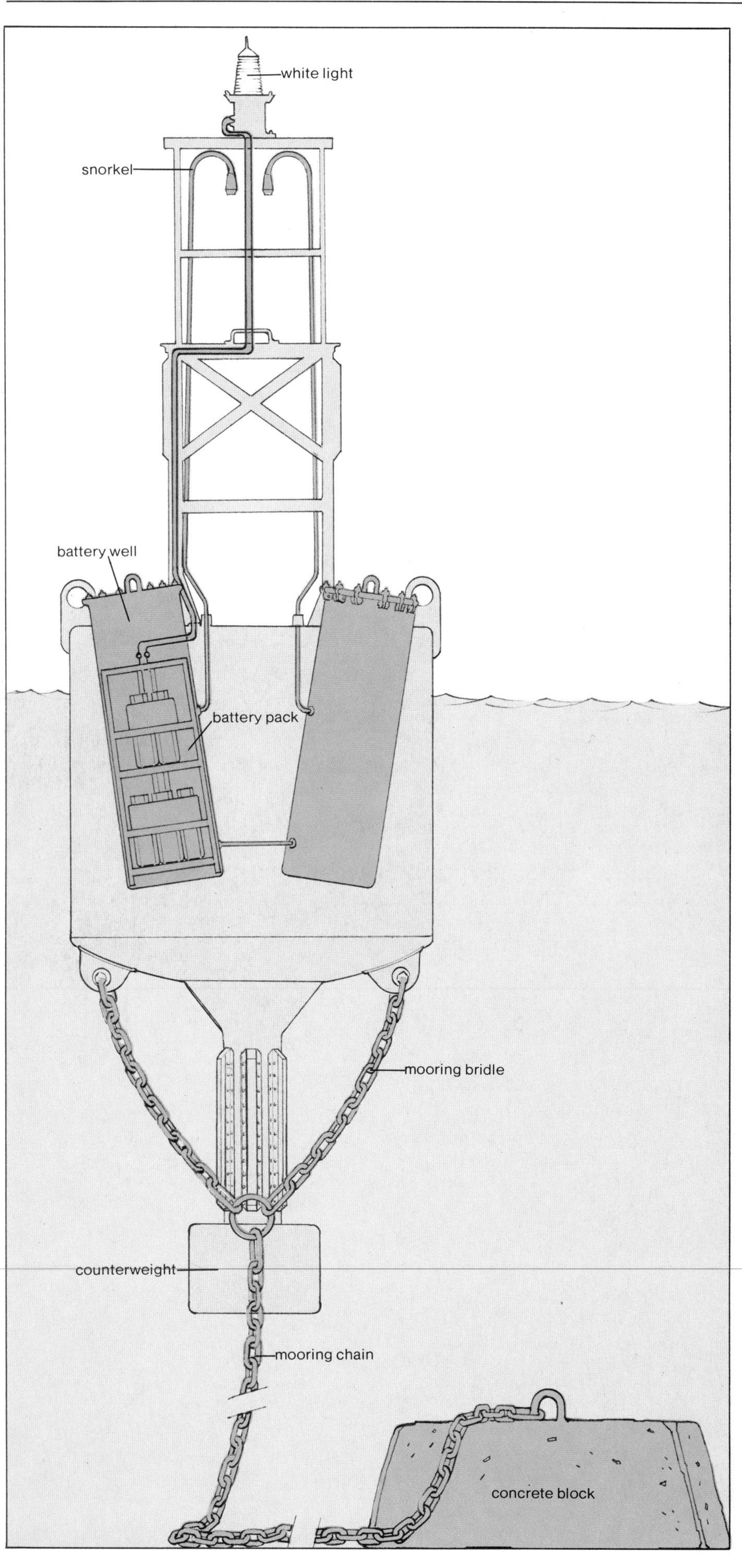

Flashers and Sounders

Buoys are the aids to navigation most commonly encountered. Some are simple metal cylinders moored to the bottom. But many, particularly those located offshore, are complex mechanisms that carry special devices for calling attention to their locations at night or in bad weather. Buoys like the one at left, a new design that is gradually replacing the traditional wasp-waisted buoy seen on page 46, light up. Lighted buoys commonly carry a blinking white light, as here; or they may emit coded signals of various colors and patterns, which are described on the following pages and on page 72. Others, like the four shown opposite, also use bells, gongs, horns or whistles to send out distinctive sound signals. Like the light signals, these noisemakers are identified both on charts and in United States government publications called light lists *(page 73)*, which help the mariner to locate buoy positions—and his own—in times of poor visibility.

Most of these aids to navigation are totally automated, and require only periodic servicing, which is done by the Coast Guard. Lights, for example, are powered by batteries housed in waterproof pockets and are capable of lasting up to three years. Light-sensitive crystals that operate in a manner similar to photoelectric cells switch on the lights automatically whenever the sunlight starts to fade below a certain intensity.

Sound buoys are operated in the main by wave action; the motion of the sea causes their bells and gongs to ring, or air to flow through carefully designed chambers to blow whistles. And though the noisemakers are of immense value to the navigator, especially along a fogbound coast, they have a limited range: the loudest of them usually can be heard no farther off than half a mile. By contrast, a lighted buoy like that at left can be seen for distances of up to seven miles.

Attached firmly to a sunken concrete block by a bridle and a slack chain, this lighted buoy is held upright by a counterweight so that its light can be seen at maximum distances. Two battery packs, mounted in waterproof wells, supply a steady 12-volt current; a snorkel from each pocket carries air to the batteries and lets gases escape.

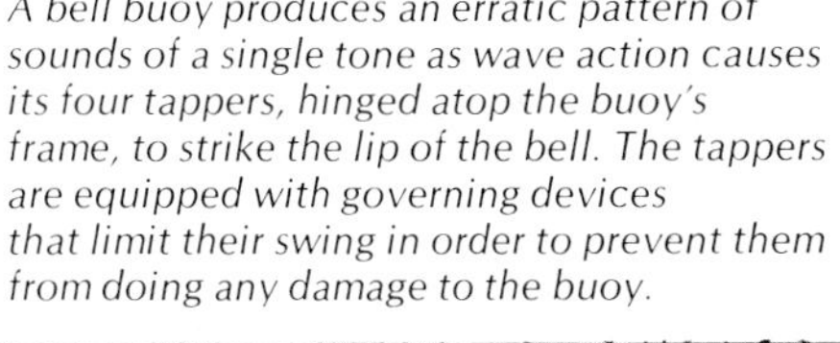

A bell buoy produces an erratic pattern of sounds of a single tone as wave action causes its four tappers, hinged atop the buoy's frame, to strike the lip of the bell. The tappers are equipped with governing devices that limit their swing in order to prevent them from doing any damage to the buoy.

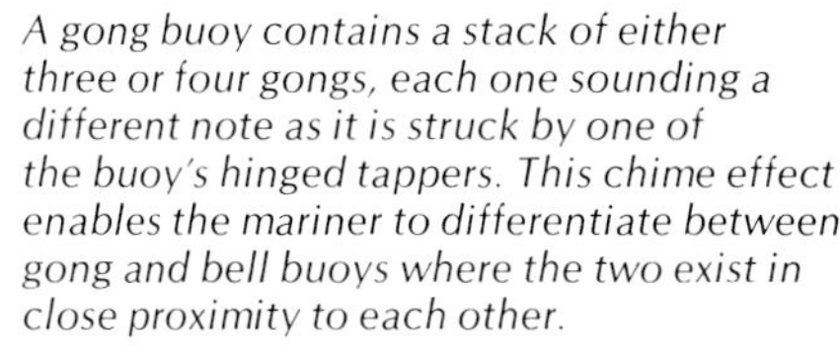

A gong buoy contains a stack of either three or four gongs, each one sounding a different note as it is struck by one of the buoy's hinged tappers. This chime effect enables the mariner to differentiate between gong and bell buoys where the two exist in close proximity to each other.

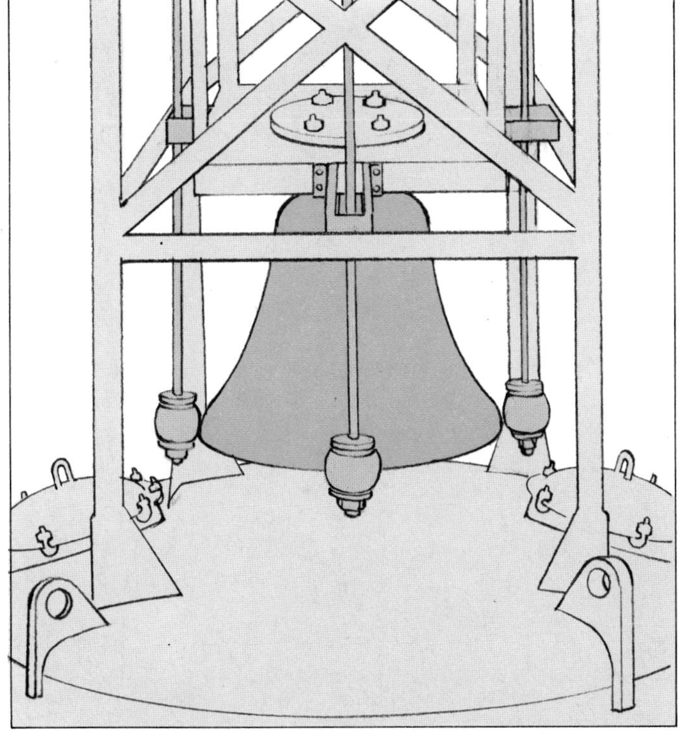

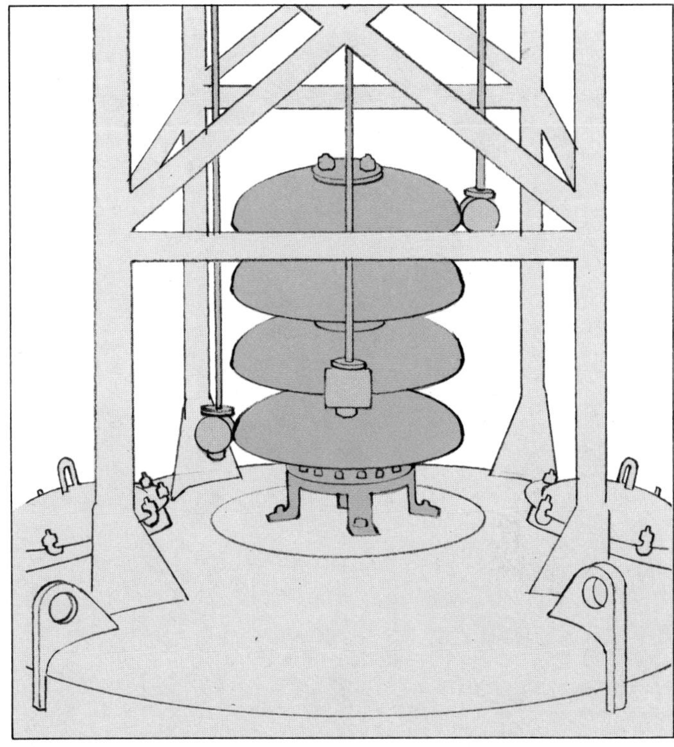

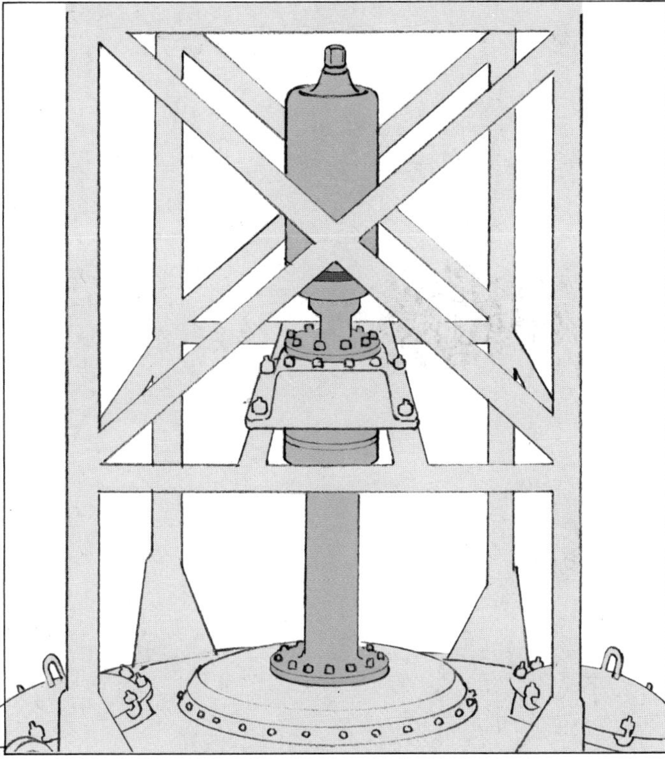

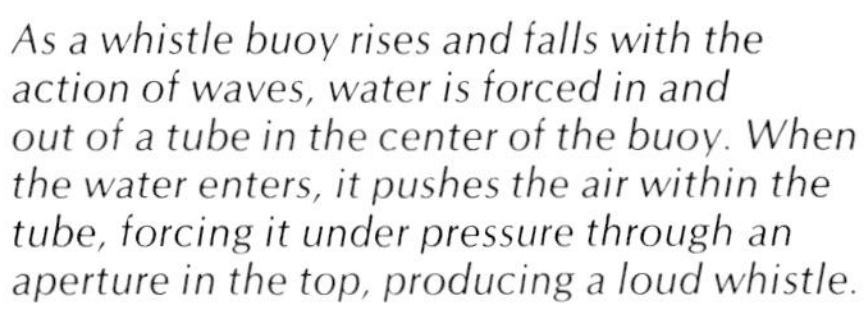

As a whistle buoy rises and falls with the action of waves, water is forced in and out of a tube in the center of the buoy. When the water enters, it pushes the air within the tube, forcing it under pressure through an aperture in the top, producing a loud whistle.

A horn buoy emits electrically energized blasts of predetermined lengths and intervals toward all points of the compass. The power comes from the same type of battery system that works the light shown opposite.

"Red, Right, Returning"

Of the four buoyage systems employed in the United States, the most important one is that used in the waters outlined at right, which are officially termed Navigable Waters by the Coast Guard. And this system of aids to navigation serves as the basis for the other three.

Essentially, the system depends upon observance of one basic rule. When returning to the land from seaward, a boat must leave all red marks to starboard and black to port, following a traditional mariner's dictum: "red, right, returning."

Such marks are coded not only by color but by number and sometimes shape —and this code is matched to a system of chart symbols (*Appendix*). Floating red marks with a conical outline—commonly known as nuns—carry even numbers. Floating black marks, or cans, are cylindrical in shape and bear odd numbers. Daymarks are affixed to stakes or pilings driven into the bottom, and convey similar messages.

Other marks in the system convey other messages: which of two channels is preferable, or where to anchor. The most common of these marks are shown here, and their typical uses are illustrated in the composite harbor scene on pages 52-53.

In the Navigable Waters buoyage system (blue outline), a boat bound inland leaves red marks to starboard. This system's arbitrary subsystem designates "inland" as southerly (or westerly) along the Atlantic Coast; on the Gulf Coast, inland is westerly and northerly; and on the Pacific, northerly.

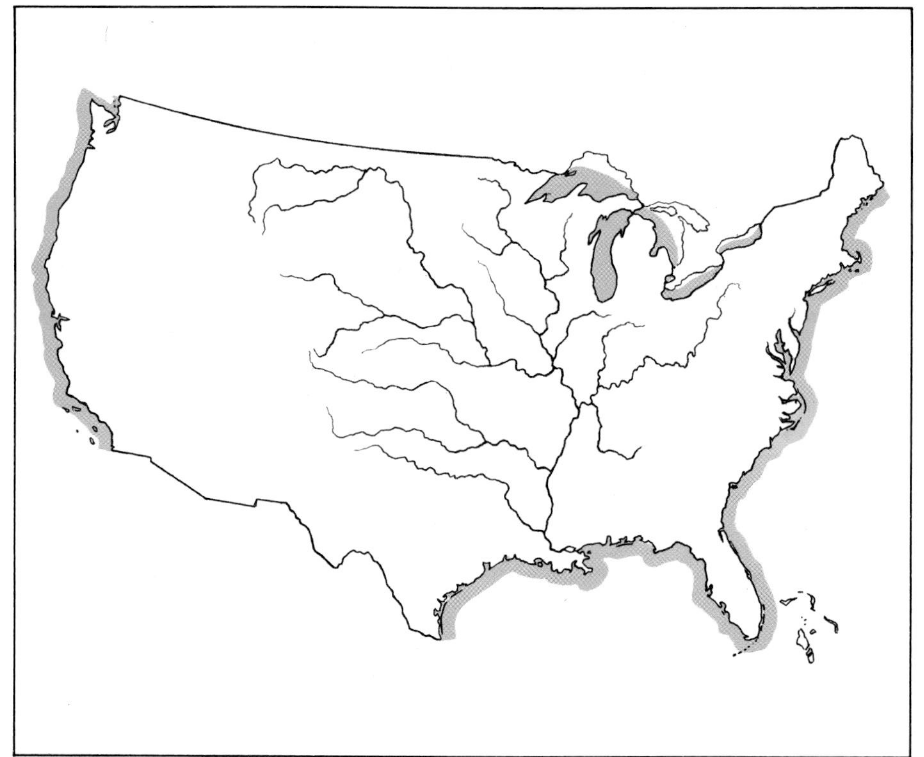

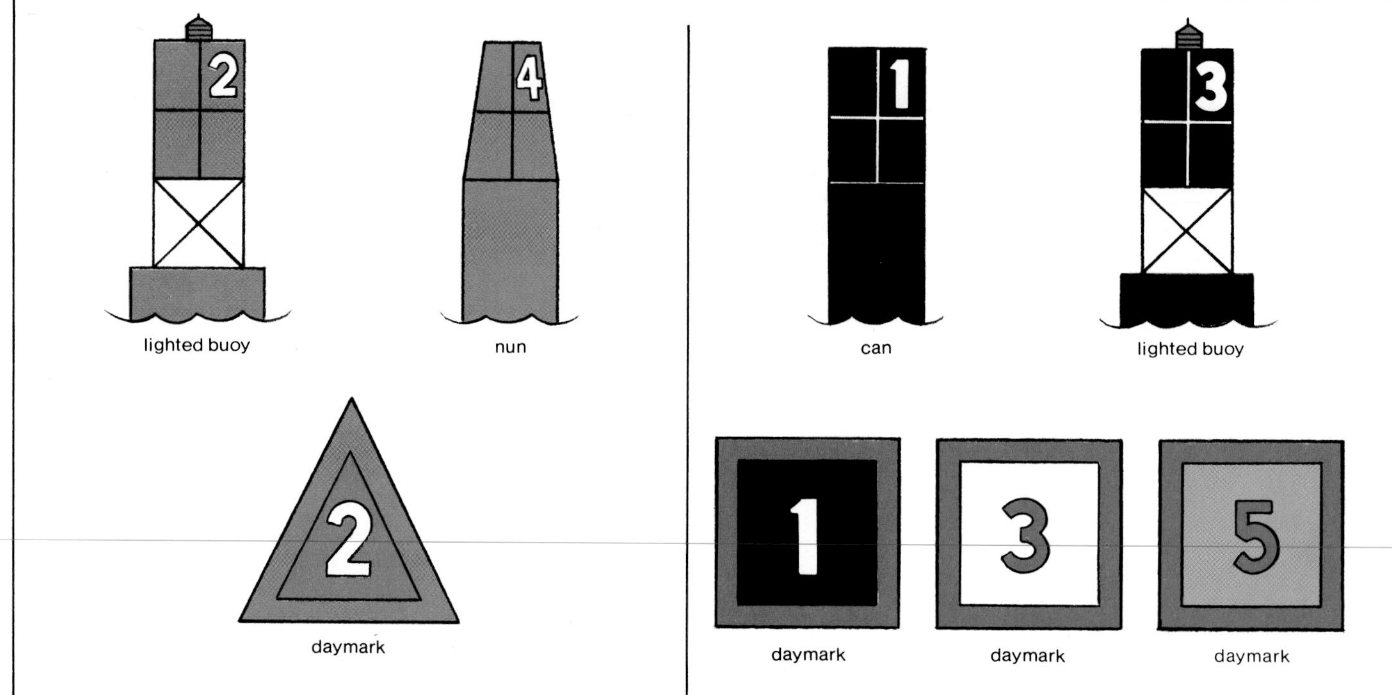

When bound inland from the sea, red even-numbered marks like the lighted buoy above and nun at upper right are kept to starboard. So are triangular red daymarks, which rest on pilings in shallower water. A lighted red buoy may flash red—or, to avoid confusion, white if there are other red lights nearby.

Heading in, black cans or lighted black buoys, which are odd-numbered, must be left to port. The buoy's light may be either green, which is the alternate color code for portside marks, or white. Square portside daymarks have green borders, although the interiors may be black, white or green.

Special-purpose buoys like those shown below can be found in all United States waters. They indicate conditions such as the presence of fish nets that might foul propellers, or quarantine areas where incoming vessels must moor until cleared. Exclusion buoys indicate extreme hazards.

Diamond-shaped daymarks like these have no special meanings. With or without notations, they are used to mark such points of navigation—or dangers—as the end of a jetty, or to call attention to a hazard around the bend of a channel. In their case, color is used only to attract a skipper's attention.

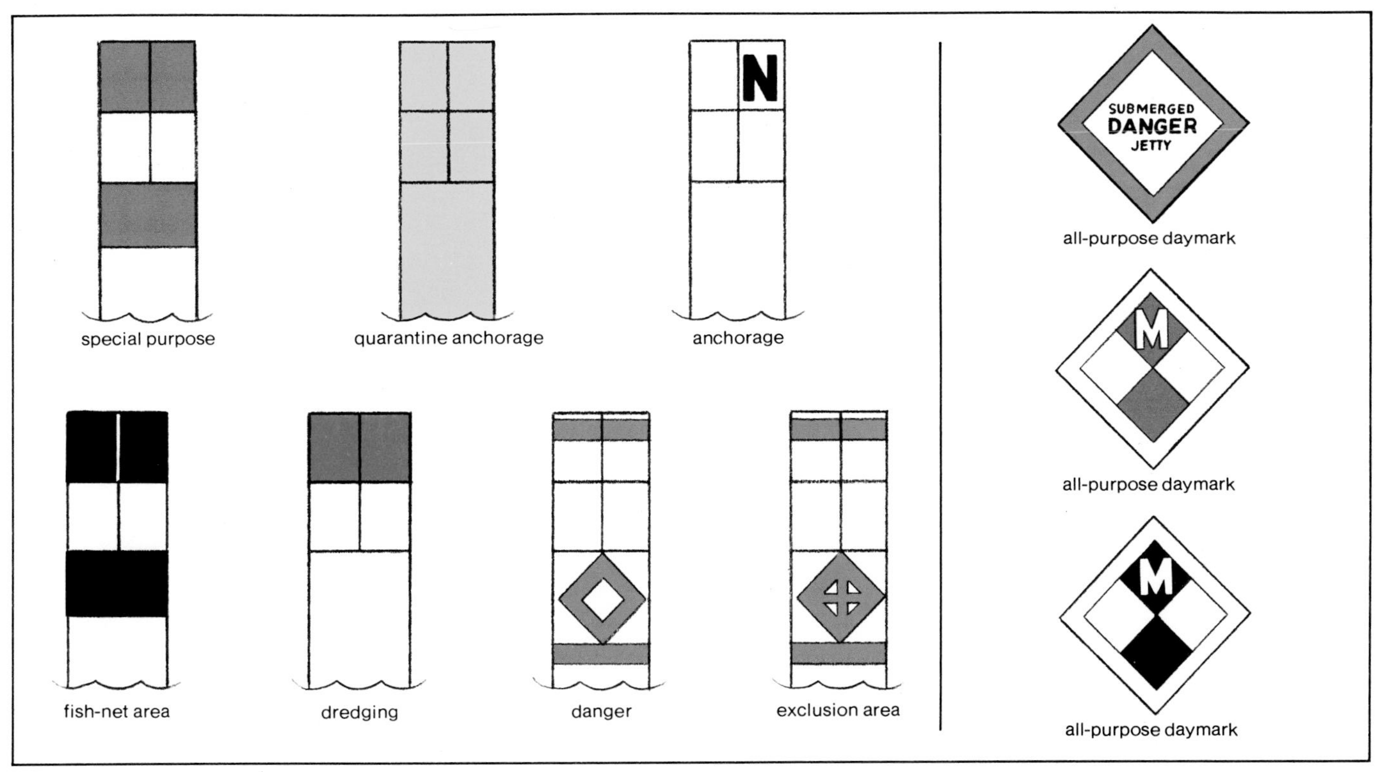

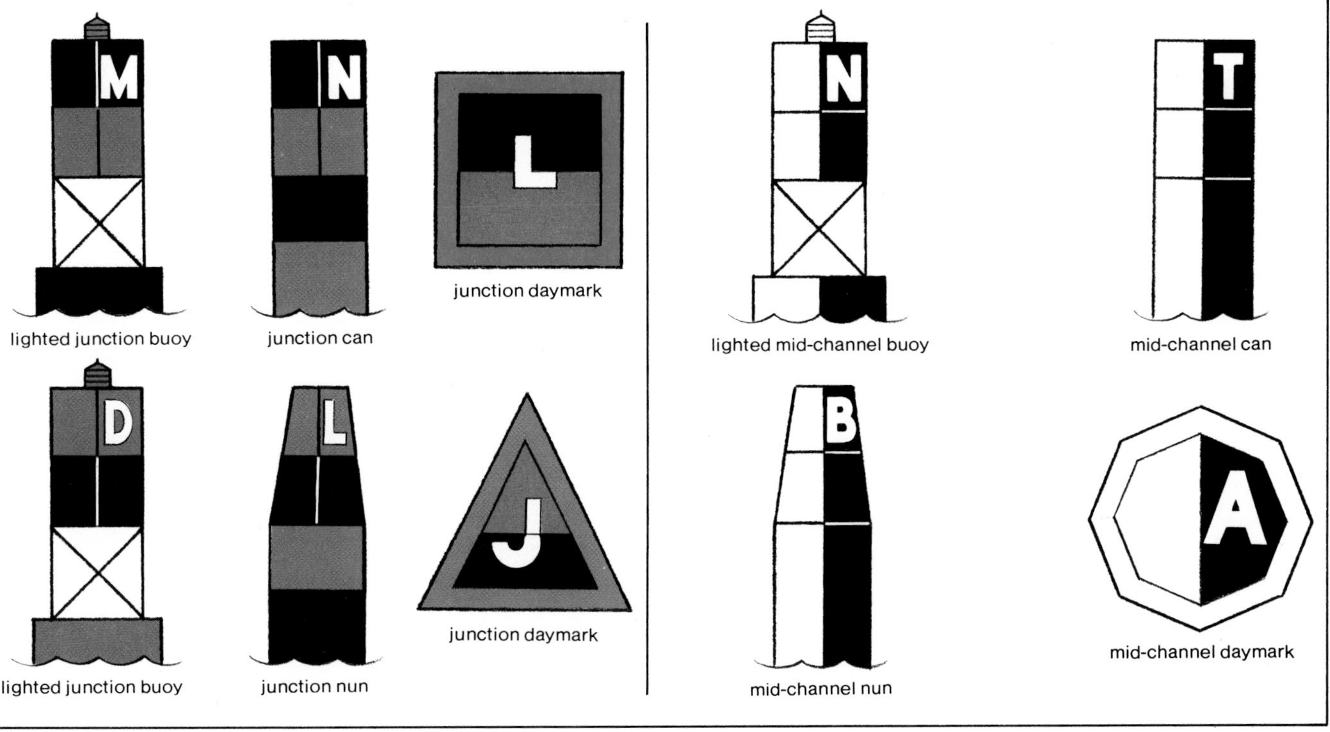

Markers like these indicate the junction of two channels and can be passed to either side. But when a black band is on top, the preferred channel is to starboard; lights may be green or white. A red band on top means the better channel is to port; lights may be red or white. The letters are for identification.

These aids indicate the middle of a channel and, like junction marks, can be passed to either side. The octagonal daymark is used only for mid-channel marks. Such aids may be equipped with white lights that signal with sequential short and long flashes. Sometimes they include identifying letters.

9A
8
10
9
N
3
2
W

The scene at left represents a mythical section of the Maine coast, whose buoys are part of the Navigable Waters system. Although buoys and markers in reality would not be as large as seen here, this view reflects a situation boatmen might encounter. Two channels and a shallow bypass lead to the same harbor. Skippers must read the buoys as detailed below. The accompanying drawings are for quick identification.

The black-and-white whistle buoy marks a channel entrance. It is passed to either side.

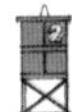

Red lighted buoy #2 is passed to the right by any boat returning from the sea—that is, in the direction indicated by the arrows.

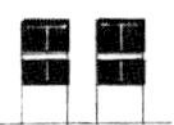

Off to starboard, black-and-white buoys warn the mariner of underwater fish nets.

An orange-rimmed diamond daymark signals an underwater hazard: a collapsed jetty.

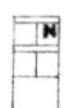

Past lighted buoy #3, anchorage buoy "N" denotes that there is a berth for vessels.

The skipper turns left around lighted black buoy #9 to head for the inner harbor.

Dead ahead, two lighted buoys—one red, one black—form the "gate" to the harbor.

At top right, red bell buoy #2 and black #3 designate the gate to the second channel.

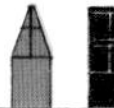

A nun to the right and a black can to the left (upper right) delineate the second channel.

A junction buoy dead ahead marks the intersection of the deepwater channel with the shallower one that lies to starboard.

A beacon, which is to starboard of a boat following the deeper channel, marks a rock. Ahead lie the buoys of the harbor gate.

Threading the Intracoastal

On the East and Gulf coasts of the United States, the Navigable Waters system described on pages 50 and 51 overlaps for long distances with another buoyage system—the Intracoastal Waterway, or ICW. The ICW consists of a series of connected natural channels that afford small boats a protected passage of 2,700 miles from Manasquan Inlet, New Jersey, to the Rio Grande in Texas. Its aids to navigation are basically identical to those of the Navigable Waters system; in fact, along most of the ICW its marks differ only in that they carry broad yellow bands.

But, wherever the Intracoastal Waterway intersects or coincides with the Navigable Waters system, the mariner must exercise special care as he proceeds. In such areas, the only navigational aids seen are those of the Navigable Waters system; they do, however, carry small yellow triangles or squares *(opposite)* that give directional signals to guide boats bound through the Intracoastal Waterway. To follow the ICW under these circumstances, a navigator must therefore ignore the meaning of the marks of the Navigable Waters system, and follow the course given to him by those small yellow triangles and squares.

The Intracoastal Waterway, outlined in blue on the chart below, intertwines along its course with the Navigable Waters system. Throughout the ICW, boats moving away from Manasquan Inlet and toward the Rio Grande are considered to be heading inland, and they must follow the special yellow ICW code.

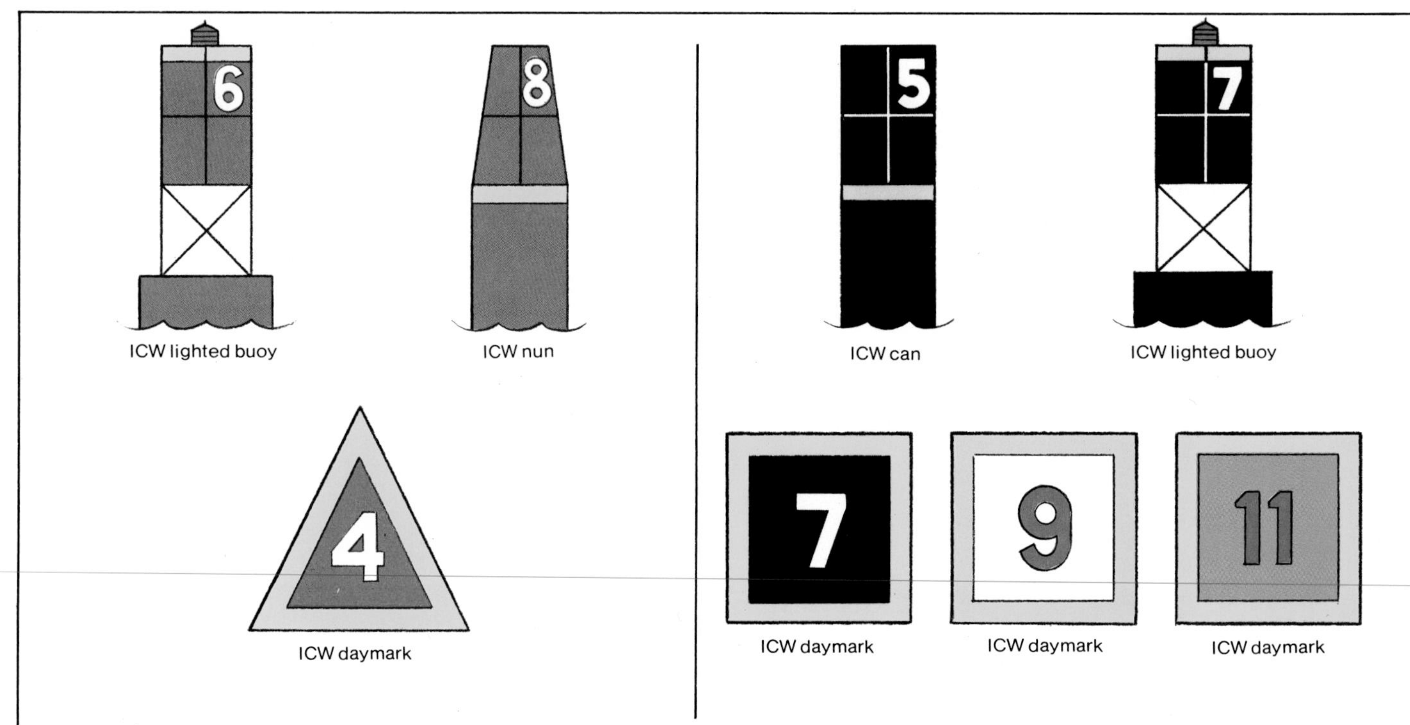

Even-numbered red buoys and triangular daymarks, which also carry the ICW's yellow bands, are kept to starboard when bound inland—as defined in the chart above. Lights are red, as here, or white. Starting at Manasquan Inlet, mark numbers usually run only up to 99, then begin again at 1.

A boat moving down the ICW from New Jersey toward Texas leaves these odd-numbered yellow-banded black buoys (with green or white lights) and square daymarks to port. The green, black or white colors of the daymarks serve as additional reminders that they are to be left to port.

So-called dual-purpose marks like those shown below are primarily part of the Navigable Waters system, and their shapes and colors give directions for its channels. Secondarily, they indicate the course of the ICW. A yellow square means that a boat following the ICW should leave the mark to port.

dual-purpose daymark

dual-purpose daymark

dual-purpose daymark

dual-purpose daymark

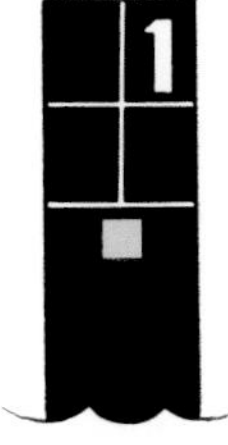

dual-purpose can

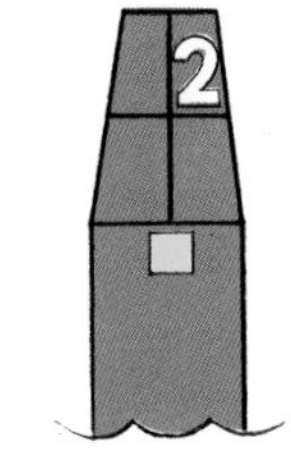

dual-purpose nun

The yellow triangles on these dual-purpose marks say that they should be kept to starboard by a boat running in the Intracoastal Waterway. The numbers on such marks are a part of the odd-left, even-right coding of the Navigable Waters system, and have no relation to the Intracoastal.

dual-purpose daymark

dual-purpose daymark

dual-purpose daymark

dual-purpose daymark

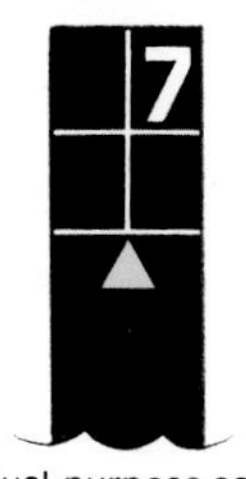

dual-purpose can

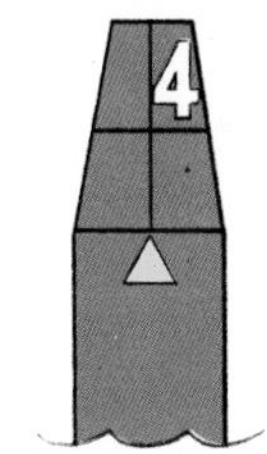

dual-purpose nun

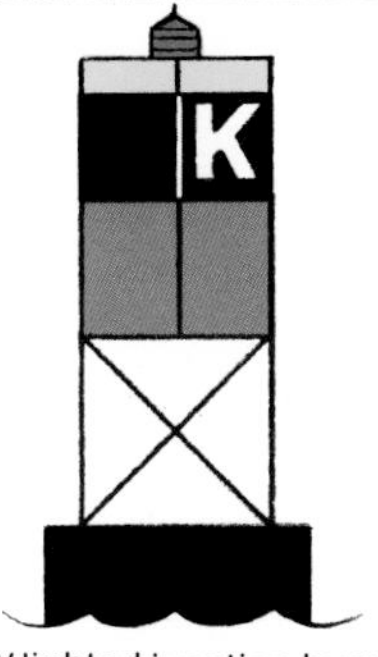

ICW lighted junction buoy

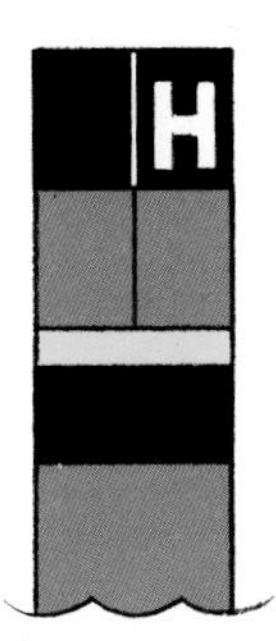

ICW junction can

ICW junction daymark

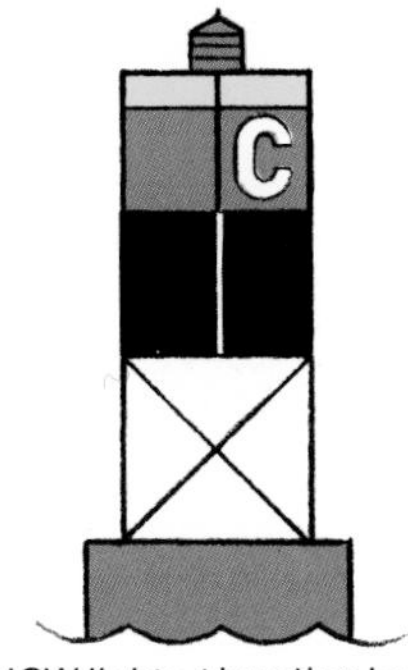

ICW lighted junction buoy

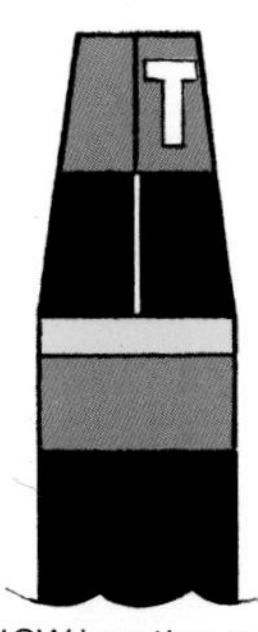

ICW junction nun

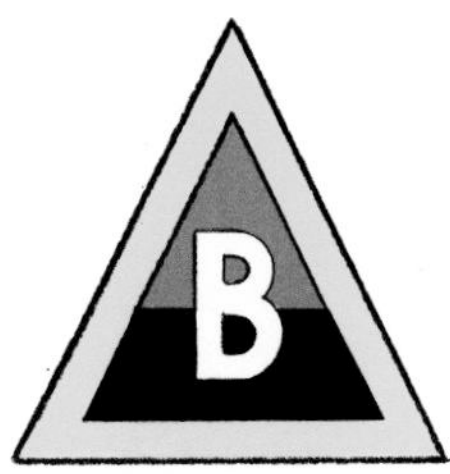

ICW junction daymark

Yellow-banded ICW junction marks indicate intersecting channels. A black band on top means the preferred channel is to starboard (the light can be green or white), red on top that it lies to port (the light is red or white). The better channel is to starboard of the square daymark, to port of the triangle.

ICW mid-channel daymark

The octagonal shape, black and white interior and yellow border of this daymark signal the center of the ICW channel. It can be passed to either side. Such mid-channel daymarks often bear white lights. The letter "E" identifies the mark when compared to its identically lettered chart symbol.

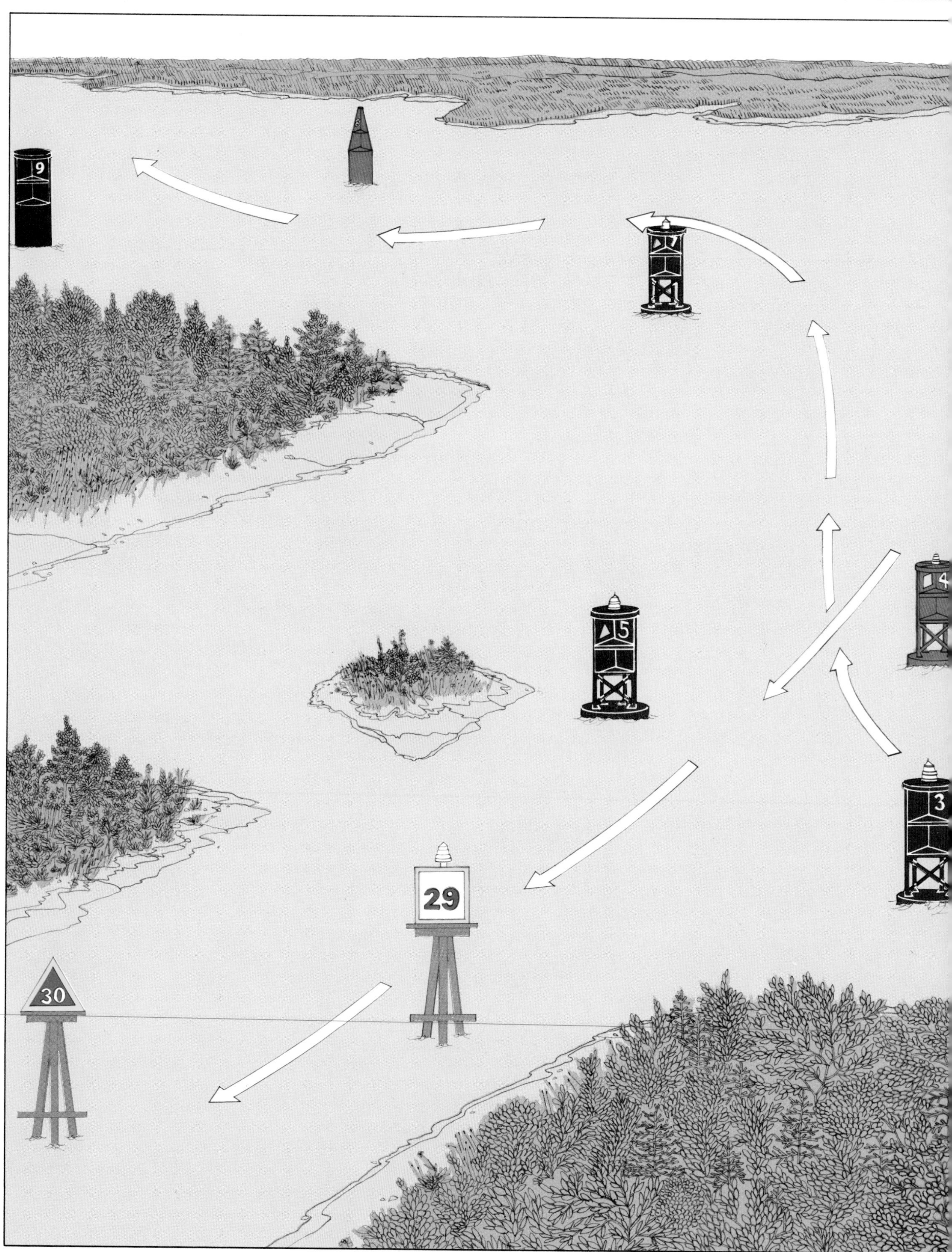
9
8
7
5
4
3
29
30

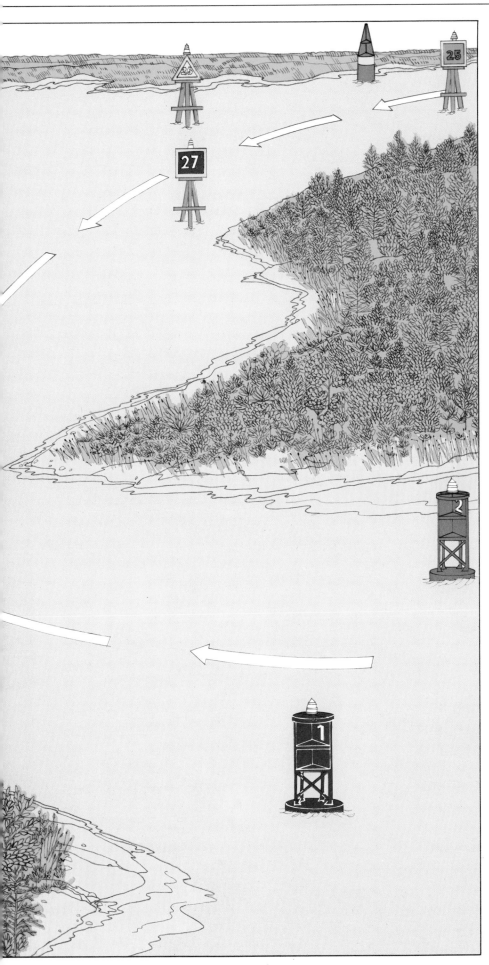

A typical intersection of two buoyage systems—the Intracoastal Waterway and Navigable Waters—is diagramed here. The ICW channel begins at top right; to travel in it, a skipper must be aware of the principle of dual-purpose marks (page 55). The Navigable channel, entered from seaward at bottom right and crossing the Intracoastal channel, is relatively simple to follow.

Cruising down the ICW, the skipper leaves square daymark #25 (top right) to port.

Red nun #24, carrying the ICW's distinctive yellow band, is kept to starboard.

The yellow triangle on dual-purpose buoy #6 tells the ICW skipper to leave it to starboard.

Although buoy #7 is black, the yellow triangle indicates that Intracoastal Waterway traffic must leave it to starboard.

Despite the red color of buoy #4, the yellow square tells the skipper to leave it to port.

Navigable Waters traffic entering from seaward leaves red lighted buoy #2 to starboard, and black buoy #1 to port.

Crossing the ICW channel, Navigable Waters traffic ignores yellow markers on red #4 and #6, and on black #5 and #7, leaving them to starboard and port respectively. Red #8 and black can #9 mark the channel continuation.

Running the Rivers

The Western Rivers buoyage system employs certain specialized aids to deal with the peculiarities of river navigation. Notable among these are "passing" and "crossing" daymarks *(below)*. The passing daymarks are set down where the river channel runs close along one of its banks. As with other aids used in all the systems, their colors, shapes and lights indicate on which side they are to be passed. Crossing daymarks are positioned in places where the river channel crosses to the opposite bank.

In addition, the system frequently employs aids called ranges. These are two marks used together. A skipper positions his boat to line up the range nearer to him with another range farther away, and follows an imaginary line drawn through them to keep on course. Such ranges are also used in other systems, but they are seen most often on Western Rivers.

Western Rivers has a few additional distinctions. Since the changing velocity of river currents causes buoys to vary position more than elsewhere, most Western Rivers marks are not charted. Aids are not numbered or lettered. Occasionally, a mark will, however, show the distance *(opposite)* from one point to another.

Outlined in blue below, the Western Rivers buoyage system is employed on the Mississippi and its tributaries (most other major rivers in the United States are governed by the Navigable Waters system). Here, as elsewhere, leave red marks to starboard when proceeding inland—that is, moving upstream.

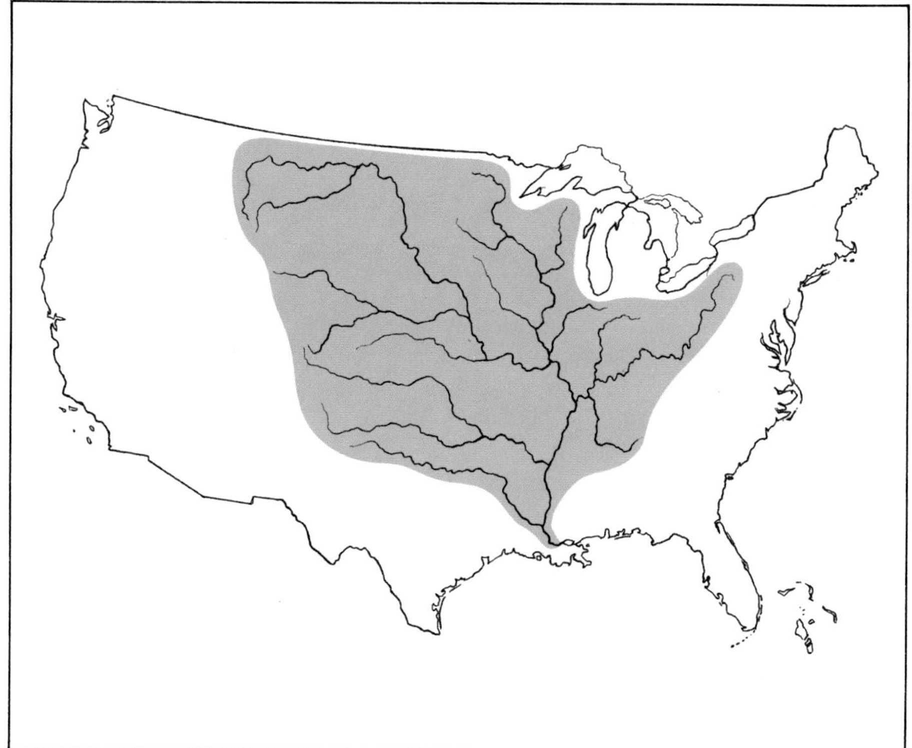

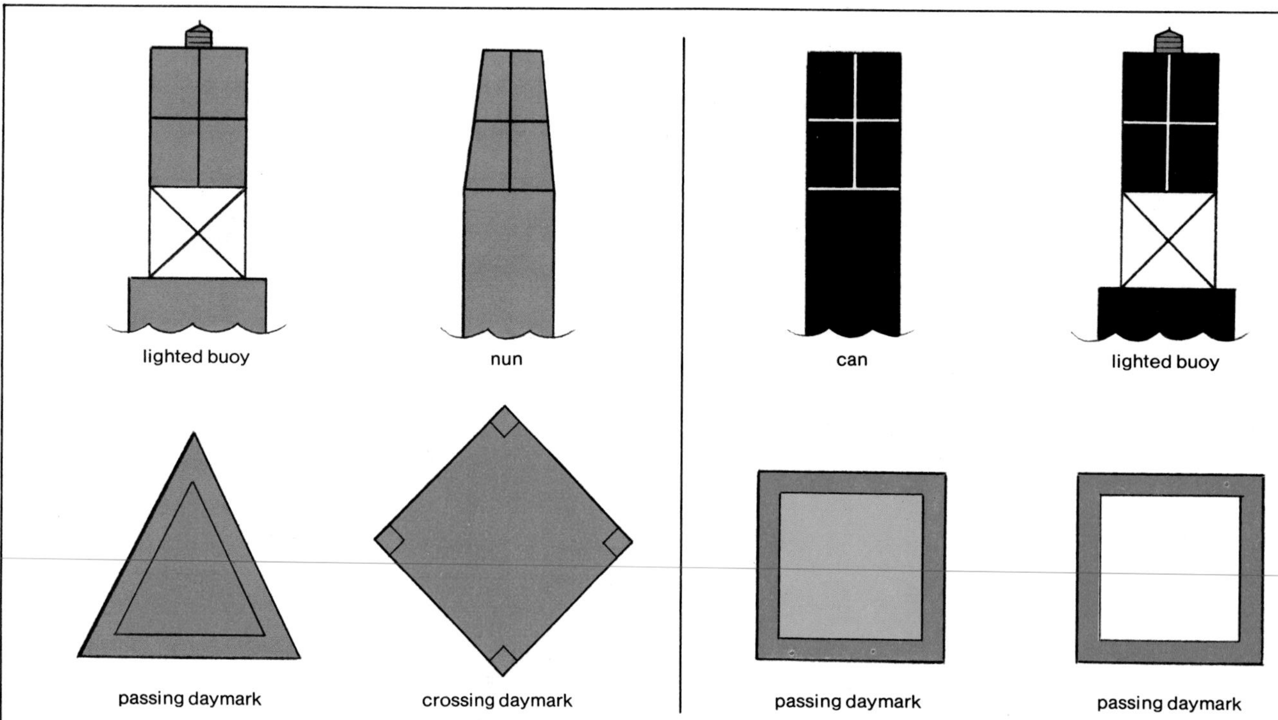

Moving upriver, a boat leaves the red nun and red-lighted (or white-lighted) buoy at top to starboard. The triangular red passing daymark, marking a channel near a riverbank, is also left to starboard—as is the red crossing diamond, which indicates that the channel is shifting to the other bank.

Black cans and lighted buoys are left to port en route upriver, as are green or white, green-bordered passing daymarks. As elsewhere, buoy lights are green or white, predominantly green. The green or white diamond-shaped crossing daymarks (near right) are also passed to port. There are no black daymarks.

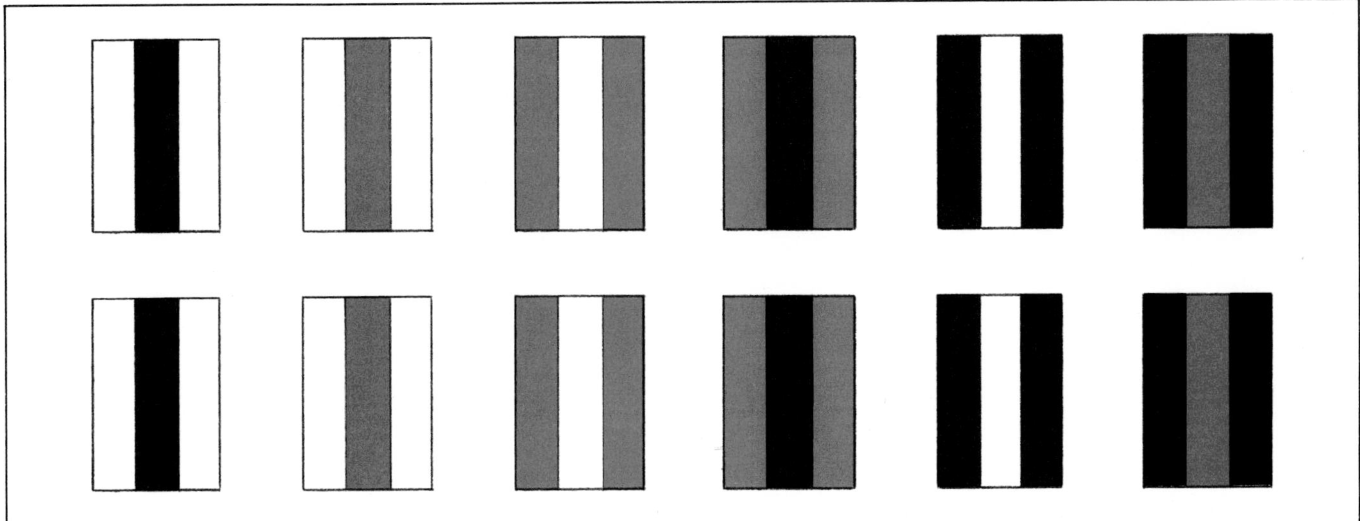

Range marks used on Western Rivers—and in the Navigable Waters—are shown above. The Intracoastal Waterway uses similar range marks, which also carry that system's distinctive yellow bands. In all systems, the basic colors serve to make the marks stand out against their backgrounds. Red, for example, might be used when green farmlands line the shore. Many ranges carry lights; again, the colors do not indicate direction but are selected for maximum visibility against the night landscape.

131.4

mile board

Mile boards on the Western Rivers mark the distance upstream from a given spot—either the river's mouth or the point of its confluence with another river. This one might be telling the mariner that he is 131.4 miles upstream from the Mississippi's Gulf outlet.

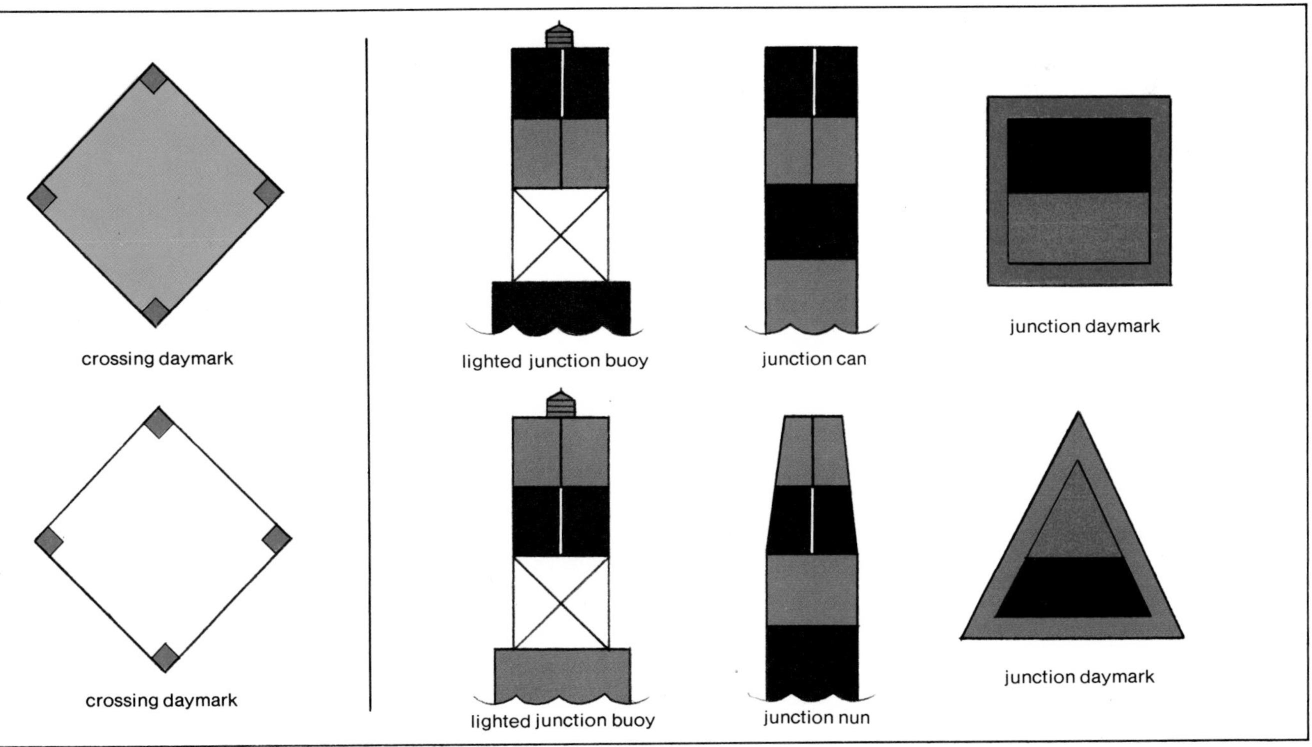

These buoys and daymarks, like those on pages 51 and 55, signal the convergence of two channels. And their color coding is the same: a black band on top says the preferred channel is to starboard (its light, if any, is green or white); a red band (or a red or white light) says that the channel is to port.

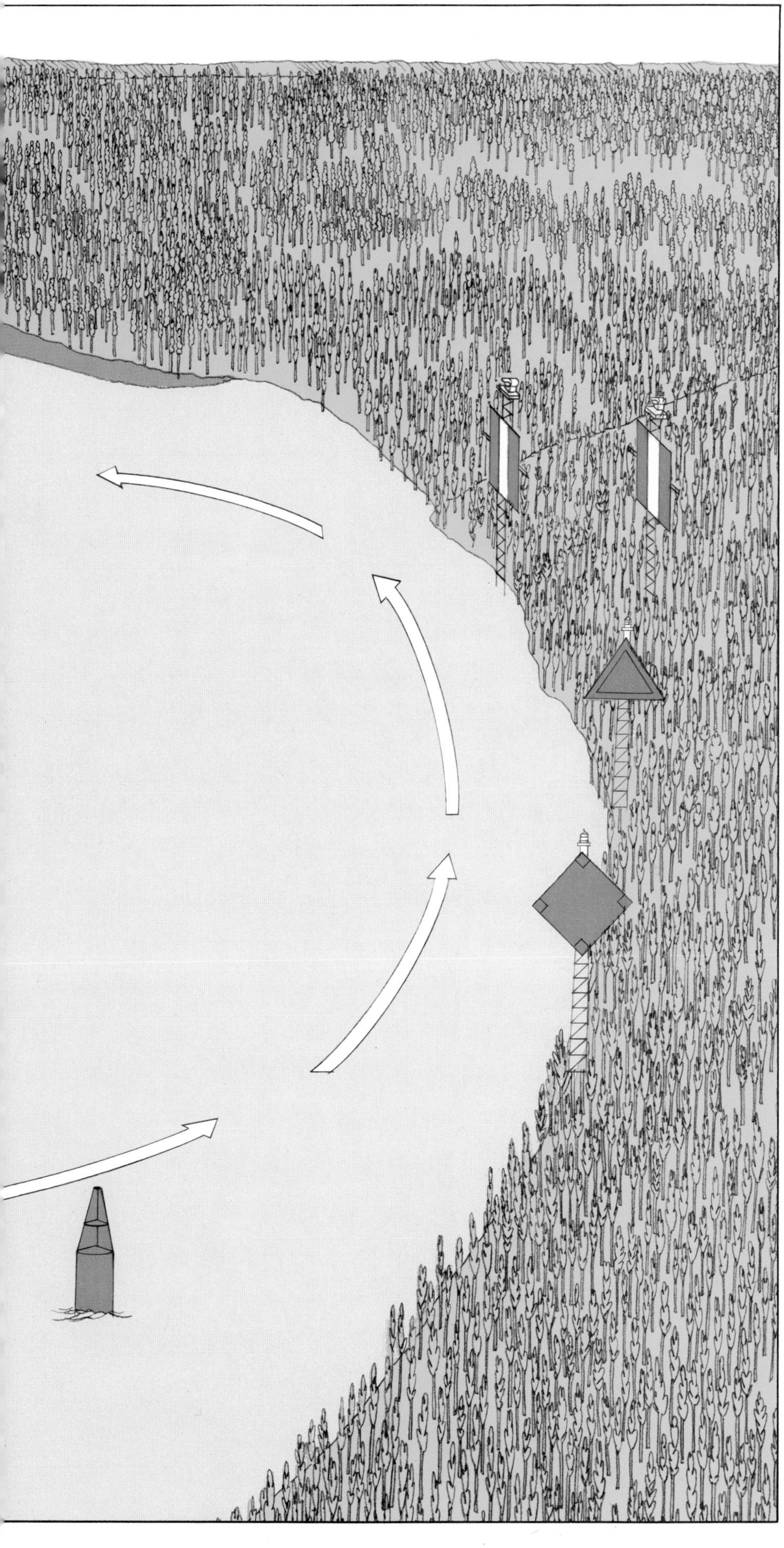

The scene at left represents an imaginary section of the Mississippi, whose traffic is governed by the Western Rivers buoyage system (pages 58-59). Traveling upriver, a skipper would follow the buoys and other marks in the manner described below.

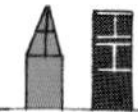

Red nuns and black cans—which are laid down in abundance because flood currents often move them or sweep them away altogether—mark mudbanks to the right and left sides, respectively, of the river channel.

A red diamond-shaped crossing daymark signals deep-draft upstream traffic to cross the river and head toward it in order to stay in the deepest water of the mainstream. Shallow-draft vessels might cut the corner to avoid the mainstream's strong current.

A triangular red passing daymark indicates that the mainstream channel continues to run closely along the right-hand bank.

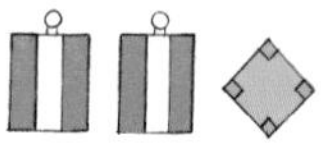

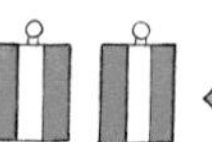

A pair of ranges, when aligned astern, directs traffic toward a green crossing daymark, farther upriver and on the opposite bank.

At a fork in the river, a red-and-black junction daymark signals by the red upper sector that the preferred channel is to port.

Square passing daymarks on the mainstream arm of the fork indicate that the deepwater channel is close by the left-hand bank.

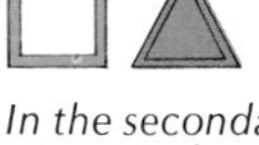

In the secondary channel, square and triangular passing daymarks show that either bank is suitable for navigation.

A System for the States

In virtually all United States waters not under federal jurisdiction, a fourth buoyage system takes over. This is the Uniform State Waterway Marking System (USWMS) used on large bodies of water that lie wholly within the borders of a state—e.g., Lake George in New York.

The system uses two special types of marks: "regulatory" and "cardinal." Regulatory marks are painted with orange crossed diamonds, diamonds, circles or rectangles *(right)* that convey specific messages; they may carry white lights.

Cardinal marks *(bottom right)* are used in areas where there is no well-defined channel—or where the mark might be approached from any one of several points. Their color coding indicates the direction of safe water and the course the boat should take to reach it. For example, the black-topped buoy tells the boatman to stay to the north or east of it, the red-topped to the south or west. The red-and-white-striped buoy signals an obstruction between it and the nearest shore. Cardinal marks, too, carry white lights, or none.

The USWMS uses black and red odd- and even-numbered channel buoys that employ the "red, right, returning" code—and one other distinctive mark, a mooring buoy *(below)*, is colored blue.

The shapes and patterns of these orange-and-white regulatory emblems give commands, warnings or information. A diamond with a cross means "keep out," a diamond alone means "beware," a circle says "obey regulations," and rectangles give directions.

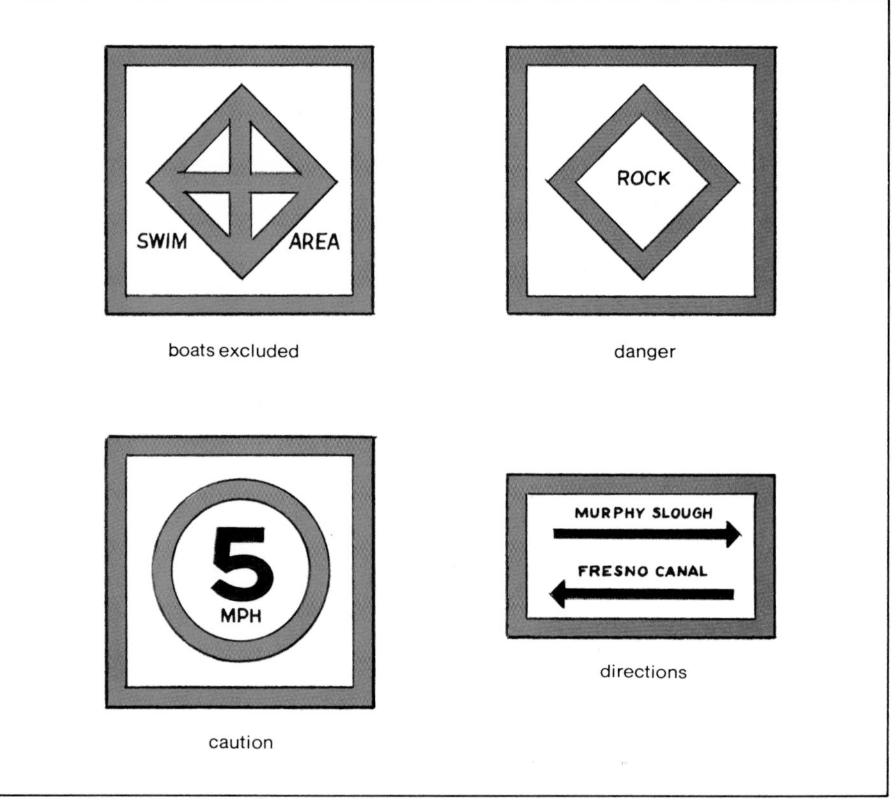

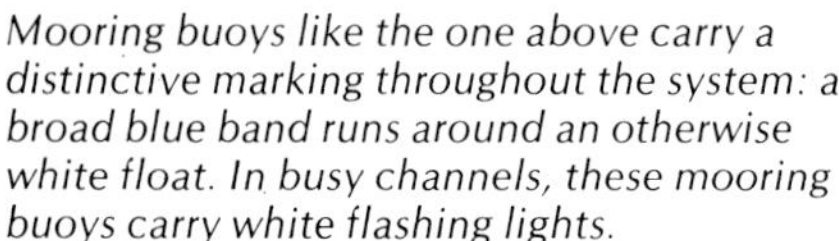

Mooring buoys like the one above carry a distinctive marking throughout the system: a broad blue band runs around an otherwise white float. In busy channels, these mooring buoys carry white flashing lights.

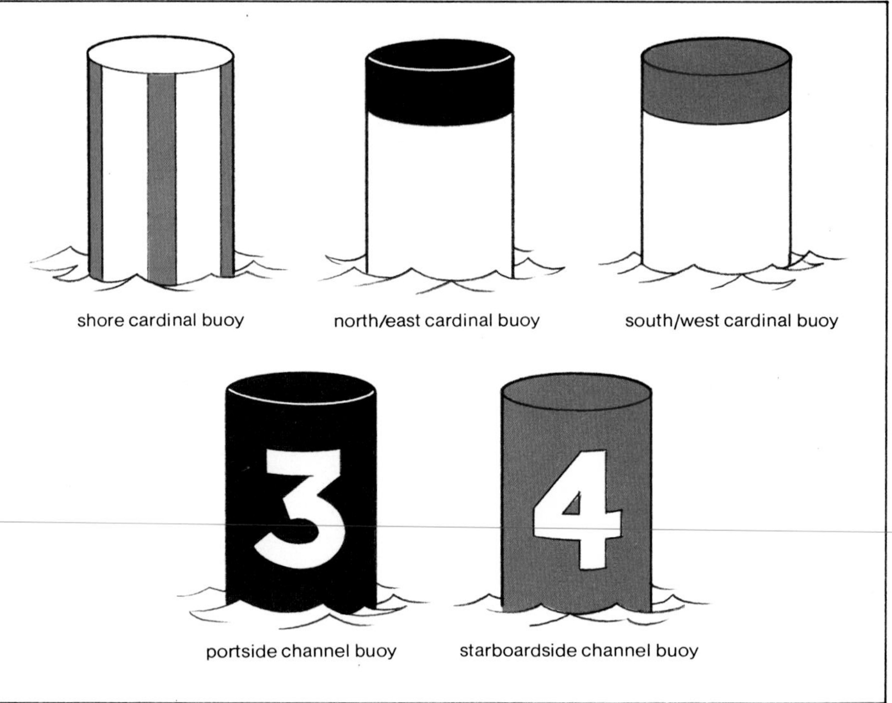

Cardinal buoys (top row) warn of hazards in different directions. A boat must not pass between shore and a red-and-white-striped buoy. It should proceed north or east of a white buoy with a black top, and south or west of one with a red top. Black channel buoys are left to port, red to starboard.

The hypothetical lake at left lies wholly within the borders of a single state and thus employs the Uniform State Waterway Marking System described opposite. In the deployment of navigation aids shown here, north is to the top of the page—as is the direction of the lake's source.

Traffic heading up the lake avoids the rocks in the foreground by passing to the north or east of the black-topped cardinal buoy.

A vertically striped shore buoy warns vessels to steer clear of the rocky hazard that lies between it and the nearest land.

Off to port, a cross-and-diamond exclusion insignia on the square daymark directs boats to keep away from a swimming beach.

To starboard, a plain diamond—indicating danger—on the daymark underscores the presence of the rocky hazard.

The red-topped cardinal buoy beyond the rock should be passed to the west by boats heading up the main channel, or to the south by a boat proceeding into the cove.

A blue-striped buoy such as the one in the cove is to be used for mooring.

A line of red buoys should be left to starboard when moving toward the lake's source.

Black buoys should be left to port when proceeding through these narrows.

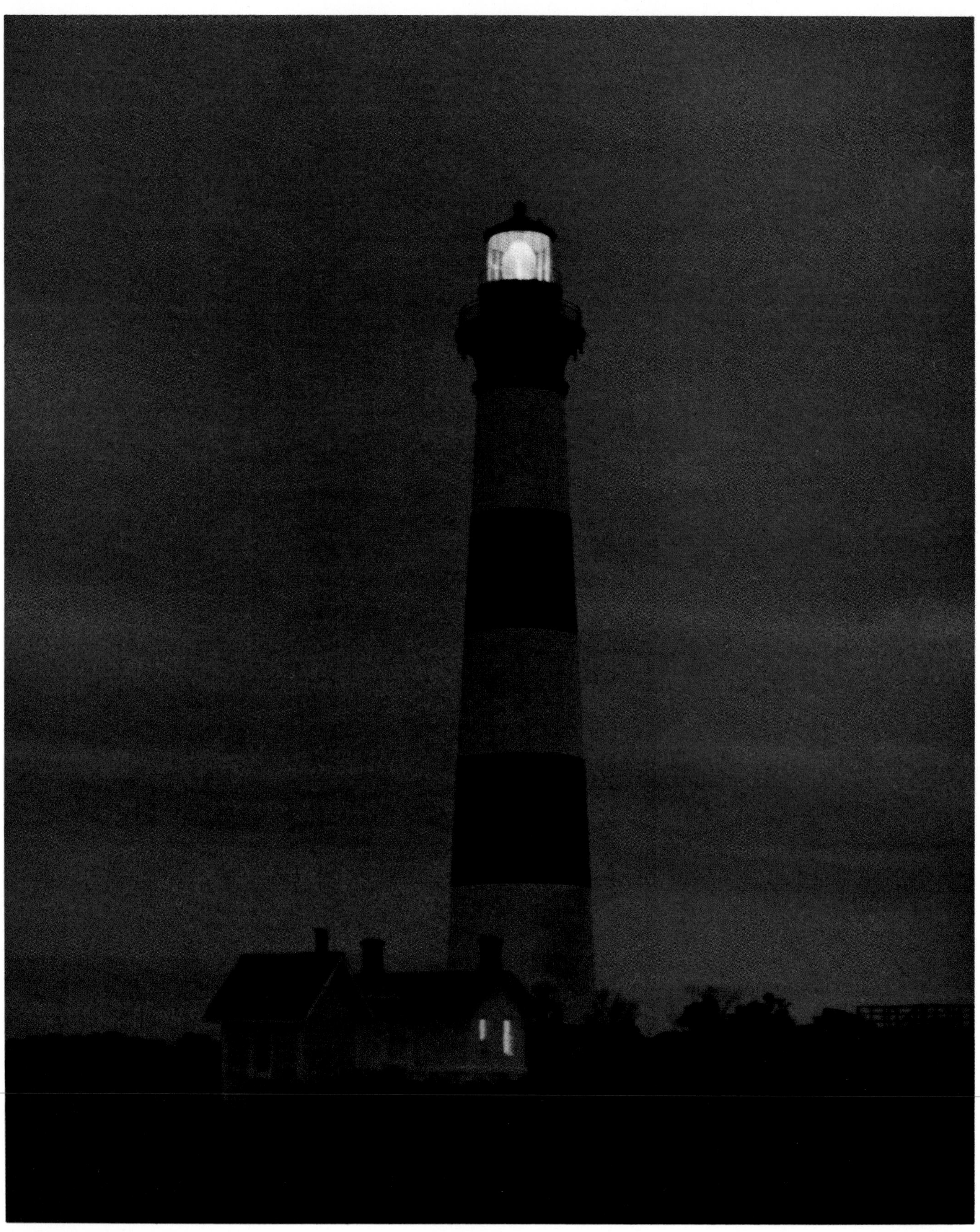

Its light gleaming beneath the crown of a 166-foot tower, the Bodie (pronounced "body") lighthouse marks dangerous shoals near Cape Hatteras, North Carolina. The island is named for the numerous bodies washed ashore after repeated shipwrecks.

Guiding Lights

By far the most visible and dramatic of all navigation aids are the large, complex structures known as light stations, whose powerful beams, frequently augmented by other warning signals, guide mariners over broad stretches of open water. The most familiar of these structures are lighthouses, such as the Bodie Island station looming above the shrubs of a North Carolina sandspit at left. The Bodie light, like scores of others perched on coastal headlands or offshore islands, casts its beam almost 20 miles over the ocean—as it has steadily for more than a century.

While a fair number of the nation's lighthouses have done similarly long service—and retain such old-fashioned features as living quarters for a resident keeper—the majority are fully automated. Besides having a complex and sophisticated lens *(overleaf)*, most of the stations now send out radio beams *(top right)* for electronic navigation by RDF *(pages 130-133)*, and are equipped with foghorns *(right, below)* that can be switched on by remote control from the nearest Coast Guard station.

On every light station, the radio beacon, the foghorn and the light itself emit their signals in characteristic, coded sequences that allow the mariner to quickly identify the source. Bodie Island Light, for example, gives two brief white flashes every 30 seconds. This identifying signal, or light phase, is noted next to the station's position on the nautical chart for the area, and is also included in a multivolume Coast Guard publication called the light lists *(page 73)*. The light lists also give the pertinent characteristics of all the foghorns and radio beacons.

Another important piece of information included in the light lists is the visible range of each station. This depends on two main factors: the height of the light above the water and the luminosity of its lamps. The listings give the distance at which the light is visible on a clear night—called the nominal range; this figure provides the navigator with a valuable clue for judging his position when the light first comes into view.

Like many light stations, the one below sends out a continuous, distinctive radio signal that can be picked up by any boat equipped with a radio direction finder (RDF). Here, the signal consists of three alternating short and long tones—symbolized by the varying widths of the stylized radio waves. While beacons on some older stations may be separate structures as here, on modern stations they are in the form of a thin antenna attached to the lighthouse.

A Fog Warning that Sometimes Goes Askew

While no warning devices announce themselves with more authority than electric foghorns, now housed in many light stations, the message they deliver is sometimes ambiguous—as shown by this schematic aerial view of a powerboat passing a light station. The reason is that the sound waves from the horn often encounter different air temperatures, which cause the waves to speed up, or slow down, and bend out of shape. The foghorn at left is surrounded by an area of cool air (tinted light blue), which transmits the sound waves in a slow, regular pulse. But when a segment of the waves meets a patch of warm air (tinted blue-gray), the warm air causes these segments to push slightly ahead. To a listener on the boat, the source of the signal then seems to be off the starboard quarter *(arrow)*, even though the foghorn's true position is directly abeam.

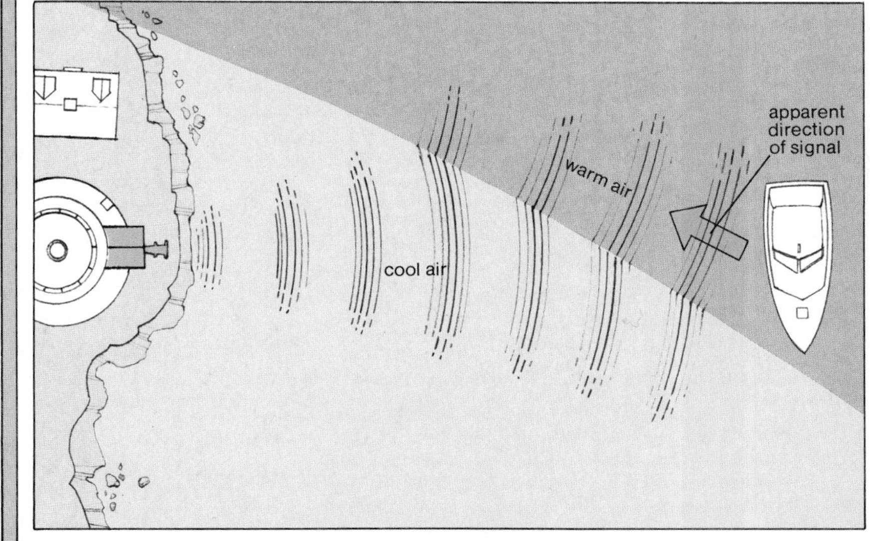

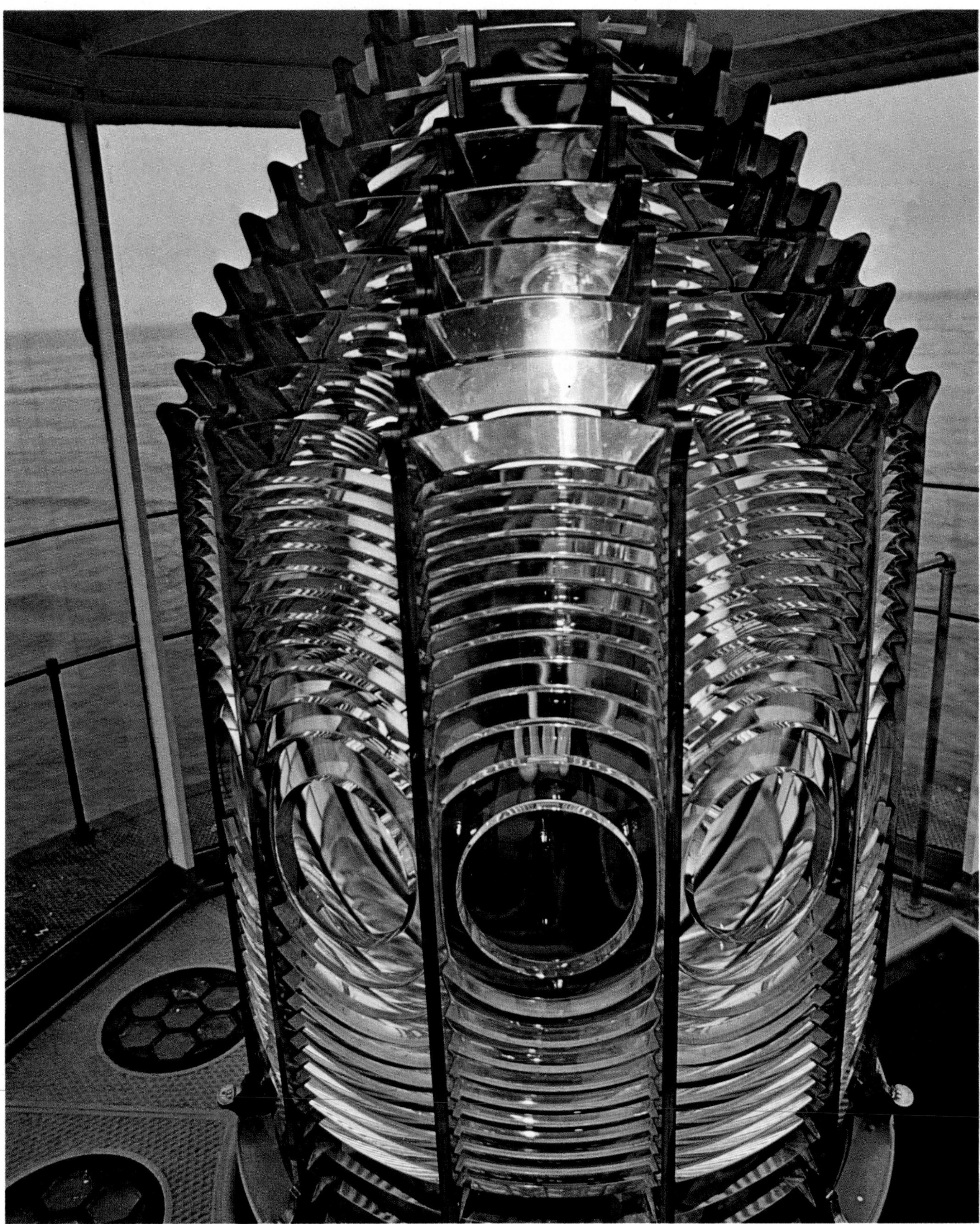

The Fresnel lens in the light station at Point Loma, California, consists of 12 vertical glass panels tapering on top into rows of prisms that form a crown. In each panel, concentric segments of prismatic rings encircle a central bull's-eye. This lens is eight feet high and weighs nearly a ton, yet because it is mounted on a friction-reducing mercury float, a relatively small electric motor can revolve it around the 1,000-watt bulb that is located inside the structure.

Mariner's Magic Lantern

The powerful beams that emanate from a typical light station owe their brilliance to a massive lens invented in 1820 by the French physicist Augustin Fresnel. A complex structure of cut-glass prisms, the Fresnel lens surrounds a light, collecting and intensifying rays so dramatically that on a clear night a 250-watt incandescent bulb may be seen 15 miles away.

This amazing optical achievement was the masterwork of an unassuming technician who lacked both a laboratory and basic scientific instruments. An engineer in Napoleon's army, Fresnel was relegated to overseeing road construction. When off duty, he pondered the nature of light, using a sheet of paper with a small hole covered by a drop of honey to serve as a makeshift lens. Despite the lack of proper equipment, Fresnel learned enough to begin authoring papers that helped establish the wave theory of light, now a basic law of physics. Eventually, Fresnel was assigned to the French Lighthouse Commission where, putting his theories into practice, he developed his lens.

Besides intensifying the strength of the light, a lighthouse lens is now so constructed that, when rotated, it sends out a characteristic coded signal *(below)*.

Crowning a steel tower that rises above the Southern California palms, the Fresnel lens at Point Loma directs its light into a predawn mist. Even though its effective range is reduced by the morning haze, the light still manages a beam strong enough to be picked up several miles out in the Pacific Ocean.

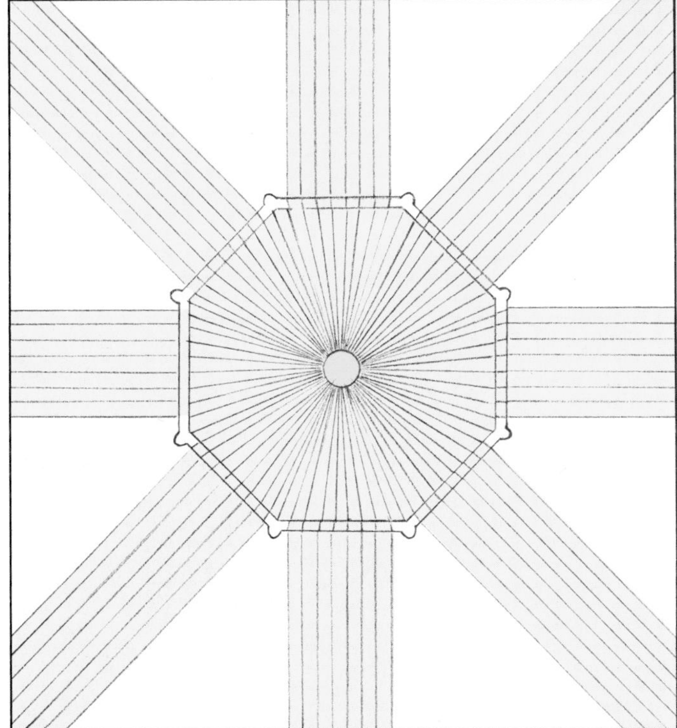

This simplified top-view drawing of a Fresnel lens shows how its panels produce a series of flashes—thereby giving a lighthouse its identifying signal. Each panel transmits light beams as a separate column. Thus, as the lens turns, light columns flash, then appear to go dark, in a recognizable pattern.

The key to the effectiveness of the Fresnel lens, illustrated here in cross section, is an ingeniously arranged set of prisms at the top and bottom of each panel; these prisms bend the light's rays so precisely and effectively that virtually all of the rays go out in orderly, intensely focused beams.

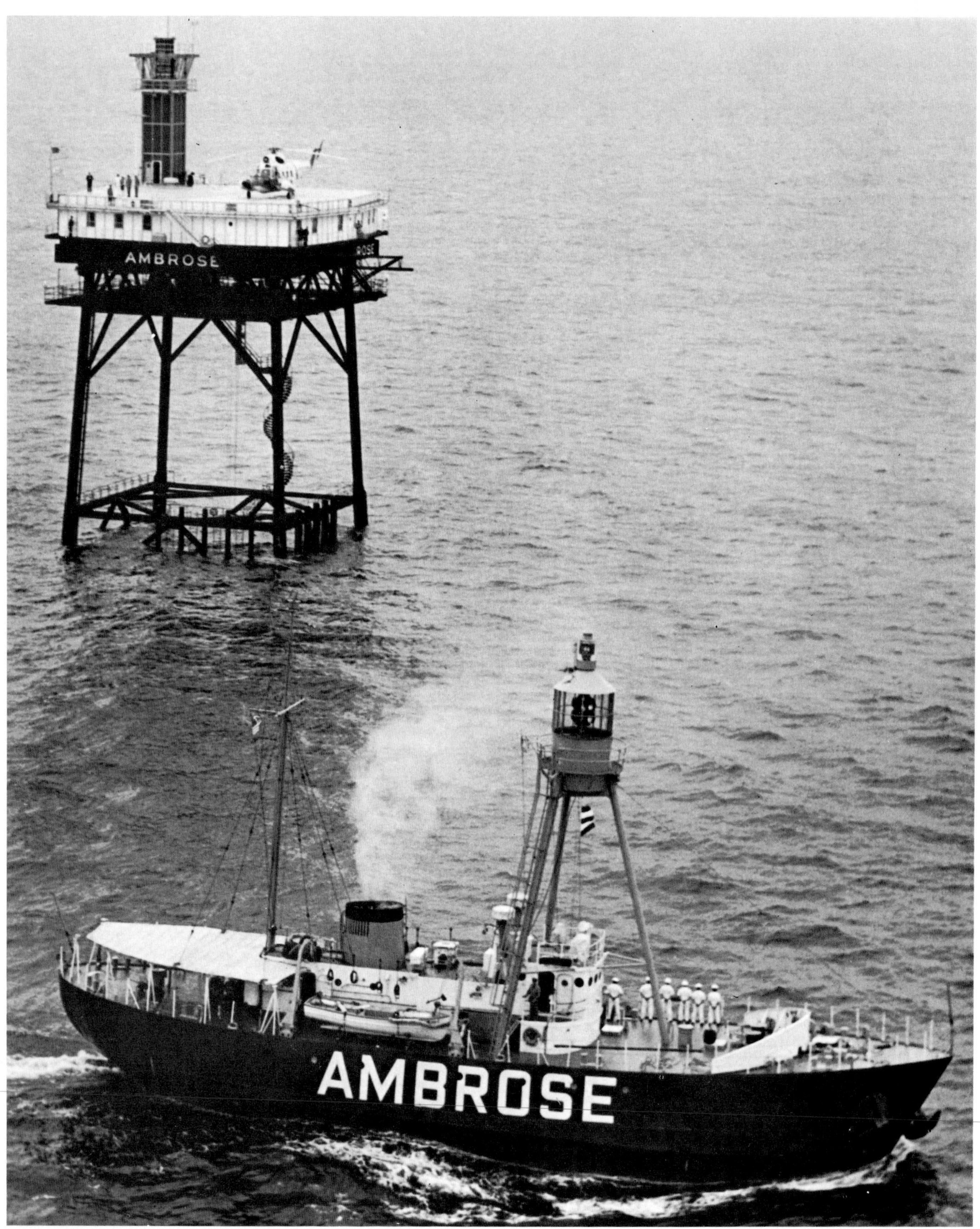

The navigational torch passes as the lightship Ambrose makes a farewell circle around its successor, an offshore light tower, in 1967. With the crew lined up on deck and signal flags flying to indicate that it is underway, the vessel leaves its post in New York harbor, where lightships had served since 1823.

Deepwater Stations

In open water where the depth is too great to construct conventional lighthouses, offshore shoals and heavily traveled seaways are marked by the three types of light stations shown here—the lightship, light tower and so-called large navigational buoy (LNB). Each of these deep-water stations has its own coded light, radio beacon and fog signal. The lightships, painted a fire-engine red, are the oldest and most colorful. But during the 10 years from 1965 to 1975 most of them were replaced either by the more modern light towers *(left)* or by LNBs. Indeed, in 1975 only two major lightships were still operating in United States waters: one off Nantucket Island in Massachusetts and the other at the mouth of the Columbia River in Washington.

Both the light towers and the LNBs represent substantial advances in efficiency and in ease of operation. The towers *(right)*, often called Texas Towers because they are adaptations of offshore oil rigs, sit firmly on bedrock: unlike the lightships, they cannot be driven out of position by storms. Some towers carry a skeleton crew of four or five men, and others need no crew at all—while the lightships demand an operating force of a dozen men or more. All the LNBs *(below)* are totally self-operating, and are cheaper to install than the towers, though the range of their lights is not as great.

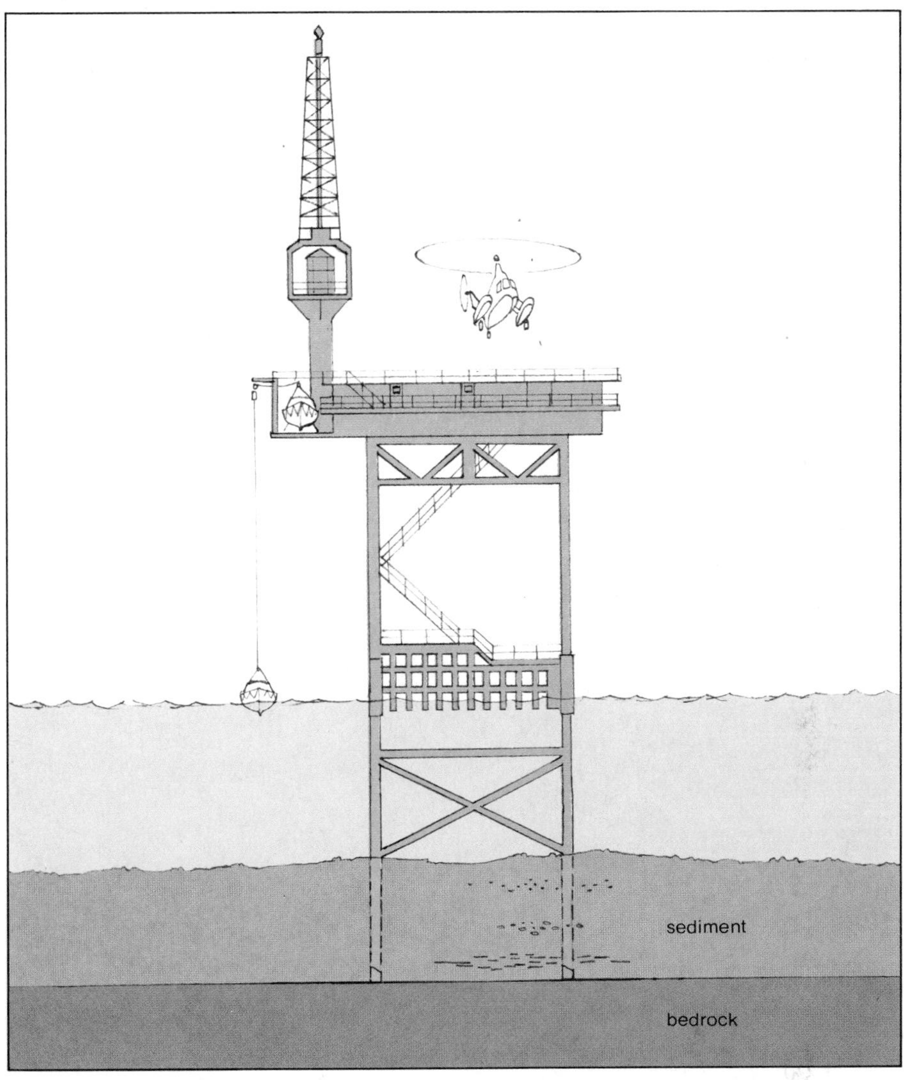

This simplified drawing of a light tower shows the station's basic structure. Pilings driven to the bedrock of the continental shelf support the tower. Its light, visible for 23 miles, is housed under the radio beacon, which transmits a coded signal 75 miles. Quarters for the five-man crew, plus storage area for supplies, are tucked into the platform on top of the girders; the roof serves as a launching pad for a supply helicopter.

Totally automated, this large navigational buoy (LNB) stands ready to be towed to its site, where it will be secured by a 10-ton concrete sinker and a 7,000-pound anchor, and then inspected quarterly by maintenance crews. Forty feet in diameter with a 42-foot tower, the LNB has a light visible 10 miles away, a radio beacon that carries 25 miles and fog signals audible at 2.5 miles. Screens around the tower act as radar reflectors.

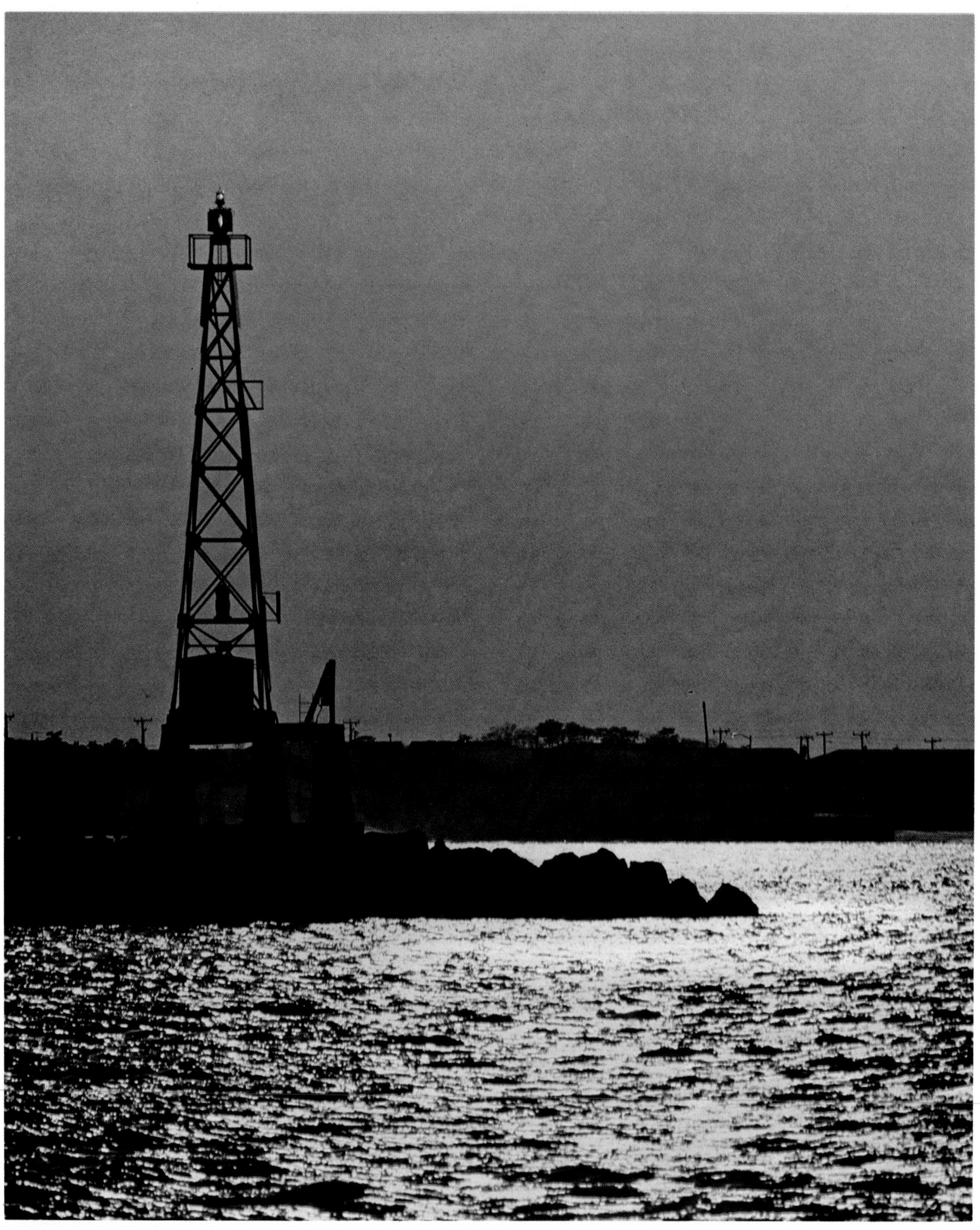

Winking a welcome—and a warning—in the dusk, a 70-foot-high beacon signals to seamen from a jetty at Little Creek Harbor, Virginia. Somewhat like a small-scale lighthouse, this beacon is equipped with its own foghorn and coded light beam, which is visible up to 12 miles at sea in perfect weather.

Beacons and Ranges

Many lighted aids to navigation are less imposing and have a shorter range than full-scale light stations—but they still rise more dramatically above the water and their signals show farther than ordinary lighted buoys. These middle-distance lights principally include beacons, such as the structure at left marking the entrance to a small harbor, and range lights, which are pairs of lighted structures (also equipped with the range daymarks shown on page 59) that indicate a main channel.

Both beacons and range lights are permanently fixed installations. Even though they are intended for fairly close-in piloting, they share important features with the larger light stations. They flash on and off with an identifying code, which is described in the light list *(overleaf)*. Both ranges and beacons carry special lenses to concentrate their beams. On beacons, the lens is generally a cylindrical, nonrotating type of Fresnel called a drum lens, while range lights, which are designed to shine in only one direction *(bottom right)*, have flat lenses similar to the kind found in theatrical spotlights. All beacons and range lights are fully automated, down to the capability of changing burned-out light bulbs *(top right)*. In addition, the larger beacons, like most light stations, may be equipped with foghorns.

A cutaway of a beacon's so-called drum lens shows the automatic bulb changer found in most small- to middle-sized navigation lights. Here, six incandescent bulbs are screwed into a hexagonal holder. When a bulb burns out, an electric current is diverted to a small motor that rotates the holder. As the spent bulb (gray) moves out of the way (arrow), a fresh one (yellow) is brought upright. At the same time, a third bulb (blue) slips into position as the next replacement.

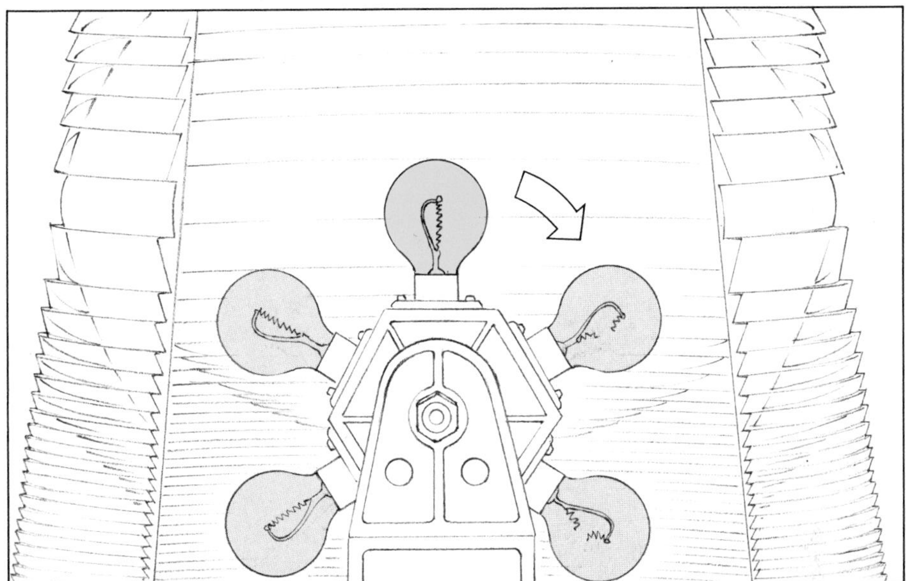

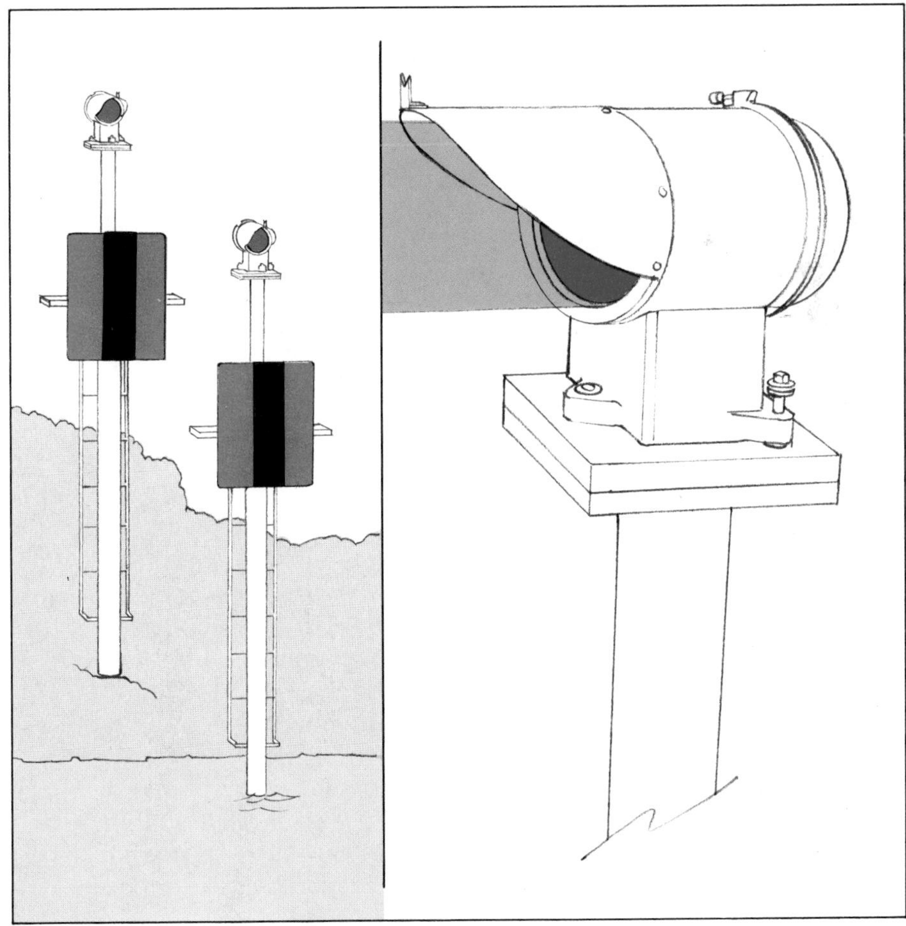

Like all range lights, the pair of lights here (above, left) are set one in front of the other—thus giving a boatman who lines them up a sure course along a channel. To assure that the nearer of the two ranges does not block the more distant one, the second range is mounted slightly higher up. For daytime identification, lighted ranges have distinctive daymarks. Each light is set in a hooded fixture (right) to create a one-directional beam that is brightest when viewed head on.

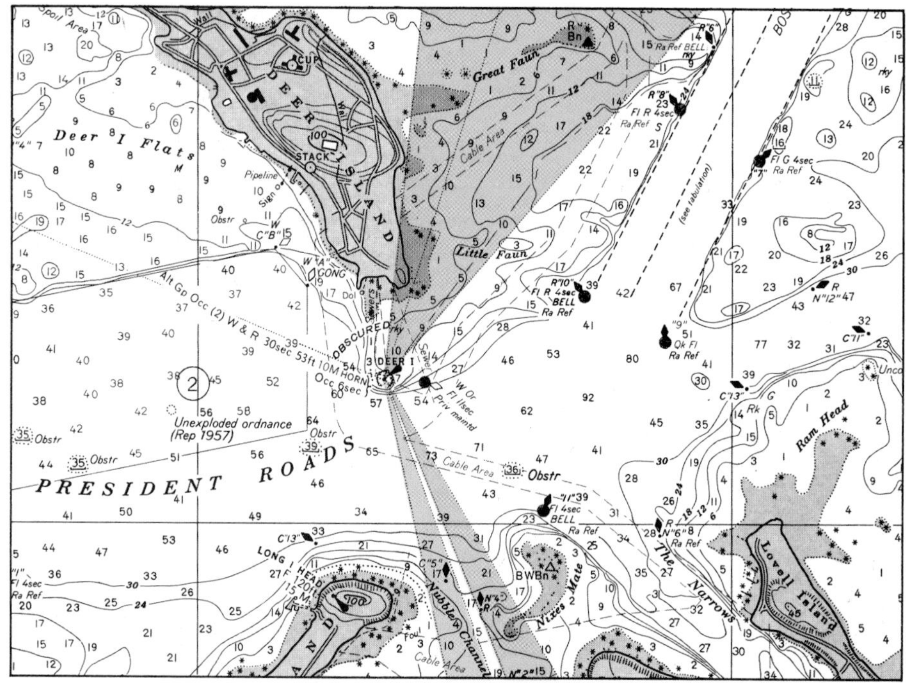

Color sectors beamed from Deer Island Light mark approaches to Boston Harbor. Shown on the chart by dotted lines, the sectors are tinted here for easy recognition. The red sector to the north warns of shoals. Below, a white sector between red and green ones signals a clear channel between two islands.

The Language of Lights

Not only is every light coded with one of 13 basic identifying characteristics *(below)*, but many also have color sectors that serve as warnings and guides *(left)*. Created by tinted filters placed in front of the light, color sectors cast hues over sweeps of water to declare danger zones and delineate navigable channels.

A navigator can decode a light's signature by watching it steadily for one minute, preferably with a watch in hand. After timing the periods of brightness and dark, and noting the color variations, if any, he then consults a book no boat should be without: a light list. Published by the Coast Guard in five volumes, the light lists index geographically every navigation aid in specified areas. The lists present information about each light *(opposite)*, including the color sectors, foghorn signals, radio-beacon data, and, of course, its coded signature using the abbreviations explained in the chart below. An additional abbreviation, Alt., for alternating, indicates that the identifying flashes in the signature alternate among two or more colors.

The Thirteen Basic Signals

In this graphic representation of basic light signatures, with their abbreviations, white triangles indicate brief flashes, white rectangles longer periods of light.

Light Pattern	Abbreviation	Description of Light
	F. = Fixed	A continuous, unblinking light.
	F. Fl. = Fixed and flashing	A continuous light, varied at regular intervals by flashes of greater brilliance.
	F. Gp. Fl. = Fixed and group flashing	A continuous light, varied by groups of two or more flashes.
	Fl. = Flashing	A light that flashes at regular intervals of not less than two seconds and whose period of darkness exceeds the period of light.
	Gp. Fl. = Group flashing	A light that sends out groups of two or more flashes at regular intervals.
	Gp. Fl. (1+2) = Composite group flashing	A flashing light in which the flashes are combined in alternating groups of different numbers.
	Mo. (A) = Morse code	A flashing light whose blinks signal letters in Morse code—in this case, dit-dah for A.
	Qk. Fl. = Quick flashing	A light that flashes 60 times or more a minute, used only on buoys and beacons.
	I. Qk. Fl. = Interrupted quick flashing	A light in which five seconds of quick flashes is followed by five seconds of darkness.
	E. Int. = Equal interval (Isophase)	A light with equal periods of light and darkness; sometimes described as an isophase light.
	Occ. = Occulting	A light that is eclipsed at regular timed intervals, but whose period of light is always greater than the duration of darkness.
	Gp. Occ. = Group occulting	A light with regularly spaced groups of two or more occultations.
	Gp. Occ. (2+3) = Composite group occulting	A light whose occultations combine in alternate groups of different numbers.

The identifying features of various lights around Lake Huron appear on this page reprinted from the Great Lakes light list. By consulting the entries in each column for Thunder Bay Island Light, for example, a navigator would discover that the light is located in a white conical tower; that it emits a white flash every 15 seconds, visible for a radius of 28 miles; that the station includes a radio beacon; and that its two-toned foghorn gives two blasts every 30 seconds.

(1) No.	(2) Name / Characteristic	(3) Location / Lat. N. Long. W.	(4) Nominal Range	(5) Ht. above water	(6) Structure / Ht. above ground / Daymark	(7) Remarks / Year
	LAKE HURON, MICHIGAN					
	WEST SIDE					
	EAST ALPENA CHANNEL					
	— Buoy 5	In 17 feet			Black can	White reflector. Private aid.
	— Buoy 6	In 16 feet			Red nun	Red reflector. Private aid.
	— Buoy 7	In 15 feet			Black can	White reflector. Private aid.
	— Buoy 8	In 14 feet			Red nun	Red reflector. Private aid.
	— Buoy 9	In 20 feet			Black can	White reflector. Private aid.
	— Buoy 10	In 14 feet			Red nun	Red reflector. Private aid.
	— Buoy 11	In 14 feet			Black can	White reflector. Private aid.
	Thunder Bay Wreck Buoy WR 2	In 18 feet. 45 03.7 83 23.6			Red nun	Red reflector.
	WEST SIDE (Chart 537) (NO 14646)					
	Middle Island Buoy 14	In 24 feet, northeast end of shoal.			Red nun	Red reflector.
1313	**Thunder Bay Island Light** Fl. W., 15ˢ	On east shore of island. 45 02.2 83 11.7	28	63	White conical tower, dwelling attached. 67	RADIOBEACON: Antenna 640 feet 181° from light tower. See p. XVIII for method of operation. DIAPHONE, two-tone; 2 blasts ev 30ˢ (2ˢbl-2ˢsi-2ˢbl-24ˢsi). 1832
1313.51	STONEYCROFT POINT LIGHT Fl. W.	45 06.4 83 18.5			TR on red skeleton tower	Private aid. Maintained from Mar. 15 to Nov. 15 1971
1314	*Nordmeer Wreck Lighted Bell Buoy WR1.* Qk. Fl. W.	In 35 feet 45 08.1 83 09.3	7		Black	Ra ref. 1,150 feet, 102.5° from last reported position of wreck.
1315	**Middle Island Light** Fl. W., 10ˢ	On east side of island, 45 11.6 83 19.3	18	78	White conical tower with orange bands in middle, dwelling detached. 71	1905
1316	STONEPOINT LIGHT Alt. Fl. W. & R., 60ˢ 3ˢ Wfl., 27ˢec. 3ˢ R fl., 27ˢec.	On end of the loading dock. 45 17.8 83 25.1	25W 21R	55	White cylindrical structure	Private aid. 1955
	Stoneport Approach Buoy 1	In 25 feet			Black can	White reflector.
	Stoneport Buoy 3	In 23 feet			Black can	Private aid.
	Stoneport Buoy 5	In 23 feet			Black can	Private aid.
	Stoneport Buoy 7	In 23 feet			Black can	Private aid.
	Presque Isle Harbor Entrance Shoal Buoy 2.	In 20 feet			Red nun	Red reflector.
1317	PRESQUE ISLE HARBOR RANGE FRONT LIGHT. F. G.	On west shore of harbor. 45 20.3 83 29.4		23	KRW on white pole 18	Higher intensity beam on bearing 274° diminishing around remainder of horizon. 1870
1318	PRESQUE ISLE HARBOR RANGE REAR LIGHT. F. G.	790 feet 274° from front light.		36	Rectangular international orange daymark with white vertical stripe. 33	1870–1967
1319	HARBOR LODGE RANGE FRONT LIGHT. F. R.	In 10 feet 45 20.5 83 29.2		16	International orange daymark on white pile.	Private aid maintained from May 15 to Oct. 31. 1957
1320	HARBOR LODGE RANGE REAR LIGHT. F. R.	In 6 feet, 500 feet 338.5° from front light.		21	International orange daymark on T. V. antenna.	Private aid maintained from May 15 to Oct. 31 1957
1321	**Presque Isle Light** Fl. W., 15ˢ (5ˢfl)	On north end of Presque Isle. 45 21.5 83 29.5	21	123	White conical tower, dwelling attached. 109	1840–1871
1322	*Adams Point Lighted Buoy 1* Fl. W., 6ˢ	In 42 feet, north of point.	7		Black	Ra ref.

91

A NOBLE LINE OF NAUTICAL SENTINELS

While automated lighting devices and electronic signals gradually assume the task of guiding mariners through darkened waters, old-fashioned lighthouses like the one at right and those on the following pages linger in the mariner's memory—and many still stand—as traditional symbols of hope and safety. These towering edifices of stone, brick, iron and wood, built in the 19th Century on lonely reefs and promontories, represent an age when men and women routinely risked their lives so that lights would beam their warning to seafarers.

Virtually every light erected in those days was an engineering triumph, a hard-won victory by daring and resourceful people. The saga of establishing a tower on Minot's Ledge *(right)* exemplifies the struggle. During lowest ebb tide, Minot's Ledge pokes only three feet above the chop of Boston Bay. In 1847 workmen began to drill holes for the pilings of a manned iron beacon. Twice waves swept all traces of their work from the ledge, both times washing men into the sea but miraculously drowning no one. Then after three years of such daredevil labor, the beacon was finished and two keepers scrambled aboard. In the spring of 1851 a raging storm crumpled the tower and the two men inside were killed.

In 1855 military engineers started construction of a new tower, this time of stone. Again tides and weather hampered work; men continually grabbed for life lines as breakers swept the rocks. Nevertheless, the workers managed to sink iron rods into holes drilled in the rock to reinforce foundation rows of granite blocks. Then the men formed sandbag dams around each block to keep the sea from washing away their mortar before it set. After five years of agonizing labor, a three-man crew rowed out to take charge of the tower—which stands to this day.

Like the builders of these lights, the men and women who lived in them were a hardy, independent breed who voluntarily consigned themselves to desolate towers and lonely lightships. They often had to row miles for food and use collected rain water to drink and bathe in.

Danger was a constant companion, and not just in the form of weather. One lightship in New York harbor was rammed by passing ships twice in one day—and survived. In Florida, light towers and lightships were attacked by Seminoles during the 1836-1837 uprisings. But the greatest threats were from storms and waves. A 35-foot wooden lighthouse on a pier at Michigan City on Lake Michigan crumpled during a storm in 1886, and the keeper, an 80-year-old woman, just managed to totter away before it fell.

Even on calm days, the keeper's lot was hard. He had to haul fuel to the lamp, and constantly clean its chimney and trim its wick. All glass surfaces of the lanterns had to be polished. And to keep down dirt that could foul the lenses, floors and walls were scrubbed weekly. To make sure the keeper never lagged in his duties, inspectors arrived unannounced.

While many keepers undertook this demanding existence alone or with buddies, others took along their wives and children. Sometimes family members found themselves joined for life not only to the keeper but to the light. Kate Walker tended a lamp in New York harbor for 35 years after her dying husband told her, "Don't forget to keep the lamp burning, Kate."

Abbie Burgess, the eldest daughter of the keeper of Matinicus Light off Maine, personified the dedication of a keeper's child. Twice, while still a teenager, Abbie found herself in charge of the light when storms stranded her father on the mainland and waves roared over the rock. Both times she kept the lamp burning nightly for almost a month. After the father retired, Abbie married his successor's son and remained for 14 more years. In 1875 she was appointed assistant keeper at White Head Light, Maine. Musing on her years in the tower, she wrote: "If I ever have a gravestone, I'd like it to be in the form of a lighthouse or beacon."

Rising 97 feet above Boston Bay, Minot's Ledge Lighthouse endures the crash of surf. The picture was made more than 50 years ago.

Built on a rock six miles off the coast of northern California, this granite tower above St. George's Reef took eight years to complete in 1892, and cost over $700,000—the most expensive lighthouse of its day. Workmen had to live on a schooner moored nearby and go to work in a cage on a wire strung from the boat's mast to the rock.

The Bluff Shoals Lighthouse in Pamlico Sound near Cape Hatteras, North Carolina, rests on pilings 12 feet above the water. At this height in relatively sheltered waters, it has seldom been hit by waves. The clapboard, houselike design of the light was typical of those first put up in Middle Atlantic bays and inlets during Victorian times.

A 19th Century wooden lightship marking the Vineyard Sound channel off Massachusetts displays oval daymarks atop its masts; at night kerosene lamps were raised below them. Keepers on lightships had arduous duty. They served 30 days without relief, were tossed about by storms and kept an anxious eye on shipping that might ram them.

The Carysfort Reef Lighthouse along Florida's Atlantic coast was designed to stand against the wind and waves of the area's frequent hurricanes by presenting only skeletal iron surfaces to the elements. The lighthouse replaced a lightship withdrawn from duty after its captain and a crewman were killed by Indians in 1837.

Served by an enclosed walkway, the Isle of Shoals Lighthouse five miles off New Hampshire looms like a fortress with a tower of granite blocks two feet thick. Originally conceived as a modest stone structure, the lighthouse was massively reinforced to protect it from anticipated attack by Confederate gunboats during the Civil War.

The ornate Racine Reef Lighthouse in Lake Michigan, embellished by a rococo frosting of ice, rises tier upon tier from an octagonal concrete foundation to spindly stovepipe and flagpole—a classic example of Victorian wedding-cake architecture, and an ultimate symbol of the austere pride of the old-time light builders and keepers.

N
30
60
E
120
240
W
300
330
DANFORTH
CONSTELLATION

3 THE BASIC PILOTING TOOLS

On a clear day a boatman traveling short distances in familiar waters can usually make intuitive judgments on all the crucial components of navigation—direction, distance, speed and time. But on any longer, more difficult journey, he must consciously apply the navigational tools—and the skills in using them—that have guided mariners for centuries. The most critical of these tools is the compass. It issues a constant report on the boat's heading, and can also be used as a sighting instrument to determine the directional relationship of the boat to some mark ashore or on the water. The boat's speedometer—or its tachometer—delivers an instant-by-instant measure of through-the-water speed. These data can be used to plot a course on a chart with the help of other tools. Parallel rules, for instance, enable a navigator to draw a line in a direction precisely defined by his chart's compass rose. Dividers help translate speed into distance on the chart. And by manipulating all these ingredients of direction, speed, time and distance, a navigator can make a plan not only for reaching a distant destination at a predetermined hour, but also for checking his position en route. Each step of the trip is recorded on the chart, creating a basis for computing the next step. Thus, a navigator gains an overview of his situation.

In theory, all these plans and devices should enable a boatman in coastal waters to determine his position with scientific precision. In practice, however, some uncertainties inevitably creep into his calculations. Taking compass sightings from a pitching deck, for instance, can be an exercise in guesswork and near frustration. Magnetic headings can be deceptive, since any piece of ferrous metal or small electric current aboard a boat may lead a compass astray—and the navigator, too, unless he has corrected or allowed for the deviation. Speedometers and tachometers faithfully record speed through the water but cannot take into account the effects that winds and currents have on a vessel's speed over the bottom.

Navigation is, thus, as much an art as a science. Nevertheless, a boatman can do a good deal to minimize uncertainty. He should install his compass with exquisite care, adjust it with precision, treat it with consideration and periodically check its accuracy. Happily, methods of verifying this vital instrument's performance have improved since the days of the "pilot's blessing" used by Columbus' navigators—raising a hand to point to the North Star and then lowering it in a steady arc onto the compass.

Today's boatman also has the aid of such conveniences as red-filtered night lights that allow him to read instruments or a chart without reducing the sensitivity of his night vision, as would happen if he were using a conventional white light. Binoculars help him to pick out the visible objects on which most of his calculations depend; a pair of 7x50 binoculars, which are hefty enough for steadiness in handling, should supply about as much magnification as the average boatman will need.

As additional help, today's naval architects usually include, in plans for boats even as small as 24 feet, a special space for the navigator to stow and use his equipment. Ideally, on a power cruiser the space will be next to the wheel; on a sailboat, belowdecks near the companionway. It should be sheltered and offer the best possible visibility all around, room to spread out charts, and secure stowage for tools. Few boats meet all these requirements. But even if a navigator has to keep his equipment in a duffel bag and unfurl his charts on the lid of the ice chest, he will quickly find that using his tools becomes second nature—and navigation an engrossing challenge that is as exciting and rewarding as any other game of skill.

In this helmsman's view of a compass, the fluid-filled dome, lighted for night steering, acts as a lens to magnify the part of the compass card that indicates the ship's heading.

As a boat turns from one heading to another, everything aboard turns with it —except the compass card. As shown at right, the card's N marking keeps pointing north no matter what the boat's heading. When a boat falls off to the right of the correct course, the lubber line does too, and both must then be steered to the left until the lubber line swings back to the proper course. Neophyte helmsmen, plagued by the illusion of a moving compass card, sometimes try to steer the card instead of the boat, thus increasing the steering error and the difficulty of getting back on course.

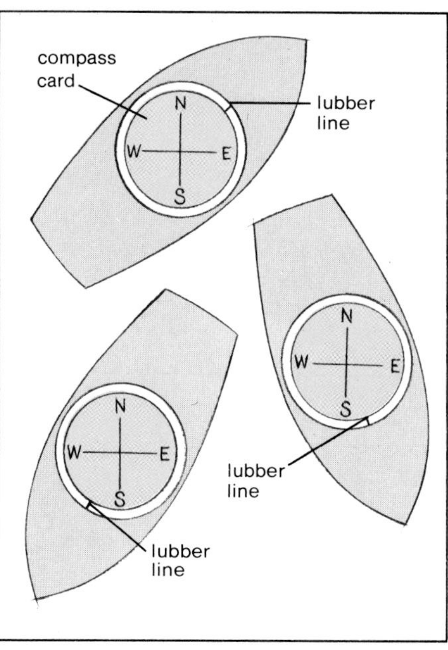

How a Compass Works

A mariner's compass, like the one at left, below, is designed to give a navigator, at a glance, his boat's correct heading relative to the direction of magnetic north. The compass' prominently displayed dial, called the compass card, is plainly marked with directions expressed in degrees, and is usually illuminated for night steering by a light with a red filter that preserves the helmsman's night vision.

On most compasses, a vertical pin called a lubber line is fixed to the compass housing—and thus, in effect, to the boat itself—to indicate the precise direction in which the boat is heading. Some compasses have similar pins—called 90° lubber lines—mounted at 90° intervals around the card for use in determining when a landmark is directly abeam or astern.

Another pin, centered on the compass card and taller than the others, is called the shadow pin. It is so named because expert navigators use the angle of its shadow to determine—by complicated calculations involving the known position of the sun—a ship's true, rather than magnetic, heading. For most boatmen, however, the shadow pin is used to determine position by taking bearings on fixed visible objects such as buoys, smokestacks and lighthouses. But sometimes, in seeking to take a bearing with the boat's steering compass, a navigator finds his view impeded by a mast or other shipboard object. In such circumstances, a hand-held bearing compass like the one on the opposite page is a great convenience.

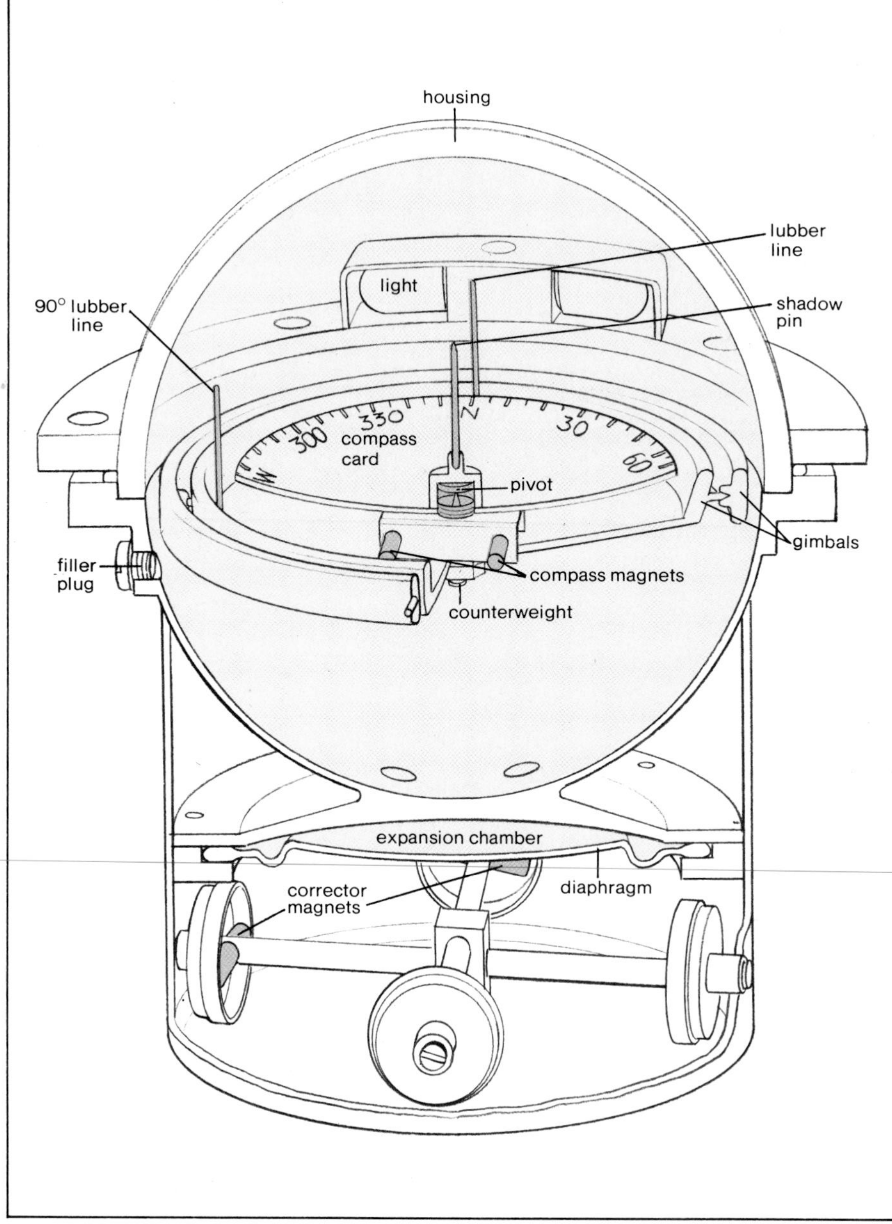

Inside a compass, as shown in the cutaway drawing, are gimbals and a counterweight to keep the card level when the boat tilts. The card—and the attached magnets aligning it with the earth's magnetic field—balance on a pivot. The housing is filled, through an opening sealed by a plug, with clear, highly refined kerosene. The fluid buoys up the card, reducing pivot friction, and damps the oscillations caused by vibration. A flexible diaphragm beneath lets the fluid expand and contract with changes in temperature. Corrector magnets in the base aid in adjusting the compass after its installation.

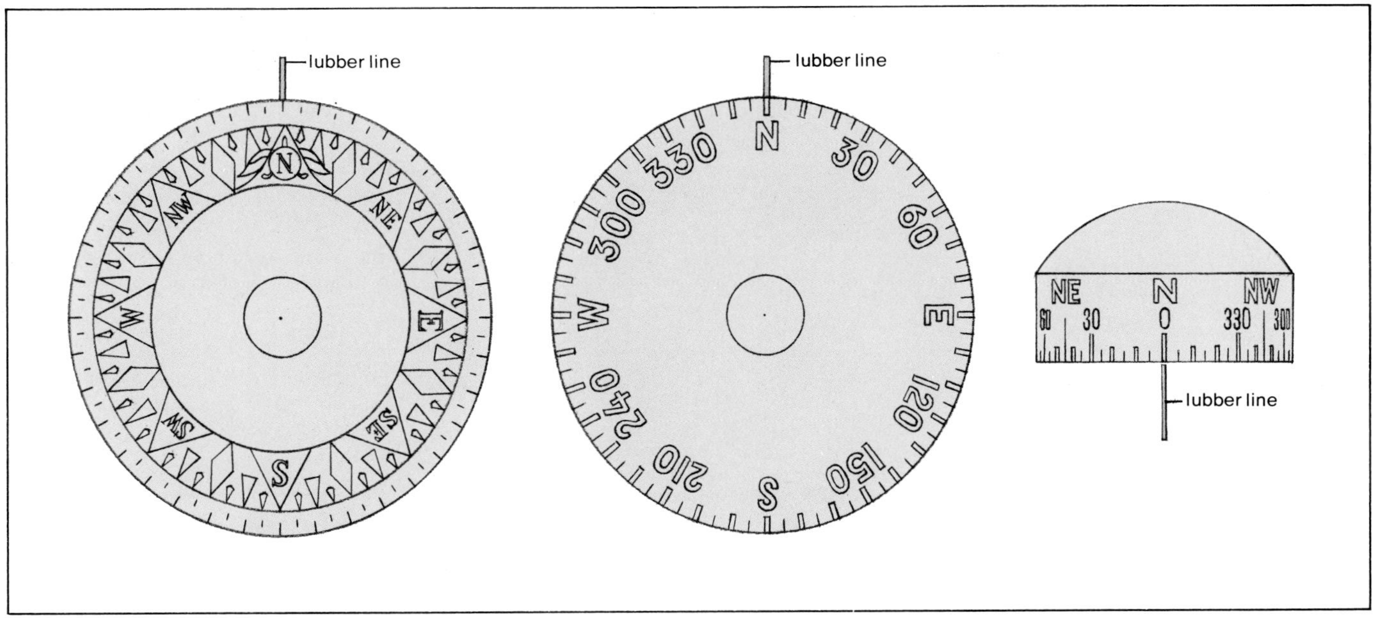

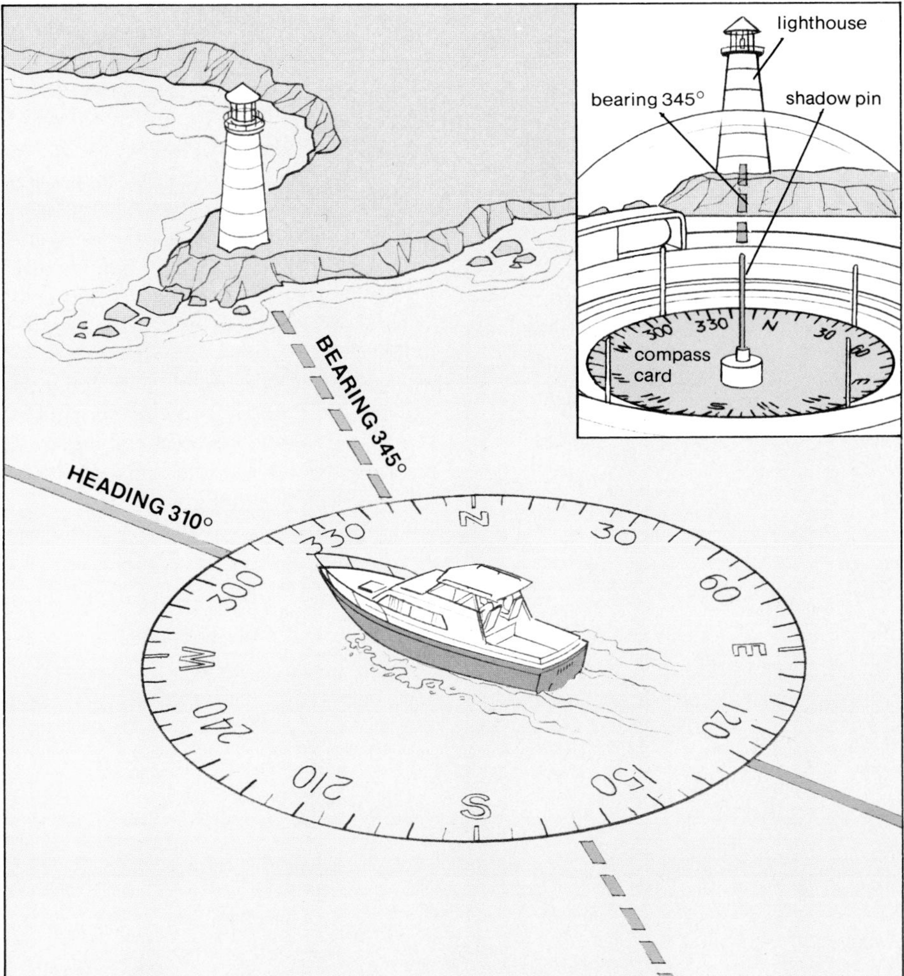

A compass not only defines the mariner's course but can also serve as an invaluable instrument for taking sightings and fixing a boat's approximate position. On the boat above, the compass shows the helmsman that he is on a course of 310° magnetic. Off to his right is a lighthouse whose position is marked on his chart. Sighting across the compass' shadow pin (inset), he determines that the bearing from the boat to the lighthouse is 345° (broken line). On his chart he draws a line from the lighthouse bearing 345°. He knows that he must be somewhere along that line, and he can reasonably assume that he is near its intersection with his 310° course line.

Until about 1900, compass cards were marked with the 64 directional points and half points shown at left, above. Most cards are now measured off by degrees (center), a system that offers greater precision and simplifies navigational calculations. Small boats are frequently equipped with an aviation-type compass (right); it features a card shaped like an inverted cup, with the degrees marked on the side and the lubber line set aft. When a boat using one of these aviation compasses strays to the left of the course, the lubber line moves to the right of the correct reading —the reverse of the usual response.

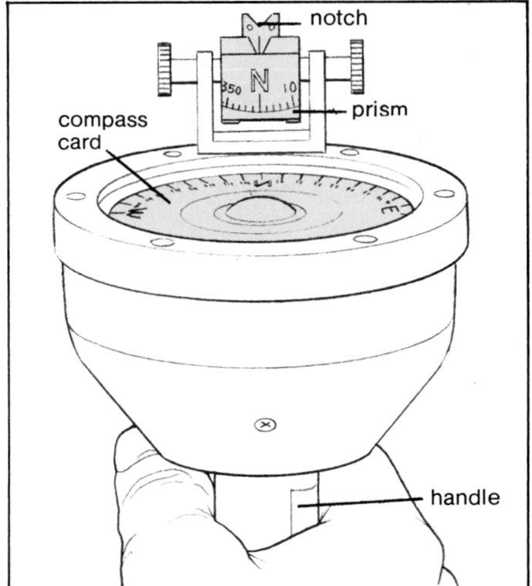

The hand-held compass above is designed for taking bearings. Holding the device at eye level, the navigator centers an object in the sighting notch and reads the bearing from the compass card through a reflecting prism. Such a compass usually contains a battery-powered light that is for night use.

To align a compass, the boatman begins by stretching a string from the center of the bow to the center of the stern, thus establishing the vessel's center line. The compass is then installed with the lubber line and shadow pin directly beneath the string. If it is necessary to offset the compass from the center line, a second line should be constructed by measuring out carefully from two points on the boat's center line, creating a parallel on which to place the compass.

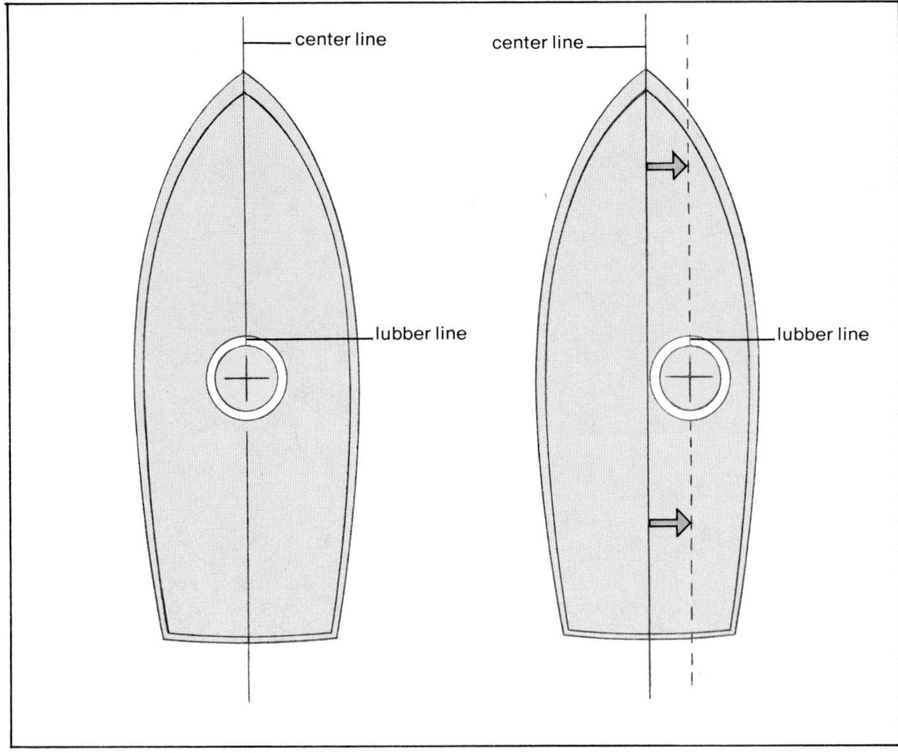

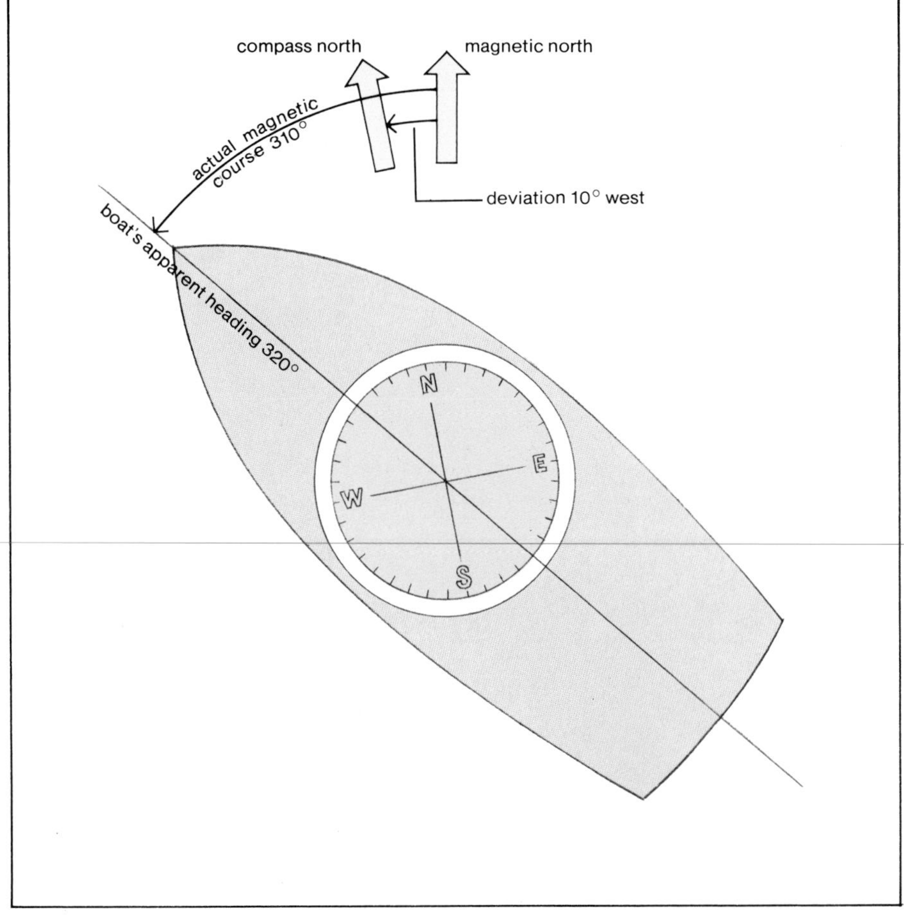

Installing and Adjusting

Two critical factors can prevent a boat's compass from helping to guide the mariner on his intended course. One is misalignment, and the other is deviation. To eliminate the former, a boatman need only be sure that the compass' lubber line and shadow pin align precisely with the boat's fore-and-aft axis, as shown at left. But to correct the latter, he must first understand the effect on the compass reading of various equipment aboard the boat, and then undertake a fairly complex set of procedures to compensate.

Ideally, the compass should be located well away from electronic equipment or any sizable piece of ferrous metal, such as the engine or a metal steering wheel. But since the prime consideration in the placement of a compass is visibility to the helmsman, some deviation may be inevitable. The extent of deviation on a boat may be so extreme that the skipper will have to call in a professional compass adjuster. Usually, however, the boatman himself, by following the procedures explained on pages 88-89, can adjust the compass so that deviation can be reduced to a minimum.

In so doing, he should run his boat along a sequence of known headings to be sure that his needle gives him an accurate reading of his boat's course. He should always begin by checking the four so-called cardinal points of the compass—north, south, east and west (beginning with north, since that is the base point of all compass calculations)—until he is certain he has established his instrument's degree of error at all points.

The compass on the boat at left has a deviation of 10° west; i.e., when the boat is headed directly toward magnetic north, or 000°, the compass points to 010°. Therefore, a helmsman steering by the faulty compass on a course of 320°, as here, will actually be on a magnetic heading of 310°. If his landfall is 20 miles away, this built-in error could cause him to miss it by nearly four miles.

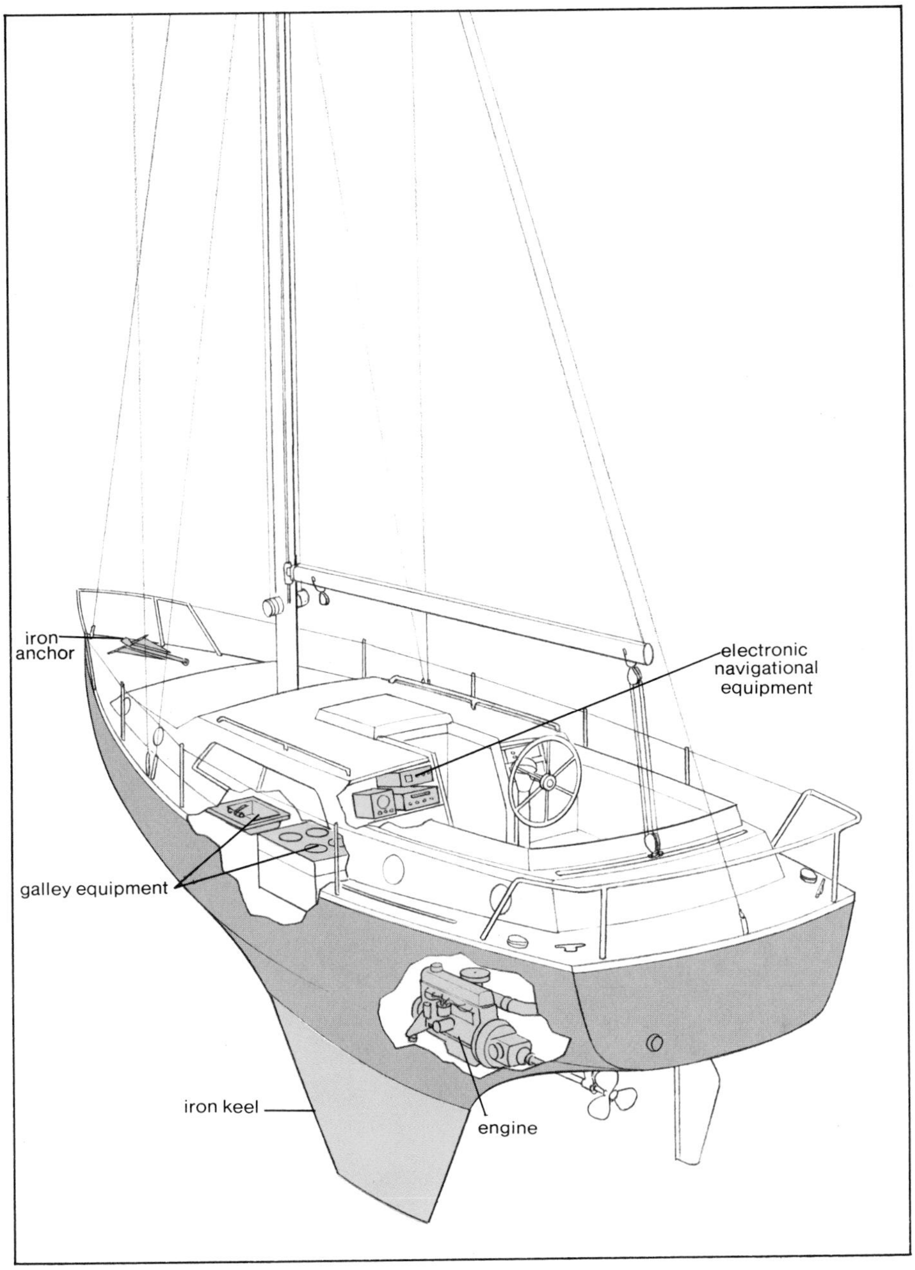

iron anchor
electronic navigational equipment
galley equipment
iron keel
engine

Any boat may be loaded with metal gear and electrical equipment likely to cause compass deviation. The effect can be minimized by using nonmagnetic metal such as bronze or the special steels that often serve for railings, standing rigging or steering wheels—and by keeping pairs of current-carrying wires close together to neutralize the effect of their electromagnetic fields. The boatman should also check his compass for changes in deviation when he turns on his engine or any electric motor, or when he brings aboard additional equipment such as a toolbox.

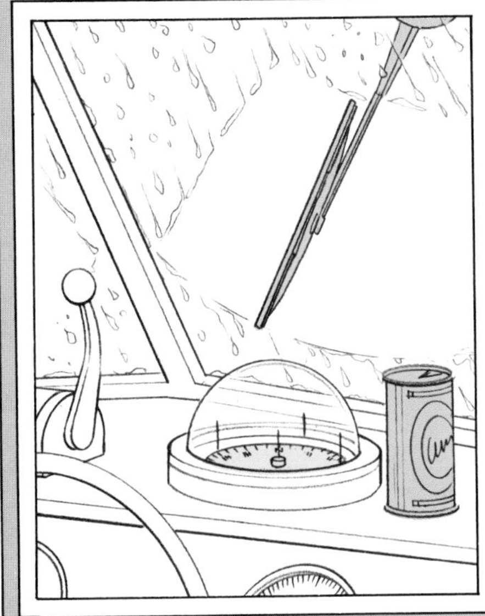

An Inclination for Beer

Small and apparently harmless items of equipment often cause compass deviations. Tiny motors and switches usually located near the compass, such as those that operate the windshield wipers, horn, lights, pump and ignition, can distract a compass. So can a beer can—or even the steel grommet on the yachting cap of a helmsman bending over the binnacle. A professional compass adjuster once struggled with an erratic compass on a boat used for fishing excursions. He finally found the trouble: an ice chest that was installed near the compass was full of canned beer at the outset of every trip and was usually empty on the return trip. His solution was to adjust the compass so that it registered due north when the chest was half full.

To reduce deviation in a typical mariner's compass to a practical minimum, a skipper uses the two pairs of corrector magnets, mounted in the compass base on brass shafts; he changes their setting with adjusting screws. On a north-south heading, the north-south corrector magnets are used to correct the compass, on an east-west heading, the other corrector magnets are employed.

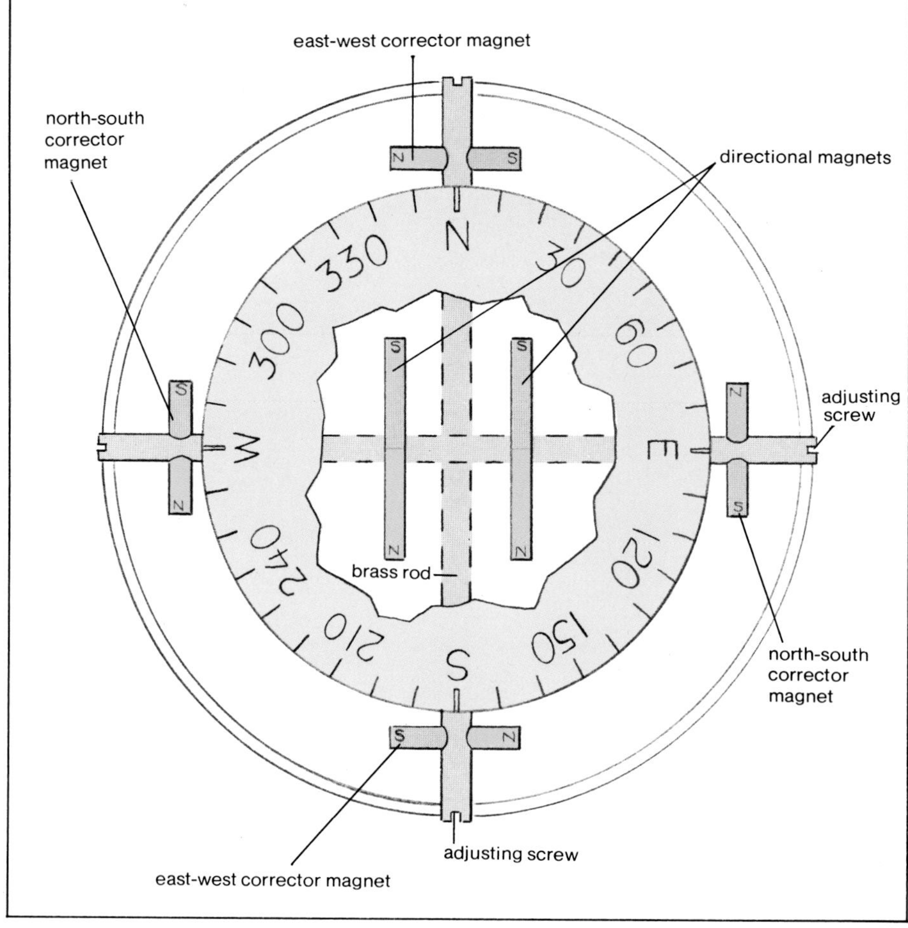

Compass corrector magnets move in pairs as their axes are turned by a key, made of brass or other nonmagnetic material. In the cutaway drawings below, the unadjusted compass at left is seen to have a deviation of 10° east. When the key is inserted in one end of the north-south corrector (right) and given a slight clockwise turn, it moves the corrector magnets, causing north on the compass card to swing onto the lubber line.

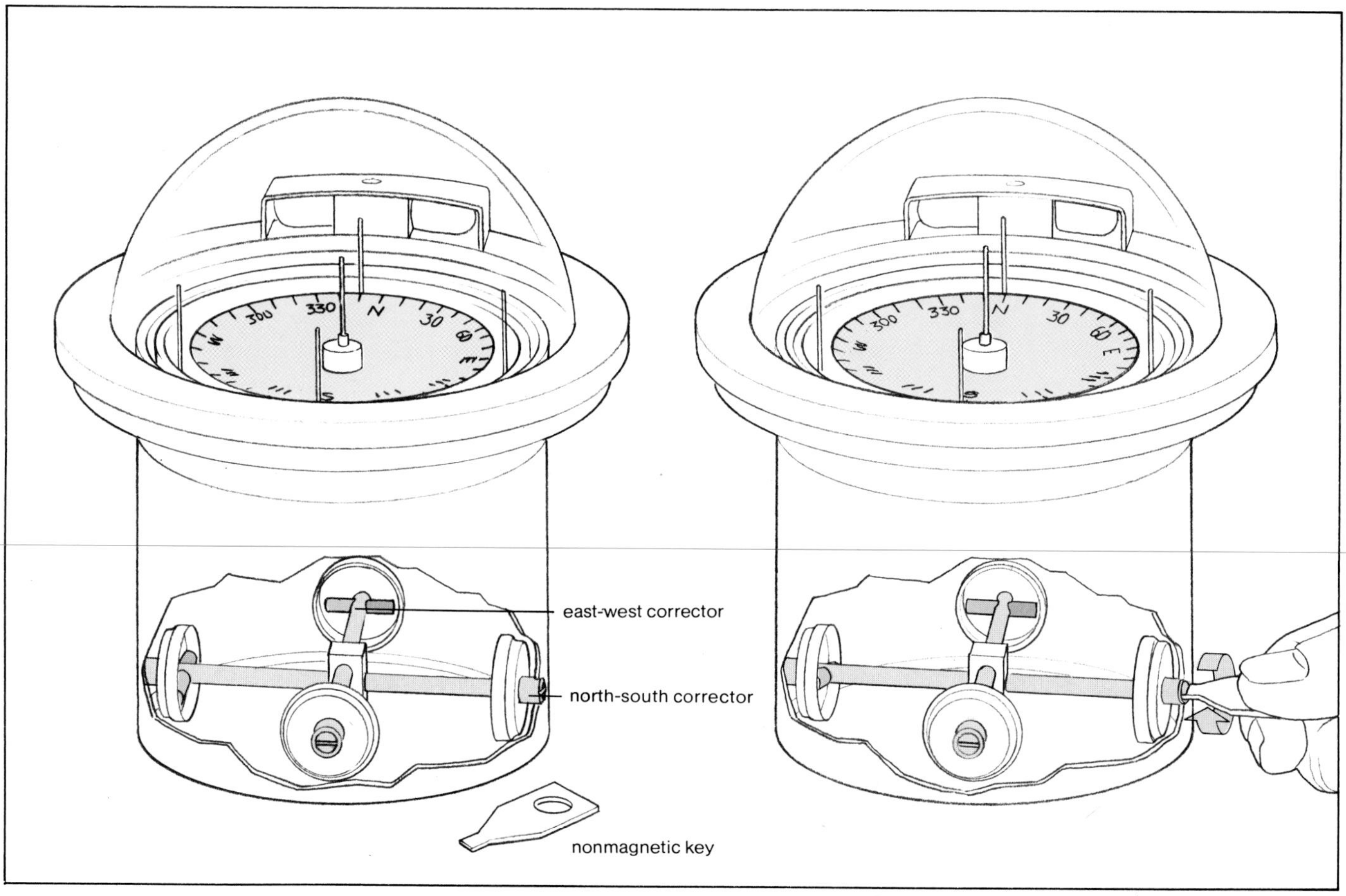

east-west corrector
north-south corrector
nonmagnetic key

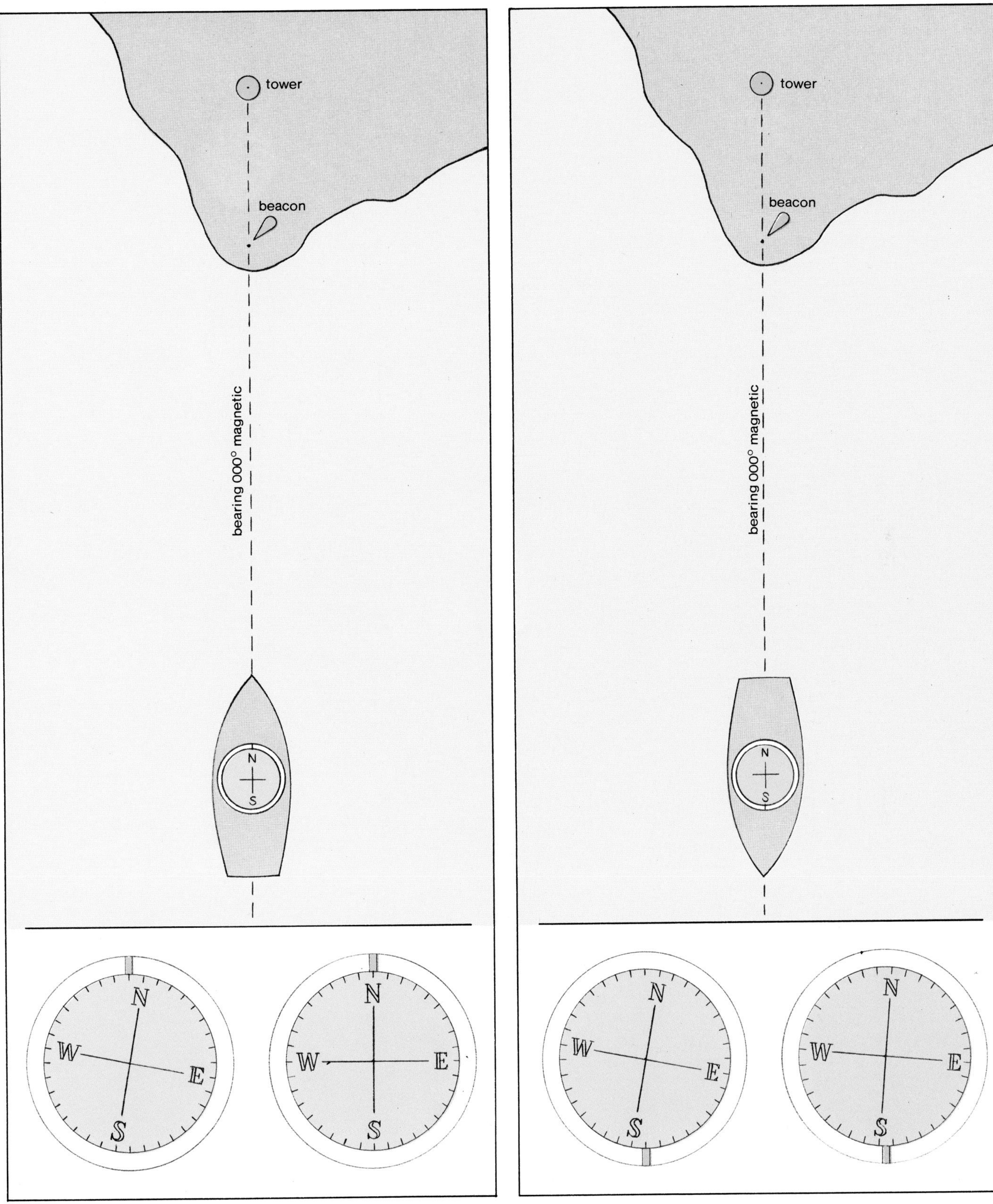

To correct deviation on a compass' first cardinal point, north, a skipper locates two fixed, charted objects that set a magnetic north-south line. When he puts his boat on that line, the compass' lubber line will be at magnetic north. If the compass is off—as it is above, by 10°—the deviation can be corrected by resetting the corrector magnets.

After correcting for deviation at a magnetic heading of north, the skipper aligns the boat's stern with the north-south range to correct deviation at south, or 180°. This will affect his north correction, so he corrects for only half the deviation at 180°. He repeats both operations, reducing deviation as much as possible. Then he can make similar adjustments on an east-west line of range.

After correcting deviation on the cardinal points (in blue, below), a skipper should check deviation at 15° intervals and keep track of the errors. He cannot make further corrections—to do so would affect his cardinal-point adjustments—but he needs to know for reference the amount of deviation. The skipper of the boat at right has begun checking by crossing the line of a range bearing 230° while steering a compass course of 015°. When the two range markers align, the range bears 229° by his compass and he knows that on a ship's heading of 015° his compass has a 1° easterly deviation.

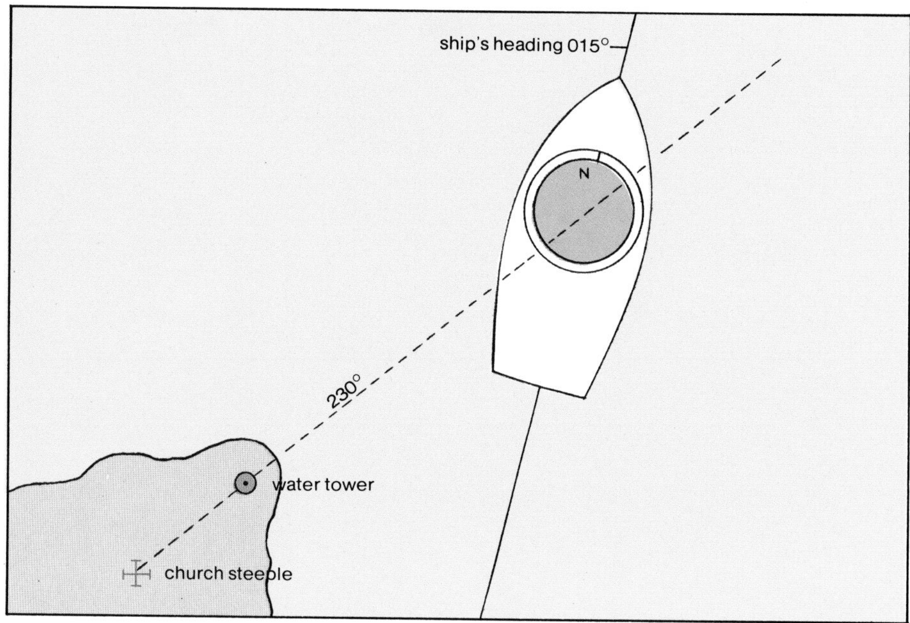

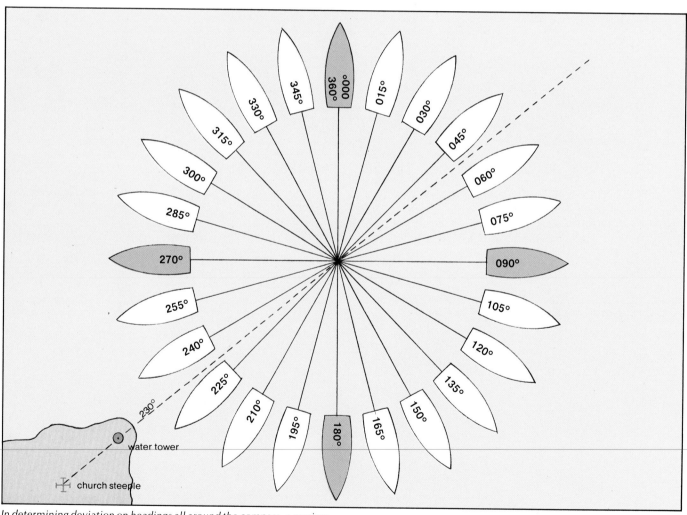

In determining deviation on headings all around the compass, a mariner must perform the maneuver illustrated at top on no less than 24 headings, including cardinals, and as a final check he must complete the circle by running a last heading on north. He can carry out this operation, called swinging ship, in various ways. He can sail his boat across the line of the range on each of the headings, as shown above. Or he can anchor his boat and warp it around from one heading to the next. If it is inconvenient to make all the deviation notations at one time or on a single range, the skipper can check deviation at some headings on one range and do the rest later on another range.

Data on compass deviation at each of the cardinal (blue) and intercardinal headings should be compiled on a table like the one below, listing the bearing of the range used, the ship's heading, the compass bearing of the range at that heading, and the amount and direction of deviation noted.

MAGNETIC COURSE	MAGNETIC BEARING OF RANGE	COMPASS BEARING OF RANGE	DEVIATION
000°	230°	230°	0
015°	230°	229°	1°E
030°	230°	228°	2°E
045°	230°	227°	3°E
060°	230°	226°	4°E
075°	230°	225°	5°E
090°	230°	225°	5°E
105°	230°	225°	5°E
120°	230°	226°	4°E
135°	230°	227°	3°E
150°	230°	228°	2°E
165°	230°	229°	1°E
180°	230°	230°	0
195°	230°	231°	1°W
210°	230°	232°	2°W
225°	230°	233°	3°W
240°	230°	234°	4°W
255°	230°	236°	6°W
270°	230°	235°	5°W
285°	230°	235°	5°W
300°	230°	234°	4°W
315°	230°	233°	3°W
330°	230°	232°	2°W
345°	230°	231°	1°W
360°	230°	230°	0

Plotting the deviation data on a graph should result in a smooth curve connecting the established points. One dot falling outside the curves—as at 255° below—can be disregarded as an error in observation. But an erratic pattern would indicate that either the data or the compass is awry.

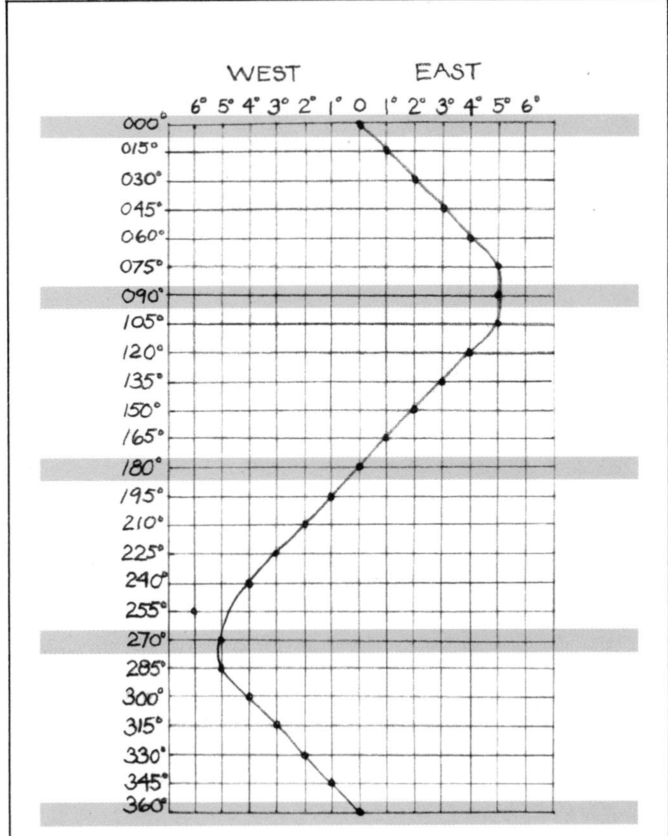

	MAGNETIC COURSE	COMPASS COURSE
NORTH	000°	000°
	015°	014°
	030°	028°
NORTH EAST	045°	042°
	060°	056°
	075°	070°
EAST	090°	085°
	105°	100°
	120°	116°
SOUTH EAST	135°	132°
	150°	148°
	165°	164°
SOUTH	180°	180°
	195°	196°
	210°	212°
SOUTH WEST	225°	228°
	240°	244°
	255°	260°
WEST	270°	275°
	285°	290°
	300°	304°
NORTH WEST	315°	318°
	330°	332°
	345°	346°
NORTH	360°	360°

Deviation data refined and corrected by being plotted on a graph, as shown above, can be converted into two columns of figures like those at left, and then posted near the compass for the helmsman's guidance. The first column lists the magnetic headings at which deviation has been observed. The figures in the second column, arrived at by adding the amount of observed deviation to, or subtracting it from, the magnetic heading, show the compass courses to be steered to achieve the correct headings. Thus, to steer a course of 015° magnetic, the helmsman puts the boat on a compass heading of 014°.

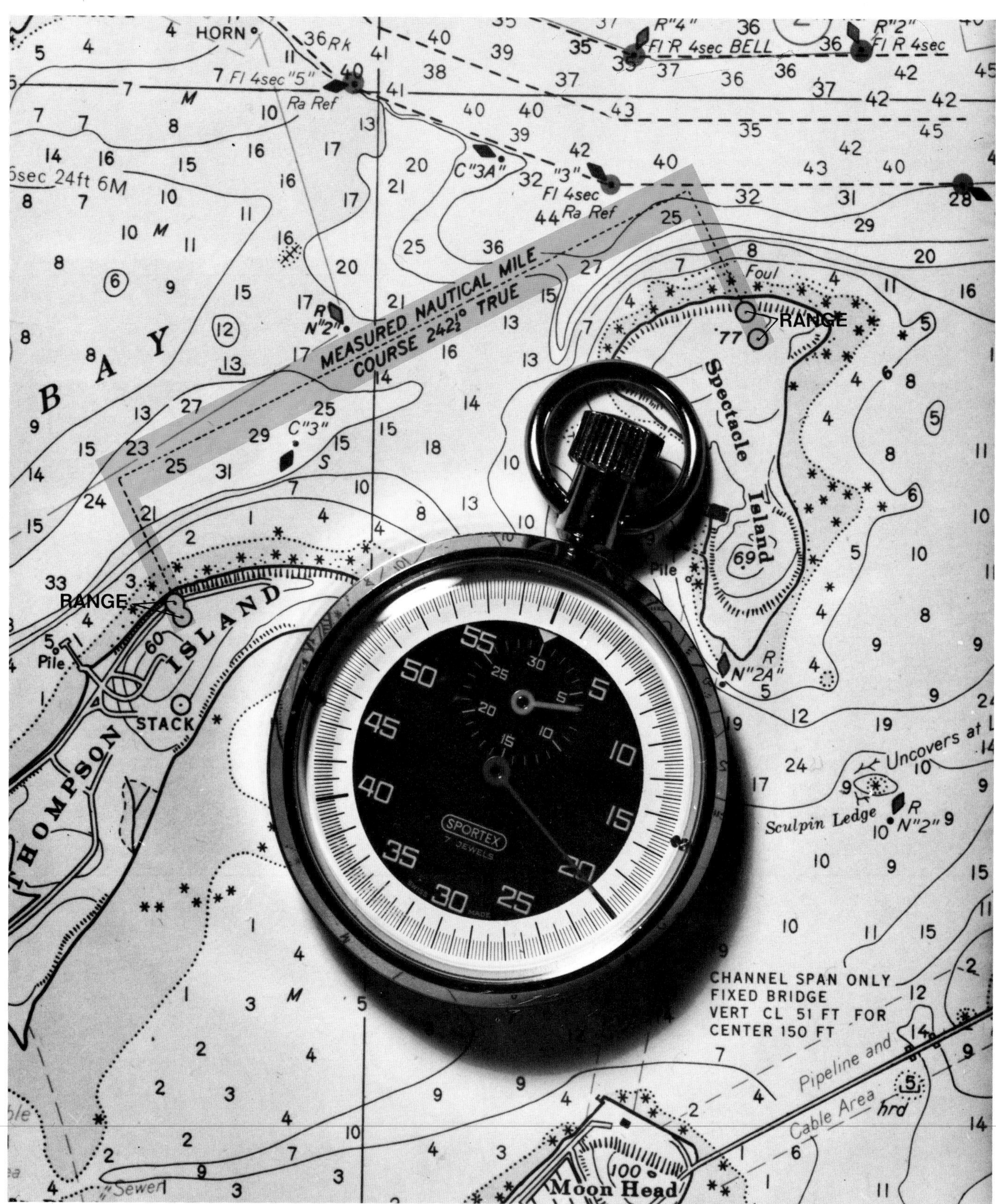

A measured mile, like the one bracketed in blue on the portion of a Boston Harbor chart shown above, can be used to check a boat's speed. It has a range at each end and is labeled with a true, rather than a magnetic, bearing since in most places magnetic north shifts slightly year by year. A skipper brings his boat up to a predetermined tachometer or speedometer reading before entering the course, starts timing at the first range and steers at a constant speed along the course's magnetic heading. At the mile's end his stopwatch reads—in this example—6 minutes 20 seconds, or 380 seconds. He divides 380 into the 3,600 seconds in an hour and gets a speed of 9.5 knots.

Time, Speed, Distance

In addition to direction, a navigator plotting a course must deal with the key elements of speed, time and distance. Time and distance are fixed and precisely measurable quantities, but a boat's speed —like its compass heading—is variable. Most modern powerboats and many sailboats have fairly accurate speedometers, but their delicate mechanisms can be affected by current, by their placement on a boat's hull, and by wear and tear. A boatman should therefore check his speedometer's accuracy periodically.

The best way to run a speed check is by measuring with a stopwatch *(left)* the time a boat takes to traverse a known distance at a steady pace, and then divide the time into the distance to get the speed. The most convenient distance is a precisely measured mile—some 90 of which have been established at various convenient locations in United States waters.

Timing a run over a measured mile is easier and more precise under power than under sail; but it is possible to sail a measured mile under reasonably constant conditions and get a good idea of a speedometer's accuracy. The skipper should run the measured mile at least once in each direction in order to balance out the accelerative or deterrent effects of wind or current, and for best results, he should do it several times at various speeds in each direction.

Most powerboats and auxiliary sailboats, whether they have speedometers or not, usually carry tachometers. By entering the results of his runs over the measured mile in a table like that at right, center, and plotting his entries on a graph, a boatman can use his tachometer as a reliable index to speed.

Thus, by one means or another, the mariner can find a way to measure his boat's speed through the water. But he must remember that, because of the effects of wind or current, this speed may be different from the boat's speed over the bottom. When making navigational calculations, he must include as a factor the speed of any current he encounters *(page 158)*, in order to establish his true speed over a given portion of the chart.

Once he knows his boat's speed, as explained in detail overleaf, he can then divide that speed into the distance indicated on his course line to compute the amount of time that will be required to reach his destination. Or, alternatively, he can multiply the speed and time to ascertain the distance the boat has traveled over some portion of a course leg.

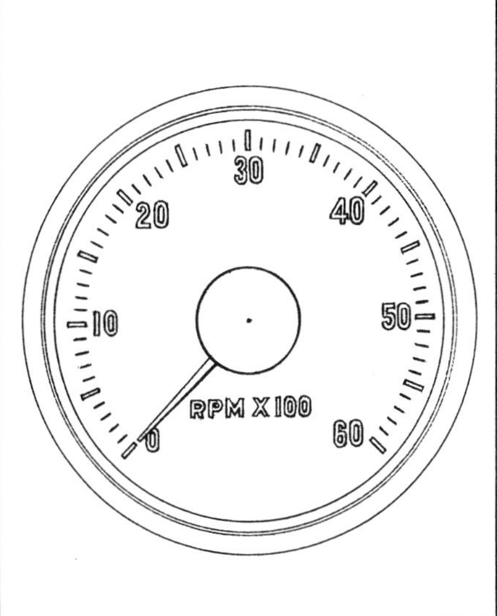

The tachometer (left), a standard device on most inboard and larger outboard craft, monitors engine revolutions per minute—in this case, zero to 6,000 in increments of 100. As set forth below, a boatman who has timed his craft over a measured mile at various tachometer readings can then use the results to gauge his speed at each setting.

The columns of figures below list the data for speed computations, obtained by running a powerboat back and forth over a measured mile at eight tachometer readings from 600 to 4,000 rpm's. Since this boat has a planing hull, which meets less water resistance above a certain speed, its velocity does not increase in a steady proportion to increased rpm's as is the case with some hull types.

RPM	NORTH - SOUTH		SOUTH - NORTH		AVERAGE SPEED
	TIME	SPEED	TIME	SPEED	
600	14 MIN. 36 SEC.	4.1	9 MIN. 40 SEC.	6.2	5.1
1500	6 MIN. 32 SEC.	9.2	5 MIN. 28 SEC.	11.0	10.1
2000	4 MIN. 14 SEC.	14.2	3 MIN. 47 SEC.	15.9	15.0
2300	3 MIN. 6 SEC.	19.4	2 MIN. 54 SEC.	20.7	20.0
2600	2 MIN. 28 SEC.	24.3	2 MIN. 20 SEC.	25.7	25.0
3000	2 MIN. 11 SEC.	27.5	2 MIN. 6 SEC.	28.6	28.0
3500	1 MIN. 58 SEC.	30.5	2 MIN. 1 SEC.	29.8	30.1
4000	1 MIN. 41 SEC.	35.6	1 MIN. 43 SEC.	35.0	35.3

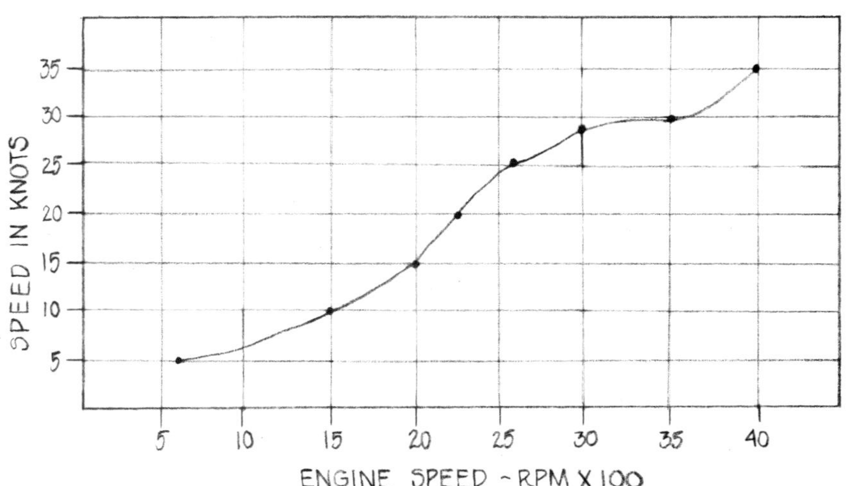

The graph above shows the last step in translating tachometer readings into speeds through the water. The skipper plots the graph from the data in the table above. Like the pilot checking his compass for deviation, he hopes to achieve a smooth curve that indicates his instrument is well calibrated, and his own observations and computations are accurate. This graph shows a jump in speed at about 2,000 rpm's—normal for a powerboat with the type of hull that begins to plane above a certain speed. Since this step-up and the other curves are relatively smooth and consistent, the pilot now has an accurate speed gauge for tachometer readings from zero to 4,000.

To measure short distances on a chart, a navigator uses a pair of dividers, opening them to span a given distance, then comparing the span to one of the scales (right) included on most charts. As an auxiliary scale he can use the latitude marks that appear along a chart's vertical edge: a minute of latitude equals one nautical mile.

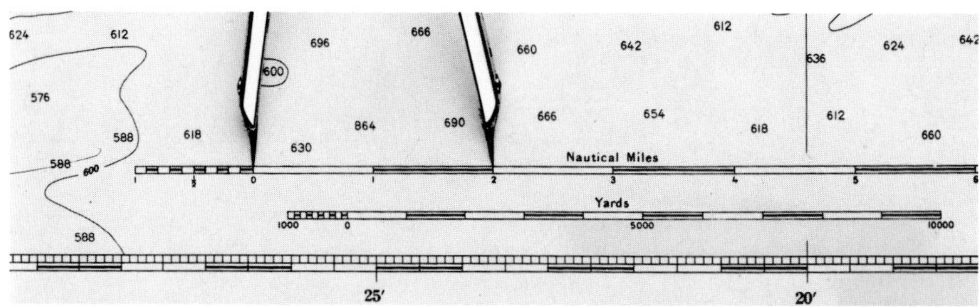

To measure course lines that are too long to be covered by the span of the dividers even when fully extended, the navigator should open them to a convenient distance—perhaps two or three miles, depending on the chart's scale—and then "walk" them as shown over the course leg for its full length. Often the dividers will not reach the end of the line on the last regular step, leaving a gap in the measurement. When this happens, pivot the dividers once more, then close them to fit the gap. Measure this shortfall on the scale and add it to the sum of the other steps.

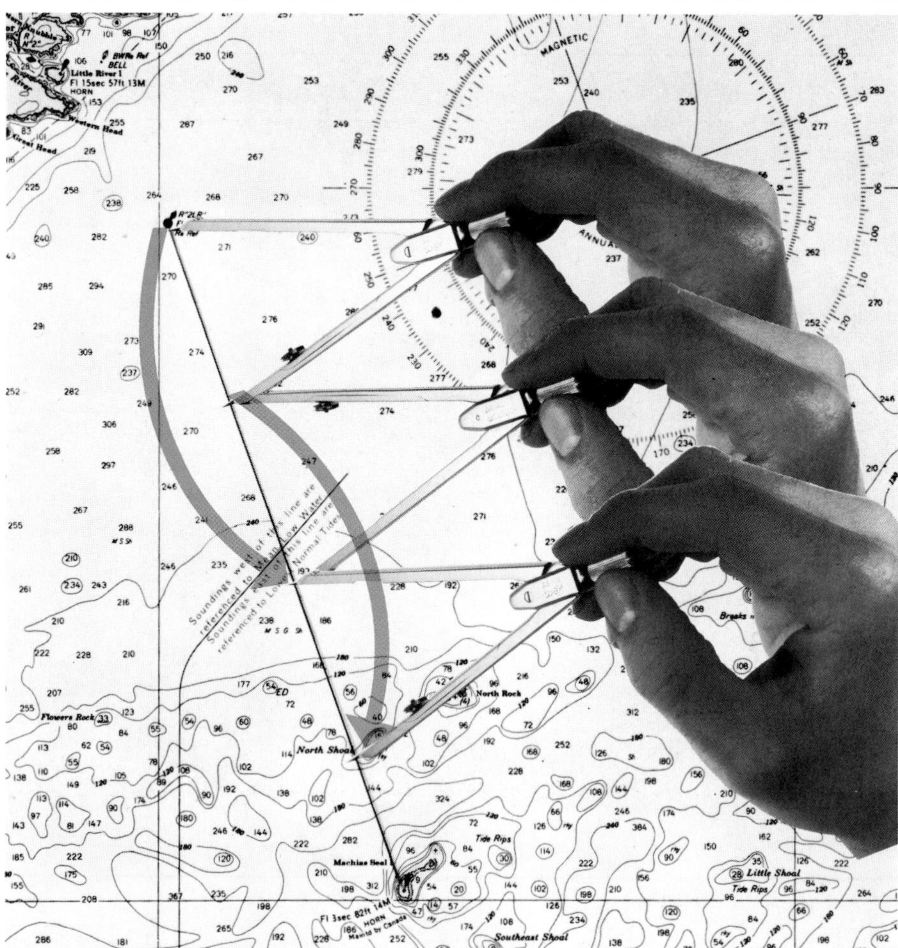

The Basic Measure

The nautical mile is based on the earth's circumference. The ancient Greeks laid the groundwork for the nautical mile when, hypothesizing that the earth was round, they divided its circumference into 360°. Sailors subsequently found that one sixtieth of a degree, called a minute of arc, was a convenient measure of shorter distances. They renamed it the nautical mile and used it as the basis for their navigating calculations—with uneven results, since the nautical mile varied depending on the prevailing estimate of the earth's size. In 1929, an international agreement permanently established the nautical mile at 1,852 meters, or about 2,000 yards.

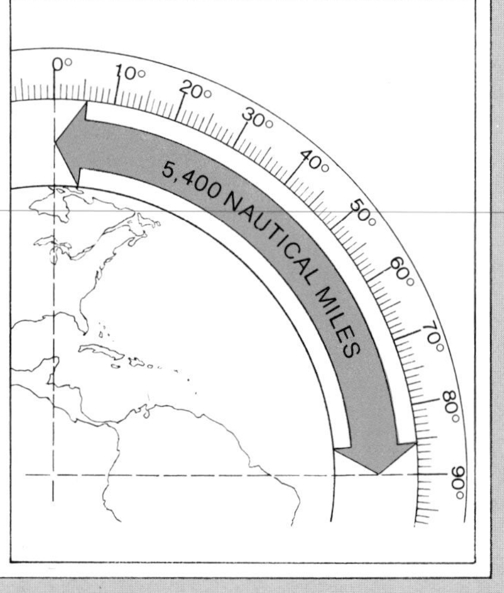

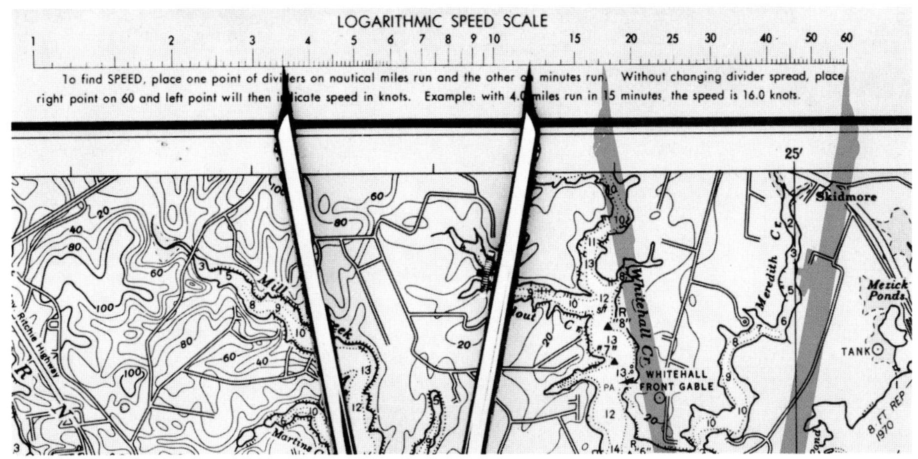

A convenient aid for determining speed, time or distance when two of the three factors are known is the logarithmic scale printed on many charts. To find the speed of a boat that has covered 3.5 nautical miles in 12 minutes, for instance, place one point of a pair of dividers at 3.5 on the scale. Open the dividers so the right point rests on 12, the elapsed time in minutes. Shift the dividers so that one point (blue dividers) precisely touches the scale at 60 minutes; the other point now lies on the speed of the boat—17.5 knots.

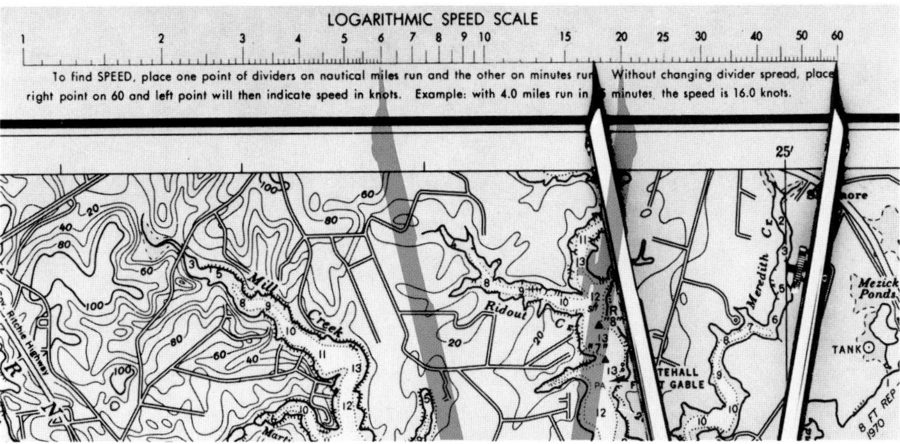

By reversing the steps above, the navigator can find out how much time it will take to cover a given distance—say, six miles—at his established speed of 17.5 knots. To do so, he places the dividers' right point at 60 on the scale and the left point on 17.5. Once again keeping the dividers set to this distance, he moves the left point to 6 (blue dividers) and reads the time, a little more than 20 minutes, from the right point. Alternatively, a pilot can estimate how far he will travel at his known speed in a specified time by setting the right point on the number of minutes, then reading the distance at the left point.

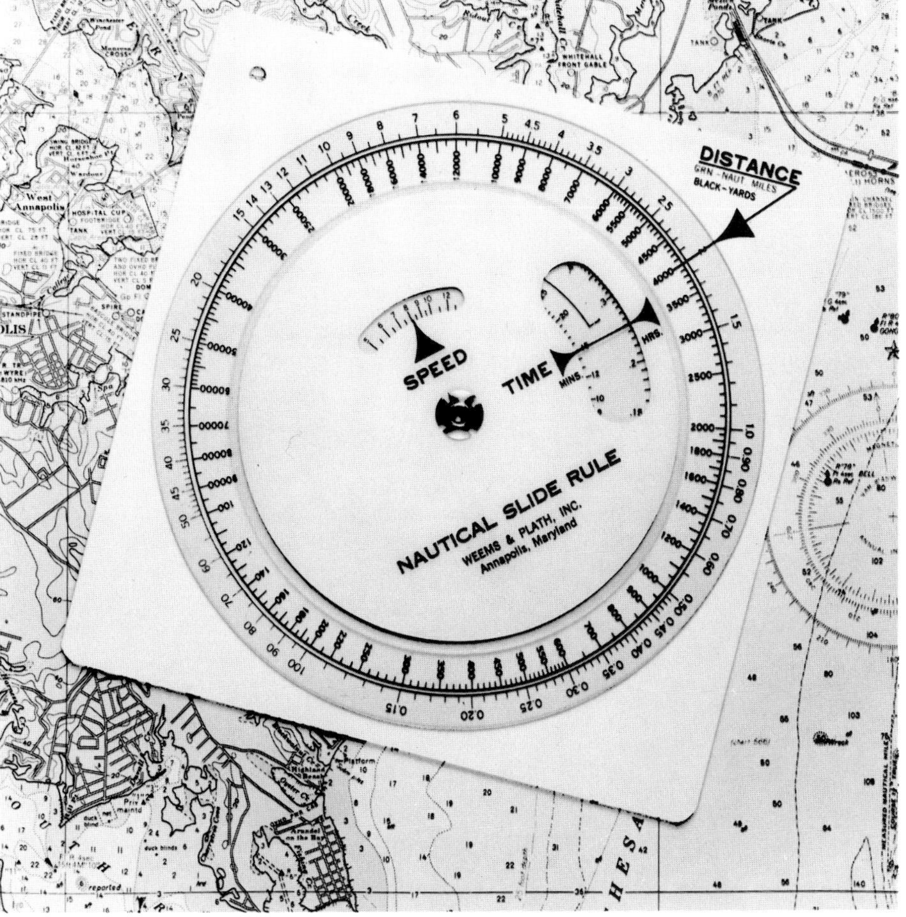

Another way to compute time, distance or speed is to use a circular slide rule, especially adapted for use by the seaman from the landsman's conventional slide rule. On the circular rule at left, distances in nautical miles and in yards appear on the rim of a large dial. A concentric smaller dial has two windows, one for reading speed in knots and one for reading time in minutes or hours. By dialing two known factors, the third can be found automatically. Here the slide rule shows that a boat traveling two nautical miles (4,000 yards) in 15 minutes (quarter of an hour) has a speed of eight knots.

Drawing a Parallel

Every pilot needs to know the exact magnetic direction of any course to be drawn on his chart. To get that information he uses the compass rose included on all charts. But since a course line drawn across a chart segment will rarely, if ever, intersect the center of a compass rose, a navigator requires some means of moving the line to the rose in order to determine its compass heading. The reverse is also true: if the navigator wishes to draw a line along a particular magnetic heading, he needs a reading from the inner—or magnetic—circle of the compass rose in order to guide his rule.

Navigators can use any one of a number of mechanical devices for making this transfer of information, and each navigator will decide for himself which tool he likes best. Shown on these pages are the two commonest, handiest and most accurate of these contrivances. The first, demonstrated at right, is a set of parallel rules, a hinged device dating from the late 16th Century. The second *(opposite)* is a more recent invention, the course protractor.

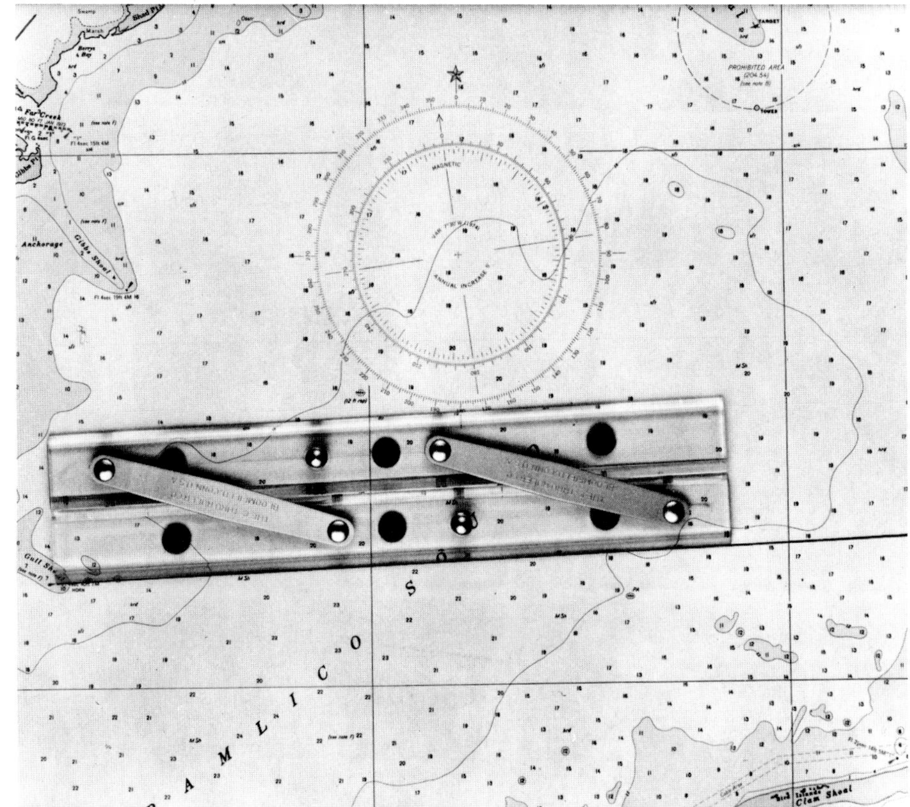

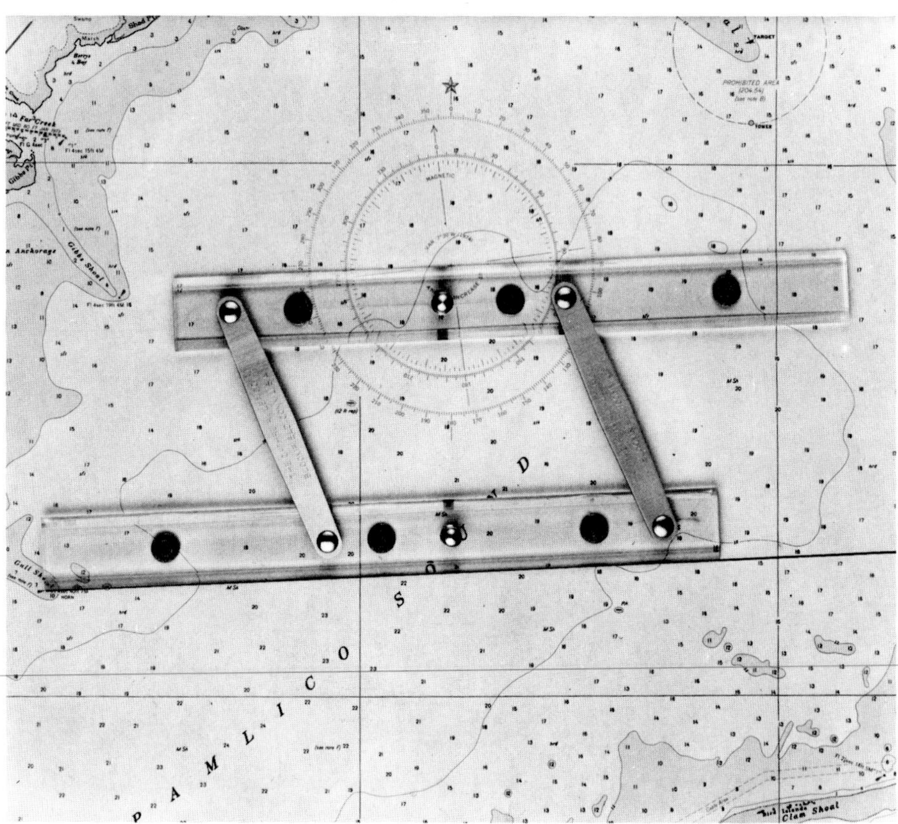

Using parallel rules to find the direction of an easterly trending course line on his chart, a navigator sets one edge—here the bottom—of the rules on the line (top picture). Then he opens the rules until the top edge intersects the rose's center. The easterly point of intersection with the inner magnetic circle—in this case 95°—is the course line's bearing. If the rose is too far from the course line to reach in one step, he "walks" the rules to the rose by opening them partway, holding the rule he has just moved firmly in place and swinging the other up to it, taking small steps to avoid slippage.

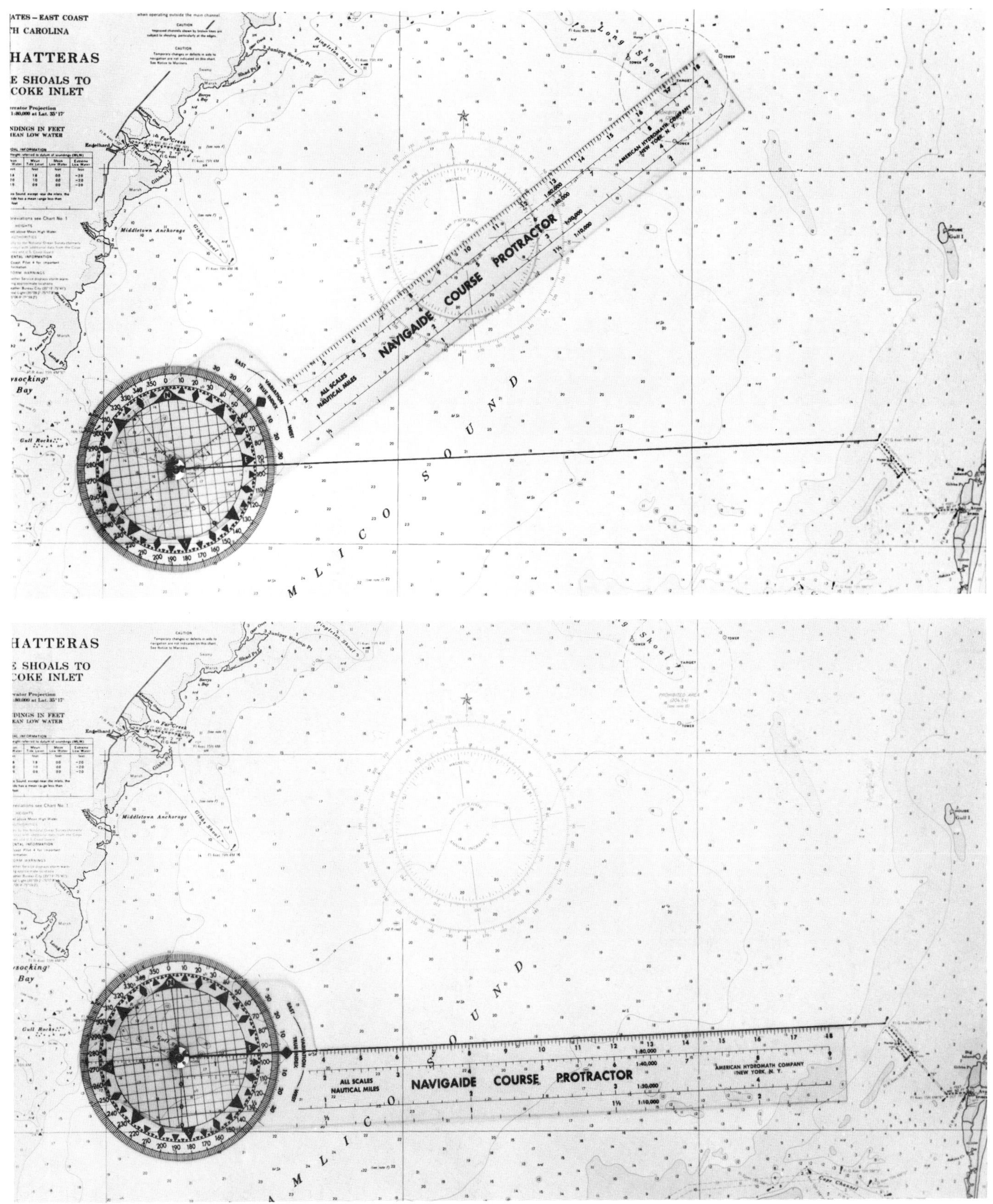

Using a course protractor to find the direction of a line of his chart, a navigator places the center hole of the disc at one end of the line with the upper edge of the arm intersecting the center of the chart's compass rose. The inner circle of the rose yields a reading of 60° magnetic. He revolves the disc until its figure 60 lines up (top picture) with the true index pointer. Holding the disc, which is oriented now with the rose, in this position, he rotates the arm until its top edge lies along the course line (lower picture). The figure on the disc opposite the true index pointer is the direction of the line—95°.

Laying Out a Course

A navigator equipped with a chart, a compass and the various devices for ascertaining speed, time and distance has all the tools needed for coastal navigation—except one. He still lacks a means of recording his course and position as he moves along, and of setting down on his chart the observations he uses in determining this critical information.

This process of marking a chart with information about a ship's movements is the culmination of the navigator's art. In practice it becomes a concise diary of a voyage, a clear record *(opposite)* of the navigator's intentions, predictions, observations, corrections and verifications.

For reasons of speed and clarity, the diary is written in a kind of navigator's shorthand *(right)*, easy to learn and easy to read. It is usually inscribed on a chart with an ordinary pencil, and an experienced navigator always has a supply of pencils, as well as a pencil sharpener, conveniently stowed by the chart table. An eraser, preferably one that works when wet, is handy, too, not only to correct mistakes but to clean old journeys from the chart so it can be used for future voyages.

The Navigator's Shorthand

Every navigator works out his own chart-notation system. The chief attributes of a good system are clarity and consistency so the navigator is never confused by his own code. The six symbols below are used almost universally by yachtsmen. They make it possible for anybody aboard a boat to figure out the chain of events on a trip like the one charted on pages 100-101, and to pilot the vessel in an emergency. A navigator may not use every symbol each time he leaves port, but he ought to be familiar with them all and know how to use them when he needs to.

C 072 MAG
D 26 S 15

A solid line represents a boat's course. Its direction is indicated by a letter C above the line, followed by three digits. MAG, for magnetic, is often omitted if all headings are magnetic. Below the line are the length of the course leg and the intended speed. This example shows a 26-nautical-mile course of 072° covered at 15 knots.

1745
195 MAG

A dashed line, easily distinguishable from a solid course line, stands for a bearing on a charted object. The direction from the boat to the object, in this case 195°, is written below the line in three digits. The time the bearing is taken—written in the four-digit form of a 24-hour nautical clock—appears above the dashed line.

1325 DR

A dot on a course line indicates a boat's position. By adding a semicircle, the time and the letters DR, the pilot specifies a dead-reckoning position. The least reliable type of position, it is entirely deduced from course, speed and time. This notation indicates where a pilot thinks he is or will be in the future.

0815 EP

A square around a dot on a course line, the letters EP and the time denote an estimated position. This symbol is used when the pilot has a bearing on a fixed object or a depth sounding *(page 129)* to combine with his projected course line. An EP is more reliable than a DR position, but is still about half guess.

1040 FIX
R FIX

An encircled dot marks a fix, a location confirmed by passing near a charted mark such as a buoy, or by taking nearly simultaneous bearings on two or more fixed objects *(below)*. The location is marked with FIX and the time. R FIX means running fix, a position derived from two bearings taken at different times.

0945 RDF FIX
RAD FIX

The navigator employs a triangle around a dot to indicate a fix based on information from electronic navigational aids *(pages 124-141)*. Each triangle is labeled to indicate both the time of the fix and the instrument used. For example, RDF FIX stands for a fix from a radio direction finder. RAD FIX means radar fix.

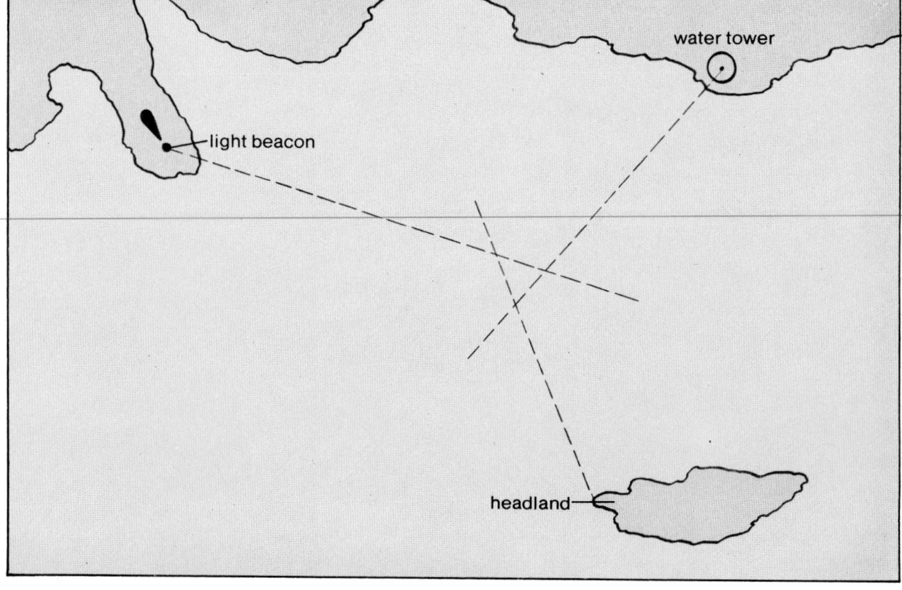

The most reliable way to determine a boat's location is by making a three-way fix (right). To make one, the boatman takes bearings on three charted objects; they should be widely separated so as to keep their bearing lines from crossing at an angle of less than 60°—but not more than 120°. Theoretically these three lines should all meet at a single point. In practice, slight errors in observation cause the lines to form a triangle, known to navigators as a cocked hat. But the boatman knows he is somewhere within the triangle, and as long as the triangle is small, the fix is usually close enough for his purposes.

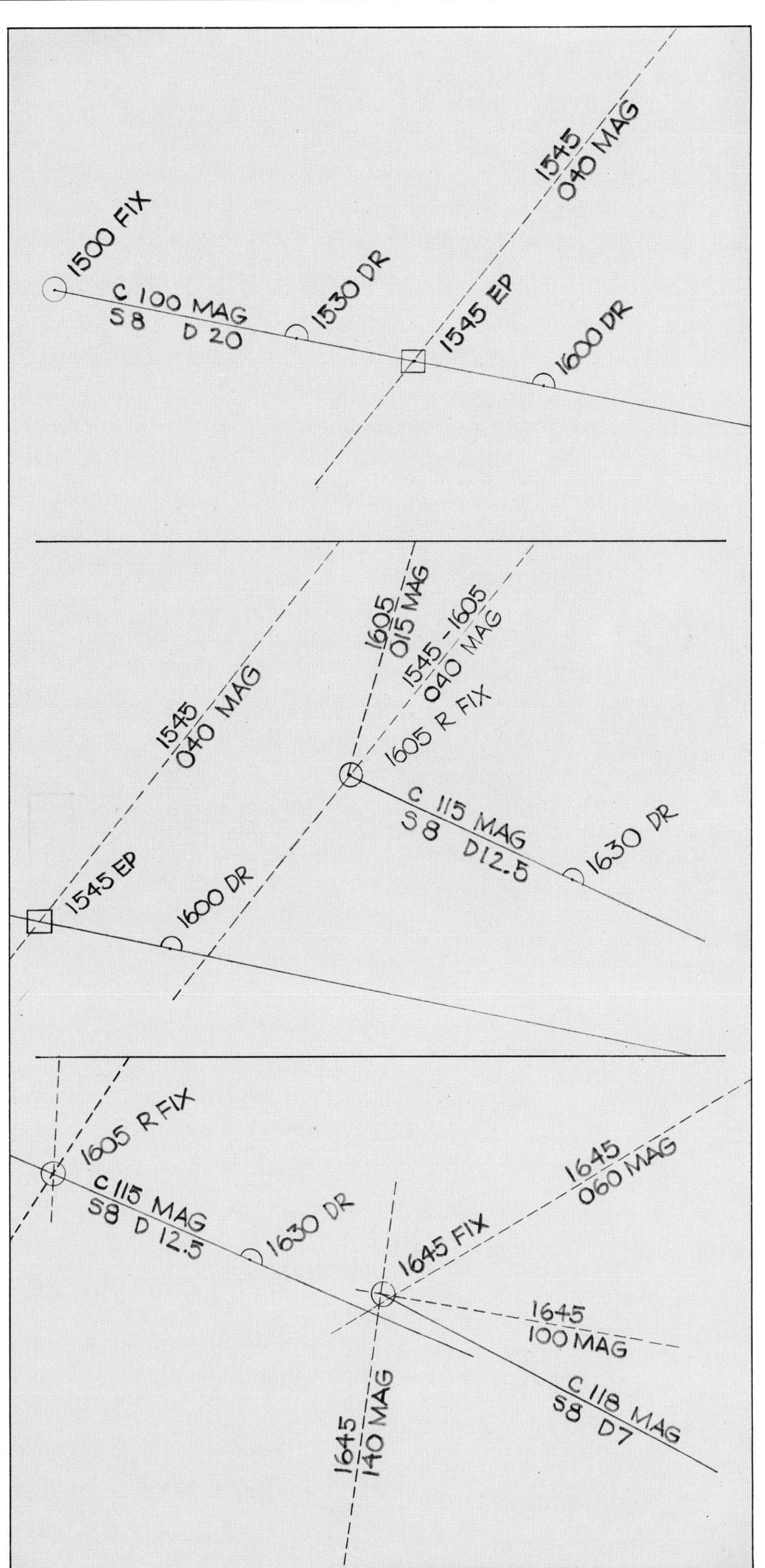

In compiling his shorthand record of a voyage, the navigator always begins with a fix. Fix data are usually written roughly perpendicular to the course line, while course data are written parallel to it. This skipper starts off at 1500 (3 p.m.), planning to go 20 miles at eight knots on a 100° course. He marks as DR positions his predicted locations for one half hour and one hour later. At 1545, he takes a bearing on a fixed, charted object, draws a dashed bearing line and labels it with time and direction. Knowing his boat is on this line, he marks its intersection with his course line as an estimated position.

At 1605, the skipper "advances" the 1545 bearing by marking off on the course line his reckoning of the distance covered in 20 minutes, then drawing a dashed line parallel to the 1545 bearing and labeling it with two time entries (1545-1605). At the same time, he takes a second bearing on the object that gave him the EP above. The intersection of this dashed line and the one representing his advanced bearing is labeled as a running fix. From this fix (which shows he is well off course), he draws a new course line to his destination—115° at eight knots for 12.5 miles—and predicts his position at 1630.

At 1645, 40 minutes after his running fix, the boatman sights three charted landmarks. He takes a bearing on each of them and draws on his chart the corresponding dashed bearing lines. He enters the resulting cocked hat as a fix; like the running fix above, it falls to one side of his plotted course line. Again, the navigator revises his course line. Beginning at his new fix, he plots a course of 118° for the seven miles remaining to his destination. He will continue to plot his position and make course adjustments that will bring him closer to his journey's safe end.

A Masterly Plot

A master navigator who can plot a proper course through multiple hazards can be as valuable to a boat as its helmsman. Shown on the chart at right is a portion of such a plot, which was compiled by navigation consultant Halsey Herreshoff one foggy summer morning as he cruised along the Maine coast.

Navigator Herreshoff first plotted a dead-reckoning course toward Flint Island, south of his anchorage in Pleasant Bay, then weighed anchor at 0945 and set out at a steady six knots.

A glimpse of the red beacon south of Norton Island through a rift in the fog at 0959 gave him a reassuring estimated position, and when at 1004 Flint Island loomed through the mist, bearings on its northern and eastern tips gave him a fix. The fog was lifting now, but in these waters morning fogs are notoriously unpredictable. Anxious, among all the rocks, to keep a constant check on his position, the skipper continued to plot every change of heading. He sprinkled his course lines with dead-reckoning positions and tested these assumptions as often as he could.

A fix at 1041 showed that he had been set, or swept off course, by a tidal current out of Western Bay. Beset again by fog and lacking a fixed visible object on which to take a bearing, he relied on a depth sounding at 1052 for an estimated position. For half an hour or so he motored east, holding closely to his plotted course, then turned 22° north. During the next hour, a string of islands off to port, glimpsed through breaks in the fog, gave him a running check on his position.

By noon the sun had burned off the fog and a fix at 1232 showed that he had been set by another tidal current. His next objective as he headed north was a clearly visible gong buoy, but midway to it, as a routine precaution, he took a bearing and noted an estimated position. From the buoy, the skipper proceeded by line of sight on up the coast (and off the chart). On the following pages are step-by-step illustrations and explanations of how an experienced pilot creates a course plot like this one, as he moves along.

On the chart at right, the course through the myriad rocky islands off the Maine coast has been marked with a blue tint for greater legibility, though in practice the navigator would have made all of his notations with a black pencil that was easily erasable.

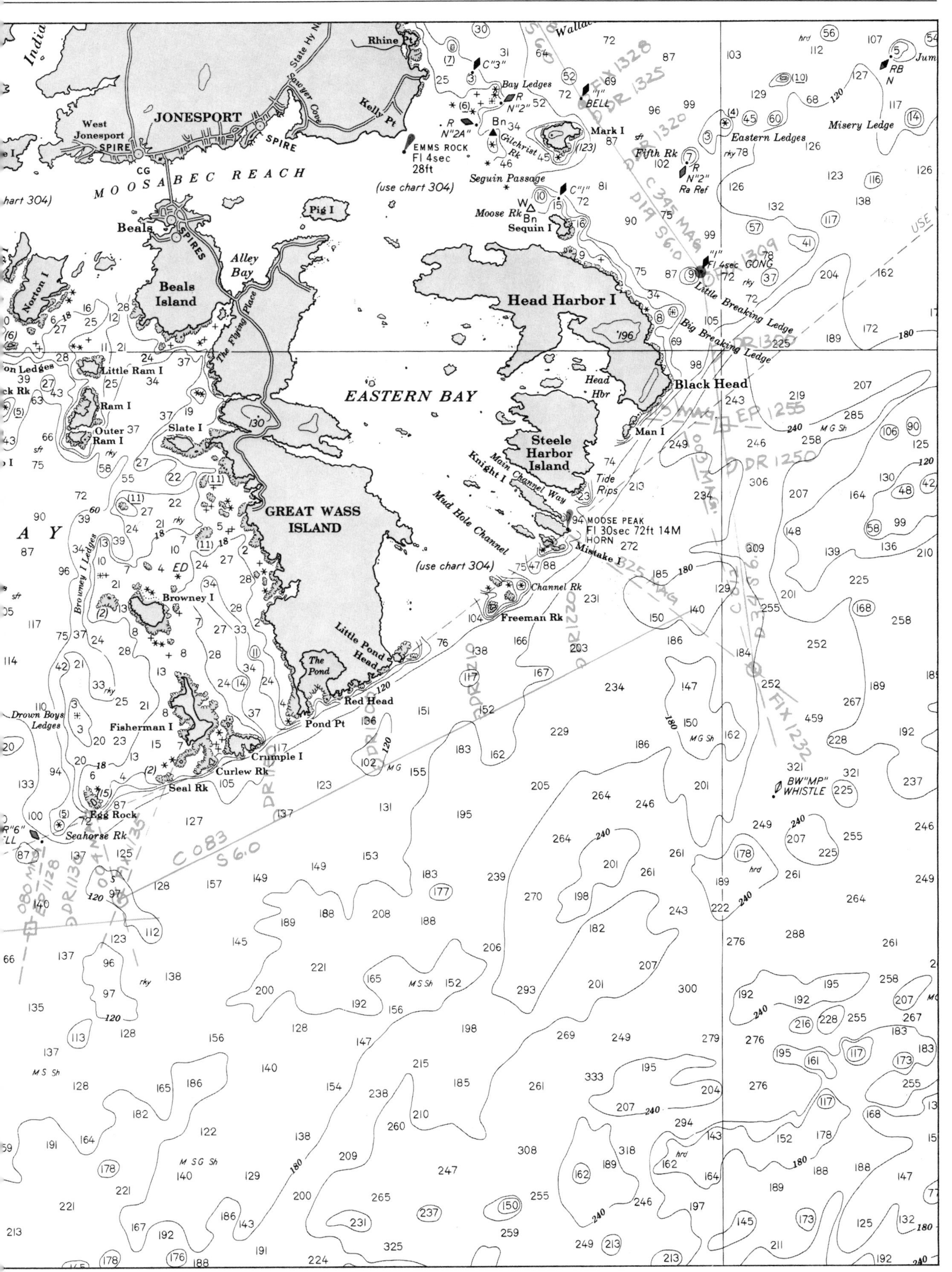
JONESPORT
West Jonesport
MOOSABEC REACH
Beals
Beals Island
Alley Bay
The Flying Place
Pig I
Head Harbor I
EASTERN BAY
Steele Harbor Island
GREAT WASS ISLAND
Black Head
Man I
Mark I
Fifth Rk
Eastern Ledges
Misery Ledge
Little Breaking Ledge
Big Breaking Ledge
Main Channel Way
Mud Hole Channel
Knight I
Mistake I
MOOSE PEAK
Fl 30sec 72ft 14M
HORN
Channel Rk
Freeman Rk
Little Pond Head
The Pond
Red Head
Pond Pt
Crumple I
Curlew Rk
Seal Rk
Fisherman I
Egg Rock
Seahorse Rk
Drown Boys Ledges
Browney I
Browney I Ledges
Slate I
Little Ram I
Ram I
Outer Ram I
Norton I
EMMS ROCK
Fl 4sec
28ft
(use chart 304)
Bay Ledges
Gilchrist Rk
Seguin Passage
Moose Rk
Sequin I
Rhine Pt
Kelly Pt
Sawyer Cove
BW"MP" WHISTLE

THE COLUMBUS

4

Before taking his boat out on a trip, especially in unfamiliar waters, a thoughtful skipper should always set aside time to ponder his course. Like the pilot of the sport fisherman at left, he may be planning no more than a 30-mile afternoon spin around Key Biscayne. Or he may be contemplating a week's cruise on the Great Lakes or along the Pacific Coast. In any case, he should consider the nature of the waters he will pass through and estimate his probable travel time; also, he should determine what navigation aids will help him on his way and how he will deal with tidal conditions or other special cruising problems he may encounter. Navigating foresight is as important

PILOTING POINT-TO-POINT

to sound boating as is checking out an engine or bringing proper safety gear.

A pilot who does his homework, and makes careful use of his findings, usually collects as dividends a safe, relatively easy trip—and the fun of exercising his piloting skills. But by failing to anticipate possible hazards, or by failing to apply the information on his chart or within his field of vision, he can easily curtail not only the pleasure of the cruise but the cruise itself. Recently, a $150,000 brand-new 48-foot cruiser fitted out with everything available for pinpoint, all-weather navigation—compass, chronometer, depth finder (or echo sounder), radar and loran—came to grinding grief in Long Island Sound because the skipper failed to read his chart and to keep an eye out ahead. Steering around the wrong side of a buoy, he hit a reef that sheared off both rudders, both struts, both shafts and both propellers.

The pilot of the sport fisherman shown on these pages, however, has made his preparations before leaving the pier: he has studied a chart of the area, chosen a route, and made mental notes of navigation aids and possible hazards. As shown on the map on the next two pages and in the photographs and chart sections that follow, his course takes him across Biscayne Bay, through a narrow channel between coral reefs, around a lighthouse, along the edge of a huge sand bar and back through a busy shipping lane to Miami.

He notes from the chart that for most of the way his path will be marked by buoys and beacons. A number of landmarks on shore may also help to keep him oriented. He makes a preliminary decision on how he will use these resources. For most of the trip he will be piloting from one point to another by line-of-sight navigation and by taking soundings. In stretches of more open water, where reference points are not always immediately visible, he will engage in a couple of dead-reckoning exercises, calculating the direction—and probable travel time—from his last accurately determined position to a further point marked on the chart but beyond his line of sight. Here and there he will use his depth finder to keep from straying into shallows, or even as a means of fixing his position.

Throughout the trip he will supplement the chart's general guidance by keeping a sharp lookout. His chart, though meticulously prepared and conscientiously updated by the National Oceanic and Atmospheric Administration, will not tell him the exact water depth in an area where dredged material is being dumped or the extent to which last week's storm shifted a sand bar.

Such close attention to the water and to his charts is not mere fussbudgeting. During his circumnavigation of Key Biscayne, the pilot of the sport fisherman will be operating on a sparkling afternoon under near-perfect conditions. If he makes a mistake, he will have time to stop and correct it. Still, he executes every maneuver with utmost precision, not only from a sense of seamanly pride, but also to prepare himself for rougher days. In fog or stormy weather, a pilot's calculations must be quick and unfailing, and may spell the difference between making port safely or not at all.

The sport fisherman rounds the first mark on the cruise: a black can marked "1," which the skipper properly leaves to starboard (page 50) as he heads out from the Miami River.

Blueprint for a Short Cruise

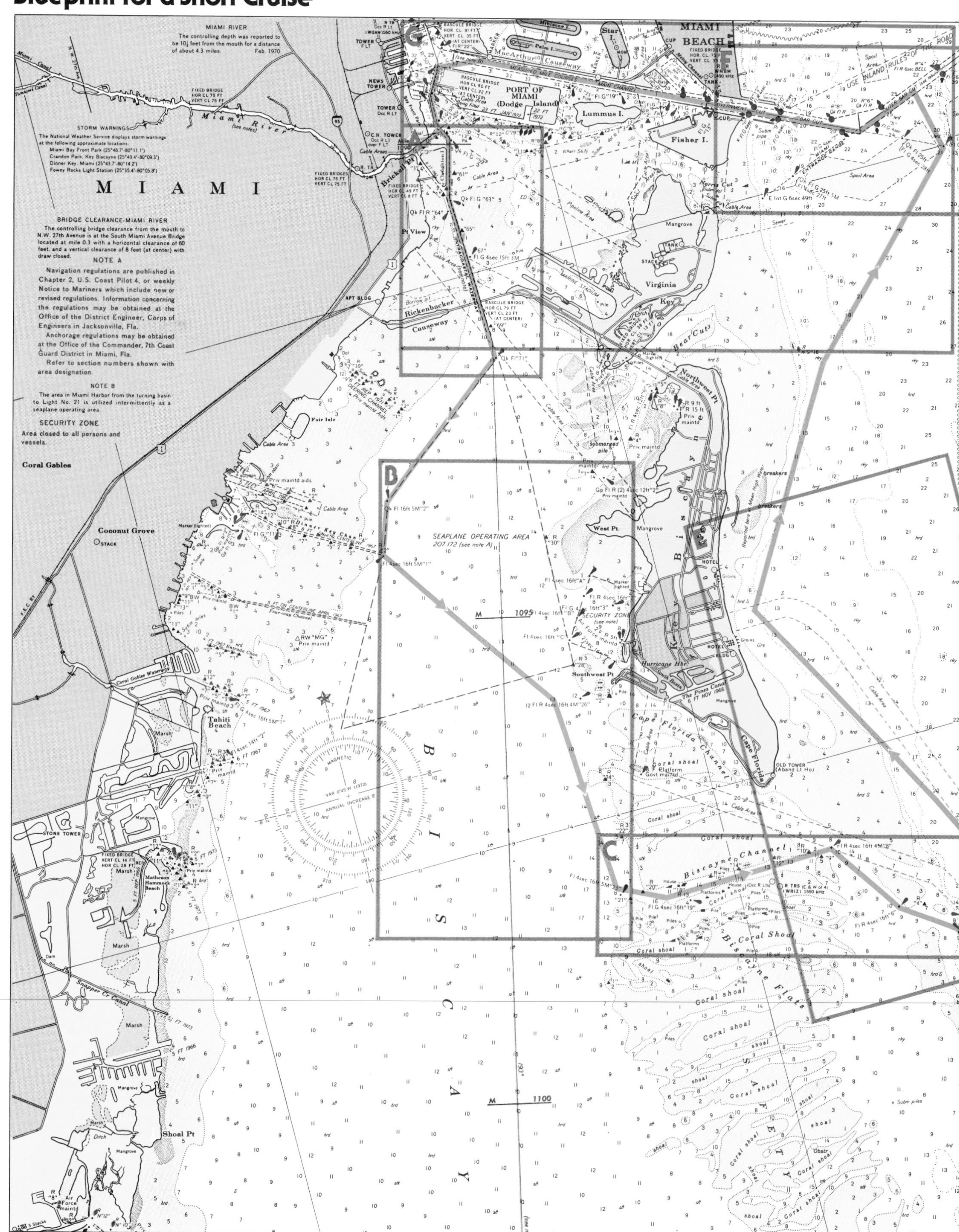

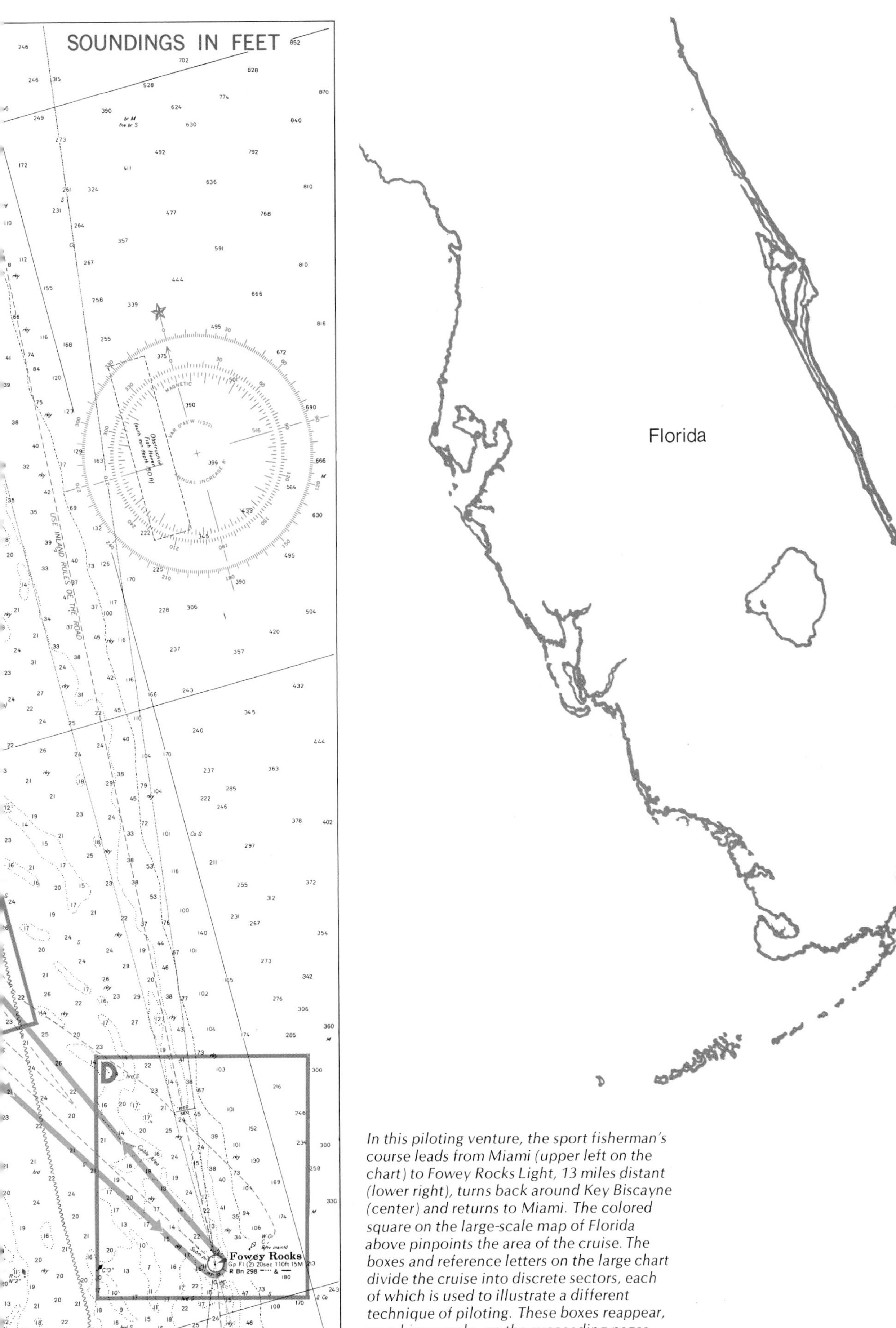

In this piloting venture, the sport fisherman's course leads from Miami (upper left on the chart) to Fowey Rocks Light, 13 miles distant (lower right), turns back around Key Biscayne (center) and returns to Miami. The colored square on the large-scale map of Florida above pinpoints the area of the cruise. The boxes and reference letters on the large chart divide the cruise into discrete sectors, each of which is used to illustrate a different technique of piloting. These boxes reappear, on a larger scale, on the succeeding pages.

First Leg of the Journey

After leaving its pier at the mouth of the Miami River, the sport fisherman making the short Florida cruise shown on these pages rounds triangular Claughton Island and enters the channel of the Intracoastal Waterway, or ICW.

In the top photograph on the opposite page, the boat is passing the spot indicated by the large figure 1 on Sector A of the chart *(right)*. Throughout this part of the journey, and until he enters the more open waters of Biscayne Bay, the pilot is guided by a series of aids to navigation lining the sides of this straight and narrow channel. As everywhere else along the ICW, the red-colored and even-numbered aids should be left to the starboard side of a boat traveling south, as here, or west. Odd-numbered and black are left to port. A part of each aid is painted yellow to show that the channel is a part of the ICW.

The channel here is kept dredged to a minimum depth—known as a controlling depth—of seven feet, and the pilot must take care to keep within the boundaries delineated by the beacons. He knows that his boat draws nearly three feet, and the numbers on the chart indicating depth in feet tell him that there are many shallower spots outside the channel.

Continuing on its southward course, the sport fisherman arrives at the point designated by the large figure 2 on the chart. Here a causeway crosses the ICW by way of the bascule bridge (a drawbridge with two counterweighted spans) shown in the lower photograph on the opposite page. The chart tells the pilot that when the bridge is closed it has a high-water vertical clearance of 23 feet. A large yellow sign on the bridge informs him that clearance is 25 feet at low tide.

If his boat carried a mast too tall to clear the bridge, he would stop short of the bridge and signal by three blasts of a horn or whistle for the bridge to be raised. However, it is illegal to request the raising of a drawbridge for a boat whose profile can be lowered enough to clear. And since this boat can clear simply by lowering its outriggers, the skipper dips them and powers through.

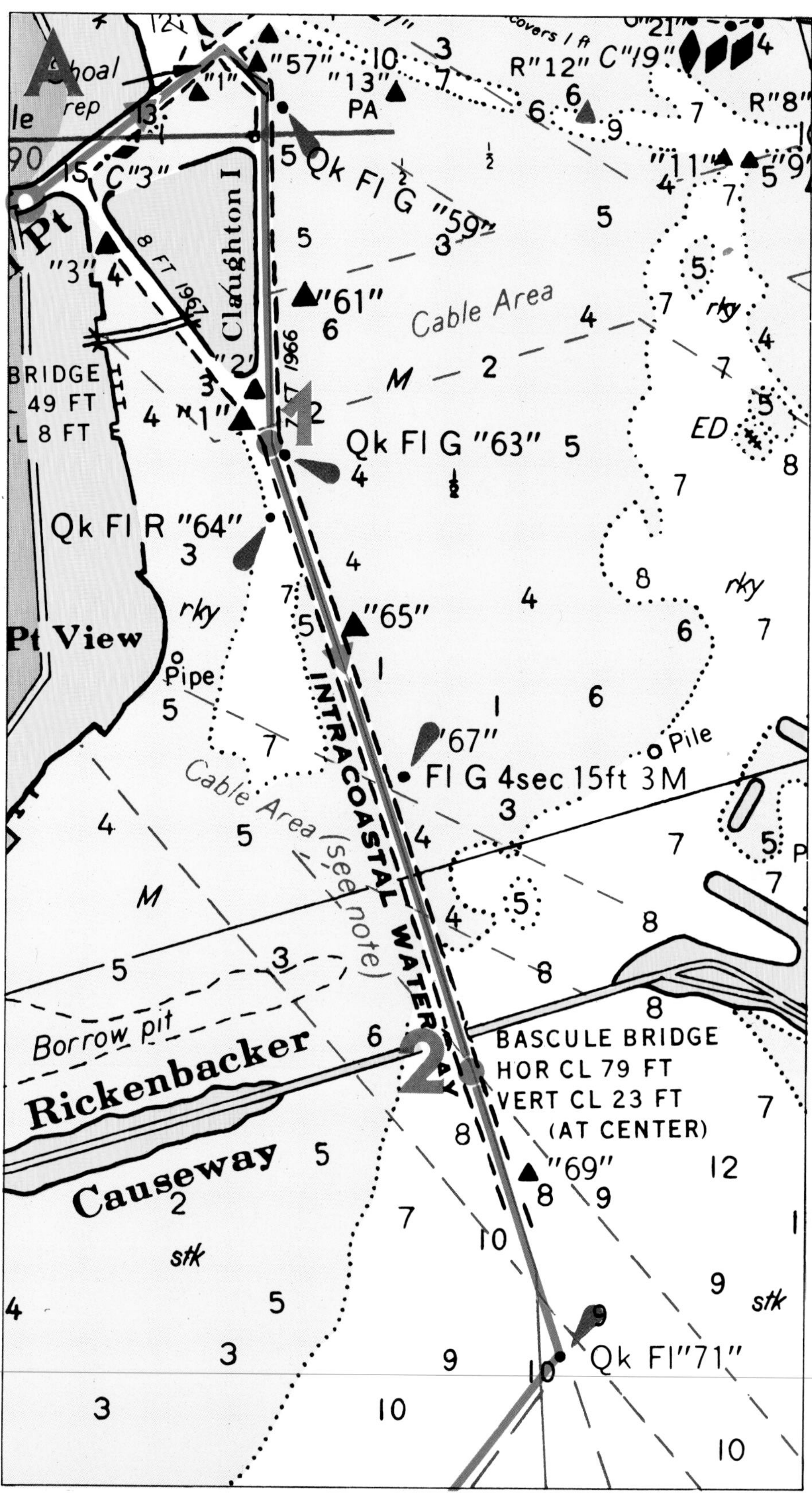

Broken lines on the chart segment above show the portion of the ICW traversed by the sport fisherman on the first leg of its voyage. The heavy green line traces the boat's course. Other information shown on the chart—and important to the pilot—includes the navigation aids marking the channel, landmarks such as bridges and prominent buildings, the depth of the ICW channel, and the horizontal and vertical clearances of the bascule bridge at figure 2. Motoring straight along this well-marked channel, the pilot can navigate visually, with no need to plot a prior course line.

1 As the powerboat churns south along the ICW channel, the skipper leaves to port the square-shaped beacon—called a daymark—that is black and odd-numbered. To his right is a small red buoy, temporarily replacing a beacon that is under repair. The yellow paint on the navigation aids identifies them as part of the Intracoastal system.

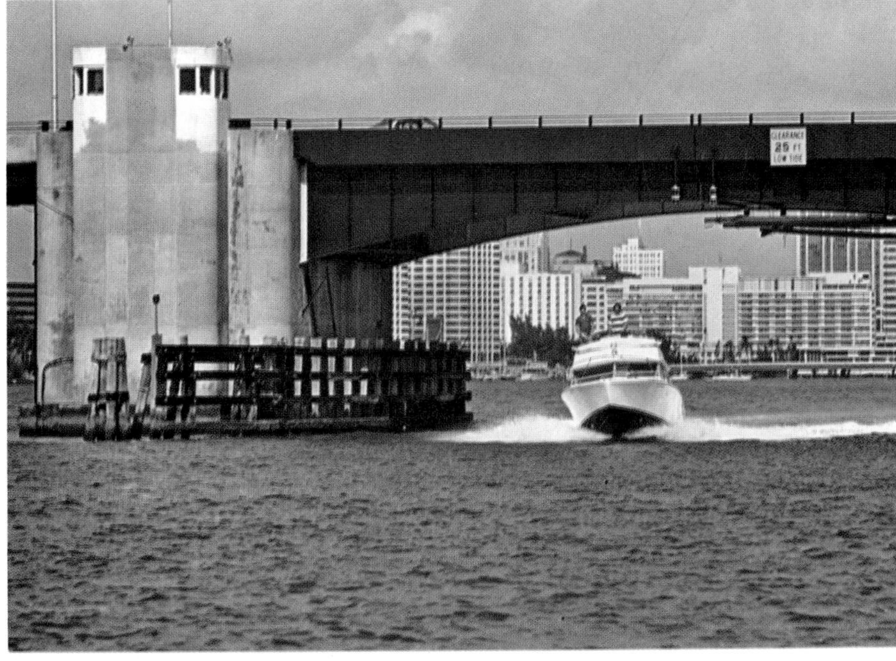

2 With outriggers lowered, the boat skims beneath the bascule bridge marked on the chart segment at left. The skipper of any sizable boat should consider before starting a trip whether he will encounter drawbridges that must be raised for his vessel. If so, he should consult the Coast Pilot as to whether there are hours during which the bridge cannot be raised for water traffic.

Plotting a dead-reckoning course, the pilot uses his parallel rules as a straight edge to draw a line on his chart from his departure position to his intended destination. Being careful to keep the rules aligned with this course, he then walks them over to the compass rose on the chart and reads that the compass heading of this course is 232° magnetic. He writes this figure, for future reference, alongside the course line, then steers his boat as close to 232° as possible.

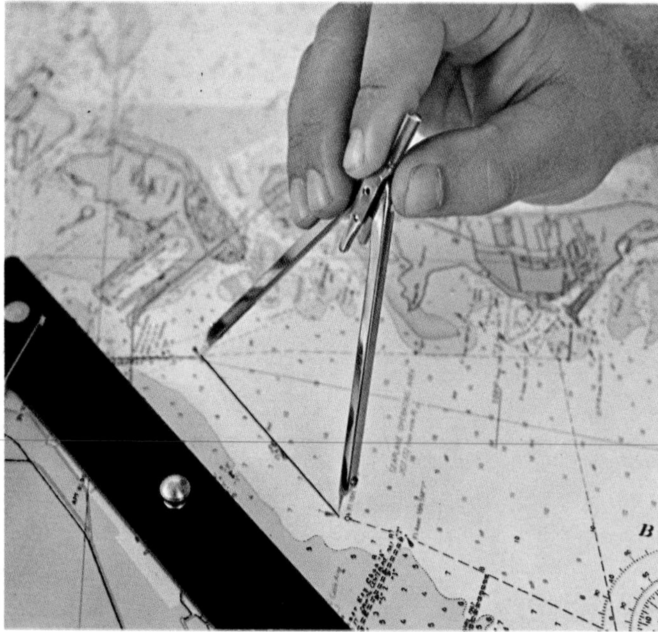

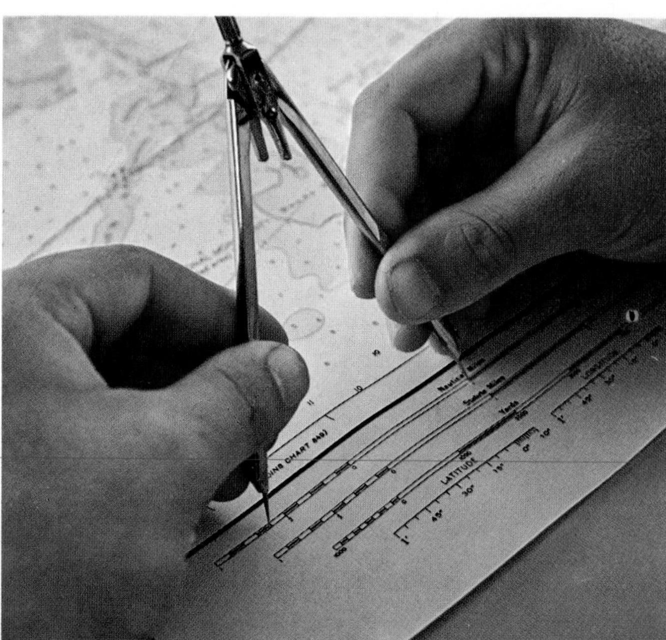

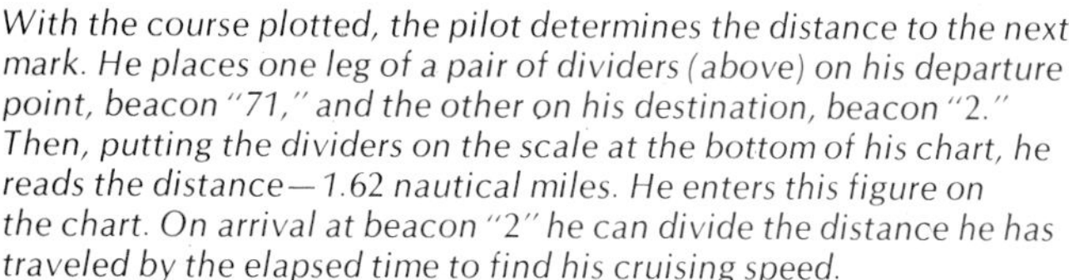

With the course plotted, the pilot determines the distance to the next mark. He places one leg of a pair of dividers (above) on his departure point, beacon "71," and the other on his destination, beacon "2." Then, putting the dividers on the scale at the bottom of his chart, he reads the distance—1.62 nautical miles. He enters this figure on the chart. On arrival at beacon "2" he can divide the distance he has traveled by the elapsed time to find his cruising speed.

Dead Reckoning

Leaving the Intracoastal Waterway sector shown on the chart on page 106 the sport fisherman's skipper is preparing to make a short run across Biscayne Bay, then around Fowey Rocks *(pages 114-115)* and home again. Before moving out where navigation aids may be spaced too widely for line-of-sight piloting, he plots a course, using the centuries-old technique called dead reckoning, or DR for short.

The objective of this leg of the trip is to get from beacon "71," shown at right, near the southern end of the ICW channel to beacon "2" *(chart, page 111)*, farther to the southwest. With a soft pencil—for easy erasure later—he draws a straight line on his chart from "71" to "2." Then using his parallel rules *(top left)*, he determines his compass heading for this course. Next he takes a measurement on the chart *(bottom left)* to find the distance between beacons. He enters both figures along the course line on his chart.

With the DR course set, the pilot notes that his departure time from beacon "71" is 12:45 p.m., or 1245 hours on the 24-hour clock used in navigation. He adds this figure to the distance and direction data he has written on the chart, and revs up the boat to a comfortable cruising speed. At this point, his tachometer—which shows the number of revolutions his engine makes per minute—reads 3,100 rpm's. Though his boat lacks a speedometer, like any careful skipper he has established from previous calibration tests *(pages 92-93)* that at those rpm's, under average conditions of wind and weather, he will be moving at about 25 knots. By keeping a close eye on his tachometer, he can try to hold a steady pace and arrive at the destination at a calculated time.

In common practice, however, winds, currents, imperfect steering and compass deviation will inevitably deflect a boat from the exact course line penciled on the chart; and the longer the run, the greater the deflection. But on the brief trip from "71" to "2," theory and practice coincide. There is almost no current here; the wind is negligible; and the distance is so short that minor steering errors have no significant effect. Within a few moments of leaving beacon "71," the pilot can see and identify beacon "2." He steers straight to it and arrives at nearly 1249 hours, having covered the 1.62 nautical miles in 3 minutes 50 seconds. By dividing the distance by the time, he can confirm that his boat is holding its speed of about 25 knots. With these data, he confidently begins the next leg of his voyage.

As he leaves "71" on his new heading of 232°, the skipper notes that the time of departure is 12:45 p.m. and enters it on his chart. He will also note on the chart the time of his arrival at beacon "2."

The tachometer on the dashboard counts the engine's rpm's, in this case 3,100. By regularly checking his tachometer, the pilot can keep his engine running steadily.

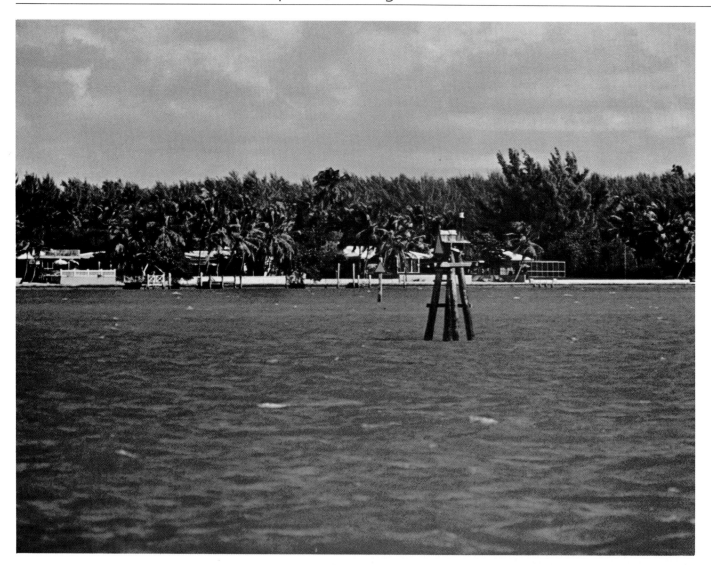

1 By lining up two fixed objects, such as the two beacons above—both are identified on the chart—a pilot gets what is called a range; that is, he knows he must be along a line running through the two objects. To find out where, he notes the intersection of this line with his boat's course line; his position is at the point of intersection.

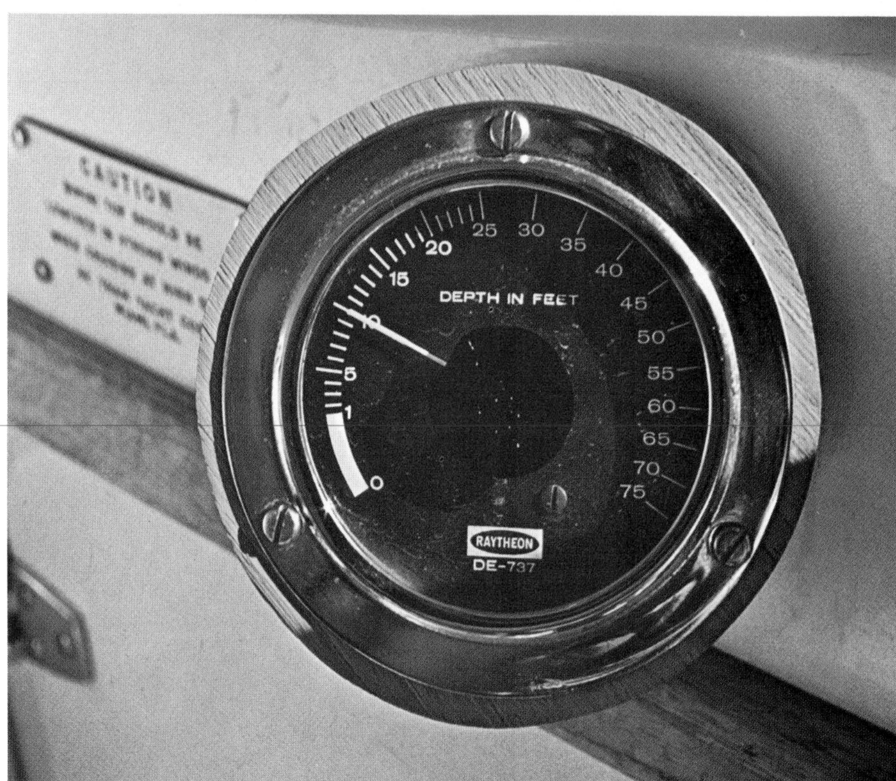

2 A reading of 10 feet on the depth finder at right confirms the sport fisherman is at large figure 2 on the chart opposite. Many boatmen use depth finders in this manner, as navigation aids to check depths en route against the chart's notation of bottom depths along their course line. Depth finders also warn of potentially dangerous shoals, such as the one shown opposite on the chart of Sector B of the Biscayne Bay voyage.

Two Checks on Position

Passing beacon "2" *(upper left corner of chart),* the sport fisherman turns toward "1," clearly visible half a mile or so to the south. While a shipmate steers toward this next point, the navigator plots a new and slightly more complicated DR course for the third leg of his short trip off Miami.

He intends to go from beacon "1" to beacon "23" at lower right in the chart, but as an exercise in piloting he decides to verify his position en route. To do so he divides the leg into two roughly equidistant parts, each with a different course heading. For the first part, he picks a heading that will bring him to a spot—large figure 1 on the chart at right—just offshore, from which he can visually line up two aids to navigation, as shown in the corresponding photograph at left.

Before arriving at this spot, the pilot draws a line to it on his chart from beacon "1." By using parallel rules, compass rose and dividers *(page 108),* he determines that his chosen spot is about two nautical miles from beacon "1" on a course of 145° magnetic, and notes these facts on the chart. As the boat rounds beacon "1" and sets off on the new course, the pilot records the time of departure as 1300. He then draws a line *(heavy broken line on chart)* that passes through the two beacons near his checkpoint and intersects his course line at large figure 1. From the point of intersection, he draws another line to beacon "23." He calculates this line as bearing 175° magnetic and the distance as 1.8 nautical miles.

Traveling at its predetermined cruising speed of about 25 knots, the boat arrives at figure 1 in just under five minutes. The pilot notes the time, looks to his left, and sees that the two beacons he has selected for his checkpoint line up like the sights on a rifle. Sailors refer to such an alignment of two charted objects as a range; and when a vessel establishes itself along a range, the craft is said to be on a line of position, or LOP. On this chart the LOP is the broken line that intersects with the boat's course, giving the pilot a so-called fix that pinpoints his position.

Noting on the chart the time of the fix, the pilot puts the boat on its new course of 175° and heads for beacon "23." Since the chart's sounding marks show that this new route skirts a shoal, the pilot switches on his depth finder *(left)* as a double check on the precision of the course he is steering. If the finder indicates depths of less than 10 feet, the skipper knows he is wandering from his proper course and must sheer off into safer water.

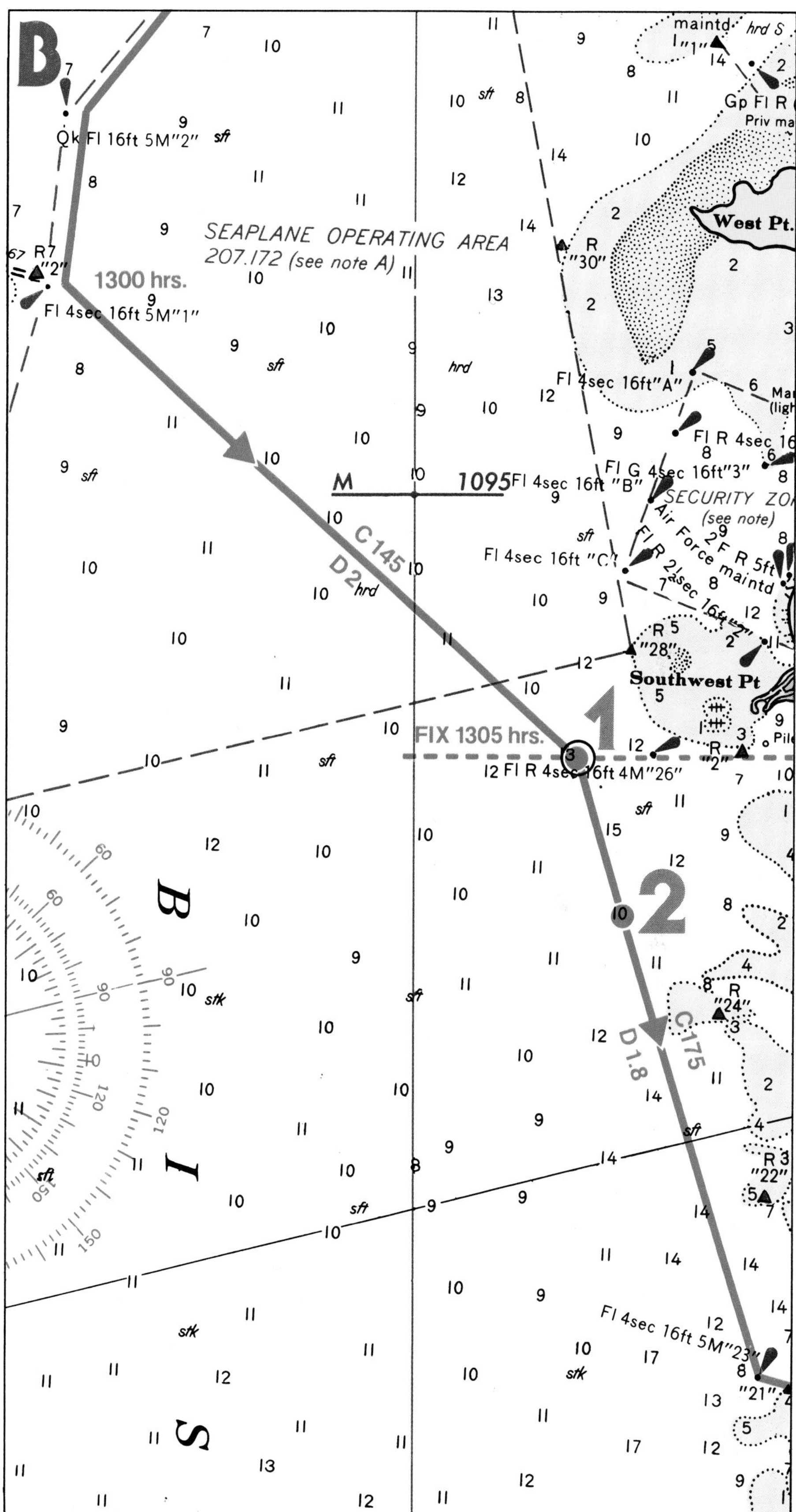

The dead-reckoning plot above is set down in boatman's shorthand (pages 98-99). Departure time from mark "1" is noted in the 24-hour system used by navigators. The course (C) is labeled according to its magnetic bearing. Distance (D) is in nautical miles; and a broken line indicates the line of position used in making a fix, with the time noted. A dot within a circle at large figure 1 marks the fix.

1 Having passed beacon "23" at the end of his course (preceding page), the pilot enters Biscayne Channel (large figure 1 on the chart below). There he follows a trail of daymarks—here fixed on unlighted beacons—that outline the channel's northern edge. Since the boat is now heading seaward, the red daymarks are to port.

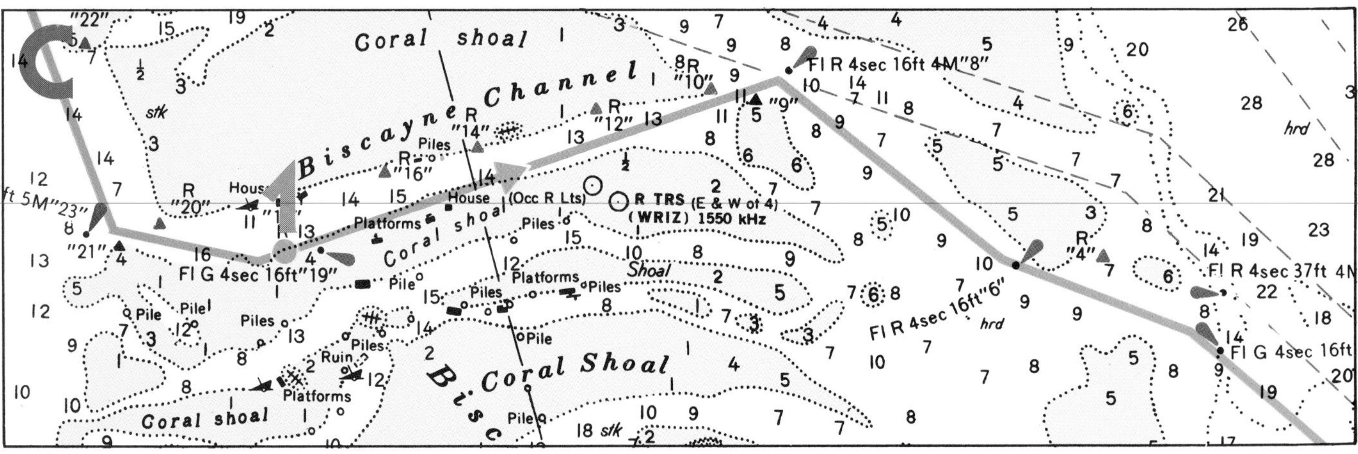

Consulting Sector C of the chart, the pilot recognizes the triangles he sees along his course (photograph at top) as the daymarks on the chart. Wrecks, pilings and houses on stilts are also indicated. But pilots should be alert for unexpected hazards; bottom contours change and new obstructions crop up oftener than do new charts.

Negotiating a Narrow Channel

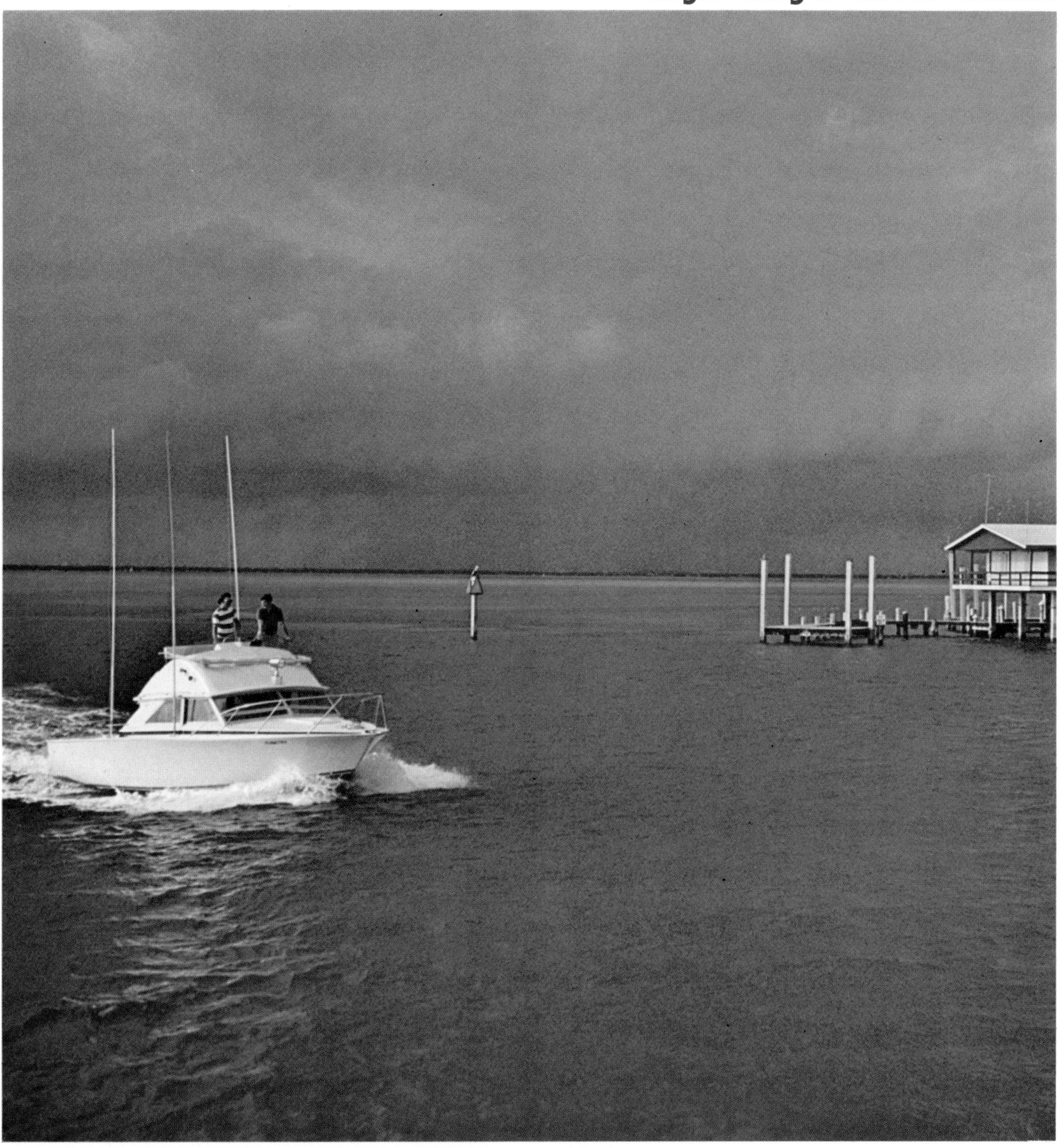

As the pilot enters Biscayne Channel just past large figure 1, he notes lighter-colored waters off to port, indicating shoal water not far outside the string of red daymarks. By keeping a sharp eye out for such signs of danger, a boatman can run safely through channels that are less clearly marked than the one off Biscayne—though he should move at a cautious pace and keep his depth finder turned on.

Rounding the Far Turn

1 *Trailing a welter of spray, the sport fisherman rounds Fowey Rocks Light (large figure 1 on chart), the outermost limit of the trip. The light's tower, erected in 1876, is a favorite homing point for local boatmen; by night, its beam can be seen for 15 nautical miles in all directions. Also at Fowey Rocks is a radio beacon whose signal can be used by a boat's radio direction finder (page 130).*

2 *The sport fisherman leaves Fowey Rocks rapidly astern as the pilot and crew head back toward Miami. In order to double-check his course at this point (large figure 2 on the chart), the pilot can take a compass bearing directly astern; the light should bear 154°–exactly 180° from the course that is being steered.*

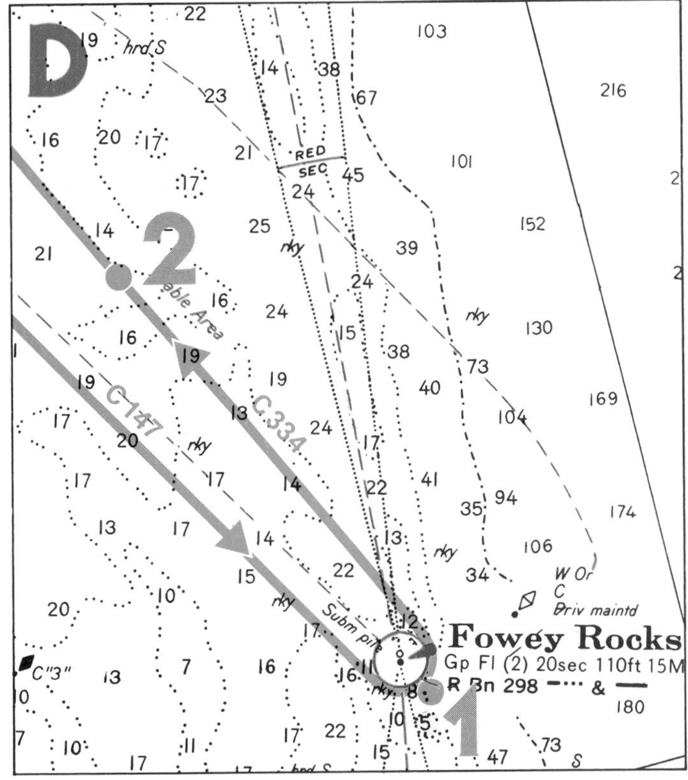

The pilot charts the course to Fowey Rocks (147° magnetic) and the homeward course (334°). Printed beneath the light's name is the key information on Fowey's characteristics. Translated, the abbreviations read: light flashes in groups of two every 20 seconds; the light, 110 feet over high water, is visible for 15 nautical miles; the frequency of the radio beacon is 298 kilohertz, broadcasting in Morse Code the letter B (dash-dot-dot-dot), plus an extended dash.

Doubling on Safety

Heading in from Fowey Rocks, the skipper sees that the dead-reckoning course he has plotted skirts a reef. To make sure he is far enough away from the reef, he computes his distance from a fixed object ashore— in this case, an abandoned lighthouse— by a technique called doubling the angle on the bow.

At large figure 1 on the chart, he takes a bearing on the lighthouse, using a hand bearing compass, a portable instrument whose face is bracketed by a sighting arrangement *(top, opposite)*. The lighthouse bears 20° west of his course of 334°. He marks this bearing *(broken line)* and the time, 1540, on his chart.

Continuing along his course, the pilot keeps checking the bearing of the lighthouse. When, at about 1544, the angle between his course and the lighthouse has doubled to 40°, he draws a second bearing on his chart. Where this second line intersects his course, he establishes a fix.

He knows from his first bearing that the interior angle at the south end of the triangle's base is 20°; the second bearing tells him the interior angle at the apex must be 140° (40° subtracted from the 180° of his straight-line course). Since the three interior angles of a triangle always add up to 180°, the other base angle must be 20°. If the base angles of a triangle are equal, its two sides are of equal length. Knowing his speed and the time elapsed, the pilot also knows that the distance from figure 1 to the fix is 1.5 nautical miles. He is, therefore, 1.5 miles off the light— enough to miss the reef.

Wishing to run close alongshore, the pilot now picks out a highly visible object on the shore ahead that will give him a bearing just skirting the shallow water. The most visible object is a large white hotel *(opposite, bottom)*, marked at the upper left corner of the chart segment. He draws a line from this fix to the hotel, and finds that its bearing is 330°. This line becomes his so-called danger bearing— so long as he stays outside it, he is safe. However, in these clear waters and in his shallow-draft boat, the pilot rightly decides (at large figure 2) that he can run along the danger bearing.

Just south of the first hotel is another hotel. By drawing a line through the second hotel, perpendicular to his course line, the pilot discovers that when the first hotel is dead ahead and the second exactly abeam he will have a fix at the point where he wants to change course again. When the moment arrives, he makes the fix and sets off on the new course.

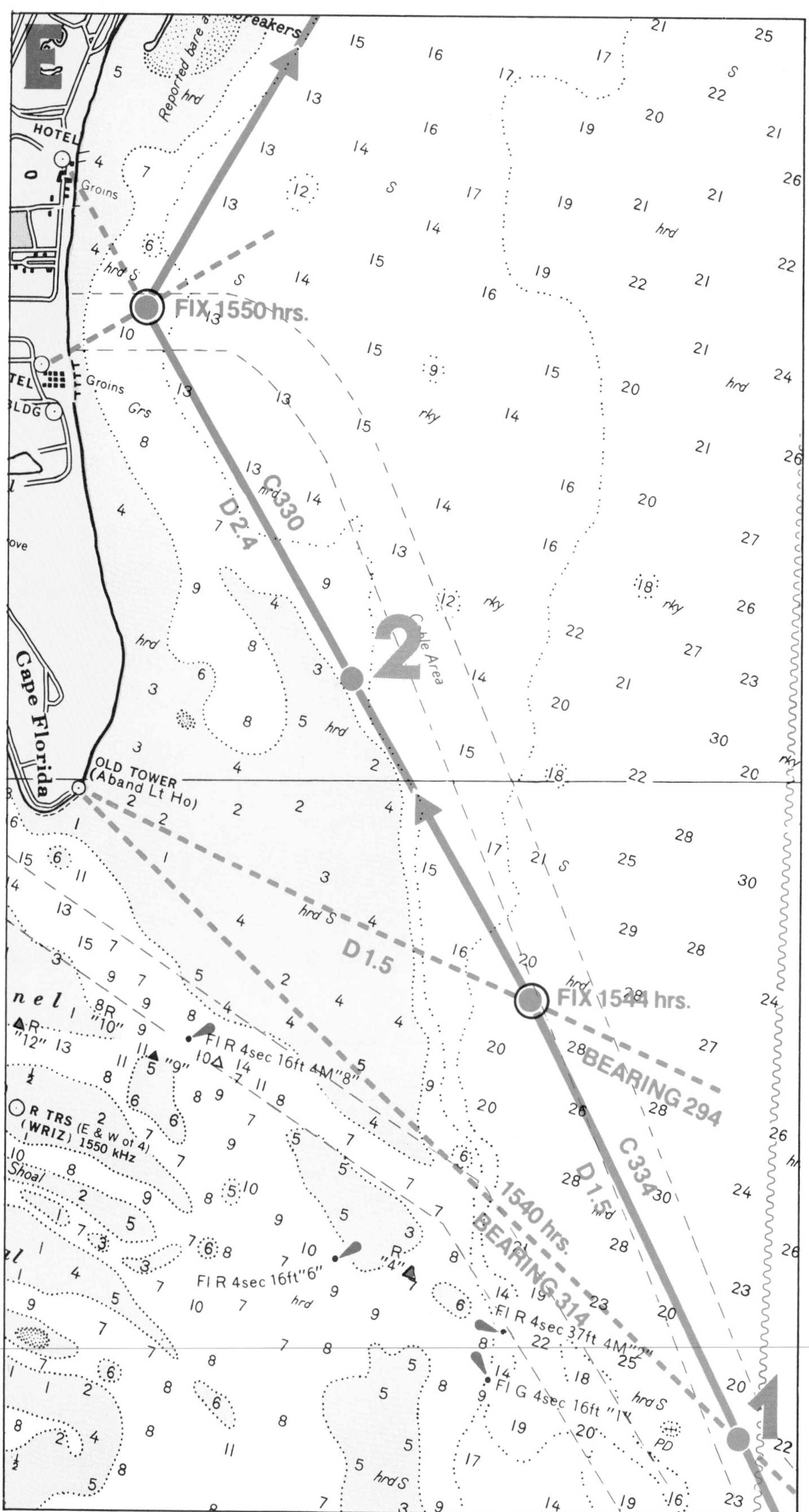

En route to Miami the skipper skirts a sand bar off Cape Florida, taking fixes to keep a safe distance away. He then heads for a hotel at top left on the chart, makes another fix and turns right to start his run up the coast.

1 *Using a hand bearing compass, the pilot notes that from figure 1 on the chart the abandoned lighthouse bears 314° and that the time (right) is 1540. A hand bearing compass should be checked with the ship's compass to make sure the readings coincide, and should not be used on a steel boat because the deviation is variable.*

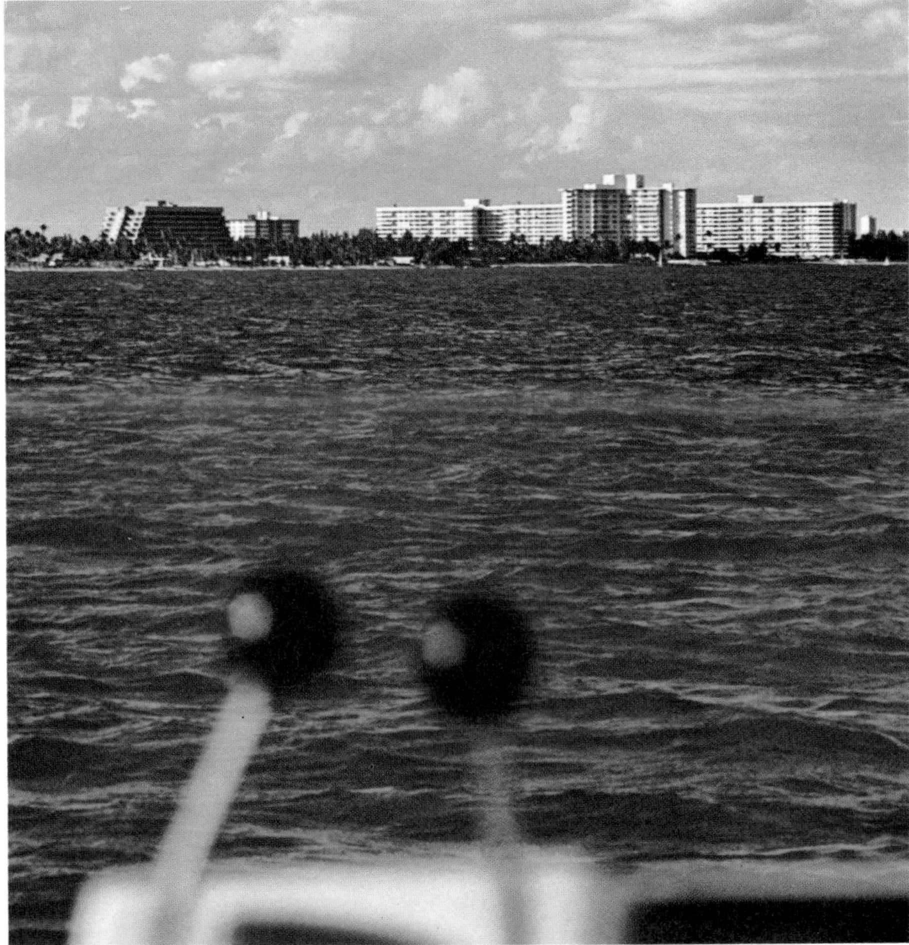

2 *The hotel shown here, seen from large figure 2 on the chart opposite, provides an excellent landmark on which to take a danger bearing and, later, to take another bearing for the fix at top left on the chart. Any large stationary object that is marked on a chart may be used for these purposes. Buoys should be shunned, if possible, as they have a tendency to shift position.*

Having powered away from his last fix (preceding page), the pilot nears a passage between two spoil areas (where dredged material is dumped). In these spoil areas, bottom depth is kept at a minimum of 16 feet—but this information is not on his chart, nor is it available in other commonly published navigational guides. Since dumping often makes water too shallow for passage, the pilot avoids these sectors as he heads for the channel that leads to the Miami harbor.

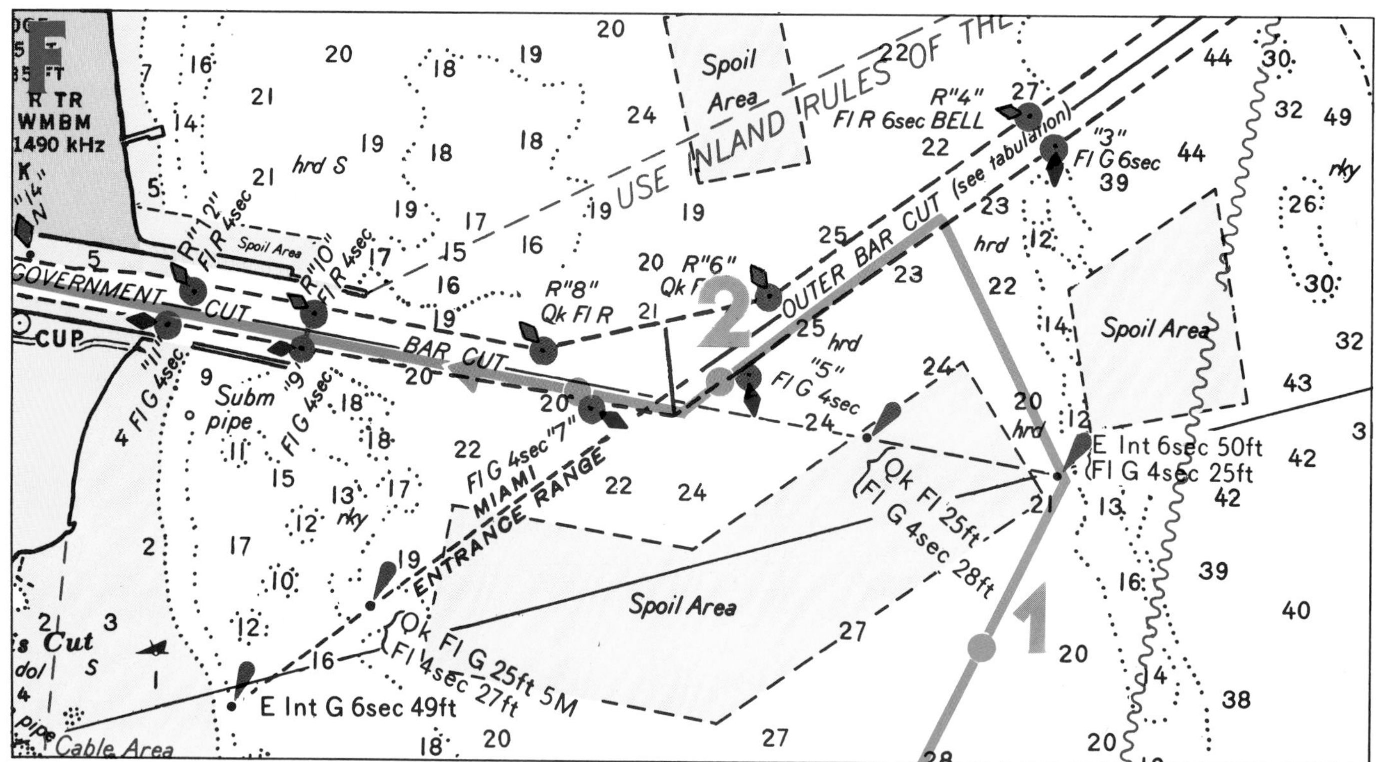

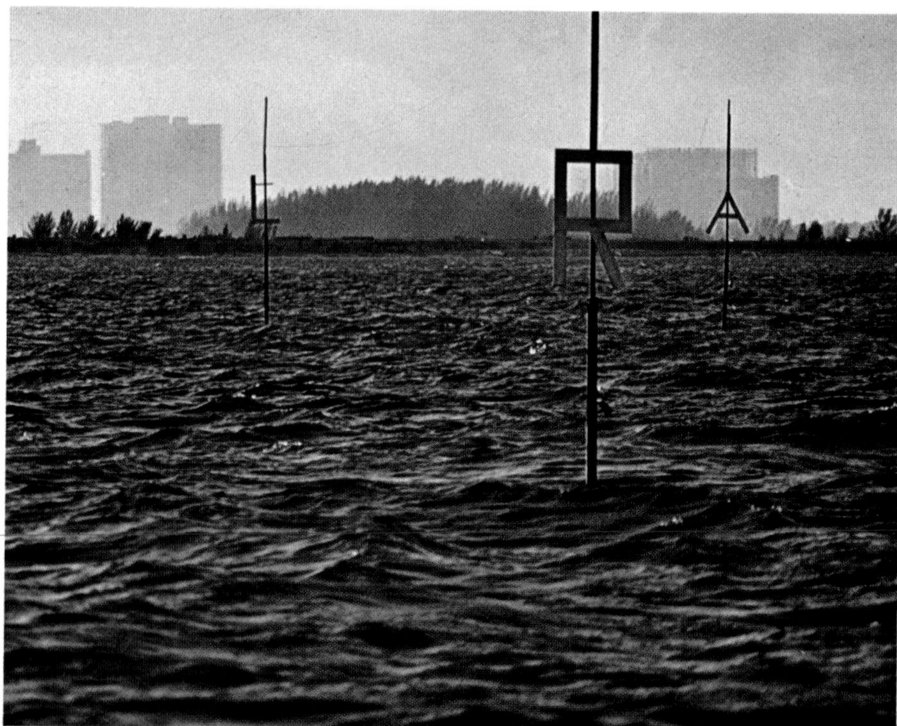

1 *As he reaches large figure 1 on the chart, the pilot sees, just to his left, stakes rising from the water to mark one of the spoil areas, which he will avoid. The letters fixed onto the stakes are some of those in the words "Great Lakes," the name of the firm commissioned to dredge the channel.*

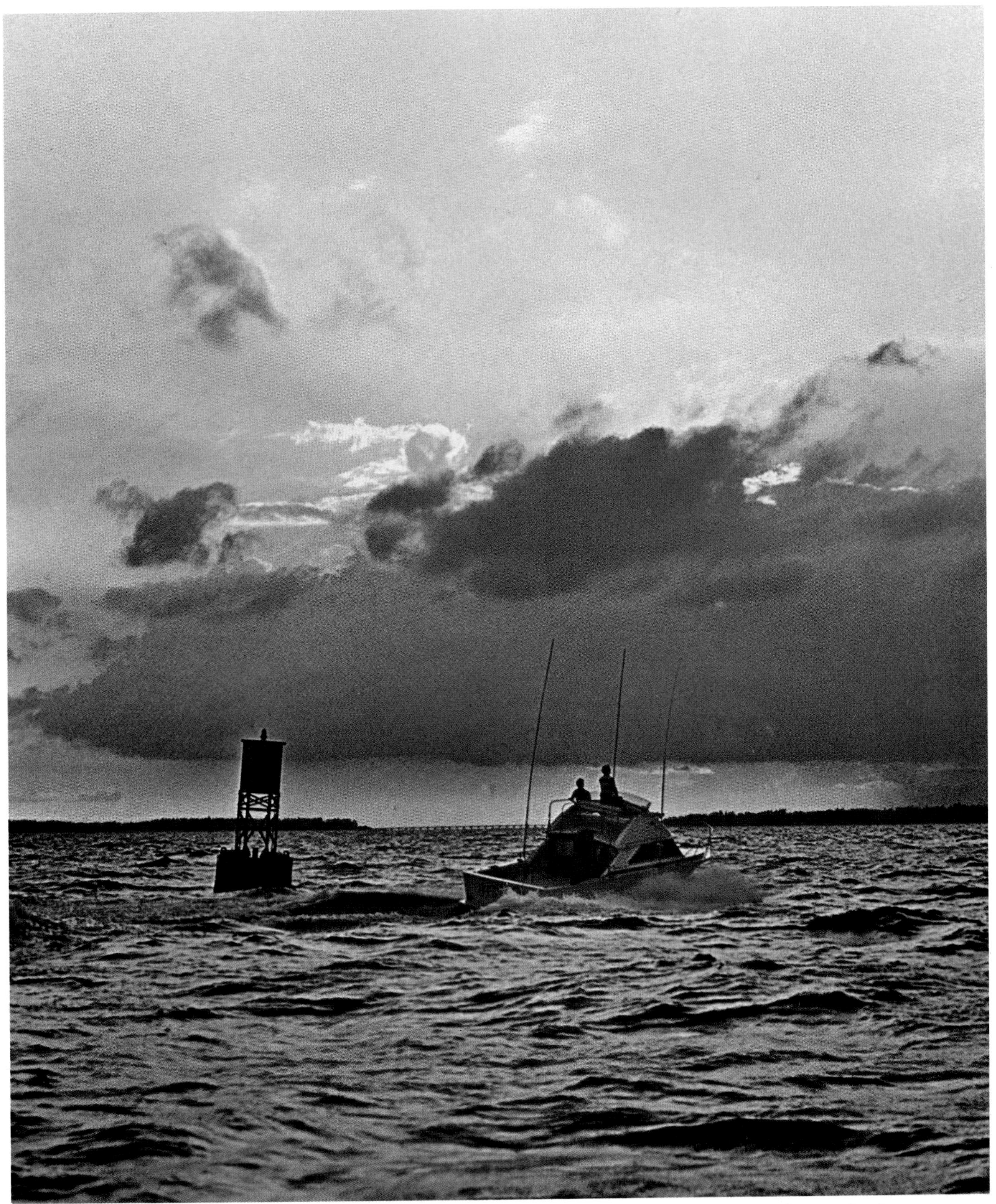

2 *At this point the pilot has entered the Outer Bar Cut segment of the main channel by turning to port after crossing the sight line between buoy "5," shown here on his port hand, and buoy "3" to starboard. The sport fisherman is now at large figure 2 on the chart at left, properly leaving the black, odd-numbered buoy to port. The square shape at the top of the buoy is a radar reflector, which helps vessels to locate the mark during times when visibility is poor.*

On the final leg of the trip, the pilot, having skirted the spoil areas and entered the dredged channel of Outer Bar Cut, now prepares for the long, straight run through Bar Cut and Government Cut. To align himself properly in the channel, he will use the range located east of the bend where Bar Cut joins Outer Bar Cut.

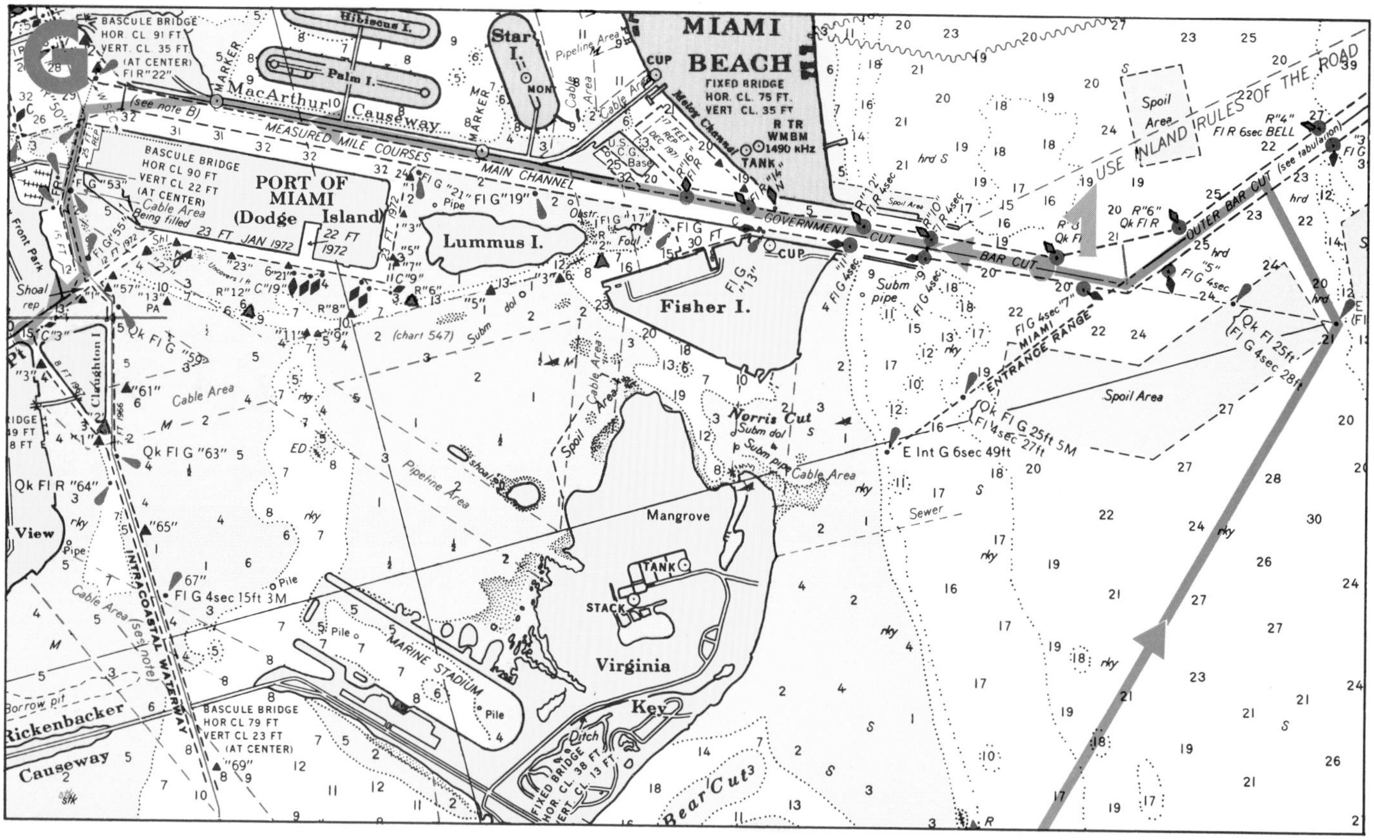

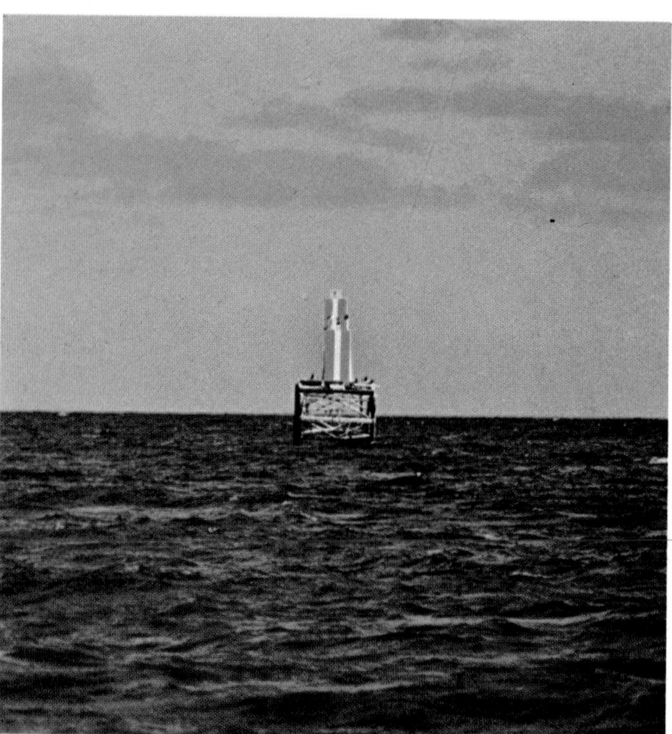

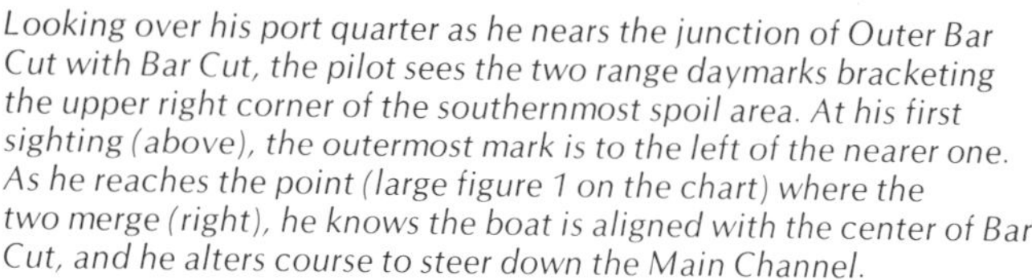

Looking over his port quarter as he nears the junction of Outer Bar Cut with Bar Cut, the pilot sees the two range daymarks bracketing the upper right corner of the southernmost spoil area. At his first sighting (above), the outermost mark is to the left of the nearer one. As he reaches the point (large figure 1 on the chart) where the two merge (right), he knows the boat is aligned with the center of Bar Cut, and he alters course to steer down the Main Channel.

Homing On the Range

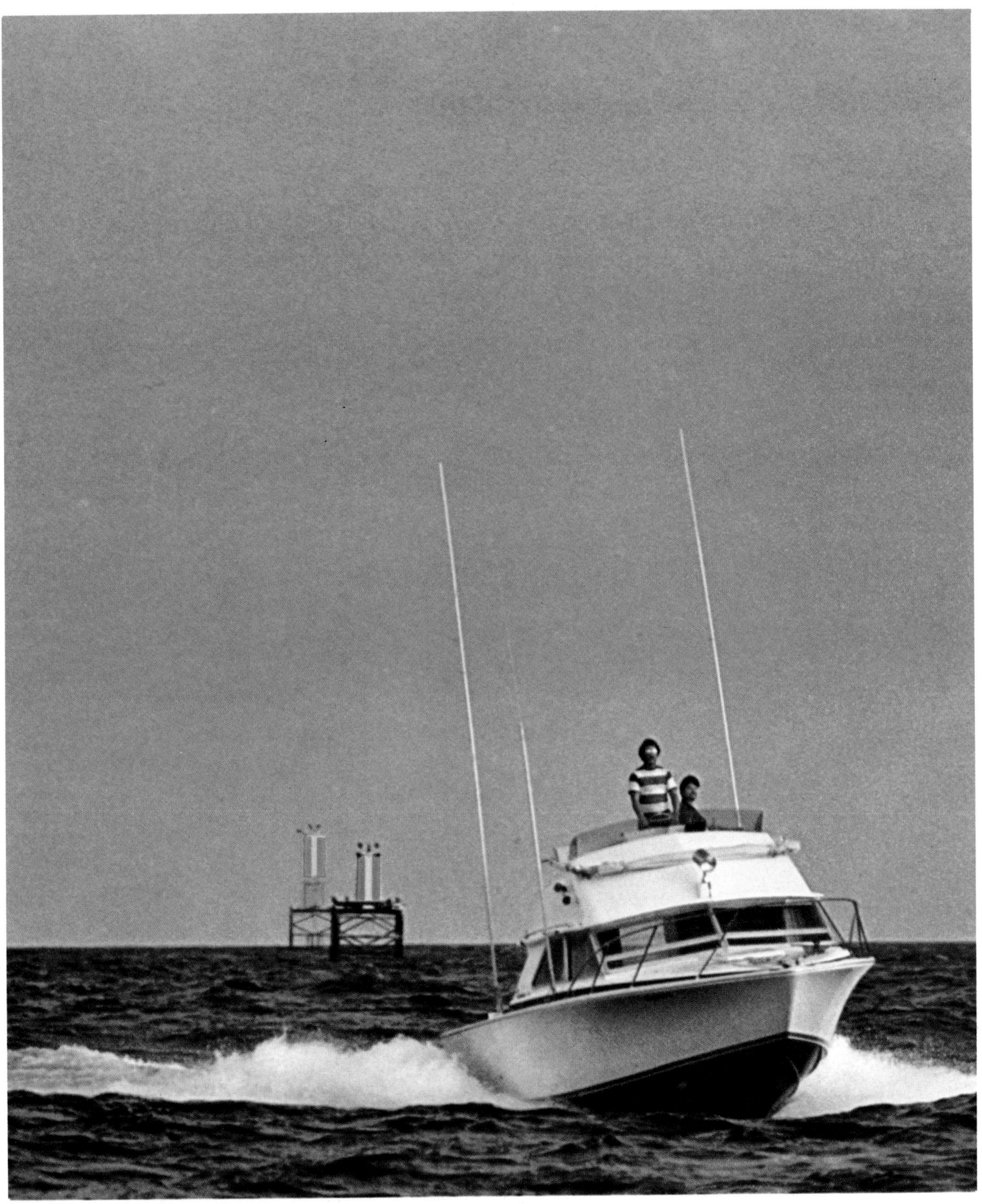

1 As the sport fisherman speeds toward Government Cut, the red-and-white-striped daymarks of the range are in line with his course, and dead astern. Later on, when darkness falls, the range will be distinguishable as flashing green lights projected down the line of the channel; the characteristics of these lights are marked on the chart. At the end of Government Cut, the skipper will turn around mark "50" (overleaf) and head back to the mouth of the Miami River.

Last Lap

The skyline of Miami lies behind the cruise's last navigational checkpoint as the pilot heads for home. The mark is Intracoastal Waterway beacon "50," and its flashing red light and flanking triangular shapes signal the skipper that he should leave it to starboard.

FATHOMS
SENSITIVITY
RAY-DF 60
BFO
GAIN
TUNING
VOLUME
L O N G I S L A N D

5

Americans love gadgets. In their daily lives they are perhaps more attracted—and better served—by gadgetry than are any other people on earth. And United States boatmen are totally in tune with this national trait. When navigating lakes and rivers and ocean waters, especially at night and in bad weather, they call on an array of electrically powered boxes to see far beyond the limits of eyesight, to hear sounds past the range of the human ear and to pinpoint a boat's position on open water.

Of these seemingly magical boxes, the most commonly used is the depth finder, or echo sounder, which bounces sound waves off the bottom and

THE BOATMAN'S MAGIC BOXES

translates the return signals into water depth—and in some cases even locates fish. Equally useful is the radio direction finder (or RDF). From distances of over 50 miles these simple receiving sets can indicate bearings on a network of Coast Guard-operated radio antennas whose locations are fixed on nautical charts. Omni (short for visual omnirange radio) is a more elaborate version of RDF equipment, transplanted to boats from aircraft cockpits. More accurate—and far more expensive—than ordinary RDF apparatus, omni picks up signals from radio beacons established for the use of aviators. On larger pleasure boats, radar listens for echoes of its own transmissions to pinpoint obstacles and to make accurate position fixes. Perhaps the most sophisticated of all the boxes is a special radio called loran (an acronym for long-range navigation) that can locate a vessel's position within a labyrinth of navigational hazards—or in the most open stretch of water.

All these devices except omni were developed to a level of practical application for military purposes during World War II. The principles of sonar, used by subchasers, are now at work in depth finders. Shipboard radar evolved from British ground radars used to intercept German aircraft.

After the war, electronic navigational aids were bulky and expensive, and thus limited to commercial vessels. In recent years, design advances—especially miniaturization—have put these electronic marvels well within the reach of many pleasure craft and their owners.

The effective use of these instruments, like the use of a compass and parallel ruler, must be keyed to nautical charts. Comparing echo-sounder readings with charted depth soundings, for example, can help identify a boat's position. The numbers appearing on the face of a loran set correspond to the numbered grid lines used for position fixes on loran charts. And RDF bearings on charted radio beacons provide lines of position.

Like all tools, even these sophisticated instruments have their limitations. During thunderstorms, for example, loran readings are difficult to make. RDF is unreliable at dawn and dusk when the sun interferes with radio waves, making accurate fixes almost impossible. Heavy rain, which bounces back radar impulses, appears on a radarscope as an opaque wall; and even on the clearest days, radar blips can be ambiguous. One man, thinking his boat was about to be crushed by what the radar showed to be a huge ship approaching from astern, rushed on deck with a life preserver to find that the threatening ship was actually a Navy blimp.

As a guide to the proper use of these sometimes puzzling gadgets, the following pages explain the functions and limitations of all the boatman's most familiar electronic boxes, from a simple depth finder costing about as much as a good camera to a sophisticated radar set whose price rivals that of a small automobile. By understanding them, and their occasional idiosyncrasies, a skipper can guide his boat safely through the most complex hazards over fog-shrouded or night-darkened waters.

The basic tools for electronic navigation include a radio direction finder, shown here on a chart table; a two-way radio on the bulkhead at right; and a depth finder affixed to a shelf.

The commonest depth-indicator box (below) is the flasher type, named for the quick-blinking neon lights that record depth on a clocklike face. The flashes show at two places on the face: at "0" for the outgoing pulse, and at the number corresponding to the water depth when the echo returns. The knob at lower left turns on the depth finder and adjusts its sensitivity to tune out any extraneous echoes. A switch at lower right sets it to read in feet or in fathoms.

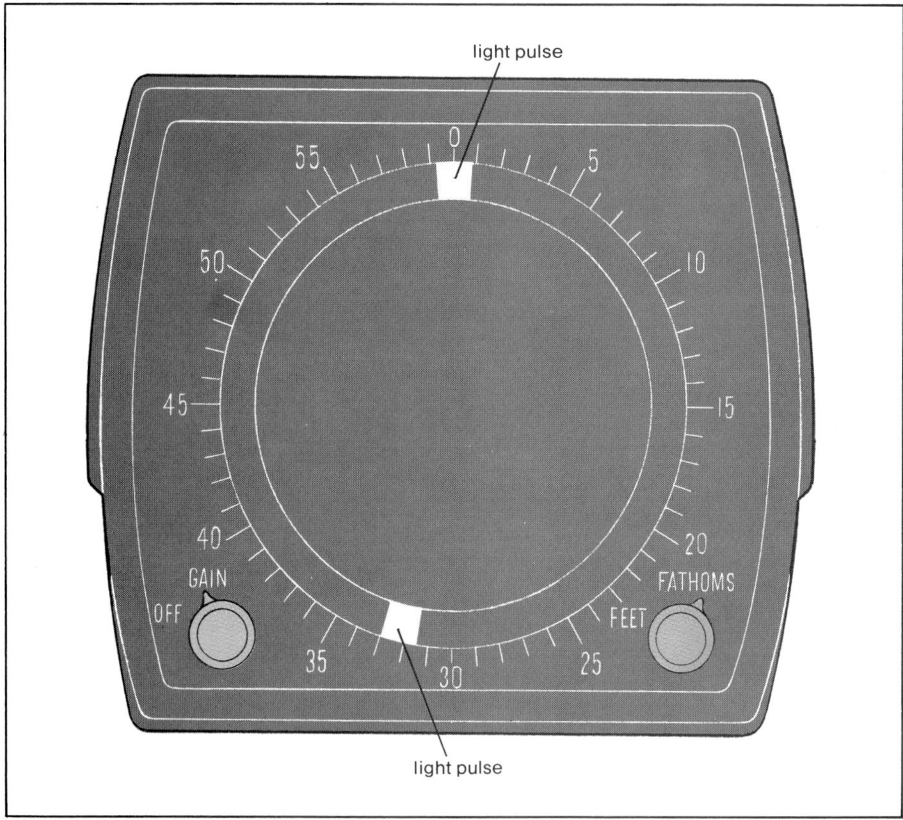

Sounding by Echo

Every skipper who cruises lakes, rivers or coastal waterways is nagged by the thought of running aground. For centuries the only defenses against this ignominy were a sharp eye and a lead line constantly wielded to take sounding on the water's depth. Nowadays, the lead line's job has been taken over by electronic sentinels called depth finders. As shown on this page, they come in different styles with different faces. But all depth finders function basically the same way: they measure the time a sound pulse takes to reach the bottom and return, and then convert the delay into a depth reading.

For sending and receiving the pulses, the echo sounder relies on a transducer *(below, left)*, which acts alternately as a loudspeaker and a microphone. It transmits as many as 20 ultrasonic pulses each second and picks up their echoes. Then a depth-indicator box *(left and below)* translates the time between transmission and echo reception into numerical readings of either feet or fathoms.

A skillful boatman can use an echo sounder in two additional ways: he can double-check his boat's position and navigate a course *(pages 128-129)* by following the bottom terrain; and if equipped with an ultrasensitive depth finder, he can even search out fish for his dinner.

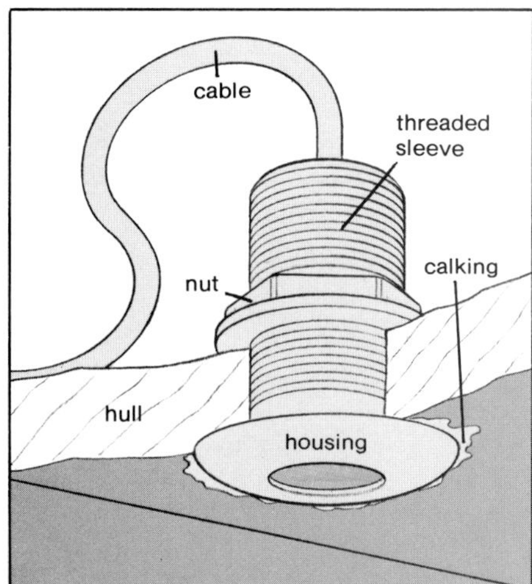

A conventional depth-finder transducer is contained in a threaded sleeve that is passed vertically through a boat's hull, calked and held tightly in place by a nut. The smoothly rounded exterior housing eliminates water turbulence—a source of false readings. The cable carries electrical impulses to this sender-receiver and back to the indicator box.

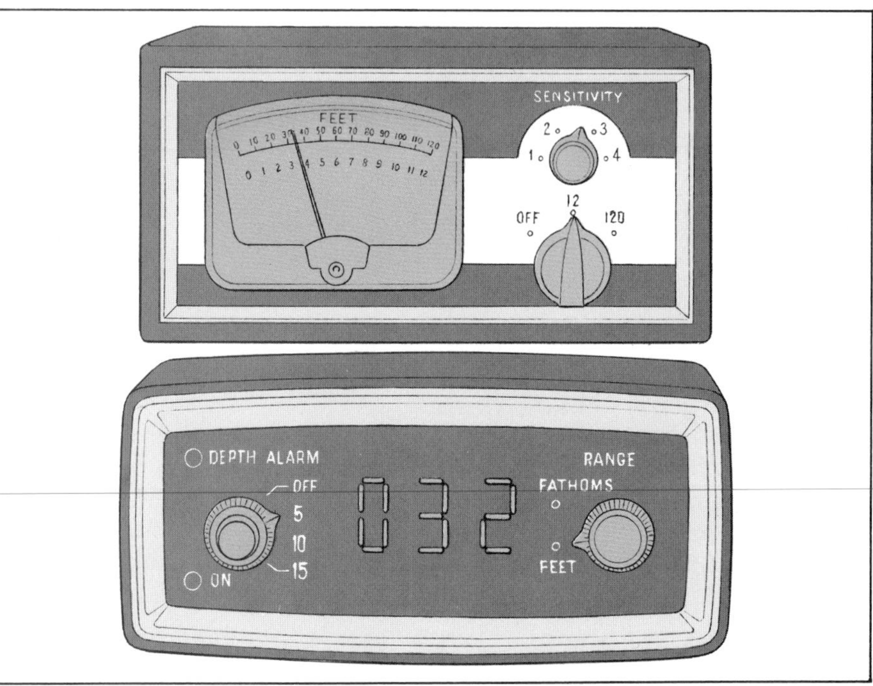

Echo sounders show depth either on a meter (top) or with lighted numbers (bottom). The meter gives accurate readings down to 12 feet —i.e., with the switch at 12; set at 120, it gives general readings to 120 feet. A sensitivity knob reduces irrelevant echoes. The digital model has a feet-fathom selector at right. At left is a base knob for an alarm that sounds when the depth reads less than a preset level; the inner knob is an on-off switch, and also adjusts brightness.

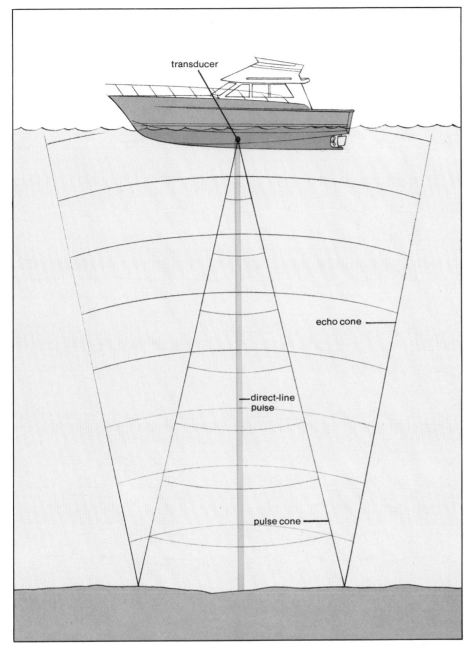

The arc-shaped sound pulses sent from a depth finder's transducer go down in a cone pattern until one portion of a pulse arc hits something. That pulse instantly rebounds, giving the depth finder a readout on the distance between the closest underwater object and the transducer. In the case of a flat bottom, as at left, all pulses except a direct-line-rebound pulse are reflected away from the transducer in an ever-widening echo cone. On a very uneven bottom, however, the transducer may pick up a rebound from a shallow ledge astern—rather than a direct-line rebound from far below.

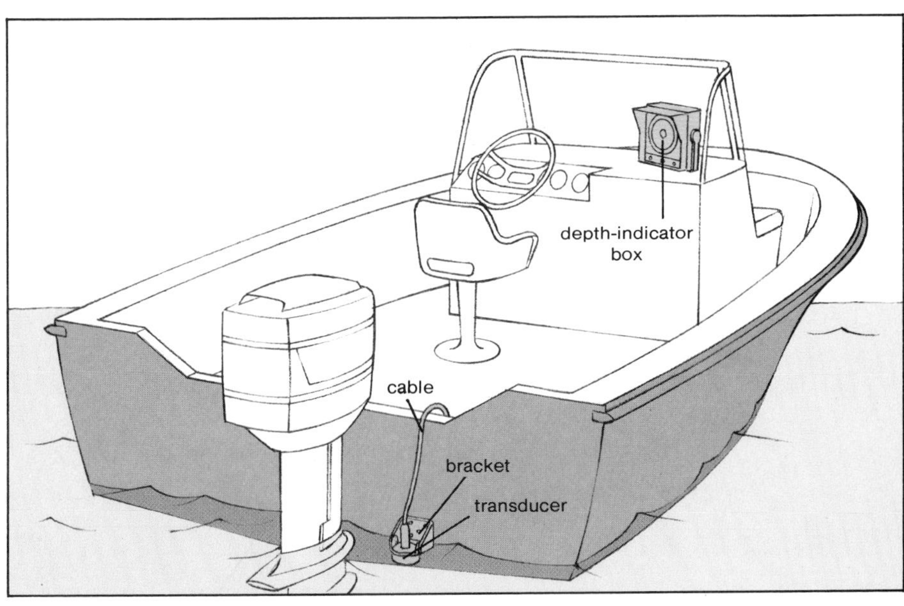

An easily demountable transducer for an outboard runabout can be attached to the transom either by a bracket, as here, or by a suction cup. The depth-finder cable should be routed as far as possible from the engine to preclude electrical interference by the spark plugs, which could distort the electronic signal. From the transom, the cable runs forward to the depth-indicator box.

When cruising a coastline with an evenly sloping sea bed, a skipper can navigate even in poor visibility by using a depth finder to match his course to charted bottom contours. Here, a pilot bound for Provincetown, Massachusetts, heads in toward Cape Cod until the depth finder tells him he has reached a 60-foot contour. Steering a course (broken line) that keeps the depth-finder reading at 60 feet, he is able to follow the contour safely around the tip of the Cape.

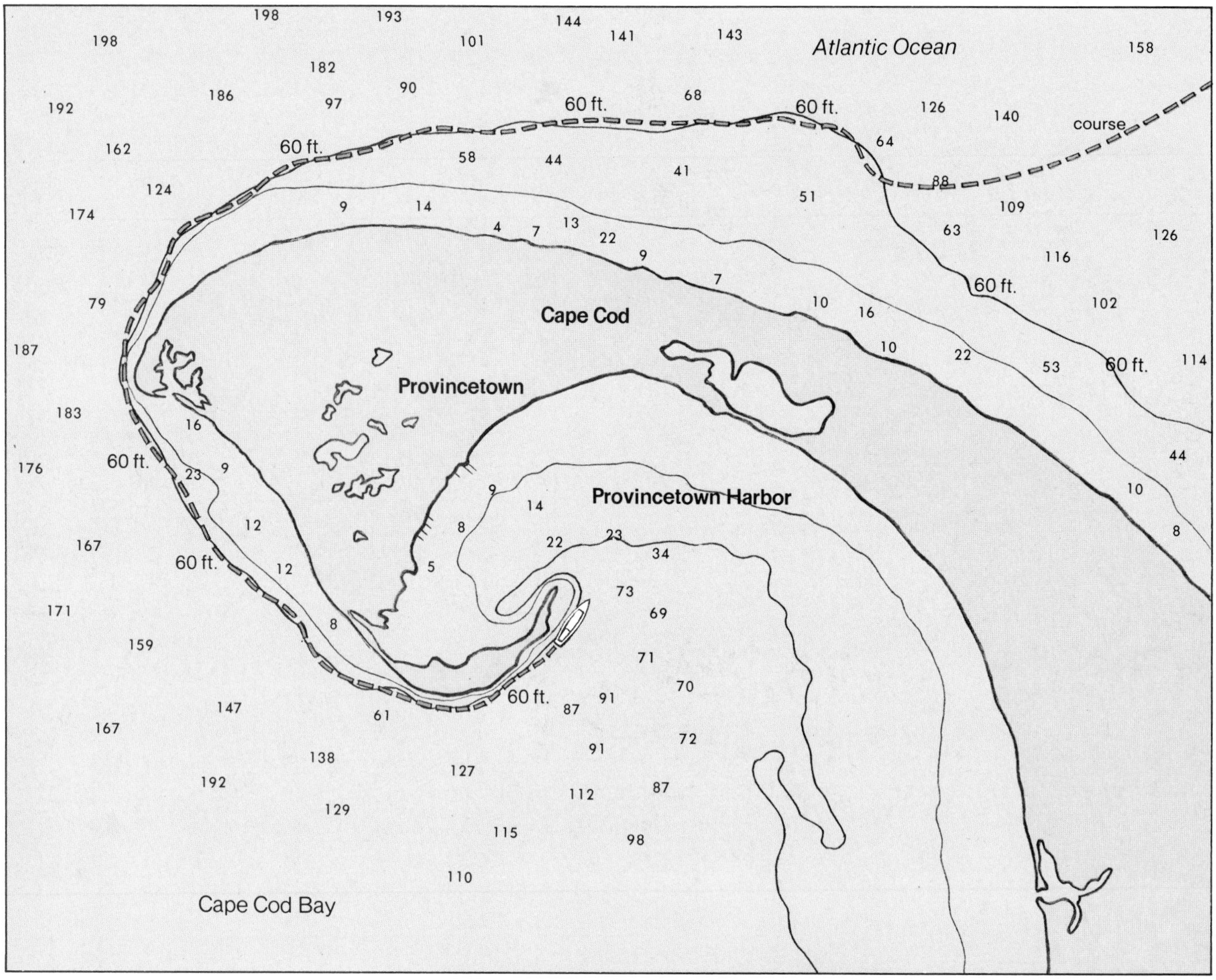

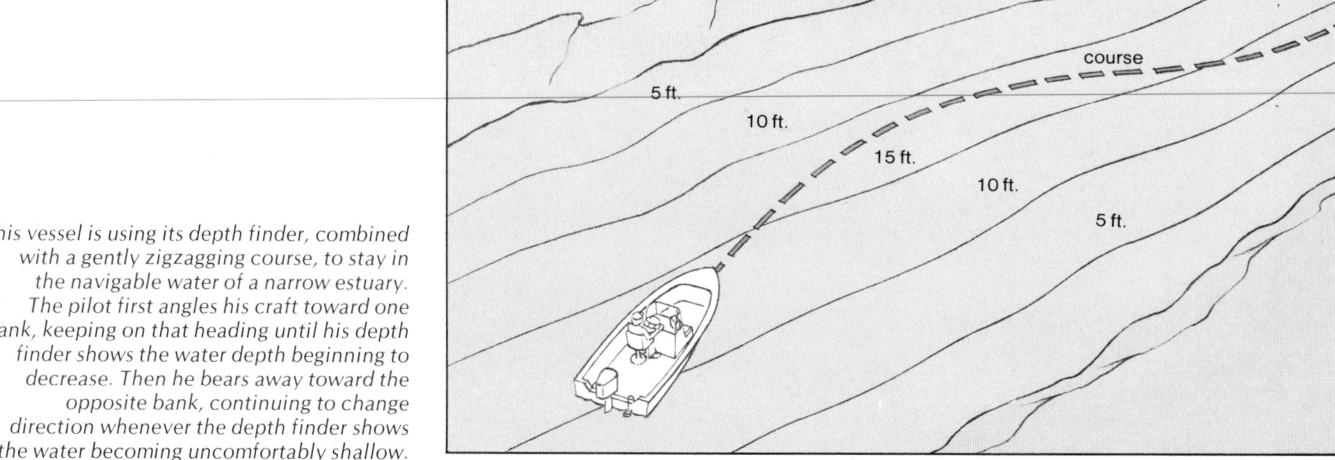

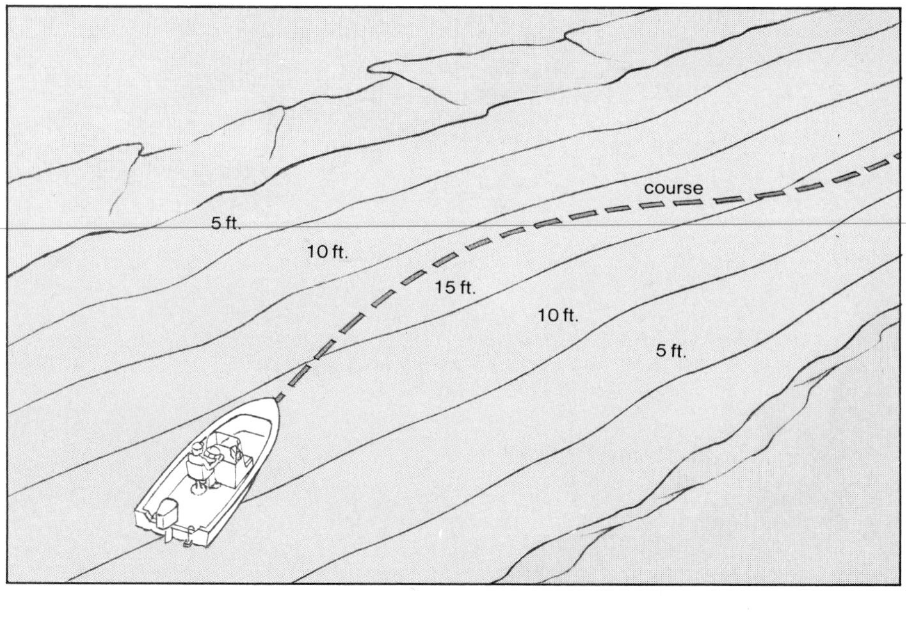

This vessel is using its depth finder, combined with a gently zigzagging course, to stay in the navigable water of a narrow estuary. The pilot first angles his craft toward one bank, keeping on that heading until his depth finder shows the water depth beginning to decrease. Then he bears away toward the opposite bank, continuing to change direction whenever the depth finder shows the water becoming uncomfortably shallow.

Where the bottom slopes irregularly offshore, such as occurs west of Moss Landing, California (below), the pilot making a blind landfall must remain alert to his depth finder's readings. Heading in, he will see his depth-finder reading increase suddenly from 25 to 88 fathoms as he passes over Monterey Canyon. Matching this increase to contour lines on his chart, he can fix his position at about three and a half miles from the harbor entrance, on a bearing of 62° magnetic.

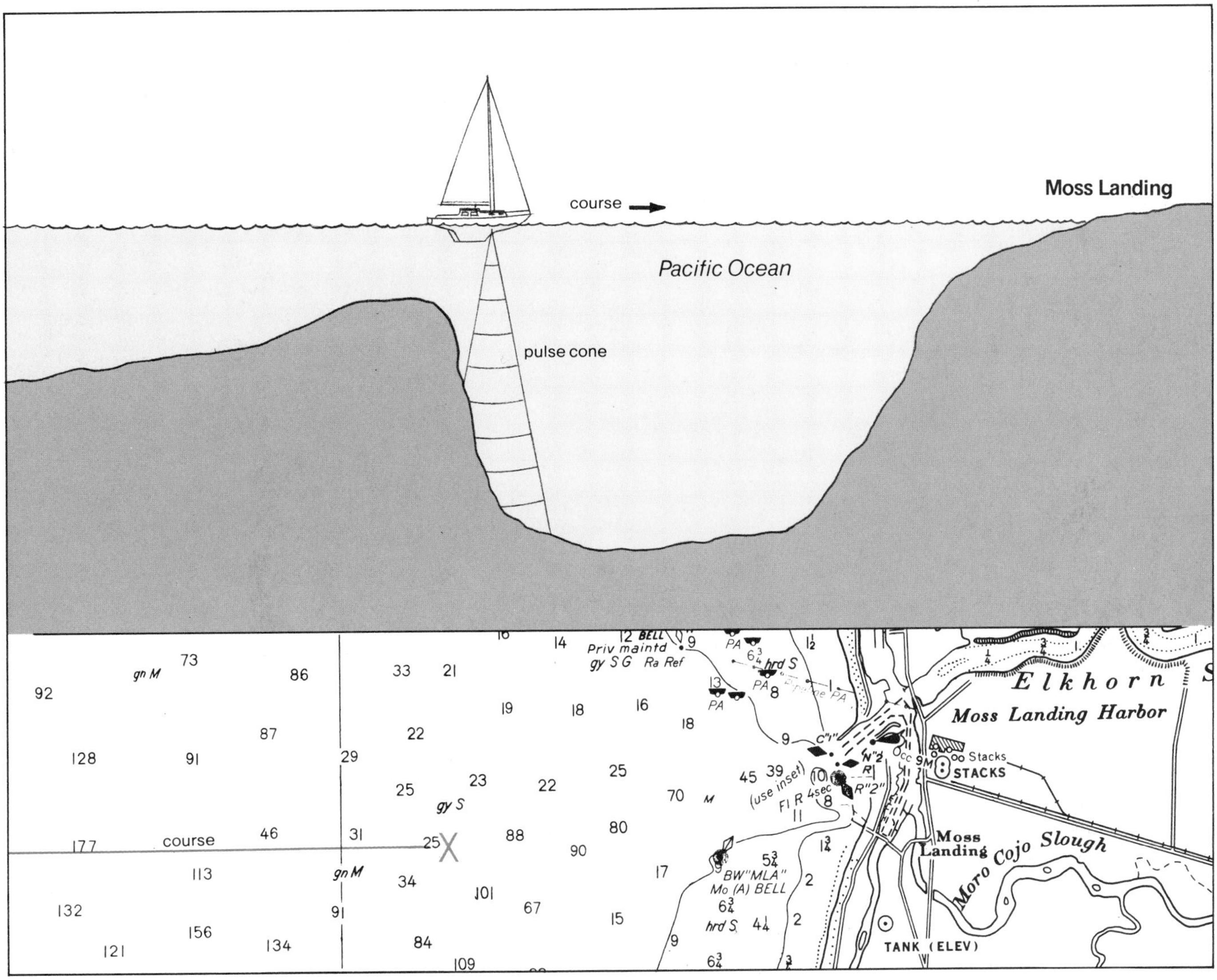

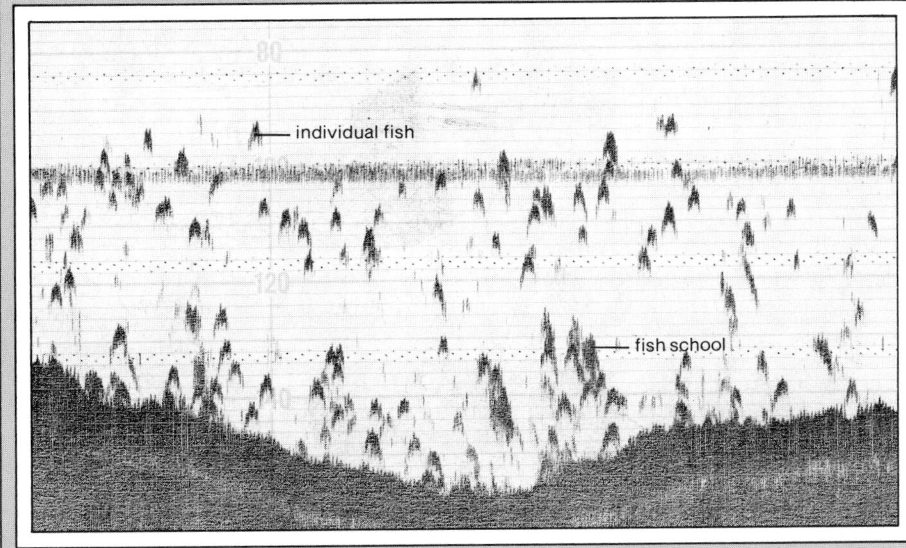

Fish by the Fathom

Though common depth finders give readings on bottom contours, some sensitive and sophisticated models can locate fish by painting pulse echoes on a moving tape. A small section of such a tape appears at left. The dark area along the lower edge represents the bottom, which a grid on the chart shows to vary from about 130 to 155 feet. The inverted-V shapes above the bottom are fish—both individuals and schools; some fishermen, with practice, claim that they can identify species. The sum total of such electronic wizardry has brought not only better fishing, but also cries of alarm from some conservationists who argue that the angler now has an unfair advantage over his quarry.

This typical RDF receiver has three bands: MARINE for ship-to-shore distress calls, and time and weather broadcasts; B.CAST for commercial stations; and BEACON for regular RDF radio beacons. The directional antenna rests inside a rotating bar. When the antenna points toward a transmitter, the needle on the null meter moves to "0." Controls on the unit's face (from left) turn on the set, switch it to direction finding, adjust its sensitivity and tune it.

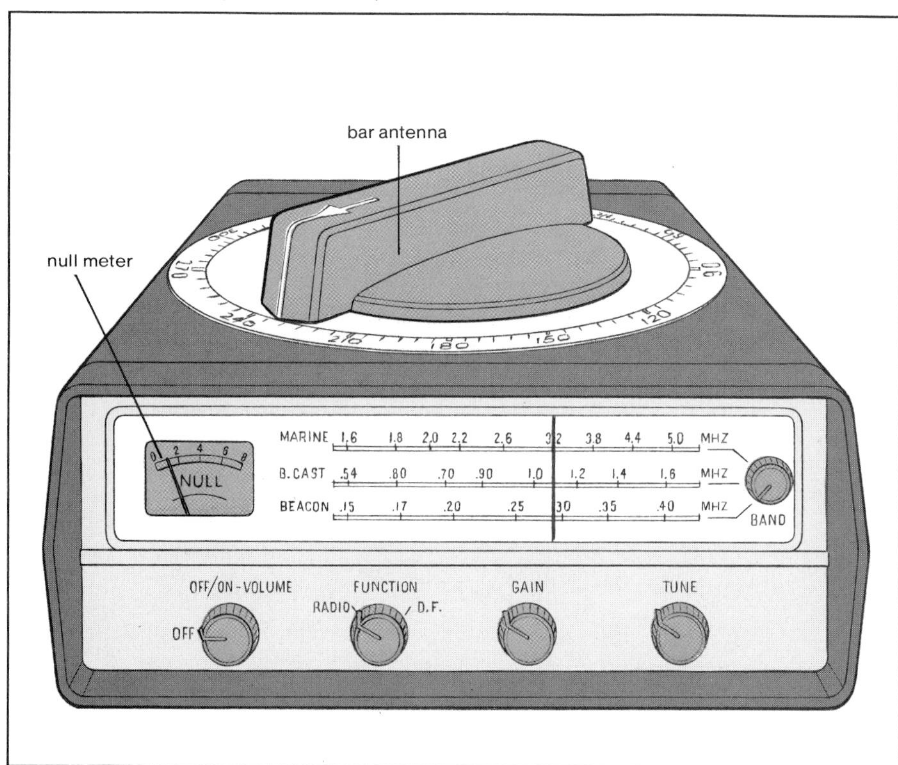

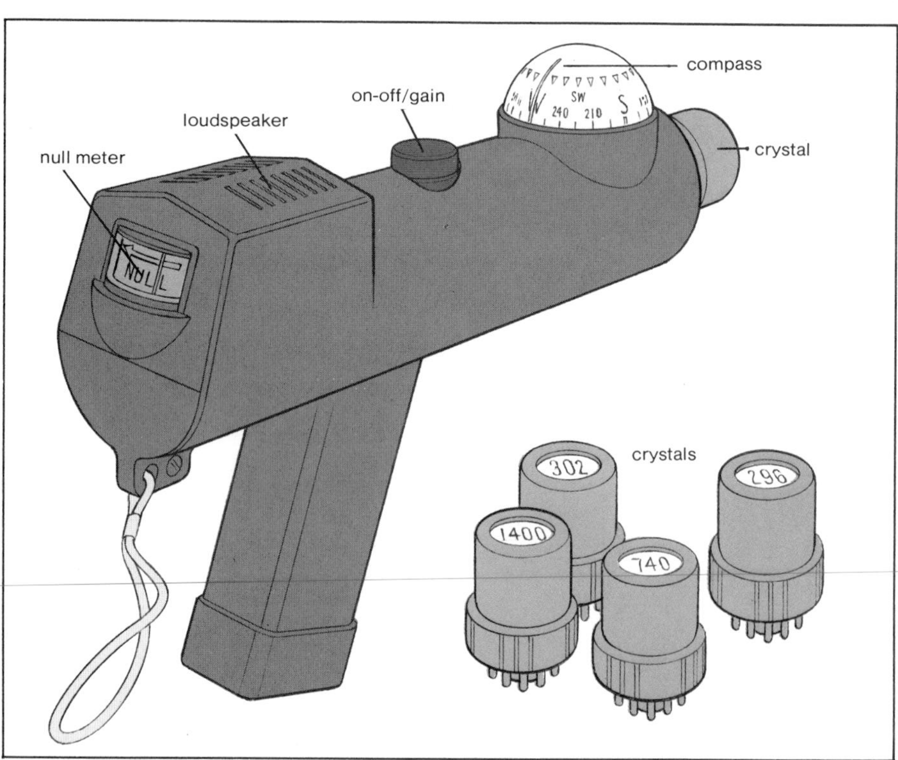

The directional antenna in this hand-held RDF set is built into its barrel; the end of the barrel accommodates plug-in radio crystals that are pretuned to fixed frequencies (note that channel numbers are marked on the spare crystals beneath the barrel). When the barrel is pointed at a transmitter, the unit registers a null on the meter at its rear. On top of the receiver are a loudspeaker for identifying the signals from beacons, an on-off switch and a compass for bearings.

Bearings by Radio Beam

After depth finders, the most widely used electronic aids to navigation are radio direction-finding (RDF) receivers. Capable of providing accurate position fixes well beyond sight of land, RDF equipment extends the yachtsman's safe horizons, while adding an extra measure of security for sailing at night and in bad weather.

As its name indicates, an RDF unit is fundamentally a radio. Sets like the one at left have faces and knobs that resemble those of everyday table radios. And the more flexible, modern hand-held units *(bottom left)*, though their design hardly calls to mind that of a conventional radio, operate on the same principle as an old-fashioned crystal set.

The heart of an RDF receiver is a bar-shaped directional antenna, made of ferrite, that is connected to a so-called null meter on the face of the set. Ferrite is an iron compound exceptionally good at picking up radio waves. It converts the radio signals into a small flow of electricity that deflects the meter according to the current's strength. The antenna produces the smallest amount of current when it is pointed directly toward a transmitter: the null position. Once a null is found, the relative bearing of its source can be converted into a compass bearing *(opposite and overleaf)* that is accurate to within three or four degrees—adequate for most piloting situations.

Though any commmercial AM radio station within the clear range of an RDF unit can be used for navigating, the most reliable source of signals is the network of special-frequency marine radio beacons maintained all around the nation's waters by the Coast Guard. The exact locations of their transmitting towers are marked on charts, and the towers are placed near the water's edge so their signals are not bent by passing over land, as is often the case with those of commercial stations. Over 200 of these radio signposts guide mariners in coastal waters and lakes. To aid in its identification, each beacon has an assigned frequency and a special signal, patterned on the Morse code, that it sends repeatedly at close intervals 24 hours a day. These, along with detailed listings of lighthouse locations, are available in booklets called light lists *(page 72)*, published by the Coast Guard.

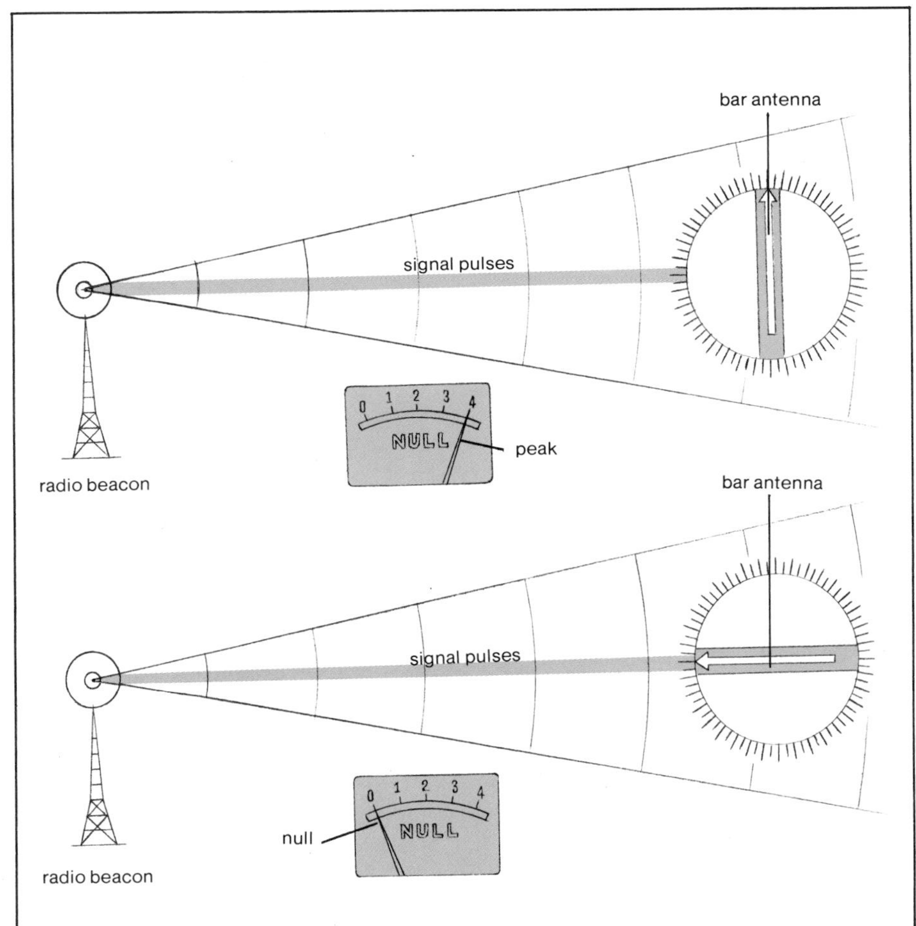

In the upper drawing, the bar antenna of an RDF unit is turned broadside to a radio beacon, and thus picks up strong signal pulses. This produces electric current within the RDF unit that deflects the null-meter pointer to the right, or peak, position. With the bar turned head-on to the beacon (lower drawing), the antenna picks up very little of the beacon's signal, and the meter pointer remains stationary at its null position.

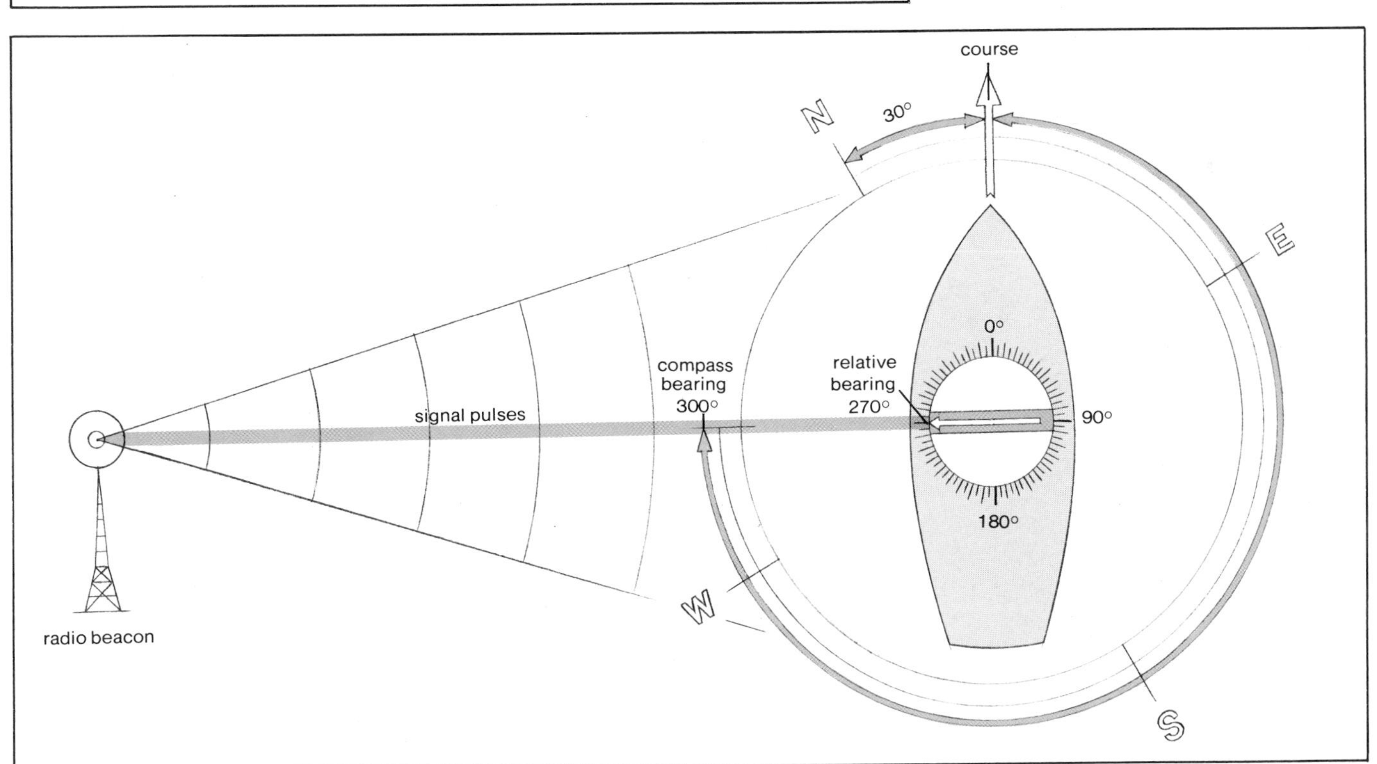

To locate a beacon, the relative bearing of all nulls must be translated into compass bearings. On hand-held RDF receivers, a built-in compass provides an instantaneous magnetic bearing. Otherwise the conversion is made by adding the vessel's compass course to the bearing given by the RDF. In this example, the RDF aboard a boat sailing a compass course of 30° shows a relative bearing to a radio beacon of 270°; thus the compass bearing to the beacon is 300°.

This stylized excerpt from the light list for Lake Michigan shows a typical network of electronic lighthouses positioned to aid navigators in taking RDF fixes. The beacons are marked here with solid blue dots and keyed to identifying boxes. Heading each box is the station's transmitting frequency. Each beacon sends for 60 seconds, rotating in the order indicated by the Roman numerals. Next are the stations' locations, the specific dot-dash code each sends and its range in miles. Short-range beacons, carrying 10 miles or less, are designated by blue circles. They send a continuous signal of half-second dashes.

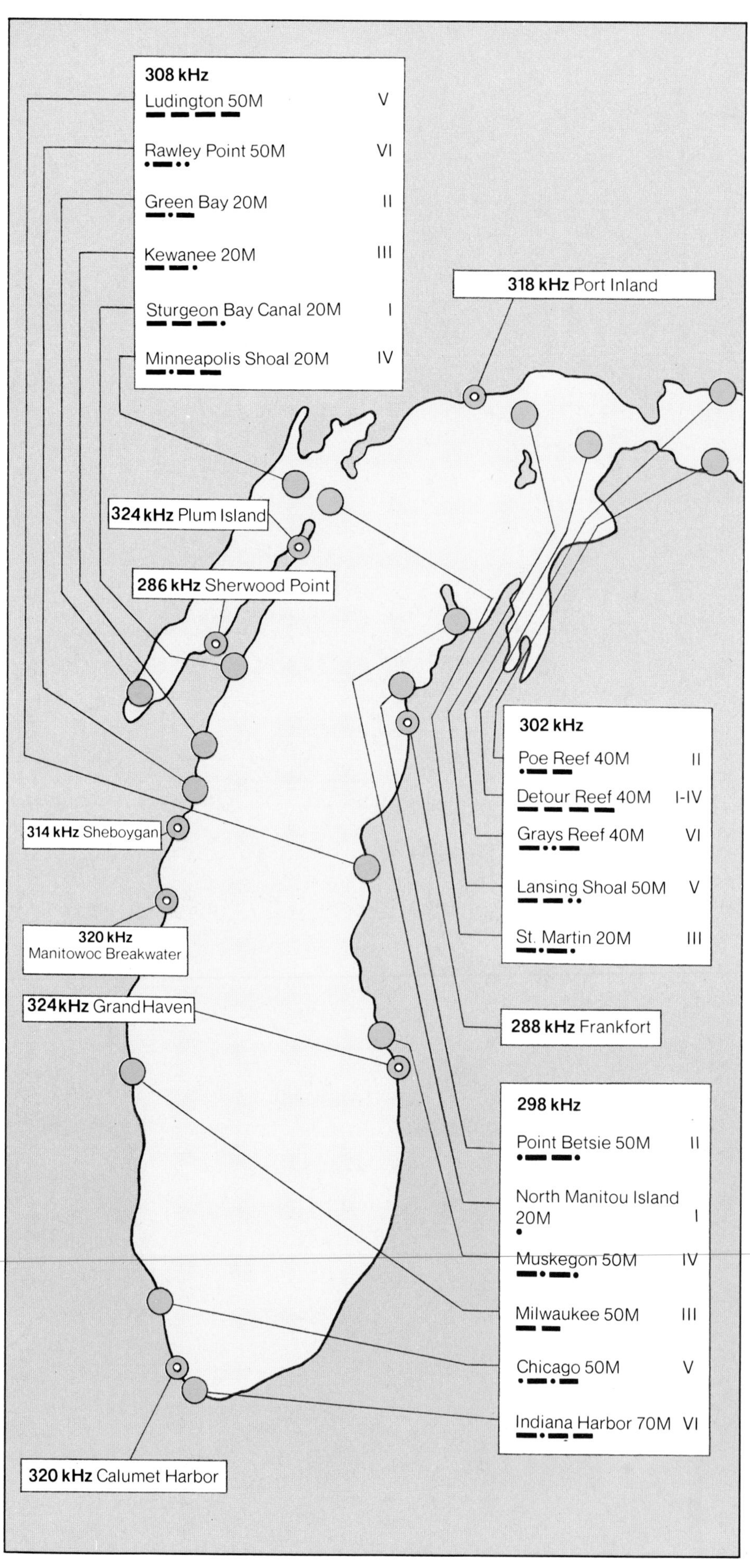

In a typical RDF exercise, a navigator crossing Lake Michigan from Milwaukee to Benton Harbor checks his course with RDF fixes, then homes in on a local radio station. At 1015, the skipper takes a fix on the Milwaukee and Muskegon radio beacons (he is out of range of Grand Haven's marker beacon) and sets a course for Benton Harbor. Two hours later, beyond the range of all the beacons along the southern part of Lake Michigan except the ones at Milwaukee and Indiana Harbor, he takes another fix. Finding himself off course, he swings to a new heading that brings him within range of Benton Harbor's commercial broadcast station—and a straight run home.

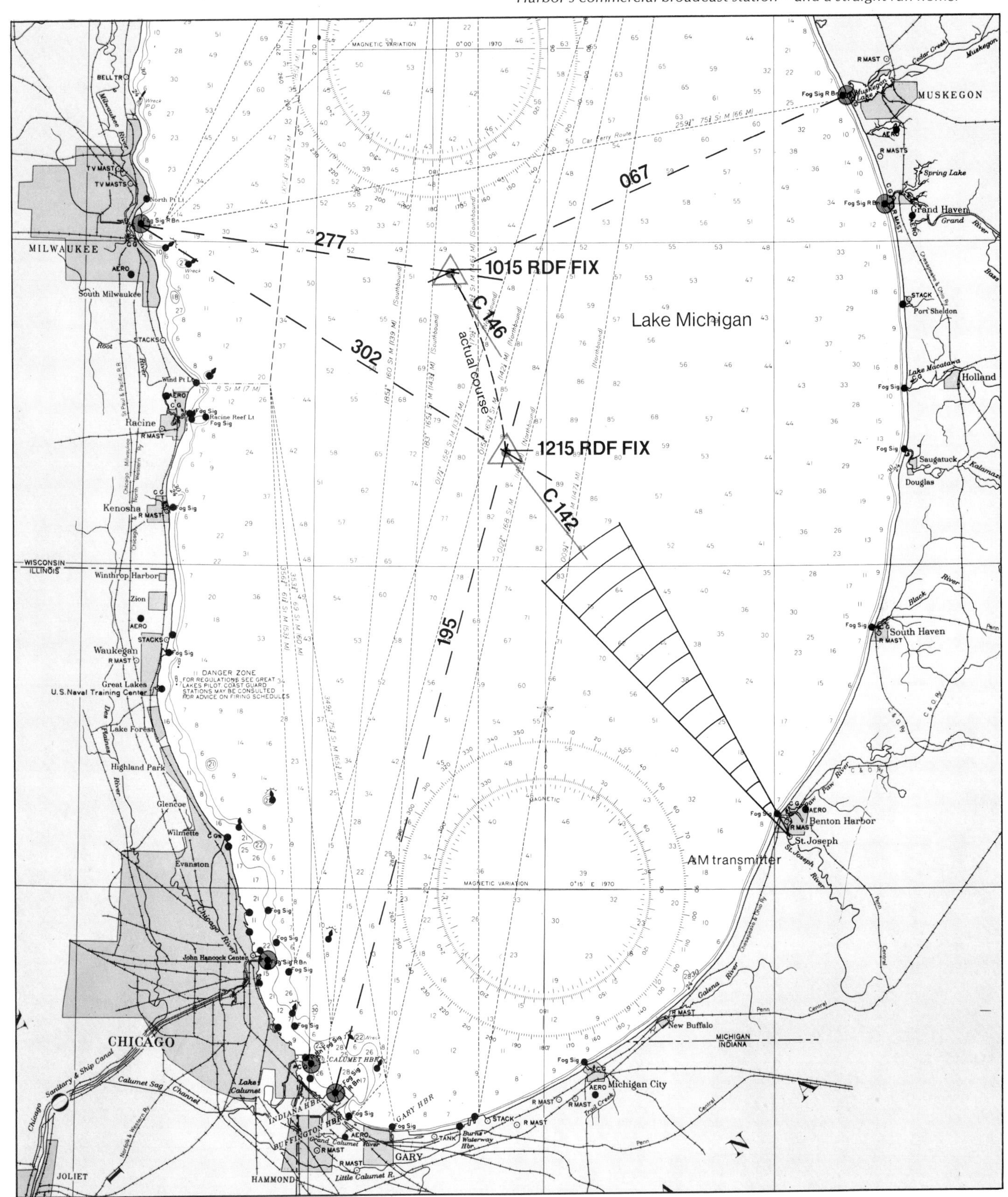

A shipboard omni unit has three simple controls: an on-off volume switch; frequency dials for tuning in on specific stations; and a knob that rotates a calibrated bearing card, marked off by degrees. When a boat homes in on the bearing that coincides with the indicator line, the hanging pointer bisects the circle. If the boat strays, the pointer swings left or right. The word FROM in the direction window means that the bearing reads from the omni station to the boat.

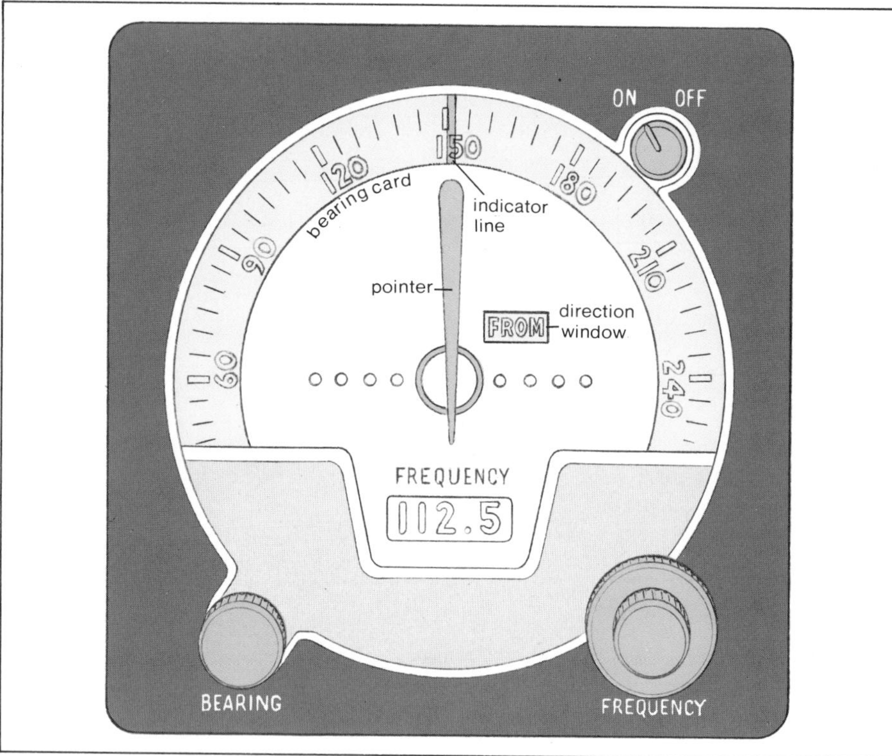

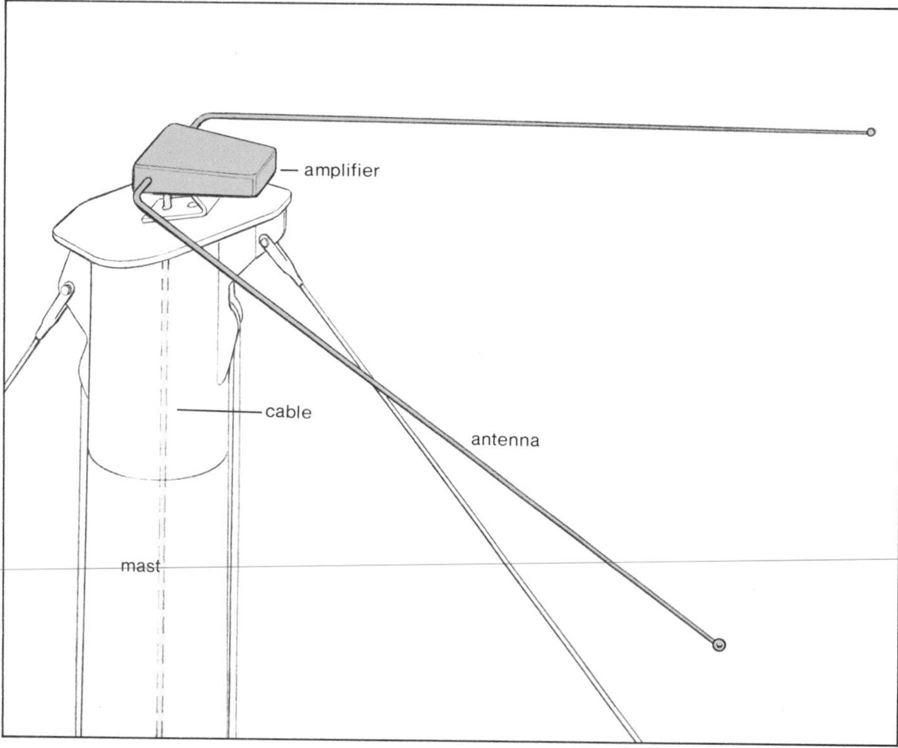

V-shaped omni antennas are permanently mounted as high as possible —on a powerboat's cabintop or, as here, on a sailboat's masthead. The antenna's arms are attached to a low-powered amplifier that boosts the strength of incoming impulses. The impulses then travel by a cable down the mast to the receiver. Because omni signals do not carry beyond the horizon, the antenna's height determines the set's range—about 60 miles for an antenna atop a 40-foot mast.

A Twist on RDF

A giant step up from conventional radio direction-finding equipment, both in accuracy and expense, is the highly sophisticated system called omni, which allows a yachtsman to tune in on specialized radio beacons that were originally designed for use by aircraft.

An omni receiver, which costs about four times as much as most RDF sets, will fix a vessel's line of position to within two compass degrees—as against almost twice that margin of error for RDF. Furthermore, omni systems are easier to use, and their signals are all but immune to atmospheric static that may disrupt RDF. Omni's major drawback is its short range; unlike ordinary radio beams, which can be bounced off the atmosphere, omni beams go in a direct line, and thus become ineffective beyond the horizon.

The key element in an omni system is the complex, very high frequency (VHF) beam sent out by each transmitting station. The beam is actually a composite of two VHF radio waves. When transmitted together, these two waves combine into a signal whose nature varies depending upon the direction in which it travels. Thus the portion of the signals that are sent out to the north differs from the signals aimed east or west.

An omni receiver detects these differences and displays them as bearings between the station and the boat. The bearings, known as radials, give the compass direction either from the station to the boat, in which case the omni receiver designates them as "from" radials *(top left)*, or, conversely, from the boat to the beacon, in which case they are designated "to" radials.

To get a bearing from an omni beacon, the yachtsman first tunes his receiver to the station's frequency; in the example at left, the frequency is 112.5 megahertz. Next he spins his bearing dial until the set's pointer hangs vertically. His bearing —shown here as 150°— appears under an indicator line at the top of the set. Then, if he wants to home in on this bearing, he simply steers his course so that the omni's pointer remains vertical.

Omni information—including the location of transmitters—is not given on standard nautical charts. But the boatman can easily add the necessary data to his charts *(right)*. Transmitter locations and beacon frequencies are available from the U.S. Department of Commerce, which publishes detailed aviation maps called sectional aeronautical charts. These charts can also be obtained at local airports.

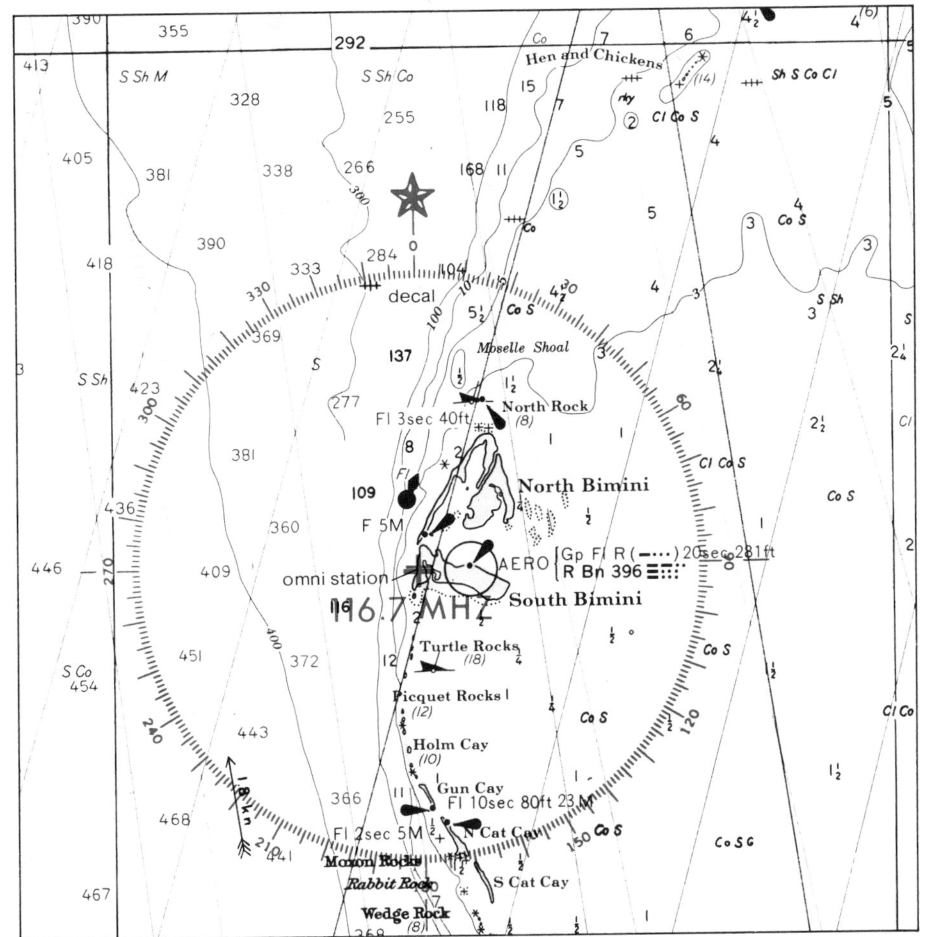

A chart segment of the Bahamas, prepared for use in omni navigation, has been marked with a cross at the precise location of the South Bimini omni station, and the station's broadcast frequency noted beside it. (The "aero" transmitter just east of the omni station is Bimini's regular airport beacon.) A transparent compass-rose decal—available at most chart stores—has been pasted down with its center on the station and its zero line on magnetic north. To find his line of position, a navigator draws a line from the station through the bearing on the decal that matches the FROM reading on his omni set.

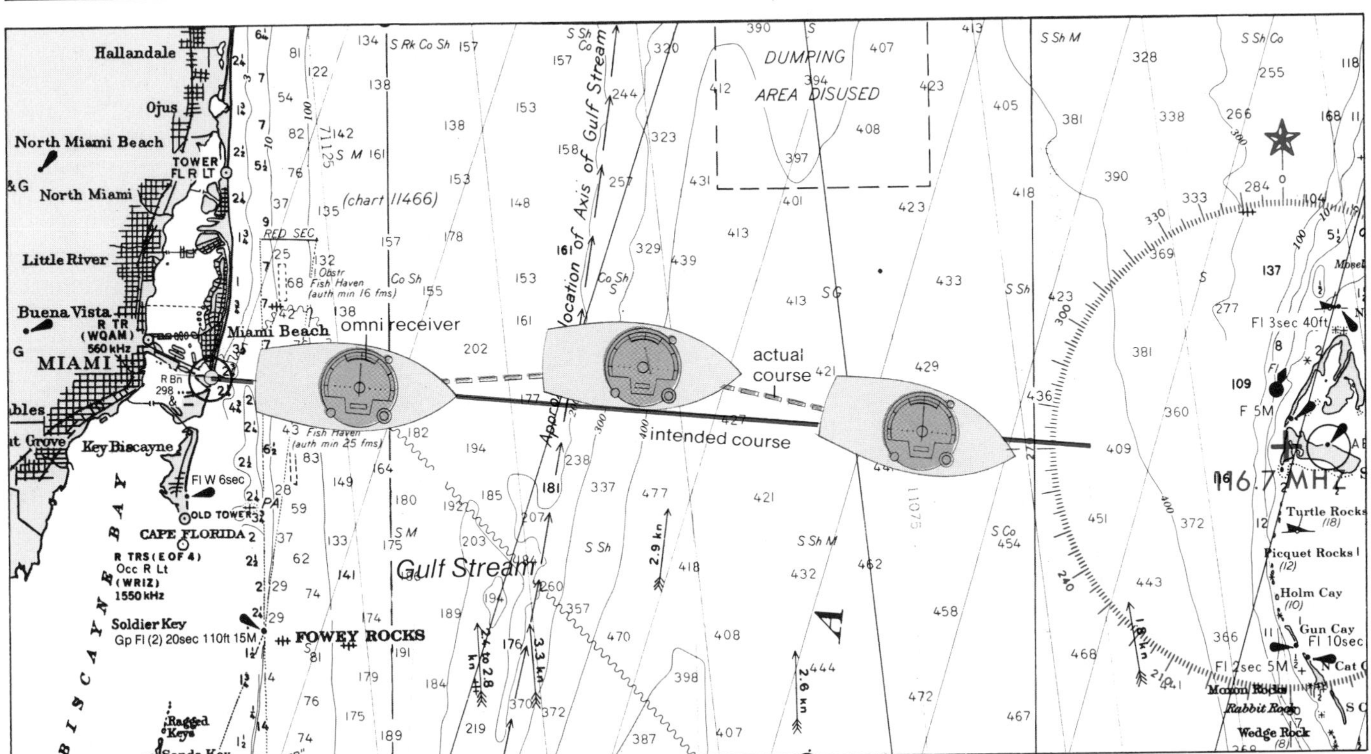

Cruising to Bimini from Miami across the north-flowing Gulf Stream (pages 164-165), a boat homes in on the Bimini omni beacon. Out of Miami, the boat heads on course along the 272 omni radial, and the receiver's pointer is centered. En route, the current carries the craft to port, causing the pointer to drift to the right. Noting the error, the skipper alters his course to starboard to line up on the radial again, thus bringing the pointer back—and keeping his boat on course.

On this simplified drawing of a radar receiver, the knobs to the right of the scope control the picture. The brilliance knob regulates the intensity of the image, while the tuning knob brings it into focus. The range knob selects the radius of the picture on the scope; the boat's own position is marked by its cross hairs. The on-off switch may be set to impose concentric range rings on the screen, and the anti-clutter and gain knobs partially block out unwanted signals.

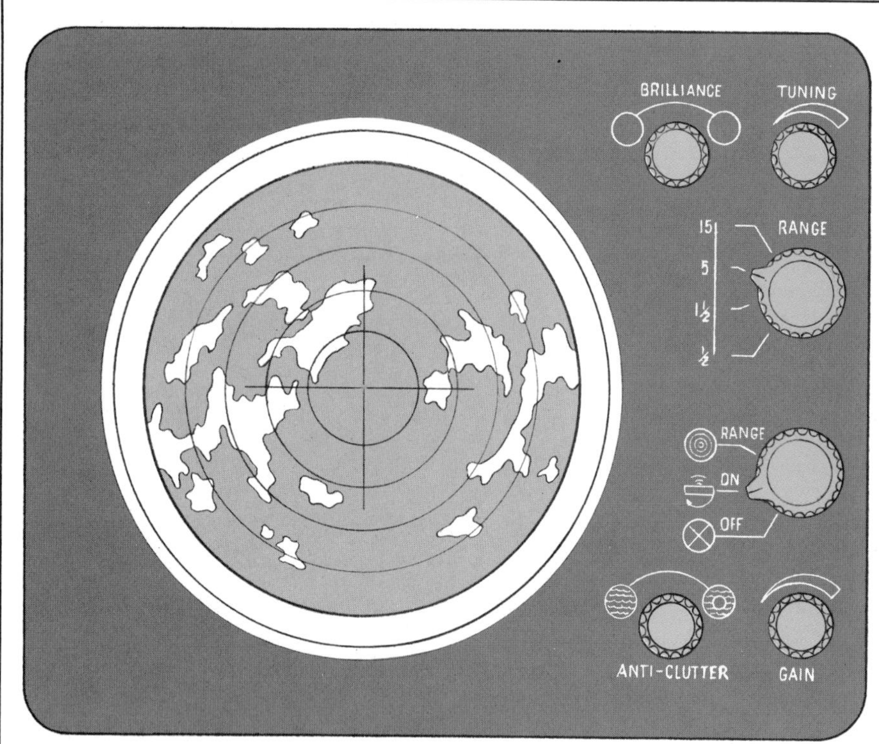

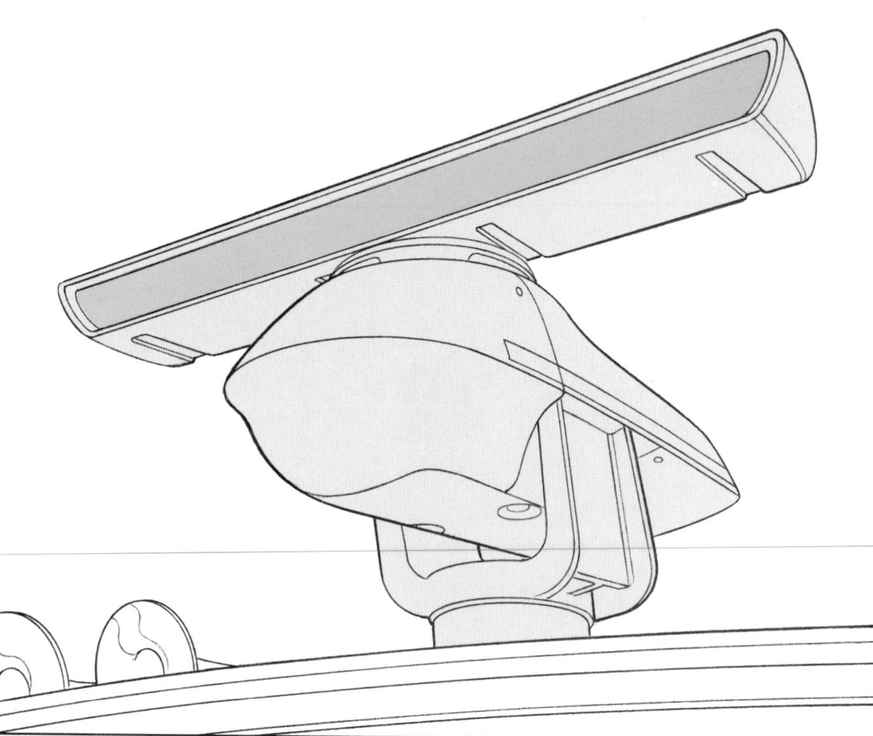

A radar's sophisticated two-way antenna consists of two major components. The slender horizontal scanner at the top, which houses the antenna's sending and receiving unit (blue), spins around at the rate of 20 times every minute, sweeping the water as far as the horizon with its SHF radio beam. The bulkier fixed unit underneath contains the driving motor and cables for carrying impulses to and from the sending and receiving unit and the scope below.

The Super Scanner

While most electronic navigating equipment delivers its message in the numerical language of directional bearings or water depths, one particular device gives the skipper a direct visual image. This is radar, whose viewing screen *(left)* reveals not only the presence, but also the distance, direction and even the shape of objects around a boat. Though some skill is needed to understand a radar picture, any navigator who learns how to read it can pilot his boat through tricky channels and heavy maritime traffic in the darkest night or the murkiest fog.

To create a radar picture, a transmitter aboard ship sends out a superhigh-frequency (SHF) radio signal from a revolving two-way antenna *(bottom left)*. As the antenna turns, scanning the water's surface, its SHF beam is reflected by nearby objects. These reflections then bounce back to the boat and the antenna picks them up. A receiver translates them into electronic images called blips that are flashed onto the radarscope, a cathode ray tube much like the tube in TV sets.

In reading a radarscope, a skipper must make some quick and expert visual interpolations, since—as on pages 138 and 139—the picture on the screen differs markedly from the world as seen by the naked eye. This is because some features—particularly objects made of metal—reflect radar beams better than others. Special buoys with metal radar reflectors, for example, show up as enormous phosphorescent splotches *(page 146)*, far out of proportion to their actual size. Other features, such as low-lying rocks, or small wood or fiberglass boats, may not appear at all. In addition, severe rain, snow or hail can mask sections of a screen with random streaks, known as clutter. And the center of the screen often blazes with a mystifying jumble of blips, called "sea return," which are simply a reflection from waves near the ship.

Experienced operators, however, interpret radar's visual quirks with relative ease. They can distinguish between the fleeting blip of a moving boat and the steady flare from a buoy. They learn to relate shapes on the scope to landmarks delineated on their charts. They keep in mind the limited range of radar waves, which are effective only to the horizon *(opposite, above)*. And since radar sets used aboard most pleasure craft produce their sharpest, most complete pictures for objects within a radius of five or six miles, most skippers use them primarily for close-in piloting in tight quarters.

The beam emanating from the radar antenna of the powerboat below sweeps out (blue) until it intercepts a sailboat on the horizon. Then part of the beam rebounds (blue-gray) back to the powerboat. The sailboat does not stop all the radar pulses. Some of them pass through nonreflecting surfaces such as the sail—and others miss the boat entirely. But since the waves travel in straight lines, they never reach the headlands at far right, which lie below the horizon.

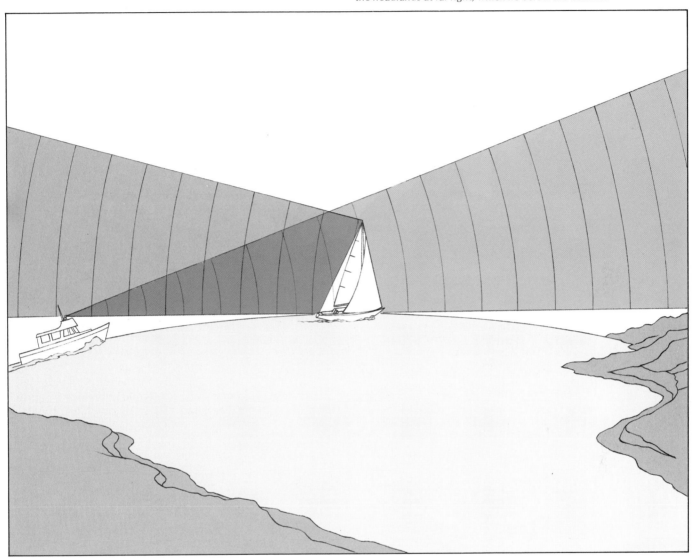

Collision Insurance

Because radar beams reflect poorly—or not at all—from wood or fiberglass boats, many small-craft skippers invest in compact but highly efficient radar reflectors like the one at right. Commonly about 15 inches in diameter, the reflectors are made of thin, interlocking metal discs from which radar waves bounce strongly no matter at what angle they strike. Usually kept folded and stowed away, they can be quickly assembled and hoisted aloft—the higher the better—for cruising at night or in bad weather. Though simple and inexpensive, these ingenious reflectors can provide an increasingly important form of anticollision insurance, as more and more vessels rely on radar to guide them through crowded waters in bad weather.

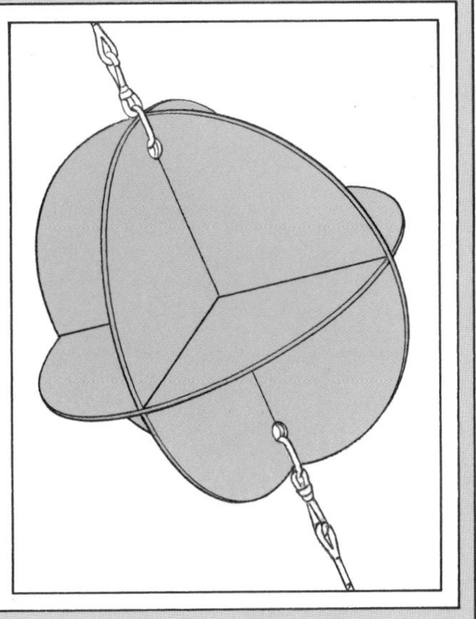

The circular pattern of glowing blips in the radarscope of a boat in Los Angeles Harbor reflects the locations—and in some cases the actual shapes—of objects around the vessel. The boat's position is marked by a bright dot at the scope's exact center. The thin white line slanting from this dot to the upper left is from the beam of the revolving antenna. The heavier, angled lines above and below the boat indicate piers and breakwaters, and the nebula of blips beyond the upper piers is from buildings on shore—as can be seen by comparing the radar picture with the chart at right. Some blips, however, have no counterparts on the chart. The spattering of light immediately surrounding the boat, for example, is reflection from nearby waves, while the small, ragged patch of brightness just below the vessel is the echo coming from a passing power cruiser.

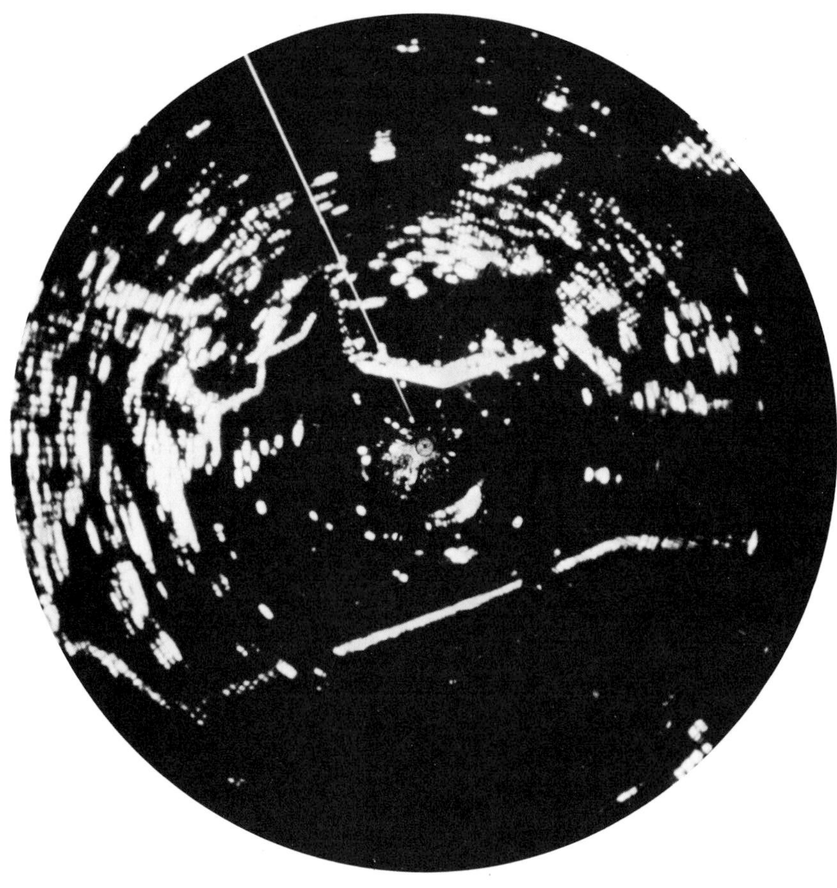

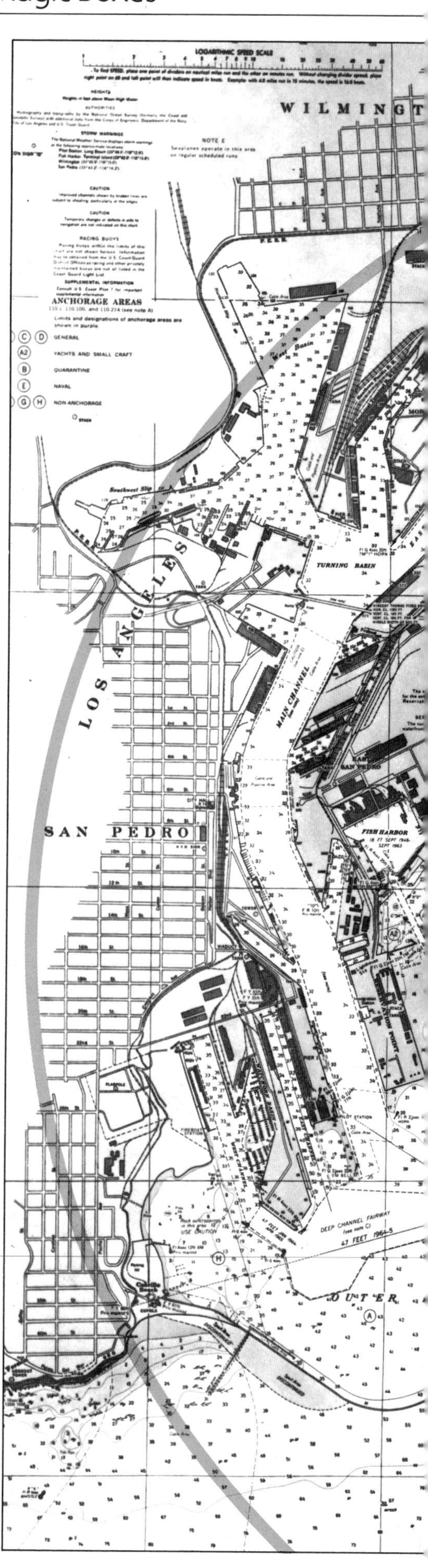

On a chart of Los Angeles Harbor, a blue circle encloses the area covered by the picture seen on the radar screen (above), and a blue X marks the position of the boat. The circle's radius is about three miles; the area of detailed radar coverage is roughly 28 square miles.

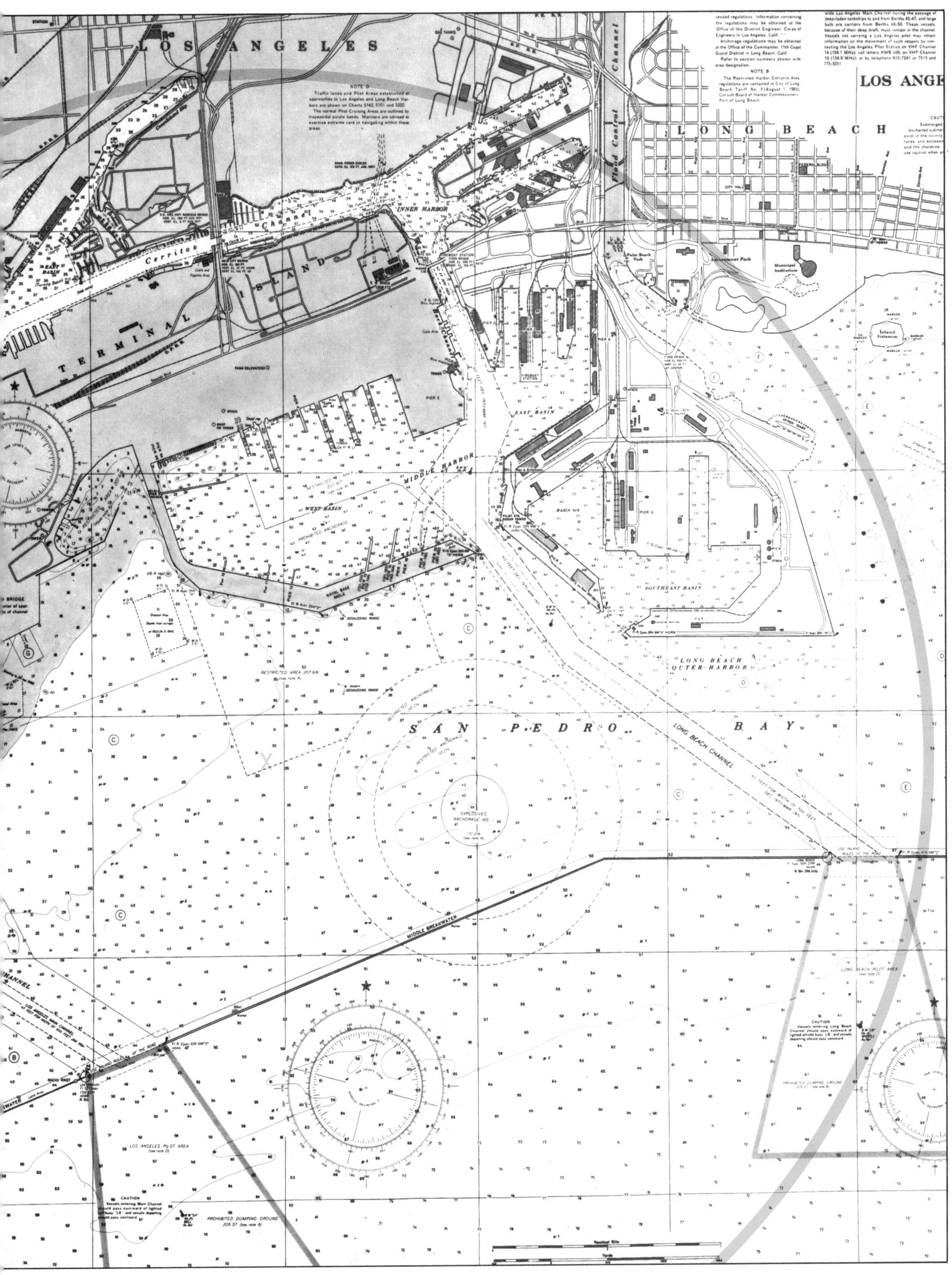
LOS ANGELES
LONG BEACH
LOS ANGE
Flood Control Channel
revised regulations. Information concerning the regulations may be obtained at the Office of the District Engineer, Corps of Engineers in Los Angeles, Calif.
Anchorage regulations may be obtained at the Office of the Commander, 11th Coast Guard District in Long Beach, Calif.
Refer to section numbers shown with area designation.
NOTE B
The Restricted Harbor Entrance Area regulations are contained in City of Long Beach Tariff No. 3 (August 1, 1965). Consult Board of Harbor Commissioners, Port of Long Beach.
wide Los Angeles Main Channel during the passage of deep-laden tankships to and from Berths 45-47, and large bulk ore carriers from Berths 48-50. These vessels, because of their deep draft, must remain in the channel. Vessels not carrying a Los Angeles pilot may obtain information on the movement of such vessels by contacting the Los Angeles Pilot Station on VHF Channel 14 (156.7 MHz), call letters KMB 406, on VHF Channel 16 (156.8 MHz); or by telephone 832-7241 or 7513 and 775-3231.
NOTE D
Traffic lanes and Pilot Areas established at approaches to Los Angeles and Long Beach Harbors are shown on Charts 5142, 5101 and 5202.
The normal Pilot Cruising Areas are outlined by trapezoidal purple bands. Mariners are advised to exercise extreme care in navigating within these areas.
TERMINAL ISLAND
Cerritos Channel
INNER HARBOR
MIDDLE HARBOR
WEST BASIN
EAST BASIN
BASIN SIX
PIER G
SOUTHEAST BASIN
LONG BEACH OUTER HARBOR
SAN PEDRO BAY
LONG BEACH CHANNEL
MIDDLE BREAKWATER
EXPLOSIVES ANCHORAGE NO.
RESTRICTED AREA 207.6
PROHIBITED ANCHORAGE
Island Grissom
Municipal Auditorium
Amusement Park
CITY HALL
FEDERAL BLDG
LONG BEACH PILOT AREA
(see note D)
CAUTION
Vessels entering Long Beach Channel should pass eastward of lighted whistle buoy LB and vessels departing should pass westward
PROHIBITED DUMPING GROUND
LOS ANGELES PILOT AREA
(see note D)
CAUTION
Vessels entering Main Channel should pass eastward of lighted bell buoy "LA" and vessels departing should pass westward
PROHIBITED DUMPING GROUND
205.57 (see note A)

By Master and Slave

Of all the magic boxes available to the yachtsman, none surpasses loran for navigational precision over great distances. Loran's wide reach is implicit in its name, which stands for long-range navigation. By means of synchronized, intersecting radio waves from a network of land-based transmitters, loran can pinpoint a boat's position with quarter-mile accuracy, even when the vessel is as far as 1,000 miles from land. Closer to shore, loran's precision is correspondingly greater. Loran receivers are compact, easy to install, consume little power and are simple to operate. But loran costs more than almost any other type of electronic gear a yachtsman can buy.

The principle of loran is essentially simple. A radio station transmits signals to two distant slave stations, which then retransmit the signals. The receiver picks up both the master transmission and the slave transmissions, and measures the elapsed time between the first signal and each of the others. These two time figures are displayed as a pair of numbers on the boat's receiver, and the boatman matches them to a loran grid, superimposed on a chart, to find his position. First, the unit picks up the master signal, which starts a pair of precision timers in the receiver. When a slave signal arrives, it stops one timer, and the elapsed time in microseconds (millionths of a second) appears on the control panel. The next slave signal stops the other timer and a second time interval flashes onto the panel.

These numbers represent specific intersecting grid lines on a loran chart. Each line is labeled with a code—SS7-Z and SS7-Y in the example on the opposite page—that identifies the particular master-slave signals. Following the code is a number that corresponds to the readings in microseconds that would appear on the loran receiver of any boat located along the line. The navigator notes the readings and finds the two intersecting grid lines—one on the SS7-Z axis, the other on the SS7-Y axis—that most nearly match the readings *(opposite)*. The point where the lines meet gives the navigator an approximate fix on his position, which he then refines by the method shown at the bottom of the opposite page.

On a loran receiver's control panel, all the controls are set for automatic operation. The knobs at bottom are tuned to one of the loran networks, in this case SS7. When the receiver locks into the network's master and slaves, the row of lights in the middle, labeled SIG, flash on. With the power switch pointing to TRACK, the set monitors the boat's progress, indicating its position in microsecond readings. Other lights and switches are for manual operation.

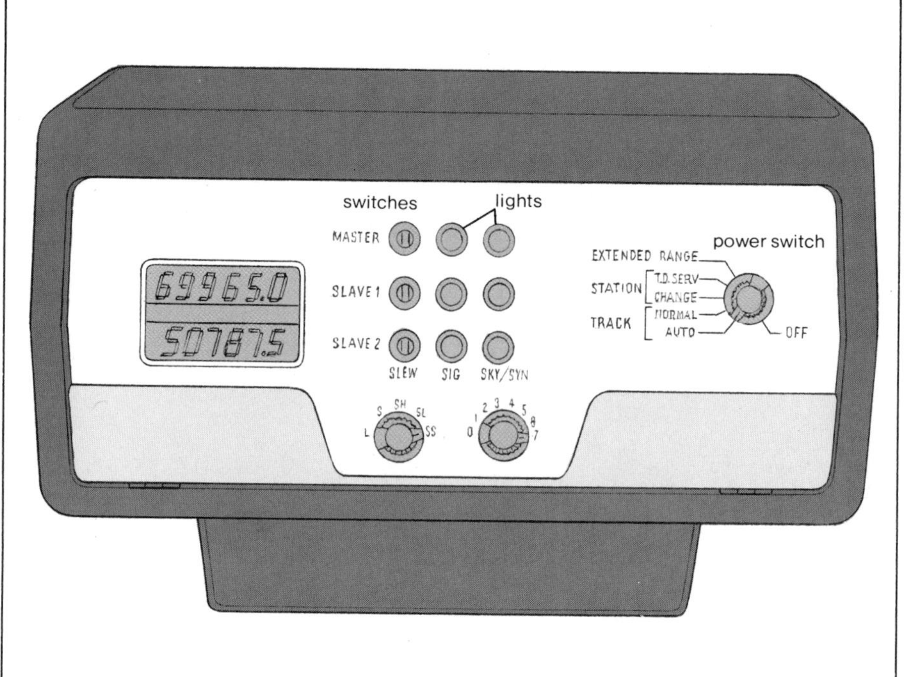

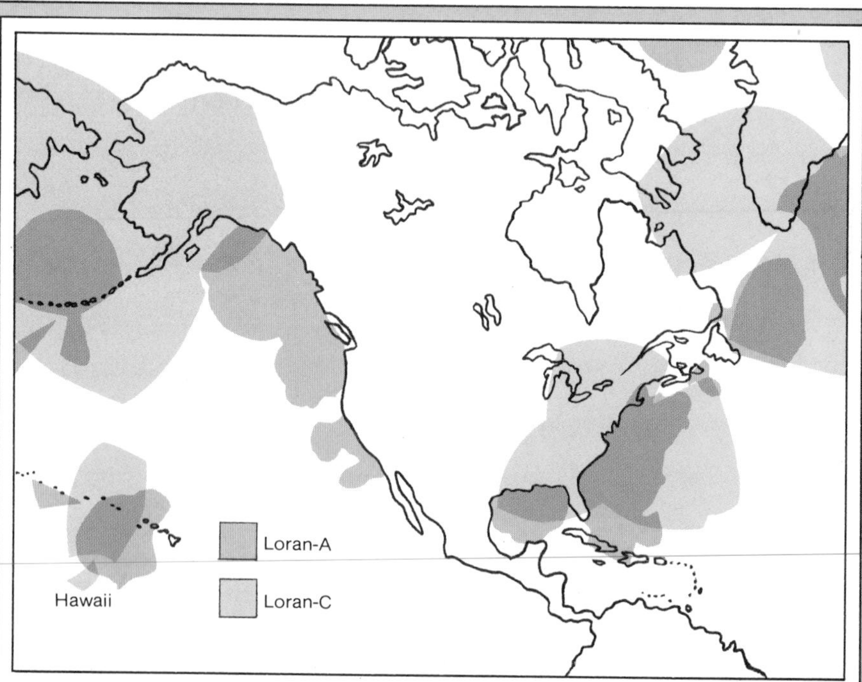

Loran's Double Standard

Two varieties of loran blanket the coastal waters of North America and Hawaii; their signals are strongest in the tinted areas. The gray patches contain networks for loran-A, the original system. But loran-A is being phased out in favor of loran-C, a more accurate version that already serves the areas shown in blue. Inside their respective zones, loran-A can fix a boat's position to within two miles, while loran-C is accurate down to 1,500 feet. With some sacrifice in precision, both systems can be used outside the shaded areas.

The first step in plotting a loran position is to match the numbers on the receiver with the loran grid of a chart. Here, a skipper following a course from Atlantic City to Montauk Point notes that the upper number on his receiver (opposite) lies between lines SS7-Z-69960.0 and SS7-Z-69980.0. Similarly, the lower number falls between lines SS7-Y-50750.0 and SS7-Y-50800.0. These four lines intersect to form a grid square, here tinted blue, that serves as a rough fix.

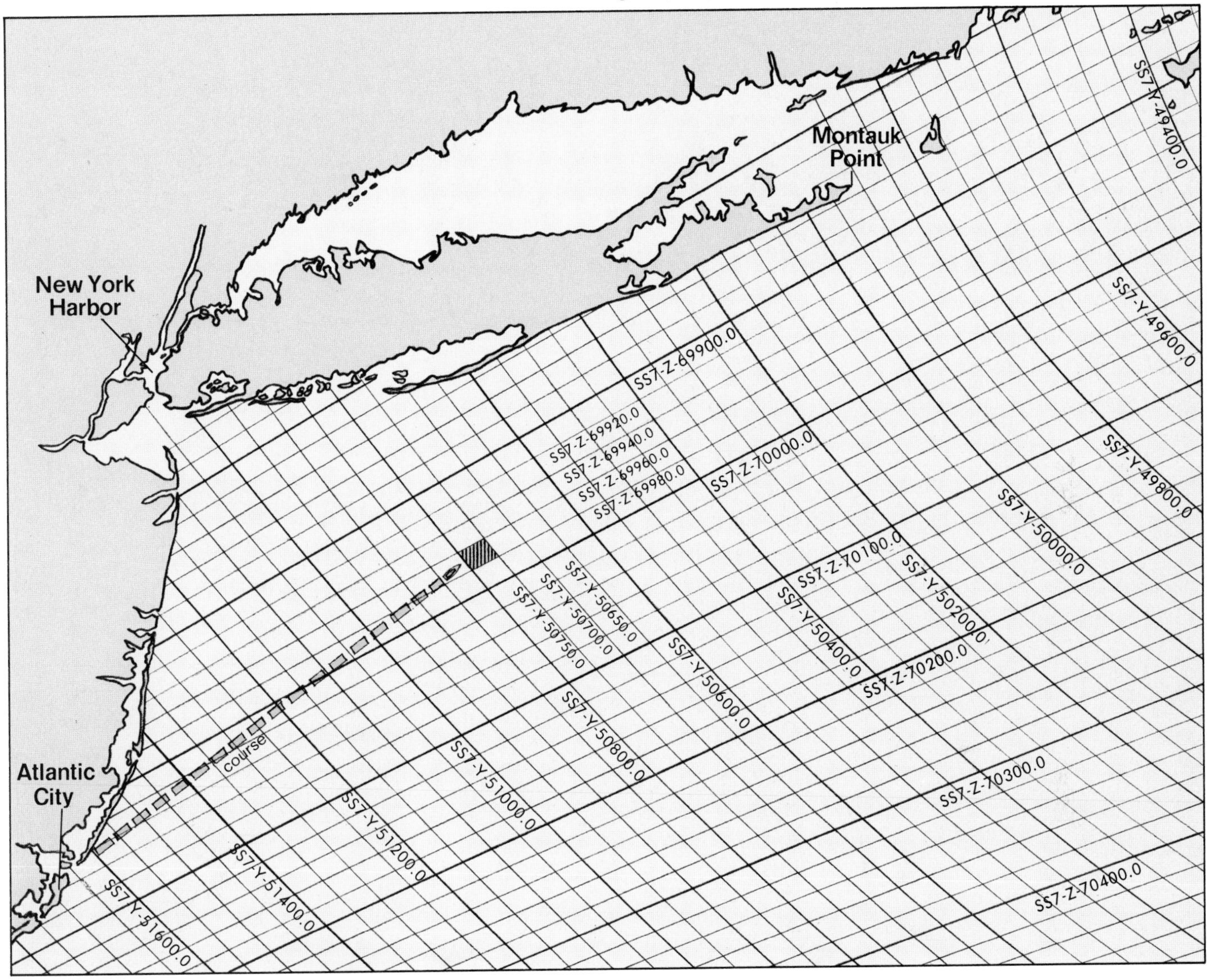

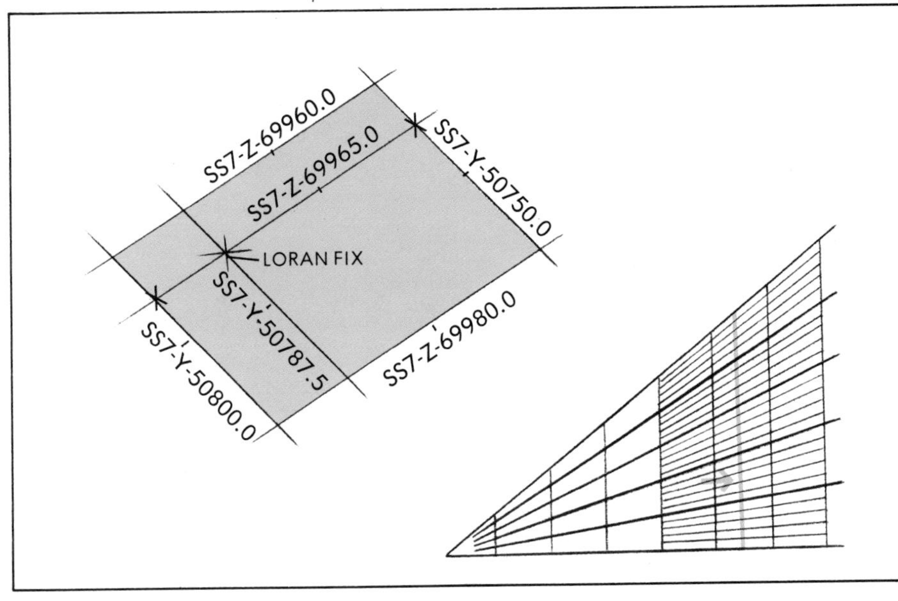

To refine his fix, the skipper measures how far along the grid square each number lies; e.g., 69965.0 on the SS7-Z axis is about one fourth of the way between the 69960.0 and 69980.0 lines. In order to find this distance the skipper refers to a wedge-shaped scale on his loran chart. He marks off the distance between the grid lines 69960.0 and 69980.0 on the chart; then, with dividers, he finds the same distance on the scale (blue line), measuring between the scale's converging boundary lines. He next takes one fourth of this distance (blue arrow) and transfers it to the grid square (black X's) for one line of position. He repeats the procedure for the second line and gets his fix.

RICH HAUL FOR AN AUTOMATED TRAWLER

The 85-foot fishing trawler *Alliance,* heading out of Point Judith, Rhode Island, on a fishing trip, is carrying the ultimate in electronic gear. Festooned atop her cabin and her superstructure is an array of antennas attesting to the presence on board of some $11,000 worth of futuristic marine technology.

Alliance's two co-owners and her three-man crew fish regularly near the edge of the continental shelf, some 50 to 75 miles away from shore. And without the electronic gear boxes, all hands could soon drift into bankruptcy.

Alliance is a lineal descendant of the sailing craft that fished New England waters for 300 years. To find their course—and the fish—those old-time sloops and schooners had only a compass, a lead line and a lookout. Often they became lost in a fog or storm, had their nets torn by unseen rocks, even sank when steamers running blind in bad weather rammed them. Amid these many perils, the catch depended primarily on chance—but, nevertheless, in those days of plentiful fish and relatively few fishing boats, the chances were generally good.

Today the picture has changed. Escalating costs, heavy competition and dwindling schools of fish force modern trawlers to search ever harder for their catch.

Despite this, *Alliance's* sophisticated electronic aids regularly guide her home with her hold bulging with 40,000 pounds of iced fish. Her radar warns of hazards, and picks out buoys and coastline contours; loran pinpoints the ship's location, guiding her to areas where fish are known to be or away from areas where wrecks endanger nets. Supersensitive depth recorders give the navigator eyes underwater, so that no school of fish hidden beneath the boat escapes his gaze. So vital have these electronic aids become that the skipper of *Alliance* says flatly, "I wouldn't go fishing without this equipment."

The fishing boat Alliance leaves her home port of Point Judith, Rhode Island, on the start of a three-day cruise to the fishing grounds near the edge of the continental shelf. Positioned on her cabin roof is a radar antenna; her superstructure carries the antennas for a wind-velocity gauge, loran, a radio and a two-way marine radiotelephone.

The skipper of Alliance steers his craft across Block Island Sound en-route to the fishing grounds. Arrayed next to him at the ready are the boat's electronic crew members. These include, from left: a wide-screen depth finder to provide a display of bottom contours; two loran sets for instant position fixes; above the lorans, an extra-sensitive depth finder that can locate fish; a radarscope with its viewing hood; and to the left of the skipper's head, two radio receivers.

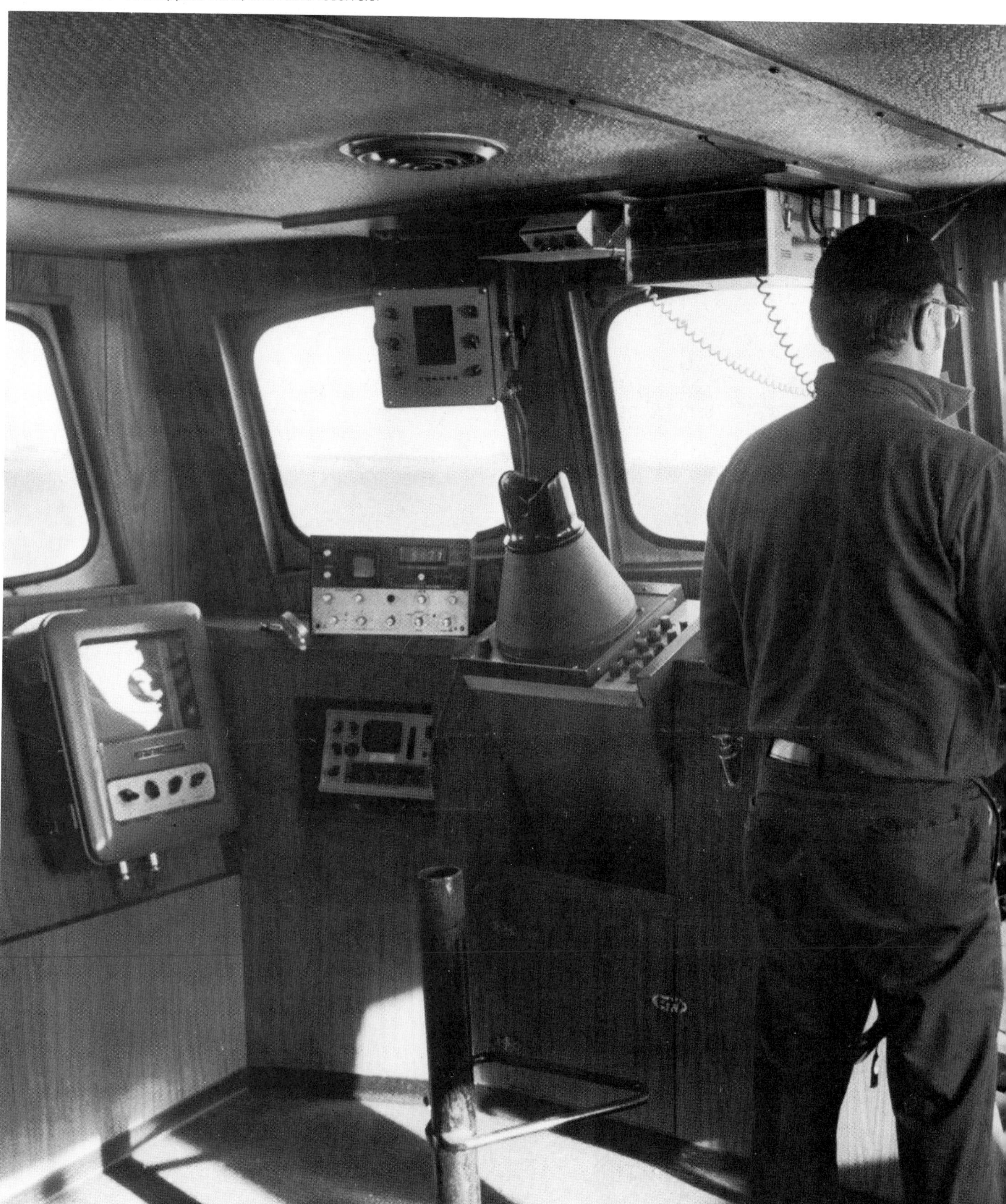

On a chart of the Atlantic Ocean off southern New England, the captain plans a triangular course to put Alliance at the edge of the continental shelf. The course's outgoing leg runs about 75 miles southeast, past Block Island. The base line cuts across a productive area for butterfish, which bring good prices.

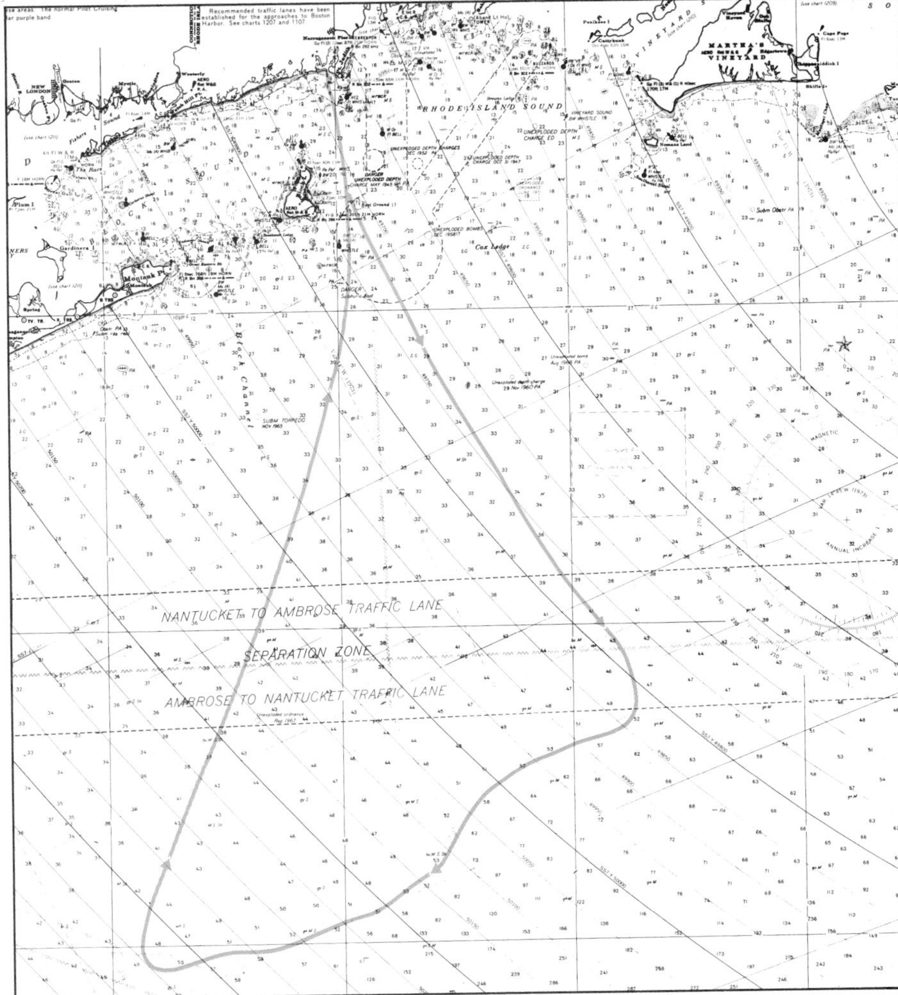

As he comes abreast of Block Island in poor visibility, the skipper of Alliance peers at his radarscope to pick up the familiar shape of the island, thus reaffirming his position and making sure no vessels are in his path. In the fleeting blips that flash on the scope, experience has taught him to recognize the shoreline, buoys, any small craft and even rain showers that may surround him. At bottom is a photographic reproduction of his view in the scope.

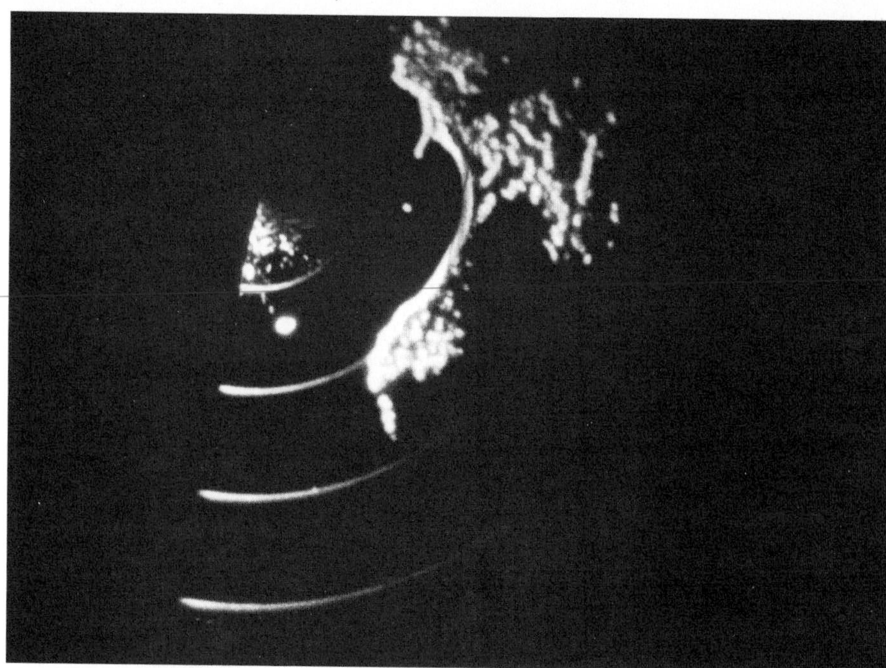

Alliance's radar shows the eastern coastline of Block Island, with the island's southern tip at the top of the screen. Alliance is at the center point of the four concentric arcs, which indicate distances of one, two, three and four nautical miles from the vessel. The mass of blips around the boat are harmless reflections from waves, which the skipper knows he can safely ignore. The small dot inside the crescent of the coast is caused by a bell buoy. The big, bright dot outside the first ring is from a radar-reflecting buoy.

Consulting his chart as he nears the fishing ground, the skipper rechecks the exact locations of bottom obstructions—marked by Xs—that would foul his nets. Next to the Xs he has noted the loran coordinate numbers (pages 140-141) that identify their locations. He has also recorded the numbers in the logbook at left. The flashing numbers on the loran set (bottom) indicate his own position; by checking the chart, he knows whether he can safely drop his nets.

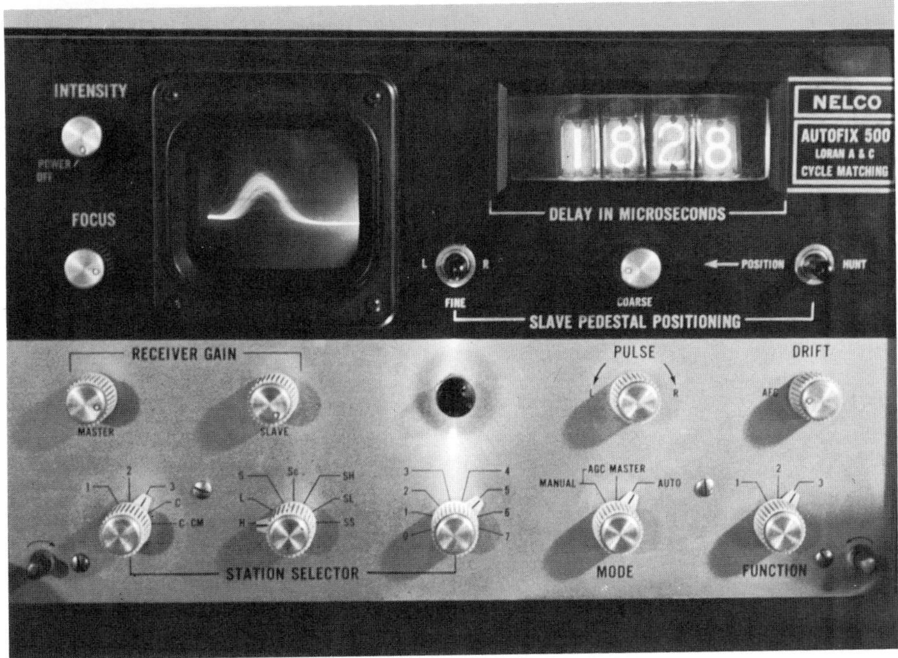

The readout panel of a loran receiver shows a four-digit number (upper right) that identifies the loran coordinate the boat is crossing. By finding the spot on the chart where this number has been printed, the captain pinpoints the location of his vessel. The wavy line on the scope (upper left) indicates that the equipment is correctly tuned to the shore-based loran broadcasting station; an incorrect tuning-dial setting would produce a line that oscillated wildly

Alliance's main depth recorder displays by print-out a profile of the smooth, sloping plain of the continental shelf. At this point the vessel is nearing the shelf's edge—which is prime fishing ground—and the skipper switches on his extra-sensitive depth indicator for any signs of fish (bottom).

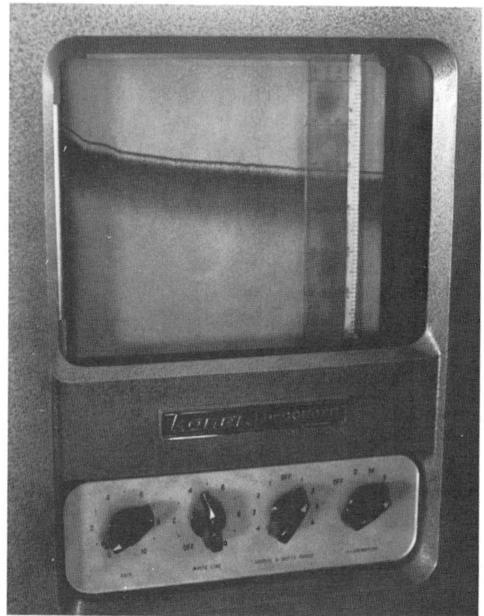

This dramatically varied light pattern on Alliance's electronic depth scope is produced by sound waves echoing off fish. The echoes, relatively weak compared with those from the bottom, are amplified by the sensitive scope. The wide base of the pattern indicates a tight grouping of fish near the bottom.

Knee-deep in the butterfish spotted on Alliance's scope, a crewman secures the vessel's net around a winch drum that hauls the net up. The enormous catch will be quickly stowed into the hold and covered with crushed ice; and Alliance will head home after another successful voyage—thanks to the lift from her electronic gear.

6

When the ocean retreats from Southend-on-Sea, England, a mile-wide mud flat uncovers in the Thames estuary *(opposite)*, as though the land had heaved up out of the sea. Some six hours later the waters return with a rush. The owner of the stranded sailboat at left knows from long observation how the local tides and currents behave, and he has prepared for them. His craft has twin keels that hold it upright when low tide dries out the estuary. The skipper also knows exactly when the tide will come in again to float him clear.

Few tidal flows are as severe or dramatic as the ones in the Thames estuary. Yet all along the world's seacoasts the tide rises and falls at least once a day,

COPING WITH CURRENT AND TIDE

and in most cases twice. This enormous movement of water generates tidal currents that swirl in and out of bays, coves, straits and estuaries, flooding when the water rises, ebbing when it recedes. Even in inland areas where the tide does not reach, water levels may fluctuate with periods of rainfall or drought, and currents of varying strength flow down rivers to the sea. Almost anywhere he sails, in fact, a boatman travels across a surface that is itself in continuous motion, a kind of watery magic carpet that carries him up and down and back and forth according to its own physical laws. To navigate across this moving surface with any degree of precision, every boatman must —like the Thames skipper—have a clear idea of the tides and currents at any given moment. For example, since the soundings on nautical charts show water depths only at the time of mean low water, a navigator using a depth finder to determine his position must calculate the tide level at the moment he takes his reading, and add it to the charted depth.

In calculating both currents and tides, the navigator's task is further complicated by the idiosyncratic time schedule of tidal movements. The exact moments of high and low water, and also the periods of flood and ebb current, vary with every location and change every day. However, these variations can be predicted with some degree of accuracy. Every year the National Ocean Survey (NOS) publishes four volumes of tide tables *(pages 152-153)* that give tide predictions for most of the navigable world. The volume entitled *East Coast of North and South America*, for example, estimates tide levels for some 2,000 places from Greenland to Tierra del Fuego. To keep each volume within manageable size, full daily predictions are listed for only a few principal points, called reference stations. All the remaining locations, or local stations, are keyed to one of the reference stations. And the tables include brief annotations that allow the navigator to compute the differences between the tides at any local station and its reference station.

Although currents in any given area generally relate to the times and extent of tidal rise and fall, the correspondence is rarely exact. The NOS, therefore, publishes a separate set of tidal current tables *(pages 154-155)* that predict current times, speeds and directions. These, too, are organized around reference stations and local stations, and allow the navigator to calculate currents for any day of the year. Also, for 13 of the nation's busiest coastal areas, the NOS issues tidal current charts *(pages 156-157)* that graphically show current patterns, hour by hour, throughout the cycle of currents.

But while the tide and current tables give fairly accurate estimates of the water's movement, their predictions are hardly ever exact. Strong winds, heavy rain, even low barometric pressure can radically alter local tide levels. And one of the world's mightiest currents, the 45-mile-wide Gulf Stream sweeping northward up the Florida coast, is caused solely by the trade winds flowing steadily across the Atlantic Ocean. Piloting through it *(pages 162-167)* is one of the supreme tests of a navigator's skill.

High and dry for the moment, a small sloop sits firmly on its twin keels, awaiting the rush of the next high water across the tidal flat in the Thames estuary at Southend-on-Sea, England.

Timetables for Tides

When coming into an area like Jekyll Sound *(right)*, which has a six-foot mid-channel shoal, a skipper needs to know how much water he will have under his hull when he gets there. To figure this, he must consult three different listings *(opposite)* in the area's tide tables and make a few quick calculations. The work sheet at right, below, simplifies this process.

In the example shown, the skipper plans to arrive at Jekyll Point on June 1, 1975, at 4:30 p.m. To figure out the tide levels, he looks up Jekyll Point in the tide tables index, and learns that the nearest reference station is Savannah River Entrance, listed in the section of the tide tables labeled Table 1 *(opposite, top)*.

From Table 1, the skipper finds the Savannah River tide levels for the afternoon of June 1 (shaded gray in this example). On his work sheet, he copies the exact times of high and low water, and the height of each (color-keyed to the table in the same gray tint). These levels will differ slightly, but significantly, from the times and heights at Jekyll Point.

To calculate the correct figures for Jekyll Point, the skipper now turns to Table 2; the figures in the first two columns labeled "differences" tell him (blue-gray tint) that the tides there occur 28 minutes later than at the reference station. He notes these figures on his work sheet, and adds them to the Savannah River data to get the Jekyll Point times. He uses the next two figures in the table to correct the height of both high and low tide.

Next, the skipper works out the figures he needs to make use of the third table, which allows him to calculate the water level at 4:30 p.m., the time at which he will pass the shoal near Jekyll Point. He gets his first figure by subtracting the high-water time (1347) from the low-water time (2007), giving him the duration of the tide fall (6 hours 20 minutes). Then he computes the time difference between high tide (1347) and his moment of arrival (1630) and notes the result (2 hours 43 minutes). Finally he subtracts the low-tide level (1.1 feet) from the high-tide level (5.7 feet) to get the tidal range (4.6 feet).

Now he finds those three figures in Table 3, as shown. This table gives the skipper a number (shaded blue) that enables him to make the key calculation; he subtracts 1.8 from the high-water height of 5.7 feet and gets the tide level at 4:30 p.m. —3.9 feet. Adding this figure to the charted depth of six feet over the shoal, he finds that he has plenty of water—9.9 feet—in which to pass with safety.

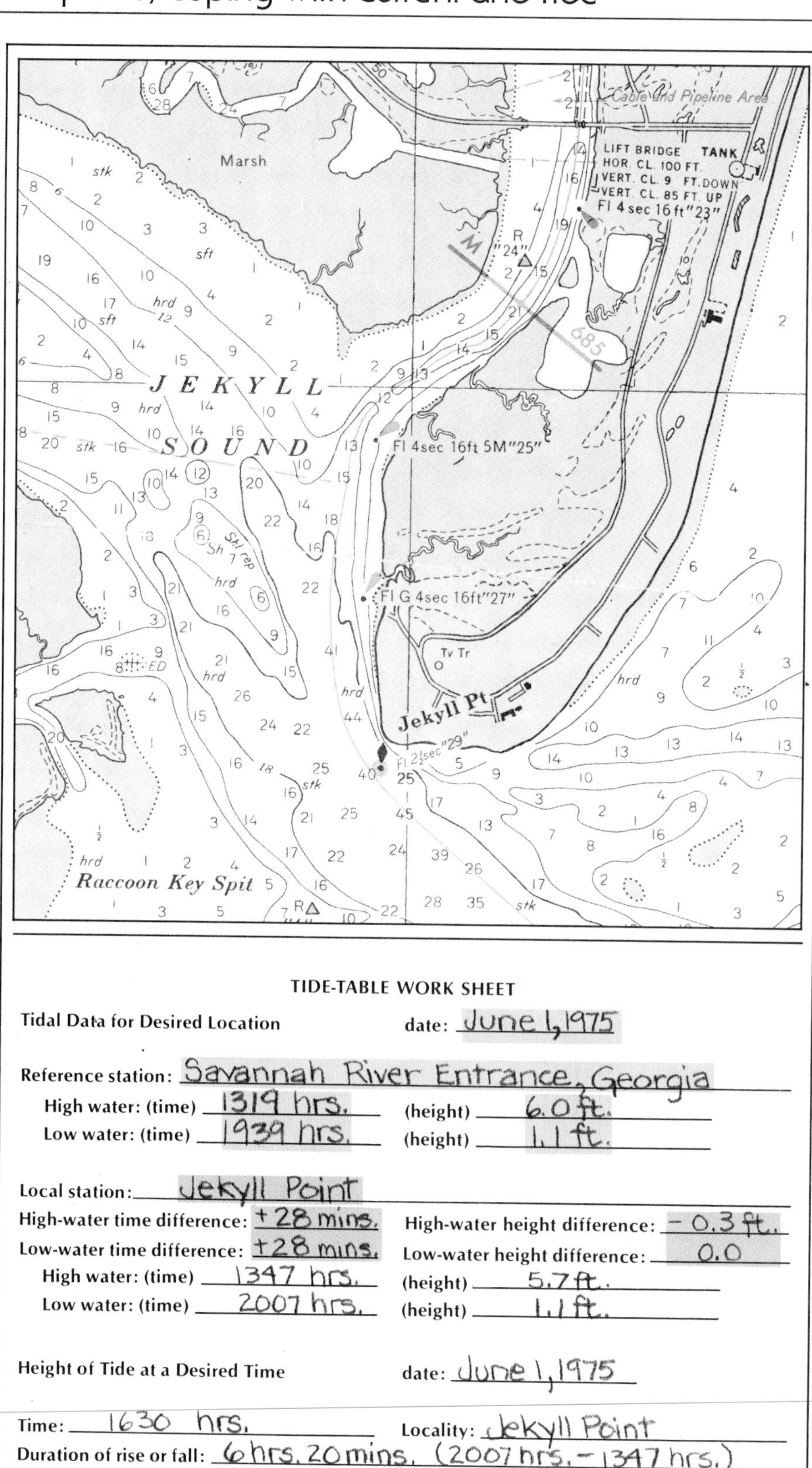

TIDE-TABLE WORK SHEET

Tidal Data for Desired Location date: June 1, 1975

Reference station: Savannah River Entrance, Georgia
High water: (time) 1319 hrs. **(height)** 6.0 ft.
Low water: (time) 1939 hrs. **(height)** 1.1 ft.

Local station: Jekyll Point
High-water time difference: +28 mins. **High-water height difference:** −0.3 ft.
Low-water time difference: +28 mins. **Low-water height difference:** 0.0
High water: (time) 1347 hrs. **(height)** 5.7 ft.
Low water: (time) 2007 hrs. **(height)** 1.1 ft.

Height of Tide at a Desired Time date: June 1, 1975

Time: 1630 hrs. **Locality:** Jekyll Point
Duration of rise or fall: 6 hrs. 20 mins. (2007 hrs. − 1347 hrs.)
Time from nearest high or low water: 2 hrs. 43 mins. (1630 hrs. − 1347 hrs.)
Range of tide: 4.6 ft. (5.7 ft. − 1.1 ft.)
Height of nearest high or low water: 5.7 ft.
Correction to height: −1.8 ft.
Height of tide at desired time: 3.9 ft. (5.7 ft − 1.8 ft.)

Height of tide at 1630 hrs.: 3.9 ft.
Charted water depth: 6.0 ft.
Depth of water at 1630 hrs.: 9.9 ft.

SAVANNAH RIVER ENTRANCE, GA., 1975 — 101

TIMES AND HEIGHTS OF HIGH AND LOW WATERS

APRIL						MAY						JUNE					
DAY	TIME H.M.	HT. FT.	DAY	TIME H.M.	HT. FT.	DAY	TIME H.M.	HT. FT.	DAY	TIME H.M.	HT. FT.	DAY	TIME H.M.	HT. FT.	DAY	TIME H.M.	HT. FT.
1	0551	-0.2	16	0503	0.3	1	0615	0.3	16	0539	0.0	1	0049	6.2	16	0044	7.1
TU	1148	6.3	W	1050	6.2	TH	1213	6.0	F	1138	6.4	SU	0719	0.5	M	0716	-0.4
	1802	0.1		1717	0.2		1826	0.7		1759	0.2		1319	6.0		1331	7.0
				2319	7.3								1939	1.1		1954	0.1
2	0025	6.9	17	0551	0.4	2	0044	6.5	17	0002	7.3	2	0137	6.0	17	0143	6.8
W	0647	0.3	TH	1145	6.1	F	0709	0.6	SA	0634	0.1	M	0811	0.5	TU	0816	-0.4
	1242	6.0		1810	0.3		1305	5.9		1239	6.5		1408	6.1		1435	7.2
	1857	0.5					1923	1.0		1903	0.3		2037	1.1		2100	0.1
3	0121	6.4	18	0017	7.1	3	0137	6.2	18	0100	7.1	3	0227	5.8	18	0246	6.6
TH	0746	0.7	F	0651	0.5	SA	0805	0.7	SU	0737	0.0	TU	0901	0.5	W	0916	-0.5
	1339	5.7		1247	6.1		1400	5.9		1343	6.7		1500	6.3		1541	7.4
	2002	0.8		1916	0.4		2025	1.1		2012	0.2		2132	1.0		2201	-0.1
4	0224	6.2	19	0118	7.0	4	0232	6.0	19	0203	7.0	4	0319	5.8	19	0351	6.5
F	0848	0.8	SA	0756	0.4	SU	0858	0.7	M	0839	-0.2	W	0951	0.3	TH	1013	-0.6
	1442	5.7		1355	6.3		1457	6.0		1452	7.0		1552	6.6		1644	7.7
	2104	0.9		2028	0.3		2122	1.0		2117	0.0		2223	0.8		2300	-0.2
5	0326	6.0	20	0222	7.0	5	0327	5.9	20	0308	6.9	5	0415	5.8	20	0454	6.5
SA	0940	0.7	SU	0902	0.1	M	0947	0.5	TU	0938	-0.5	TH	1036	0.1	F	1107	-0.7
	1543	5.8		1504	6.7		1551	6.2		1558	7.4		1644	6.9		[illegible]	

Table 1 *in the tide tables for the East Coast predicts times and heights of high and low water at 48 key points, or reference stations, such as Savannah River Entrance, Georgia (left), for every day of the year. Time listings are in standard time for the area, indicated on a 24-hour clock. On Sunday afternoon, June 1, for example, high water is at 1319, or 1:19 p.m., and low water at 1939, or 7:39 p.m. Heights for these two tides are 6.0 feet and 1.1 feet above the area's charted depths. These figures, transposed to a work sheet (opposite), provide a start for determining water levels at other spots in the area.*

No.	PLACE	POSITION Lat.	POSITION Long.	DIFFERENCES Time High water	DIFFERENCES Time Low water	DIFFERENCES Height High water	DIFFERENCES Height Low water	RANGES Mean	RANGES Spring	Mean Tide Level
		° ′	° ′	h. m.	h. m.	feet	feet	feet	feet	feet
	GEORGIA — Continued St. Catherines and Sapelo-Sounds — Continued	N.	W.							
			on SAVANNAH RIVER ENT., p. 100							
	Time meridian, 75°W.									
2756	Dallas Bluff, Julienton River-------	31 35	81 19	+0 50	+1 01	+0.7	0.0	7.6	8.9	3.8
2757	Blackbeard Island------------------	31 32	81 12	+0 20	+0 19	0.0	0.0	6.9	8.1	3.4
2758	Dog Hammock, Sapelo River----------	31 32	81 16	+0 31	+0 23	+0.2	0.0	7.1	8.3	3.6
2759	Pine Harbor, Sapelo River----------	31 33	81 22	+1 05	+1 01	+0.3	0.0	7.2	8.4	3.6
2760	Eagle Creek, Mud River-- ----------	31 31	81 17	+0 23	+0 16	+0.3	0.0	7.2	8.4	3.6
	St. Andrew Sound									
2797	Jekyll Point-----------------------	31 01	81 26	+0 28	+0 28	-0.3	0.0	6.6	7.7	3.3
2799	Jointer Island, Jointer Creek-------	31 06	81 30	+1 02	+0 49	+0.3	0.0	7.2	8.4	3.6
	Little Satilla River									
2801	2½ miles above mouth---------	31 04	81 30	+0 47	+0 49	-0.1	0.0	6.8	8.0	3.4

Table 2 *of the tide tables shows how the tides at various local stations differ in time and height from tides at the reference stations in Table 1. At Jekyll Point, high water is 28 minutes later than at Savannah River Entrance, as indicated by the "+ 28" in the high-water time-difference column. To find the moment of high water at Jekyll Point on the afternoon of June 1, this figure must be added to the time of the afternoon high water at Savannah River Entrance. In addition, high water is 0.3 feet lower than at the reference station, so this figure must be subtracted from the Savannah River Entrance tide level.*

Time from the nearest high water or low water

Duration of rise or fall h. m.	h. m.	h. m.	h. m.	h. m.	h. m.	h. m.	h. m.	h. m.	h. m.	h. m.	h. m.	h. m.	h. m.	h. m.	h. m.
4 00	0 08	0 16	0 24	0 32	0 40	0 48	0 56	1 04	1 12	1 20	1 28	1 36	1 44	1 52	2 00
4 20	0 09	0 17	0 26	0 35	0 43	0 52	1 01	1 09	1 18	1 27	1 35	1 44	1 53	2 01	2 10
4 40	0 09	0 19	0 28	0 37	0 47	0 56	1 05	1 15	1 24	1 33	1 43	1 52	2 01	2 11	2 20
5 00	0 10	0 20	0 30	0 40	0 50	1 00	1 10	1 20	1 30	1 40	1 50	2 00	2 10	2 20	2 30
5 20	0 11	0 21	0 32	0 43	0 53	1 04	1 15	1 25	1 36	1 47	1 57	2 08	2 19	2 29	2 40
5 40	0 11	0 23	0 34	0 45	0 57	1 08	1 19	1 31	1 42	1 53	2 05	2 16	2 27	2 39	2 50
6 00	0 12	0 24	0 36	0 48	1 00	1 12	1 24	1 36	1 48	2 00	2 12	2 24	2 36	2 48	3 00
6 20	0 13	0 25	0 38	0 51	1 03	1 16	1 29	1 41	1 54	2 07	2 19	2 32	2 45	2 57	3 10
6 40	0 13	0 27	0 40	0 53	1 07	1 20	1 33	1 47	2 00	2 13	2 27	2 40	2 53	3 07	3 20
7 00	0 14	0 28	0 42	0 56	1 10	1 24	1 38	1 52	2 06	2 20	2 34	2 48	3 02	3 16	3 30
7 20	0 15	0 29	0 44	0 59	1 13	1 28	1 43	1 57	2 12	2 27	2 41	2 56	3 11	3 25	3 40
7 40	0 15	0 31	0 46	1 01	1 17	1 32	1 47	2 03	2 18	2 33	2 49	3 04	3 19	3 35	3 50
8 00	0 16	0 32	0 48	1 04	1 20	1 36	1 52	2 08	2 24	2 40	2 56	3 12	3 28	3 44	4 00
8 20	0 17	0 33	0 50	1 07	1 23	1 40	1 57	2 13	2 30	2 47	3 03	3 20	3 37	3 53	4 10
8 40	0 17	0 35	0 52	1 09	1 27	1 44	2 01	2 19	2 36	2 53	3 11	3 28	3 45	4 03	4 20
9 00	0 18	0 36	0 54	1 12	1 30	1 48	2 06	2 24	2 42	3 00	3 18	3 36	3 54	4 12	4 30
9 20	0 19	0 37	0 56	1 15	1 33	1 52	2 11	2 29	2 48	3 07	3 25	3 44	4 03	4 21	4 40
9 40	0 19	0 39	0 58	1 17	1 37	1 56	2 15	2 35	2 54	3 13	3 33	3 52	4 11	4 31	4 50
10 00	0 20	0 40	1 00	1 20	1 40	2 00	2 20	2 40	3 00	3 20	3 40	4 00	4 20	4 40	5 00
10 20	0 21	0 41	1 02	1 23	1 43	2 04	2 25	2 45	3 06	3 27	3 47	4 08	4 29	4 49	5 10
10 40	0 21	0 43	1 04	1 25	1 47	2 08	2 29	2 51	3 12	3 33	3 55	4 16	4 37	4 59	5 20

Correction to height

Range of tide Ft.	Ft.	Ft.	Ft.	Ft.	Ft.	Ft.	Ft.	Ft.	Ft.	Ft.	Ft.	Ft.	Ft.	Ft.	Ft.
0.5	0.0	0.0	0.0	0.0	0.0	0.0	0.1	0.1	0.1	0.1	0.1	0.2	0.2	0.2	0.2
1.0	0.0	0.0	0.0	0.0	0.1	0.1	0.1	0.2	0.2	0.2	0.3	0.3	0.4	0.4	0.5
1.5	0.0	0.0	0.0	0.1	0.1	0.1	0.2	0.2	0.3	0.4	0.4	0.5	0.6	0.7	0.8
2.0	0.0	0.0	0.0	0.1	0.1	0.2	0.3	0.3	0.4	0.5	0.6	0.7	0.8	0.9	1.0
2.5	0.0	0.0	0.1	0.1	0.2	0.2	0.3	0.4	0.5	0.6	0.7	0.9	1.0	1.1	1.2
3.0	0.0	0.0	0.1	0.1	0.2	0.3	0.4	0.5	0.6	0.8	0.9	1.0	1.2	1.3	1.5
3.5	0.0	0.0	0.1	0.2	0.2	0.3	0.4	0.6	0.7	0.9	1.0	1.2	1.4	1.6	1.8
4.0	0.0	0.0	0.1	0.2	0.3	0.4	0.5	0.7	0.8	1.0	1.2	1.4	1.6	1.8	2.0
4.5	0.0	0.0	0.1	0.2	0.3	0.4	0.6	0.7	0.9	1.1	1.3	1.6	1.8	2.0	2.2
5.0	0.0	0.1	0.1	0.2	0.3	0.5	0.6	0.8	1.0	1.2	1.5	1.7	2.0	2.2	2.5
5.5	0.0	0.1	0.1	0.2	0.4	0.5	0.7	0.9	1.1	1.4	1.6	1.9	2.2	2.5	2.8
6.0	0.0	0.1	0.1	0.3	0.4	0.6	0.8	1.0	1.2	1.5	1.8	2.1	2.4	2.7	3.0
6.5	0.0	0.1	0.2	0.3	0.4	0.6	0.8	1.1	1.3	1.6	1.9	2.2	2.6	2.9	3.2
7.0	0.0	0.1	0.2	0.3	0.5	0.7	0.9	1.2	1.4	1.8	2.1	2.4	2.8	3.1	3.5
7.5	0.0	[illegible]	0.2	0.3	0.5	0.7	1.0	[illegible]	1.5	[illegible]	[illegible]	[illegible]	3.0	[illegible]	3.8

Table 3 *provides the navigator with the "correction to height" that allows him to determine the tide level at a particular spot at any time. On the work sheet opposite, he has calculated the duration of rise or fall, time from nearest high or low water, and range of tide as 6 hours 20 minutes, 2 hours 43 minutes, and 4.6 feet, respectively. He finds the 6:20 figure in the left-hand column, tracks it across to 2:43 in the table (the closest figure is actually 2:45), then follows that column down until it intersects the line from 4.5 (the nearest range figure to 4.6). The lines meet at the desired correction number—1.8. Since the tide is falling, he subtracts 1.8 from high water to arrive at the Jekyll Point tide level—3.9 feet.*

Forecasting Currents

Just as tide tables and work sheets help sailors figure out the heights of tides, so the tidal current tables help them forecast the speed and time of currents.

Suppose a skipper wants to cut into Blynman Canal in Gloucester, Massachusetts *(right)*, on June 18, 1975. If the current is flowing out of the canal with any force when he gets there, he may have trouble entering. So to establish the time, strength and direction of the various currents at the canal he refers to the tidal current tables and makes some quick calculations on the work sheet below.

He begins by consulting the nearest reference station, in this case Boston Harbor. Looking up Boston Harbor in Table 1 *(opposite, top)* under the column for June, he finds the periods of slack water, and also the times and velocities of the maximum ebb and flood currents. He expects to arrive at Blynman Canal around midday on June 18, but he is not sure precisely when. So he copies down all the figures for the various daytime currents (shaded gray, to key them to the work sheet).

Next, referring to Table 2, the skipper looks up the differences between the Blynman Canal currents (shaded blue-gray) and those at Boston Harbor. Following the steps described on the opposite page, he calculates the times of the two slack-water periods at Blynman, and the time and velocity of the maximum ebb and flood currents. He also notes down the directions of the ebb and flood—listed in degrees relative to true north.

As soon as the skipper nears the canal and can predict his exact arrival time—in this case 1400 hours, or 2 p.m.—he can turn to Table 3 and figure out what the current will be doing at that moment. He must first calculate two key figures from the data he has already entered on his work sheet. He determines the interval between his arrival time (1400) and the nearest slack water (1147); it is 2 hours 13 minutes. Now he wants to find the interval between the nearest slack water (1147) and the nearest maximum current (1507); it is 3 hours 20 minutes. Plotting these two intervals on Table 3, he finds the correction factor: 0.9 (blue shading). From his work sheet, the skipper notes that the maximum current will be flooding at 3.42 knots. He multiplies this figure by the correction factor to obtain the velocity when he reaches the canal: 3.07 knots. From Table 2 he has found that the current will be flowing at 310° true—the westerly bearing of the canal—giving him a welcome three-knot push through the channel.

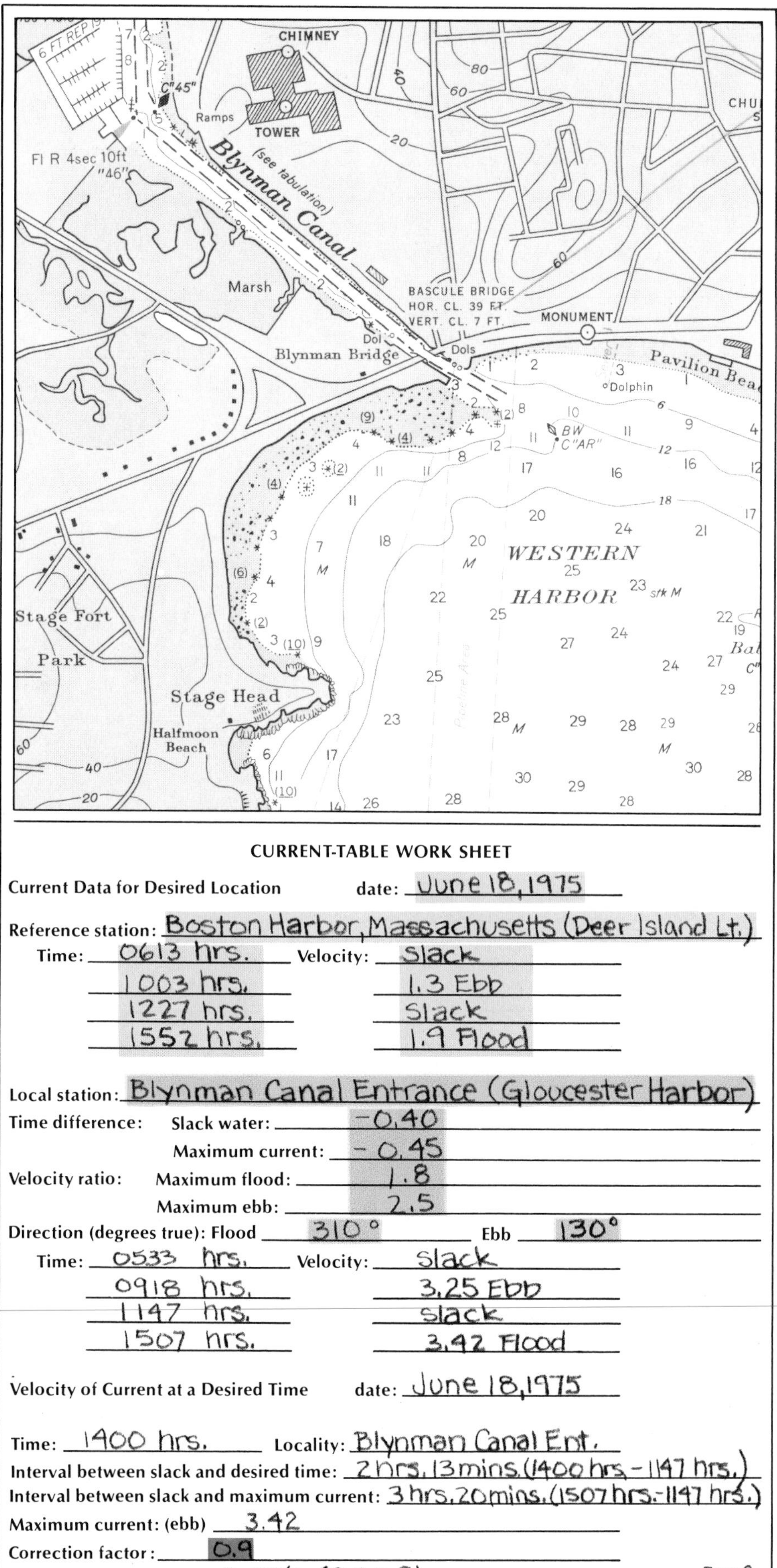

CURRENT-TABLE WORK SHEET

Current Data for Desired Location date: June 18, 1975

Reference station: Boston Harbor, Massachusetts (Deer Island Lt.)

Time	Velocity
0613 hrs.	Slack
1003 hrs.	1.3 Ebb
1227 hrs.	Slack
1552 hrs.	1.9 Flood

Local station: Blynman Canal Entrance (Gloucester Harbor)

Time difference: Slack water: −0.40
Maximum current: −0.45

Velocity ratio: Maximum flood: 1.8
Maximum ebb: 2.5

Direction (degrees true): Flood 310° **Ebb** 130°

Time	Velocity
0533 hrs.	Slack
0918 hrs.	3.25 Ebb
1147 hrs.	Slack
1507 hrs.	3.42 Flood

Velocity of Current at a Desired Time date: June 18, 1975

Time: 1400 hrs. **Locality:** Blynman Canal Ent.

Interval between slack and desired time: 2 hrs. 13 mins. (1400 hrs. − 1147 hrs.)

Interval between slack and maximum current: 3 hrs. 20 mins. (1507 hrs. − 1147 hrs.)

Maximum current: (ebb) 3.42

Correction factor: 0.9

Velocity at desired time: 3.07 (3.42 X 0.9) **Direction (degrees true):** 310°

BOSTON HARBOR (DEER ISLAND LIGHT), MASS., 1975

F-FLOOD, DIR. 260° TRUE   E-EBB, DIR. 085° TRUE

MAY								JUNE			
DAY	SLACK WATER TIME H.M.	MAXIMUM CURRENT TIME H.M.	VEL. KNOTS	DAY	SLACK WATER TIME H.M.	MAXIMUM CURRENT TIME H.M.	VEL. KNOTS	DAY	SLACK WATER TIME H.M.	MAXIMUM CURRENT TIME H.M.	VEL. KNOTS	DAY	SLACK WATER TIME H.M.	MAXIMUM CURRENT TIME H.M.	VEL. KNOTS
1		0021	1.7F	16	0236	0517	1.3E	1		0137	1.4F	16		0120	1.8F
TH	0308	0703	1.4E	F	0903	1218	1.7F	SU	0416	0822	.1.1E	M	0410	0751	1.4E
	0936	1255	1.6F		1511	1739	1.1E		1040	1405	1.4F		1031	1354	1.9F
	1546	1934	1.1E		2118				1654	2052	1.0E		1644	2030	1.4E
	2152								2308				2303		
2		0115	1.5F	17		0036	1.6F	2		0229	1.3F	17		0224	1.8F
F	0400	0802	1.2E	SA	0330	0618	1.3E	M	0508	0916	1.0E	TU	0510	0859	1.3E
	1029	1348	1.5F		0956	1315	1.7F		1130	1457	1.4F		1128	1452	1.9F
	1641	2036	1.0E		1606	1918	1.1E		1745	2147	1.0E		1743	2135	1.4E
	2249				2217										
3		0212	1.4F	18		0139	1.6F	3	0003	0324	1.3F	18	0007	0326	1.8F
SA	0456	0901	1.1E	SU	0428	0803	1.2E	TU	0603	1007	1.0E	W	0613	1003	1.3E
	1123	1444	1.4F		1053	1415	1.7F		1221	1549	1.4F		1227	1552	1.9F
	1739	2131	1.0E		1704	2049	1.2E		1836	2238	1.0E		1844	2237	1.5E
	2347				2321										
4		0307	1.3F	19		0243	1.7F	4	0057	0417	1.3F	19	0111	0427	1.8F
SU	0554	0954	1.1E	M	0530	0920	1.3E	W	0657	1058	1.0E	TH	0718	1104	1.4E
	1217	1539	1.4F		1152	1516	1.8F		1310	1639	1.4F		1327	1651	1.9F
	1835	2226	1.1E		1805	2156	1.3E		1926	2328	1.1E		1945	2338	1.7E
5	0045	0405	1.3F	20	0025	0347	1.7F	5	0150	0508	1.4F	20	0213	0527	1.8F
M	0652	1050	1.1E	TU	0633	1024	1.3E	TH	0751	1147	1.0E	F	0821	1202	1.4E
	1310	1630	1.4F		1251	1616	1.9F		1359	1728	1.5F		1425	1747	2.0F
	1928	2319	1.1E		1905	2257	1.5E		2013				2044		
6	0140	0456	1.4F	21	0128	0448	1.8F	6		0015	1.2E	21		0031	1.7E
TU	0747	1139	1.1E	W	0736	1125	1.4E	F	0240	0557	1.4F	SA	0312	0622	1.9F
	1359	1719	1.5F		1349	1712	2.0F		0842	1236	1.0E		0922	1257	1.5E
	2016				2004	[illegible]	1.7F		[illegible]	[illegible]	1.6F		1520	[illegible]	[illegible]

No.	PLACE	POSITION		TIME DIFFERENCES		VELOCITY RATIOS		MAXIMUM CURRENTS			
								Flood		Ebb	
		Lat.	Long.	Slack water	Maximum current	Maximum flood	Maximum ebb	Direction (true)	Average velocity	Direction (true)	Average velocity
		° ′	° ′	*h. m.*	*h. m.*			*deg.*	*knots*	*deg.*	*knots*
	MASSACHUSETTS COAST—Continued *Time meridian, 75°W.*	N.	W.	on BOSTON HARBOR, p.16							
390	Merrimack River entrance	42 49	70 49	+0 40	(*)	1.3	1.1	285	2.2	105	1.4
395	Newburyport, Merrimack River	42 49	70 52	+1 10	+0 40	0.9	1.1	290	1.5	100	1.4
400	Plum Island Sound entrance	42 42	70 47	+0 15	-0 10	0.9	1.2	315	1.6	185	1.5
405	Annisquam Harbor Light	42 40	70 41	+0 20	-0 05	0.8	0.8	200	1.0	015	1.3
410	Gloucester Harbor entrance	42 35	70 40	*Current too weak and variable to be predicted.*							
415	Blynman Canal ent., Gloucester Hbr	42 37	70 40	-0 40	-0 45	1.8	2.5	310	3.0	130	3.3
420	Marblehead Channel	42 30	70 49	+0 40	+0 40	0.3	0.2	285	0.4	105	0.4
425	Nahant, off East Point	42 25	70 54	-0 20	-0 20	0.5	0.5	235	0.8	085	0.7
430	Lynn Harbor entrance	42 25	70 57	-0 05	-0 05	0.3	0.3	325	0.5	170	0.5
435	Winthrop Beach, 1.2 miles east of	42 23	70 57	-0 05	-0 30	0.2	0.2	195	0.4	095	0.2
	BOSTON HARBOR APPROACHES										
440	Stellwagen Bank	42 24	70 24	*Current too weak and variable to be predicted.*							
445	Boston Lightship, 3 miles SSE. of	42 20	70 45	*Current too weak and variable to be predicted.*							
450	North Channel, off Great Faun	42 21	70 56	-0 05	-0 25	0.7	1.1	200	1.2	025	1.4
455	Hypocrite Channel	42 21	70 54	-0 30	-0 30	0.7	0.7	255	1.2	070	1.0
460	Nantasket Roads entrance	42 19	70 53	0 00	-0 20	1.0	1.0	260	1.4	085	1.5
465	[illegible] Rock Channel	[illegible]	[illegible]	[illegible]	[illegible]	0.7	0.9	220	1.2	[illegible]	[illegible]

TABLE A

Interval between slack and desired time	Interval between slack and maximum current													
	h. m. 1 20	*h. m.* 1 40	*h. m.* 2 00	*h. m.* 2 20	*h. m.* 2 40	*h. m.* 3 00	*h. m.* 3 20	*h. m.* 3 40	*h. m.* 4 00	*h. m.* 4 20	*h. m.* 4 40	*h. m.* 5 00	*h. m.* 5 20	*h. m.* 5 40
h. m.	*f.*	*f.*	*f.*	*f.*	*f.*	*f.*	*f.*	*f.*	*f.*	*f.*	*f.*	*f.*	*f.*	*f.*
0 20	0.4	0.3	0.3	0.2	0.2	0.2	0.2	0.1	0.1	0.1	0.1	0.1	0.1	0.1
0 40	0.7	0.6	0.5	0.4	0.4	0.3	0.3	0.3	0.3	0.2	0.2	0.2	0.2	0.2
1 00	0.9	0.8	0.7	0.6	0.6	0.5	0.5	0.4	0.4	0.4	0.3	0.3	0.3	0.3
1 20	1.0	1.0	0.9	0.8	0.7	0.6	0.6	0.5	0.5	0.5	0.4	0.4	0.4	0.4
1 40	---	1.0	1.0	0.9	0.8	0.8	0.7	0.7	0.6	0.6	0.5	0.5	0.5	0.4
2 00	---	---	1.0	1.0	0.9	0.9	0.8	0.8	0.7	0.7	0.6	0.6	0.6	0.5
2 20	---	---	---	1.0	1.0	0.9	0.9	0.8	0.8	0.7	0.7	0.7	0.6	0.6
2 40	---	---	---	---	1.0	1.0	1.0	0.9	0.9	0.8	0.8	0.7	0.7	0.7
3 00	---	---	---	---	---	1.0	1.0	1.0	0.9	0.9	0.8	0.8	0.8	0.7
3 20	---	---	---	---	---	---	1.0	1.0	1.0	0.9	0.9	0.9	0.8	0.8
3 40	---	---	---	---	---	---	---	1.0	1.0	1.0	0.9	0.9	0.9	0.9
4 00	---	---	---	---	---	---	---	---	1.0	1.0	1.0	1.0	0.9	0.9
4 20	---	---	---	---	---	---	---	---	---	1.0	1.0	1.0	1.0	0.9
4 40	---	---	---	---	---	---	---	---	---	---	1.0	1.0	1.0	1.0
5 00	---	---	---	---	---	---	---	---	---	---	---	1.0	1.0	1.0
5 20	---	---	---	---	---	---	---	---	---	---	---	---	1.0	1.0
5 40	---	---	---	---	---	---	---	---	---	---	---	---	---	1.0

Table 1 *of the tidal current tables lists the four daily periods of slack water at Boston, and the times and velocities of the peak flood (F) and ebb (E) currents. The boatman refers to the entries in the table that correspond to his approximate arrival time at his local station—in this case the daytime hours of June 18 (gray shading). Thus he notes that the morning slack water is at 0613 hours, and that at 1003 hours there will be an ebb current of 1.3 knots. He then transfers these figures to the work sheet on the opposite page, along with the figures for the afternoon slack water and flood current.*

Table 2 *shows the differences between the Boston Harbor currents and those at Blynman Canal (blue-gray shading). In the first time-difference column, the boatman finds that slack water at Blynman is 40 minutes earlier; thus the Blynman slack occurs at 0533 and 1147. The next column indicates that maximum currents are earlier by 45 minutes; so the Blynman ebb is 0918, the flood 1507. From the two velocity-ratio columns he finds that the Blynman ebb will be stronger by a multiple of 2.5 knots, the flood by a multiple of 1.8 knots. Thus the maximum ebb current at Blynman is 3.25 knots, the flood 3.42.*

Table 3, *part A (or in certain special cases part B), of the tidal current tables furnishes a correction factor that allows the navigator to find the current velocities at any time not accounted for by Tables 1 and 2. First he determines the interval between slack and desired time (2 hours 13 minutes), then finds the closest approximation in the left column (2:20). Now he figures the interval between slack and maximum current (3 hours 20 minutes). Reading across from 2:20 and down from 3:20, he finds the correction factor —0.9. That enables him to get the current velocity at the time he wants—3.07 knots.*

Patterns of Flow

For certain heavily traveled boating areas the National Ocean Survey has prepared annotated charts providing instant readings on the speed and direction of tidal currents. These tidal current charts are issued in booklets containing sets of 12, one for each hour of the current cycle. The four charts on these pages are from the set for Block Island Sound, near Connecticut. The data on such charts are based on the current at the area's reference station—in this case a tide-ripped narrows called The Race. To determine what the current is doing at a specific hour of a particular day, the navigator must check the tidal current tables *(pages 154-155)* for that day's listings at the reference station.

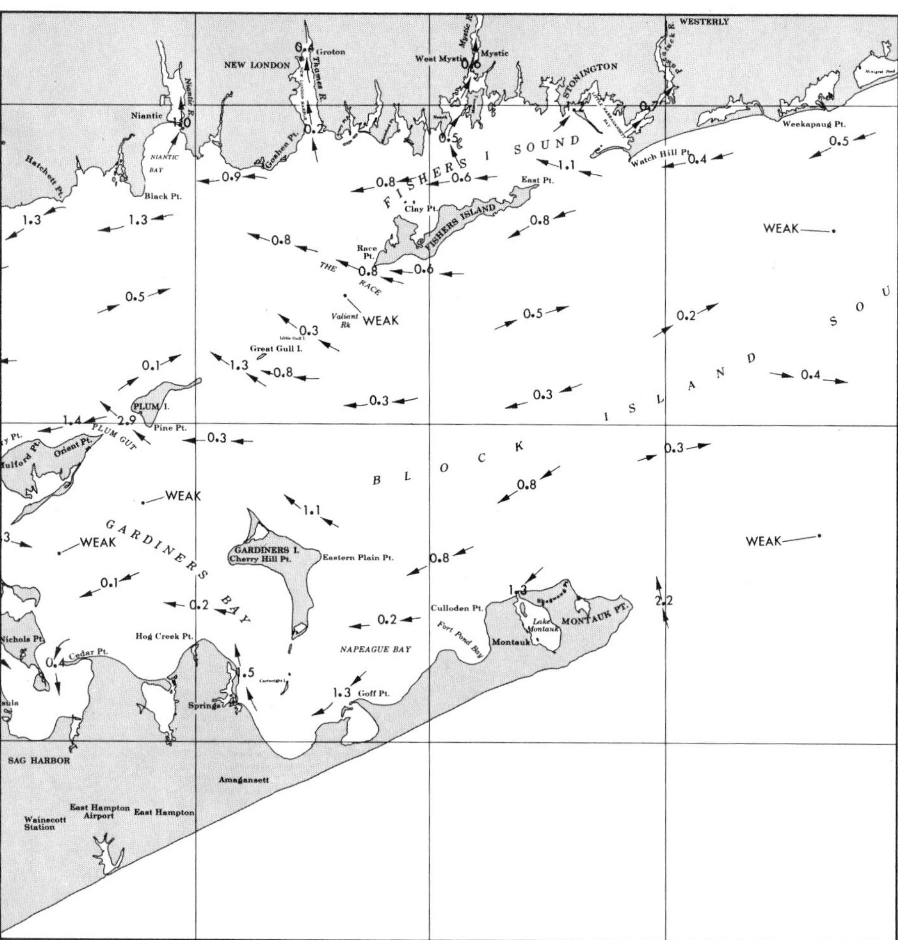

Slack water; flood begins. *When currents are slowest at The Race (top center, running southwest of Fishers Island), there are weak and conflicting currents all across the surrounding waters, as indicated by the labeled arrows. But a 2.9-knot current has already begun to stream northwest into Long Island Sound through a narrow channel that is called Plum Gut (left, middle).*

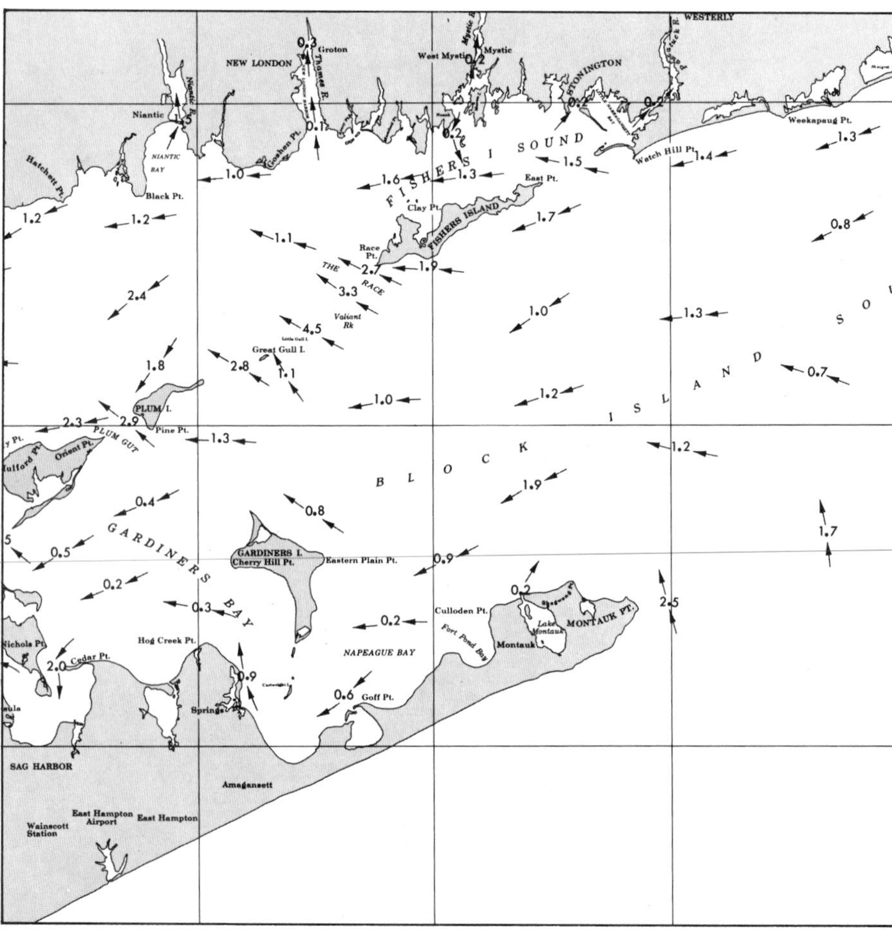

Maximum flood. *Three hours after slack water at The Race, currents flood into Long Island Sound at speeds up to 4.5 knots. As in all current charts, designated velocities are for the twice-monthly periods of spring tides, when currents run strongest. To adjust the figures for periods of weaker currents, the boatman can refer to the front of the current-chart booklet, where there is a correction table and instructions for using it.*

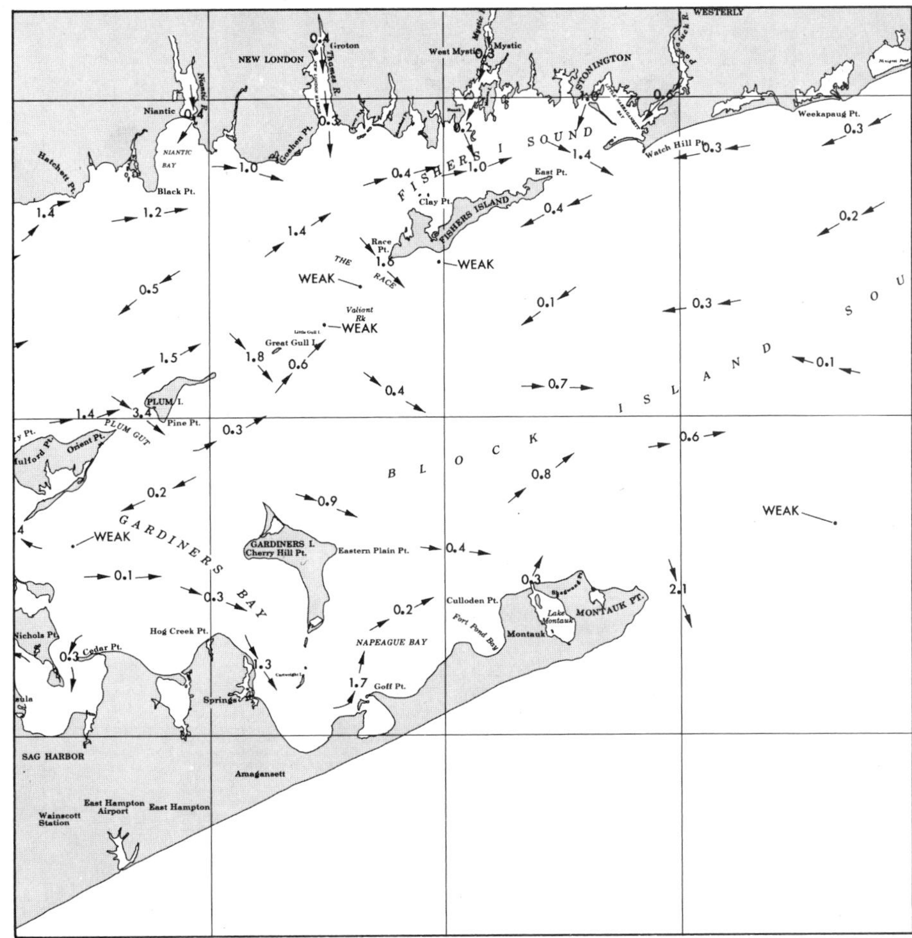

Slack water; ebb begins. *Just as the current turns at The Race, flows are weak and contrary throughout most of the nearby area. But along the north and south shores of Long Island Sound (top left corner), eastward-running currents have begun to quicken, and in the narrow sluice of Plum Gut, the ebb current has already reached 3.4 knots.*

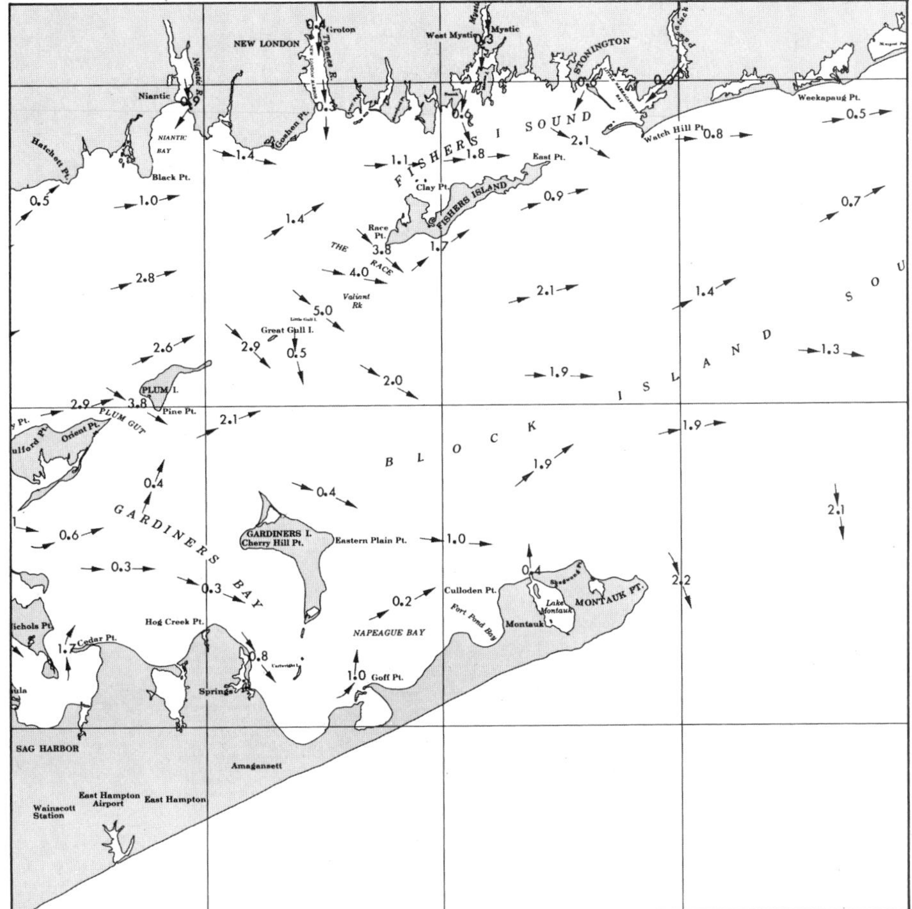

Maximum ebb. *Three hours after slack water at The Race, the ebb current surges southeasterly at speeds up to five knots, and the water now empties through Plum Gut at 3.8 knots. But at one channel, between Plum and Great Gull islands, the flow is only 2.9 knots, making this the easiest passage for a boat heading west into Long Island Sound.*

Working the Angles

Once the strength and direction of the current in a given place on a given day and hour have been calculated, as in the work sheet on page 154, they become vital statistics in plotting a course.

When a boat is running directly with or against the current, figuring the effect is a matter of simple arithmetic: running with a four-knot current adds four knots to the craft's progress over the bottom; bucking the current cuts progress by four knots. In either case, the skipper simply points his bow in the direction of his next mark and sails ahead.

More commonly, however, navigators must contend with a current that runs at an angle to the boat's intended path. The crosscurrent sweeps the boat sideways—and the longer the vessel stays in the current, the farther off course it will be carried, as shown in the diagram at right. So the skipper must adjust his heading in advance to compensate.

Some skippers are experienced enough at traveling through currents to make the proper adjustment by means of an educated guess, especially where distances are short. Over long distances, however—or when visibility is poor or navigational hazards threaten—more accurate methods are essential. One common approach is to work out a current triangle like that at the top of the opposite page.

The triangle is a graphic representation of the strength and direction of the current, and its effect on a moving boat. One line indicates the boat's intended path, or track, and the distance it travels in a given period of time. Since this distance depends on how fast the boat is moving, the length of the line also serves to represent the boat's speed (that is, a line covering 10 miles of chart and two hours of travel time indicates a speed of five knots). A second line, laid down from the destination end of the first line, shows the direction of the current and—by its length—the current's speed. The triangle's third leg provides the answer: the new heading the boat must take and the speed at which it must travel.

In practice, the current triangle may be plotted directly on a chart *(opposite, below)*. Note that the current's direction is shown in degrees relative to true north—the way it is reported in the tidal current tables; the navigator should therefore refer to the compass rose's outer circle when plotting the current on his chart. Other directions—for his course and track—are plotted in degrees magnetic, using the rose's inner circle.

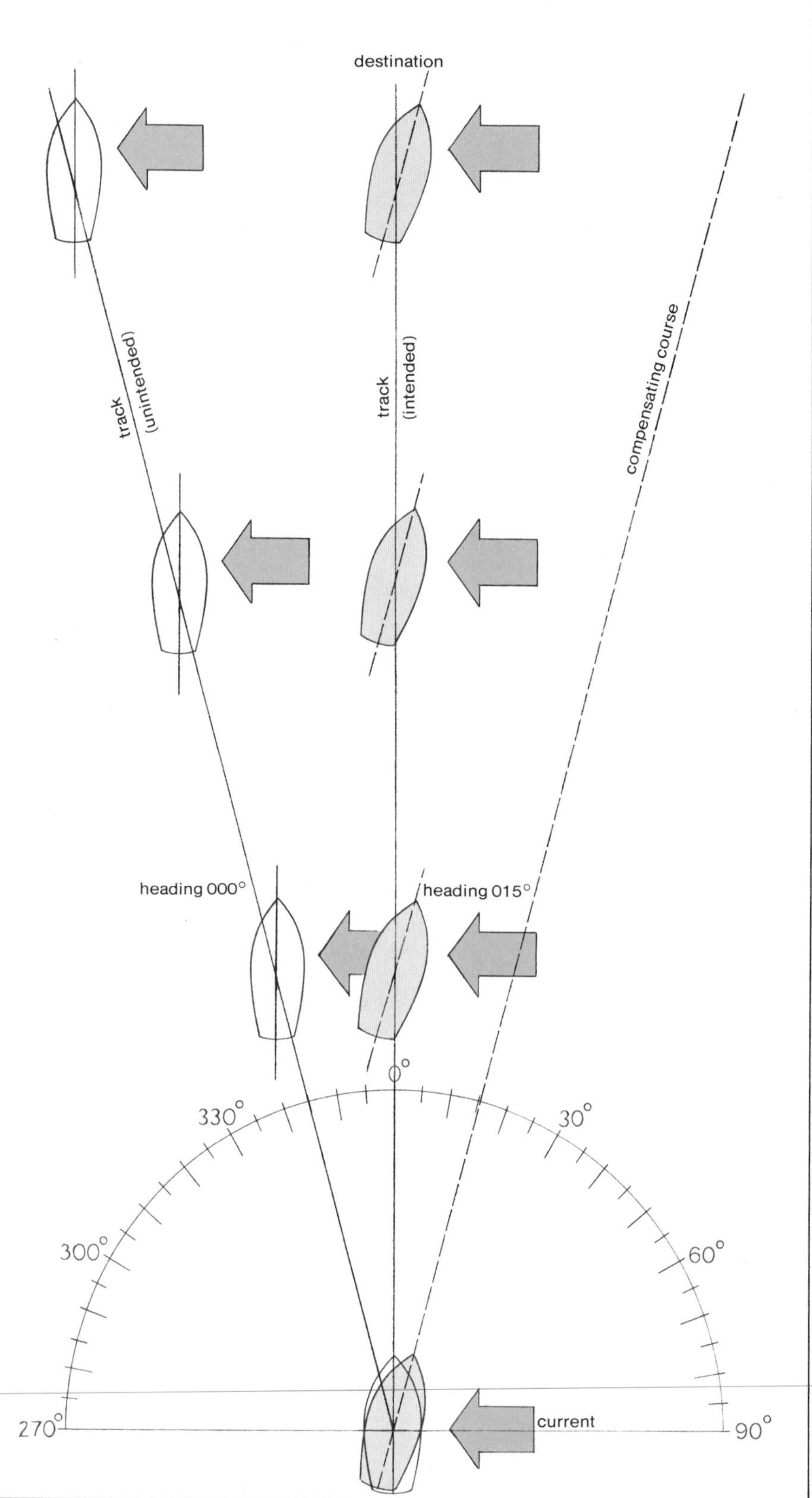

The effect of current on a boat's progress—and the way to correct for it—is shown by the diverging tracks of the two vessels in this diagram. Both are bound for a destination that bears 000°; and both move through a crosscurrent. The white boat heads straight for its objective, making no allowance for this flow; consequently, the current carries it progressively to port of its intended track. The gray boat, however, has anticipated the current, and heads into it slightly, at about 15°. Though the vessel's bow will always be pointed a bit to starboard of its goal, its actual track will lead right there.

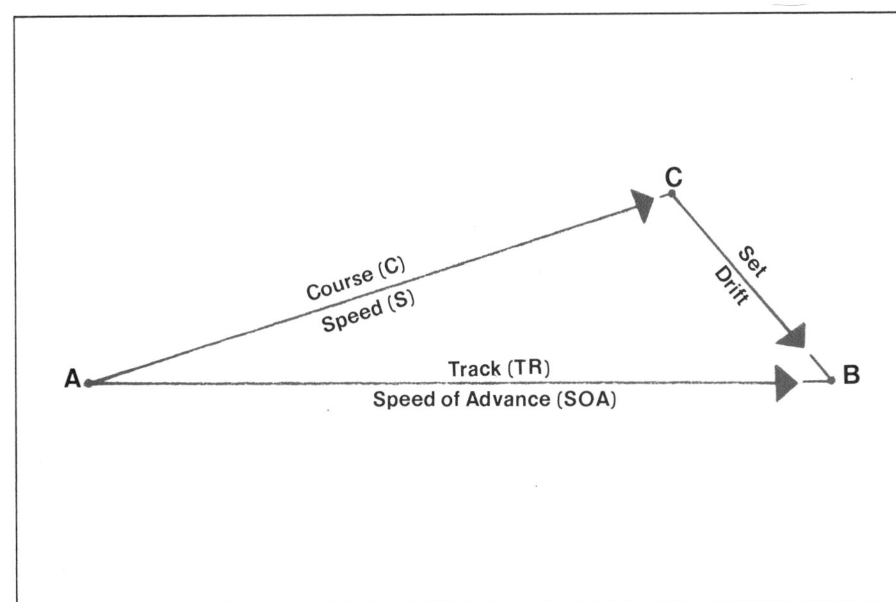

On this current triangle—with its own special shorthand—point A is the boat's starting position, B its destination. Line AB represents the boat's intended track (TR) and speed of advance (SOA); BC shows the current's speed, or drift, and its direction, or set; AC gives the boat's corrected course and speed.

Using a current triangle, the navigator has figured his corrected course from nun "2" to gong "3." He drew his intended track (TR) and measured the distance (three miles). He entered his cruising speed (six knots) as his SOA, and his estimated travel time (30 minutes). He then drew his current line in degrees true (T) and measured off the distance the two-knot current will travel in a half hour (one mile). Lastly, he drew a line from nun "2" to the outer end of the current line to get his heading. The current will push him forward, as well as sideways, so he can cut his speed through the water to five knots.

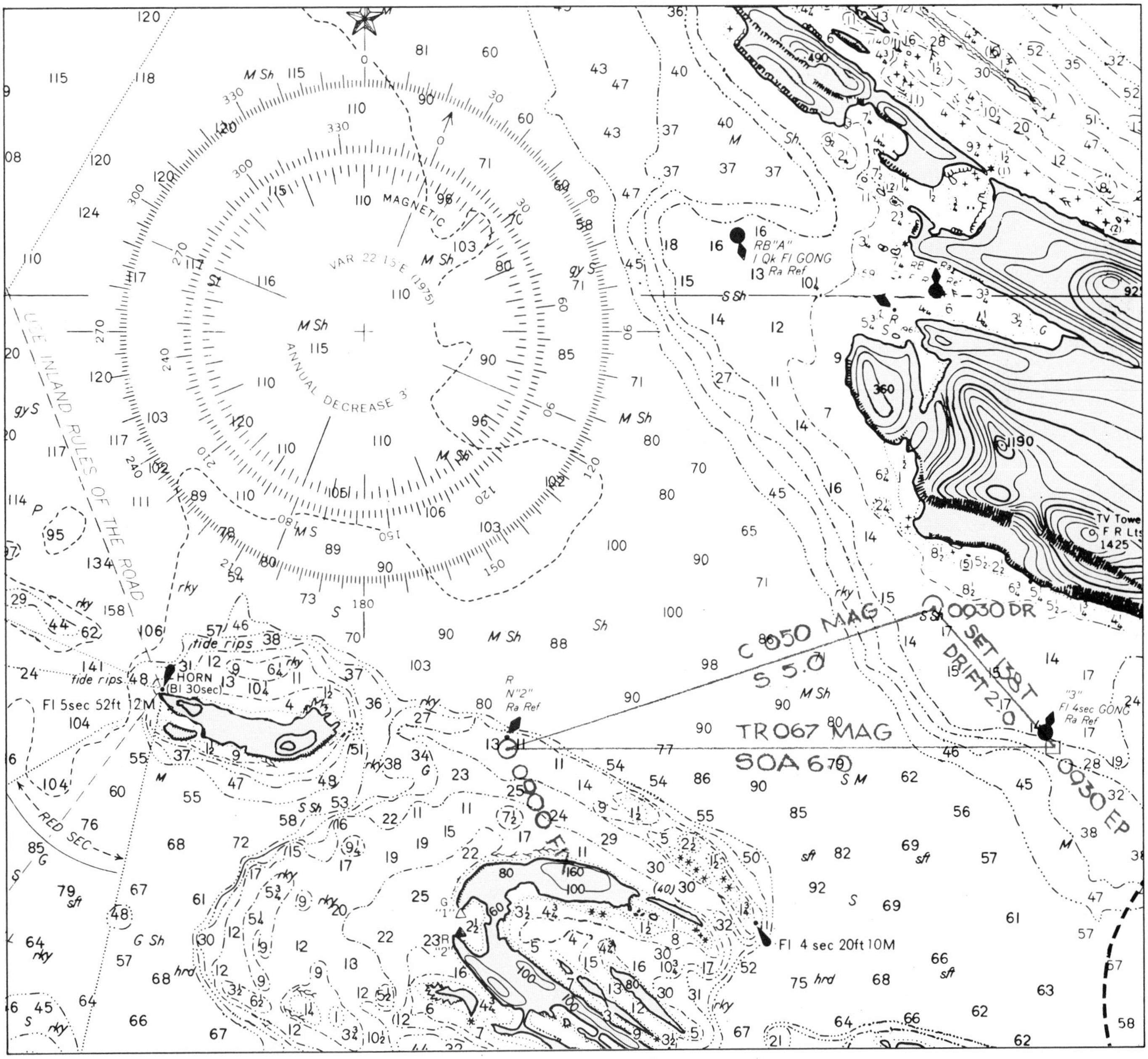

How to Read a River

Unlike currents in tidal channels, which may reverse themselves as often as four times a day, a fresh-water river flows in only one main direction. Yet from bank to bank the internal dynamics of a river at any point can be extremely complex. As the illustrations on these pages show, the flow of every stream, whether it is the lordly Mississippi *(right)* or an unnamed creek in the New Jersey Pine Barrens, varies from spot to spot, depending on the bends and twists the river takes, and on the conformation of its bottom.

The current is strongest along a river's main channel, where the water is deepest. In the shallows near shore, the current tends to grow weaker; as the river bottom rises, it creates an increasing degree of drag on the water, slowing it down. Depending on a river bed's particular contours, the forward flow may stop altogether near the bank, or it may even be sent into a reverse spin, eddying upstream before being pulled back into the faster downriver current.

If the river is fairly straight, the main current is usually in the middle. But wherever the river curves, the main current is thrown as though by centrifugal force to the outside bank *(opposite, below)*. There, the current's impact erodes the bank and deepens the bottom just under it; as a result, the current speeds up. Along the inside of the curve, however, the current slackens, leaving deposits of silt that build up into shoals. Because of this constant erosion and sedimentation, the river's bottom conformation continually changes; the boatman cruising along the stream should pay special attention both to navigation aids and to his depth finder.

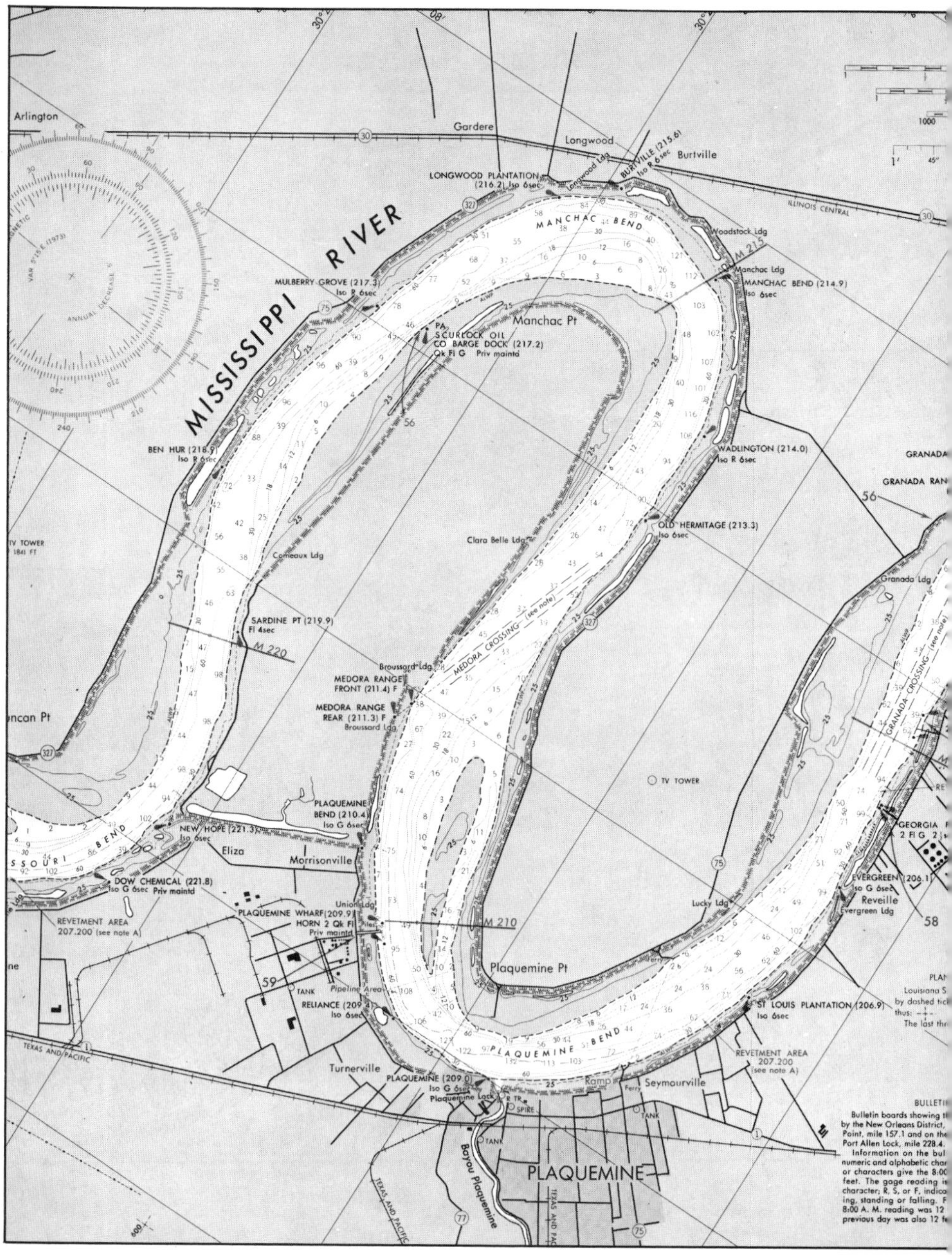

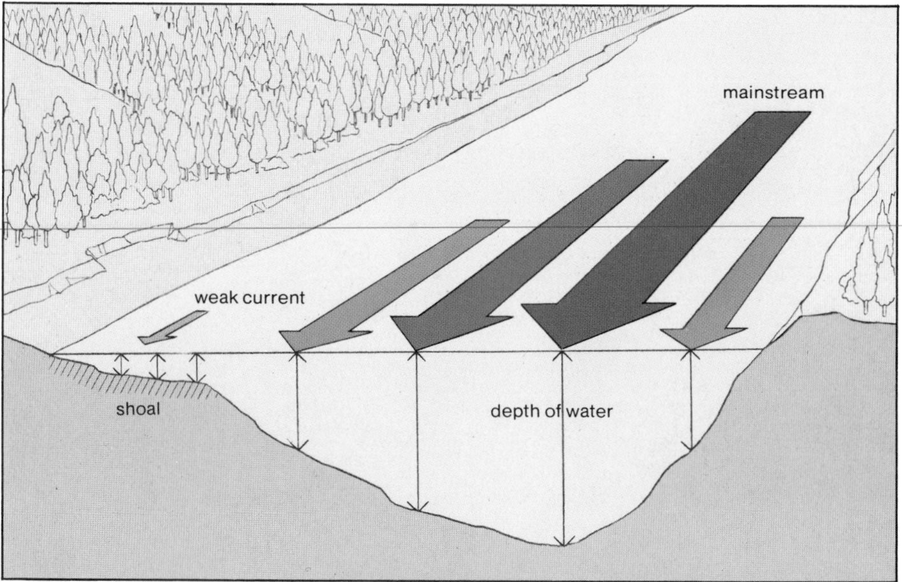

As a river flows along its bed, contours of the bottom and the banks constantly modify the speed of the current, as represented by the arrows in the diagram at right. The mainstream (wide, dark-tinted arrow) moves deepest and fastest; the skipper traveling downriver may add several knots to his forward speed by riding it. Conversely, a boatman who is headed upriver can stay in shallower water where there are weaker currents (paler arrows) to go against.

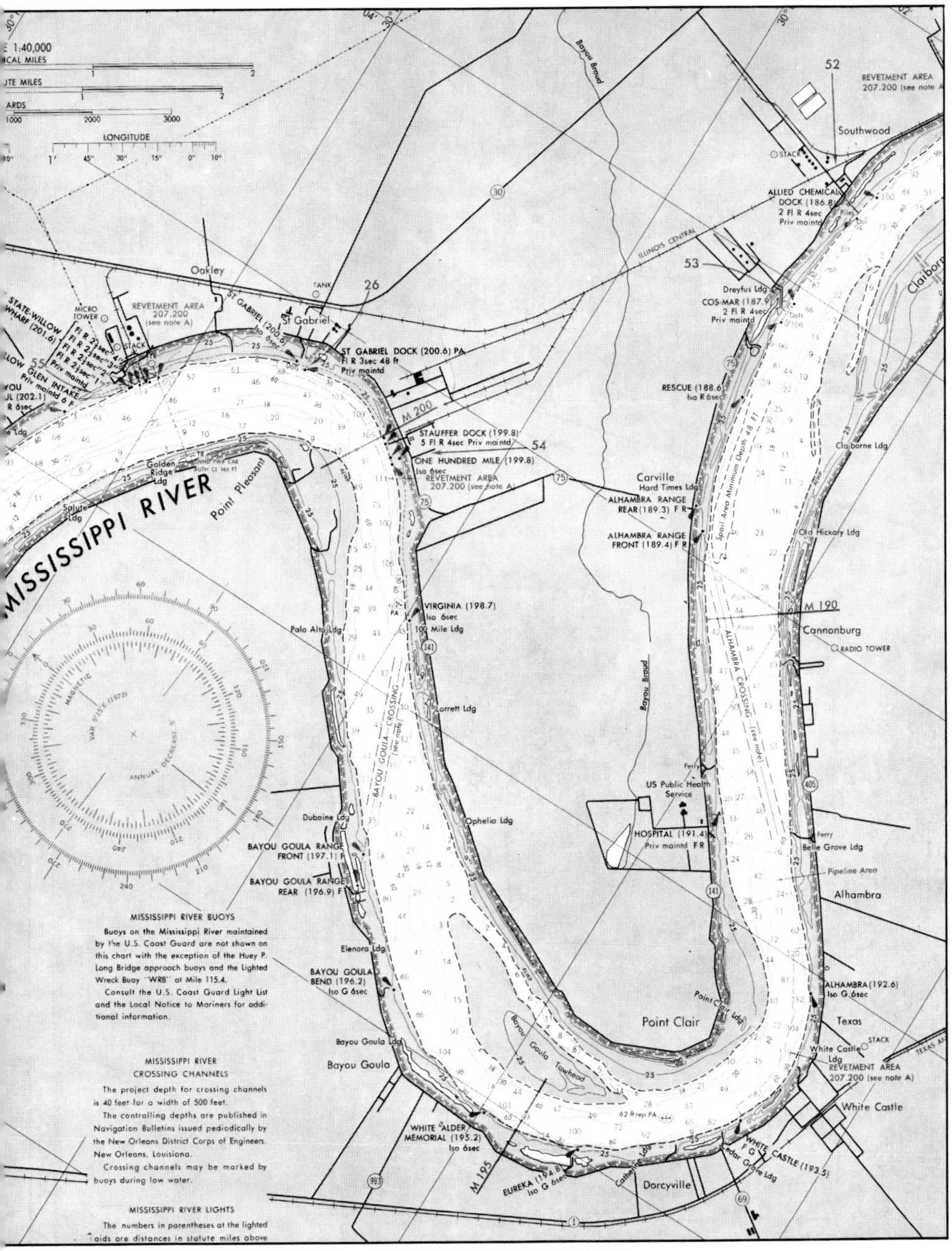

MISSISSIPPI RIVER BUOYS

Buoys on the Mississippi River maintained by the U.S. Coast Guard are not shown on this chart with the exception of the Huey P. Long Bridge approach buoys and the Lighted Wreck Buoy "WRB" at Mile 115.4.

Consult the U.S. Coast Guard Light List and the Local Notice to Mariners for additional information.

MISSISSIPPI RIVER CROSSING CHANNELS

The project depth for crossing channels is 40 feet for a width of 500 feet.

The controlling depths are published in Navigation Bulletins issued pediodically by the New Orleans District Corps of Engineers, New Orleans, Louisiana.

Crossing channels may be marked by buoys during low water.

MISSISSIPPI RIVER LIGHTS

The numbers in parentheses at the lighted aids are distances in statute miles above

A charted stretch of the Mississippi River just south of Baton Rouge, Louisiana, demonstrates the typical placement of deep and shoal water as a river rounds each bend. Although this graphic information, when translated into current patterns (below), can save a boatman hours of travel time, he should remember that river depths are unstable at curves, where the antagonistic forces of shoal building and erosion are at constant war. In hugging the insides, therefore, he should factor in a judicious safety margin in using charted river depths.

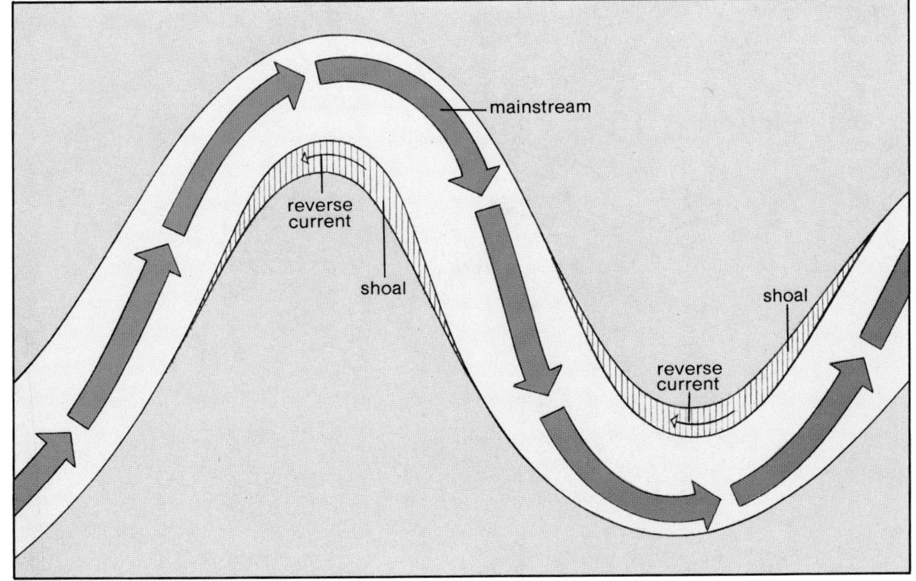

When flowing through a series of curves a river's mainstream, represented here by heavy blue arrows, caroms from the outer wall of one bend to the outer wall of the next. Currents on the inside of each bend move considerably slower and may occasionally swing around completely to create a backwater over shoals, as shown. By keeping to the inside while traveling upstream, the boatman not only can avoid the main current —which can move at five and a half knots along the Mississippi during the spring runoff —but may even get a lift from the eddies.

Catching a bone in her teeth, the 79-foot ketch Kialoa churns through Gulf Stream waters off Florida. Built by California racing enthusiast Jim Kilroy, the vessel is equipped with the finest in navigation gear, including omni, loran and a sea thermometer that registered Kialoa's entry into the warm flow of the Stream itself.

Racing the Gulf Stream

No condition of tide or current challenges a navigator's skill more thoroughly than does the broad river of wind-driven tropical water known as the Gulf Stream, which sweeps up the eastern coast of North America and out into the Atlantic. The speed of this current—and even its exact location—changes in often mystifying and unpredictable ways. But for the navigator of a sleek ocean racer like the one at left, a knowledge of just where the main flow of the Gulf Stream may be and how fast it is moving on any given day can mean the difference between winning a trophy or finishing somewhere in the ruck.

The vessel challenging the Stream on these pages is the ketch *Kialoa,* shown during her run in the 1975 Ocean Triangle Race between Florida and the Great Bahama Bank. The navigator, Scott Perry *(right, standing),* had to contend with light, fluky winds at the start, and an unexpected westward shift in the Gulf Stream's axis. To prepare for the current's erratic behavior, Perry armed himself with a sheaf of information on the flow in past years that helped him estimate its probable strength and position. To determine just when *Kialoa* entered the Stream, he referred to a simple but effective device—a sea thermometer that jumped a telltale 4° in the current's warm waters. In addition, Perry closely monitored *Kialoa's* progress through the Stream's path with a steady sequence of omni and loran fixes. Perry's careful navigating paid off, as *Kialoa* sailed the 132-mile course in just 15 and a half hours, bringing her home well ahead of the fleet.

Minutes before the 9 a.m. starting gun, helmsman Kilroy and navigator Scott Perry, holding a stopwatch, prepare for a dual struggle with the Gulf Stream and competing boats. In any race whose course crosses the Stream, the boat that best calculates—or guesses—the current's speed and location may receive a boost that means victory.

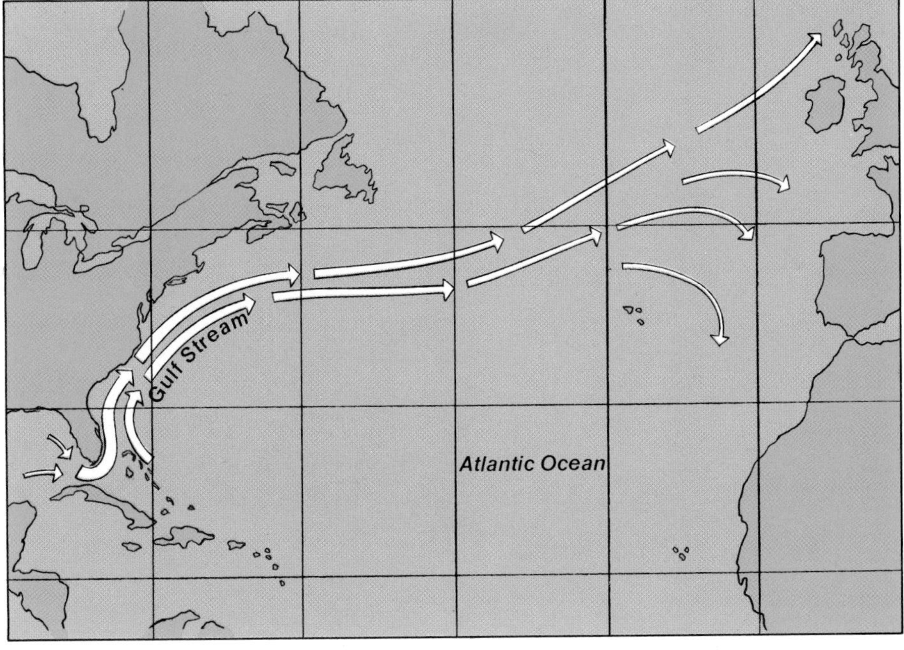

The Gulf Stream begins where wind-driven feeder currents from the Gulf of Mexico and surrounding tropical waters funnel through the narrow straits between Florida and Cuba. From there the Stream surges northward up the Atlantic coast, saltier and significantly warmer than the sea around it. Diminishing to a sluggish drift as it veers eastward across the Atlantic, the Stream splits into subsidiary currents and then finally dissipates against the coasts of Europe and West Africa.

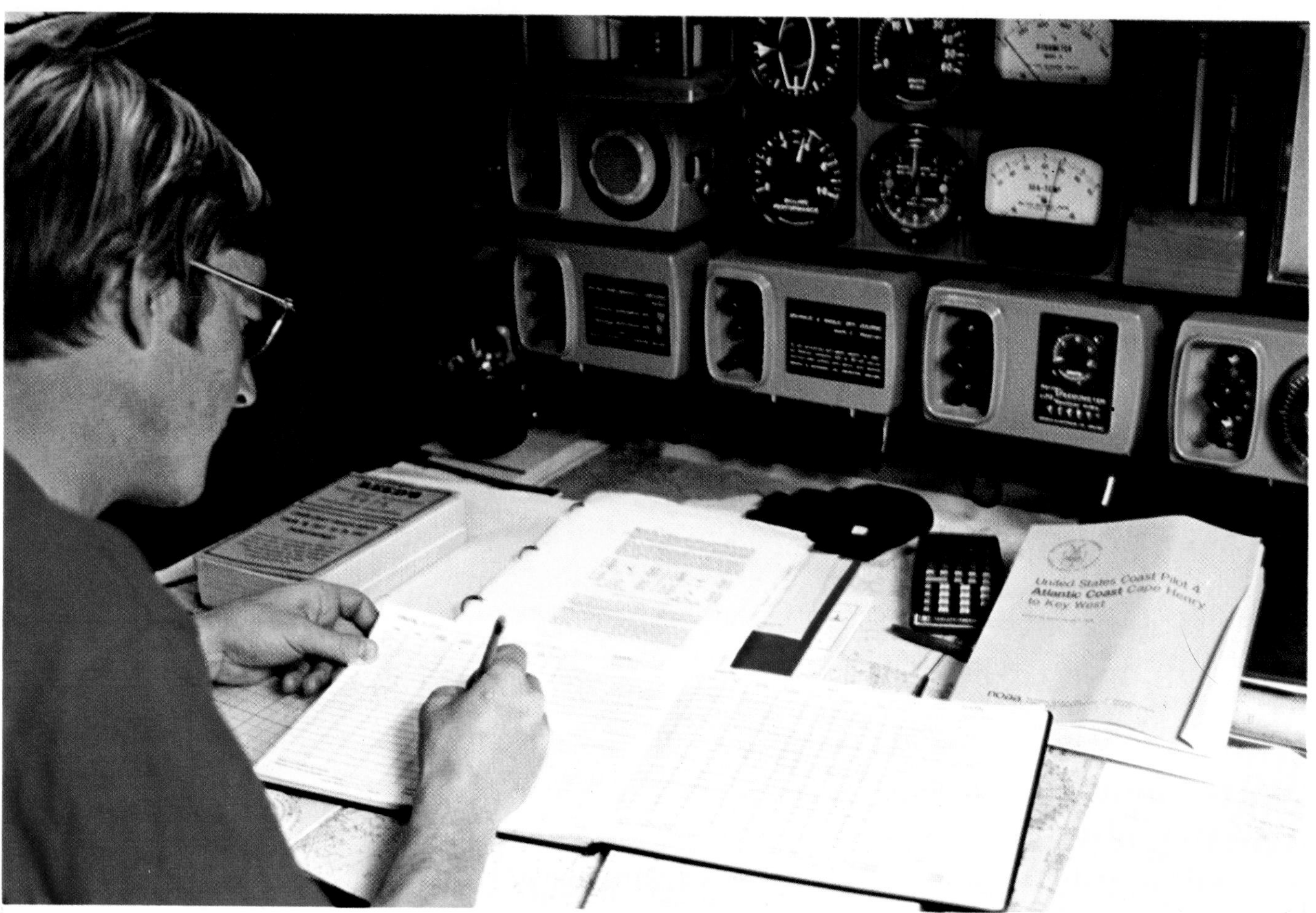

Tucked belowdecks in the navigator's nook, Perry keeps a running record of Kialoa's progress in a logbook. Depth soundings, wind direction and speed, boat speed, and sea temperatures can be instantly assessed by reading the various dials and gauges in the console behind the chart table. On the table, next to a blue-jacketed NOS Coast Pilot volume for the Florida area, is a pocket computer that allows Perry to test in advance the effect of different headings on Kialoa's forward progress toward the next mark.

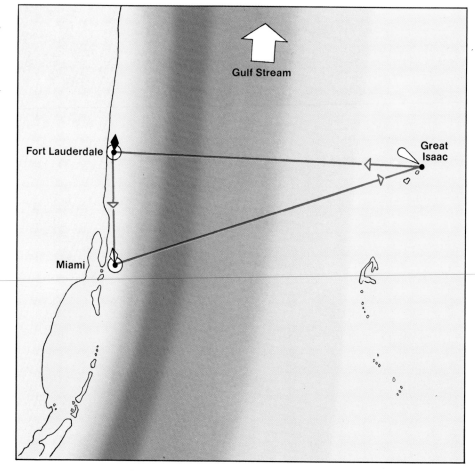

The course of the Ocean Triangle Race runs east-northeast from the Miami sea buoy, around Great Isaac Light, west to the Fort Lauderdale sea buoy and south again to the starting point. The Gulf Stream, tinted in progressively darker shades of blue to indicate the strength of its flow, is a major factor throughout the race, but especially on the first two long legs. About 45 miles wide at this point, the current runs north at an average three to four knots along its strongest axis, slightly to the west of center, and diminishes by about a knot along the edges.

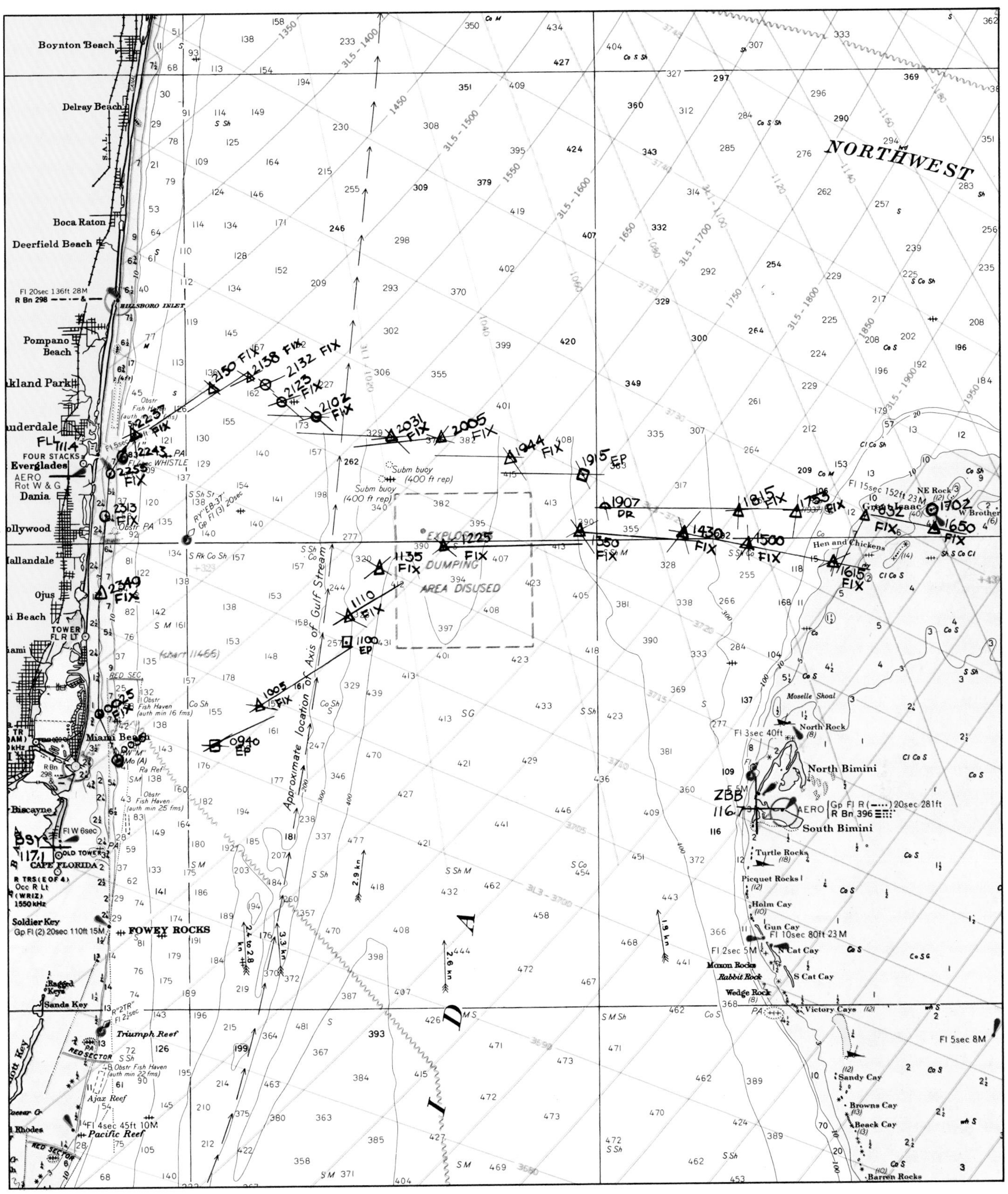

On this chart of Kialoa's progress, the sequence of Perry's fixes shows that even the best-laid plots often need revising to account for wind and current shifts. Sailing in light air for the first half of the outbound leg, and carried steadily north by the Gulf Stream, Kialoa edged well above the direct course line. Then, at 1150, she picked up a strong northeasterly wind that carried her to the first mark. On the second leg, to offset the current, Perry called for a heading slightly south of the straight-line, or rhumb-line, course. But an unexpected one-knot increase in the current's strength and a five-mile westward shift of its axis sent Kialoa north again as she neared the second mark.

Driving hard into a 22-knot wind, helmsman Kilroy urges Kialoa on through choppy Gulf Stream seas. The crew has taken a reef in the mizzen, and now checks the trim of the main. The strong breeze held steady until the end of the race, giving the 42-ton Kialoa a powerful push toward the finish line.

As Kialoa nears the Miami sea buoy—and the finish line—Scott Perry reports her position to the race committee. The clock on the bulkhead behind him shows the time to be 12:25, shortly after midnight. Kialoa crossed the line 10 minutes later, the first to finish out of a fleet of 86 boats.

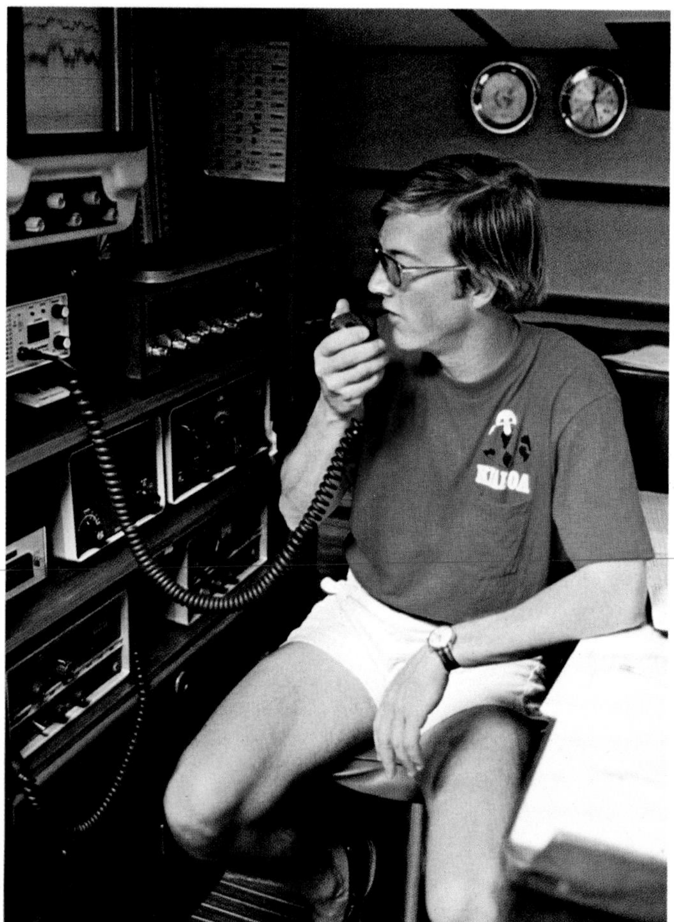

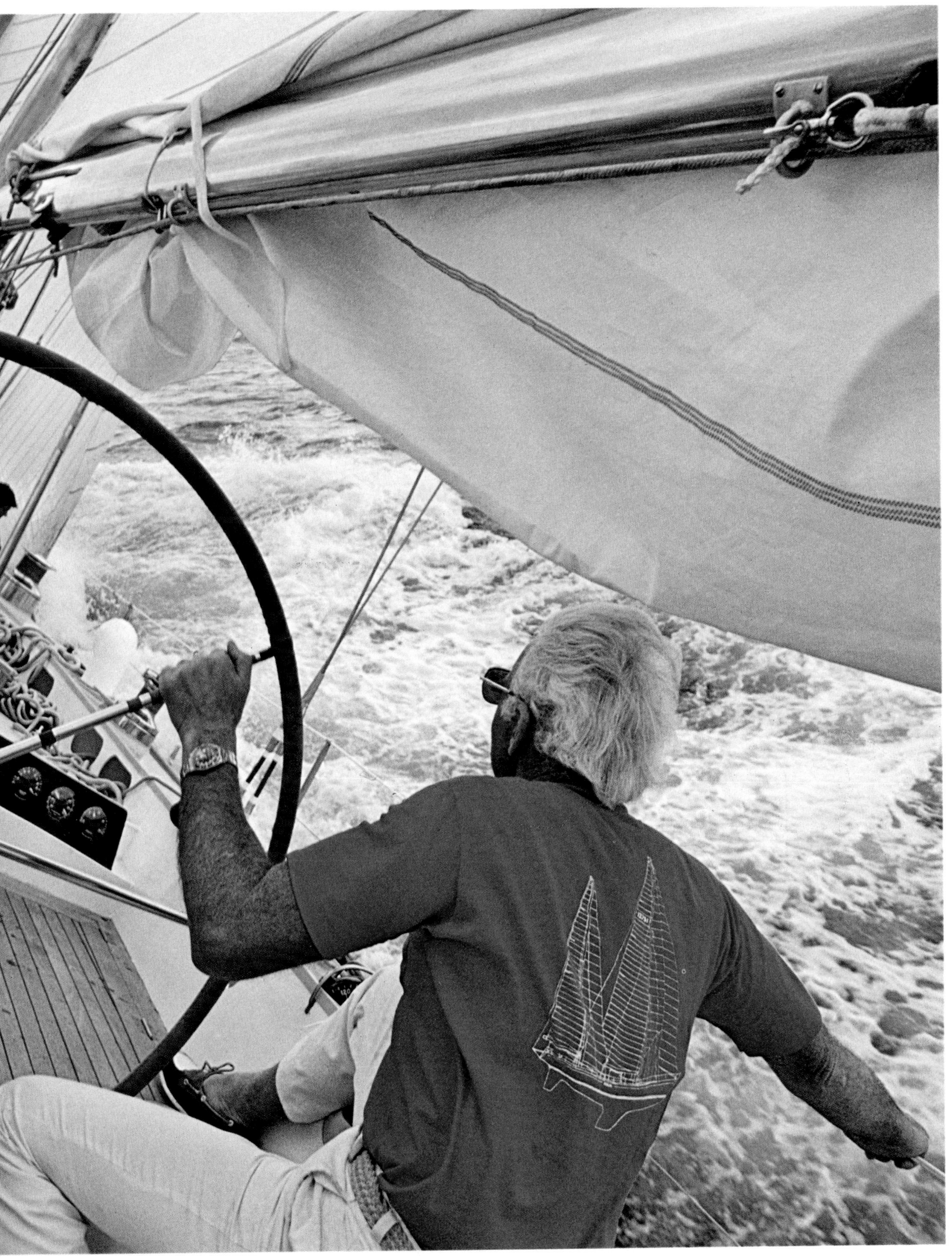

Pilot's Guide to Navigation Aids

The position and pertinent features of any aid to navigation, from the smallest buoy to the tallest light station, are marked on charts in a concise language of symbols, abbreviations and terse notations. Each symbol has its own distinctive shape, and is exaggerated in scale for easy recognition. Often the symbols are colored in significant ways, e.g., reddish-purple for a red nun. A complete listing of symbols is included in the light lists and Chart No. 1; samples of the most common are given below.

Lights

A magenta teardrop or disc indicates a lighted aid. Abbreviated labels, and sometimes additional symbols, define the light's particular nature.

Position of Light

Indicated by a black dot beneath the teardrop, or at the center of the disc.

Riprap around Light

Boulders called riprap, piled around a light's base to protect the structure from waves.

Light Beacon

A beacon equipped with an identifying light.

Aeronautical Light

A light intended to guide airplane pilots, but that can also be used by mariners.

Lightship

A permanently anchored ship that serves as a lighted aid to navigation.

Sector Light

A colored light shining over a precise area, usually of danger, shown by dotted lines.

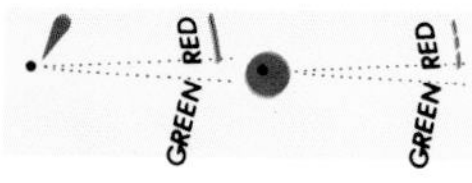

Directional Light

A light that marks a safe channel (dotted lines) by bracketing it with two color sectors.

Buoys and Day Beacons

Buoys are symbolized by an elongated diamond shape, which may be color coded and labeled. Triangles indicate day beacons.

Position of Buoy

Indicated by a black dot—or sometimes by a circle—just below the diamond.

Light Buoy

Indicated by a magenta teardrop or disc accompanying the buoy's position mark.

Nun

A buoy with a conical top.

Can

A buoy that is cylindrical in shape.

R "2" R "2" **Starboard-Hand Buoy**

A red even-numbered buoy, left to starboard by a boat returning to harbor; the diamond may be tinted or uncolored.

"1" **Port-Hand Buoy**

A black odd-numbered buoy, left to port by a returning boat; the diamond is tinted black.

BW **Mid-Channel Buoy**

A buoy with black and white vertical stripes, used to mark the center of a channel.

Junction Buoy

A buoy with horizontal bands of red and black, marking the junction of two channels; may also mark wrecks or other obstructions.

Y **Quarantine Buoy**

A yellow buoy designating an anchorage where boats from foreign ports await clearance.

BW **Fish-Net Buoy**

A buoy with black and white horizontal bands that warns of commercial fish nets.

W **Anchorage Buoy**

A solid-white buoy, indicating that portion of a congested area where boats may anchor.

Priv maintd **Private Aid to Navigation**

A privately owned and maintained buoy.

Bn **Day Beacon**

A fixed, unlighted aid to navigation.

MARKER **Range Marker**

Sometimes accompanied by a dotted line that shows the direction of the range.

W Or W Or **Special-Purpose Buoy**

An orange-and-white buoy—used mainly by the government—to mark restricted areas.

Radio Installations

A small circle with an interior dot pinpoints radio towers or beacons. A larger magenta circle marks radio beacons intended specifically for navigation.

Radio Beacon

A beacon for taking bearings by RDF.

R TR (WBAL) 1090 kHz **Commercial Broadcasting Station**

Radio tower; the station's call letters and broadcast frequency are indicated.

AERO R Bn 302 **Aeronautical Radio Beacon**

A beacon for airline pilots, also usable by boatmen equipped with RDF; always accompanied by the beacon's broadcast frequency and its Morse-code signal.

Fog Signals

These warning sounds can be identified by the characteristics of their noisemaking device—which is always noted on the chart.

DIA **Diaphone**
A signal activated by compressed air that begins with a high-pitched blast and ends with a deeper tone.

SIREN **Siren**
Similar to the whine of a police siren.

HORN **Horn**
Electrically powered signal with a slightly higher pitch than that of an automobile horn.

WHIS **Whistle**
A low-pitched, mournful hoot that is activated by wave motion.

BELL **Bell**
A single tone, irregularly repeated, similar in sound to a church bell.

GONG **Gong**
A multitoned signal produced by four separate gongs striking at random.

Supplementary Notations

Besides the standard abbreviations that are given above, some aids are accompanied on the chart with other abbreviated information. For example, 10 M means that a light's range is 10 nautical miles. And Alt. Fl. W 30sec, R 30sec describes a light's signature as alternating 30-second flashes of white and red.

Alt	**Alternating**	B	**Black**
M	**Nautical mile**	Bu	**Blue**
m; min	**Minutes of time**	G	**Green**
Ra Ref	**Radar reflector**	Or	**Orange**
Rot	**Rotating**	R	**Red**
sec	**Seconds of time**	W	**White**
SEC	**Sector**	Y	**Yellow**

Glossary

Abeam A direction at right angles to the centerline of the boat.

Back The wind is said to back when it changes in a counterclockwise direction, as from northeast to northwest. The opposite is to veer.

Beacon A freestanding or fixed aid to navigation, smaller than a light station.

Beam The width of the boat at its widest part. A boat is "on her beam ends" when heeled over 90°.

Bear To lie in a specified direction from a designated reference point; also, to move or tend to move in a certain direction.

Bearing The direction in which an object is seen, or the direction of one object from another, expressed in compass points or degrees. A true bearing is one expressed in degrees relative to true north; a magnetic bearing is one expressed in degrees relative to magnetic north.

Binnacle Housing of the compass.

Bone in her teeth A colloquial phrase implying that a boat is moving through the water at considerable speed. The "bone" is the bow wave thus produced.

Bow The forward part of the boat. (The word prow, cherished by poets, describes a ship's ornamented stem and is otherwise avoided by seamen.)

Box the compass To name the 32 points of the compass in sequence from north through east, south, west, back to north.

Buoy A floating aid to navigation used to mark the navigable limits of channels, indicate hazards, define anchorages, post local regulations, etc.

Can An unlighted cylindrical buoy.

Cardinal mark A navigation aid—used in the Uniform State Waterway Marking System—that is color-coded to indicate the compass direction around which it should be passed. A red-topped cardinal mark may be passed to the south or west, a black-topped one to north or east.

Chart recorder A highly sensitive depth finder in which the readings are noted by stylus traces on moving tape, often used by fishermen to locate schools of fish.

Clutter Unwanted reflections on a radar screen, commonly from rain, snow or sleet.

Cocked hat A small polygon formed by three or more bearing lines intersecting on a chart. The position of the ship from which the bearings have been taken is assumed to be within that polygon.

Compass card A circular card marked either in degrees or compass points to indicate the direction a boat is heading in—or that an object bears from the boat.

Compass point One of 32 divisions of the compass card equal to an arc of 11¼ degrees. The cardinal points are north, east, south and west; the intercardinal points are northeast, southeast, southwest and northwest.

Compass rose Two concentric circles, each divided into 360 degrees or 32 points, printed on nautical charts and used for laying off courses or bearings. The outer circle is graduated in degrees true, the inner circle in degrees magnetic.

Contour line A line on a chart connecting points of equal depth or elevation.

Controlling depth The minimum depth of a specified channel.

Countercurrent A current flowing in a direction opposite to that of the principal current.

Course The direction in which a ship is steering in making her way from point to point during a voyage. A magnetic course is the direction of the ship's heading relative to magnetic north; a compass course is the direction of the ship's heading based on the ship's compass (including errors of deviation and variation).

Course line The graphic representation on a chart of a ship's course, normally used in constructing a dead-reckoning plot.

Danger bearing A line drawn on a chart from a visible, charted object to a navigational hazard. The navigator uses the magnetic bearing of this line to warn him when his course is leading him too close to the danger.

Day beacon An unlit beacon.

Daymark The colored and numbered or lettered sign placed on many beacons to identify them. Most daymarks are coated with reflective material to make them visible in a searchlight beam at night.

Dead reckoning The process of projecting a ship's position based on the course steered and the distance run since the vessel's last known position; commonly abbreviated as DR.

Depth finder An instrument for measuring the depth of the water by means of a timed sonic pulse; also known as depth sounder or echo sounder.

Deviation The error in a magnetic compass caused by magnetic influences on board a boat. Deviation is described as being easterly or westerly according to whether the ship's compass is deflected east or west of magnetic north.

Diaphone A compressed-air sound-signal apparatus used in light stations to produce warning signals during fog.

Directional antenna A bar antenna used by radio direction finders to locate the bearing of a radio station.

Dividers An instrument with two pointed legs, hinged where the upper ends join; used to measure distances on a scale and transfer them to a chart, or vice versa.

Doubling the angle on the bow A method of obtaining a running fix by measuring the angles in a triangle formed by the boat's course line and two successive bearings taken on the same object.

Draft The depth a vessel extends below the waterline.

Drift The speed, in knots, of a current.

Drum lens A nonrotating Fresnel-type lens often used on lighted buoys.

Ebb The tidal movement of water away from the land and toward the sea, as in ebb current; the falling of the water level from high tide to low tide, as in ebb tide.

Estimated position (EP) In piloting, an approximate position obtained from incomplete data; less accurate than a fix.

Fathom A nautical measure equal to six feet; used for measuring water depths, and also for indicating the lengths of lead lines, cordage and anchor chains.

Fathom line A line on a chart connecting equal water depths and thereby marking the contours of underwater geographical features.

Fetch The distance along open water or land over which the wind blows; to achieve a desired destination under sail, particularly with an adverse wind or tide.

Fix A boat's position as marked on a chart, established by taking bearings on two or more known landmarks (visual fix) or two or more radio sources (electronic fix).

Flashing Description of a light—fixed on a navigation aid—that flashes on and off. The period of light is always briefer than the period of darkness.

Flood The movement of water toward the land and away from the sea; the rising of the water level from low tide to high tide.

Fore and aft A boat's longitudinal axis.

Fresnel lens A glass lens composed of an aggregation of prisms that concentrate and direct light in horizontal beams.

Gain control A device installed on marine radio receivers to improve the clarity of radio signals; also used for the same purpose on radar sets.

Genoa A large headsail set on the headstay and overlapping the mainsail.

Hand bearing compass A hand-held compass incorporating a sighting apparatus and used primarily for taking bearings.

Head The forward part of a boat, including the bow and adjacent areas; the uppermost corner of a triangular sail; a seagoing lavatory.

Heading The direction in which a boat's head is pointed.

Height of tide The amount of water above or below mean low water at any given time in the tide cycle.

Helm The device, usually a tiller or wheel, connected to the rudder, by which a boat is steered.

Intracoastal Waterway The system of inland waterway channels running along the Atlantic and Gulf coasts of the United States from Manasquan Inlet, New Jersey, to the Mexican border in Texas; commonly abbreviated as ICW.

Isophase Description of a light—fixed on a navigation aid—that flashes on and off at equal intervals.

Jibe To turn a boat's stern through the wind so that the sails swing from one side of the boat to the other, putting the boat on another tack.

Ketch A boat with a two-masted rig in which the larger, or mainmast, is forward, and the smaller mizzenmast is stepped aft—but forward of the rudder and usually of the helm.

KiloHertz (kHz) A unit, equal to one thousand cycles per second, used to describe radio frequency.

Knot A nautical mile equal in distance to one minute of latitude, or 1.15 statute miles; a common contraction for speed expressed in nautical miles per hour.

Landfall A sighting of or coming to land, also the land so approached or reached; the land first sighted at the end of a sea voyage.

Lead When pronounced "leed," the direction of a line; when pronounced "led," the metal weight at the end of a line used for taking soundings.

Lead line A line marked off in fathoms and weighted at one end with a lead, used for measuring water depths; also called a sounding line.

Leeway The lateral movement of a ship caused by the force of the wind.

Leg A section of a vessel's track or plotted course along a single heading; in a race, one of the marked portions of the course; also, the path a sailboat takes between tacks when beating to windward.

Life lines Safety lines and guardrails rigged around a boat's deck to prevent the crew from being washed overboard.

Line of position A straight line somewhere along which a ship is presumed to be. The line may be determined either by ranges, or by visual or electronic bearings.

Log A device for measuring the rate of a ship's motion through the water; also, a ship's journal or written record of the vessel's day-by-day performance, listing speeds, distances traveled, weather conditions, landfalls and other information.

Loran A radio positioning system that allows navigators to make position fixes by the reception of synchronized low-frequency radio transmissions. The word loran is an acronym for *lo*ng-*ra*nge *n*avigation.

Lubber line A mark on the inside of the compass bowl that indicates the fore-and-aft—or athwartships—line of a boat.

Magnetic north The spot on the earth toward which magnetic compass needles tend to point.

Mainsail The sail set on the after side of the mainmast, usually the biggest working sail; often called simply the main.

Mark The generic term for navigation aids such as buoys and beacons.

Mean high water The average level of high tide for any area.

Mean low water The average level of low tide for any area.

MegaHertz (mHz) A unit, equal to one million cycles per second, used to describe radio frequency.

Mizzen The sail set on the aftermast of a yawl or ketch.

Neap tide A tide of less than average range, occurring at the first and third quarters of the moon.

Null The compass point at which a radio direction finder's directional antenna receives the weakest signal from a given RDF station, thereby indicating the station's bearing.

Nun A partially conical, unlighted buoy.

Occulting Description of a light—fixed on a navigation aid—that is eclipsed at regular intervals. The duration of light is always greater than the duration of darkness.

Omni A navigation system that provides bearings by means of a VHF radio signal; also known as visual omni range (VOR). The system was originally designed for aviators, but is also used by mariners.

Parallel rules Two rulers connected by metal straps that allow the rules to separate but remain parallel; used in chart work to apply the readings on a compass rose to various plotted course and bearing lines, or vice versa.

Piloting The act of guiding a vessel, and fixing her position, by means of visible landmarks and aids to navigation, charts and various instruments.

Port The left side of a boat, when looking forward.

Quarter Either side of a boat's stern.

Radar A means of locating objects by reflected superhigh-frequency radio pulses. The word radar is an acronym for *ra*dio *d*etection *a*nd *r*anging.

Radial A term used by operators of omni sets to designate bearings either to or from an omni transmitter.

Radio beacon Marine radio transmitters operated by the Coast Guard and positioned along U.S. coastal waters and the Great Lakes to aid boatmen in piloting by means of radio direction-finding equipment; designated R Bn on nautical charts.

Radio direction finder (RDF) A specialized marine radio capable of establishing the bearing of the station whose signal it is receiving.

Range The alignment of two prominent objects or landmarks that gives a navigator a line of position; two fixed navigation aids whose alignment helps to guide a vessel through a channel; the distance at which a lighted navigation aid may be seen.

Range lights Two navigation lights, one higher than the other and located some distance apart, set upon ranges.

Reef To reduce sail area without removing the sail entirely, done by partially lowering the sail and securing loose fabric along the foot of the sail or the boom.

Relative bearing A bearing stated as a direction relative to the ship's fore-and-aft line, expressed in compass points or degrees from her bow, beam or quarter, as in "two points off the starboard bow."

Rhumb line The path a boat follows when sailing toward a specific point on the compass; on a Mercator chart, a straight line.

Run To sail before the wind; also, the narrowing part of the hull, aft, underwater.

Running fix A position determined by the intersection of two lines of position obtained from bearings taken at different times, often on the same object.

Sea buoys The first buoys a mariner encounters when approaching a channel or harbor entrance from the sea.

Sea return A term used to describe radar reflections from waves around the boat. Most radar sets have sensitivity knobs to reduce sea return.

Sector A colored segment in the sweep of a navigation light. A red sector, for example, warns of dangerous waters.

Set The direction in which a current is moving, expressed in compass degrees; also, the direction in which a boat is pushed by current or wind.

Shadow pin A vertical pin mounted at the center of a compass card, used in taking bearings.

Slack water The period of little or no current about halfway between maximum flood and maximum ebb currents.

Sounding Water depth at a given spot, measured in feet or fathoms; a chart notation of water depth, at mean low water; the act of measuring water depth with a lead line or a depth finder.

Speed of advance (SOA) The average speed in knots needed to cover a given distance over the bottom in a given amount of time.

Spring tide A tide of greater than average range, occurring around the times of new and full moons.

Starboard The right side of a boat, looking forward.

Superhigh frequency (SHF) A designated band of the radio spectrum, from 3,000 to 30,000 mHz.

Swinging ship The process of determining the deviation of a ship's compass by putting the vessel through a sequence of headings.

Tidal current The horizontal movement of water caused by the ebbing and flooding of the tide.

Tidal range The amount of change in an area's water level from low tide to high tide; e.g., an area covered by two feet of water at low tide and six feet of water at high tide has a tidal range of four feet.

Tide The alternate rising and falling of the surface level in bodies of water, caused primarily by the gravitational forces of the sun and the moon on the earth. Tide is always the vertical movement of water (as opposed to the horizontal movement of tidal currents), although, colloquially, tide is used to refer to both currents and changes in water level.

Track (TR) The path a boat actually travels over the bottom.

Transducer The sending-receiving device of a depth finder that transmits sonic pulses to the bottom, and then picks up the echoes.

Trim To adjust the set of a sail relative to the wind.

True north The geographic North Pole; the chart direction to the North Pole, where, on a globe, the lines of longitude converge.

Variation The difference, expressed in degrees of an angle, between the direction of true north and magnetic north at any point on the surface of the earth. Variation is designated as east or west depending on whether the magnetic needle is deflected east or west of true north.

Veer The wind is said to veer when it shifts in a clockwise direction, as from north to northeast. When the wind shifts counterclockwise, it is said to back.

Very high frequency (VHF) A designated band of the radio spectrum, ranging from 30 to 300 mHz.

Bibliography

Navigation

Bowditch, Nathaniel:
American Practical Navigator. U.S. Navy Hydrographic Office, 1962.
American Practical Navigator. U.S. Government, 1966.

Dunlap, G. D., *Navigation and Finding Fish with Electronics.* International Marine Publishing Company, 1972.

Dunlap, G. D., and H. H. Shufeldt, *Dutton's Navigation and Piloting.* Naval Institute Press, 1972.

Hobbs, Richard R., *Marine Navigation 1: Piloting,* Fundamentals of Naval Science Series. Naval Institute Press, 1974.

Kals, W. S., *Practical Navigation.* Doubleday & Company, Inc., 1972.

Mixter, George W., *Primer of Navigation.* D. Van Nostrand Co., Inc., 1960.

Shufeldt, H. H., and G. D. Dunlap, *Piloting and Dead Reckoning.* Naval Institute Press, 1970.

Simonsen, Capt. Svend T., *Simonsen's Navigation.* Prentice-Hall, Inc., 1973.

Taylor, E. G. R., *The Haven-finding Art.* Hollis & Carter, 1958.

Townsend, Sallie, and Virginia Ericson, *The American Navigator's Handbook.* Thomas Y. Crowell Co., 1974.

Charts

Bagrow, Leo, *History of Cartography.* Translated by D. L. Paisley, revised and enlarged by R. A. Skelton. Harvard University Press, 1964.

Brindze, Ruth, *Charting the Oceans.* The Vanguard Press, Inc., 1972.

Brown, Lloyd A., *The Story of Maps.* Little, Brown and Company, 1949.

Greenhood, David, *Down to Earth: Mapping for Everybody.* Holiday House, 1944.

Howse, Derek, and Michael Sanderson, *The Sea Chart.* Fletcher & Son Ltd. (England), 1973.

General

Andrews, Howard L., and Alexander L. Russell, *Basic Boating: Piloting and Seamanship.* Prentice-Hall, 1964.

Brindze, Ruth, ed., *The Experts' Book of Boating.* Prentice-Hall, Inc., 1959.

Chapman, Charles F., *Piloting, Seamanship, & Small Boat Handling.* Motor Boating and Sailing, 1972.

French, John, *Electrical and Electronic Equipment for Yachts.* Dodd, Mead & Co., 1974.

Freuchen, Peter, *Peter Freuchen's Book of the Seven Seas.* Julian Messner, Inc., 1957.

Gaskell, T. F., *The Gulf Stream.* The John Day Company, 1973.

Marchaj, C. A., *Sailing Theory and Practice.* Dodd, Mead & Company, 1964.

History

Beaver, Patrick, *A History of Lighthouses.* The Citadel Press, 1973.

Cotter, Charles H., *A History of Nautical Astronomy.* American Elsevier Publishing Company Inc., 1968.

Hale, John R., *Age of Exploration.* TIME-LIFE BOOKS, 1966.

May, Commander W. E., *A History of Marine Navigation.* W. W. Norton & Company, Inc., 1973.

Morison, Samuel Eliot:
Admiral of the Ocean Sea: A Life of Christopher Columbus. Little, Brown and Company, 1942.
The European Discovery of America: The Southern Voyages. Oxford University Press, 1974.

Morison, Samuel Eliot, trans. and ed., *Journals and Other Documents on the Life and Voyages of Christopher Columbus.* The Heritage Press, 1963.

Government Publications

Chart No. 1: United States of America, Nautical Chart Symbols and Abbreviations. Prepared jointly by Defense Mapping Agency Hydrographic Center and National Ocean Survey (Department of Commerce, National Oceanic and Atmospheric Administration). Published by Defense Mapping Agency Hydrographic Center. Washington: 1974.

Significant Aspects of the Tides. U.S. Department of Commerce, National Ocean Survey, Educational Pamphlet #5, January 1971.

Tidal Currents. U.S. Department of Commerce, National Ocean Survey, Educational Pamphlet #4, February 1972.

Where to Buy Charts

Most marine supply stores carry a full complement of the government charts, tables, light lists and piloting guides needed to navigate local waters. If the boatman finds that the store is out of stock, however, or if he requires charts or other publications for distant areas, he can obtain the necessary materials by writing directly to the appropriate issuing office, as listed below.

1. National Ocean Survey, Distribution Division, C44, 6501 Lafayette Avenue, Riverdale, Maryland 20840. Telephone: (301) 436-6990. Publishes charts for all U.S. coastal areas, the Great Lakes, sections of major rivers; *Coast Pilots,* tide tables, tidal current tables, tidal current charts, *Chart No. 1;* catalogues of NOS charts. Distributes *Notice to Mariners.*

2. Defense Mapping Agency Depot, 5801 Tabor Avenue, Philadelphia, Pennsylvania 19120. Telephone: (215) 697-4262. Issues charts of foreign waters, a chart catalogue and *Notice to Mariners.* Distributes *Chart No. 1.*

3. U.S. Army Corps of Engineers. The district office in each state issues charts and chart lists for inland lakes and waterways.

4. Superintendent of Documents, Government Printing Office, Washington, D.C. 20402. Distributes light lists.

5. Hydrographic Chart Distribution Office, Department of the Environment, 1675 Russell Road, Ottawa, Ontario, Canada, K1A0E6. Distributes Canadian charts and marine publications.

Acknowledgments

For help given in the preparation of this book the editors wish to thank the following: Aqua Meter Instrument Corp., Roseland, New Jersey; Stanley Baldwin, Fairhaven, Massachusetts; The Bertram Yacht Company, Miami, Florida; Commander Ransom K. Boyce, First Coast Guard District, Boston, Massachusetts; Chris-Craft Industries, New York, New York; Goldberg Marine Distributors, Incorporated, New York, New York; Theodore Haendel, U.S. Merchant Marine Academy, Kings Point, New York; Hammond Map Store, New York, New York; Fred Hernandez, Bertram Yacht Co., Miami, Florida; Richard Humphrey, Staten Island, New York; P. S. Iskowitz, Aids to Navigation School, Governors Island, New York; Kenyon Marine, Guilford, Connecticut; H. Lewkowitz, New York, New York; Lion Yachts, Stamford, Connecticut; James McCauley, Nelson Bourret, Paul Bennet, Point Judith Fishing Cooperative, Point Judith, Rhode Island; Robert Merriam, Merriam Electronics, Point Judith, Rhode Island; National Oceanic and Atmospheric Administration, National Ocean Survey, Department of Commerce, Washington, D.C.; New York Nautical Instrument & Service Corp., New York, New York; Robert D. Ogg, Danforth, Portland, Maine; Henry E. Olsen, City Island, New York; Scott Perry, Lexington, Kentucky; E. S. Ritchie & Sons, Inc., Pembroke, Massachusetts; J. J. Scholz, Sun Electric Corporation, Crystal Lake, Illinois; E. M. Volek, Aids to Navigation School, Governors Island, New York; James Woodward, Ninth Coast Guard District, Federal Office Building, Cleveland, Ohio.

Picture Credits *Credits from left to right are separated by semicolons, from top to bottom by dashes.*

Cover—Richard Meek for SPORTS ILLUSTRATED. 6,7—Paul A. Darling. 9—Jim Molloy for *The Providence Journal.* 12—Photo by Dennis L. Crow, background chart by National Oceanic and Atmospheric Administration (NOAA), National Ocean Survey (NOS). 14,15,16—NOAA, NOS. 17—NOAA, NOS; chart symbols drawn by Nicholas Fasciano. 18,19—NOAA, NOS. 20—Chart symbols drawn by Fred Wolff. 21—Drawings by Nicholas Fasciano. 22,23—Photos by John Zimmerman—chart by NOAA, NOS. 24—Maps drawn by Nicholas Fasciano. 25—NOAA, NOS. 26—From *Mapmaking: The Art That Became a Science* by Lloyd A. Brown by permission of Little, Brown & Co., redrawn by Nicholas Fasciano. 27—Defense Mapping Agency Hydrographic Center. 28 through 31—NOAA, NOS. 32,33—NOAA, NOS—Defense Mapping Agency Hydrographic Center; U.S. Army Corps of Engineers, Little Rock and Tulsa Districts. 34 through 37—Enrico Ferorelli. 38,39—National Maritime Museum, Greenwich, England. 40,41—Photo Bibliotèque Nationale, courtesy of the Département des Cartes et Plans, Bibliotèque Nationale, Paris. 42 through 45—Derek Bayes, courtesy of the National Maritime Museum, Greenwich, England. 46—B. Evans from Sea Library. 48,49—Drawings by William G. Teodecki. 50,51—Drawings by Dale Gustafson. 52,53—Drawing by Nicholas Fasciano. 54,55—Drawings by Dale Gustafson. 56,57—Drawings by Nicholas Fasciano. 58,59—Drawings by Dale Gustafson. 60,61—Drawings by Nicholas Fasciano. 62—Drawings by Dale Gustafson. 63—Drawing by Nicholas Fasciano. 64—Bruce Roberts from Rapho/Photo Researchers. 65—Drawings by William G. Teodecki. 66—Roy Porello. 67—Thomas E. Mahnken Jr.—drawings by William G. Teodecki. 68—U.S. Coast Guard. 69—Drawing by William G. Teodecki—U.S. Coast Guard. 70—John Chang McCurdy. 71—Drawings by William G. Teodecki. 72—NOAA, NOS—signal chart drawn by Walter Johnson. 73—U.S. Coast Guard. 75—Peabody Museum of Salem. 76,77—U.S. Coast Guard, courtesy Brown Brothers; U.S. Coast Guard, courtesy Mariner's Museum. 78,79—Nathaniel Stebbins from The Society for the Preservation of New England Antiquities; Wide World. 80—Peabody Museum of Salem. 81—No credit. 82—Ken Kay. 84—Drawing by Roger Metcalf—drawing by Dale Gustafson. 85—Drawing by Roger Metcalf—drawings by Dale Gustafson (3). 86—Drawings by Roger Metcalf. 87,88—Drawings by Dale Gustafson. 89,90—Drawings by Roger Metcalf. 91—Tables and graph drawn by Rosi Cassano. 92—Photo by Ken Kay, chart by NOAA, NOS. 93—Drawing by Roger Metcalf—chart and graph drawn by Rosi Cassano. 94—Photo by Ken Kay, chart by NOAA, NOS—drawing by Fred Wolff. 95,96,97—Photos by Ken Kay, chart by NOAA, NOS. 98,99—Drawings by Rosi Cassano. 100,101—NOAA, NOS. 102 through 123—Photos by Stephen Green-Armytage, charts by NOAA, NOS. Map on 105 drawn by Nicholas Fasciano. 124—Enrico Ferorelli. 126—Drawings by Fred Wolff. 127, 128—Drawings by Roger Metcalf. 129—Drawing by Roger Metcalf—NOAA, NOS—Ross Laboratories. 130—Drawings by Fred Wolff. 131,132—Drawings by Roger Metcalf. 133—NOAA, NOS. 134—Drawings by Fred Wolff. 135—NOAA, NOS, bottom inset drawing by Roger Metcalf. 136—Drawings by Fred Wolff. 137—Drawing by Roger Metcalf—drawing by Fred Wolff. 138,139—John Zimmerman; NOAA, NOS. 140—Drawing by Fred Wolff—map by Roger Metcalf. 141—Drawings by Roger Metcalf. 142 through 149—Marvin Newman, charts on 145 and 147 by NOAA, NOS. 150—Sue Cummings. 152—NOAA, NOS—work sheet drawn by Rosi Cassano. 153—NOAA, NOS. 154—NOAA, NOS—work sheet drawn by Rosi Cassano. 155,156,157—NOAA, NOS. 158—Drawing by Fred Wolff. 159—Composite from NOAA, NOS charts, current triangle drawn by Rosi Cassano. 160,161—NOAA, NOS—drawings by Fred Wolff. 162—Eric Schweikardt for SPORTS ILLUSTRATED. 163, 164—Eric Schweikardt—drawings by Fred Wolff. 165—NOAA, NOS, inset course drawn by Rosi Cassano. 166, 167—Eric Schweikardt. 168—Drawings by Fred Wolff.

Index

Page numbers in italics indicate illustrations.

Printed in U.S.A.